Advanced Praise for
The Unified Modeling Language Reference Manual, Second Edition

"If you are a serious user of UML, there is no other book quite like this one. I have been involved with the UML specification process for some time, but I still found myself learning things while reading through this book—especially on the changes and new capabilities that have come with UML 2.0. The intimate involvement of the author in the creation and continuing evolution of UML, and the encyclopedic scope of his book, make the work a unique contribution to the UML 2.0 literature, as the first edition was for UML 1.0."

—Ed Seidewitz, Chief Architect, InteliData Technologies Corporation

"In addition to the documents of the OMG UML 2.0 Standard, this book is probably the most important source for the Unified Modeling Language. It is a detailed reference, covering the mainstream ideas as well as the delicate niches of the language. The Dictionary of Terms offers precise, comprehensive and, perhaps most important, systematic information on all aspects of the UML 2.0."

—Martin Gogolla, Professor for Computer Science, University of Bremen

"Comprehensive and instructive, written by a person with the insights of not only the technical matters, but also the processes that led to the UML language and its version 2.0. This book should be a companion for every serious UML modeler."

—Øystein Haugen, Ericsson Representative in the OMG UML 2.0 Standardization, Associate Professor, University of Oslo

"This book provides an authoritative and user-oriented account of UML 2.0."

—Dr. Robert France, Department of Computer Science, Colorado State University.

"This is so far the most comprehensive book on UML 2.0. It gives you what the specification does not: real introductions to the various parts of UML, annotated examples, discussions on how to use the new features, and an insight into how and why the new features entered UML 2.0. As one of the persons who was involved in the making of UML 2.0, I can tell that the book is faithful to the specification and to the ideas behind the new features. Read this book instead or as a complement to the specification."

—Birger Møller-Pedersen, Professor, University of Oslo

The Unified Modeling Language Reference Manual

Second Edition

The Addison-Wesley Object Technology Series

Grady Booch, Ivar Jacobson, and James Rumbaugh, Series Editors

For more information, check out the series web site at www.awprofessional.com/otseries.

Ahmed/Umrysh, *Developing Enterprise Java Applications with J2EE™ and UML*

Arlow/Neustadt, *Enterprise Patterns and MDA: Building Better Software with Archetype Patterns and UML*

Arlow/Neustadt, *UML and the Unified Process: Practical Object-Oriented Analysis and Design*

Armour/Miller, *Advanced Use Case Modeling: Software Systems*

Bellin/Simone, *The CRC Card Book*

Bergström/Råberg, *Adopting the Rational Unified Process: Success with the RUP*

Binder, *Testing Object-Oriented Systems: Models, Patterns, and Tools*

Bittner/Spence, *Use Case Modeling*

Booch, *Object Solutions: Managing the Object-Oriented Project*

Booch, *Object-Oriented Analysis and Design with Applications, 2E*

Booch/Bryan, *Software Engineering with ADA, 3E*

Booch/Rumbaugh/Jacobson, *The Unified Modeling Language User Guide*

Box/Brown/Ewald/Sells, *Effective COM: 50 Ways to Improve Your COM and MTS-based Applications*

Carlson, *Modeling XML Applications with UML: Practical e-Business Applications*

Collins, *Designing Object-Oriented User Interfaces*

Conallen, *Building Web Applications with UML, 2E*

D'Souza/Wills, *Objects, Components, and Frameworks with UML: The Catalysis(SM) Approach*

Douglass, *Doing Hard Time: Developing Real-Time Systems with UML, Objects, Frameworks, and Patterns*

Douglass, *Real-Time Design Patterns: Robust Scalable Architecture for Real-Time Systems*

Douglass, *Real Time UML, 3E: Advances in The UML for Real-Time Systems*

Eeles/Houston/Kozaczynski, *Building J2EE™ Applications with the Rational Unified Process*

Fontoura/Pree/Rumpe, *The UML Profile for Framework Architectures*

Fowler, *Analysis Patterns: Reusable Object Models*

Fowler et al., *Refactoring: Improving the Design of Existing Code*

Fowler, *UML Distilled, 3E: A Brief Guide to the Standard Object Modeling Language*

Gomaa, *Designing Concurrent, Distributed, and Real-Time Applications with UML*

Gomaa, *Designing Software Product Lines with UML*

Graham, *Object-Oriented Methods, 3E: Principles and Practice*

Heinckiens, *Building Scalable Database Applications: Object-Oriented Design, Architectures, and Implementations*

Hofmeister/Nord/Dilip, *Applied Software Architecture*

Jacobson/Booch/Rumbaugh, *The Unified Software Development Process*

Jordan, *C++ Object Databases: Programming with the ODMG Standard*

Kleppe/Warmer/Bast, *MDA Explained: The Model Driven Architecture™: Practice and Promise*

Kroll/Kruchten, *The Rational Unified Process Made Easy: A Practitioner's Guide to the RUP*

Kruchten, *The Rational Unified Process, 3E: An Introduction*

Lau, *The Art of Objects: Object-Oriented Design and Architecture*

Leffingwell/Widrig, *Managing Software Requirements, 2E: A Use Case Approach*

Manassis, *Practical Software Engineering: Analysis and Design for the .NET Platform*

Marshall, *Enterprise Modeling with UML: Designing Successful Software through Business Analysis*

McGregor/Sykes, *A Practical Guide to Testing Object-Oriented Software*

Mellor/Balcer, *Executable UML: A Foundation for Model-Driven Architecture*

Mellor et al., *MDA Distilled: Principles of Model-Driven Architecture*

Naiburg/Maksimchuk, *UML for Database Design*

Oestereich, *Developing Software with UML, 2E: Object-Oriented Analysis and Design in Practice*

Page-Jones, *Fundamentals of Object-Oriented Design in UML*

Pohl, *Object-Oriented Programming Using C++, 2E*

Pollice et al. *Software Development for Small Teams: A RUP-Centric Approach*

Quatrani, *Visual Modeling with Rational Rose 2002 and UML*

Rector/Sells, *ATL Internals*

Reed, *Developing Applications with Visual Basic and UML*

Rosenberg/Scott, *Applying Use Case Driven Object Modeling with UML: An Annotated e-Commerce Example*

Rosenberg/Scott, *Use Case Driven Object Modeling with UML: A Practical Approach*

Royce, *Software Project Management: A Unified Framework*

Rumbaugh/Jacobson/Booch, *The Unified Modeling Language Reference Manual*

Schneider/Winters, *Applying Use Cases, 2E: A Practical Guide*

Smith/Williams, *Performance Solutions: A Practical Guide to Creating Responsive, Scalable Software*

Stevens/Pooley, *Using UML, Updated Edition: Software Engineering with Objects and Components*

Unhelkar, *Process Quality Assurance for UML-Based Projects*

van Harmelen, *Object Modeling and User Interface Design: Designing Interactive Systems*

Wake, *Refactoring Workbook*

Warmer/Kleppe, *The Object Constraint Language, 2E: Getting Your Models Ready for MDA*

White, *Software Configuration Management Strategies and Rational ClearCase®: A Practical Introduction*

The Component Software Series

Clemens Szyperski, Series Editor

For more information, check out the series web site at www.awprofessional.com/csseries.

Allen, *Realizing eBusiness with Components*

Apperly et al., *Service- and Component-based Development: Using the Select Perspective™ and UML*

Atkinson et al., *Component-Based Product Line Engineering with UML*

Cheesman/Daniels, *UML Components: A Simple Process for Specifying Component-Based Software*

Szyperski, *Component Software, 2E: Beyond Object-Oriented Programming*

Whitehead, *Component-Based Development: Principles and Planning for Business Systems*

The Unified Modeling Language Reference Manual

Second Edition

James Rumbaugh
Ivar Jacobson
Grady Booch

✦ Addison-Wesley

Boston • San Francisco • New York • Toronto • Montreal
London • Munich • Paris • Madrid
Capetown • Sydney • Tokyo • Singapore • Mexico City

The publisher offers discounts on this book when ordered in quantity for bulk purchases and special sales. For more information, please contact:

U.S. Corporate and Government Sales
(800) 382-3419
corpsales@pearsontechgroup.com

For sales outside of the U.S., please contact:
International Sales
(317) 581-3793
international@pearsontechgroup.com

Visit Addison-Wesley on the Web: www.awprofessional.com

Library of Congress Cataloging-in-Publication Data

Rumbaugh, James.
   The unified modeling language reference manual / James Rumbaugh, Ivar Jacobson, Grady Booch.-- 2nd ed.
      p. cm.
   ISBN 0-321-24562-8
   1. Computer software--Development. 2. UML (Computer science) I. Jacobson, Ivar. II. Booch, Grady. III. Title.

   QA76.76.D47R86 2004
   005.3--dc22

   2004012580

ISBN 0-321-24562-8

Text printed on recycled paper.

1 2 3 4 5 6 7 8 9 10—CRW—09 08 07 06 05 04

First printing, July 2004

For Madeline, Nick, and Alex

—Jim

Contents

Preface

Goals

This book is intended to be a complete, useful reference to the Unified Modeling Language (UML) for the developer, architect, project manager, system engineer, programmer, analyst, contracting officer, customer, and anyone else who needs to specify, design, build, or understand complex software systems. It provides a full reference to the concepts and constructs of UML, including their semantics, notation, and purpose. It is organized to be a convenient but thorough reference for the working professional developer. It also attempts to provide additional detail about issues that may not be clear from the standards documents and to provide a rationale for many decisions that went into the UML.

This book is not intended as a guide to the UML standards documents or to the internal structure of the metamodel contained in them. The details of the metamodel are of interest to methodologists and UML tool builders, but most other developers have little need for the arcane details of the Object Management Group (OMG) documents. This book provides all the details of UML that most developers need; in many cases, it makes information explicit that must otherwise be sought between the lines of the original documents. For those who wish to consult the source documents, they are on the OMG web site (www.omg.org).

This book is intended as a reference for those who already have some understanding of object-oriented technology. For beginners, the original books by us and by other authors are listed in the bibliography; although some of the notation has changed, books such as [Rumbaugh-91], [Jacobson-92], [Booch-94], and [Meyer-88] provide an introduction to object-oriented concepts that is still valid and therefore unnecessary to duplicate here. [Blaha-05] updates [Rumbaugh-91] using UML notation. For a tutorial introduction to UML that shows how to model a number of common problems, see *The Unified Modeling Language User Guide* [Booch-99] or *UML Distilled* [Fowler-04].

UML does not require a particular development process. Although UML may be used with a variety of development processes, it was designed to support an iterative, incremental, use-case–driven process with a strong architectural focus—the kind we feel is most suitable for the development of modern, complex systems. To place UML in its context as a tool for software development, this book defines the stages of such a process, but they are not part of the UML standard. *The Unified Software Development Process* [Jacobson-99] describes in detail the kind of process we believe complements the UML and best supports software development.

Second Edition and UML Version

This second edition has been extensively modified from the first edition, which was published in 1999. This edition is based on the OMG "adopted" specification of UML version 2.0, with anticipated changes to the "available" specification being prepared by an OMG Finalization Task Force. Corrections to the book due to changes in the OMG UML specification will be posted on the publisher's web site for this book at www.awprofessional.com/titles/0321245628. The information in the book is accurate as of June 2004.

Original specification documents and up-to-date information about work on UML and related topics can be found on the OMG web site at www.omg.org.

Reference Manual and OMG Specification

UML is a large modeling language with many features. A reference manual that just repeats the original specification documents would not help readers much. As in any dictionary or encyclopedia, we have had to summarize information as clearly as possible while reducing the amount of material included. We have frequently chosen to emphasize common usages by omitting obscure special cases or redundant means of representing some concepts. This does not mean that those capabilities are useless, but most readers should be able to succeed without using them. The *Reference Manual* should not be regarded as the final authority on the UML language, however. As with any standard, the final authority rests with the official specifications, and these should be consulted to resolve disputes.

We have tried to follow these principles:

- Explain the main intent of a concept without getting lost in the details of the metamodel representation.

- Avoid discussion of abstract metaclasses. Modelers must ultimately use concrete metaclasses, which can be described more simply if the internal abstract layers are collapsed.

- Avoid discussion of the packaging of the metamodel. The packages may be important to tool builders, but modelers don't need to know them most of the time. If you need to know, you need to look at the specification in detail anyway.

- Describe concepts from the complete specification. The OMG specification has a number of intermediate layers and compliance points that greatly complicate understanding of UML. We describe UML with all of its features. If your tool does not implement all of the facilities, then some of the features may be unavailable to you, but it doesn't usually hurt to know about them.

- Describe concepts from the viewpoint of their normal usage. Often the OMG specification goes to considerable trouble to express concepts in a general way. This is proper for a specification, but we feel that readers often understand concepts better if they are presented in a specific context and then generalized. If you are worried about the application of a concept in a complex, ambiguous situation and you feel that the *Reference Manual* explanation may be inadequate, check the original specification. Unfortunately, however, even the OMG specification is sometimes ambiguous in complex situations.

Outline of the Book

The UML Reference Manual is organized into four parts: (1) an overview of UML history and of modeling, (2) a survey of UML concepts, (3) an alphabetical dictionary of UML terms and concepts, and (4) brief appendices.

The first part is an overview of UML—its history, purposes, and uses—to help you understand the origin of UML and the need it tries to fill.

The second part is a brief survey of UML concepts so that you can put all the features into perspective. The survey provides a brief overview of the views UML supports and shows how the various constructs work together. This part uses an example that walks through various UML views. It contains one chapter for each kind of UML view. This survey is not intended as a full tutorial or as a comprehensive description of concepts. It serves mainly to summarize and relate the various UML concepts, providing starting points for detailed readings in the dictionary.

The third part contains the reference material organized for easy access to each topic. The bulk of the book is an alphabetical dictionary of all of the concepts and constructs in UML. Each UML term of any importance has its own entry in the dictionary. The dictionary is meant to be complete; therefore, everything in the concept overview in Part 2 is repeated in more detail in the dictionary. The same or similar information has sometimes been repeated in multiple dictionary articles so that the reader can conveniently find it. Some common object-oriented terms that are not official UML concepts are included to provide context in examples and discussions.

Appendices show the UML metamodel and a summary of UML notation. There is a brief bibliography of major object-oriented books, but no attempt has been made to include a comprehensive citation of sources of ideas for UML or other approaches. Many of the books in the bibliography contain excellent lists of references to books and journal articles for those interested in tracking the development of the ideas.

Dictionary Entry Formatting Conventions

The dictionary part of the book is organized as an alphabetical list of entries, each describing one concept in some detail. The articles represent a flat list of UML concepts at various conceptual levels. A high-level concept typically contains a summary of its subordinate concepts, each of which is fully described in a separate article. The articles are highly cross-referenced. The flat dictionary organization permits the description of each concept to be presented at a fairly uniform level of detail, without constant shifts in level for the nested descriptions that would be necessary for a sequential presentation. The hypertext format of the document should also make it convenient for reference. It should not be necessary to use the index much; instead, go directly to the main article in the dictionary for any term of interest and follow cross-references. This format is not necessarily ideal for learning the language; beginners are advised to read the overview description of UML found in Part 2 or to read introductory books on UML, such as the *UML User Guide* [Booch-99].

Dictionary articles have the following divisions, although not all divisions appear in all articles.

Headword and brief definition

The name of the concept appears in boldface, set to the left of the body of the article. A brief definition follows in normal type. This definition is intended to capture the main idea of the concept, but it may simplify the concept for concise presentation. Refer to the main article for precise semantics.

Predefined stereotypes are included as entries. A comment in parentheses following the entry name identifies the modeling element to which they apply.

Semantics

This section contains a detailed description of the meaning of the concept, including constraints on its uses and its execution consequences. Notation is not covered in this section, although examples use the appropriate notation. General semantics are given first. For concepts with subordinate structural properties, a list of the properties follows the general semantics, often under the subheading *Structure*. In most cases, properties appear as a table in alphabetical order by property name, with the description of each property on the right. If a property has an enumerated list of choices, they may be given as an indented sublist. In more complicated cases, a property is given its own article to avoid excessive nesting. When properties require more explanation than permitted by a table, they are described in normal text with run-in headers in boldface italics. In certain cases, the main concept is best described under several logical subdivisions rather than one list. In such cases, additional sections follow or replace the *Structure* subsection. Although several

entry name   Dictionary entry format

A brief description of the concept in one or two sentences.
  See also related concept.

Semantics

A description of the semantics in several paragraphs.

Structure

A list of the subordinate concepts within the main concept.

item	Description of an item. UML metamodel names are usually converted into plain English.
enumerated item	An enumeration with several values. List of values:
value	The meaning of this value of the item.

Another item. More complicated topics are described in separate paragraphs.

Example

An example may be included in semantics, notation, or stand alone.

Notation

Description of the notation, usually including a diagram or syntax.

Presentation options

Describes variant forms of notation, usually optional.

Style guidelines

States recommended practice although not mandatory.

Discussion

The author's opinions or background explanations beyond UML.

History

Changes from UML version 1.x.

stereotype entry (stereotype of Class)

Description of the meaning of the stereotype.

organizational mechanisms have been used, their structure should be obvious to the reader. The names of properties are usually stated in plain language rather than using internal identifiers from the UML metamodel, but the correspondence is meant to be obvious.

Notation

This section contains a detailed description of the notation for the concept. Usually, the notation section has a form that parallels the preceding semantics section, which it references, and it often has the same divisions. The notation section usually includes one or more diagrams to illustrate the concept. The actual notation is printed in black. To help the reader understand the notation, many diagrams contain annotations in blue. Any material in blue is commentary and is not part of the actual notation.

Style guidelines

This optional section describes widespread style conventions. They are not mandatory, but they are followed within the UML specification itself. Recommended presentation guidelines may also be given in a separate section.

Example

This subsection contains examples of notation or illustrations of the use of the concept. Frequently, the examples also treat complicated or potentially confusing situations. If the examples are brief, they may be folded in with another section.

Discussion

This section describes subtle issues, clarifies tricky and frequently confused points, and contains other details that would otherwise digress from the more descriptive semantics section. A minority of articles have a discussion section.

This section also explains certain design decisions that were made in the development of the UML, particularly those that may appear counterintuitive or that have provoked strong controversy. Simple differences in taste are generally not covered.

Sometimes we express an opinion on the value (or lack thereof) of certain concepts. We recognize that others may disagree with these assessments. We have tried to confine opinions to the discussion section.

History

This section describes changes from UML1 to UML2, sometimes including reasons for the changes. Minor changes are not usually listed. Absence of this section does not mean that no changes have occurred.

Syntax Conventions

Syntax expressions. Syntax expressions are given in a modified BNF format in a sans serif font (Myriad). Literal values that appear in the target sentence are printed in black, and the names of syntax variables and special syntax operators are printed in blue.

Text printed in black appears literally in the target string.

Punctuation marks (always printed in black) appear literally in the target string.

Any word printed in blue ink represents a variable that must be replaced by another string or another syntax production in the target string. Words may contain letters and hyphens. If a blue word is italicized or underlined, the actual replacement string must be italicized or underlined.

In code examples, comments are printed in blue to the right of the code text.

Subscripts and L-brackets are used as syntax operators as follows:

expression$_{opt}$	The expression is optional.
expression$_{list,}$	A comma-separated list of the expression may appear. If there is zero or one repetition, there is no separator. If a different punctuation mark than a comma appears in the subscript, then it is the separator.
$\lfloor$= expression$\rfloor_{opt}$	A pair of right angles ties together two or more terms that are considered a unit for optional or repeated occurrences. In this example, the equal sign and the expression form one unit that may be omitted or included.

Two-level nesting is avoided. Particularly convoluted syntax may be simplified somewhat for presentation, but use of such convoluted syntax is likely to be confusing for humans anyway and should be avoided.

Literal strings. In running text, language keywords, names of model elements, and sample strings from models are shown in a sans serif font (Myriad).

Diagrams. In diagrams, blue text and arrows are annotations, that is, explanations of the diagram notation that do not appear in an actual diagram. Any text and symbols in black are actual diagram notation.

CD

This book is accompanied by a CD containing the full text of the book in Adobe® Reader® (PDF) format. Using Adobe Reader, the viewer can easily search the book for a word or phrase. The CD version also contains a clickable table of contents, index, Adobe Reader bookmarks, and extensive hot links (in red) in the bodies of the articles. Simply click on one of the links to jump to the dictionary article for a word or phrase. We hope that this CD will be a useful reference aid for readers.

Creators of UML

We wish to thank the many collaborators who built the UML specification through years of meetings, heated discussions, writing, and implementation of ideas. The list of contributors has grown significantly since UML1, and the OMG specification no longer lists the major contributors, who number between twenty and fifty depending on the threshold for inclusion, and even more if work influencing UML is included. It no longer appears possible to compile a complete list without overlooking many persons.

Most of all, we want to celebrate the hundreds of persons who contributed to the community of ideas from which UML was drawn—ideas in object-oriented technology, software methodology, programming languages, user interfaces, visual programming, and numerous other areas of computer science. It is impossible to list them all, or indeed to track even the major chains of influence, without a major scholarly effort, and this is an engineering book, not a historical review. Many of them are well known, but many good ideas also came from those who did not have the good fortune to become widely recognized. The bibliography includes a few of the lesser-known books that influenced the authors.

Acknowledgments

We would like to acknowledge the reviewers who made this book possible. For the second edition, they include Conrad Bock, Martin Gogolla, Øystein Haugen, Birger Møller-Pedersen, and Ed Seidewitz. For the first edition, we received feedback from Mike Blaha, Conrad Bock, Perry Cole, Bruce Douglass, Martin Fowler, Eran Gery, Pete McBreen, Gunnar Övergaard, Karin Palmkvist, Guus Ramackers, Tom Schultz, Ed Seidewitz, and Bran Selic.

On a more personal note, I wish to thank Professor Jack Dennis, who inspired my work in modeling and the work of many other students more than thirty years ago. The ideas from his Computations Structures Group at MIT have borne much fruit, and they are not the least of the sources of UML. I must also thank Mary Loomis and Ashwin Shah, with whom I developed the original ideas of OMT, and my former colleagues at GE R&D Center, Mike Blaha, Bill Premerlani, Fred Eddy, and Bill Lorensen, with whom I wrote the OMT book.

Finally, without the patience of my wife, Madeline, and my sons, Nick and Alex, there would have been no UML and no book about it.

James Rumbaugh
Cupertino, California
June 2004

Part 1: Background

This part describes general principles underlying UML, including the nature and purpose of modeling and those aspects of the UML that pervade all functional areas.

1
UML Overview

This chapter is a quick overview of UML and what it is good for.

Brief Summary of UML

The Unified Modeling Language (UML) is a general-purpose visual modeling language that is used to specify, visualize, construct, and document the artifacts of a software system. It captures decisions and understanding about systems that must be constructed. It is used to understand, design, browse, configure, maintain, and control information about such systems. It is intended for use with all development methods, lifecycle stages, application domains, and media. The modeling language is intended to unify past experience about modeling techniques and to incorporate current software best practices into a standard approach. UML includes semantic concepts, notation, and guidelines. It has static, dynamic, environmental, and organizational parts. It is intended to be supported by interactive visual modeling tools that have code generators and report writers. The UML specification does not define a standard process but is intended to be useful with an iterative development process. It is intended to support most existing object-oriented development processes.

The UML captures information about the static structure and dynamic behavior of a system. A system is modeled as a collection of discrete objects that interact to perform work that ultimately benefits an outside user. The static structure defines the kinds of objects important to a system and to its implementation, as well as the relationships among the objects. The dynamic behavior defines the history of objects over time and the communications among objects to accomplish goals. Modeling a system from several separate but related viewpoints permits it to be understood for different purposes.

The UML also contains organizational constructs for arranging models into packages that permit software teams to partition large systems into workable pieces, to understand and control dependencies among the packages, and to manage the versioning of model units in a complex development environment. It contains constructs for representing implementation decisions and for organizing run-time elements into components.

UML is not primarily a programming language. It can be used to write programs, but it lacks the syntactic and semantic conveniences that most programming languages provide to ease the task of programming. Tools can provide code generators from UML into a variety of programming languages, as well as construct reverse-engineered models from existing programs. The UML is not a highly formal language intended for theorem proving. There are a number of such languages, but they are not easy to understand or to use for most purposes. The UML is a general-purpose modeling language. For specialized domains, such as GUI layout, VLSI circuit design, or rule-based artificial intelligence, a more specialized tool with a special language might be appropriate. UML is a discrete modeling language. It is not intended to model continuous systems such as those found in engineering and physics. UML is intended to be a universal general-purpose modeling language for discrete systems such as those made of software, firmware, or digital logic.

UML History

UML was developed in an effort to simplify and consolidate the large number of object-oriented development methods that had emerged.

Object-oriented development methods

Development methods for traditional programming languages, such as Cobol and Fortran, emerged in the 1970s and became widespread in the 1980s. Foremost among them was Structured Analysis and Structured Design [Yourdon-79] and its variants, such as Real-Time Structured Design [Ward-85] and others. These methods, originally developed by Constantine, DeMarco, Mellor, Ward, Yourdon, and others, achieved some penetration into the large system area, especially for government-contracted systems in the aerospace and defense fields, in which contracting officers insisted on an organized development process and ample documentation of the system design and implementation. The results were not always as good as hoped for—many computer-aided software engineering (CASE) systems were little more than report generators that extracted designs after the implementation was complete—but the methods included good ideas that were occasionally used effectively in the construction of large systems. Commercial applications were more reluctant to adopt large CASE systems and development methods. Most businesses developed software internally for their own needs, without the adversarial relationship between customer and contractors that characterized large government projects. Commercial systems were perceived to be simpler, whether or not this was actually true, and there was less need for review by outside organizations.

The first object-oriented language is generally acknowledged to be Simula-67 [Birtwistle-75], developed in Norway in 1967. This language never had a significant following, although it greatly influenced the developers of several of the later object-oriented languages. The work of Dahl and Nygaard had a profound influence on the development of object orientation. The object-oriented movement became active with the widespread availability of Smalltalk in the early 1980s, followed by other object-oriented languages, such as Objective C, C++, Eiffel, and CLOS. The actual usage of object-oriented languages was limited at first, but object-orientation attracted a lot of attention. About five years after Smalltalk became widely known, the first object-oriented development methods were published by Shlaer/Mellor [Shlaer-88] and Coad/Yourdon [Coad-91], followed soon thereafter by Booch [Booch-94], Rumbaugh/Blaha/Premerlani/Eddy/Lorensen [Rumbaugh-91] (updated as [Blaha-05]), and Wirfs-Brock/Wilkerson/Wiener [Wirfs-Brock-90] (note that copyright years often begin in July of the previous calendar year). These books, added to earlier programming-language design books by Goldberg/Robson [Goldberg-83], Cox [Cox-86], and Meyer [Meyer-88], started the field of object-oriented methodology. The first phase was complete by the end of 1990. The Objectory book [Jacobson-92] was published slightly later, based on work that had appeared in earlier papers. This book took a somewhat different approach, with its focus on use cases and the development process.

Over the next five years, a plethora of books on object-oriented methodology appeared, each with its own set of concepts, definitions, notation, terminology, and process. Some added useful new concepts, but overall there was a great similarity among the concepts proposed by different authors. Many of the newer books started from one or more of the existing methods and made extensions or minor changes. The original authors were not idle either; most of them updated their original work, often incorporating good ideas from other authors. In general, there emerged a pool of common core concepts, together with a wide variety of concepts embraced by one or two authors but not widely used. Even in the core concepts, there were minor discrepancies among methods that made detailed comparison somewhat treacherous, especially for the casual reader.

Unification effort

There were some early attempts to unify concepts among methods. A notable example was Fusion by Coleman and his colleagues [Coleman-94], which included concepts from OMT [Rumbaugh-91], Booch [Booch-94], and CRC [Wirfs-Brock-90]. As it did not involve the original authors, it must be regarded as another new method rather than as a replacement of several existing methods. The first successful attempt to combine and replace existing approaches came when

Rumbaugh joined Booch at Rational Software Corporation in 1994. They began combining the concepts from the OMT and Booch methods, resulting in a first proposal in 1995. At that time, Jacobson also joined Rational and began working with Booch and Rumbaugh. Their joint work was called the Unified Modeling Language (UML). The momentum gained by having the authors of three of the top methods working together to unify their approaches shifted the balance in the object-oriented methodology field, where there had previously been little incentive (or at least little willingness) for methodologists to abandon some of their own concepts to achieve harmony.

In 1996, the Object Management Group (OMG) issued a request for proposals for a standard approach to object-oriented modeling. UML authors Booch, Jacobson, and Rumbaugh began working with methodologists and developers from other companies to produce a proposal attractive to the membership of OMG, as well as a modeling language that would be widely accepted by tool makers, methodologists, and developers who would be the eventual users. Several competing efforts also were started. Eventually, all the proposals coalesced in the final UML proposal that was submitted to the OMG in September 1997. The final product is a collaboration among many people. We began the UML effort and contributed a few good ideas, but the ideas in it are the product of many minds.

Standardization

The Unified Modeling Language was adopted unanimously by the membership of the OMG as a standard in November 1997 [UML-98]. The OMG assumed responsibility for the further development of the UML standard. Even before final adoption, a number of books were published outlining the highlights of the UML. Many tool vendors announced support or planned support for the UML, and several methodologists announced that they would use UML notation for further work. UML has now supplanted most, if not all, of the previous modeling notations in development processes, modeling tools, and articles in the technical literature. The emergence of the UML appears to have been attractive to the general computing public because it consolidates the experiences of many authors with an official status that has reduced gratuitous divergence among tools.

Noteworthy is a series of international research conferences with the title *UML yyyy*, where yyyy is a year starting with 1998 and continuing annually [UMLConf]. Also note the yearly [ECOOP] and [OOPSLA] conferences dealing with object-oriented technology in general.

UML2

After several years of experience using UML, the OMG issued requests for proposals to upgrade UML to fix problems uncovered by experience of use and to extend it with additional capabilities that were desired in several application domains. Proposals were developed from November 2000 to July 2003, with a specification of UML version 2.0 being adopted by the OMG membership shortly thereafter [UML-04]. The adopted specification underwent the normal OMG finalization process to fix bugs and problems encountered in initial implementation, with a final available specification expected at the end of 2004 or beginning of 2005.

In this book, we use the term *UML1* to refer to UML specification versions 1.1 to 1.5 and *UML2* to refer to UML specification versions 2.0 and higher.

New features. In general, UML2 is mostly the same as UML1, especially regarding the most commonly used, central features. Some problem areas have been modified, a few major enhancements have been added, and many small bugs have been fixed, but users of UML1 should have little trouble using UML2. The new version may be considered like a new version of a programming language or an application. Some of the most important changes visible to users are:

- Sequence diagram constructs and notation based largely on the ITU Message Sequence Chart standard, adapted to make it more object-oriented.

- Decoupling of activity modeling concepts from state machines and the use of notation popular in the business modeling community.

- Unification of activity modeling with the action modeling added in UML version 1.5, to provide a more complete procedural model.

- Contextual modeling constructs for the internal composition of classes and collaborations. These constructs permit both loose and strict encapsulation and the wiring of internal structures from smaller parts.

- Repositioning of components as design constructs and artifacts as physical entities that are deployed.

Internal mechanisms. Other changes affect the internal representation of UML constructs (the metamodel) and its relationship to other specifications. These changes will not concern most users directly, but they are important to toolmakers because they affect interoperability across multiple specifications, therefore they will affect users indirectly:

- Unification of the core of UML with the conceptual modeling parts of MOF (Meta-Object Facility). This permits UML models to be handled by generic MOF tools and repositories.

- Restructuring of the UML metamodel to eliminate redundant constructs and to permit reuse of well-defined subsets by other specifications.

- Availability of profiles to define domain and technology-specific extensions of UML.

Other sources

In addition to the various development methods cited above and a number of others that came a bit later, certain UML views show strong influences from particular non-object-oriented sources.

The static view, with classes connected by various relationships, is strongly influenced by Peter Chen's Entity-Relationship (ER) model originally developed in 1976. The influence came into UML through most of the early object-oriented methods. The ER model also heavily influenced database systems. The programming language world and the database world have unfortunately mostly gone their separate ways.

State machine models have been used in computer science and electrical engineering for many years. David Harel's statecharts are an important extension to classical state machines that add the concept of nested and orthogonal states. Harel's ideas were adapted by OMT, and from there into other methods and eventually into UML, where they form the basis of the state machine view.

The sequence diagram notation of UML2 is taken from the ITU Message Sequence Chart (MSC) standard [ITU-T Z.120], adapted to make it match other UML concepts better. This standard, which has been widely used in the telecommunications industry, replaces the sequence diagram notation of UML1 by adding a number of structured constructs to overcome problems in the previous UML1 notation. The ITU is considering whether to adopt some or all of the changes into the ITU standard.

The structured classifier concepts of UML2 were strongly influenced by the real-time engineering constructs of SDL [ITU-T Z.100], MSC, and the ROOM method [Selic-94].

The activity diagram notation of UML1, and even more that of UML2, is heavily influenced by various business process modeling notations. Because no single business process modeling notation was dominant, the UML notation was selected from various sources.

There are many other influences of UML, and often the original source of an idea precedes the person who is famous for popularizing it. About 20 persons were major contributors to the UML1 specification, with many others participating in a lesser way. Maybe 30 or so played major roles in the development of UML2, with scores of others submitting suggestions, reviewing proposals, and writing books. It is impossible to list everyone who contributed to UML, and the brief references that we have included undoubtedly overlook some important contributors, for which we ask understanding.

What does *unified* mean?

The word *unified* has the following relevant meanings for UML.

Across historical methods and notations. The UML combines the commonly accepted concepts from many object-oriented methods, selecting a clear definition for each concept, as well as a notation and terminology. The UML can represent most existing models as well as or better than the original methods can.

Across the development lifecycle. The UML is seamless from requirements to deployment. The same set of concepts and notation can be used in different stages of development and even mixed within a single model. It is unnecessary to translate from one stage to another. This seamlessness is critical for iterative, incremental development.

Across application domains. The UML is intended to model most application domains, including those involving systems that are large, complex, real-time, distributed, data or computation intensive, among other properties. There may be specialized areas in which a special-purpose language is more useful, but UML is intended to be as good as or better than any other general-purpose modeling language for most application areas.

Across implementation languages and platforms. The UML is intended to be usable for systems implemented in various implementation languages and platforms, including programming languages, databases, 4GLs, organization documents, firmware, and so on. The front-end work should be identical or similar in all cases, while the back-end work will differ somewhat for each medium.

Across development processes. The UML is a modeling language, not a description of a detailed development process. It is intended to be usable as the modeling language underlying most existing or new development processes, just as a general-purpose programming language can be used in many styles of programming. It is particularly intended to support the iterative, incremental style of development that we recommend.

Across internal concepts. In constructing the UML metamodel, we made a deliberate effort to discover and represent underlying relationships among various concepts, trying to capture modeling concepts in a broad way applicable to many known and unknown situations. This process led to a better understanding of the concepts and a more general applicability of them. This was not the original purpose of the unification work, but it was one of the most important results.

Goals of UML

There were a number of goals behind the development of UML. First and most important, UML is a general-purpose modeling language that all modelers can use. It is nonproprietary and based on common agreement by much of the computing community. It is meant to include the concepts of the leading methods so that it can be used as their modeling language. At the very least, it was intended to supersede the models of OMT, Booch, and Objectory, as well as those of other participants of the proposal. It was intended to be as familiar as possible; whenever possible, we used notation from OMT, Booch, Objectory, and other leading methods. It is meant to support good practices for design, such as encapsulation, separation of concerns, and capture of the intent of a model construct. It is intended to address current software development issues, such as large scale, distribution, concurrency, patterns, and team development.

UML is not intended to be a complete development method. It does not include a step-by-step development process. We believe that a good development process is crucial to the success of a software development effort, and we propose one in a companion book [Jacobson-99]. It is important to realize that UML and a process for using UML are two separate things. UML is intended to support all, or at least most, of the existing development processes. UML includes the concepts that we believe are necessary to support a modern iterative process based on building a strong architecture to solve user-case–driven requirements.

A final goal of UML was to be as simple as possible while still being capable of modeling the full range of practical systems that need to be built. UML needs to be expressive enough to handle all the concepts that arise in a modern system, such as concurrency and distribution, as well as software engineering mechanisms, such as encapsulation and components. It must be a universal language, like any general-purpose programming language. Unfortunately, that means that it cannot be small if we want it to handle things other than toy systems. Modern languages and modern operating systems are more complicated than those of 50 years ago because we expect much more of them. UML has several kinds of models; it is not something you can master in one day. It is more complicated than some of its antecedents because it is intended to be more comprehensive. But you don't have to learn it all at once, any more than you would a programming language, an operating system, or a complex user application, not to mention a natural language or skill.

Complexity of UML

UML is a large and varied modeling language intended for use on many different levels and at many stages of the development lifecycle. It has been criticized for being large and complex, but complexity is inherent in any universal application that is intended for realistic use on real-world problems, such as operating systems, programming languages, multimedia editing applications, spreadsheet editors, and desktop publishing systems. Such applications can be kept small only at the cost of making them toys, and the developers of UML did not wish it to be a toy.

The complexity of UML must be understood in light of its history:

- UML is a product of consensus of persons with varied goals and interests. It shares the qualities of the product of a democratic process. It is not as clean or coherent as the product of a single will. It contains superfluous features (but different persons might disagree about exactly what is superfluous). It contains overlapping features that are not always well integrated. Most of all, it lacks a consistent viewpoint. Unlike a programming language, which has a fairly narrow usage, it is intended for all kinds of things, from business modeling to graphical programming. Wide breadth of applicability usually comes at the expense of specificity.

- It was originally the merger of four or five leading modeling approaches, and later has been the target for accommodating a number of existing notations, such as SDL (Specification and Description Language, [ITU-T Z.100]), various business modeling languages (which themselves had no single standard), action languages, state machine notations, and so on. The desire to preserve previous notation often creates inconsistencies across features and includes redundant notation intended to cater to the familiarities of certain usage groups.

- The official specification documents have been written by teams of uneven ability. There is a wide variation in style, completeness, precision, and consistency among various sections of the documents.

- UML is not a precise specification in the manner of a formal language. Although the computer science community holds formality to be a virtue, few mainstream programming languages are precisely defined, and formal languages are often inaccessible even to experts. It should also be noted that modeling is not the same as coding. In the construction industry, blueprints are written in an informal style using many conventions that depend on the common sense of the craftsperson, but buildings are built from them successfully.

- The semantics sections sometimes contain vague statements without adequate explanation and examples. Terms are introduced in metamodels and not well distinguished from other terms. There are too many fine distinctions that someone thought important but did not explain clearly.

- There is far too much use of generalization at the expense of essential distinctions. The myth that inheritance is always good has been a curse of object-orientation from its earliest days.

- There is a tension between concepts for conceptual modeling and programming language representation, with no consistent guidelines.

UML Assessment

- UML is messy, imprecise, complex, and sprawling. That is both a fault and a virtue. Anything intended for such widespread usage is going to be messy.

- You don't have to know or use every feature of UML any more than you need to know or use every feature of a large software application or programming language. There is a small set of central concepts that are widely used. Other features can be learned gradually and used when needed.

- UML can be and has been used in many different ways in real-world development projects.

- UML is more than a visual notation. UML models can be used to generate code and test cases. This requires an appropriate UML profile, use of tools matched to the target platform, and choices among various implementation trade-offs.

- It is unnecessary to listen too much to UML language lawyers. There is no single right way to use it. It is one of many tools that a good developer uses. It doesn't have to be used for everything. You can modify it to suit your own needs provided you have the cooperation of your colleagues and software tools.

UML Concept Areas

UML concepts and models can be grouped into the following concept areas.

Static structure. Any precise model must first define the universe of discourse, that is, the key concepts from the application, their internal properties, and their relationships to each other. This group of constructs is the static view. Application concepts are modeled as classes, each of which describes discrete objects that hold information and communicate to implement behavior. The information they hold is modeled as attributes; the behavior they perform is modeled as operations. Several classes can share their common structure using generalization. A child class adds incremental structure and behavior to the structure and behavior that it obtains by inheritance from the common parent class. Objects also have run-time connections to other individual objects. Such object-to-object relationships are modeled as associations among classes. Some relationships among elements are grouped together as dependency relationships, including relationships among levels of abstraction, binding of template parameters, granting of permission, and usage of one element by another. Classes may have interfaces, which describe their externally-visible behavior. Other relationships are include and extend dependencies of use cases. The static view is notated using class diagrams and its variants. The static view can be used to generate most data structure declarations in a program. There are several other kinds of elements in UML diagrams, such as interfaces, data types, use cases, and signals. Collectively, these are called classifiers, and they behave much like classes with certain additions and restrictions on each kind of classifier.

Design constructs. UML models are meant for both logical analysis and designs intended for implementation. Certain constructs represent design items. A structured classifier expands a class into its implementation as a collection of parts held together by connectors. A class can encapsulate its internal structure behind externally visible ports. A collaboration models a collection of objects that play roles within a transient context. A component is a replaceable part of a system that conforms to and provides the realization of a set of interfaces. It is intended to be easily substitutable for other components that meet the same specification.

Deployment constructs. A node is a run-time computing resource that defines a location. An artifact is a physical unit of information or behavior description in a computing system. Artifacts are deployed on nodes. An artifact can be a manifestation, that is, an implementation, of a component. The deployment view describes the configuration of nodes in a running system and the arrangement of artifacts on them, including manifestation relationships to components.

Dynamic behavior. There are three ways to model behavior. One is the life history of one object as it interacts with the rest of the world; another is the communication patterns of a set of connected objects as they interact to implement behavior; the third is the evolution of the execution process as it passes through various activities.

The view of an object in isolation is a state machine—a view of an object as it responds to events based on its current state, performs actions as part of its response, and transitions to a new state. State machines are displayed in state machine diagrams.

An interaction overlays a structured classifier or collaboration with the flow of messages between parts. Interactions are shown in sequence diagrams and communication diagrams. Sequence diagrams emphasize time sequences, whereas communication diagrams emphasize object relationships.

An activity represents the execution of a computation. It is modeled as a set of activity nodes connected by control flows and data flows. Activities can model both sequential and concurrent behavior. They include traditional flow-of-control constructs, such as decisions and loops. Activity diagrams may be used to show computations as well as workflows in human organizations.

Guiding all the behavior views is a set of use cases, each a description of a slice of system functionality as visible to an actor, an external user of the system. The use case view includes both the static structure of the use cases and their actors as well as the dynamic sequences of messages among actors and system, usually expressed as sequence diagrams or just text.

Model organization. Computers can deal with large flat models, but humans cannot. In a large system, the modeling information must be divided into coherent pieces so that teams can work on different parts concurrently. Even on a smaller system, human understanding requires the organization of model content into packages of modest size. Packages are general-purpose hierarchical organizational units of UML models. They can be used for storage, access control, configuration management, and constructing libraries that contain reusable model fragments. A dependency between packages summarizes the dependencies among the package contents. A dependency among packages can be imposed by the overall system architecture. Then the contents of the packages must conform to the package dependencies and to the imposed system architecture.

Profiles. No matter how complete the facilities in a language, people will want to make extensions. UML contains a limited extensibility capability that should accommodate most of the day-to-day needs for extensions, without requiring a change to the basic language. A stereotype is a new kind of model element with the same structure as an existing element, but with additional constraints, a different interpretation and icon, and different treatment by code generators and other back-end tools. A stereotype defines a set of tagged values. A tagged value is a user-defined attribute that applies to model elements themselves, rather than objects in the run-time system. For example, tagged values may indicate project management information, code generator guidance, and domain-specific information. A constraint is a well-formedness condition expressed as a text string in some constraint language, such as a programming language, special constraint language, or natural language. UML includes a constraint language called OCL. A profile is a set of stereotypes and constraints for a particular purpose that can be applied to user packages. Profiles can be developed for particular purposes and stored in libraries for use in user models. As with any extensibility mechanism, these mechanisms must be used with care because of the risk of producing a private dialect unintelligible to others. But they can avoid the need for more radical changes.

2
The Nature and Purpose of Models

This chapter explains what models are, what they are good for, and how they are used. It also explains the various grades of models: ideal, partial, and tool-based.

What Is a Model?

A model is a representation in a certain medium of something in the same or another medium. The model captures the important aspects of the thing being modeled from a certain point of view and simplifies or omits the rest. Engineering, architecture, and many other creative fields use models.

A model is expressed in a medium that is convenient for working. Models of buildings may be drawings on paper, 3-D figures made of cardboard and papier-mâché, or finite-element equations in a computer. A construction model of a building shows the appearance of the building but can also be used to make engineering and cost calculations.

A model of a software system is made in a modeling language, such as UML. The model has both semantics and notation and can take various forms that include both pictures and text. The model is intended to be easier to use for certain purposes than the final system.

What Are Models For?

Models are used for several purposes.

To capture and precisely state requirements and domain knowledge so that all stakeholders may understand and agree on them. Various models of a building capture requirements about the appearance, traffic patterns, various kinds of utility services, strength against wind and earthquakes, cost, and many other things. Stakeholders include the architect, structural engineer, general contractor, various subcontractors, owner, renters, and the city.

Different models of a software system may capture requirements about its application domain, the ways users will use it, its breakdown into modules, common patterns used in its construction, and other things. Stakeholders include the architect, analysts, programmers, project manager, customers, funders, end users, and operators. Various kinds of UML models are used.

To think about the design of a system. An architect uses models on paper, on a computer, or as 3-D constructs to visualize and experiment with possible designs. The simplicity of creating and modifying small models permits creative thought and innovation at little cost.

A model of a software system helps developers explore several architectures and design solutions easily before writing code. A good modeling language allows the designer to get the overall architecture right before detailed design begins.

To capture design decisions in a mutable form separate from the requirements. One model of a building shows the external appearance agreed to with the customer. Another model shows the internal routing of wires, pipes, and ventilation ducts. There are many ways to implement these services. The final model shows a design that the architect believes is a good one. The customer may verify this information, but often customers are not concerned about the details, as long as they work.

One model of a software system can capture the external behavior of a system and the real-world domain information represented by the system. Another model shows the internal classes and operations that implement the external behavior. There are many ways to implement the behavior; the final design model shows one approach that the designer believes is a good one.

To generate usable work products. A model of a building can be used to generate various kinds of products. These include a bill of materials, a simulated animated walkthrough, a table of deflections at various wind speeds, and a visualization of strain at various points in the frame.

A model of a software system can be used to generate class declarations, procedure bodies, user interfaces, databases, scenarios of legal use, configuration scripts, and lists of race conditions.

To organize, find, filter, retrieve, examine, and edit information about large systems. A model of a building organizes information by service: structural, electrical, plumbing, ventilation, decoration, and so on. Unless the model is on a computer, however, finding things and modifying them are not so easy. If it is on a computer, changes can be made and recalled easily, and multiple designs can be easily explored while sharing some common elements.

A model of a software system organizes information into several views: static structure, state machines, interactions, requirements, and so on. Each view is a projection of the information in the complete model as selected for a purpose.

Keeping a model of any size accurate is impossible without having an editing tool that manages the model. An interactive graphical model editor can present information in different formats, hide information that is unnecessary for a given purpose and show it again later, group related operations together, make changes to individual elements, as well as change groups of elements with one command, and so on.

To explore multiple solutions economically. The advantages and risks of different design methods for buildings may not be clear at first. For example, different substructures may interact in complicated ways that cannot be evaluated in an engineer's head. Models can explore the various designs and permit calculations of costs and risks before the actual building is constructed.

Models of a large software system permit several designs to be proposed and compared. The models are not constructed in full detail, of course, but even a rough model can expose many issues the final design must deal with. Modeling permits several designs to be considered, at a small cost of implementing any one design.

To master complex systems. An engineering model of a tornado approaching a building provides understanding that is not possible from a real-world building. A real tornado cannot be produced on demand, and it would destroy the measuring instruments, anyway. Many fast, small, or violent physical processes can now be understood using physical models.

A model of a large software system permits dealing with complexity that is too difficult to deal with directly. A model can abstract to a level that is comprehensible to humans, without getting lost in details. A computer can perform complicated analyses on a model in an effort to find possible trouble spots, such as timing errors and resource overruns. A model can determine the potential impact of a change before it is made, by exploring dependencies in the system. A model can also show how to restructure a system to reduce such effects.

Levels of Models

Models take on different forms for various purposes and appear at different levels of abstraction. The amount of detail in the model must be adapted to one of the following purposes.

Guides to the thought process. High-level models built early in a project serve to focus the thought process of the stakeholders and highlight options. They capture requirements and represent a starting point toward a system design. The early models help the originators explore possible options before converging on a system concept. As design progresses, the early models are replaced by more accurate models. There is no need to preserve every twist and turn of the early exploratory process. Its purpose is to produce ideas. The final "thinking models" should be preserved even after the focus shifts to design issues, however. Early models do not require the detail or precision of an implementation model, and they do not require a full range of implementation concepts. Such models use a subset of UML constructs, a more limited subset than later design models.

When an early model is a complete view of a system at a given precision—for example, an analysis model of what must be done—then it should be preserved when development shifts to the next stage. There is an important difference between adding detail (in which case, the chain of reasoning should be preserved) and the normal random-walk process of exploring many dead ends before arriving at the right solution. In the latter case, it is usually overwhelming and unnecessary to save the entire history except in extraordinary situations in which complete traceability is required.

Abstract specifications of the essential structure of a system. Models in the analysis or preliminary design stages focus on the key concepts and mechanisms of the eventual system. They correspond in certain ways with the final system. But details are missing from the model, which must be added explicitly during the design process. The purpose of the abstract models is to get the high-level pervasive issues correct before tackling the more localized details. These models are intended to be evolved into the final models by a careful process that guarantees that the final system correctly implements the intent of the earlier models. There must be traceability from these essential models to the full models; otherwise, there is no assurance that the final system correctly incorporates the key properties that the essential model sought to show. Essential models focus on semantic intent. They do not need the full range of implementation options. Indeed, low-level performance distinctions often obscure the logical semantics. The path from an essential model to a complete implementation model must be clear and straightforward, however, whether it is generated automatically by a code generator or evolved manually by a designer.

Full specifications of a final system. An implementation model includes enough information to build the system. It must include not only the logical semantics of the system and the algorithms, data structures, and mechanisms that ensure proper performance, but also organizational decisions about the system artifacts that are necessary for cooperative work by humans and processing by tools. This kind of model must include constructs for packaging the model for human understanding and for computer convenience. These are not properties of the target application itself. Rather, they are properties of the construction process.

Exemplars of typical or possible systems. Well-chosen examples can give insight to humans and can validate system specifications and implementations. Even a large collection of examples, however, necessarily falls short of a definitive description.

Ultimately, we need models that specify the general case; that is what a program is, after all. Examples of typical data structures, interaction sequences, or object histories can help a human trying to understand a complicated situation, however. Examples must be used with some care. It is logically impossible to induce the general case from a set of examples, but well-chosen prototypes are the way most people think. An example model includes instances rather than general descriptors. It therefore tends to have a different feel than a generic descriptive model. Example models usually use only a subset of the UML constructs, those that deal with instances. Both descriptive models and exemplar models are useful in modeling a system.

Complete or partial descriptions of systems. A model can be a complete description of a single system with no outside references. More often, it is organized as a set of distinct, discrete units, each of which may be stored and manipulated separately as a part of the entire description. Such models have "loose ends" that must be bound to other models in a complete system. Because the pieces have coherence and meaning, they can be combined with other pieces in various ways to produce many different systems. Achieving reuse is an important goal of good modeling.

Models evolve over time. Models with greater degrees of detail are derived from more abstract models, and more concrete models are derived from more logical models. For example, a model might start as a high-level view of the entire system, with a few key services in brief detail and no embellishments. Over time, much more detail is added and variations are introduced. Also over time, the focus shifts from a front-end, user-centered logical view to a back-end, implementation-centered physical view. As the developers work with a system and understand it better, the model must be iterated at all levels to capture that understanding; it is impossible to understand a large system in a single, linear pass. There is no one "right" form for a model.

What Is in a Model?

Semantics and presentation. Models have two major aspects: semantic information (semantics) and visual presentation (notation).

The semantic aspect captures the meaning of an application as a network of logical constructs, such as classes, associations, states, use cases, and messages. Semantic model elements carry the meaning of the model—that is, they convey the semantics. The semantic modeling elements are used for code generation, validity checking, complexity metrics, and so on. The visual appearance is irrelevant to most tools that process models. The semantic information is often called *the model*. A semantic model has a syntactic structure, well-formedness rules, and execution dynamics. These aspects are often described separately (as in the UML definition documents), but they are tightly interrelated parts of a single coherent model.

The visual presentation shows semantic information in a form that can be seen, browsed, and edited by humans. Presentation elements carry the visual presentation of the model—that is, they show it in a form directly apprehensible by humans. They do not add meaning, but they do organize the presentation to emphasize the arrangement of the model in a usable way. They therefore guide human understanding of a model. Presentation elements derive their semantics from semantic model elements. But inasmuch as the layout of the diagrams is supplied by humans, presentation elements are not completely derivable from logical elements. The arrangement of presentation elements may convey connotations about semantic relationships that are too weak or ambiguous to formalize in the semantic model but are nevertheless suggestive to humans.

Context. Models are themselves artifacts in a computer system, and they are used within a larger context that gives them their full meaning. This context includes the internal organization of the model, annotations about the use of each model in the overall development process, a set of defaults and assumptions for element creation and manipulation, and a relationship to the environment in which they are used.

Models require an internal organization that permits simultaneous use by multiple work groups without undue interference. This decomposition is not needed for semantic reasons—a large monolithic model would be as precise as a set of models organized into coherent packages, maybe even more precise because the organizational boundaries complicate the job of defining precise semantics. But teams of workers could not work effectively on a large monolithic model without constantly getting in each other's way. Moreover, a monolithic model has no pieces that can be reused in other situations. Finally, changes to a large model have consequences that are difficult to determine. Changes to a small, isolated piece of a large model can be tractable if the model is properly structured into subsystems with well-defined interfaces. In any case, dividing large systems into a hierarchy of well-chosen pieces is the most reliable way to design large systems that humans have invented over thousands of years.

Models capture semantic information about an application system, but they also need to record many kinds of information about the development process itself, such as the author of a class, the debug status of a procedure, and who is permitted to edit a diagram. Such information is, at best, peripheral to the semantics of the system, but it is important to the development process. A model of a system therefore needs to include both viewpoints. This is most easily achieved by regarding the project management information as annotations to the semantic model—that is, arbitrary descriptions attached to model elements but whose meaning is outside the modeling language. In UML these annotations are implemented as text strings whose usage is defined by optional profiles.

The commands used to create and modify a model are not part of the semantics of the modeling language any more than the commands of a text editor or browser are part of the semantics of a programming language. Model element properties do not have *default* values; in a particular model, they simply have *values*. For practical development, however, humans need to build and modify models without having to specify everything in full detail. Default values exist in the boundary between the modeling language and the editing tool that supports it. They are really defaults on the tool commands that create a model, although they may transcend an individual tool and become user expectations about the implementation of the language by tools in general.

Models are not built and used in isolation. They are part of a larger environment that includes modeling tools, languages and compilers, operating systems, networks of computers, implementation constraints, and so on. The information about a system includes information about all parts of the environment. Some of it will be stored in a model even though it is not semantic information. Examples include project management annotations (discussed above), code generation hints and directives, model packaging, and default command settings for an editor tool. Other information may be stored separately. Examples include program source code and operating system configuration commands. Even if some information is part of a model, the responsibility for interpreting it may lie in various places, including the modeling language, the modeling tool, the code generator, the compiler, a command language, and so on. This book describes the interpretation of models that is defined in the UML specification, and which therefore applies to all uses of UML. But when operating in a physical development environment, other sources may add additional interpretations beyond that given in the UML specification.

What Does a Model Mean?

A model is a *generator* of potential configurations of systems; the possible systems are its *extent*, or values. Ideally, all configurations consistent with the model should be possible. Sometimes, however, it is not possible to represent all constraints within a model. A model is also a description of the generic structure and meaning of a system. The descriptions are its *intent*, or meaning. A model is always an abstraction at some level. It captures the *essential* aspects of a system and ignores some of the details. The following aspects must be considered for models.

Abstraction versus detail. A model captures the essential aspects of a system and ignores others. Which ones are essential is a matter of judgment that depends on the purpose of the model. This is not a dichotomy; there may be a spectrum of models of increasing precision. A modeling language is not a programming language. A modeling language may permit models to be specified at various levels of detail. An early model or a high-level model may not require full detail, because additional detail may be irrelevant for the purpose at hand. Models at different levels of precision can be used across the life of a project. A model intended for code generation requires at least some programming language issues to be addressed. Typically, models have low precision during early analysis. They gain detail as the development cycle progresses, so the final models have considerable detail and precision.

Specification versus implementation. A model can tell *what* something does (*specification*) as well as *how* the function is accomplished (*implementation*). These aspects should be separated in modeling. It is important to get the *what* correct before investing much time in the *how*. Abstracting away from implementation is an important facet of modeling. There may be a chain of several specification-implementation relationships, in which each implementation defines the specifications for the next layer.

Description versus instance. Models are descriptions. The things they describe are instances, which usually appear in models only as examples. Most instances exist only as part of the run-time execution. Sometimes, however, run-time instances are themselves descriptions of other things. We call these hybrid objects *metadata*. Looked at more deeply, it is unrealistic to insist that everything is either an instance or a description. Something is an instance or a description not in isolation but only in relation to something else, and most things can be approached from multiple viewpoints.

Variations in interpretation. There are many possible interpretations of models in a modeling language. One can define certain *semantic variation points*—places at which different interpretations are possible—and assign each interpretation a name as a *semantic variation* so that one can state which variation is being used. For example, the Self language has a different mechanism for finding methods than the Smalltalk language; a semantic variation point on the method resolution mechanism allows either programming language to be supported. Semantic variation points permit different execution models to be supported.

Part 2: UML Concepts ————

This part contains an overview of UML concepts to show how they fit together in modeling a system. This part is not meant to describe concepts in full detail. For full details about a UML concept, see the encyclopedia section of this book.

3

UML Walkthrough

This chapter presents a brief walkthrough of UML concepts and diagrams using a simple example. The purpose of the chapter is to organize the high-level UML concepts into a small set of views and diagrams that present the concepts visually. It shows how the various concepts are used to describe a system and how the views fit together. This summary is not intended to be comprehensive; many concepts are omitted. For more details, see the subsequent chapters that outline the UML semantic views, as well as the detailed reference material in the encyclopedia chapter.

The example used here is a theater box office that has computerized its operations. This is a contrived example, the purpose of which is to highlight various UML constructs in a brief space. It is deliberately simplified and is not presented in full detail. Presentation of a full model from an implemented system would neither fit in a small space nor highlight a sufficient range of constructs without excessive repetition.

UML Views

There is no sharp line between the various concepts and constructs in UML, but, for convenience, we divide them into several views. A view is simply a subset of UML modeling constructs that represents one aspect of a system. The division into different views is somewhat arbitrary, but we hope it is intuitive. One or two kinds of diagrams provide a visual notation for the concepts in each view. The views used in this book are not part of the UML specification, but we use them as an aid to organizing and presenting the UML concepts.

At the top level, views can be divided into these areas: structural classification, dynamic behavior, physical layout, and model management.

Table 3-1 shows the UML views and the diagrams that display them, as well as the main concepts relevant to each view. This table should not be taken as a rigid set of rules but merely as a guide to normal usage, as mixing of views is permitted.

Structural classification describes the things in the system and their relationships to other things. The classifier concept models things in a system. Classifiers include class, use case, actor, node, collaboration, and component.

Classifiers provide the basis on top of which dynamic behavior is built. Structural views include the static view, design view, and use case view.

Dynamic behavior describes the behavior of a system or other classifier over time. Behavior can be described as a series of changes to snapshots of the system drawn from the static view. Dynamic behavior views include the state machine view, activity view, and interaction view.

Physical layout describes the computational resources in the system and the deployment of artifacts on them. This includes the deployment view.

Model management describes the organization of the models themselves into hierarchical units. The package is the generic organizational unit for models. A model is a package hierarchy that provides a semantically complete abstraction of a system from a particular viewpoint. The model management view crosses the other views and organizes them for development work and configuration control.

Table 3-1: *UML Views and Diagrams*

Major Area	View	Diagram	Main Concepts
structural	static view	class diagram	association, class, dependency, generalization, interface, realization
	design view	internal structure	connector, interface, part, port, provided interface, role, required interface
		collaboration diagram	connector, collaboration, collaboration use, role
		component diagram	component, dependency, port, provided interface, realization, required interface, subsystem
	use case view	use case diagram	actor, association, extend, include, use case, use case generalization

Table 3-1: *UML Views and Diagrams (continued)*

Major Area	View	Diagram	Main Concepts
dynamic	state machine view	state machine diagram	completion transition, do activity, effect, event, region, state, transition, trigger
	activity view	activity diagram	action, activity, control flow, control node, data flow, exception, expansion region, fork, join, object node, pin
	interaction view	sequence diagram	occurrence specification, execution specification, interaction, interaction fragment, interaction operand, lifeline, message, signal
		communication diagram	collaboration, guard condition, message, role, sequence number
physical	deployment view	deployment diagram	artifact, dependency, manifestation, node
model management	model management view	package diagram	import, model, package
	profile	package diagram	constraint, profile, stereotype, tagged value

Extensions to UML are organized into profiles. UML profiles declare several constructs intended to provide a limited but useful extensibility capability. These constructs include constraints, stereotypes, and tag definitions. Profiles are declared on class diagrams and applied on package diagrams. Stereotypes are usually applied on class diagrams, although they can appear in other places also. Profiles may also include libraries of domain-specific classes.

Static View

The static view models concepts in the application domain as well as internal concepts invented as part of the implementation of an application. This view is static because it does not describe the time-dependent behavior of the system, which is described in other views. The main constituents of the static view are classes and their relationships: association, generalization, and various kinds of dependency, such as realization and usage. A class is the description of a concept from the application domain or the application solution. Classes are the center around which the class view is organized; other elements are owned by or attached to classes. The static view is displayed in class diagrams, so called because their main focus is the description of classes.

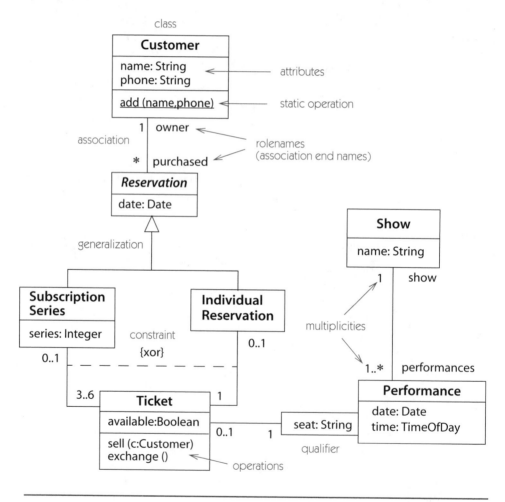

Figure 3-1. *Class diagram*

Classes are drawn as rectangles. Lists of attributes and operations are shown in separate compartments. The compartments can be suppressed when full detail is not needed. A class may appear on several diagrams. The attributes and operations are often shown on one diagram (the "home" diagram) and suppressed on other diagrams.

Relationships among classes are drawn as paths connecting class rectangles. The different kinds of relationships are distinguished by line texture and by adornments on the paths or their ends.

Figure 3-1 shows a class diagram from the box office application. This diagram contains part of a ticket-selling domain model. It shows several important classes, such as **Customer**, **Reservation**, **Ticket**, and **Performance**. Customers may have many reservations, but each reservation is made by one customer. Reservations are of two kinds: subscription series and individual reservations. Both reserve tickets: in one case, only one ticket; in the other case, several tickets. Every ticket is part of a subscription series or an individual reservation, but not both. Every performance has many tickets available, each with a unique seat number. A performance can be identified by a show, date, and time.

Classes can be described at various levels of precision and concreteness. In the early stages of design, the model captures the more logical aspects of the problem. In the later stages, the model also captures design decisions and implementation details. Most of the views have a similar evolutionary quality.

Design Views

The previous views model the concepts in the application from a logical viewpoint. The design views model the design structure of the application itself, such as its expansion into structured classifiers, the collaborations that provide functionality, and its assembly from components with well-defined interfaces. These views provide an opportunity to map classes onto implementation components and expand high-level classes into supporting structure. Implementation diagrams include the internal structure diagram, the collaboration diagram, and the component diagram.

Internal structure diagram

Once the design process begins, classes must be decomposed into collections of connected parts that may be further decomposed in turn. A structured classifier models the parts of a class and their contextual connectors. A structured class can be encapsulated by forcing communications from outside to pass through ports obeying declared interfaces.

An internal structure diagram shows the decomposition of a class. Figure 3-2 shows a internal structure diagram for the box office in the ticketing system. This class is decomposed into three parts: a ticket seller interface, a performance guide that retrieves performances according to date and other criteria, and a set of databases that contain the data on the performances and the tickets. Each part interacts through a well-defined interface specified by its ports. The entire box office interacts with the outside through a port. Messages on this port are dispatched to the ticket seller class, but the internal structure of the box office class is hidden from outside clients.

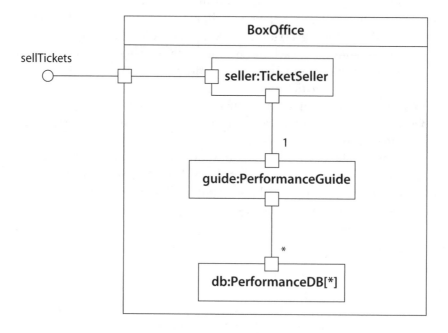

Figure 3-2. *Internal structure diagram*

Collaboration diagram

A collaboration is a contextual relationship among a set of objects that work together to fulfill some purpose. It contains a collection of roles—contextual slots within a generic pattern that can be played by, or bound to, individual objects. There may be connectors providing contextual relationships among the roles.

Figure 3-3 shows a collaboration diagram for the theater sales system. Three kinds of separate components interact to provide the functionality of the system: kiosks, sales terminals, and the box office application. These distinct components are not owned by a single overall class, but they cooperate in well-defined ways to provide services to the users.

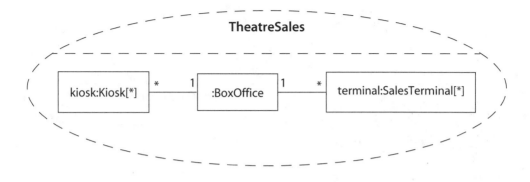

Figure 3-3. *Collaboration diagram*

Component diagram

A component is a kind of structured classifier, so its internal structure may be defined on an internal structure diagram. Figure 3-4 shows the internal structure of the theater sales system. The theater sales system is defined as a component whose internal structure contains uses of other components. There are three user interfaces: one each for customers using a kiosk, clerks using the on-line reservation system, and supervisors making queries about ticket sales. There is a ticket seller component that sequentializes requests from both kiosks and clerks, a component that processes credit card charges, and the repository containing the ticket information. The component definition diagram provides the structure of a kind of component; a particular configuration of the application may use more than one copy of a component.

A small circle attached to a component or a class is a provided interface—a coherent set of services made available by a component or class. A small semicircle attached to a component or a class is a required interface—a statement that the component or class needs to obtain services from an element that provides them. For example, subscription sales and group sales are both provided by the ticket seller component; subscription sales are accessible from both kiosks and clerks, but group sales are only accessible from a clerk. Nesting a provided interface and a required interface indicates that one component will call on the other to obtain the needed services. Note that interfaces may be used on all classifiers, not just components.

A component diagram shows the components in a system—that is, the software units from which the application is constructed—as well as the dependencies among components so that the impact of a proposed change can be assessed. Figure 3-5 shows a component diagram for the components used in the credit card

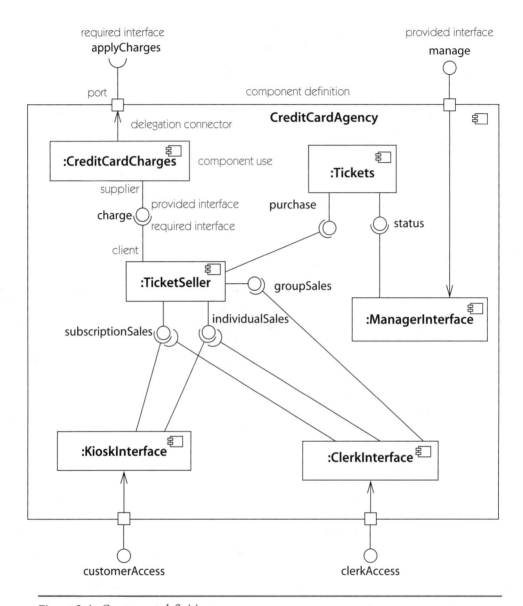

Figure 3-4. *Component definition*

agency component. The dashed dependency lines show compatible provided and required interfaces, but when the interfaces have the same names the dependency lines are redundant. In this example, the component diagram adds little to the internal structure diagram. In a larger example, the component diagram would combine components used in many different places.

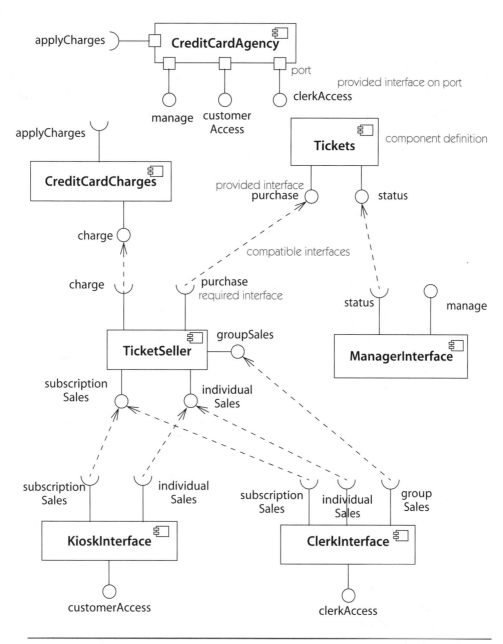

Figure 3-5. *Component diagram*

Use Case View

The use case view models the functionality of a subject (such as a system) as perceived by outside agents, called actors, that interact with the subject from a particular viewpoint. A use case is a unit of functionality expressed as a transaction among actors and the subject. The purpose of the use case view is to list the actors and use cases and show which actors participate in each use case. The behavior of use cases is expressed using dynamic views, particularly the interaction view.

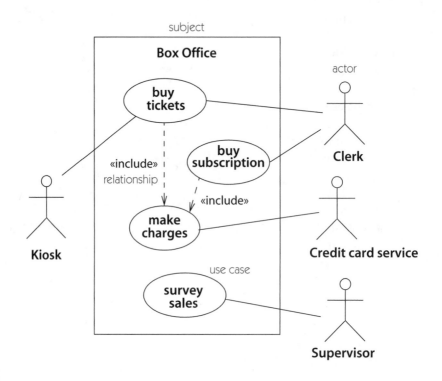

Figure 3-6. *Use case diagram*

Figure 3-6 shows a use case diagram for the box office example. Actors include the clerk, supervisor, and kiosk. The kiosk is a separate system that accepts orders from a customer. The box office class is the subject of the use cases, that is, the class whose behavior they describe. The customer is not an actor in the box office application because the customer is not directly connected to the application. Use cases include buying tickets through the kiosk or the clerk, buying subscriptions (only through the clerk), and surveying total sales (at the request of the supervisor). Buying tickets and buying subscriptions include a common fragment—that is, making charges to the credit card service. (A complete description of a box office system would involve a number of other use cases, such as exchanging tickets and checking availability.)

Use cases can also be described at various levels of detail. They can be factored and described in terms of other, simpler use cases. A use case is implemented as a collaboration in the interaction view.

State Machine View

A state machine models the possible life histories of an object of a class. A state machine contains states connected by transitions. Each state models a period of time during the life of an object during which it satisfies certain conditions. When an event occurs, it may cause the firing of a transition that takes the object to a new state. When a transition fires, an effect (action or activity) attached to the transition may be executed. State machines are shown as state machine diagrams.

Figure 3-7 shows a state machine diagram for the history of a ticket to a performance. The initial state of a ticket (shown by the black dot) is the **Available** state. Before the season starts, seats for season subscribers are assigned. Individual tickets purchased interactively are first locked while the customer makes a selection. After that, they are either sold or unlocked if they are rejected. If the customer takes too long to make a selection, the transaction times out and the seat is unlocked. Seats sold to season subscribers may be exchanged for other performances, in which case they become available again.

State machines may be used to describe user interfaces, device controllers, and other reactive subsystems. They may also be used to describe passive objects that go through several qualitatively distinct phases during their lifetime, each of which has its own special behavior.

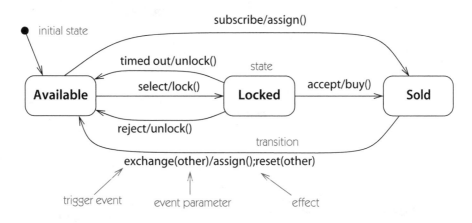

Figure 3-7. *State machine diagram*

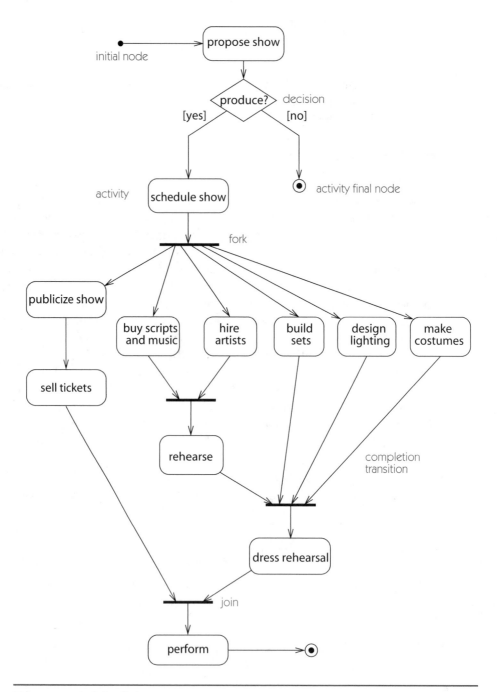

Figure 3-8. *Activity diagram*

Activity View

An activity shows the flow of control among the computational activities involved in performing a calculation or a workflow. An action is a primitive computational step. An activity node is a group of actions or subactivities. An activity describes both sequential and concurrent computation. Activities are shown on activity diagrams.

Figure 3-8 shows an activity diagram for the box office. This diagram shows the activities involved in mounting a show. (Don't take this example too seriously if you have theater experience!) Arrows show sequential dependencies. For example, shows must be picked before they are scheduled. Heavy bars show forks or joins of control. For example, after the show is scheduled, the theater can begin to publicize it, buy scripts, hire artists, build sets, design lighting, and make costumes, all concurrently. Before rehearsal can begin, however, the scripts must be ordered and the artists must be hired.

This example shows an activity diagram the purpose of which is to model the real-world workflows of a human organization. Such business modeling is a major purpose of activity diagrams, but activity diagrams can also be used for modeling software activities. An activity diagram is helpful in understanding the high-level execution behavior of a system, without getting involved in the internal details of message passing required by a collaboration diagram.

The input and output parameters of an activity can be shown using flow relationships connecting the action and object nodes.

Interaction View

The interaction view describes sequences of message exchanges among the parts of a system. An interaction is based on a structured classifier or a collaboration. A role is a slot that may be filled by objects in a particular use of an interaction. This view provides a holistic view of behavior in a system—that is, it shows the flow of control across many objects. The interaction view is displayed in two diagrams focused on different aspects: sequence diagrams (Figure 3-9) and communication diagrams (Figure 3-10).

Sequence diagram

A sequence diagram shows a set of messages arranged in time sequence. Each role is shown as a lifeline—that is, a vertical line that represents the role over time through the entire interaction. Messages are shown as arrows between lifelines. A sequence diagram can show a scenario—that is, an individual history of a transaction. Structured control constructs, such as loops, conditionals, and parallel execution, are shown as nested rectangles with keywords and one or more regions.

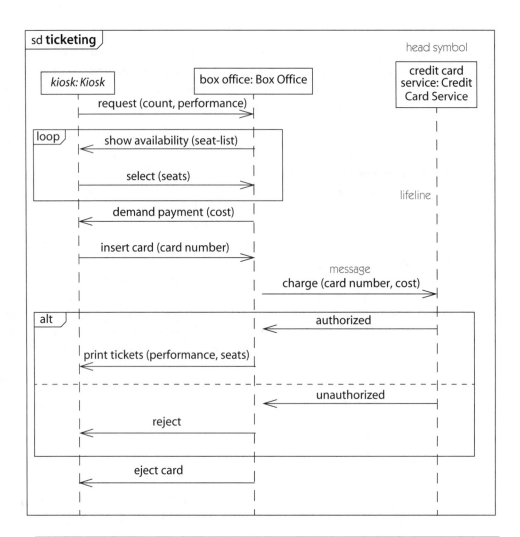

Figure 3-9. *Sequence diagram*

One use of a sequence diagram is to show the behavior sequence of a use case. When the behavior is implemented, each message on a sequence diagram corresponds to an operation on a class or an event trigger on a transition in a state machine.

Figure 3-9 shows a sequence diagram for the **buy tickets** use case. The context of the use case execution is a collaboration involving three roles: one each of types **Kiosk**, **Box Office**, and **Credit Card Service**. This use case is initiated by the customer at the kiosk communicating with the box office. The steps for the **make charges** use case are included within the sequence, which involves communication with both the kiosk and the credit card service. Both a successful and an unsuccessful scenario are shown as alternatives. This sequence diagram is at an early stage of development and does not show the full details of the user interface. For example, the exact form of the seat list and the mechanism of specifying seats must still be determined, but the essential communication of the interaction has been specified by the use case.

Communication diagram

A communication diagram shows roles in an interaction as a geometric arrangement (Figure 3-10). Each rectangle shows a role—more precisely, a lifeline representing the life of an object over time. The messages among objects playing roles are shown as arrows attached to connectors. The sequence of messages is indicated by sequence numbers prepended to message descriptions.

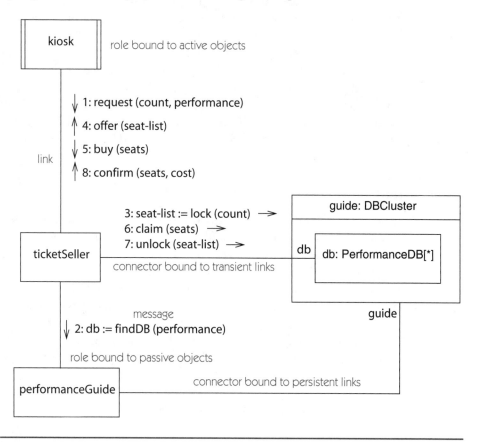

Figure 3-10. *Communication diagram*

One use of a communication diagram is to show the implementation of an operation. A collaboration shows the parameters and local variables of the operation as roles, as well as more permanent associations. When the behavior is implemented, the message sequencing on a communication diagram corresponds to the nested calling structure and signal passing of the program.

Figure 3-10 shows a communication diagram for part of the reserve tickets interaction at a later stage of development. It shows the interaction among internal objects in the application to reserve tickets. The request arrives from the kiosk and is used to find the database for the particular performance from the set of all performances. The pointer **db** that is returned to the **ticketSeller** object represents a local transient link to a performance database that is maintained during the interaction and then discarded. The ticket seller requests a number of seats to the performance; a selection of seats in various price ranges is found, temporarily locked, and returned to the kiosk for the customer's selection. When the customer makes a selection from the list of seats, the selected seats are claimed and the rest are unlocked.

Both sequence diagrams and communication diagrams show interactions, but they emphasize different aspects. A sequence diagram shows time sequence as a geometric dimension, but the relationships among roles are implicit. A communication diagram shows the relationships among roles geometrically and relates messages to the connectors, but time sequences are less clear because they are implied by the sequence numbers. Each diagram should be used when its main aspect is the focus of attention.

Deployment View

A deployment diagram represents the deployment of run-time artifacts on nodes. An artifact is a physical implementation unit, such as a file. A node is a run-time resource, such as a computer, device, or memory. An artifact may be a manifestation (implementation) of one or more components. This view permits the consequences of distribution and resource allocation to be assessed.

Figure 3-11 shows a descriptor-level deployment diagram for the box office system. This diagram shows the kinds of nodes in the system and the kinds of artifacts they hold. A node is shown as a cube symbol. An artifact is shown as a rectangle with a keyword. The manifestation relationship shows which artifacts implement which components.

An artifact type can be located on different kinds of nodes, and different artifact types can manifest the same kind of component.

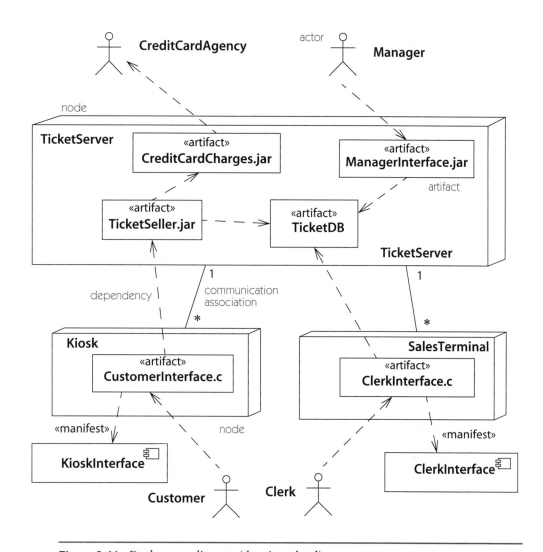

Figure 3-11. *Deployment diagram (descriptor level)*

Figure 3-12 shows an instance-level deployment diagram for the box office system. The diagram shows the individual nodes and their links in a particular configuration of the system. The information in this model is consistent with the descriptor-level information in Figure 3-11.

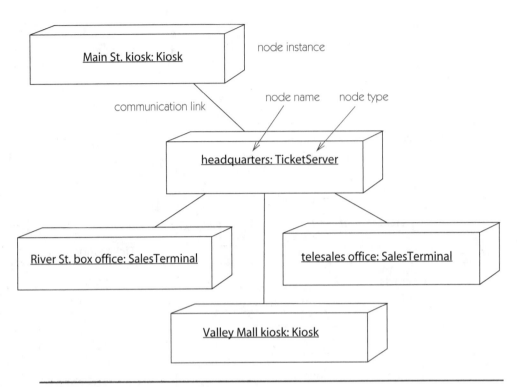

Figure 3-12. *Deployment diagram (instance level)*

Model Management View

The model management view models the organization of the model itself. A model comprises a set of packages that hold model elements, such as classes, state machines, and use cases. Packages may contain other packages: therefore, a model starts with a root package that indirectly contains all the contents of the model. Packages are units for manipulating the contents of a model, as well as units for access control and configuration control. Every model element is owned by one package or one other element.

A model is a complete description of a system at a given precision from one viewpoint. There may be several models of a system from various viewpoints—for example, an analysis model as well as a design model. A model may be shown as a special kind of package, but usually it is sufficient to show only the packages.

Model management information is usually shown on package diagrams, which are a variety of class diagram.

Figure 3-13 shows the breakdown of the entire theater system into packages and their dependency relationships. The box office package contains packages for the

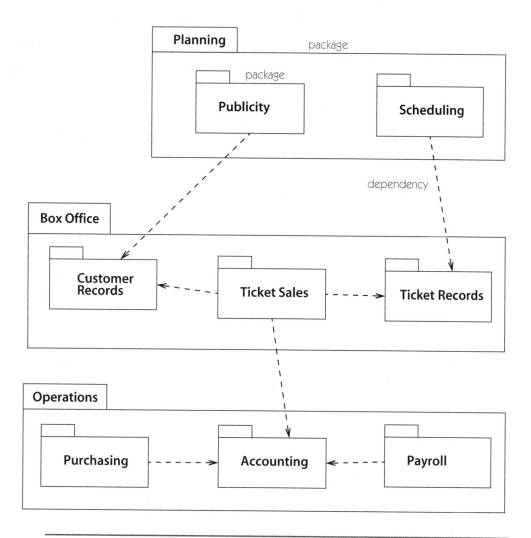

Figure 3-13. *Package diagram*

previous examples in this chapter; the full application also includes theater operations and planning subsystems. Each subsystem consists of several packages.

Profiles

UML is defined using a metamodel, that is, a model of the modeling language itself. The metamodel is complicated and dangerous to change. In addition, many tools will be built upon the standard metamodel, and they could not operate correctly with a different metamodel. The profile mechanism permits limited changes to UML without modifying the underlying metamodel. Profiles and constraints permit UML to be tailored to specific domains or platforms while maintaining interoperability across tools.

UML includes three main extensibility constructs: constraints, stereotypes, and tagged values. A constraint is a textual statement of a semantic relationship expressed in some formal language or in natural language. A stereotype is a new kind of model element devised by the modeler and based on an existing kind of model element. A tagged value is a named piece of information attached to any model element.

These constructs permit many kinds of extensions to UML without requiring changes to the basic UML metamodel itself. They may be used to create tailored versions of the UML for an application area. A coherent set of stereotypes with their tag definition and constraints is modeled as a profile.

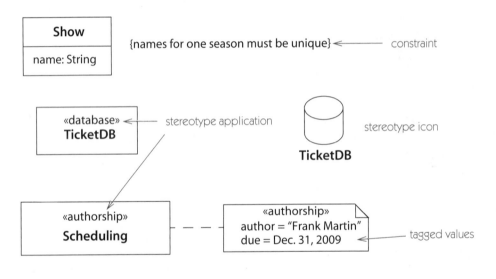

Figure 3-14. *Extensibility constructs*

Figure 3-14 shows examples of constraints, stereotypes, and tagged values. The constraint on class **Show** ensures that the names of shows are unique. Figure 3-1 shows an **xor** constraint on two associations; an object can have a link from one of them at a time. Constraints are useful for making statements that can be expressed in a text language but which are not directly supported by UML constructs.

The stereotype on component **TicketDB** indicates that the component is a database, which permits the interfaces supported by the component to be omitted as they are the interfaces supported by all databases. Modelers can add new stereotypes to represent special elements. A set of implied constraints, tagged values, or code generation properties can be attached to a stereotype. A modeler can define an icon for a given stereotype name as a visual aid, as shown in the diagram. The textual form may always be used, however.

The tagged values on package **Scheduling** show that Frank Martin is responsible for finishing it before the end of the decade. This project management information is defined in the **authorship** stereotype that has been applied to the **Scheduling** class. Tagged values are especially useful for project management information and for code generation parameters. Most tagged values would be stored as pop-up information within an editing tool and would not usually be displayed on printed pictures.

Stereotypes and their tags are defined in profiles. A profile is a package to group extensions intended to tailor the model toward a particular domain, technology, or implementation. Profiles will usually be predefined and stored in libraries. Profiles can be applied to packages to extend the elements in them.

4

Static View

Overview

The static view is the foundation of UML. The elements of the static view of a model are the concepts that are meaningful in an application, including real-world concepts, abstract concepts, implementation concepts, computer concepts—all kinds of concepts found in systems. For example, a ticket system for a theater has concepts such as tickets, reservations, subscription plans, seat assignment algorithms, interactive web pages for ordering, and archival data for redundancy.

The static view captures object structure. An object-oriented system unifies data structure and behavioral features into a single object structure. The static view includes all the traditional data structure concerns, as well as the organization of the operations on the data. Both data and operations are quantized into classes. In the object-oriented perspective, data and behavior are closely related. For example, a **Ticket** object carries data, such as its price, date of performance, and seat number, as well as operations on it, such as reserving itself or computing its price with a special discount.

The static view describes behavioral declarations, such as operations, as discrete modeling elements, but it does not contain the details of their dynamic behavior. It treats them as things to be named, owned by classes, and invoked. Their dynamic execution is described by other views that describe the internal details of their dynamics. These other views include the interaction view and the state machine view. Dynamic views require the static view to describe the things that interact dynamically—you can't say *how* something interacts without first saying *what* is interacting. The static view is the foundation on which the other views are built.

Key elements in the static view are classifiers and their relationships. A classifier is a modeling element that describes things containing values. There are several kinds of classifiers, including classes, interfaces, and data types. Behavioral things, such as use cases and signals, are also reified as classifiers. Implementation purposes are behind some classifiers, such as components, collaborations, and nodes.

Large models must be organized into smaller units for human understanding and reusability. A package is a general-purpose organizational unit for owning and managing the contents of a model. Every element is owned by some package. A model is a set of packages that describes a complete view of a system and can be used more or less independently of other models; it designates a root package that indirectly owns the packages describing the system.

An object is a discrete unit out from which the modeler understands and constructs a system. It is an instance of a class—that is, an individual with identity whose structure and behavior are described by the class. An object has an identifiable piece of state with well-defined behavior that can be invoked.

Relationships among classifiers are association, generalization, and various kinds of dependency, including realization and usage.

Classifier

A classifier models a discrete concept that describes things (objects) having identity, state, behavior, relationships, and an optional internal structure. Kinds of classifiers include class, interface, and data type. Other kinds of classifiers are reifications of behavioral concepts, things in the environment, or implementation structures. These classifiers include use case, actor, collaboration, component, and node, as well as various kinds of behavior. Table 4-1 lists the various kinds of classifiers and their functions. The metamodel term classifier includes all these concepts, but as class is the most familiar term, we will discuss it first and define the other concepts by difference from it.

Table 4-1: *Kinds of Classifiers*

Classifier	Function	Notation
actor	An outside user of a system	(actor figure)
artifact	A physical piece of system information	«artifact» Name
class	A concept from the modeled system	Name

Table 4-1: *Kinds of Classifiers (continued)*

Classifier	Function	Notation
collaboration	A contextual relationship among objects playing roles	(Name)
component	A modular part of a system with well-defined interfaces	Name
enumeration	A data type with predefined literal values	«enumeration» Name
primitive type	A descriptor of a set of primitive values that lack identity	Name
interface	A named set of operations that characterize behavior	«interface» Name
node	A computational resource	
role	An internal part in the context of a collaboration or structured classifier	role:Name
signal	An asynchronous communication among objects	«signal» Name
structured classifier	A classifier with internal structure	
use case	A specification of the behavior of an entity in its interaction with outside agents	

Class. A class represents a discrete concept within the application being modeled representing things of a particular kind—a physical thing (such as an airplane), a business thing (such as an order), a logical thing (such as a broadcasting schedule), an application thing (such as a cancel button), a computer thing (such as a hash table), or a behavioral thing (such as a task). A class is the descriptor for a set of objects with similar structure, behavior, and relationships. All attributes and operations are attached to classes or other classifiers. Classes are the foci around which object-oriented systems are organized.

An object is a discrete entity with identity, state, and invocable behavior. Objects are the individual pieces in a run-time system; classes are the individual concepts by which to understand and describe the multitude of individual objects.

A class defines a set of objects that have state and behavior. State is described by attributes and associations. Attributes are generally used for pure data values without identity, such as numbers and strings, and associations are used for connections among objects with identity. Individual pieces of invocable behavior are described by operations; a method is the implementation of an operation. The lifetime history of an object is described by a state machine attached to a class. The notation for a class is a rectangle with compartments for the name of the class, attributes, and operations, as shown in Figure 4-1.

A set of classes may use the generalization relationship and the inheritance mechanism built on it to share common pieces of state and behavior description. Generalization relates more specific classes (subclasses) to more general classes (superclasses) that contain properties common to several subclasses. A class may have zero or more parents (superclasses) and zero or more children (subclasses). A class inherits descriptions of state and behavior from its parents and other ancestors, and it defines state and behavior descriptions that its children and other descendants inherit.

A class has a unique name within its container, which is usually a package but is sometimes another class. The class has a visibility with respect to its container; the visibility specifies how it may be used by other classes outside the container.

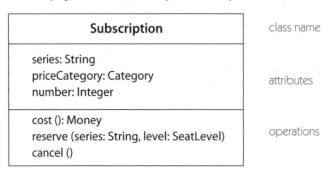

Figure 4-1. *Class notation*

Interface. An interface is the description of behavior of objects without giving their implementation or state. One or more classes or components may realize an interface, and each class implements the operations found in the interface.

Data types. A primitive type is the description of primitive values that lack identity (independent existence and the possibility of side effects). Primitive types include numbers and strings. Primitive types are passed by value and are immutable entities. A primitive type has no attributes but may have operations. Operations do not modify data values, but they may return data values as results.

User models may also declare enumeration types. An enumeration type declares a set of enumeration literals that may be used as values.

Levels of meaning. Classes can exist at several levels of meaning in a model, including the analysis, design, and implementation levels. When representing real-world concepts, it is important to capture the real-world state, relationships, and behavior. But implementation concepts, such as information hiding, efficiency, visibility, and methods, are not relevant real-world concepts. They *are* relevant design concepts. Many potential properties of a class are simply irrelevant at the analysis level. An analysis-level class represents a logical concept in the application domain or in the application itself. The analysis model should be a minimal representation of the system being modeled, sufficient to capture the essential logic of the system without getting into issues of performance or construction.

When representing a high-level design, concepts such as localization of state to particular classes, efficiency of navigating among objects, separation of external behavior and internal implementation, and specification of the precise operations are relevant to a class. A design-level class represents the decision to package state information and the operations on it into a discrete unit. It captures the key design decision, the localization of information and functionality to objects. Design-level classes contain both real-world content and computer system content.

Finally, when representing programming-language code, the form of a class closely matches the chosen programming language, and some abilities of a general class may be forgone if they have no direct implementation in the language. An implementation-level class maps directly into programming-language code.

The same system can be modeled from multiple viewpoints, such as a logical model capturing real-world information and a design model capturing internal representation decisions. An implementation-oriented class may realize a logical class in from another model. A logical class captures the attributes and relationships of the real-world information. An implementation class represents the declaration of a class as found in a particular programming language. It captures the exact form of a class, as needed by the language. In many cases, however, analysis, design, and implementation information can be nested into a single class.

Relationships

Relationships among classifiers are association, generalization, and various kinds of dependency, including realization and usage (see Table 4-2).

Table 4-2: *Kinds of Relationships*

Relationship	Function	Notation
association	A description of a connection among instances of classes	————
dependency	A relationship between two model elements	- - - -≫
generalization	A relationship between a more specific and a more general description, used for inheritance and polymorphic type declarations	———▷
realization	Relationship between a specification and its implementation	- - - -▷
usage	A situation in which one element requires another for its correct functioning	«kind» - - - -≫

The association relationship describes semantic connections among individual objects of given classes. Associations provide the connections with which objects of different classes can interact. The remaining relationships relate the descriptions of classifiers themselves, not their instances.

The generalization relationship relates general descriptions of parent classifiers (superclasses) to more specialized child classifiers (subclasses). Generalization facilitates the description of classifiers out of incremental declaration pieces, each of which adds to the description inherited from its ancestors. The inheritance mechanism constructs complete descriptions of classifiers from incremental descriptions using generalization relationships. Generalization and inheritance permit different classifiers to share the attributes, operations, and relationships that they have in common, without repetition.

The realization relationship relates a specification to an implementation. An interface is a specification of behavior without implementation; a class includes implementation structure. One or more classes may realize an interface, and each class implements the operations found in the interface.

The dependency relationship relates classes whose behavior or implementation affects other classes. There are several kinds of dependency in addition to realization, including trace dependency (a loose connection among elements in different models), refinement (a mapping between two levels of meaning), usage (a requirement for the presence of another element within a single model), and binding (the assignment of values to template parameters). Usage dependency is frequently used to represent implementation relationships, such as code-level relationships. Dependency is particularly useful when summarized on model organization units, such as packages, on which it shows the architectural structure of a system. Compilation constraints can be shown by dependencies, for example.

Association

An association describes discrete connections among objects or other instances in a system. An association relates an ordered list (tuple) of two or more classifiers, with repetitions permitted. The most common kind of association is a binary association between a pair of classifiers. An instance of an association is a link. A link comprises a tuple (an ordered list) of objects, each drawn from its corresponding class. A binary link comprises a pair of objects.

Associations carry information about relationships among objects in a system. As a system executes, links among objects are created and destroyed. Associations are the "glue" that ties a system together. Without associations, there are nothing but isolated classes that don't work together.

A single object may be associated with itself if the same class appears more than once in an association. If the same class appears twice in an association, the two instances do not have to be the same object, and usually they are not.

Each connection of an association to a class is called an association end. Most information about an association is attached to one of its ends. Association ends can have names (rolenames) and visibility. The most important property they have is multiplicity—how many instances of one class can be related to one instance of the other class. Multiplicity is most useful for binary associations because its definition for n-ary associations is complicated. If the multiplicity upper bound is greater than one, the ordering and uniqueness of associated values may be specified on an association end.

The notation for a binary association is a line or path connecting the participating classes. The association name is placed along the line with the rolename and multiplicity at each end, as shown in Figure 4-2.

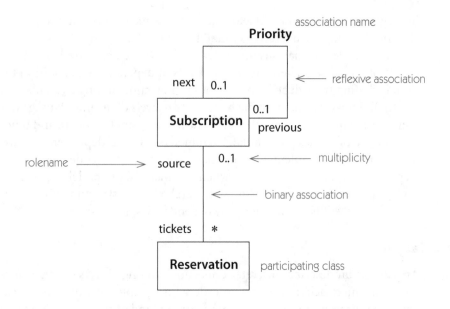

Figure 4-2. *Association notation*

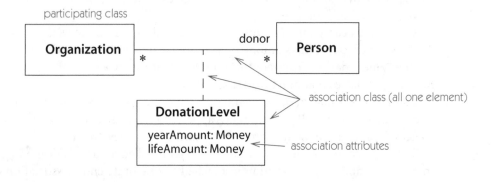

Figure 4-3. *Association class*

An association can also have attributes of its own, in which case it is both an association and a class—an association class (see Figure 4-3). If the value of an association attribute is unique within a set of related objects, then it is a qualifier, and the association is a qualified association (see Figure 4-4). A qualifier is a value that selects a unique object from the set of related objects across an association. Lookup tables and arrays may be modeled as qualified associations. Qualifiers are important for modeling names and identification codes. Qualifiers also model indexes in a design model.

Figure 4-4. *Qualified association*

During analysis, associations represent logical relationships among objects. There is no great need to impose direction or to be concerned about how to implement them. Redundant associations should be avoided because they add no logical information. During design, associations capture design decisions about data structure, as well as separation of responsibilities among classes. Directionality of associations is important, and redundant associations may be included for efficiency of object access, as well as to localize information in a particular class. Nevertheless, at this stage of modeling, associations should not be equated with C++ pointers. A navigable association at the design stage represents state information available to a class, but it can be mapped into programming-language code in various ways. The implementation can be a pointer, a container class embedded in a class, or even a completely separate table object. Other kinds of design properties include visibility and changeability of links. Figure 4-5 shows some design properties of associations.

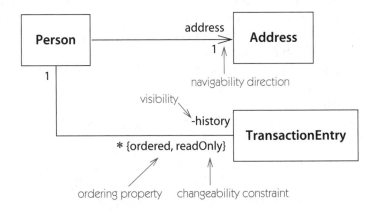

Figure 4-5. *Design properties of association*

Aggregation and composition. An aggregation is an association that represents a part-whole relationship. It is shown by a hollow-diamond adornment on the end of the path attached to the aggregate class. A composition is a stronger form of association in which the composite has sole responsibility for managing its parts, such as their allocation and deallocation. It is shown by a filled-diamond adornment on the composite end. An object may belong to at most one composition. There is a separate association between each class representing a part and the class representing the whole, but for convenience the paths attached to the whole may be joined together so that the entire set of associations is drawn as a tree. Figure 4-6 shows an aggregate and a composite.

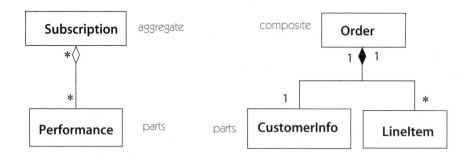

Figure 4-6. *Aggregation and composition*

Links. An instance of an association is a link. A link is an ordered list (tuple) of object references, each of which must be an instance of the corresponding class in the association or an instance of a descendant of the class. The links in a system constitute part of the system state. Links do not exist independently of objects; they take their identity from the objects they relate (in database terms, the list of objects is the *key* for the link). In the case of bags, there may be multiple links corresponding to a tuple of objects, however. Conceptually, an association is distinct from the classes that it relates. In practice, associations are often implemented using pointers in the participating classes, but they can be implemented as container objects separate from the classes they connect.

Bidirectionality. The different ends of an association are distinguishable, even if two of them involve the same class. This simply means that different objects of the same class can be related. Because the ends are distinguishable, an association is not symmetric (except in special cases); the ends cannot be interchanged. In ordinary discourse, this is only common sense; the subject and the object of a verb are not interchangeable. An association is sometimes said to be bidirectional. This means that the logical relationships work both ways. This statement is frequently misunderstood, even by some methodologists. It does not mean that each class "knows" the other class, or that, in an implementation, it is possible to access each class from the other. It simply means that any logical relationship has an inverse, whether or not the inverse is easy to compute. To assert the ability to traverse an association in one direction but not the other as a design decision, associations can be marked with navigability.

Why is the basic model relational, rather than the pointer model prevalent in programming languages? The reason is that a model attempts to capture the intent behind an implementation. If a relationship between two classes is modeled as a pair of pointers, the pointers are nevertheless related. The association approach acknowledges that relationships are meaningful in both directions, regardless of how they are implemented. It is simple to convert an association into a pair of pointers for implementation, but very difficult to recognize that two pointers are inverses of each other unless this fact is part of the model.

Generalization

The generalization relationship is a taxonomic relationship between a more general description and a more specific description that builds on it and extends it. The more specific description is fully consistent with the more general one (it has all its properties, members, and relationships) and may contain additional information. For example, a mortgage is a more specific kind of loan. A mortgage keeps the basic characteristics of a loan but adds additional characteristics, such as a house as security for the loan. The more general description is called the parent; an element in the transitive closure is an ancestor. The more specific description is called the child; an element in the transitive closure is a descendant. In the example, **Loan** is the parent class and **Mortgage** is the child class. Generalization is used for classifiers (classes, interfaces, data types, use cases, actors, signals, and so on). For classes, the terms superclass and subclass are used for parent and child.

A generalization is drawn as an arrow from the child to the parent, with a large hollow triangle on the end connected to the parent (Figure 4-7). Several generalization relationships can be drawn as a tree with one arrowhead branching into several lines to the children.

Purpose of generalization. Generalization has two purposes. The first is to define the conditions under which an instance of one class (or other element) can be used when a variable (such as a parameter or procedure variable) is declared as holding values of a given class. This is called the substitutability principle (from Barbara Liskov). The rule is that an instance of a descendant may be used wherever the ancestor is declared. For example, if a variable is declared to hold loans, then a mortgage object is a legal value.

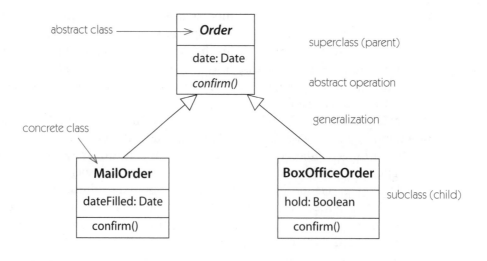

Figure 4-7. *Generalization notation*

   Generalization enables polymorphic operations—that is, operations whose implementation (method) is determined by the class of object they are applied to rather than being explicitly stated by the caller. This works because a parent class may have many possible children, each of which implements its own variation of an operation, which is defined across the entire set of classes. For example, computing interest would work differently for a mortgage and an automobile loan, but each of them is a variation on computing interest on the parent **Loan** class. A variable is declared to hold the parent class, and then an object of any child class can be used, any of which has its own particular operations. This is particularly useful because new classes can be added later, without the need to modify existing polymorphic calls. For example, a new kind of loan could be added later, and existing code that uses the **compute interest** operation would still work. A polymorphic operation can be declared without an implementation in a parent class with the intent that an implementation must be supplied by each descendant class. Such an incomplete operation is abstract (shown by italicizing its name).

   The other purpose of generalization is to permit the incremental description of an element by sharing the descriptions of its ancestors. This is called inheritance. Inheritance is the mechanism by which a description of the objects of a class is assembled out of declaration fragments from the class and its ancestors. Inheritance permits shared parts of the description to be declared once and shared by many classes, rather than be repeated in each class that uses it. This sharing reduces the size of a model. More importantly, it reduces the number of changes that must be made on an update to the model and reduces the chance of accidental inconsistency. Inheritance works in a similar way for other kinds of elements, such as states, signals, and use cases.

Inheritance

Each kind of generalizable element has a set of inheritable properties. For any model element, these include constraints. For classifiers, they also include features (attributes, operations, and signal reception) and participation in associations. A child inherits all the inheritable properties of all its ancestors. Its complete set of properties is the set of inherited properties together with the properties that it declares directly.

For a classifier, no attribute with the same signature may be declared more than once (directly or inherited). Otherwise, there is a conflict, and the model is ill formed. In other words, an attribute declared in an ancestor may not be redeclared in a descendant. An operation may be declared in more than one classifier, provided the specifications are consistent (same parameters, constraints, and meaning). Additional declarations are simply redundant. A method may be declared by multiple classes in a hierarchy. A method attached to a descendant supersedes and replaces (overrides) a method with the same signature declared in any ancestor. If two or more distinct copies of a method are nevertheless inherited by a class (via multiple inheritance from different classes), then they conflict and the model is ill formed. (Some programming languages permit one of the methods to be explicitly chosen. We find it simpler and safer just to redefine the method in the child class.) Constraints on an element are the union of the constraints on the element itself and all its ancestors; if any of them is inconsistent, then the model is ill formed.

In a concrete class, each inherited or declared operation must have a method defined, either directly or by inheritance from an ancestor.

Under some circumstances, a redefinition of an inherited definition may be declared in a subclass. Redefinition can change the name or some of the properties of a feature, but it can create confusion and should be used sparingly.

Multiple inheritance

If a classifier has more than one parent, it inherits from each one (Figure 4-8). Its features (attributes, operations, and signals) are the union of those of its parents. If the same class appears as an ancestor by more than one path, it nevertheless contributes only one copy of each of its members. If a feature with the same signature is declared by two classes that do not inherit it from a common ancestor (independent declarations), then the declarations conflict and the model is ill formed. UML does not provide a conflict resolution rule for this situation because experience has shown that the designer should explicitly resolve it. Some languages, such as Eiffel, permit conflicts to be explicitly resolved by the programmer, which is much safer than implicit conflict resolution rules, which frequently lead to surprises for the developer.

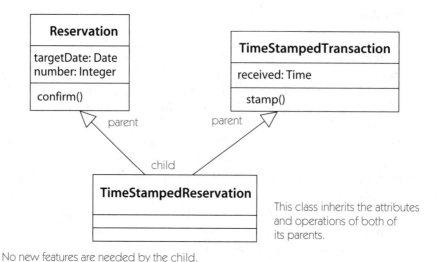

Figure 4-8. *Multiple inheritance*

Single and multiple classification

Many object-oriented languages assume single classification—an object has only one direct class. There is no logical necessity that an object have a single class. We typically look at real-world objects from many angles simultaneously. In the general formulation of UML, an object may have one or more direct classes—multiple classification. The object behaves as if it belonged to an implicit class that was a child of each of the direct classes—effectively, multiple inheritance without the need to actually declare the new class.

Static and dynamic classification

In the simplest formulation, an object may not change its class after it is created (static classification). Again, there is no logical necessity for this restriction. It is primarily intended to make the implementation of object-oriented programming languages easier. In the more general formulation, an object may change its direct class dynamically (dynamic classification). In doing so, it may lose or gain attributes or associations. If it loses them, the information in them is lost and cannot be recovered later, even if it changes back to the original class. If it gains attributes or associations, then they must be initialized at the time of the change, in a similar manner to the initialization of a new object.

When multiple classification is combined with dynamic classification, an object can add and remove classes to its classification during its life. The dynamic classes are sometimes called roles or types. One common modeling pattern is to require that each object have a single static inherent class (one that cannot change during the life of the object) plus zero or more role classes that may be added or removed over the lifetime of the object. The inherent class describes its fundamental properties, and the role classes describe properties that are transient. Although many programming languages do not support multiple dynamic classification in the class declaration hierarchy, it is nevertheless a valuable modeling concept that can be mapped into associations.

Realization

The realization relationship (Figure 4-9) connects a model element, such as a class, to another model element, such as an interface, that supplies its behavioral specification but not its structure or implementation. The client must support (by inheritance or by direct declaration) at least all the operations that the supplier has. Although realization is meant to be used with specification elements, such as interfaces, it can also be used with a concrete implementation element to indicate that its specification (but not its implementation) must be supported. This might be used to show the relationship of an optimized version of a class to a simpler but inefficient version, for example.

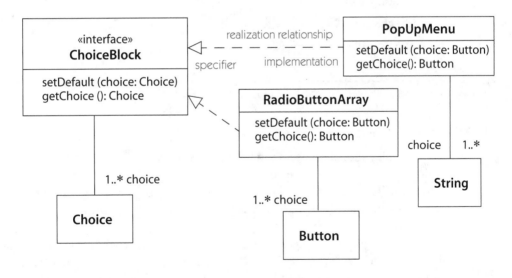

Figure 4-9. *Realization relationship*

Both generalization and realization relate a more general description to more complete versions of it. Generalization relates two elements at the same semantic level (at the same level of abstraction, for example), usually within the same model; realization relates two elements at different semantic levels (an analysis class and a design class, for example, or an interface and a class), often found in different models. There may be two or more entire class hierarchies at different stages of development whose elements are related by realization. The two hierarchies need not have the same form because the realizing classes may have implementation dependencies that are not relevant to the specifying classes.

Realization is displayed as a dashed arrow with a closed hollow arrowhead (Figure 4-9) on the more general class. It is similar to the generalization symbol with a dashed line, to indicate that it is similar to a kind of inheritance.

An interface realized by a class is called a provided interface, because the class provides the services of the interface to outside callers. This relationship may be shown by attaching a small circle to the class rectangle by a line; the circle is labeled with the name of the interface. An interface that a class uses to implement its internal behavior is called a required interface. This relationship may be shown by attaching a small semicircle to the class rectangle by a line. This notation is not used to declare interfaces, but rather to show their relationships to classes. See Figure 4-10.

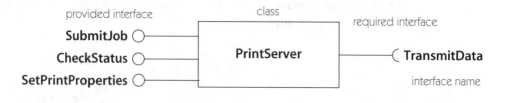

Figure 4-10. *Provided and required interfaces*

Dependency

A dependency indicates a semantic relationship between two or more model elements. It relates the model elements themselves and does not require a set of instances for its meaning. It indicates a situation in which a change to the supplier element may require a change to or indicate a change in meaning of the client element in the dependency.

The association and generalization relationships are dependencies by this definition, but they have specific semantics with important consequences. Therefore, they have their own names and detailed semantics. We normally use the word dependency for all the other relationships that don't fit the sharper categories. Table 4-3 lists the kinds of dependencies applicable to the static view.

A trace dependency is a conceptual connection among elements in different models, often models at different stages of development. It lacks detailed semantics. It is typically used to trace system requirements across models and to keep track of changes made to models that may affect other models.

Table 4-3: *Kinds of Dependencies*

Dependency	Function	Keyword
access	A private import of the contents of another package	access
binding	Assignment of values to the parameters of a template to generate a new model element	bind
call	Statement that a method of one class calls an operation of another class	call
creation	Statement that one class creates instances of another class	create
derivation	Statement that one instance can be computed from another instance	derive
instantiation	Statement that a method of one class creates instances of another class	instantiate
permission	Permission for an element to use the contents of another element	permit
realization	Mapping between a specification and an implementation of it	realize
refinement	Statement that a mapping exists between elements at two different semantic levels	refine
send	Relationship between the sender of a signal and the receiver of the signal	send
substitution	Statement that the source class supports the interfaces and contracts of the target class and may be substituted for it	substitute
trace dependency	Statement that some connection exists between elements in different models, but less precise than a mapping	trace
usage	Statement that one element requires the presence of another element for its correct functioning (includes call, creation, instantiation, send, and potentially others)	use

A refinement is a relationship between two versions of a concept at different stages of development or at different levels of abstraction, expressed as two separate model elements. The two model elements are not meant to coexist in the final detailed model. One of them is usually a less finished version of the other. In principle, there is a mapping from the less finished model element to the more finished model element. This does not mean that translation is automatic. Usually, the more detailed element contains design decisions that have been made by the designer, decisions that might be made in many ways. In principle, changes to one model could be validated against the other, with deviations flagged. In practice, tools cannot do all this today, although some simpler mappings can be enforced. Therefore a refinement is mostly a reminder to the modeler that multiple models are related in a predictable way.

A derivation dependency indicates that one element can be computed from another element (but the derived element may be explicitly included in the system to avoid a costly recomputation). Derivation, realization, refinement, and trace are abstraction dependencies—they relate two versions of the same underlying thing.

A usage dependency is a statement that the behavior or implementation of one element affects the behavior or implementation of another element. Frequently, this comes from implementation concerns, such as compiler requirements that the definition of one class is needed to compile another class. Most usage dependencies can be derived from the code and do not need to be explicitly declared, unless they are part of a top-down design style that constrains the organization of the system (for example, by using predefined components and libraries). The specific kind of usage dependency can be specified, but this is often omitted because the purpose of the relationship is to highlight the dependency. The exact details can often be obtained from the implementation code. Stereotypes of usage include call and instantiation. The call dependency indicates that a method on one class calls an operation on another class; instantiation indicates that a method on one class creates an instance of another class.

Several varieties of dependency add elements to a namespace. The import dependency adds the names within the target namespace contents to the importing namespace. The access dependency also adds names to a namespace, but the added names are not visible outside of the namespace to which they are added.

A binding is the assignment of values to the parameters of a template. It is a highly structured relationship with precise semantics obtained by substituting the arguments for the parameters in a copy of the template.

Usage and binding dependencies involve strong semantics among elements at the same semantic level. They must connect elements in the same level of model (both analysis or both design, and at the same level of abstraction). Trace and refinement dependencies are vaguer and can connect elements from different models or levels of abstraction.

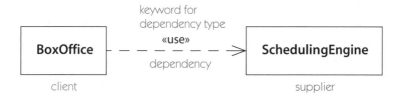

Figure 4-11. *Dependencies*

A dependency is drawn as a dashed arrow from the client to the supplier, with a stereotype keyword to distinguish its kind, as shown in Figure 4-11.

Constraint

UML supplies a set of concepts and relationships for modeling systems as graphs of modeling elements. Some things, however, are better expressed linguistically—that is, using the power of a textual language. A constraint is a Boolean expression represented as a string to be interpreted in a designated language. Natural language, set theoretic notation, constraint languages, or various programming languages may be used to express constraints. The UML includes the definition of a constraint language, called OCL, that is convenient for expressing UML constraints and is expected to be widely supported. See the entry for OCL and the book [Warmer-99] for more information on OCL.

Figure 4-12 shows constraints.

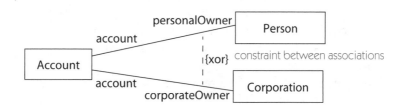

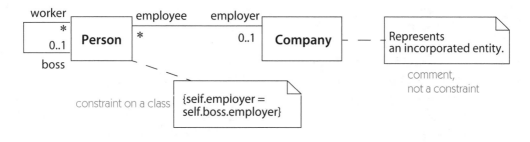

Figure 4-12. *Constraints*

Constraints can be used to state various nonlocal relationships, such as restrictions on paths of associations. In particular, constraints can be used to state existence properties (*there exists an X such that condition C is true*) and universal properties (*for all y in Y, condition D must be true*).

Some standard constraints are predefined as UML standard elements, including associations in an exclusive-or relationship and various constraints on the relationships of subclasses in generalization.

A constraint is shown as a text expression in braces. It may be written in a formal language or natural language. The text string may be placed in a note or attached to a dependency arrow.

Predefined constraints can be expressed in OCL. For example, the xor constraint in Figure 4-12 can be written in OCL as:

```
context Account inv :
    personalOwner -> size > 0  xor  corporateOwner -> size > 0
```

Instance

An instance is a run-time entity with identity, that is, something that can be distinguished from other run-time entities. It has a value at any moment in time. Over time the value can change in response to operations on it.

One purpose of a model is to describe the possible states of a system and their behavior. A model is a statement of potentiality, of the possible collections of objects that might exist and the possible behavior history that the objects might undergo. The static view defines and constrains the possible configurations of values that an executing system may assume. The dynamic view defines the ways in which an executing system may pass from one configuration to another. Together, the static view and the various dynamic views based on it define the structure and behavior of a system.

A particular static configuration of a system at one instant is called a snapshot. A snapshot comprises objects and other instances, values, and links. An object is an instance of a class. Each object is a direct instance of the class that completely describes it and an indirect instance of the ancestors of that class. (If multiple classification is allowed, then an object may be the direct instance of more than one class.) Similarly, each link is an instance of an association, and each value is an instance of a data type.

An object has one data value for each attribute in its class. The value of each attribute must be consistent with the data type of the attribute. If the attribute has optional or multiple multiplicity, then the attribute may hold zero or multiple values. A link comprises a tuple of values, each of which is a reference to an object of a given class (or one of its descendants). Objects and links must obey any constraints on the classes or associations of which they are instances (including both explicit constraints and built-in constraints, such as multiplicity).

The state of a system is a *valid system instance* if every instance in it is an instance of some element in a well-formed system model and if all the constraints imposed by the model are satisfied by the instances.

The static view defines the set of objects, values, and links that can exist in a single snapshot. In principle, any combination of objects and links that is consistent with a static view is a possible configuration of the model. This does not mean that every possible snapshot can or will occur. Some snapshots may be legal statically but may not be dynamically reachable under the dynamic views in the system.

The behavioral parts of UML describe the valid sequences of snapshots that may occur as a result of both external and internal behavioral effects. The dynamic views define how the system moves from one snapshot to another.

Object diagram

A diagram of a snapshot is an image of a system at a point in time. Because it contains images of objects, it is called an object diagram. It can be useful as an example of the system, for example, to illustrate complicated data structures or to show behavior through a sequence of snapshots over time (Figure 4-13). An object diagram is not restricted to specific objects. It may also include value specifications of objects in which some of the values may be incompletely specified, for example, by indicating a range of values rather than a specific value.

Snapshots are examples of systems, not definitions of systems. The definition of system structure and behavior is the goal of modeling and design. Examples can help to clarify meaning to humans, but they are not definitions.

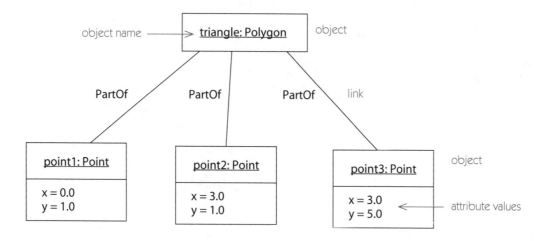

Figure 4-13. *Object diagram*

5

Design View

Overview

Much of a system model is intended to show the logical and design aspects of the system independent of its final packaging in an implementation medium. The implementation aspects are important, however, for both reusability and performance purposes. The design view shows decisions about decomposition of a system into modular units with encapsulation boundaries and external interfaces. Although the elements in the design view are more abstract than the final code, they do require knowledge of implementation trade-offs that will eventually be reflected in the code.

Complex systems require multiple levels of structure. During early modeling, a class is defined by its external properties. During design modeling, the internal design of a high-level class may be expanded into constituent parts. A structured classifier is a classifier with internal parts that are connected within the context of the classifier. A structured classifier may have a loose boundary or a tight boundary where all communications occur over well-defined interaction points called ports. The types of the internal parts may themselves be structured classifiers; therefore the decomposition of the system can span several levels.

In a design, independent objects often work together to perform operations and other behaviors. For a limited time, objects are related by their participation in a shared context. A collaboration is a description of a group of objects that have a temporary relationship within the context of performing a behavior. A collaboration is a conceptual relationship, not a concrete object, although there may be objects in an implementation related to it. The connections among the objects may include various kinds of transient relationships, such as parameters, variables, and derived relationships, as well as ordinary associations.

The design view shows the logical organization of the reusable pieces of the system into substitutable units, called components. A component has a set of external interfaces and a hidden, internal implementation. Components interact through interfaces so that dependencies on specific other components are avoided. During implementation, any component that supports an interface can be substituted for it, allowing different parts of a system to be developed without dependency on internal implementation.

Structured Classifier

A structured classifier is a classifier with internal structure. It contains a set of parts connected by connectors. An instance of a structured class contains an object or set of objects corresponding to each part. A part has a type and a multiplicity within its container. An object that is a part may only belong to one structured object. All of the objects in a single structured object are implicitly related by their containment in the same object. This implicit relationship may be exploited in the implementation of behavior on the structured class.

A connector is a contextual relationship between two parts in a structured classifier. It defines a relationship between objects serving as parts of the same structured object. A connector among two parts of a structured class is different from an association between two classes that are associated by composition to the same class. In the association, there is no requirement that the association connects two objects that are contained in the same composite object. Each association to a single class is independent, whereas all the connectors in a single structured class share a single context at run time. Connectors may be implemented by ordinary associations or by transient relationships, such as procedure parameters, variables, global values, or other mechanisms.

Figure 5-1 shows an example of a ticket order that contains parts.

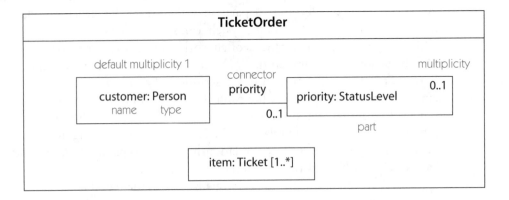

Figure 5-1. *Structured class*

Structured classifiers may be tightly encapsulated by forcing all interactions between the external environment and the internal parts to pass through ports. A port is an interaction point with a well-defined interface. The port may be connected to internal parts or ports on internal parts, or it may be connected directly to the main behavior of the structured classifier. Messages received by a port are automatically forwarded to the part or behavior (or vice versa on output). Each port has a set of provided interfaces and required interfaces that define its external interactions. A provided interface specifies the services that a message to the port may request. A required interface specifies the services that a message from the port may require from the external environment. External connections to an encapsulated classifier may only go to ports. An external connection is legal if the interfaces match. In the case of input requests, the provided interface must support at least the services requested by the external connection. In the case of output requests, the required interface must request no more than the services provided by the external connection.

Figure 5-2 shows the ports and interfaces for a camcorder.

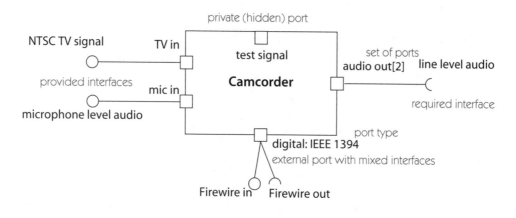

Figure 5-2. *Structured class with ports*

Collaboration

A collaboration is a description of a collection of objects that interact to implement some behavior within a context. It describes a society of cooperating objects assembled to carry out some purpose. A collaboration contains roles that are filled by objects at run time. A role represents a description of the objects that can participate in an execution of the collaboration. A connector represents a description of associations among roles of the collaboration. Relationships among roles and connectors inside a collaboration are only meaningful in that context. Roles and connectors may have types (classifiers and associations) that specify which objects can be bound to them. The association types are optional, because the relationships in a collaboration may be transient and implemented using other mechanisms, such as parameters. The relationships described by a collaboration apply only to objects bound to roles within a particular collaboration instance; they do not apply to the underlying classifiers and associations apart from the collaboration.

The static view describes the inherent properties of a class. For example, a **Ticket** has a show and a set associated with it. This relationship applies to all instances of the class. A collaboration describes the properties that an instance of a class has when it plays a particular role in a collaboration. For example, a **ticket** in a Ticket-Sale collaboration has a **seller**, something that is not relevant to a **Ticket** in general but is an essential part of the ticket sale collaboration.

An object in a system may participate in more than one collaboration. Collaborations in which it appears need not be directly related, although their execution is connected (perhaps incidentally) through the shared object. For example, one person may be a **buyer** in one collaboration and a **seller** in another collaboration. Somewhat less often, an object may play more than one role in the same collaboration.

A collaboration is a kind of structured classifier.

Figure 5-3 shows a collaboration for a ticket sale.

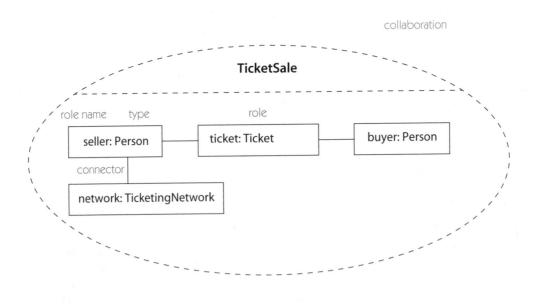

Figure 5-3. *Collaboration definition*

Patterns

A pattern is a parameterized collaboration, together with guidelines about when to use it. A parameter can be replaced by different values to produce different collaborations. The parameters usually designate slots for classes. When a pattern is instantiated, its parameters are bound to actual classes within a class diagram or to roles within a larger collaboration.

The use of a pattern is shown as a dashed ellipse connected to each of its classes by a dashed line that is labeled with the name of the role. For example, Figure 5-4 shows the use of the **Observer** pattern from [Gamma-95]. In this use of the pattern, **CallQueue** replaces the **Subject** role and **SlidingBarIcon** replaces the **Observer** role.

Patterns may appear at the analysis, architecture, detailed design, and implementation levels. They are a way to capture frequently occurring structures for reuse. Figure 5-4 shows a use of the Observer pattern.

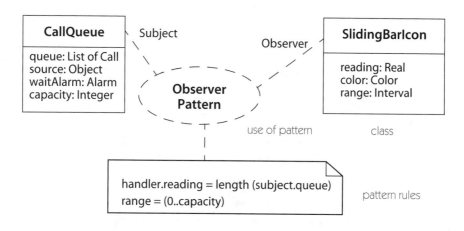

Figure 5-4. *Pattern usage*

Component

A component represents a modular piece of a logical or physical system whose externally visible behavior can be described much more concisely than its implementation. Components do not depend directly on other components but on interfaces that components support. A component in a model can be replaced by another component that supports the proper interfaces, and a component instance within a system configuration can be replaced by an instance of any component that supports the same interfaces.

Components (because they are classes) have interfaces they support (provided interfaces) and interfaces they require from other components (required interfaces). The use of named interfaces permits direct dependencies among components to be avoided, facilitating easier substitution of new components. A component diagram shows the network of dependencies among components. The component view can appear in two forms. It can show a set of available components (a component library) with their dependencies; this is the material out of which a system can be assembled. It can also show a configured system, with the selection of components (out of the entire library) used to build it. In this form, each component is wired to other components whose services it uses; these connections must be consistent with the interfaces of the components.

A component icon is drawn as a rectangle with two small rectangles on its side. A component is drawn as a rectangle with a small component icon in its upper right corner. The rectangle contains the name of the component. A provided interfaces is drawn as a small circle connected to the component by a line. A required interface is drawn as a small semicircle connected to the component by a line. Figure 5-5 shows an example.

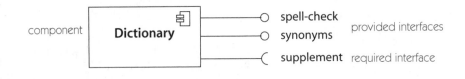

Figure 5-5. *Component with interfaces*

Components may have ports. Messages received on different ports are distinguishable by the component and may be implemented differently. A port is shown by a small square on the boundary of a component symbol. Interface symbols may be attached to a port.

Components may contain other components as their implementation. The "wiring" of two components in an implementation is shown by nesting the circle of a provided interface in the semicircle of another required interface in a "ball and socket" notation (Figure 5-6).

A component is a structured classifier. The semantic distinction between a structured classifier and a component is not very great. A component is more of a statement of design intent than a semantic difference.

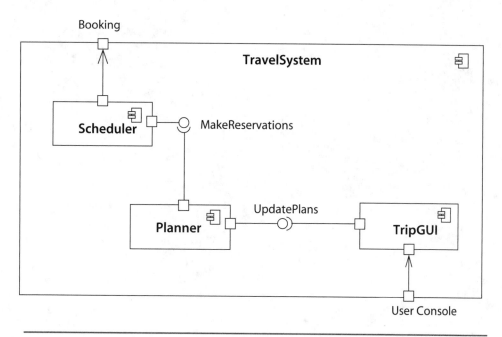

Figure 5-6. *Component internal structure*

6

Use Case View

Overview

The use case view captures the behavior of a system, subsystem, class, or component as it appears to an outside user. It partitions the system functionality into transactions meaningful to actors—idealized users of a system. The pieces of interactive functionality are called use cases. A use case describes an interaction with actors as a sequence of messages between the system and one or more actors. The term *actor* includes humans, as well as other computer systems and processes. Figure 6-1 shows a use case diagram for a telephone catalog sales application. The model has been simplified as an example.

Actor

An actor is an idealization of a role played by an external person, process, or thing interacting with a system, subsystem, or class. An actor characterizes the interactions that a class of outside users may have with the system. At run time, one physical user may be bound to multiple actors within the system. Different users may be bound to the same actor and therefore represent multiple instances of the same actor definition. For example, one person may be a customer and a cashier of a store at different times.

Each actor participates in one or more use cases. It interacts with the use case (and therefore with the system or class that owns the use case) by exchanging messages. The internal implementation of an actor is not relevant in the use case; an actor may be characterized sufficiently by a set of attributes that define its state.

Actors may be defined in generalization hierarchies, in which an abstract actor description is shared and augmented by one or more specific actor descriptions.

An actor may be a human, a computer system, or some executable process.

An actor is drawn as a small stick person with the name below it.

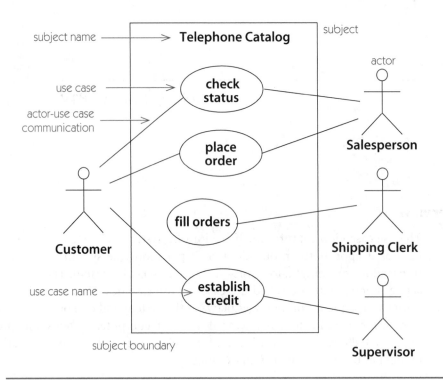

Figure 6-1. *Use case diagram*

Use Case

A use case is a coherent unit of externally visible functionality provided by a classifier (called the subject) and expressed by sequences of messages exchanged by the
subject and one or more actors of the system unit. The purpose of a use case is to
define a piece of coherent behavior without revealing the internal structure of the
subject. The definition of a use case includes all the behavior it entails—the mainline sequences, different variations on normal behavior, and all the exceptional
conditions that can occur with such behavior, together with the desired response.
From the user's point of view, these may be abnormal situations. From the system's
point of view, they are additional variations that must be described and handled.

In the model, the execution of each use case is independent of the others, although an implementation of the use cases may create implicit dependencies
among them due to shared objects. Each use case represents an orthogonal piece of
functionality whose execution can be mixed with the execution of other use cases.

The dynamics of a use case may be specified by UML interactions, shown as
statechart diagrams, sequence diagrams, communication diagrams, or informal
text descriptions. When use cases are implemented, they are realized by collabora-

tions among classes in the system. One class may participate in multiple collaborations and therefore in multiple use cases.

At the system level, use cases represent external behavior of the subject as visible to outside users. A use case is somewhat like an operation, an operation invocable by an outside user. Unlike an operation, however, a use case can continue to receive input from its actors during its execution. Use cases can be applied to an entire system and can also be applied internally to smaller units of a system, such as subsystems and individual classes. An internal use case represents behavior that a subsystem presents to the rest of the system. For example, a use case for a class represents a coherent chunk of functionality that a class provides to other classes that play certain roles within the system. A class can have more than one use case.

A use case is a logical description of a slice of functionality. It is not a manifest construct in the implementation of a system. Instead, each use case must be mapped onto the classes that implement a system. The behavior of the use case is mapped onto the transitions and operations of the classes. Inasmuch as a class can play multiple roles in the implementation of a system, it may therefore realize portions of multiple use cases. Part of the design task is to find implementation classes that cleanly combine the proper roles to implement all the use cases, without introducing unnecessary complications. The implementation of a use case can be modeled as a set of one or more collaborations. A collaboration is a realization of a use case.

A use case can participate in several relationships, in addition to association with actors (Table 6-1).

Table 6-1: *Kinds of Use Case Relationships*

Relationship	Function	Notation
association	The communication path between an actor and a use case that it participates in	————
extend	The insertion of additional behavior into a base use case that does not know about it	«extend» - - - -≫
include	The insertion of additional behavior into a base use case that explicitly describes the insertion	«include» - - - -≫
use case generalization	A relationship between a general use case and a more specific use case that inherits and adds features to it	———▷

A use case is drawn as an ellipse with its name inside or below it. It is connected by solid lines to actors that communicate with it.

The description of a large use case can be factored into other, simpler use cases. This is similar to the way the description of a class can be defined incrementally from the description of a superclass. A use case can incorporate the behavior of other use cases as fragments of its own behavior. This is called an include relationship. The included use case is not a specialization of the original use case and cannot be substituted for it.

A use case can also be defined as an incremental extension to a base use case. This is called an extend relationship. There may be several extensions of the same base use case that may all be applied together. The extensions to a base use case add to its semantics; it is the base use case that is instantiated, not the extension use cases.

The include and extend relationships are drawn as dashed arrows with the keyword «include» or «extend». The include relationship points at the use case to be included; the extend relationship points at the use case to be extended.

A use case can also be specialized into one or more child use cases. This is use case generalization. Any child use case may be used in a situation in which the parent use case is expected.

Use case generalization is drawn the same as any generalization, as a line from the child use case to the parent use case with a large triangular arrowhead on the parent end. Figure 6-2 shows use case relationships in the catalog sales application.

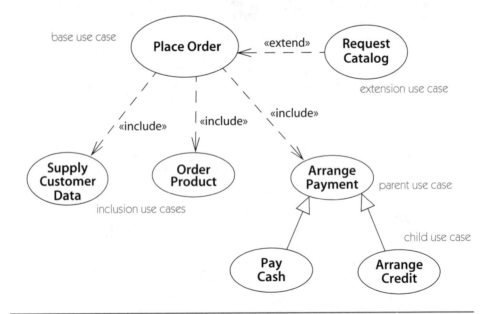

Figure 6-2. *Use case relationships*

7

State Machine View

Overview

The state machine view describes the dynamic behavior of objects over time by modeling the lifecycles of objects of each class. Each object is treated as an isolated entity that communicates with the rest of the world by detecting events and responding to them. Events represent the kinds of changes that an object can detect—the receipt of calls or explicit signals from one object to another, a change in certain values, or the passage of time. Anything that can affect an object can be characterized as an event. Real-world happenings are modeled as signals from the outside world to the system.

A state is a set of object values for a given class that have the same qualitative response to events that occur. In other words, all objects with the same state react in the same general way to an event, so all objects in a given state execute the same effect—an action or activity—when they receive the same event. Objects in different states, however, may react differently to the same event, by performing different effects. A state machine describes a small number of states that an object may hold. For each state, the state machine specifies the consequences of receiving each kind of event as an effect and a change to a new state. For example, an automatic teller machine reacts to the cancel button one way when it is processing a transaction and another way when it is idle.

State machines describe the behavior of classes, but they also describe the dynamic behavior of use cases, collaborations, and methods. For one of these objects, a state represents a step in its execution. We talk mostly in terms of classes and objects in describing state machines, but they can be applied to other elements in a straightforward way.

State Machine

A state machine is a graph of states and transitions. Usually a state machine is attached to a class and describes the response of an instance of the class to events that it receives. State machines may also be attached to behaviors, use cases, and collaborations to describe their execution.

A state machine is a model of all possible life histories of an object of a class. The object is examined in isolation. Any external influence from the rest of the world is summarized as an event. When the object detects an event, it responds in a way that depends on its current state. The response may include the execution of an effect and a change to a new state. State machines can be structured to share transitions, and they can model concurrency.

A state machine is a localized view of an object, a view that separates it from the rest of the world and examines its behavior in isolation. It is a reductionist view of a system. This is a good way to specify behavior precisely, but often it is not a good way to understand the overall operation of a system. For a better idea of the system-wide effects of behavior, interaction views are often more useful. State machines are useful for understanding control mechanisms, however, such as user interfaces and device controllers.

Event

An event is a type of noteworthy occurrence that has a location in time and space. It occurs at a point in time; it does not have duration. Model something as an event if its occurrence has consequences. When we use the word *event* by itself, we usually mean an event descriptor—that is, a description of all the individual event occurrences that have the same general form, just as the word *class* means all the individual objects that have the same structure. A specific occurrence of an event is called an occurrence. Events may have parameters that characterize each individual event occurrence, just as classes have attributes that characterize each object. Events can be divided into various explicit and implicit kinds: signal events, call events, change events, and time events. Table 7-1 is a list of event types and their descriptions.

Table 7-1: *Kinds of Events*

Event Type	Description	Syntax
call event	Receipt of an explicit synchronous call request by an object	op (a:T)
change event	A change in value of a Boolean expression	**when** (exp)
signal event	Receipt of an explicit, named, asynchronous communication among objects	sname (a:T)
time event	The arrival of an absolute time or the passage of a relative amount of time	**after** (time)

Signal. A signal is kind of classifier that is explicitly intended as a communication vehicle between two objects; the reception of a signal is an event for the receiving object. The sending object explicitly creates and initializes a signal instance and sends it to one or a set of explicit objects. Signals embody asynchronous one-way communication, the most fundamental kind. The sender does not wait for the receiver to deal with the signal but continues with its own work independently. To model two-way communication, multiple signals can be used, at least one in each direction. The sender and the receiver can be the same object.

Signals may be declared in class diagrams as classifiers, using the keyword «signal»; the parameters of the signal are declared as attributes. As classifiers, signals can have generalization relationships. Signals may be children of other signals; they inherit the attributes of their parents, and they trigger transitions that contain the parent signal type (Figure 7-1).

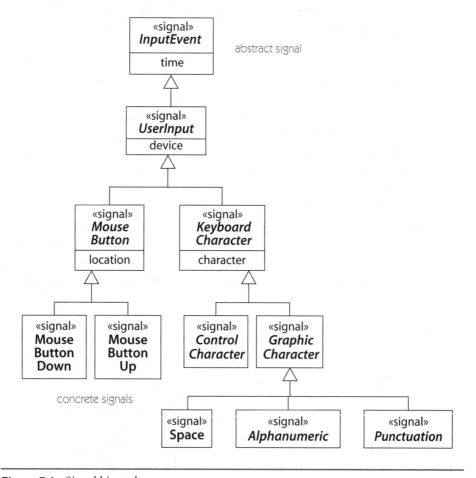

Figure 7-1. *Signal hierarchy*

Call event. A call event is the reception of a call of an operation by an object. The receiving class chooses whether an operation will be implemented as a method or a call event trigger in a state machine (or possibly both). The parameters of the operation are the parameters of the call event. Once the receiving object processes the call event by taking a transition triggered by the event or failing to take any transition, control returns to the calling object. Unlike a method, however, a state machine transition triggered by a call event may continue its own execution in parallel with the caller.

Change event. A change event is the satisfaction of a Boolean expression that depends on designated attribute values. This is a declarative way to wait until a condition is satisfied, but it must be used with care, because it represents a continuous and potentially nonlocal computation (action at a distance, because the value or values tested may be distant). This is both good and bad. It is good because it focuses the model on the true dependency—an effect that occurs when a given condition is satisfied—rather than on the mechanics of testing the condition. It is bad because it obscures the cause-and-effect relationship between the action that changes an underlying value and the eventual effect. The cost of testing a change event is potentially large, because in principle it is continuous. In practice, however, there are optimizations that avoid unnecessary computation. Change events should be used only when a more explicit form of communication is unnatural.

Note the difference between a guard condition and a change event. A guard condition is evaluated once when the trigger event on the transition occurs and the receiver handles the event. If it is false, the transition does not fire and the condition is not reevaluated. A change event is evaluated continuously until it becomes true, at which time the transition fires.

Time event. Time events represent the passage of time. A time event can be specified either in absolute mode (time of day) or relative mode (time elapsed since a given event). In a high-level model, time events can be thought of as events from the universe; in an implementation model, they are caused by signals from some specific object, either the operating system or an object in the application.

State

A state machine defines a small number of named states. A state can be characterized in three complementary ways: as a set of object values that are qualitatively similar in some respect; as a period of time during which an object waits for some event or events to occur; or as a period of time during which an object performs some ongoing do activity. A state may have a name, although often it is anonymous and is described simply by its effects and relationships. In effects, states are the units of control from which state machines are constructed.

In a state machine, a set of states is connected by transitions. A transition connects two states (or more, if there is a fork or join of control). A transition is processed by the state that it leaves. When an object is in a state, it is sensitive to the trigger events on transitions leaving the state.

A state is shown as a rectangle with rounded corners (Figure 7-2).

Confirm Credit

Figure 7-2. *State*

Transition

A transition leaving a state defines the response of an object in the state to the occurrence of an event. In general, a transition has an event trigger, a guard condition, an effect, and a target state. Table 7-2 shows kinds of transitions and implicit effects invoked by transitions.

Table 7-2: *Kinds of Transitions and Implicit Effects*

Transition Kind	Description	Syntax
entry transition	The specification of an entry activity that is executed when a state is entered	**entry/** activity
exit transition	The specification of an exit activity that is executed when a state is exited	**exit/** activity
external transition	A response to an event that causes a change of state or a self-transition, together with a specified effect. It may also cause the execution of exit and/ or entry activities for states that are exited or entered.	e(a:T)[guard]/activity
internal transition	A response to an event that causes the execution of an effect but does not cause a change of state or execution of exit or entry activities	e(a:T)[guard]/activity

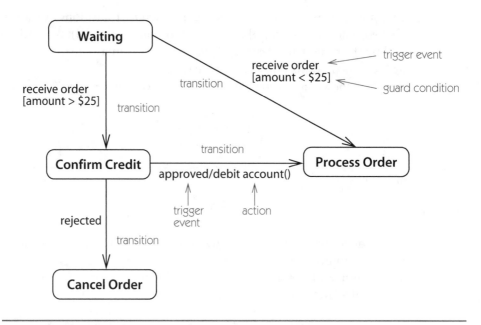

Figure 7-3. *External transitions*

External transition. An *external transition* is a transition that changes the active state. This is the most common kind of transition. It is drawn as an arrow from the source state to the target state, with other properties shown as a text string attached to the arrow (Figure 7-3).

Trigger event. The trigger specifies the event that enables a transition. The event may have parameters, which are available to an effect specified as part of the transition. If a signal has descendants, receipt of any descendant of the signal enables the transition. For example, if a transition has signal **MouseButton** as a trigger (see Figure 7-1), then receipt of **MouseButtonDown** will trigger the transition.

An event is not a continuous thing; it occurs at a point in time. When an object receives an event occurrence, the event occurrence is placed into an event pool for the object. An object handles one event occurrence at a time. When the object is free, an event occurrence is removed from the pool. A transition must fire at the time the object handles the event; the event occurrence is not "remembered" until later (except in the special case of deferred events, which remain in the event pool until they trigger a transition or until the object enters a state where they are no longer deferred). If two events occur simultaneously, they are handled one at a time. An event occurrence that does not trigger any transition is simply ignored and lost. This is not an error. It is much easier to ignore unwanted events than to try to specify all of them.

Guard condition. A transition may have a guard condition, which is a Boolean expression. It may reference attributes of the object that owns the state machine, as well as parameters of the trigger event. The guard condition is evaluated when the trigger event occurs. If the expression evaluates as true, then the transition fires—that is, its effects occur. If the expression evaluates as false, then the transition does not fire. The guard condition is evaluated only once, at the time the trigger event occurs. If the condition is false and later becomes true, it is too late to fire the transition.

The same event can be a trigger for more than one transition leaving a single state. Each transition with the same event must have a different guard condition. If the event occurs, a transition triggered by the event may fire if its condition is true. Often, the set of guard conditions covers all possibilities so that the occurrence of the event is guaranteed to fire some transition. If all possibilities are not covered and no transition is enabled, then an event is simply ignored. Only one transition may fire (within one thread of control) in response to one event occurrence. If an event enables more than one transition, only one of them fires. A transition on a nested state takes precedence over a transition on one of its enclosing states. If two conflicting transitions are enabled at the same time, one of them fires nondeterministically. The choice may be random or it may depend on implementation details, but the modeler should not count on a predicable result.

If an orthogonal state is active, each region in it is active, meaning that multiple states (at least one in each region) may be active concurrently. If multiple states are active, a single event occurrence may trigger a transition in each orthogonal region. The concurrent transitions are executed concurrently and do not interact, except possibly indirectly because of effects on shared objects.

Completion transition. A transition that lacks an explicit trigger event is triggered by the completion of activity in the state that it leaves (this is a completion transition). A completion transition may have a guard condition, which is evaluated at the time the activity in the state completes (and not thereafter). Completion transitions take priority over ordinary events and do not wait for a normal run-to-completion step.

Effect. When a transition fires, its effect (if any) is executed. An effect may be an action or an activity. An action is a primitive computation, such as an assignment statement or simple arithmetic computation. Other actions include sending a signal to another object, calling an operation, creating or destroying an object, and getting and setting attribute values. An effect may also be an activity—that is, a list of simpler actions or activities. An action or activity cannot be terminated or affected by simultaneous effects. (An advanced profile might add an action that terminates or interrupts other activities.) Conceptually, one activity is processed at a time; therefore, a second event cannot be handled during the execution of an effect.

The overall system can perform multiple activities simultaneously. An implementation system can process hardware interrupts and time share between several actions. An activity is noninterruptible within its own thread of control. Once started, it must complete and it must not interact with other simultaneously active effects. This is called run-to-completion semantics. But effects should not be used as a long transaction mechanism. Their duration should be brief compared to the response time needed for external events. Otherwise, the system might be unable to respond in a timely manner.

An effect may use parameters of the trigger event and attributes of the owning object as part of its expression.

Change of state. When the execution of the effect is complete, the target state of the transition becomes active. This may trigger an exit activity or an entry activity (or several if the state machine traverses several nested states from the source to the target state).

Nested states. States may be nested inside other composite states (see following entry). A transition leaving an outer state is applicable to all states nested within it. The transition is eligible to fire whenever any nested state is active. If the transition fires, the target state of the transition becomes active. Composite states are useful for expressing exception and error conditions, because transitions on them apply to all nested states without the need for each nested state to handle the exception explicitly.

Entry and exit activities. A transition across one or more levels of nesting may exit and enter states. A state may specify activities that are performed whenever the state is entered or exited. Entering the target state executes an entry activity attached to the state. If the transition leaves the original state, then its exit activity is executed before the effect on the transition and the entry activity on the new state.

Entry activities are often used to perform setup needed within a state. Because an entry activity cannot be evaded, any actions that occur inside the state can assume that the setup has occurred, regardless of how the state is entered. Similarly, an exit activity is an activity that occurs whenever the state is exited, an opportunity to perform clean up. It is particularly useful when there are high-level transitions that represent error conditions that abort nested states. The exit activity can clean up such cases so that the state of the object remains consistent. Entry and exit activities could in principle be attached to incoming and outgoing transitions, but declaring them as special effects of the state permits the state to be defined independently of its transitions and therefore encapsulated.

Internal transition. An internal transition has a source state but no target state. The firing rules for an internal transition are the same as for a transition that changes state. An internal transition has no target state, so the active state does not change as a result of its firing. If an internal transition has an effect, the effect is executed, but no change of state occurs, and therefore no exit or entry activities are executed. Internal transitions are useful for modeling interrupt situations that do not change the state (such as counting occurrences of an event or putting up a help screen).

Entry and exit activities use the same notation as internal transitions, except they use the reserved words **entry** and **exit** in place of the event trigger name, although these effects are triggered by external transitions that enter or leave the state.

A self-transition invokes exit and entry activities on its state (conceptually, it exits and then reenters the state); therefore, it is not equivalent to an internal transition. Figure 7-4 shows entry and exit activities as well as internal transitions.

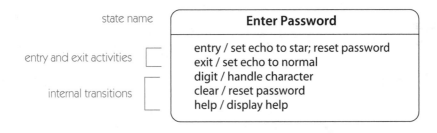

Figure 7-4. *Internal transitions, and entry and exit actions*

Composite State

A simple state has no substructure, just a set of transitions and possible entry and exit activities. A composite state is one that has been decomposed into regions, each of which contains one or more direct substates. Table 7-3 lists the various kinds of states.

A decomposition of a nonorthogonal state into direct substates is similar to specialization of a class. An outer state is decomposed into several inner states, each of which inherits the transitions of the outer state. Only one direct substate per nonorthogonal state can be active at one time. The outer state represents the condition of being in any one of the inner states.

Transitions into or out of a composite state invoke any entry activity or exit activity of the state. If there are several composite states, a transition across several levels may invoke multiple entry activities (outermost first) or several exit activities (innermost first). If there is an effect on the transition itself, the effect is executed after any exit activities and before any entry activities are executed.

Table 7-3: *Kinds of States*

State Kind	Description	Notation
simple state	A state with no substructure	S
orthogonal state	A state that is divided into two or more regions. One direct substate from each region is concurrently active when the composite state is active.	
nonorthogonal state	A composite state that contains one or more direct substates, exactly one of which is active at one time when the composite state is active	S
initial state	A pseudostate that indicates the starting state when the enclosing state is invoked	●
final state	A special state whose activation indicates the enclosing state has completed activity	◉
terminate	A special state whose activation terminates execution of the object owning the state machine	✕
junction	A pseudostate that chains transition segments into a single run-to-completion transition	●
choice	A pseudostate that performs a dynamic branch within a single run-to-completion transition	◇
history state	A pseudostate whose activation restores the previously active state within a composite state	H

Table 7-3: *Kinds of States*

State Kind	Description	Notation
submachine state	A state that references a state machine definition, which conceptually replaces the submachine state	s: M
entry point	A externally visible pseudostate within a state machine that identifies an internal state as a target	a → T
exit point	A externally visible pseudostate within a state machine that identifies an internal state as a source	U ⊗ b →

Each region of a composite state may have an initial state. A transition to the composite state boundary is implicitly a transition to the initial state. A new object starts at the initial state of its outermost state. Similarly, a composite state can have a final state. A transition to the final state triggers a completion transition on the composite state. If an object reaches the final state of its outermost state, it is destroyed. Initial states, final states, entry activities, and exit activities permit the definition of a state to be encapsulated independent of transitions to and from it.

Figure 7-5 shows a sequential decomposition of a state, including an initial state. This is the control for a ticket-selling machine.

A decomposition of an orthogonal state into orthogonal regions represents independent computation. When an orthogonal state is entered, the number of control threads increases as a direct substate in each orthogonal region becomes active. When the orthogonal state is exited, the number of control threads decreases. Often, concurrency is implemented by a distinct object for each substate, but orthogonal states can also represent logical concurrency within a single object. Figure 7-6 shows the concurrent decomposition of taking a university class.

It is often convenient to reuse a fragment of a state machine in other state machines. A state machine can be given a name and referenced from a state of one or more other machines. The target state machine is a submachine, and the state referencing it is called a submachine state. It implies the (conceptual) substitution of a copy of the referenced state machine at the place of reference, a kind of state machine subroutine. A submachine can define named entry points and exit points that connect to internal states. Transitions to a submachine state can use connection points that reference these entry and exit points, hiding the internal structure

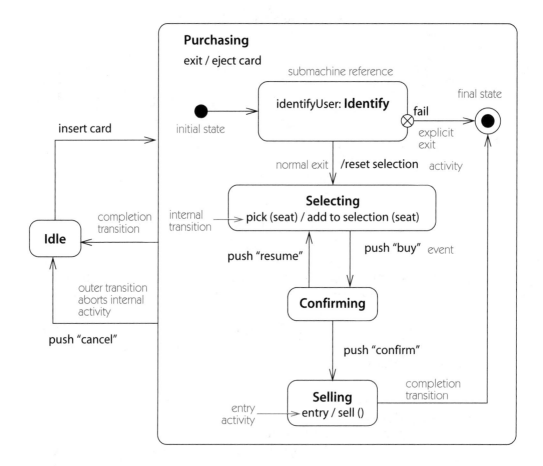

Figure 7-5. *State machine*

of the submachine from external clients. Instead of a submachine, a state can contain an do activity—that is, a computation or continuous activity that takes time to complete and that may be interrupted by events. Figure 7-7 shows a submachine reference.

A transition to a submachine state causes activation of the initial state of the target submachine. To enter a submachine at other states, an entry point can be referenced. A entry point identifies a state in the submachine without exposing the contents of the submachine.

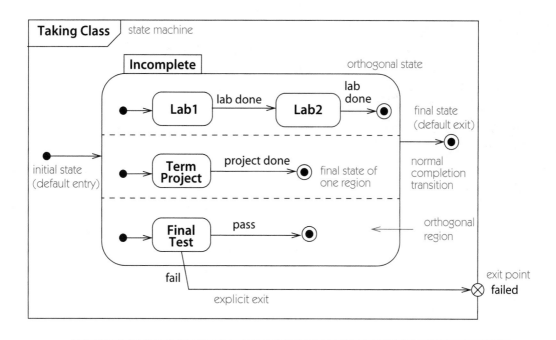

Figure 7-6. *State machine with orthogonal composite state*

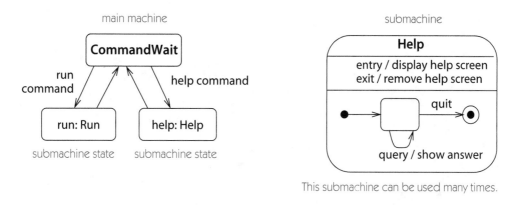

Figure 7-7. *Submachine state*

8

Activity View

Overview

An activity is a graph of nodes and flows that shows the flow of control (and optionally data) through the steps of a computation. Execution of steps can be both concurrent and sequential. An activity involves both synchronization and branching constructs, similar to but more powerful than a traditional flow chart, which only supports sequential and branching constructs.

An activity definition contains activity nodes. An activity node represents the execution of a statement in a procedure or the performance of a step in a workflow. Nodes are connected by control flows and data flows. An activity node normally begins execution when there are tokens (indicators of control) on each of its input flows. An activity node waits for the completion of its computation. When the execution of the node completes, then execution proceeds to nodes found on its output flows. Activity flows are like completion transitions—they occur when execution completes—but actions may be included that wait for specific events.

Activity nodes may be nested. An activity diagram may contain branches, as well as forking of control into concurrent threads. Concurrent threads represent activities that can be performed concurrently by different objects or persons in an organization. Frequently concurrency arises from aggregation, in which each object has its own concurrent thread. Concurrent activities can be performed simultaneously or in any order. An activity graph is like a traditional flow chart except it permits concurrent control in addition to sequential control—a big difference.

There are also predefined control nodes that support various forms of control, such as decisions (branches) and merges. Concurrent execution is modeled using forks and joins. There are also control constructs to support exception handling and the parallel application of an activity to the elements of a set.

Ultimately the leaves of an activity graph are actions. An action is a basic, predefined activity, such as accessing or modifying attribute or link values, creating or destroying objects, calling operations, and sending signals.

Activity

An activity definition is shown in an activity diagram (Figure 8-1).

An activity node is shown as a box with rounded corners containing a description of the activity. A control flow is shown as an arrow. Branches are shown as guard conditions on control flows or as diamonds with multiple labeled exit arrows. A fork or join of control is shown by multiple arrows entering or leaving a heavy synchronization bar. Figure 8-1 shows an activity diagram for processing an order by the box office.

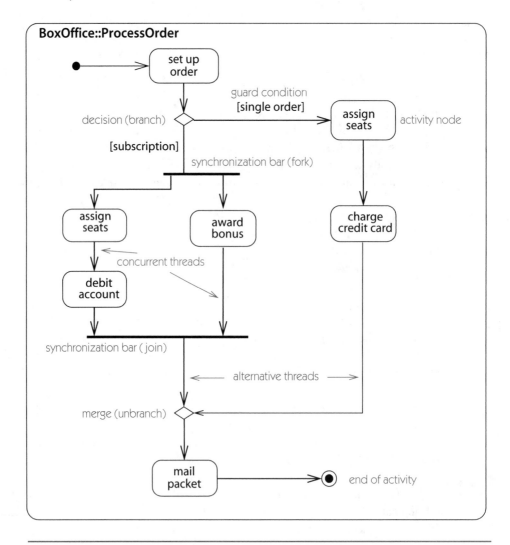

Figure 8-1. *Activity diagram*

For those situations in which external events must be included, the receipt of an event can be shown as an action that denotes waiting for a signal. A similar notation shows sending a signal.

Partitions. It is often useful to organize the activities in a model according to responsibility—for example, by grouping together all the activities handled by one business organization. This kind of assignment can be shown by organizing the activities into distinct regions (called partitions) separated by lines in the diagram. Because of the appearance, a region is sometimes called a swimlane. Figure 8-2 shows partitions.

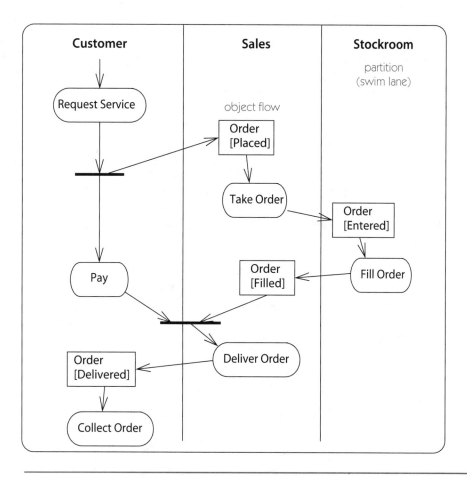

Figure 8-2. *Partitions and object flows*

Object flows. An activity diagram can show the flow of object values, as well as the flow of control. An object flow represents an object that is the input or output of an activity. For an output value, a solid arrow is drawn from an activity to an object flow. For an input value, a solid arrow is drawn from an object flow to an activity. If an activity has more than one output value or successor control flow, the arrows are drawn from a fork symbol. Similarly, multiple inputs are drawn to a join symbol.

Figure 8-2 shows an activity diagram in which both activities and object flows have been assigned to swimlanes.

Activities and Other Views

Activity graphs do not show the full detail of a computation. They show the flow of activities but not the objects that perform the activities. Activity graphs are a starting point for design. To complete a design, each activity must be implemented as one or more operations, each of which is assigned to a specific class to implement. Such an assignment results in the design of a collaboration that implements the activity graph.

Action

UML has a set of primitive actions that model manipulation of objects and links as well as computation and communication among objects. UML does not define a syntax for actions because it is expected that most models will use an existing action language or programming language. Table 8-1 shows the various kinds of actions.

Table 8-1: *Kinds of actions*

Category	Actions	Purpose
classification	readIsClassifiedObject reclassifyObject testIdentity	test classification change classification test object identity
communication	broadcastSignal callOperation reply (implicit) return sendObject sendSignal	broadcast normal call reply after explicit accept implicit action on activity end send signal as object send signal as argument list

Table 8-1: *Kinds of actions (continued)*

Category	Actions	Purpose
computation	accept call accept event addVariableValue applyFunction callBehavior clearVariable readSelf readVariable removeVariableValue writeVariable	inline wait for call inline wait for event add additional value to set mathematical computation nested behavior reset value in procedure obtain owning object identity obtain value in procedure remove value from set set value in procedure
control	startOwnedBehavior	explicit control
creation	createLinkObject createObject	create object from association create normal object
destruction	destroyObject	destroy object
exception	raiseException	raise exception in procedure
read	readExtent readLink readLinkObjectEnd readLinkObject- EndQualifier readStructuralFeature	get all objects get link value get value from association class get qualifier value get attribute value
time	durationObservation timeObservation	measure time interval get current time

write	addStructuralFeature-
	  Value
	clearAssociation
	clearStructuralFeature
	createLink
	destroyLink
	removeStructural-
	  FeatureValue
		set attribute value
		
		clear links
		clear attribute value
		add a link
		remove a link
		remove value from set

9

Interaction View

Overview

Objects interact to implement behavior. This interaction can be described in two complementary ways, one of them centered on individual objects and the other on a collection of cooperating objects.

A state machine is a narrow, deep view of behavior, a reductionist view that looks at each object individually. A state machine specification is precise and leads immediately to code. It can be difficult to understand the overall functioning of a system, however, because a state machine focuses on a single object at a time, and the effects of many state machines must be combined to determine the behavior of an entire system. The interaction view provides a more holistic view of the behavior of a set of objects. This view is modeled by interactions acting on structured classifiers and collaborations.

Interaction

A structured classifier defines a contextual relationship. A structured classifier (including a collaboration) may have a set of attached behaviors that apply to a set of objects bound to a single instance of the context. One kind of behavior description is a sequence of messages exchanged by the objects bound to the roles. A description of message sequences on a structured class or collaboration is called an interaction. A structured class or collaboration can have any number of interactions, each of which describes a series of messages exchanged among the objects in the context to perform a goal. Very commonly, interactions describe the execution of operations. The parameters of the operation serve as the roles of a collaboration that represents the operation execution.

An interaction is a set of messages within a structured classifier or collaboration that are exchanged by roles across connectors. An instance of an interaction corresponds to an instance of its context, with objects bound to roles exchanging message instances across links bound to connectors. An interaction often models the execution of an operation, use case, or other behavioral entity.

A message is a one-way communication between two objects, a flow of control with information from a sender to a receiver. A message may have arguments that convey values from the sender to the receiver. A message can be a signal (an explicit, named, asynchronous interobject communication) or a call (the synchronous or asynchronous invocation of an operation with a mechanism for later returning control to the sender of a synchronous call).

The creation of a new object may be modeled as a message sent by the creator object and received by the class itself. The creation event is available to the new instance as the current event on the transition from the top-level initial state.

Events (including the sending and receipt of messages) on a single role are ordered in time. Other events are concurrent unless they are related by a chain of intermediate messages or they are explicitly ordered. Two messages are ordered if the receive event of one precedes the send event of the other. Otherwise they may be concurrent.

Sequencing of events and messages can be shown in two kinds of diagrams: a sequence diagram (focusing on the time sequences of the messages) and a communication diagram (focusing on the relationships among the objects that exchange the messages).

Sequence Diagram

A sequence diagram displays an interaction as a two-dimensional chart. The vertical dimension is the time axis; time proceeds down the page. The horizontal dimension shows the roles that represent individual objects in the collaboration. Each role is represented by a vertical column containing a head symbol and a vertical line—a lifeline. During the time an object exists, it is shown by a dashed line. During the time an execution specification of a procedure on the object is active, the lifeline is drawn as a double line.

In general, a sequence diagram shows only sequences of messages and not exact time intervals. A timing diagram can be used when metric time is important, but for understanding the semantics of interactions, sequence diagrams are usually sufficient.

A message is shown as an arrow from the lifeline of one object to that of another. The arrows are arranged in time sequence down the diagram. An asynchronous message is shown with a stick arrowhead.

Figure 9-1 shows a typical sequence diagram with asynchronous messages.

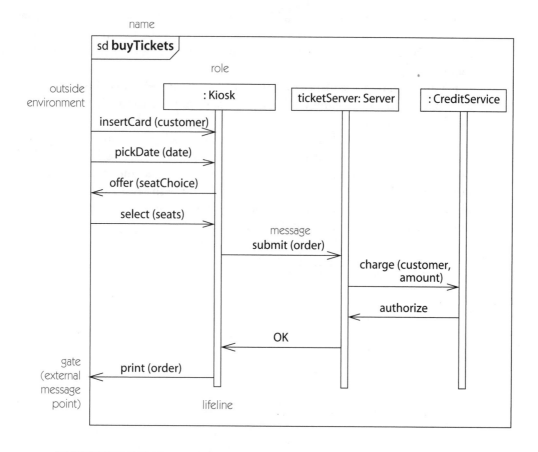

Figure 9-1. *Sequence diagram*

Execution Specification

An execution specification (activation) is the execution of a procedure, including any time it waits for nested procedures to execute. It is shown by a double line replacing part of the lifeline in a sequence diagram.

A call is shown by an arrow leading to the top of the execution specification the call initiates. A synchronous call is shown with a filled triangular arrowhead.

A recursive call occurs when control reenters an operation on an object, but the second call is a separate execution specification from the first. Recursion or a nested call to another operation on the same object is shown in a sequence diagram by stacking the activation lines.

The return of control from a call is shown by a dashed arrow with a stick arrowhead. In a procedural environment, return arrows may be omitted, because they are implicit at the end of an execution specification, but it is much clearer to show them.

Figure 9-2 shows a sequence diagram with procedural flow of control, including a second call to an object nested in another call and the creation of an object during the computation.

An active object is one that holds the root of a stack of executions. Each active object has its own event-driven thread of control that executes in parallel with other active objects. An active object is shown by a double line on each side of its head symbol. This indication is often omitted as it doesn't really mean much. The objects that are called by an active object are passive objects; they receive control only when called, and they yield it up when they return.

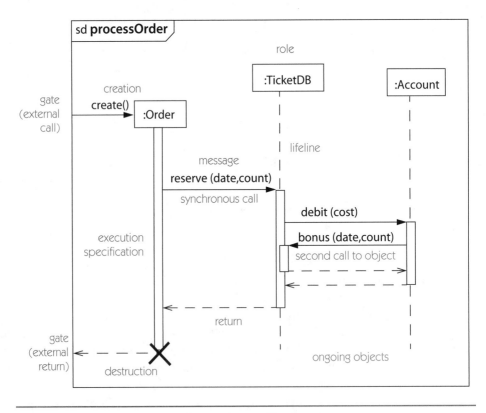

Figure 9-2. *Sequence diagram with execution specifications*

Structured Control Constructs

Sequential flow of control is easily shown in a sequence diagram as a sequence of messages (that's why it's called a *sequence diagram*). More complex flow of control may be shown using combined fragments. A combined fragment has a keyword and one or more subfragments (called interaction operands). The number and meaning of the subfragments depends on the keyword. See Figure 9-3.

An interaction use is a reference to another interaction, which is usually defined in its own sequence diagram.

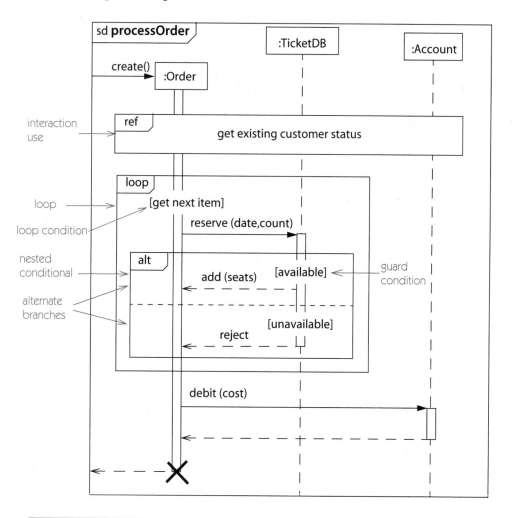

Figure 9-3. *Structured control constructs*

A loop has one subfragment, which is executed as long as the first guard condition in the subfragment is true.

A conditional fragment (keyword alt) has two or more subfragments, each having an initial guard condition. When the conditional is reached, a subfragment whose guard condition is true is executed. If more than one is true, one of them is selected nondeterministically for execution. If none is true, no execution is consistent with the specification. The optional fragment (keyword opt) is a special case with a single subfragment that is executed if its guard condition is true and omitted if the condition is false.

A parallel fragment (keyword par) has two or more subfragments. When the fragment is reached, all of the subfragments are executed concurrently. The relative sequence of messages in different subfragments is indeterminate and the messages can be interleaved in any possible order. When all subfragments have completed execution, the concurrent executions join together again into a single flow.

There are a number of other, more specialized structured constructs.

Figure 9-3 shows a sequence diagram containing a loop with a nested conditional.

Communication Diagram

A communication diagram is based on the context supplied by a structured classifier (including a collaboration). Roles and connectors describe the configuration of objects and links that may occur when an instance of a the context is executed. When the context is instantiated, objects are bound to the roles and links are bound to the connectors. Connectors may also be bound to various kinds of temporary links, such as procedure arguments or local procedure variables. Only objects that are involved in the context are modeled, although there may be others in the entire system. In other words, a communication diagram models the objects and links involved in the implementation of an interaction and ignores the others.

Messages among roles are shown as labeled arrows attached to connectors. Each message has a sequence number, an optional guard condition, a name and argument list, and an optional return value name. The sequence number includes the (optional) name of a thread. All messages in the same thread are sequentially ordered. Messages in different threads are concurrent unless there is an explicit sequencing dependency. Various implementation details may be added, such as a distinction between asynchronous and synchronous messages.

Figure 9-4 shows a communication diagram.

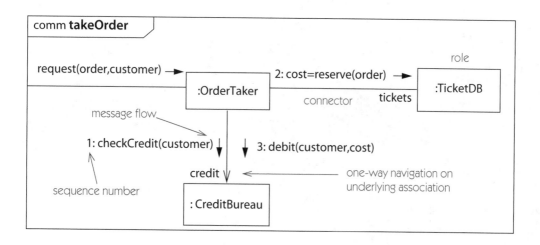

Figure 9-4. *Communication diagram*

Communication and sequence diagrams. Communication diagrams and sequence diagrams both show interactions, but they emphasize different aspects. Sequence diagrams show time sequences clearly but do not show object relationships explicitly. Communication diagrams show object relationships clearly, but time sequences must be obtained from sequence numbers. Sequence diagrams are often most useful for showing scenarios; communication diagrams are often more useful for showing detailed design of procedures. Once the structure of a procedure is defined, however, a sequence diagram may be more useful for planning fine details of control.

10

Deployment View

Overview

The deployment view shows the physical arrangement of nodes. A node is a run-time computational resource, such as a computers or other device. At run time, nodes can contain artifacts, physical entities such as files. The manifestation relationship shows the relationship between design elements, such as components, and the artifacts that embody them in the software system. The deployment view may highlight performance bottlenecks due to placement of artifacts manifesting interdependent components on different nodes.

Node

A node models a run-time computational resource, generally having at least a memory and often processing capability as well. Nodes may have stereotypes to distinguish different kinds of resources, such as CPUs, devices, and memories. Nodes may hold artifacts.

A node type is shown as a stylized cube with its name embedded. A node instance is shown as a cube with an underlined name string with a name and node type (Figure 10-1).

Associations between nodes represent communication paths. The associations can have stereotypes to distinguish different kinds of paths.

Nodes may have generalization relationships to relate a general description of a node to a more specific variation.

Artifact

An artifact models a physical entity such as a file. An artifact is shown by a rectangle with the keyword «artifact». The presence of an artifact on a node is shown by physically nesting the artifact symbol inside the node symbol.

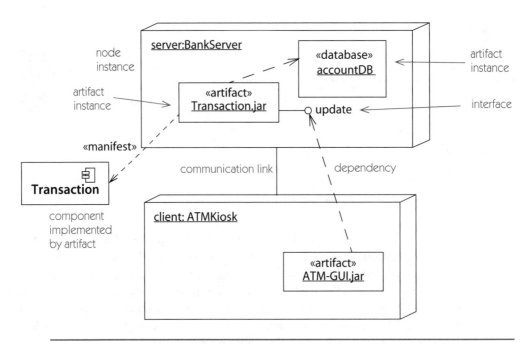

Figure 10-1. *Deployment diagram*

Various kinds of artifacts, such as databases, web pages, executables, or scripts, can be marked with stereotypes.

If an artifact implements a component or other class, a dashed arrow with the keyword «manifest» is drawn from the artifact symbol to the symbol of the component that it implements. This relationship is called manifestation.

11

Model Management View

Overview

Any large system must be divided into smaller units so that humans can work with a limited amount of information at one time and so that work teams do not interfere with each other's work. Model management consists of packages (including special kinds of packages) and dependency relationships among packages.

Package

A package is a piece of a model. Every part of a model must belong to one package. The modeler may allocate the contents of a model to a set of packages. But to be workable, the allocation must follow some rational principle, such as common functionality, tightly coupled implementation, and a common viewpoint. UML does not impose a rule for composing packages, but a good decomposition into packages will greatly enhance model maintainability.

Packages contain top-level model elements, such as classes and their relationships, state machines, use case graphs, interactions, and collaborations—anything not contained in some other element. Elements such as attributes, operations, states, lifelines, and messages are contained in other elements and do not appear as direct contents of packages. Every top-level element has one package in which it is declared. This is its "home" package. It may be referenced in other packages, but the contents of the element are owned by the home package. In a configuration control system, a modeler must have access to the home package to modify the contents of an element. This provides an access control mechanism for working with large models. Packages are also the units for any versioning mechanisms.

Packages may contain other packages. There is a root package that indirectly contains the entire model of a system. There are several possible ways to organize the packages for a system. They may be arranged by view, by functionality, or by any other basis that the modeler chooses. Packages are general-purpose hierarchical organizational units of UML models. They can be used for storage, access control, configuration management, and constructing libraries containing reusable model fragments.

If the packages are well chosen, so that the organization structures (packages) correspond to design structures (components), they reflect the high-level architecture of a system—its decomposition into subsystems and their dependencies. Packages that cut across subsystems often cause troubles among teams of designers. A dependency among packages summarizes the dependencies among the package contents.

Dependencies on Packages

Dependencies arise among individual elements, but in a system of any size, they must be viewed at a higher level. Dependencies among packages summarize dependencies among elements in them—that is, package dependencies are derivable from the dependencies among individual elements.

The presence of a dependency among packages implies that there exists in a bottom-up approach (an existence statement), or is permitted to exist later in a top-down approach (a constraint on future design), at least one relationship element of the given kind of dependency among individual elements within the corresponding packages. It is an "existence statement" and does not imply that all elements of the package have the dependency. It is a flag to the modeler that there exists further information, but the package-level dependency does not contain the further information itself; it is only a summary.

Figure 11-1 shows the package structure for a ticket-ordering subsystem. It has dependencies on outside packages.

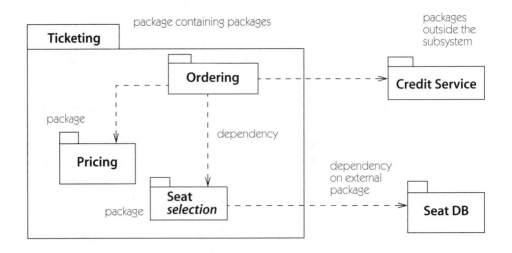

Figure 11-1. *Packages and their relationships*

The top-down approach reflects the overall system architecture. The bottom-up approach can be automatically generated from the individual elements. Both approaches have their place in modeling, even on a single system.

Multiple dependencies of the same kind among individual elements are aggregated to a single package-level dependency among the packages containing the elements. If the dependencies among individual elements contain stereotypes (such as different kinds of usage), the stereotype may be omitted in the package-level dependency in order to yield a single high-level dependency.

Packages are drawn as rectangles with tabs on them (desktop "folder" icons). Dependencies are shown as dashed arrows.

Visibility

A package is a namespace for its elements. It establishes visibility of its elements. Elements directed owned by packages can have public or private visibility. A package can see only the elements of other packages that have been given public visibility by the package containing them. Elements with private visibility are visible only in the package containing them and any packages nested inside that package.

Visibility also applies to the features of classes (attributes and operations). An element with public visibility can be seen by other classes within the same package or within other packages that can see the class and by descendants of the class. A feature with private visibility can only be seen by its own class. A feature with protected visibility can be seen by the class or a descendant of a class. A feature with package visibility can be seen by other classes within the same package, but not by classes in other packages, even if they can see the class.

A package nested within another package is part of the container and has full access to its contents (transitively). A container, however, may not see inside its nested packages without proper visibility; the contents are encapsulated.

Import

A package may import elements from another package to add their names to its namespace (Figure 11-2). Importing does not add any modeling power, but it does simplify text expressions that appear in constraints and eventually code. An element can be imported if it is visible to the importing package. A package may also import an entire package, which is equivalent to importing all the visible elements within it.

An imported element becomes a visible element of the importing package under its imported name (which may differ from the original name, although they are usually the same). The access relationship adds an element to the namespace without making it public in the importing package.

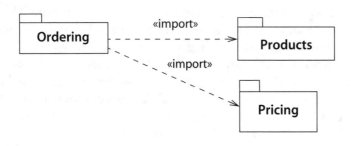

Figure 11-2. *Package import*

Model

A model is a package that encompasses a complete description of a particular view of a system. It provides a closed description of a system from one viewpoint. It does not have strong dependencies on other packages, such as implementation dependencies or inheritance dependencies. The trace relationship is a weak form of dependency among elements in different models that notes the presence of some connection without specific semantic implications.

Usually, a model is tree-structured. The root package contains in itself nested packages that constitute the full detail of the system from the given viewpoint. A model can be shown as a package with a triangle adornment but usually there is little point in showing models as symbols.

12

Profiles

Overview

UML provides several extension mechanisms to allow modelers to make some common extensions without having to modify the underlying modeling language. These extension mechanisms have been designed so that tools can store and manipulate the extensions without understanding their full semantics or purpose. It is expected that back-end tools and add-ins will be written to process various kinds of extensions. These tools will define a particular syntax and semantics for their extensions that only they need understand.

Extensions are organized into profiles. A profile is coherent set of extensions applicable to a given domain or purpose. By their nature, profiles are not applicable in all circumstances, and different profiles may or may not be compatible with one another.

This approach to extensions probably will not meet every need that arises, but it should accommodate a large portion of the tailoring needed by most modelers in a simple manner that is easy to implement.

The extensibility mechanisms are stereotype, tagged values, and constraints.

Keep in mind that an extension, by definition, deviates from the standard form of UML and may therefore lead to interoperability problems. The modeler should carefully weigh benefits and costs before using extensions, especially when existing mechanisms will work reasonably well. Typically, extensions are intended for particular application domains or programming environments, but they result in a UML dialect, with the advantages and disadvantages of all dialects.

Stereotype

Many modelers wish to tailor a modeling language for a particular application domain. This carries some risk, because the tailored language will not be universally understandable, but people nevertheless attempt to do it.

A stereotype is a kind of model element defined in the model itself. The information content and form of a stereotype are the same as those of an existing kind of base model element, but its meaning and usage is different. For example, modelers in the business modeling area often wish to distinguish business objects and business processes as special kinds of modeling elements whose usage is distinct within a given development process. These can be treated as special kinds of classes—they have attributes and operations, but they have special constraints on their relationships to other elements and on their usage.

A stereotype is based on an existing model element. The information content of the stereotyped element is the same as the existing model element. This permits a tool to store and manipulate the new element the same way it does the existing element. The stereotyped element may have its own distinct icon—this is easy for a tool to support. For example, a "business organization" might have an icon that looks like a group of persons. The stereotype may also have a list of constraints that apply to its usage. For example, perhaps a "business organization" can be associated only with another "business organization" and not with any class. Not all constraints can be automatically verified by a general-purpose tool, but they can be enforced manually or verified by an add-in tool that understands the stereotype.

Stereotypes may define tagged values to store additional properties that are not supported by the base element.

Stereotypes are shown as text strings surrounded by guillemets («») placed in or near the symbol for the base model element. The modeler may also create an icon for a particular stereotype, which replaces the base element symbol (Figure 12-1).

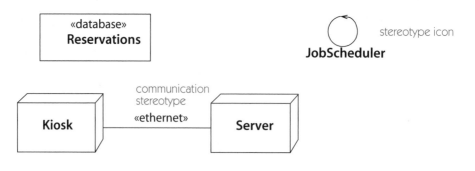

Figure 12-1. *Stereotypes*

Tagged Value

A tag definition is a definition of an attribute for a modeling element itself, that is, the definition of a metaatribute. It defines properties of elements in user models, rather than properties of run-time objects. It has a name and a type. A tag definition is owned by a stereotype.

When a stereotype is applied to a model element, the model element gains the tags defined in the stereotype (Figure 12-2). For each tag, the modeler may specify a tagged value. Tagged values are shown as strings with the tag name, an equal sign, and the value within notes attached to a model element (Figure 12-2). They will often be omitted on diagrams but shown on pop-up lists and forms.

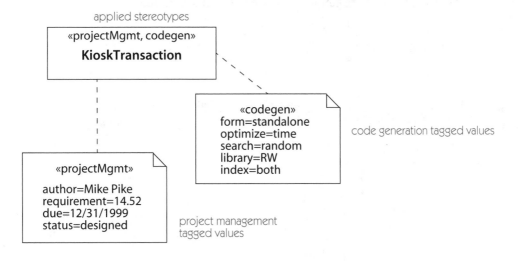

Figure 12-2. *Stereotypes and tagged values*

In defining a stereotype, each tag is a name of some property the modeler wants to record, and the value in a model element is the value of that property for the given element. For example, the tag might be **author**, and the value might be the name of the person responsible for the element, such as **Charles Babbage**.

Tags can be defined to store arbitrary information about elements. They are particularly useful for storing project management information, such as the creation date of an element, its development status, due dates, and test status. Any string may be used as a tag name, except that the names of built-in metamodel attributes should be avoided (because tags and attributes together can be considered properties of an element and accessed uniformly in a tool), and a number of tag names are predefined.

Tagged values also provide a way to attach implementation-dependent add-in information to elements. For example, a code generator may need additional information about the kind of code to generate from a model. Often, there are several possible ways to correctly implement a model; the modeler must provide guidance about which choices to make. Certain tags can be used as flags to tell the code generator which implementation to use. Other tags can be used for other kinds of add-in tools, such as project planners and report writers.

Profile

A profile is a package that identifies a subset of an existing base metamodel (possibly including all of it) and defines stereotypes and constraints that may be applied to the selected metamodel subset (Figure 12-3). It is intended to make limited extensions to UML to tailor it to a specific domain, technology, or implementation.

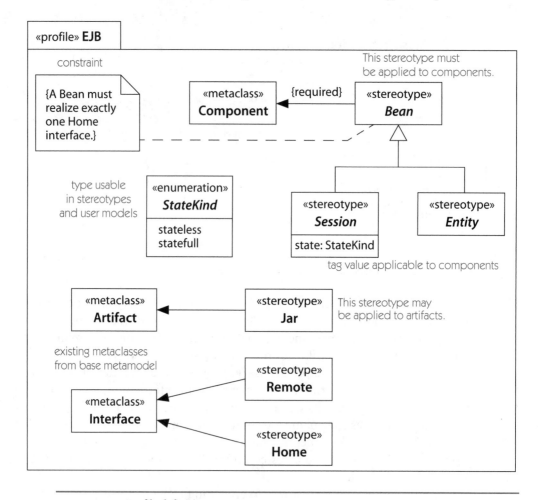

Figure 12-3. *Profile definition*

A profile is made available to a use model by profile application on a package. The constraints on the profile apply to the elements of the package, and the stereotypes defined in the profile can be used by model elements in the package. Figure 12-4 shows the application of profiles to a package.

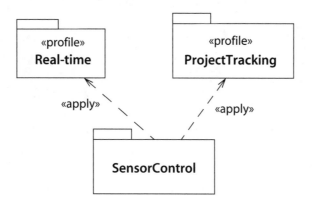

Figure 12-4. *Profile application*

13
UML Environment

Overview

UML models are used within an environment. Most people use modeling as a means to an end—namely, the development of good systems—and not an end in itself. The purpose and interpretation of the model are affected by the rest of the environment. Other facilities in the wider environment include metamodels that cross many languages, model-editing tools, programming languages, operating systems and major system components, and the business and engineering world within which systems are used. The responsibility for giving meaning to a model and implementing its intent lies with all these facilities, including UML.

Models occur at various levels of concreteness. UML is a general-purpose modeling language that includes semantics and notation but is usable with different tools and implementation languages. Each level of usage introduces certain modeling considerations that appear in the UML to various degrees.

Semantics Responsibilities

A metamodel is the description of a model. A modeling language describes models; therefore, it can be described by a metamodel. A metamodel attempts to make a language precise by defining its semantics, but there is a tension to permit extensions for new situations. The actual form of the metamodel is important to tool implementation and model interchange but not very important to most users. We therefore have not covered it in this book. Those who are interested can consult the original standards documents available on the OMG web site (www.omg.org).

A metamodel and a language must cover a lot of ground and accommodate many interpretations. Existing systems have differing execution and memory models. It is impossible to choose one of them as the right interpretation. In fact, it is probably misleading to even consider such a choice. Instead, one can think of the different interpretations of execution models as semantic variation points. A semantic variation point is a point of difference about the detailed semantics of execution, but one that is orthogonal to other aspects of a system. For example, an environment may or may not choose to support dynamic classification, the ability of an object to change class at run time. Today, most programming languages do not permit it, mainly for programming-language implementation reasons, but some do. The difference is indistinguishable in the static semantics. The choice of static classification or dynamic classification can be identified as a semantic variation point with two options: static classification or dynamic classification. When such choices exist, people often argue about which is the right interpretation. Realize instead that this is a choice, and give it a name so that either choice can be used.

A metamodel describes the contents of a model that is well formed, just as a programming language describes a well-formed program. Only a well-formed model has a meaning and proper semantics; it does not make sense to ask the meaning of a model that is ill formed. Much of the time, however, models under development are not well formed. They are incomplete and possibly inconsistent. But that is what model-editing tools must support—incomplete models, not just finished models. The UML metamodel describes correct, well-formed models. A separate metamodel could describe possible model fragments. We leave it to the tool makers to decide where to draw the line on supporting model fragments and what kind of semantic support to give to ill-formed models.

UML includes profiles to tailor its use in specialized domains. The profile mechanism includes the ability to define stereotypes with tagged values. Profiles can be used to tailor a UML variant by defining a set of stereotypes and tags and adopting conventions for their use in order to build a model. For example, variants could be developed that are focused on the implementation semantics of various programming languages. Adding extensions can be powerful, but it carries some inherent dangers. Because their semantics are not defined within UML, UML cannot supply their meaning; the interpretation is up to the modeler. Furthermore, if you are not careful, some meanings may be ambiguous or even inconsistent. Modeling tools can provide automated support for stereotypes and tags defined by the tools, but not for user-defined extensions. Regardless of the support for extensions, any extension pulls the user away from the common center that the language standard provides and undercuts the goals of interchangeability of models and of the understandability of models. Some profiles may be standardized by OMG or industry groups, which reduces the danger of incompatibility. Of course, whenever you use a particular class library, you diverge from the perfect interchangeability of nothingness. So don't worry about it in the abstract. Use the profiles when they help, but avoid them when they are not needed.

Notation Responsibilities

Notation does not add meaning to a model, but it does help the user to understand the meaning in it. Notation does not have semantics, but it often adds connotations for a user, such as the perceived affinity of two concepts based on their nearness in a diagram.

The UML specifications and this book define a canonical UML notation, what might be called the publication format for models. This is similar to many programming languages in which programs within journal articles are printed in an attractive format with careful layout, reserved words in boldface, and separate figures for each procedure. Real compilers have to accept messier input. We expect that editing tools will extend the notation to a screen format, including such things as the use of fonts and color to highlight items; the ability to easily suppress and filter items that are not currently of interest, to zoom into a diagram to show nested elements, to traverse hot links to other models or views; and animation. It would be hopeless to try to standardize all these possibilities and foolish to try, because there is no need and it would limit useful innovation. This kind of notational extension is the responsibility of a tool builder. In an interactive tool, there is less danger from ambiguity, because the user can always ask for a clarification. This is probably more useful than insisting on a notation that is totally unambiguous at first glance. A tool must be able to produce the canonical notation when requested, especially in printed form, but reasonable extensions should be expected in an interactive tool.

We expect that tools will also permit users to extend notation in limited but useful ways. We have specified that stereotypes can have their own icons. Other kinds of notational extensions might be permitted, but users need to use some discretion.

Note that notation is more than pictures; it includes information in text-based forms and the invisible hyperlinks among presentation elements.

Programming Language Responsibilities

UML must work with various implementation languages without incorporating them explicitly. UML should permit the use of any (or at least many) programming languages, for both specification and target-code generation. The problem is that each programming language has many semantic issues should not be absorbed into UML, because they are better handled as programming-language issues, and there is considerable variation in execution semantics. For example, the semantics of concurrency are handled in diverse ways among the languages (if they are handled at all). Profiles can be defined for different programming languages.

Primitive data types are not described in detail in UML. This is deliberate to avoid incorporating the semantics of one programming language in preference to all others. For most modeling purposes, this is not a problem. Use the semantic model applicable to your target language. This is an example of a semantic variation point that can be addressed in a language profile.

The representation of detailed language properties for implementation raises the problem of capturing information about implementation properties without building their semantics into UML. One approach is to capture language properties that go beyond UML's built-in capabilities by defining profiles containing stereotypes and tagged values for various programming language properties. A generic editor need not understand them. Indeed a user could create a model using a tool that did not support the target language and transfer the final model to another tool, such as a code generator, for final processing. The code generator would understand the stereotypes. Of course, if the generic tool does not understand the stereotypes and tags, it cannot check them for consistency. But this is no worse than normal practice with text editors and compilers.

Code generation and reverse engineering for the foreseeable future will require input from the designer in addition to a UML model. Directives and hints to the code generator can be supplied as tagged values and stereotypes. For example, the modeler could indicate which kind of container class should be used to implement an association. Of course, this means that code-generation settings in tools might be incompatible, but we do not believe there currently is sufficient agreement on the right approach to standardize the language settings. In any case, different tools will use their code generators as their competitive advantage. Eventually, default settings may emerge and become ripe for standardization.

Modeling with Tools

Models require tool support for realistic-sized systems. Tools provide interactive ways to view and edit models. They provide a level of organization that is outside the scope of the UML itself but that conveys understanding to the user and helps in accessing information. Tools help to find information in large models by searching and filtering what is presented.

Tool issues

Tools deal with the physical organization and storage of models. These must support multiple work teams on a single project, as well as reuse across projects. The following issues are outside the scope of canonical UML, but must be considered for actual tool usage.

Ambiguities and unspecified information. At early stages, many things are still unsaid. Tools must be able to adjust the precision of a model and not force every value to be specific. See the following sections "Inconsistent models for work in progress" and "Null and unspecified values."

Presentation options. Users do not want to see all the information all the time. Tools must support filtering and hiding of information that is unwanted at a given time. Tools will also add support for alternate visualizations by using the capabilities of the display hardware. This has been covered above in the section "Notation Responsibilities."

Model management. Configuration control, access control, and versioning of model units are outside the scope of UML, but they are crucial to the software engineering process and go on top of the metamodel.

Interfaces to other tools. Models need to be handled by code generators, metrics calculators, report writers, execution engines, and other back-end tools. Information for other tools needs to be included in the models, but it is not UML information. Profiles with stereotypes and tagged values are suitable for holding this information.

Inconsistent models for work in progress

The ultimate goal of modeling is to produce a description of a system at some level of detail. The final model must satisfy various validity constraints to be meaningful. As in any creative process, however, the result is not necessarily produced in a linear fashion. Intermediate products will not satisfy all the validity constraints at every step. In practice, a tool must handle not only semantically valid models, which satisfy the validity constraints, but also syntactically valid models, which satisfy certain construction rules but may violate some validity constraints. Semantically invalid models are not directly usable. Instead they may be thought of as "works in progress" that represent paths to the final result.

Null and unspecified values

A complete model must have values for all the attributes of its elements. In many cases, null (no value) is one of the possible values, but whether a value may be null is a part of the type description of the attribute; many types do not have a natural null value within their range of values. For example, null makes no sense as the upper bound on the size of a set. Either the set has a fixed upper size or there is no bound, in which case its maximum size is unlimited. Nullability is really just an augmentation to the range of possible values of a data type.

On the other hand, during early stages of design, a developer may not care about the value of a particular property. It might be a value that is not meaningful at a particular stage, for example, visibility when making a domain model. Or the value may be meaningful but the modeler may not have specified it yet, and the developer needs to remember that it still needs to be chosen. In this case, the value is unspecified. This indicates that a value will eventually be needed but that it has not yet been specified. It is not the same as a null value, which may be a legitimate value in the final model. In many cases, particularly with strings, a null value is a good way to indicate an unspecified value, but they are not the same. An unspecified value is not meaningful in a well-formed model. The UML definition does not handle unspecified values. They are the responsibility of tools that support UML and are considered part of a "work in progress" model that, by necessity, has no semantic meaning.

Part 3: Reference ———————————

14

Dictionary of Terms

abstract

A class, use case, signal, or other classifier that cannot be instantiated. Also used to describe an operation that has no implementation. Antonym: concrete.

See abstract operation, generalizable element.

Semantics

An abstract class is a class that is not instantiable—that is, it may not have direct instances, either because its description is incomplete (such as lacking methods for one or more operations) or because it is not intended to be instantiated even though its description is complete. An abstract class is intended for specialization. To be useful, an abstract class must have descendants that may have instances; an abstract leaf class is useless. (It can appear as a leaf in a framework, but eventually, it must be specialized.)

An operation lacking an implementation (a method) is abstract. A concrete class may not have any abstract operations (otherwise, it is necessarily abstract), but an abstract class may have concrete operations. Concrete operations are those that can be implemented once and used the same across all subclasses. In their implementation, concrete operations may use only features (attributes and operations) known to the class in which they are declared. One of the purposes of inheritance is to factor such operations into abstract superclasses so that they can be shared by all subclasses. A concrete operation may be polymorphic—that is, it can be overridden by a method in a descendant class—but it need not be polymorphic (it may be a leaf operation). A class, all of whose operations are implemented, may be abstract, but it must be explicitly declared as such. A class with one or more unimplemented operations is automatically abstract.

Similar semantics apply to use cases. An abstract use case defines a fragment of behavior that cannot appear by itself, but it can appear in the definition of concrete use cases by the generalization, include, or extend relationships. By factoring the common behavior into an abstract use case, the model is made smaller and easier to understand.

Notation

The name of an abstract classifier or an abstract operation is shown in italics. Alternately, the keyword **abstract** may be placed in a property list below or after the name, for example, Account {abstract}.

See also class name.

Example

Figure 14-1 shows an abstract class Account with one abstract operation, computeInterest, and one concrete operation, deposit. Two concrete subclasses have been declared. Because the subclasses are concrete, each of them must implement the operation computeInterest. Attributes are always concrete.

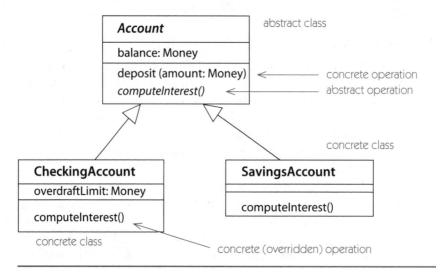

Figure 14-1. *Abstract and concrete classes*

History

In UML2, generalization has been restricted to classifiers. However, an operation in a classifier may be considered declared abstract or concrete even though operations themselves are not generalizable.

Discussion

The distinction between modeling a class as abstract or concrete is not as fundamental or clear-cut as it might first appear. It is more a design decision about a model than an inherent property. During the evolution of a design, the status of a class may change. A concrete class may be modeled as abstract if subclasses that enumerate all its possibilities are added. An abstract class may be modeled as concrete if distinctions among subclasses are found to be unnecessary and removed or are represented by attribute values instead of distinct subclasses.

One way to simplify the decision is to adopt the design principle that all nonleaf classes must be abstract (and all leaf classes must of necessity be concrete, except for an abstract leaf class intended for future specialization). This is not a UML rule; it is a style that may or may not be adopted. The reason for this "abstract superclasses" rule is that an inheritable method on a superclass and a method on a concrete class often have different needs that are not well served by a single method. The method on the superclass is forced to do two things: define the general case to be observed by all descendants and implement the general case for the specific class. These goals frequently conflict. Instead, any nonabstract superclass can be separated mechanically into an abstract superclass and a concrete leaf subclass. The abstract superclass contains all methods intended to be inherited by all subclasses; the concrete subclass contains methods that are needed for the specific instantiable class. Following the abstract superclass rule also allows a clean distinction between a variable or parameter that must hold the specific concrete type and one that can hold any descendant of the superclass.

In Figure 14-2, consider the declaration of class Letter that does not follow the abstract superclass rule. This class has an operation, getNextSentence, that returns the text for the next unread sentence, as well as an operation, resetCursor, that sets the cursor to the beginning. However, the subclass EncryptedLetter represents a letter that has been encrypted. The operation getNextSentence has been overridden because the text must be decrypted before it is returned. The implementation of the operation is completely different. Because Letter is a concrete superclass, it is impossible to distinguish a parameter that must be an ordinary Letter (nonoverridable) from one that could be either an ordinary Letter or an EncryptedLetter.

The abstract superclass approach is to distinguish abstract class Letter (which might be an encrypted letter or a nonencrypted letter) and to add class NonEncryptedLetter to represent the concrete case, as shown in Figure 14-3. In this case, getNextSentence is an abstract operation that is implemented by each subclass and resetCursor is a concrete operation that is the same for all subclasses. The model is symmetrical.

If the abstract superclass rule is followed, the declaration of abstract classes can be determined automatically from the class hierarchy and showing it on diagrams is redundant.

There is an exception to the statement that an abstract leaf class is useless: An abstract class may be declared in order to be a common namespace for a set of

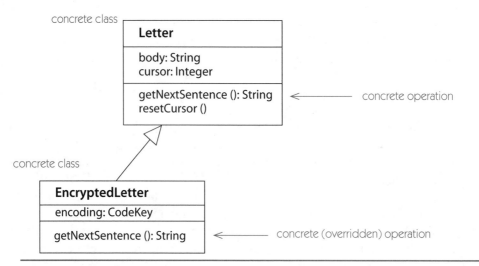

Figure 14-2. *Concrete superclass leads to ambiguity*

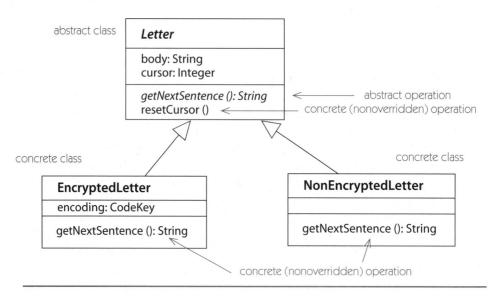

Figure 14-3. *Abstract superclass avoids ambiguity*

global class-scope attributes and operations. This is a relatively minor usage, mainly for programming convenience when dealing with non-object-oriented languages, and users are advised to avoid it in most cases. Global values violate the spirit of object-oriented design by introducing global dependencies. A singleton class can often provide the same functionality in a more extensible way.

See [Gamma-95], Singleton pattern.

abstract class

A class that may not be instantiated.
See abstract.

Semantics

An abstract class may not have direct instances. It may have indirect instances through its concrete descendants.
See abstract for a discussion.

abstract operation

An operation that lacks an implementation—that is, one that has a specification but no method. An implementation must be supplied by any concrete descendant class.
See abstract, generalizable element, inheritance, polymorphic.

Semantics

If an operation is declared as abstract in a class, it lacks an implementation (a method or a trigger) in the class, and the class itself is necessarily abstract. An implementation must be supplied for the operation by a concrete descendant. If the class inherits an implementation of the operation but declares the operation as abstract, the abstract declaration invalidates the inherited implementation in the class. If an operation is declared as concrete in a class, then the class must supply or inherit an implementation (a method or a trigger) from an ancestor. If an operation is not declared at all in a class, then it inherits the operation declaration and implementation (or lack thereof) from its ancestors.

An operation may be implemented as a method or as a state machine trigger. Each class may declare its own implementation for an operation or inherit a definition from an ancestor.

Notation

The name of an abstract operation is shown in italics (Figure 14-4). Alternately, the keyword **abstract** may be placed in a property list after the operation signature.

Discussion

The most important use for the concept of inheritance is to support abstract operations that can be implemented differently by each concrete descendant class. An abstract operation permits a caller to invoke an operation without knowing precisely which class of object is the target, provided the target object is known to support the operation by being an indirect instance of an abstract class that has a

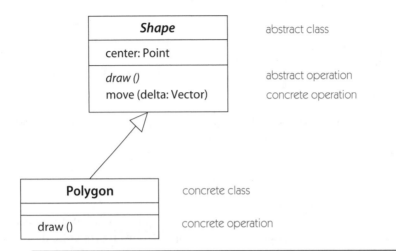

Figure 14-4. *Abstract operation and class*

declaration of the abstract operation. The significance of such polymorphic operations is that the responsibility for determining the kind of object is shifted from
the caller to the inheritance mechanism. Not only is the caller freed of the bother
and cost of writing case statements, but the caller need not even be aware of which
possible subclasses of an abstract class exist. This means that additional subclasses
may be added later with new operation implementations. Abstract operations,
polymorphism, and inheritance thereby facilitate updating of systems to add new
kinds of objects and behaviors without having to modify the code that invokes the
generic behavior. This greatly reduces the time needed to update a system and,
even more important, it reduces the possibility of accidental inconsistencies.

abstraction

1. The act of identifying the essential characteristics of a thing that distinguish it
from all other kinds of things and omitting details that are unimportant from a
certain viewpoint. Abstraction involves looking for similarities across sets of things
by focusing on their essential common characteristics. An abstraction always involves the perspective and purpose of the viewer; different purposes result in
different abstractions for the same things. All modeling involves abstraction, often
at many levels for various purposes. The higher the level of abstraction, the less detail included.

2. A kind of dependency that relates two elements that represent the same concept
at different abstraction levels.

See derivation, realization, refinement, trace dependency.

Semantics

An abstraction dependency is a relationship between two elements at different abstraction levels, such as representations in different models, at different levels of precision, at different levels of concreteness, or at different levels of optimization. Generally the two representations would not be used simultaneously. Normally one element is more detailed than the other; the more detailed element is the client and the less detailed element is the supplier. If there is no clear understanding that either element is more detailed, then either element can be modeled as the client.

Variations of abstraction dependency are trace dependency, refinement, derivation, and realization.

Notation

An abstraction dependency is shown as a dashed arrow from the client element to the supplier element with the keyword «trace», «refine», or «derive». The realization dependency has its own special notation as a dashed arrow with a closed triangular arrowhead on the supplier element.

The mapping between elements can be attached to the relationship as a constraint symbol.

Discussion

The phrase abstract class follows from the first definition. An abstract class focuses on a few essential details that apply to a range of concrete classes. Changing the viewpoint moves one up or down the generalization hierarchy.

accept action

An action whose execution blocks until a specified kind of event is recognized by the executing object. A specialized version waits for the receipt of a call of a specified operation.

See action for details.

History

This action is new to UML2.

access

A variation on the import dependency that permits one package to use names from another namespace to reference elements from that namespace. The imported names are private within the importing package and may not be referenced or reimported by external packages.

See import for full details.

action

A primitive activity node whose execution results in a change in the state of the system or the return of a value.

Semantics

An action is a primitive activity node—that it, it is the smallest computation that can be expressed in UML. An action is an activity node that *does* something to the state of the system or extracts information from it. If a high-level activity is viewed as a tree of nested activity nodes, the leaves of the tree are actions. Actions include arithmetic and string functions, manipulations of objects and their values, communications among objects, and similar things. Note that flow-of-control constructs, such as conditionals and loops, are not considered actions, because they are activities that contain smaller parts. Calls of operations, however, are considered actions. Although the execution of a call may be recursive, the call action itself is a leaf node within the specification of a particular activity and has no embedded structure within that activity. A call action references another activity definition, but that activity definition is distinct from the one containing the call.

Typical actions include assignment of values to attributes, accessing values of attributes or links, creation of new objects or links, simple arithmetic, and sending signals to other objects. Actions are the discrete steps out of which behavior is built.

An action has a number of input pins and output pins that model input and output values. The number and types of pins depends on the kind of action. For example, a subtract action has two input pins and one output pin, all of numerical type.

An action may begin execution when input values are available on all its input pins and control tokens are available on all incoming control edges. When execution begins, the input values and tokens are consumed so that no other action can use them. When the execution of an action is complete, output values are produced on all its output pins and control tokens are placed on all outgoing control edges.

Actions are usually felt to be "fast" computations that take minimal time to execute. In particular, with a few exceptions, the execution of an action has no relevant internal structure that can be modeled. If execution of the action is interrupted before it is complete, it has no effect on the system state; there are no externally visible intermediate effects. The exception is the call action. After a call request is transmitted, the execution of this action blocks until a reply is received from the initiated activity; execution of a call action can take an indefinite length of time. The execution model might be slightly cleaner if the call action were broken into two parts, one to issue the call and one to wait for the response, but this would introduce unnecessary complications.

The system can execute several actions concurrently, but their execution has no direct interaction; there may be indirect dependencies through the use of shared objects, however. The provision for concurrent action execution does not constrain the implementation of a model. Concurrency can be implemented by a single processor time-sharing among multiple executions or it can be implemented by multiple execution units.

Some kinds of actions can terminate abnormally and raise exceptions rather than completing normally. See exception for a discussion of this issue.

Execution of actions may be forcibly terminated by certain mechanisms. See interrupt for a discussion of this issue.

The full UML specification permits specification of streaming behavior and non-reentrant action execution. These are advanced features that must be used with care to avoid ill-formed models. They can be avoided in most logical models.

Structure

An action has a list of input pins and output pins. The number of pins depends on the specific kind of action. Most kinds of actions have a fixed number of pins holding values of specified types; a few kinds of actions have a variable number of pins of arbitrary types. During execution, each input pin holds a value that is an argument of the action. After execution, each output pin holds a value that is a result of the action.

Precondition and postcondition. An action may have local preconditions and postconditions. A precondition is an assertion by the modeler that a particular condition is supposed to be true when an action becomes enabled. It is not intended as a guard condition that may or may not be true. If a precondition is violated, the model is ill formed. Enforcement of preconditions is a semantic variation point determined by the implementation environment.

A postcondition is an assertion that a particular condition is supposed to be true at the completion of execution of an action. Its enforcement is similar to a precondition.

Kinds of actions

Accept call action. This is a variant of the accept event action. The trigger is the receipt of a call of a specified operation. The call is usually synchronous and the calling execution is blocked waiting for a reply. The output of this action provides an opaque piece of information that identifies the execution of the action that called the current object. This information may be copied and passed to other actions, but it may be used only once in a reply action to transmit a reply to the caller. If the call was asynchronous, the return information is empty, and a subsequent attempt to reply to it is a programming error with undefined consequences. (A particular implementation profile might specify the consequences.)

Accept event action. Execution of this action blocks execution of the current execution thread until the owning object detects a specified kind of event, often the receipt of a specified signal. The parameters of the event are included in the output of the action. This action is intended for asynchronous invocations. If it is triggered by a synchronous call with no return parameters, an immediate return is performed but the execution of the current thread continues. It is a semantic error if the action is triggered by a synchronous call with return parameters, because the accept event action is unable to provide them. The accept call action is intended for that situation.

Apply function action. Execution of this action produces a list of output values as a a function of a list of input values. There are absolutely no side effects on part of the system; the only effect is the production of the output values themselves. The transformation is specified as a primitive function. A primitive function is a mathematical function; that is, it defines each output value in terms of the list of input values without any internal effects or side-effects. The specification of primitive functions is outside the scope of UML itself; they must be specified using some external language, such as mathematical notation. The intent is that any particular implementation of a system would have a predefined set of primitive functions that could be used. It is not the intent to permit user definition of new primitive functions in a convenient way. Examples of primitive functions include arithmetic operations, Boolean operations, and string operations. Other examples appropriate for particular systems include operations on time and dates.

The number and types of the input and output values must be compatible with the specified function. In most cases, a particular primitive function has a fixed number of input and output pins.

The purpose of providing primitive functions in UML is to avoid selecting certain primitive operations as "fundamental." Every programming language selects a different set of primitive operations.

Primitive functions are intended for specifying the built-in, predefined computational actions of a system, such as arithmetic, Boolean functions, or basic string processing, which cannot usefully be reduced to procedure calls. It is expected that they would be defined by profile builders and not by most modelers. A primitive function is not meant to be used instead of procedure definition for ordinary algorithmic computation.

Broadcast event action. Execution of this action creates an instance of the specified signal, using the input values of the action to fill attribute values of the signal, and transmits a copy of the signal instance to an implementation-dependent set of system target objects. Execution of the action is complete when all the signal instances have been transmitted (and possible before they are received by their targets). Transmission of each signal instance and the subsequent behavior of each target object all proceed concurrently.

Call action. There are two varieties: a call operation action and a call behavior action.

Execution of a call operation action results in the invocation of an operation on an object. The action specifies an operation. As inputs, it has a list of argument values and a target object. The input values must be compatible with the operation parameters and the class that owns the operation. As outputs, the actions has a list of result values. The action also has a flag stating whether the call is synchronous or asynchronous.

When the action is executed, the input values and operation kind are formed into a message that is transmitted to the target object. If the call is asynchronous, the action is complete and the caller may proceed; if the called operation later attempts to return values, they are ignored. If the call is synchronous, the caller is blocked during the execution of the operation.

Receipt of the message by the target object causes an effect on the target object, usually the execution of a method, but other effects can be specified by the model, such as triggering a state machine transition. The mechanism of determining which behavior to perform based on an operation and target object is called resolution.

If the call is synchronous, the system saves information sufficient to eventually return control to the calling action execution. This return information is opaque to the user model and may not be manipulated in any way. When the execution of the called method is complete, the output values of the behavior (usually an activity) are assembled into a reply message that is transmitted to the action execution that issued the call.

The call behavior action is a variant that references an activity directly rather than an operation. This variant is similar to a conventional procedure call in that there is no method lookup needed; the referenced activity is executed using the input values of the action as arguments. In other respects, it is similar to the call operation action.

Classification actions. The classified action determines whether an object is classified by a given classifier. The reclassify action adds and/or removes classifiers from a given object. These actions are intended to be used in systems that support dynamic classification.

Create action. Execution of a create action results in the instantiation of an object (see creation). The class to be instantiated is a parameter of the action. There are no input pins. Execution of the action creates a new instance of the class. The identity of the instance is placed on the output pin of the action. The created object is a "raw" object that has not been initialized; initialization must be modeled separately. However, it is expected that implementation profiles will be defined that include various initialization protocols.

Destroy action. Execution of a destroy action results in the destruction of a target object. The identity of the object is an input of the action. There are no outputs. The result of executing the action is the destruction of the object. All links involving the object are invalid and must be destroyed, but they may or may not be automatically destroyed by an implementation. There is a flag on the action that indicates that participating links and composite parts of the object (see composition) are to be destroyed as part of the action; otherwise their destruction must be modeled explicitly using additional actions. It is expected that implementation profiles will be defined that include various destruction protocols.

There is also an action that explicitly destroys links and link objects.

Raise exception action. Execution of a raise exception action causes an exception to occur. The value on the single input pin is an object that becomes the exception value. Raising of the exception causes the normal execution of the action to be terminated and begins a search of the action and its enclosing activities for an exception handler whose exception type includes the class of the exception object. See exception handler for details.

Read action. There is a family of read actions. Execution of a read action reads the value of a slot and places the value on the output pin of the action. Depending on the specific kind of action, the slot may be a local variable of the containing activity, an attribute of an object supplied as in input value, or the value of a link or one of its attributes. As inputs, the action has an expression for a target variable, object, or link, as well as the name of a property of the object (if applicable). A navigation statement is modeled as a read action.

Reply action. A reply action transmits a message in response to the previous receipt of an accept call action. The output of the accept call action provides the information needed to decode the sending of the accept call action; that information may not be used in any other way. The reply action may have a list of reply values, which are transmitted as part of the reply message. After executing a reply action, the execution of the current thread proceeds. Meanwhile, the reply message is transmitted to the execution of the call action that triggered the accept call action by the current object. Usually this execution belongs to a different object. When the reply message is received by the caller, it is treated as a normal return from a called operation and execution of the caller proceeds.

A reply to an accepted call must be made once. An attempt to reply to the same call twice is a semantic error. If no reply is even made, the caller will hang up forever (assuming that no interrupts occur).

Read extent action. Execution of a read extent action produces a set containing all the instances of a specified classifier on the single output pin. The set of instances produced may depend on implementation considerations, and an implementation may support multiple extents. Some implementations may choose to not support it. By its nature, this action is depends on the assumption that the system has a well-defined boundary within which objects can be retrieved systematically. It is most appropriate in closed systems in which there is a central record of instances, such as database systems. It is less likely to be useful in highly distributed systems with open boundaries.

Return action. There is no explicit action to return from an ordinary call. When the execution of a called activity is complete, its output values are packaged into a reply message that is transmitted to the execution that called the activity. Receipt of that message unblocks the calling execution. Return statements in conventional programming languages are modeled by using break constructs to return control to the top level of the activity when it just falls off the end of the activity.

To return from a call that has been captured asynchronously by an accept action, use an explicit reply action. In UML, either the receipt of the call and its reply are both implicit (as in an ordinary activity serving as a method) or they are both explicit.

Send action. A send action creates a message object and transmits it to a target object, where it may trigger behavior. There are two variants: The send object action has two input pins, one for the target object and one for the message object. A copy of the object on the message object input is transmitted to the target object. The send signal action specifies a class as the signal type. The action has an input pin for the target object plus a list of input pins equal in number to the number of attributes of the signal type. Execution of this action creates a message object of the given signal type, using the values of the input pins as attribute values. Otherwise the two variants behave the same.

A copy of the message object is transmitted to the target object. The identity of the message object is not preserved by the transmission. The sender execution keeps its own thread of control and proceeds concurrently with the transmission of the message and any induced effects; sending a message is asynchronous. If a synchronous activity is triggered by the receipt of a message, any attempts at replying or returning control or return values are silently ignored. The sender has no further connection with the sent signal or its effects.

Start owned behavior action. This action has one input value, the target object. Execution of this action causes the owned behavior of the target object to begin. Owned behavior may be a state machine or an activity. This is a very low-level action that exposes the implementation engine. Many models will avoid this action and simply assume that owned behavior starts automatically when an object is created. The choice is a semantic variation point. Programming languages have a wide variety of initialization semantics, therefore no specific high-level initialization semantic was included in UML.

Test identity action. This action compares the identity of two input objects and outputs a Boolean value telling whether they are the same object.

Time action. There are actions to return the current time and to return the duration between sending and receiving a message.

Write action. A write action sets the value of a slot to a run-time value received as input by the action. Depending on the specific kind of action, the slot may correspond to a local variable of the containing activity, an attribute of the class of an object supplied as in input value, or the value of a link or one of its attributes. As inputs, the action has an expression for a target variable, object, or link; the name of a property of the object (if applicable); and a value to be assigned to the slot. An assignment statement is modeled as a write action. For slots with multiple values, write actions have variations to add or remove single values and to replace or clear all values.

Notation

An action is shown as part of an activity diagram. An action is drawn as a rectangle with rounded corners (Figure 14-5). The name of the action or a text description of the action appears inside the rounded rectangle. In addition to the predefined kinds of actions, real-world models and high-level models may use an action to represent external real-world effects or informal system behavior by just naming the action in words.

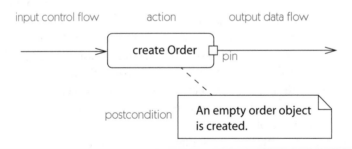

Figure 14-5. *Action*

Flow arrows are drawn to and from the boundary of the rectangle. Input and output pins may be shown as small squares straddling the boundary of the rectangle, in which case the flow arrows connect to the squares representing the pins.

If an implementation uses a particular programming language or action language, the actions may be expressed in the syntax of that language, as specified in an implementation profile. The UML specification does not include a predefined text syntax for the various kinds of actions.

Preconditions and postconditions may be shown as note symbols (dog-eared rectangles) connected to the action symbol by a dashed line.

Some communication actions have special notation. These include accept event action, accept time event action, and send signal action. Figure 14-6 shows some of these.

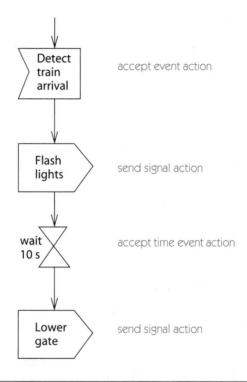

Figure 14-6. *Special notation for communication actions*

UML does not define notation for the bulk of the actions. The modeler can notate an action using a rounded box, with the action written in the syntax of some chosen language or pseudolanguage.

History

In UML1, actions included in their structure some flow-of-control mechanisms, such as a recurrence expression and an object set expression, greatly increasing their complexity. In UML2, actions have been repositioned as primitive activity nodes, with the flow-of-control and higher-level mechanisms moved to the activity model. In UML 1.1 and UML 1.3, all actions were regarded as invocations sent to objects. A full action model was introduced in UML 1.5, but it was not widely used because it was soon superseded by UML 2.0. In UML2, invocations have been distinguished from other kinds of actions, simplifying the specification of each kind of action. UML1.1 and UML 1.3 included a motley selection of actions, with some curious omissions. UML 1.5 included a more balanced set of actions. UML2 attempts to include a complete base set of actions.

Discussion

All programming languages have different sets of base actions built into their definitions and style of use, and it is impossible to include them all without clashes in semantics. The UML specification defines a set of fairly low-level actions sufficient to describe behavior. High-level semantics of complex effects, such as initialization, cascading destruction, and reflective control mechanisms, were avoided in the UML semantics and left for implementation profiles. This decision was a result of a trade-off between the desire for precision and the need for developers to work with various target languages, which have a wide range of semantic concepts. There is much more variation in execution semantics among programming languages than there is in data structure or in the set of available control constructs. Subtle differences are difficult to map in a practical way among languages, regardless of whether it is possible in theory. The selection of one programming language as the basis for an action language would, therefore, have the effect of discouraging the others, which the designers did not want to do. The semantics of actions have therefore been left low level and free of implementation concerns within UML itself. For many practical uses, such as code generation, UML must be augmented with the action language (often a standard programming language) that is being used. Some critics have complained that UML is imprecise because of this freedom, but it is imprecise only to the degree that the chosen action language is imprecise. The real defect is that UML does not impose a lingua franca of actions and other expressions, but this is hardly possible in today's polyglot world of computation, regardless of the emotional appeal of such unity.

There is an unevenness in the selection of UML actions. A number of actions, such as the start owned behavior action, might have been better left to implementation profiles, as they have an unmistakable implementation flavor.

action expression

An obsolete UML1 term, mostly superseded by behavior and do activity.

action sequence

An obsolete UML1 term. Sequences of actions may now be connected by activity edges.

activation

A UML1 term replaced by execution specification.

active

A state that has been entered and has not yet been exited; one that is held by an object.

See also active class, active object.

Semantics

A state becomes active when a transition entering it fires. An active state ceases to be active when a transition leaving it fires. If an object is active, then at least one state is active. (In the degenerate case, a class may have only a single state. In that case, the response to an event is always the same.) If a state is active within the state machine for an object's class, the object is said to *hold* the state.

An object may hold multiple states at one time. The set of active states is called the active state configuration. If a nested state is active, then all states that contain it are active. If the object permits concurrency, then more than one orthogonal region may be active. Each transition affects, at most, a few states in the active state configuration. On a transition, unaffected active states remain active.

A composite state may be sequential or orthogonal. If it is sequential and active, then exactly one of its immediate substates is active. If it is orthogonal and active, then exactly one substate in each of its immediate regions is active. In other words, a composite state expands into an AND-OR tree of active substates; at each level, certain states are active.

A transition across a composite state boundary must be structured to maintain these concurrency constraints. A transition into a sequential composite state usually has one source state and one destination state. Firing such a transition does not change the number of active states. A transition into an orthogonal composite state usually has one source state and one destination state for each subregion of the orthogonal composite state. Such a transition is called a fork. If one or more regions are omitted as destinations, the initial state from each omitted region is implicitly a destination; if one of the regions lacks an initial state, then the model is ill formed. Firing such a forked transition increases the number of active states. The situation is reversed on exit from an orthogonal composite state.

See state machine, which contains a full discussion of the semantics of orthogonal states and complex transitions.

Example

The top of Figure 14-7 shows a sample state machine with both sequential and orthogonal composite states. The transitions have been omitted to focus on the

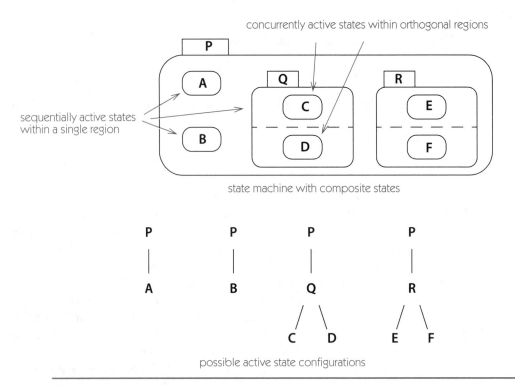

Figure 14-7. *Concurrently active states*

states. The bottom of the figure shows the various configurations of states that can be active concurrently. In this example, there are four possible configurations of active states. Only the leaf states are concrete; the higher states are abstract—that is, an object may not be in one of them without also being in a nested leaf state. For instance, the object may not be in state Q without being in the substates of Q. Because Q is orthogonal, both C and D must be active if Q is active. Each leaf state corresponds to a thread of control. In a larger example, the number of possible configurations may grow exponentially and it may be impossible to show them all, hence the advantage of the notation.

active class

A class whose instances are active objects.
    See active object for details.

Semantics

An active class is a class whose instances are active objects.

Notation

An active class is shown as a rectangle with doubled vertical lines on the left and right sides. The notation has changed in UML2.

Example

Figure 14-8 shows a class diagram with an active class and its passive parts. Figure 14-9 shows a collaboration that contains active objects corresponding to this model.

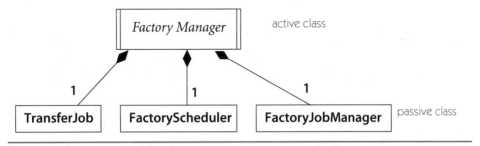

Figure 14-8. *Active class and passive parts*

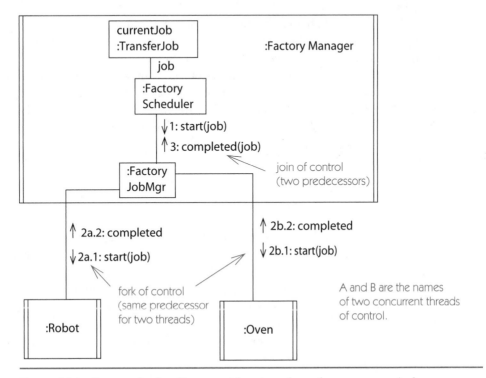

Figure 14-9. *Communication diagram with active roles and concurrent control*

active object

An object that owns a thread of control and can initiate control activity; an instance of an active class.

See also passive object.

Semantics

An active object does not run within another thread, stack frame, or state machine. It has an independent locus of control within the overall execution of a system. In a sense, it *is* the thread. Each active object is a distinct locus of execution; active objects are not reentrant, and recursive execution is not possible without the creation of additional objects.

An active object is the root of an execution stack frame in conventional computational terms. The creation of an active object initiates a new instance of a state machine. When the state machine performs a transition, an execution stack frame is created and continues until the action of the transition runs to its completion and the object waits for external input. An active object, therefore, does not run in the scope of another object. It can be created by an action of another object, but once created, it has an independent existence. The creator may be an active or a passive object. An active object is driven by events. Operations on it by other objects should be implemented by the active object as call events.

A passive object may be created as part of an action by another object. It has its own address space. A passive object has no thread of control. Its operations are called within the stack frame of an active object. It may be modeled by a state machine, however, to show the changes in its state caused by operations on it.

A conventional operating system process is best equated with an active object. An operating system thread may or may not be implemented by an active object.

The active-passive distinction is primarily a design decision and does not constrain the semantics of the objects. Both active and passive objects may have state machines and may exchange events.

Notation

A collaboration role for an active object is shown on a collaboration diagram as a rectangle with doubled vertical lines at the left and right sides. Frequently, active object roles are shown as composites with embedded parts.

An active object is also shown as an object symbol with doubled edges, with the name underlined, but active objects appear only within examples of execution and therefore are not so common.

The property keyword {active} may also be used to indicate an active object.

Example

Figure 14-9 shows three active objects in a factory automation system: a robot; an oven; and a factory manager, which is a control object. All three objects exist and execute concurrently. The factory manager initiates a thread of control at step 1, which then forks into two concurrent threads of control (2a and 2b) that are executed by the oven and the robot, respectively. When each has finished its execution, the threads join at step 3, in the factory manager. Each object remains alive and preserves its state until the next event arrives for it.

History

The notation has changed in UML2.

active state configuration

The set of states that are active at one time within a state machine. The firing of a transition changes a few states in the set; the others remain unchanged.

See active, complex transition, state machine.

Semantics

In general, a system can have multiple active states concurrently. The entire set of active states is called the *active state configuration*. The transition firing rules of state machines define which states must be active for a transition to fire and what changes occur to the active state configuration as a result of a transition firing.

A state machine is a tree of states. If a composite state is active, exactly one direct substate in each of its regions must be active. If a submachine state is active, one top-level state within its referenced state machine must be active. If a simple state is active, it has no substructure. Starting with the entire state machines, these rules may be applied recursively to determine legal active state configurations.

activity

A specification of executable behavior as the coordinated sequential and concurrent execution of subordinate units, including nested activities and ultimately individual actions connected by flows from outputs of one node to inputs of another. Activities can be invoked by actions and as constituents of other behaviors, such as state machine transitions. Activities are shown as activity diagrams.

See also state machine.

Semantics

An activity is a behavioral specification that describes the sequential and concurrent steps of a computational procedure. Workflows, algorithms, and computer code are examples of procedures that are often modeled as activities. Activities focus on the process of computation rather than the objects performing the computation or the data values involved, although these can be represented as part of an activity. State machines and activities are similar, in that both describe sequences of states that occur over time and the conditions that cause changes among the states. The difference is that a state machine concerns the states of an object performing or undergoing a computation, whereas an activity concerns the states of the computation itself, possibly across many objects, and explicitly models the flow of control and information among the activity nodes.

Structure. An activity is modeled as a graph of activity nodes connected by control and object flows. Activity nodes represent nested activities, actions, data locations, and control constructs. Actions model effects on the system. The flows among the nodes model the flow of control and data within the activity. Control construct nodes provide more complicated ways of specifying flow of control. Flow of control may be implemented in various ways, including changes of state of objects and messages transmitted among objects.

An activity has input and output parameters that represent values supplied to and produced by an execution of it. An activity can be attached to various other behaviors as a piece of parameterized behavior. For example, an activity may be attached to a state machine transition as an effect; to the entry, exit, or presence in a state; to an operation as a method; as the implementation of a use case; and as an invocation within another activity. Each specific construct provides syntax to supply the input and output arguments that bind to each of the parameters of the activity. When one of the constructs that invokes an activity is executed, an execution of the activity is created and initialized by copies of the input arguments. When execution of the activity is complete, the result values from the activity become the output values of the invoking construct.

An activity may be marked as being read-only. This is an assertion that its execution will not modify any variables or objects outside the activity itself, except possibly for temporary variables that disappear before completion of execution. This kind of assertion may be useful for code generators, but it may be difficult or impossible to check automatically, so the modeler must be careful.

Execution semantics. The graph structure of activities and their semantics are loosely based on Petri nets, an important area in the theory of computation since the 1960s. Each activity is a graph of nodes connected by directed flows. Nodes include actions, nested activities, data locations, and various control constructs.

Flows represent the flow of information within the execution of an activity, including the flow of control and the flow of data.

An execution of an activity may be imagined as proceeding on a copy of the activity graph containing tokens. A token is a marker indicating the presence of control or data at the point in the computation represented by a node or flow. Control tokens have no internal structure. Data tokens contain data values representing intermediate results at that point in the computation. The model is similar to a traditional flow chart, but activity graphs may contain concurrent subcomputations, therefore they may have multiple tokens at a given time.

The basic computation rule is simple: An action node is enabled to execute if tokens are present on its input flows (or on data nodes at the source ends of the input flows). In other words, an input flow indicates a dependency on the completion of a previous stage of the activity, and a token on the input flow indicates that the previous stage has been completed. When a node is enabled to execute, it may begin execution. If other nodes involving the same tokens are also enabled, only one of them will execute; the choice may be nondeterministic. When a node begins execution, it consumes its input tokens; that is, they are removed from the input flows and their values become available within the execution. Consumption of tokens prevents another node from executing using the same tokens. Each kind of node has its own execution rules, described in the glossary entry for that node. When execution of a node is complete, output tokens are produced and placed on the output flows of the node. The tokens can then enable the execution of subsequent nodes.

Actions require tokens on all inputs and produce tokens on all outputs. Other activity elements provide various flow-of-control behaviors, such as decisions, loops, forks and joins of control, parallel execution, and so on. In general, an activity node begins execution when tokens are present on a specified set of its input nodes, it executes concurrently with other nodes, and it produces tokens on a specified set of its output nodes. Many kinds of activity nodes require tokens on a subset of inputs or produce tokens on a subset of outputs. There are also advanced kinds of actions that allow execution based on a subset of inputs.

The execution rules are fundamentally concurrent. If two activity nodes are enabled by different sets of tokens, they can execute concurrently. This means that there is no inherent execution ordering among the nodes. It does not mean that the implementation must be parallel or involve multiple computation units, although it can be. It does mean that the implementation may sequence the executions in any order, including parallel, without altering the correctness of the computation. Sequential execution is fundamentally deterministic, but concurrent execution can introduce indeterminacy, which can be an important part of some models.

Context. An activity executes within a context. The context includes its input parameter values, the owning object on whose behalf it executes, and its place in the execution invocation hierarchy. Nodes in the activity have access to the input parameters and to the attributes and associations of the owning object. If an activity is attached to a classifier directly, it begins execution when an instance of the classifier is created and ceases when it is destroyed. If an activity is attached to a operation a method, it begins execution when its operation is invoked.

Exceptions. An exception is a type of occurrence that stops the normal execution sequence and initiates a search for an exception handler on the currently executing node or on a node within which it is nested. The execution handler must be declared to handle the type of the exception. The node having the execution handler is called the protected node. All activity contained within the protected node ceases, and the execution handler is executed using the exception parameters as input. When the execution handler completes execution, execution resumes as if the protected node had completed execution. In most cases, the node raising the exception is nested (at some level) within the protected node.

Interrupts. An interruptible activity region is a region from which one or more interruptible activity edges depart. If an interruptible activity edge passes a token, all activity within the region is terminated.

Multiple tokens. The simplest and most usual form of activity allows at most a single token on any edge. A more complicated variant allows multiple tokens on edges and in buffers (object nodes that collect and possibly sequence tokens). It is also possible to distinguish activities in which a single execution handles all invocations from the more usual activities in which each invocation creates an independent execution. A single-execution activity is similar to a C-family static function.

Object flow. Sometimes it is useful to see the relationships between a node and the objects that are its argument values or results. The input to and the outputs from a node may be shown as an object flow. This is an edge in the activity graph that represents the flow of data (including objects) within the computation. The data itself is modeled as an object node. Various constraints can be placed on the flow of data; see object flow for details.

Partitions. The activities of an activity graph can be partitioned into groups based on various criteria. Each group represents some meaningful partition of the responsibilities for the activities—for example, the business organization responsible for a given workflow step or the objects that execute nodes within an activity. Because of their graphical notation, the groups are sometimes called swimlanes.

Notation

An activity is notated as an activity diagram. An activity definition is shown as a large rounded border containing a graph of node symbols and flow arrows representing the decomposition of the activity into its constituents. The name of the activity is usually shown in the upper left corner. Preconditions and postconditions are shown as text strings preceded by the keywords «precondition» or «postcondition». Input and output parameter nodes are shown as small rectangles straddling the border; the name of the parameter may be placed within the rectangle. A parameter may also be listed under the activity name in the format name: Type.

Activity diagrams include various node symbols: actions, decisions, forks, joins, merges, and object nodes. An arrow represents both control flow and object flow; an object flow must connect to an object node at one or both ends, therefore the distinction is clear from context. The interior of an activity definition may be tiled into partitions by heavy lines. See these various entries for more details.

See control node for some optional symbols that can be useful in activity diagrams.

The keyword «singleExecution» is placed within an activity that has a single shared execution.

Example

Figure 14-10 shows a workflow of the activities involved in processing an order at a theater box office. It includes a branch and subsequent merge based on whether the order is for a subscription or for individual tickets. The fork initiates concurrent activities that logically occur at the same time. Their actual execution may or may not overlap. The concurrency is terminated by a subsequent matching join. If there is only one person involved, then concurrent activities can be performed in any order (presuming they cannot be performed simultaneously, which is permitted by the model, but might be difficult in practice). For example, the box office personnel could assign the seats, then award the bonus, then debit the account; or they could award the bonus, assign the seats, then debit the account—but they cannot debit the account until after the seats have been assigned.

Partitions. The activities in an activity graph can be partitioned into regions, which are called swimlanes from their visual appearance as regions on a diagram separated by solid lines. A partition is an organizational unit for the contents of an activity graph. Often, each partition represents an organizational unit within a real-world organization. Partitions can also be used to specify the classes responsible for implementing the actions included within each partition.

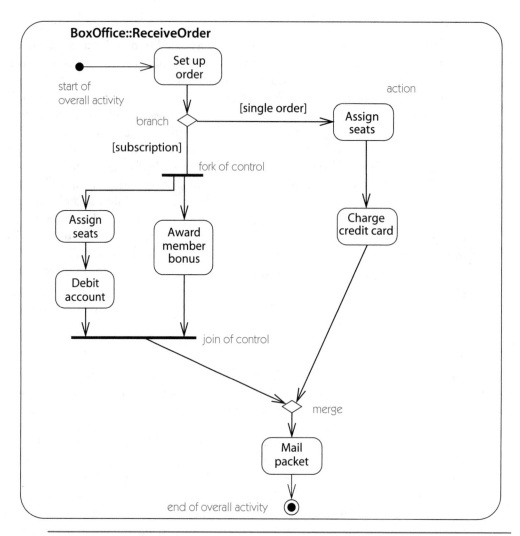

Figure 14-10. *Activity diagram*

Example

In Figure 14-11, the activities are divided into three partitions, each one corresponding to a different stakeholder. There is no UML requirement that the partitions correspond to objects, although in this example there are obvious classes that would fall under each partition, and those classes would be the ones that perform the operations to implement each activity in the finished model.

The figure also shows the use of object flow symbols. The object flows correspond to different states of an order object as it works its way through a network of activities. The symbol **Order[placed]**, for example, means that at that place in the

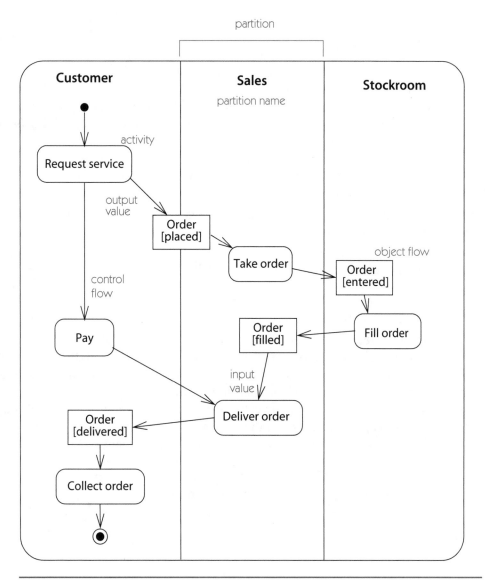

Figure 14-11. *Activity diagram with swimlanes*

computation, an order has been advanced to the **placed** state in the **Request Ser-vice** activity but has not yet been consumed by the **Take Order** activity. After the **Take Order** activity completes, the order is then in the **entered** state, as shown by the object flow symbol on the output of the **Take Order** activity. All the object flows in this example represent the same object at different times in its life. Be-cause they represent the same object, they cannot exist at the same time. A sequen-tial control path can be drawn through all of them, as is apparent in the diagram.

Object flow. Objects that are input to or output by an action may be shown as object symbols. The symbol represents the object at the point in the computation at which it is suitable as an input or just produced as an output (usually an object does both). An object flow arrow is drawn from an activity node to an object node that is one of its outputs, and an object flow arrow is drawn from an object node to an activity node that uses the object as one of its inputs. The same object may be (and usually is) the output of one node and the input of one or more subsequent nodes.

Control flow arrows may be omitted when object flow arrows supply a redundant constraint. In other words, when an action produces an output that is input by a subsequent action, that object flow relationship implies a control constraint.

Class in state. Frequently, the same object is manipulated by a number of successive activities that change its state. For greater precision, the object may be displayed multiple times on a diagram, each appearance denoting a different state during its life. To distinguish the various appearances of the same object, the state of the object at each point may be placed in brackets and appended to the name of the class—for example, PurchaseOrder[approved].

See also control node for other symbols that can be used in activity diagrams.

Expansion region. An expansion region is the expansion of computation containing a multiple value into a set of computations executed in parallel (Figure 14-12). This indicates that multiple copies of the activity occur concurrently. Each input to the expansion region receives collection value, shown by the segmented-box icon. If there are multiple inputs, all collections must be the same size. Scalar inputs are also allowed. One execution of the expansion region is performed for each element of the collections. For each output position in the expansion region, the output

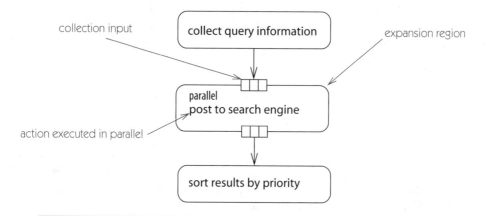

Figure 14-12. *Expansion region*

values from all of the executions are assembled into a single collection value. An expansion region represents a "forall" construct.

In addition to parallel execution, as shown in the example, execution may be iterative (sequential) or streaming (multiple pipelined tokens in a single execution).

History

Activity modeling underwent a major expansion in UML2, with many additional constructs and many convenience options added motivated by the business modeling community. In UML1, activities had been considered variants of state machines, which ensured well-formedness but imposed severe constraints on their form. In UML2, the metamodels were separated and activity semantics were basely (loosely) on Petri net semantics. Additionally, the syntax of activity composition was greatly loosened, permitting much freer form but also making it easier to construct ill-formed models.

Discussion

Much of the optional notation added in UML2 is based on notation used in various business process modeling approaches (although there is no single standard). A modeler must understand the target audience of a model before deciding whether to use this and other optional notation oriented toward a particular community.

activity diagram

A diagram that shows the decomposition of an activity into its constituents.
    See activity.

activity edge

A sequencing relationship between two activity nodes, possibly including data.

Semantics

An activity edge is a sequencing relationship between a source activity node and a target activity node. The target node cannot execute until the source node has completed execution and emitted a token onto the activity edge. If a node has multiple edges of which it is the target, it cannot execute until all of them have tokens, unless the rules for the particular kind of activity node specify that a subset of input edges may enable execution. An edge may represent simple flow of control (control flow) or it may represent the flow of data (data flow), including the implicit flow of control that indicates that the data value has been produced.

Structure

Guard. A guard is a Boolean expression attached to an edge that determines whether the edge may enable a target activity node. If the value of the expression is true, the node may be enabled; otherwise it may not be enabled.

Weight. A weight indicates the number of tokens consumed when a target node executes. The default is one when no weight is specified. See weight.

Notation

See control flow and data flow for notation.

activity expression

This UML1 term is now obsolete. Activities are now directly modeled as first-class constructs.

activity final node

A node in an activity specification whose execution causes the forced termination of all flows in the activity and the termination of execution of the activity.
See final node.

Semantics

An activity final node represents the completion of execution of an activity. If there is any concurrent execution when a token reaches the node, all other execution in the activity is forcibly terminated and the tokens removed. In the most common case, the token reaching the node is the only active one.

Outputs of the activity that have previously been generated are released for delivery.

If the activity was invoked by another activity, a token is returned to the invoking activity. If the activity represents the life of an object, the object is destroyed.

Notation

An activity final node is shown as a small circle with a smaller black dot inside it (a bull's eye symbol).

Example

Figure 14-13 shows a simple activity. Activity begins at the initial node. Activity ends at the activity final node.

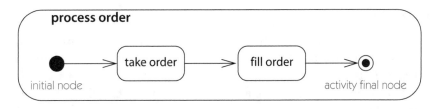

Figure 14-13. *Activity final node and initial node*

activity group

An arbitrary subset of nodes and edges within an activity specification. Partitions and structured nodes are kinds of activity groups.

activity node

A kind of element in an activity that can be connected by flows. This is an abstract element type whose specific varieties include actions, control nodes, object nodes (including pins and parameter nodes), and structured nodes.

Semantics

An activity decomposition comprises activity nodes connected by flows. The various kinds of activity nodes are described under their own entries.

Activity nodes may be grouped into structured nodes and partitions. Structured nodes provide a hierarchical organization of nodes that includes structured control constructs.

Nodes may be redefined as part of the specialization of an activity definition.

The *mustIsolate* flag specifies that actions in a structured node execute without conflict with actions from other nodes. A conflict is an attempt to access the same information, such as the attribute slot of an object, when at least one of the accesses modifies the information, thereby leading to the possibility of indeterminacy. If the possibility of conflict exists, the node must be executed without interleaving any execution of conflicting nodes. Any implementation technique that supports this objective is acceptable.

Notation

The notation depends on the specific kind of activity node. Usually it is a rectangle with rounded corners or some variation of that.

activity partition

A partition on activity graphs for organizing responsibilities for activities. Activity partitions do not have a fixed meaning, but they often correspond to organizational units in a business model. They can also be used to specify the class responsible for implementing a set of tasks. Sometimes called *swimlane* because of its notation.

See also activity.

Semantics

The activity nodes within an activity may be organized into partitions, often called *swimlanes* because of their notation. Activity partitions are groupings of activity nodes for organizing an activity graph. Each activity partition represents some meaningful characteristic of the nodes—for example, the business organization responsible for a workflow step. Activity partitions may be used in any way that suits the modeler. If they are present, they partition the nodes of the activity graph among them.

If a class is attached to a partition, the class is responsible for implementing the behavior of the nodes contained within the partition.

Each activity partition has a name that is distinct from other partitions.

Notation

An activity diagram may be divided into sections, each separated from its neighbor by solid lines (Figure 14-14). Although the lines are most often vertical and straight, they may be horizontal or curved, or they may form a grid. Each section corresponds to an activity partition. Each partition represents high-level responsibility for part of the overall activity, which may eventually be implemented by one or more objects. The relative ordering of the activity partitions on a diagram has no semantic significance but might indicate some real-world relationship. Each activity node is assigned to one partition, and its symbol is placed within its section. Flows may cross lanes; there is no significance to the routing of a flow arrow.

Because activity partitions are arbitrary categories, they may be indicated by other means if a geometrical arrangement into sections is impractical. Possibilities include the use of color or simply the use of tagged values to show the partition. Alternately, activity nodes may be labeled with their partitions.

History

Partitions in UML2 can be two-dimensional, unlike UML1.

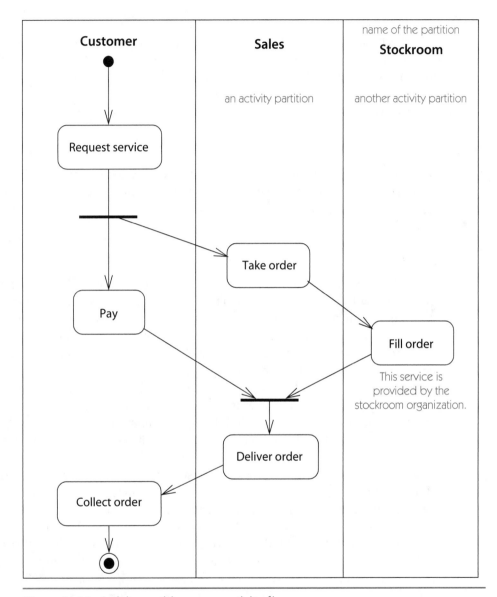

Figure 14-14. *Activity partitions on an activity diagram*

activity view

That aspect of the system dealing with the specification of behavior as activities connected by control flows. This view contains activity specifications and is shown on activity diagrams. It is loosely grouped with other behavioral views as the dynamic view.

See activity.

actor

A classifier for entities outside a subject that interact directly with the subject. An actor participates in a use case or coherent set of use cases to accomplish an overall purpose.

See also use case.

Semantics

An actor is a classifier that characterizes a role played by an outside user or related set of users with respect to a subject. The subject is also a classifier. An actor is an idealization with a focused purpose and meaning and might not correspond exactly to physical objects. One physical object may combine disparate purposes and therefore be characterized by several actors. Different physical objects may include the same purpose, and that aspect of them would be modeled by the same actor. The user object may be a human, a computer system, a device, another subsystem, or another kind of object. For example, actors in a computer network system might include **Operator, System Administrator, Database Administrator**, and plain **User**. There can also be nonhuman actors, such as **RemoteClient, MasterSequencer**, and **NetworkPrinter**.

Each actor defines a role that users of a subject may assume when interacting with the subject. The complete set of actors describes all the ways in which outside users communicate with the subject. When a system is implemented, the actors are implemented by physical objects. One physical object can implement more than one actor if it can fulfill all their roles. For example, one person can be both a salesclerk and a customer of a store. These actors are not inherently related, but they can both be implemented by a person. When the design of a subject is implemented, the various actors inside the system are realized by design classes (see realization).

The various interactions of actors with a subject are quantized into use cases. A use case is a coherent piece of functionality involving a subject and its actors to accomplish something meaningful to the actors. A use case may involve one or more actors. One actor may participate in one or more use cases. Ultimately, the actors are determined by the use cases and the roles that actors play in various use cases. An actor that participates in no use cases would be pointless.

Actor instances communicate with the system by sending and receiving message instances (signals and calls) to and from use case instances and, at realization level, to and from the objects that implement the use case. This is expressed by associations between the actor and the use case.

An actor is external to its subject and therefore is not owned by or defined within the subject. An actor is usually defined in the same package as its subjects. It is inappropriate to show associations among actors in a use case model; actors may have associations to their subjects and to use cases.

Actors may have associations with use cases, components, and classes.

Generalization

Two or more actors may have similarities; that is, they may communicate with the same set of use cases in the same way. This similarity is expressed with generalization to another (possibly abstract) actor, which models the common aspects of the actors. The descendant actors inherit the roles and the relationships to use cases held by the ancestor actor. An instance of a descendant actor can always be used in cases in which an instance of the ancestor is expected (substitutability principle). A descendant includes the attributes and operations of its ancestors.

Notation

An actor may be shown as a class symbol (rectangle) with the stereotype «actor». The standard stereotype icon for an actor is the "stick man" figure, with the name of the actor below the figure. The actor may have compartments that show attributes and events that it receives, and it may have dependencies to show events that it sends. These are capabilities of a normal classifier (Figure 14-15).

Special icons may be defined for actors or sets of actors.

The name of an abstract actor is shown using italics.

Figure 14-15. *Actor symbol*

actual parameter

See argument.

aggregate

A class that represents the whole in an aggregation (whole-part) association.

aggregation

A form of association that specifies a whole-part relationship between an aggregate (a whole) and a constituent part. It is also applicable to attributes and parameters.

See also composition.

Semantics

A binary association may be declared an aggregation—that is, a whole-part relationship. One end of the association is designated the aggregate while the other end is unmarked. Both ends may not be aggregates (or composites), but both ends can be unmarked (in which case, it is not an aggregation).

The links instantiated from aggregation associations obey certain rules. The aggregation relationship is transitive and antisymmetric across all aggregation links, even across those from different aggregation associations. Transitivity means that it makes sense to say that "B is part of A" if there is a path of aggregation links from B to A in the direction of traversal (in this example, from part to whole). Antisymmetry means that there are no cycles in the directed paths of aggregation links. That is, an object may not be directly or indirectly part of itself. Putting the two rules together, the graph of aggregation links from all aggregation associations forms a partial order graph, a graph without cycles (a tree is a special and common case of a partial order). Figure 14-16 shows an example.

A directed path of links from object B to object A implies that there is a directed path of aggregation associations from the class of B to the class of A, but the path of associations may involve cycles in which the same class appears more than once. A directed path of aggregation associations from a class to itself is a *recursive assembly*.

There is a stronger form of aggregation, called composition. A composite is an aggregate with the additional constraints that an object may be part of only one composite and that the composite object has responsibility for the disposition of all its parts—that is, for their creation and destruction. An aggregation that is not a composition is called a shared aggregation, because parts may be shared among more than one whole.

See composition for details.

In shared aggregation, a part may belong to more than one aggregate, and it may exist independently of the aggregate. Often the aggregate "needs" the parts, in the sense that it may be regarded as a collection of parts. But the parts can exist by themselves, without being regarded only as parts. For example, a path is little more than a collection of segments. But a segment can exist by itself whether or not it is part of a path, and the same segment may appear in different paths.

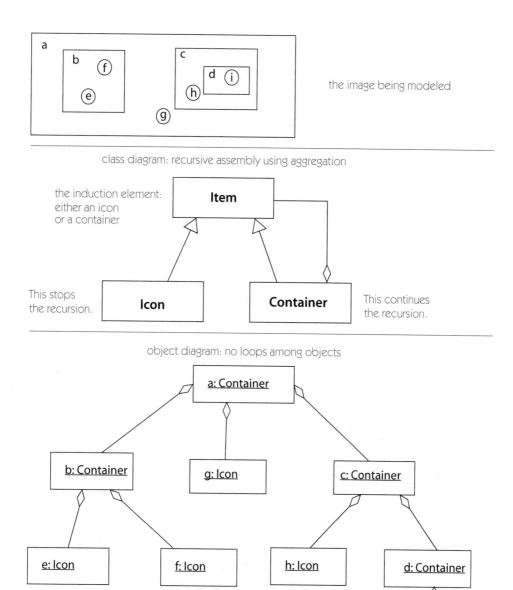

the image being modeled

class diagram: recursive assembly using aggregation

the induction element:
either an icon
or a container

Item

This stops
the recursion.

Icon

Container

This continues
the recursion.

object diagram: no loops among objects

a: Container

b: Container

g: Icon

c: Container

e: Icon

f: Icon

h: Icon

d: Container

i: Icon

Figure 14-16. *Aggregations of objects are acyclic*

Composition is also applicable to attributes and parameters. In this situation, the object owning the attribute or parameter is the whole, and the values of the attribute or parameter are the parts.

See association and association end for most of the properties of aggregation.

Notation

A shared aggregation is shown as a hollow diamond adornment on the end of an association line at which it connects to the aggregate class (Figure 14-17). If the aggregation is a composition, then the diamond is filled (Figure 14-82). The ends in an association may not both have aggregation indicators.

An aggregate class can have multiple parts. The relation between the aggregate class and each part class is a separate association (Figure 14-18).

If there are two or more aggregation associations to the same aggregate class, they may be drawn as a tree by combining the aggregation ends into a single segment (Figure 14-19). This requires that all the adornments on the aggregation ends be consistent; for example, they must all have the same multiplicity. Drawing aggregations as a tree is purely a presentation option; there are no additional semantics to it.

To indicate a composite attribute, use the property string {composite} following the rest of the attribute string. There is no particular notation for a shared aggregation in an attribute. If the distinction is important, the relationship can be shown as an association.

Discussion

The distinction between aggregation and association is often a matter of taste rather than a difference in semantics. Keep in mind that aggregation is association. Aggregation conveys the thought that the aggregate is inherently the sum of its parts. In fact, the only real semantics that it adds to association is the constraint that chains of aggregate links may not form cycles, which is often important to know, however. Other constraints, such as existence dependency, are specified by the multiplicity, not the aggregation marker. In spite of the few semantics attached to aggregation, everybody thinks it is necessary (for different reasons). Think of it as a modeling placebo.

Several secondary properties are connected with aggregation, but not reliably enough to make them part of its required definition. These include propagation of operations from aggregate to parts (such as a move operation) and compact memory assignment (so that the aggregate and its recursive parts can be efficiently loaded with one memory transfer). Some authors have distinguished several kinds of aggregation, but the distinctions are fairly subtle and probably unnecessary for general modeling.

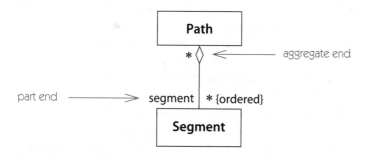

Figure 14-17. *Aggregation notation*

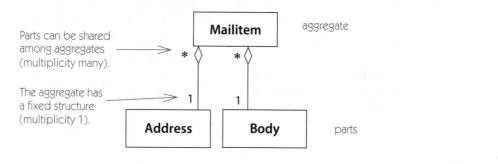

Figure 14-18. *One aggregate with several parts*

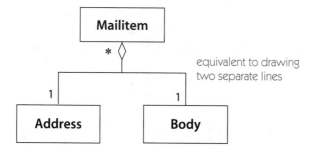

Figure 14-19. *Tree form of notation for multiple aggregations to the same class*

Aggregation is a property that transcends a particular association. One can compose aggregations over different pairs of classes, and the result is an aggregation. Aggregation imposes a constraint on the instances of all aggregation associations (including composition associations) that there may be no cycles of aggregation links, including links from different associations. In a sense, aggregation is a kind of generalization of association in which constraints and some operations apply to associations of many specific kinds.

Composition has more specific semantics that correspond to physical containment and various notions of ownership. Composition is appropriate when each part is owned by one object and when the part does not have an independent life separate from its owner. It is most useful when parts must be allocated and initialized at the time the owner is created, and the parts do not survive the destruction of their owner. Attributes of a class are usually assumed to have these properties. By using composition, the burden of memory management and the danger of dangling pointers or orphaned objects can be avoided. It is also appropriate for situations in which a bundle of attributes has been isolated into a distinct class for encapsulation and manipulation reasons, but the attributes really apply to the main class. Container classes used to implement associations are also obvious candidates for composite parts, although normally they should be generated by a code generator and not modeled explicitly. Note that a composite part, such as a container class, may contain references (pointers) to noncomposite parts, but the referenced objects are not destroyed when the referencing object is destroyed.

The distinction between associations and attributes is also more a matter of taste or implementation language than semantics. Attributes inherently have a feel of aggregation about them.

alt

Keyword indicating a conditional construct in an interaction, such as a sequence diagram. See conditional.

alternative

A conditional construct in an interaction, such as a sequence diagram. See conditional.

analysis

That stage of system development that captures requirements and the problem domain. Analysis focuses on what to do; design focuses on how to do it. In an iterative process, the stages need not be performed sequentially. The results of this stage are represented by analysis-level models, especially the use case view and the static view. Contrast analysis, design, implementation, and deployment (phase).

See stages of modeling, development process.

analysis time

A time during which an analysis activity of the software development process is performed. Do not assume that all the analysis for a system occurs at the same time or precedes other activities, such as design and implementation. The various activities are sequential for any single element, but different activities may be intermixed for the entire system.

See design time, modeling time.

ancestor

An element found by following a path of one or more parent relationships.

See generalization, parent.

any trigger

A trigger on a state machine transition that is satisfied by the occurrence of any event that does not trigger another transition on the same state.

Semantics

This is an "else" construct for transitions. It is, of course, incorrect to have multiple any-triggers on the same state.

It is probably allowable to have any-triggers on a state and a containing state, with the most specific transition taking precedence, but the specification is silent on this point.

Notation

The keyword **all** is used for the name of the trigger in place of an event name.

application

See profile application.

apply

Keyword on a dashed arrow between a package and a profile indicating application of the profile to the package. See profile application.

apply function action

An action whose execution evaluates a predefined mathematical function to compute one or more output values. It is a pure function evaluation and has no side effects or interaction with the state of the system except through the input and output values.

See action for details.

architecture

The organizational structure of a system, including its decomposition into parts, their connectivity, interaction mechanisms, and the guiding principles that inform the design of a system.

See also package.

Semantics

Architecture is the set of significant decisions about the organization of a software system. It includes the selection of structural elements and the interfaces through which they are connected, the large-scale organization of structural elements and the topology of their connection, their behavior as specified in the collaborations among those elements, the important mechanisms that are available across the system, and the architectural style that guides their organization. For example, the decision to construct a system from two layers in which each layer contains a small number of subsystems that communicate in a particular way is an architectural decision. Software architecture is not only concerned with structure and behavior, but also with usage, functionality, performance, resilience, reuse, comprehensibility, economic and technology constraints and trade-offs, and aesthetic concerns.

Discussion

Architectural decisions about the decomposition of a system into parts can be captured using models, subsystems, packages, and components. The dependencies among these elements are key indicators of the flexibility of the architecture and the difficulty of modifying the system in the future.

Another major part of an architecture is the mechanisms that it provides to build upon. These may be captured with collaborations and patterns.

Nonstructural decisions can be captured using tagged values.

argument

A specific value corresponding to a parameter.

See also binding, parameter, substitutability principle.

Semantics

A run-time instance of a parameterized element, such as an operation or an action, has a list of argument values, each of which is a value whose type must be consistent with the declared type of the matching parameter. A value is consistent if its class or data type is the same or a descendant of the declared type of the parameter. By the substitutability principle, a value of a descendant may be used anywhere an ancestor type is declared.

An occurrence of a broadcast action, a call action, or a send action requires arguments for the parameters, unless the signal or operation lacks attributes or parameters.

In a template binding, however, arguments appear within a UML model at modeling time. Template arguments can include not only ordinary data values, objects, and expressions, but also classifiers. In the latter case, the corresponding parameter type must be **Classifier** or some other metatype. The value of a template argument must be fixed at modeling time; it may not be used to represent a run-time argument. Do not use templates if the parameters are not bound at modeling time.

artifact

The specification of a physical piece of information that is used or produced by a software development process, such as an external document or a work product, or by the deployment and operation of a system. An artifact can be a model, description, or software.

Semantics

An artifact corresponds to a concrete real-world element. An instance of an artifact is deployed to a node instance. Artifacts often represent files or documents. They are inherently connected to the implementation of a system. An artifact may be associated with a component.

Profiles are expected to define various kinds of artifacts suitable for different implementation environments. Standard stereotypes of artifacts include source and executable.

Structure

Deployment. An artifact may be deployable on a node. This indicates that instances of the artifact may be deployed on instances of the node.

Nested artifacts. An artifact may contain other artifacts. The nested artifacts are deployed on the same node instance as the contained artifact or on a contained node instance.

Manifestation. An artifact may manifest, that is, result from and implement, a set of model elements. This relationship captures links between design elements and their physical manifestation. For example, a design class may generate as artifacts a source file, an executable file, and a documentation file.

Notation

An artifact is shown as a rectangle with the keyword «artifact» above the artifact name. An artifact instance is shown with its name underlined. The manifestation relationship is shown by a dashed arrow from the artifact to the elements that it manifests; the keyword «manifest» is placed next to the arrow. Deployment of an artifact to a node (or instances of them) is shown by placing the artifact symbol inside the boundary of the node symbol.

Figure 14-20 shows an artifact located in a node and manifesting a component.

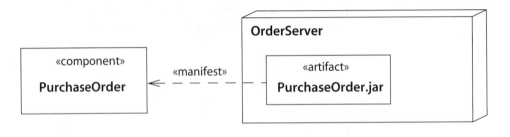

Figure 14-20. *Artifact notation*

History

Artifacts in UML2 can manifest any kind of element, not just components as in UML1. A number of things that were considered components in UML1 have been reclassified as artifacts.

assembly connector

A connector between two elements (parts or ports) in the internal implementation specification of a structured classifier or component.

See connector, delegation connector.

assert

Keyword in a sequence diagram indicating an assertion.

assertion

A combined fragment in an interaction indicating that the behavior described by the contents is the only valid behavior at that point in the execution. Any other behavior contradicts the meaning.

Semantics

In general, an interaction is a specification of permissible behavior, which does not include all possible behavior. An assertion is a statement that the specified behavior of the assertion region is the only possible behavior at that point in the execution. Note, however, that the ignore and consider operators can be used to filter the behavior under consideration. If certain kinds of events are explicitly ignored, their occurrence or nonoccurrence will not affect an assertion.

For example, use an assertion fragment containing a conditional fragment to indicate that the alternatives explicitly provided in the conditional are the only possible outcomes and that any other outcomes may not happen.

Notation

An assertion is shown as a tagged region in a sequence diagram with the keyword **assert**. Figure 14-21 shows an assertion. It states that after the motor receives a start message from the controller, the next message must be a stop message. The assertion makes no statement about messages involving any other objects.

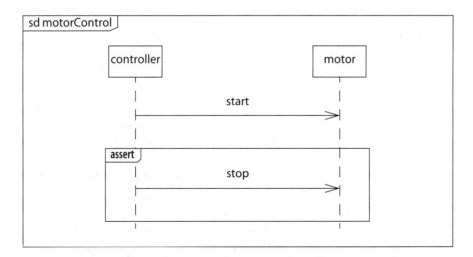

Figure 14-21. *Assertion*

association

The semantic relationship between two or more classifiers that involves connections among their instances.

See also association class, association end, association generalization, binary association, multiplicity (association), *n*-ary association.

Semantics

An association is a relationship among two or more specified classifiers that describes connections among their instances. The participating classifiers have ordered positions within the association. The same class may appear in more than one position in an association. Each instance of an association (a link) is a tuple (an ordered list) of references to objects. The extent of the association is a collection of such links. The collection may be a set (no duplicate entries) or a bag (duplicate entries allowed), and the elements may be unordered (set) or ordered (list). A given object may appear more than once within the set of links, or even more than once within the same link (in different positions) if the definition of the association permits. Associations are the "glue" that holds together a system model. Without associations, there is only a set of isolated classes.

Structure

An association has a optional name, but most of its description is found in a list of association ends, each of which describes the participation of objects of a class in the association. Note that an association end is simply part of the description of an association and not a separable semantic or notational concept.

Name. An association has an optional name, a string that must be unique among associations and classes within the containing package. (An association class is both an association and a class; therefore, associations and classes share a single namespace). An association is not required to have a name; rolenames on its ends provide an alternate way of distinguishing multiple associations among the same classes. By convention, the name is read in the order that participating classes appear in the list: WorksFor (Person, Company) = a Person works for a Company; Sells (Person, Car, Customer) = a Salesman sells a Car to a Customer.

Association ends. An association contains an ordered list of two or more association ends. (By ordered, we mean that the ends are distinguishable and are not interchangeable.) Each association end defines the participation of one class at a given position (role) in the association. The same class may appear in more than one position; the positions are, in general, not interchangeable. Each association end specifies properties that apply to the participation of the corresponding objects, such as how many times a single object may appear in links in the association (multiplicity). Certain properties, such as navigability, apply only to binary associations, but most apply to both binary and *n*-ary associations.

Association ends and attributes are alternate ways to specify the same underlying relationships. Attributes are slightly more restrictive than associations, and are always owned by their classes.

See association end for full details.

Derivation. An association may be specified as being derived from other elements, such as associations, attributes, or constraints.

Specialization. Associations may be specialized. Each link of the more specific association must also appear in the more general association.

Associations may also be redefined. See redefinition.

Instantiation

A link is an instance of an association. It contains one slot for each association end. Each slot contains a reference to an object that is an instance (direct or indirect) of the class specified as the class of the corresponding association end. A link has no identity apart from the list of objects in it. The links in the extent of an association form a collection which can be a set, bag, ordered set, or sequence, depending on the uniqueness and ordering settings on the multiplicity. The number of appearances of an object in the set of links must be compatible with the multiplicity on each end of the association. For example, if association **SoldTickets** connects many tickets to one performance, then each ticket may appear only once in a link, but each performance can appear many times, each time with a different ticket. (Presumably multiple copies of the same identical link can appear in bags or sequences. This does not require distinct identity, but the UML specification is somewhat vague on this.)

Links may be created and destroyed as the execution of a system proceeds, subject to restrictions on changeability of each end of the association. In some cases, a link can be created or changed from an object on one end of an association but not the other end. A link is created from a list of object references. A link has no identity of its own. It therefore makes no sense to talk about changing its value. It may be destroyed, and a new link may be created to take its place, however. A link of an association class does have one or more attribute values in addition to the list of objects that define its identity, and the attribute values can be modified by operations while preserving the references to the participating objects.

Notation

A binary association is shown as a solid path connecting the borders of two classes (Figure 14-22). An *n*-ary association is shown as a diamond connected by paths to each of its participant classes (Figure 14-191). (In the binary association, the

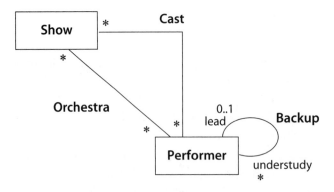

Figure 14-22. *Associations*

diamond is suppressed as extraneous.) More than one end of the path may connect to a single class.

A path consists of one or more connected solid segments—usually straight line segments, but arcs and other curves are allowed, especially to show a self-association (an association in which one class appears more than once). The individual segments have no semantic significance. The choice of a particular set of line styles is a user choice. See path.

To avoid ambiguity, a line crossing may be drawn using a small semicircle to pass one line over another line that it crosses (Figure 14-23). This notation is optional.

Figure 14-23. *Line crossing notation*

The ends of the paths have adornments that describe the participation of a class in the association. Some adornments are displayed on the end of the path, between the line segment and the class box. If there are multiple adornments, they are placed in sequence from the end of the line to the class symbol—navigation arrow, aggregation/composition diamond, qualifier (Figure 14-24).

Other adornments, such as name labels, are placed near the thing they identify. Rolenames are placed near an end of the path.

See association end for full details on the notation of adornments.

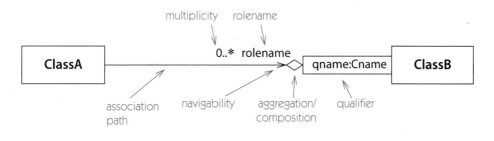

Figure 14-24. *Adornment order on association end*

Association name

A name for the association is placed near the path but far enough from an end so that there is no danger of confusion. (The danger of confusion is purely visual for a human. Within a graphic tool, the related symbols can be connected with unambiguous internal hyperlinks. It is a tool responsibility to determine how far is far enough.) The association name can be dragged from segment to segment of a multisegment association with no semantic impact. The association name may have a small filled triangle near it to show the ordering of the classes in the list. Intuitively, the name arrow shows which way to "read" the name. In Figure 14-25, the association **WorksFor** between class **Person** and class **Company** would have the name triangle pointing from **Person** to **Company** and would be read "Person works for Company." Note that the ordering triangle on the name is purely a notational device to indicate the ordering of the association ends. In the model itself, the ends are inherently ordered; therefore, the name in the model does not require or have an ordering property.

Figure 14-25. *Association name*

A stereotype on the association is indicated by showing the stereotype name in guillemets (« ») in front of or instead of the association name. A property string may be placed after or below the association name.

A derived association is noted by placing a slash (/) in front of its name.

Association class

An association class is shown by attaching a class symbol to the association path with a dashed line. For an *n*-ary association, the dashed line is connected to the association diamond. The class-like properties of the association are shown in the class symbol, and the association-like properties are shown on the path. Note, however, that the underlying modeling construct is a single element, even though the image is drawn using two graphic constructs.

See association class for more details.

Xor constraint

The constraint {xor} connects two or more associations that are connected to a single class (the base class) at one end. An instance of the base class may participate in exactly one association connected by the constraint. The multiplicity of the chosen association must be observed. If any association multiplicity includes the cardinality 0, then an instance of the base class might have no link from the association; otherwise, it must have one.

An xor-constraint is shown as a dashed line connecting two or more associations, all of which must have a class in common, with the constraint string {xor} labeling the dashed line (Figure 14-26). The rolenames on the ends away from the common class must be different.

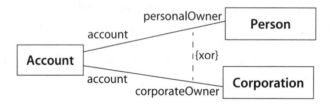

Figure 14-26. *Xor association*

Generalization

Generalization between associations is shown with a generalization arrow between the association path lines (large closed arrowhead on the more general end). See association generalization.

History

In UML1, the extent of an association was always a set, that is, there were no duplicates. This created problems with the normal use of lists, because modelers expected (and needed) duplicate entries to be possible. UML2 allows duplicate links to be included. More frequently, models will include sets (unordered with no duplicates) and lists (ordered with duplicates), but it is also possible to have bags (unordered with duplicates) and ordered sets (ordered with no duplicates).

The distinction between attributes and association ends has been weakened in UML2, therefore it is easier to shift viewpoints in a model. Association ends may be owned by associations or participating classifiers, which permits alternate ways of packaging.

Discussion

An association need not have a name. Usually, rolenames are more convenient because they provide names for navigation and code generation and avoid the problem of which way to read the name. If it has a name, the name must be unique within its package. If it does not have a name and there is more than one association between a pair (or set) of classes, then rolenames must be present to distinguish the associations. If there is only one association between a pair of classes, then the class names are sufficient to identify the association.

An argument can be made that association names are most useful when the real-world concept has a name, such as **Marriage** or **Job**. When an association name is "directed" by reading in a given direction, it is usually better simply to use rolenames, which are unambiguous in the way they are read.

See transient link for a discussion of modeling instance relationships that exist only during procedure execution.

See composition for an example of generalization involving two associations.

association (binary)

See binary association.

association (*n*-ary)

See *n*-ary association.

association class

An association class is an association that is also a class. An association class has both association and class properties. Its instances are links that have attribute values as well as references to other objects. Even though its notation consists of the symbols for both an association and a class, it is really a single model element.

See also association, class.

Semantics

An association class has the properties of both associations and classes—it connects two or more classes, and it also has attributes and operations. An association class is useful when each link must have its own attribute values, operations, or references to objects. It may be regarded as a class with an extra class reference for each association end, which is the obvious and normal way to implement it. Each instance of the association class has object references as well as the attribute values specified by the class part.

An association class C connecting classes A and B is not the same as a class D with binary associations to A and B (see the discussion section). Like all links, a link of an association class such as C takes its identity from the object references in it. The attribute values are not involved in providing identity. Therefore, two links of C must not have the same pair of (a, b) objects, even if their attribute values differ, unless the uniqueness setting on the association ends is nonunique, that is, unless the links form a bag. See the discussion.

Association classes may have operations that modify the attributes of the link or add or remove links to the link itself. Because an association class is a class, it may participate in associations itself.

An association class may not have itself as one of its participating classes (although someone could undoubtedly find a meaning for this kind of recursive structure).

Notation

An association class is shown as a class symbol (rectangle) attached by a dashed line to an association path (Figure 14-27). The name in the class symbol and the name string attached to the association path are redundant. The association path may have the usual association end adornments. The class symbol may have attributes and operations, as well as participate in associations of its own as a class. There are no adornments on the dashed line; it is not a relationship but simply part of the overall association class symbol.

Style guidelines

The attachment point should not be near enough to either end of the path that it appears to be attached to the end of the path or to any of the role adornments.

Note that the association path and the association class are a single model element and therefore have a single name. The name can be shown on the path or the class symbol or both. If an association class has only attributes but no operations or other associations, then the name may be displayed on the association path and omitted from the association class symbol to emphasize its "association nature." If it has operations and other associations, then the name may be omitted from the path and placed in the class rectangle to emphasize its "class nature." In neither case is the actual semantics different.

Discussion

Figure 14-27 shows an association class representing employment. The employment relationship between a company and a person is many-to-many. A person may have more than one job, but only one job for a given company. The salary is not an attribute of either the company or the person because the association is many-to-many. It must be an attribute of the relationship itself.

The boss-worker relationship is not just a relationship between two people. It is a relationship between a person in one job and a person in another job—it is an association (**Manages**) between the association class and itself.

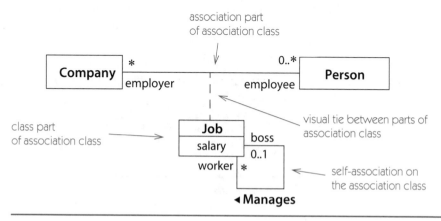

Figure 14-27. *Association class*

The following example shows the difference between an association class and a reified relationship modeled as a class. In Figure 14-28, the ownership of stock is modeled as an association between Person and Company. The association class attribute **quantity** represents the number of shares held. This relationship is modeled as an association class because there should be only one entry for any pairing of **Person** and **Company**.

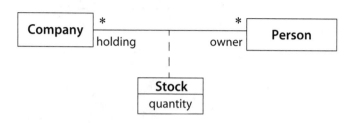

Figure 14-28. *Association class with attribute*

To model purchases of stock, as shown in Figure 14-29, there can be multiple purchases with the same Person and Company. Yet they must be distinguished because each purchase is distinct and has its own date and cost in addition to quantity. The keyword {bag} is placed on each association end to indicate that there may be multiple links, and therefore multiple link objects, involving the same pairs of objects. Alternately, as shown in Figure 14-30, the relationship can be *reified*—that is, made into distinct objects with their own identity. An ordinary class is the used to model this case, because each purchase has its own identity, independent of the **Person** and **Company** classes that it relates.Although the models are not identical, they model the same information. Finally, it can be modeled as a ternary association, as shown in Figure 14-31. This is an inferior choice, however, because a lot uniquely determines a tuple from the association and therefore the company

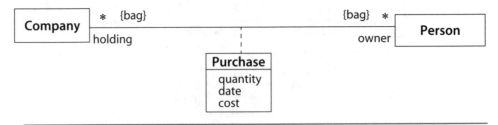

Figure 14-29. *Nonunique association class*

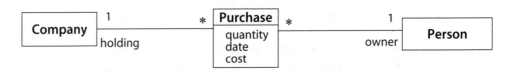

Figure 14-30. *Reified association*

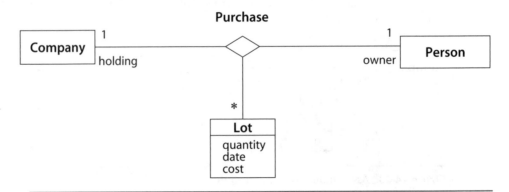

Figure 14-31. *Ternary association*

and person. Ternary associations are usually not useful unless the multiplicity is many on all ends; otherwise a binary association shows more information about the multiplicity constraints.

association end

A part of an association that defines the participation of a class in the association. One class may be connected to more than one end in the same association. The association ends within an association have distinct positions, have names, and, in general, are not interchangeable. An association end has no independent existence or meaning apart from its association.

See also association.

Semantics

Structure

An association end holds a reference to a target classifier. It defines the participation of the classifier in the association. An instance of the association (a link) must contain an instance of the given classifier or one of its descendants in the given position. Participation in an association is inherited by children of a classifier.

An attribute is a degenerate association in which one association end is owned by a classifier that is conceptually at the other, unmodeled end of the association. In a modeling situation in which all the participant classifiers are of fairly even importance or the relationship may be viewed in more than one direction, an association is more appropriate. In a situation in which the relationship is always viewed in a single direction, an attribute may be more appropriate.

Because of the underlying similarity of association ends and attributes, most of their modeling properties are combined into a single modeling element, called a structural property. See property for a full list of modeling settings for both association end and attribute.

Notation

See property for most of the notation for association ends. Properties of association ends are shown by placing graphical or text adornments on or near the line ends (Figure 14-32).

If there are multiple adornments on a single association end, they are presented in the following order, reading from the end of the path attached to the class outward toward the bulk of the path (Figure 14-24):

qualifier

aggregation or composition symbol

navigation arrow

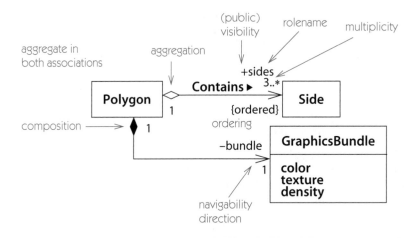

Figure 14-32. *Various adornments on association ends*

End names and multiplicity strings should be placed near the end of the path so that they are not confused with a different association. They may be placed on either side of the line. It is tempting to require that they always be placed on one side of the line (clockwise or counterclockwise), but this is sometimes overridden by the need for clarity in a crowded layout. An end name and a multiplicity may be placed on opposite sides of the same role, or they may be placed together (for example, * employee).

Other settings are shown as property strings in braces ({}). Multiple property strings may be placed in the same pair of braces, separated by commas, or they may be shown separately. The property string labels should be placed near the ends of the path so that they do not interfere with end names or multiplicity strings.

association generalization

A generalization relationship between two associations.

See also association, generalization.

Semantics

Generalization among associations is permitted, although it is somewhat uncommon. As with any generalization relationship, the child element must add to the intent (defining rules) of the parent and must subset the extent (set of instances) of the parent. Adding to the intent means adding additional constraints. A child association is more constrained than its parent. For example, in Figure 14-33, if the parent association connects classes **Subject** and **Symbol**, then the child association may connect classes **Order** and **OrderSymbol**, where **Order** is a child of

Subject and OrderSymbol is a child of Symbol. Subsetting the extent means that every link of the child association is a link of the parent association, but not the reverse. The example obeys this rule. Any link connecting Order and OrderSymbol will also connect Subject and Symbol, but not all links connecting Subject and Symbol will connect Order and OrderSymbol.

Notation

A generalization arrow symbol (solid body, triangular hollow arrowhead) connects the child association to the parent association. The arrowhead is on the parent. Because of the lines connecting other lines, association generalization notation can be confusing and should be used with care.

Example

Figure 14-33 shows two specializations of the general model-view association between Subject and Symbol: The association between Order and OrderSymbol is a specialization, as is the association between Customer and CustomerSymbol. Each of these connects a Subject class to a Symbol class. The general Subject-Symbol association may be regarded as an abstract association whereas the two child associations are concrete.

This pattern of paired class hierarchies connected by associations is fairly common.

Discussion

The distinction between subsetting and specializing an association is not clearly described in the UML2 specification.

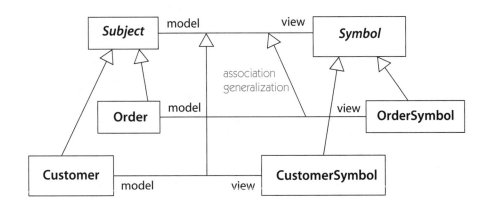

Figure 14-33. *Association generalization*

asynchronous action

A request in which the sending object does not pause to wait for results; a send.
See send, synchronous action.

atomic

An action or operation whose execution must be completed as a unit; one that may not be partially executed or terminated by an external event or interrupt. Usually, atomic operations are small and simple, such as assignments and simple arithmetic or string calculations. An atomic computation occurs at a definite point in the execution sequence.

This is not a precise UML term.

See also action, do activity, run-to-completion.

Semantics

Conceptually, atomic actions that do not access shared resources simply require concurrent execution. There are many ways to map such actions onto shared processor resources as part of an implementation.

If actions access shared resources (memory, devices, or external interactions), they can hardly be considered atomic. The term is sometimes used to mean noninterleavable on a global basis, but such kinds of global interactions require a more detailed, implementation-specific model.

attribute

An attribute is the description of a named element of a specified type in a class; each object of the class separately holds a value of the type.

Semantics

An attribute is a named element within a classifier that describes the values that instances of the classifier may hold. Every instance of the classifier or one of its descendants has a slot holding a value of the given type. All the slots are distinct and independent of each other (except for class-scope attributes, which are described later). As execution proceeds, the value held by a slot within an instance may be replaced by a different value of the type, provided the attribute is changeable.

A classifier forms a namespace for its attributes. Also included in the namespace are other properties, such as the rolenames of associations leaving the classifier and internal parts.

An attribute can be redefined. See redefinition (property).

Structure

Attributes and association ends contain the same information and can be inter-changed relatively easily. An attribute may be regarded as an association end that is owned by a classifier and is navigable from the classifier to the attribute value. A piece of information may be modeling as an attribute, an association end, or both.

For a list of the modeling settings for an attribute, see property.

Notation

An attribute is shown as a text string that can be parsed into various properties. The default syntax is:

$$\lfloor\text{«stereotype»}\rfloor_{opt}\ \text{visibility}_{opt}\ /_{opt}\ \text{name}\ \lfloor\text{:type}\rfloor_{opt}\ \text{multiplicity}_{opt}$$
$$\lfloor=\text{initial-value}\rfloor_{opt}\ \lfloor\{\text{property-string}\}\rfloor_{opt}$$

Visibility. The visibility is shown as a punctuation mark. Alternately, the visibility can be shown as a keyword within the property string. The latter form must be used for user-defined or language-dependent choices. The predefined choices are

+ (public)	Any class that can see the class can also see the attribute.
# (protected)	The class or any of its descendants can see the attribute.
– (private)	Only the class itself can see the attribute.
~ (package)	Any class in the same package can see the attribute.

Name. The name is shown as an identifier string.

Type. The type is shown as an expression string denoting a classifier. The name of a class or a data type is a legitimate expression string indicating that the values of the attribute must be of the given type. Additional type syntax depends on the language of the expression. Each language has syntax for constructing new data types out of simple ones. For example, C++ has syntax for pointers, arrays, and functions. Ada also has syntax for subranges. The language of the expression is part of the internal model, but it is not usually shown on a diagram. It is assumed that it is known for the entire diagram or obvious from its syntax.

The type string may be suppressed (but it still exists in the model).

Multiplicity. The multiplicity is shown as a multiplicity expression (see below) enclosed in square brackets ([ ]) placed after the type name. If the multiplicity is "exactly one," then the expression, including the brackets, may be omitted. This indicates that each object has exactly one slot holding a value of the given type (the most common case). Otherwise, the multiplicity must be shown. See multiplicity for a full discussion of its syntax. For example:

colors : Saturation [3]	An array of 3 saturations
points : Point [2..*]	An array of 2 or more points

Note that a multiplicity of 0..1 provides for the possibility of null values—the absence of a value, as opposed to a particular value from the range. A null value is not a value within the domain of most data types; it extends that domain with an extra value outside the domain. For pointers, however, the null value is often part of the implementation (although, even then, it is usually by convention—for example, the value 0 in C or C++, an artifact of memory addressing conventions). The following declaration permits a distinction between the *null* value and the empty string, a distinction supported by C++ and other languages.

name : String [0..1]   If the name is missing, it is a null value.

If the upper bound is greater than one, then ordering and uniqueness settings can be specified as property strings. Keyword choices include **ordered**, **bag**, **seq**, **sequence**, and **list**. See property for details.

Derivation. A derived attribute is indicated by a slash (/) in front of the name.

Initial value. The default initial value is shown as a string. The language of evaluation is usually not shown explicitly (but it is present in the model). If there is no default value, then both the string and the equal sign are omitted. If the attribute multiplicity includes the value 0 (that is, optional) and no explicit initial value is given, then the attribute starts with an empty value (zero repetitions).

Changeability. The property string {**readOnly**} indicates that the value may not be changed after initialization. If no choice is given, then the setting is **changeable**.

Redefinition and subsetting. These settings can be specified by property strings. See property and redefinition (property) for details.

Tagged value. Zero or more tagged values may be attached to an attribute (as to any model element). Each tagged value is shown in the form tag = value, where tag is the name of a tag and value is a literal value. Tagged values are included with property keywords as a comma-separated property list enclosed in braces.

Static. A static attribute (class scope) is shown by underlining the name and type expression string; otherwise, the attribute is instance-scope.

static-attribute

Figure 14-34 shows the declaration of some attributes.

+size: Area = (100,100)	public, initial value
#visibility: Boolean = invisible	protected, initial value
+default-size: Rectangle	public
maximum-size: Rectangle	static
–xptr: XWindowPtr {requirement=4.3}	private, tagged value

Figure 14-34. *Attributes*

Presentation options

Programming-language syntax. The syntax of the attribute string can be that of a programming language, such as C++ or Smalltalk. Specific tagged properties may be included in the string.

Style guidelines

Attribute names are shown in normal typeface.

Discussion

A similar syntax is used to specify qualifiers, template parameters, operation parameters, and so on (some of these omit certain terms).

Note that an attribute is semantically equivalent to a composition association. (There may be some doubt about this. The specification includes a notation for composition of attributes. The use of attributes in the metamodel included in the specification, however, indicates that this is not meant to be taken seriously.) However, the intent and usage of attributes and associations are usually different. Use attributes for data types—that is, for values with no identity. Use associations for classes—that is, for values with identity. The reason is that for objects with identity, it is important to see the relationship in both directions; for data types, the data type is usually subordinate to the object and has no knowledge of it.

History

Attributes and association ends have been semantically unified in UML2, so that it is much easier to convert among them in a model.

The multiplicity setting now appears after the type name, rather than after the attribute name. This makes it possible to treat the multiplicity as part of the overall type specification. Redefinition and subsetting have been added. The concept of target scope has been dropped.

auxiliary (stereotype of Class)

A class that supports another, more central *focus* class, typically by providing control mechanisms.

See focus.

background information

Each appearance of a symbol for a class on a diagram or on different diagrams may have its own presentation choices. For example, one symbol for a class may show the attributes and operations, and another symbol for the same class may suppress them. Tools may provide style sheets attached to either individual symbols or entire diagrams. Style sheets would specify the presentation choices, and they would be applicable to most kinds of symbols, not just classes.

Not all modeling information is most usefully presented in a graphical notation. Some information is best presented in a textual or tabular format. For example, detailed programming information is often best presented as text lists. UML does not assume that all the information in a model will be expressed as diagrams; some of it may be available only as tables. The UML2 Appendix D describes a tabular format for sequence diagrams, but there is nothing special about either sequence diagrams or the particular format listed in the appendix that prevents the use of tables for any modeling information. That is because the underlying information is adequately described in the UML metamodel, and the responsibility for presenting tabular information is a tool responsibility. Hidden links may exist from graphical items to tabular items within tools.

bag

A collection of elements that may have multiple copies of identical elements, as opposed to a set, in which each element must be unique.

Semantics

Bags may be indicated on multiplicity specifications using the uniqueness flag with a value of false. In combination with the ordering flag, modelers may specify unordered sets, ordered sets, unordered bags, and ordered bags. Ordered bags are called sequences or lists. Multiplicity is applicable to attribute values, association ends, parameters, and other elements.

History

Support for bags on multiplicity is new in UML2.

become

This UML1 dependency has been retired in UML2.

behavior

A specification of how the state of a classifier changes over time. Behavior is specialized into activity, interaction, and state machine. A behavior describes the dynamics of an entire classifier as a unit. A classifier also owns a set of behavioral features (such as operations) that may be invoked independently as part of its overall semantics.

Semantics

Behavior is a generic term for the specification of how the state of an instance of a classifier changes over time in response to external events and internal computations. The classifier may be a concrete entity (such as a class) or a collaboration. Behavior may be specified for the instance as a whole or for individual operations that may be invoked on an instance. It includes activity, interaction, and state state machine. Each of these has its own detailed structure, semantics, and usages, which are described in separate entries.

A behavior may have parameters, which must correspond to the parameters of an operation it implements. A behavior attached to an operation takes effect when the operation is invoked and continues until the execution of the operation is complete. A behavior attached to an entire classifier takes effect when an instance of the classifier is instantiated and continues while the instance exists.

A behavior may reentrant or non-reentrant. A reentrant behavior may be invoked within an existing execution of the same behavior.

A behavior may redefine another behavior. The rules for redefinition are specified under each kind of behavior.

Preconditions and postconditions may be attached to behaviors. These are constraints that must be satisfied when the behavior begins and finishes. These are meant to be assertions whose failure indicates a modeling or implementation error, not executable parts of the behavior specification.

A behavior is modeled as a classifier, but most often it describes the execution of a distinct classifier, which is called the context for the behavior. Messages are not sent to the behavior directly but to the context. Sometimes, however, a behavior may serve as its own context. In this situation, an instance of the behavior can directly receive messages from other instances. A behavior-as-context may be used to model things such as operating system processes, tasks in a workflow, and other kinds of reified behavior.

The behavior for a classifier can be redefined. A behavior can be specialized as with any classifier. See redefinition (behavior).

Execution semantics

On the instantiation of a classifier, an instance is created and initialized according to default and explicit initialization rules. A behavior attached to the classifier describes the subsequent execution of the instance. An execution of the behavior corresponding to the instance has its own state space for local variables and for the state of the behavior occurrence itself, unshared with any other behavior occurrences. An execution of a behavior has a reference to its context, that is, the instance whose execution it represents. If the behavior execution reaches a terminal state, the instance of the classifier is destroyed and ceases to exist.

On the invocation of an operation, an execution of the behavior attached to the operation is created with copies of the actual arguments to the invocation. The behavior execution has its own state space for local variables and its own state, independent of any other invocations of the same instance. The execution of each behavior proceeds independently of other executions, except to the extent that they explicitly exchange messages or implicitly access data from shared objects. When the execution of an operation is completed, the behavior execution emits return values (if the operation is synchronous) and ceases to exist.

behavioral feature

A named model element specifying dynamic behavior, such as an operation or reception, that is part of a classifier. It also has a list of exceptions that might be raised during the execution of the behavior specified by the feature.

See operation, reception.

Semantics

A behavioral feature has a list of parameters, including zero or more return parameters. It may also have a concurrency kind specification that specifies whether concurrent invocations are permitted to the same passive instance. The concurrency specification on a behavioral feature is ignored for an active instance, which controls its own concurrency.

A behavioral feature is owned by a classifier. A behavior may be attached to a behavioral feature as a method within that classifier or any number of its descendants. A method is an implementation of a behavioral feature. The method declared in a classifier for a behavioral feature is inherited by descendant classifiers unless it is replaced by a new method.

A behavioral feature may be abstract or concrete with respect to a particular classifier. If it is abstract, it has no method within the classifier and must not be invoked on a direct instance of the classifier. If it is concrete, it must have an implementation in the classifier or an ancestor class. An abstract behavioral feature in one classifier becomes concrete in a subclassifier if a method is specified in the subclass. More rarely, a concrete behavioral feature in one classifier may be declared as abstract in a subclassifier, in which case it cannot be used until a still further descendant classifier makes it concrete again by supplying a method.

behavioral state machine

A state machine used to express the behavior of objects of a class (including an entire system), as opposed to the specification of a legal sequence of operation invocations.

See state machine. Compare with protocol state machine.

Semantics

A behavioral state machine is an executable behavior intended to specify the execution of objects of a class as triggered by the occurrence of events. A behavioral state machine must be prepared to accept any sequence of legal events. In contrast, a protocol state machine is the specification of the legal sequences of invocation of operations. It is not directly executable and is not intended to handle arbitrary sequences of events; rather, it is intended to constrain the overall system to avoid nonlegal sequences.

Discussion

The mechanism used in UML is based on (but not identical to) the statechart formalism invented by computer scientist David Harel. This kind of specification can be transformed into code in various ways for implementation.

behavioral view

A view of a model that emphasizes the behavior of the instances in a system, including their methods, collaborations, and state histories.

binary association

An association between exactly two classes.
    See also association, *n*-ary association.

Semantics

A binary association is an association with exactly two association ends, by far the most common kind of association. Because an end in a binary association has a unique other end, binary associations are particularly useful for specifying navigation paths from object to object. An association is navigable in a given direction if it can be traversed in that direction. Some other properties, such as multiplicity, are defined for *n*-ary associations, but they are more intuitive and useful for binary associations.

Notation

A binary association is shown as a solid path connecting two class symbols. Adornments can be attached to each end, and an association name may be placed near the line, far enough from either end so that it is not mistaken for a rolename. The notation for a binary association is the same as the notation for an *n*-ary association except for the suppression of the central diamond symbol. Binary associations, however, can have adornments that are not applicable to *n*-ary associations, such as aggregation. See association for details.

bind

Keyword for a binding dependency in the notation.
See binding.

binding

The matching of values to parameters to produce an individual element from a parameterized element. The binding relationship is a directed relationship between a model element and a parameter within the context of an invocation or use of a template.
See also bound element, template.

Semantics

A parameterized definition, such as an operation, signal, or template, defines the form of an element. A parameterized element cannot be used directly, however, because its parameters do not have specific values. Binding is a directed relationship that assigns values to parameters to produce a new, usable element. Binding acts on operations to produce calls, on signals to produce messages, and on templates to produce new model elements. The first two are bound during execution to produce run-time entities. These do not usually figure in models except as examples or simulation results. The argument values are defined within the execution system.

A template is bound at modeling time, however, to produce new model elements for use within the model. The argument values can be other model elements, such as classes, in addition to data values, such as strings and integers. The binding relationship binds values to a template, producing an actual model element that can be used directly within the model.

A binding relationship has a supplier element (the template), a client element (the newly generated bound element), and a list of values to bind to template parameters. The bound element is defined by substituting each argument value for its corresponding parameter within a copy of the template body. The classification of each argument must be the same as or a descendant of the declared classification of its parameter.

A binding does not affect the template itself. Each template can be bound many times, each time producing a new bound element.

Notation

Template binding is indicated with the keyword «bind» attached to a dashed arrow that connects the generated element (on the tail of the arrow) to the template (on the arrowhead). See Figure 14-35. The actual argument values are shown as a

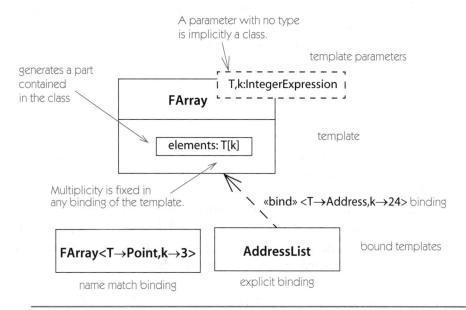

Figure 14-35. *Template declaration and binding*

comma-separated list of text expressions enclosed in angle brackets following the «bind» keyword on the arrow:

«bind» <argument$_{list,}$>

where each argument has the form:

parameter-name → value

If the parameters are ordered (as is usual with operations), only the value need be included. Note that the value can include types, if appropriate for the parameter.

An alternative and more compact notation for binding uses name matching to avoid the need for arrows. To indicate a bound (generated) element, the name of a template is followed by a comma-separated list of text expressions enclosed in angle brackets:

template-name <argument$_{list,}$>

In either case, each argument is stated as a text string that is evaluated statically at model-building time. It is not evaluated dynamically as an operation or signal argument is.

In Figure 14-35, the explicit form using the arrow declares a new class **Address-List**, whose name can be used in models and expressions. The implicit inline form **Farray<T→Point,k→3>** declares an "anonymous class" without a name of its own. The inline syntax may be used in expressions.

Additional attributes or operations can be added to the bound class; the interpretation is that an anonymous class is created by the binding and the new class with the additional features is a subclass of the anonymous class.

History

The notation for binding has changed in UML2.

Discussion

Template parameters and operation parameters are at different semantic levels, but they represent related semantic concepts, at least conceptually.

The specification uses an arrow composed from a hyphen and a right angle bracket (->) but that may be regarded as an example of typographical cowardice in light of the availability modern character sets and the death of the punch card.

The notation for template binding has been changed slightly in UML2, and templates have been restricted to elements for which they make sense.

Boolean

An enumeration whose values are **true** and **false**.

Boolean expression

An expression that evaluates to a Boolean value. Useful in guard conditions.

bound element

A model element produced by binding argument values to the parameters of a template.

See also binding, template.

Semantics

A template is a parameterized description of a group of potential elements. To obtain an actual element, the template's parameters must be *bound* to actual values. The actual value for each parameter is an expression supplied by the scope within which the binding occurs. Most arguments are classes or integers.

If the scope is itself a template, then the parameters of the outer template can be used as arguments in binding the original template, in effect reparameterizing it. But parameter names from one template have no meaning outside its body. Parameters in two templates cannot be assumed to correspond just because they have the same names, any more than subroutine parameters could be assumed to match based only on their names.

A bound element is fully specified by its template. As a convenience, additional attributes can be declared in a bound class. This is equivalent to declaring an anonymous class that performs the binding, then declaring the bound class as a subclass of it and adding the new attributes to the bound class. See template for an example.

Example

Figure 14-36 shows the rebinding of a template. **Polygon** is a template with a single parameter—the size **n**. We want to build it using an existing template **FArray**, which has two parameters—the type of element **T** and the size **k**. To build it, the parameter k from the **FArray** template is bound to the parameter n from the Polygon template. The parameter T from the **FArray** template is bound to the class **Point**. This has the effect of removing one parameter from the original template. To use the **Polygon** template to make a **Triangle** class, the size parameter **n** is bound to the value 3. To make a **Quadrilateral** class, it is bound to the value 4.

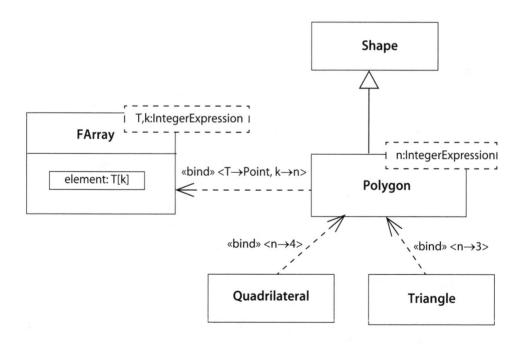

Figure 14-36. *Rebinding a template*

Figure 14-36 also shows the template **Polygon** as a child of class **Shape**. This means that each class bound from **Template** is a subclass of **Shape**—**Triangle** and **Quadrilateral** are both subclasses of Shape.

Notation

A bound element can be shown using a dashed arrow from the template to the bound element; the arrow has the keyword «**bind**». Alternately, it can be shown using the text syntax TemplateName<argument$_{list,}$>, using name matching to identify the template. The text form avoids the need to show the template or to draw an arrow to it; this form is particularly useful when the bound element is used as a classifier for an attribute or operation parameter.

See binding for details. Figure 14-35 shows an example.

The attribute and operation compartments are usually suppressed within a bound class because they must not be modified in a bound element.

A bound element name (either the inline "anonymous" form using angle brackets or the explicit "binding arrow" form) may be used anywhere an element name of the parameterized kind could be used. For example, a bound class name could be used as an attribute type or as part of an operation signature within a class symbol on a class diagram. Figure 14-37 shows an example.

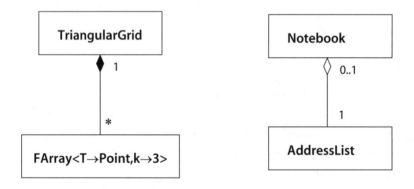

Figure 14-37. *Use of bound templates in associations*

Discussion

Classifiers are obvious candidates for parameterization. The types of their attributes, operations, or associated classifiers are common parameters in templates. Parameterized collaborations are patterns. Operations, in a sense, are inherently parameterized. Packages can be parameterized. The usefulness of parameterization of other elements is not so clear, but uses will likely be found.

branch

A situation in a state machine in which a single trigger leads to more than one possible outcome, each with its own guard condition. Branches may be static and dynamic.

A situation in an activity in which an input flow may lead to one of several possible output flows, each with its own guard condition.

See also choice, decision node, fork, join, junction, merge.

Semantics

State machine. If the same event can have different effects that depend on different guard conditions, then they can be modeled as separate transitions with the same event trigger. In practice, however, it is convenient to permit a single trigger to drive multiple transitions. This is especially true in the common case in which the guard conditions cover every possibility, so that an occurrence of the event is guaranteed to trigger one of the transitions. A *branch* is a part of a transition that splits the transition path into two or more segments, each with a separate guard condition. The event trigger is placed on the first, common segment of the transition. The output of one branch segment can be connected to the input of another branch to form a tree. Each path through the tree represents a distinct transition.

The branch can be static or dynamic. In the static case, the branch point is modeled using a junction vertex. The conjunction of all the conditions on a path in a transition is equivalent to a single condition that is conceptually evaluated before the transition fires. If there is no path for which all conditions are true, no transition fires. The chosen path is unaffected by changes to values caused by actions executed during transition. A transition fires in a single step, despite its appearance as a tree of branches. The tree is merely a modeling convenience. One path leading from each vertex may be labeled with the pseudocondition else. This path is enabled to fire if and only if no other path is enabled.

In the dynamic case, the branch point is modeled using a choice vertex. A choice vertex represents a temporary state. If all of the conditions on a path leading to a choice vertex are true, the transition may fire up to the choice vertex. Any effects on the path are executed and affect conditions in the remainder of the transition beyond the choice point. Conditions on subsequent segments are then evaluated and a path is selected to complete the transition. (It may lead to another choice.) If no path is enabled, the state machine is ill formed. (It is impossible to undo the effects of the partially executed path.) To avoid this situation, it is recommended that an else condition be included, unless it is certain that a path will be enabled.

A choice vertex can be considered a "real" state in which an immediate transition must be enabled to another state, whereas a junction vertex is merely a syntactic convenience in organizing paths that share some conditions.

Activity. Branches are modeled as decision nodes. A decision node has one input flow and several possible output flows, each with its own guard condition. Decision nodes are always active. Any effects of a behavior on the input flow may affect the guard conditions on the output flows. It is important that the guard conditions cover all possibilities, similar to a choice in a state machine, otherwise the activity is ill formed. An else condition may be used in an activity graph to guarantee that a guard condition will be true.

Notation

State machine. A static branch may be shown by repeating an event trigger on multiple transition arcs with different guard conditions. This may also be done with completion transitions, as in an activity diagram.

For greater convenience, however, the head of a transition arrow may be connected to a small black circle, which indicates a junction. The transition arrow is labeled with the trigger event, if any, but it should not have an action on it. Any actions go on the final segment of the transition (unless they are shared by all paths).

The effect of a tree of branches is the same as expanding the tree into a separate transition arc for each path through the tree, all sharing the same trigger event but each with its own conjunction of guard conditions, action, and target state. Figure 14-38 shows two ways to draw the same situation. Note that the conditions may include parameters of the trigger event.

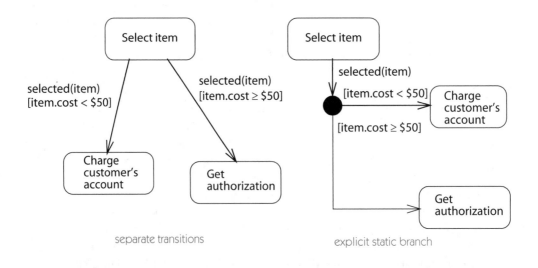

Figure 14-38. *Two ways to show a static branch*

A dynamic branch may be shown by connecting the head of a transition arrow to a diamond, which indicates a choice. The incoming arrow may have conditions and actions, which are executed before the choice occurs.

A diamond symbol may have two or more arrows leaving it. Each arrow is labeled with a guard condition. The reserved word **else** can be used as a guard condition. Its value is true if all the other (explicit) guard conditions are false. The head of each arrow may be connected to another branch or to a state. An arrow connected to a state may have an action label attached. No arrow leaving a choice may have an event trigger.

Figure 14-39 shows a variation on the previous example, this time using a choice. In this case, the priceItem action is performed as part of the transition to compute the price. Because the price is not known before the initial transition segment fires, the branch must be dynamic, so a choice vertex is used. It is easy to verify that the conditions cover all possibilities, therefore an else path is unnecessary.

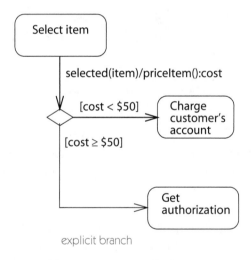

Figure 14-39. *Dynamic branch*

Activity diagram. Both decisions (dynamic branches) and merges (the inverse of a branch) can be shown as diamonds, as shown in Figure 14-40. In the case of a merge, there are two or more input arrows and a single output arrow. No guard conditions are necessary on a merge.

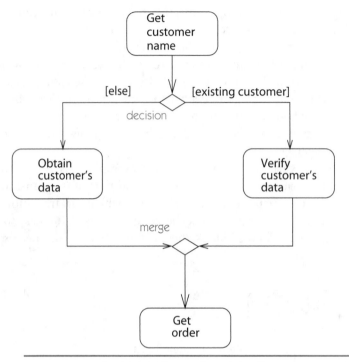

Figure 14-40. *Decision and merge in activity diagram*

break

A kind of interaction operator, indicating that the operand subfragment is performed and the rest of the enclosing fragment is not performed.

Semantics

The break operator has an operand subfragment with a guard condition. If the guard condition is true, the operand is executed and the remainder of the enclosing fragment is omitted. If the guard condition is false, the operand is not executed and the remainder of the enclosing fragment is executed. This operator may be regarded as a shorthand for an alternative operator in which the remainder of the enclosing fragment need not be an explicit subfragment.

The break operand must cover all lifelines of the enclosing fragment.

Notation

The keyword **break** appears as the interaction operator label.

Figure 14-41 shows an example of break. If the user presses the cancel button after receiving an identification request, the remainder of the sequence is ignored Otherwise, the user presents identification, and the validation sequence proceeds.

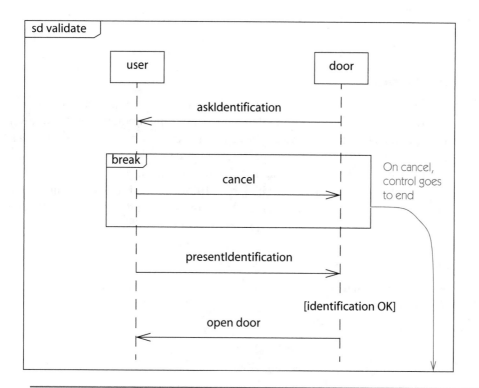

Figure 14-41. *Break*

broadcast

An asynchronous signal sent to an implicit set of target objects associated with the current system.

See action.

Semantics

A broadcast action has a signal type and a list of arguments as parameters, but no target object. The signal is sent to all of the objects in a system-dependent implicit set. The intent is that all objects reachable from the system be sent the signal, but in practice this is impractical, and a broadcast will usually go to a subset of objects on the local node.

Discussion

The concept of broadcast is theoretically problematic, because the set of nodes may be open, so it must be regarded as a fundamentally implementation-specific action associated with some concept of locality and a closed universe of objects.

buffer

See central buffer node.

Semantics

Buffering capability is assumed in the handling of messages received by objects, but the details of this capability depend on the implementation. Careful design of models can avoid the need for buffers in many common cases, but there are situations in which it is semantically necessary.

Buffering capability is implicit in the handling of tokens within an activity, particularly if streaming tokens are included. In many common cases, only one token at a time can exist at a location, so buffering is not always needed. An explicit, shared buffer can be modeled using a central buffer node.

buildComponent (stereotype of Component)

A component that defines a set of components for organizational or system-level development purposes.

call

To invoke an operation or a behavior.
See also action, call trigger.

Semantics

A call is an action that invokes an operation on a target object. A call supplies actual values for the parameters of the operation. Each value must be compatible with its corresponding parameter; that is, it must be of the same type or of a descendant type. If the operation has default parameters, they may be omitted from the call and the default values will be automatically supplied. The call operation action has the operation as a static parameter of the action and has run-time input values for the target object and arguments.

Information about the call, including the argument values and, for a synchronous call, information sufficient to return control to the caller, is transmitted to the target object. The manner of transmitting the information is not constrained and may be implementation dependent. In particular, the target object may be on the same system or a remote system; there is no distinction between local and remote calls. In the case of concurrent or asynchronous calls, no assumptions should be made about the order in which different calls are received. System profiles are free to constrain some of these possibilities.

The invoked operation is used to cause an effect on the target object, using the operation resolution rules of the underlying system. For example, an object-oriented method lookup rule would examine the class of the target object for a method attached to the operation; if a method is not found, it would examine ancestor classes until a method is found. However, the UML2 specification does not mandate a specific operation resolution rule. Other kinds of method lookup are possible, including delegation (as in the self language), before-and-after methods, various forms of inheritance, and triggering state machine transitions (see below). Unfortunately, the UML specification does not list or name the various resolution rules. Most modelers will probably use the object-oriented rules familiar from Smalltalk and Java, so any other approaches should be clearly stated comments attached to a model.

Activity effect. In this style, methods are modeled as activities. Using the object-oriented resolution rule, if the operation cannot be resolved to an activity, there is an error. The UML2 specification does not state whether such an error should be handled at run time as an exception or whether the model is considered ill formed. This choice is a semantic variation point that is an implementation choice.

Once a method is determined, an execution of it is created, with the target object and argument values supplied to it. Execution of the activity continues until it terminates. During execution of the activity, any return values that are produced are preserved.

A call may be asynchronous or synchronous. On an asynchronous call, the execution of the caller continues immediately after the call is issued, and the execution of the invoked operation continues concurrently with the execution of the caller. When the execution of an asynchronous call completes, it simply terminates. If there are any return values, they are ignored. There is no flow of control back to the caller.

On a synchronous call, the execution of the caller is blocked during the call. Along with the argument values, sufficient information about the calling execution is transmitted to enable the caller to be awakened when the execution of the invoked operation is complete. The form of this return control information is not specified and an implementation is free to use any approach that works. The return control information is not explicitly available to the invoked operation. When the execution of the invoked procedure is complete, the fact of completion together with any return values generated by the invoked operation are transmitted to the caller, which is awakened and allowed to continue execution.

Alternate method semantics. The UML2 specification permits the definition of arbitrary semantics for the effect of receiving an operation call, but it does not provide any formal way to define such semantics, nor does it provide many guidelines on meaningful rules. The following guidelines seem reasonable but are not in the specification document. A resolution rule may depend on the target object and the operation. It should probably not depend on the argument values. In the conventional object-oriented case, the method depends on the type of the object and nothing else about the object. In this case, methods would be attached to classes and not to objects. In a delegation approach (as used in the Self language), methods can be attached directly to objects, and method lookup uses delegation pointers rather than superclass pointers. For synchronous calls, it is necessary that the resolved effect reach an explicit return point, at which time control can be returned to the caller, although it is not necessary that the invoked effect cease execution immediately. Any return values must be specified somehow and available at the point of return. It is possible for a call to invoke more than one activity. In that case, the rules must make clear what order the various activities are executed, including the possibility of concurrent execution. Also, in a synchronous call, the return point must be clear, either because it is explicitly in one of the activities or because it implicitly follows the completion of a designated set of activities. If there are multiple activities for a synchronous call with return values, it must be clear how the return values are produced. Probably the simplest approach is to designate a single activity as the main activity whose termination will supply return values and cause a return of control to the caller. More complicated return rules are possible, but they risk semantic meaninglessness as well as unimplementability. In all likelihood, most modelers will use the traditional object-oriented class-based single-method resolution semantics for most modeling.

State machine transition effect. The receipt of a call request by an object with an active state machine may cause the firing of a transition triggered by the operation. The parameters of the operation are available to any effect attached to the transition. It is possible for a call to trigger both a method and a transition, if both are defined for a given class. In that case, the method is executed first. Execution of the method may affect the state of the object, and the new state will be available to the state machine in evaluating guard conditions and executing attached activities. If the call is synchronous, any return values from the method are returned to the caller at the completion of the method, at which time the caller is unblocked and continues execution. At that point (or if there is no method), the call may enable transitions triggered by the operation. Regardless of whether the call was synchronous, execution of state machine transitions is asynchronous and cannot return values. If there is no method, execution of a synchronous call proceeds immediately, but any transitions triggered by it may proceed concurrently with subsequent execution of the caller.

Explicit acceptance of a call. There is an accept action that explicitly waits for the receipt of a call on a particular operation. When the owning object receives a call on the given operation, the receiving action receives a copy of the argument values of the call. If the call was synchronous, the caller is blocked and the receiving action delivers an opaque output value that contains sufficient information to later return control to the caller. The receiving procedure may not examine or manipulate this information in any way, but it may be copied, stored, and passed along.

When a subsequent action executes a reply action on the same operation, it must supply a copy of the opaque return information as an argument, together with the return values specified by the operation. At that time, the return values are transmitted to the caller and the caller is allowed to continue execution. Execution of the receiving procedure continues after the reply action until it performs another receive action, terminates, or performs a call of its own. If the call is asynchronous, the caller continues immediately and no reply action is necessary. If a reply is nevertheless attempted using the return information supplied in the receive action on the asynchronous call, there is no effect and execution continues without error.

If a class has a method on a given operation, execution of the method will take precedence over the receive action (which would therefore never get executed). If two or more receive actions on the same operation are outstanding for a single object, it is indeterminate which one will receive the call, but one and only one will receive the call.

Ports. A call to a structured classifier may include a port on the target object. The object receiving the call can distinguish which port received the call and use this information within a method or to choose among methods.

Direct call of a procedure. There is an action to call a behavior directly. Most of the time the behavior is a procedure (in UML terms, an activity). There is no target object. The action has input values for the behavior arguments. The call may be asynchronous or synchronous. If synchronous, it may have return values.

A direct call represents a way to model a non-object-oriented call to a specific procedure and also a way to structure large activities into manageable pieces.

Dependencies. A call usage dependency models a situation in which an operation of the client class (or the operation itself) calls an operation of the supplier class (or the operation itself). It is represented with the «call» stereotype.

Notation

On a sequence diagram or a communication diagram, a call is shown as a text message directed to a target object or class.

On an activity diagram, a call is shown as a rounded box containing the name of the operation. An argument list in parentheses may optionally be shown. A call to a port uses the syntax:

```
operation-name via port-name
```

A call dependency is shown as a dashed arrow from the caller to the called class or operation with the stereotype «call».

Most calls will be represented as part of text procedures in a programming language.

Discussion

See resolution for a discussion of the various effects that calls may invoke. These include execution of procedures and enabling of state machine transitions.

Many programming languages treat remote procedure calls differently from local procedure calls, primarily for historical reasons of performance and hardware limitations. There is no longer any reason to distinguish them in models and UML does not do so. It is not necessary that a called procedure run in the same environment space as the calling procedure, as long as some control information passes between the environments.

Note that the apply function action is not a call, but the execution of a primitive predefined mathematical function, such as a numerical computation.

call (stereotype of Usage dependency)

A stereotyped dependency, the source of which is an operation and the target of which is an operation. A call dependency specifies that the source invokes the target operation. A call dependency may connect a source operation to any target operation that is within scope, including, but not limited to, operations of the enclosing classifier and operations of other visible classifiers.

See call, usage.

Discussion

This stereotype is badly conceived. Operations do not call operations; methods (implementations of operations) call operations. An operation is a specification of behavior and does not imply any particular implementation. This stereotype mistakenly conflates specification and implementation. Avoid it.

call event

The event of receiving a call for an operation by a target object. It may be implemented by methods on the class of the object, by actions on state machine transitions, or by other ways as determined by the resolution rule for the target.

See call, call trigger.

call trigger

The specification of the effect caused by the reception of a call by an active object. If an object (through its class) has no trigger for an operation, the receipt of a call causes an immediate effect. That is, an effect occurs concurrently with any other effect in the system, in particular, concurrently with any activity by the target object itself. The most common immediate effect is the execution of a method in the thread of control of the caller. Note that many methods may execute concurrently on the same target object if they are invoked from independent threads of control. There is no synchronization of these executions with each other or with any main activity by the target object.

In contrast, if an active object has a trigger on an operation, a call does not cause an immediate effect. Instead, a call event is placed in the event pool for the target object. A trigger implies the synchronization of multiple calls on a single object. When the object finishes a run-to-completion step and requires another trigger, the call event may be selected. (UML does not specify any generic ordering rules for choosing events from the event pool, but it is expected that profiles associated with particular execution environments may establish such rules, such as first-in first-out.) Once a call event is selected, it undergoes the resolution process to establish an effect. This effect may be the execution of a method, the enabling of a state machine transition, or something else. This is for generality. In the vast majority of models, resolution will be object oriented. If the trigger is associated with a method, the method will be executed first and may return values to the caller. When the method is completed, the caller is free to proceed. If there is no method, the caller may proceed immediately (even if the call is synchronous) and there are no return values. If the trigger is associated with a state machine transition, the transition is enabled (subject to guard conditions) after a possible method executes and proceeds concurrently with the subsequent execution of the caller.

Example

Figure 14-42 shows calls to operations that are implemented as triggers on state machine internal transitions. An account can be **Locked** and **Unlocked**. The **deposit** operation always adds money to the account, regardless of its state. The **withdraw** operation takes all of the money if the account is unlocked or none of

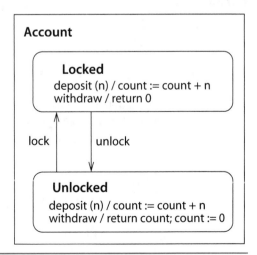

Figure 14-42. *Call events*

the money if it is locked. The **withdraw** operation is implemented as a call event that triggers internal transitions in each state. When the call occurs, one or the other action sequence is executed, depending on the active state. If the system is locked, zero is returned; if the system is unlocked, all of the money in the account is returned and the count is reset to zero.

History

The concept of allowing a call to trigger transitions was named *call event* in UML1, but it has been broadened and integrated better with signals and other kinds of behaviors in UML2 in a major change.

canonical notation

UML defines a canonical notation that uses monochromatic line drawings and text for displaying any model. This is the standard "publication format" of UML models and is suitable for printed diagrams.

Graphical editing tools can extend the canonical notation for convenience and to provide interactive capabilities. For example, a tool might provide the capability to highlight selected elements on the screen. Other interactive capabilities include navigation within the model and filtering of the displayed model according to selected properties. This kind of formatting is ephemeral and is not mandated by UML. With an interactive display, there is little danger of ambiguity as the user can simply ask for a clarification. Therefore, the focus of the UML standard is the printed canonical form, which every tool must support, with the understanding that an interactive tool may and should provide interactive extensions.

cardinality

The number of elements in a set. It is a specific number. Contrast with multiplicity, which is the range of possible cardinalities a set may hold.

Discussion

Note that the term *cardinality* is misused by many authors to mean what we call multiplicity, but the term cardinality has a long-standing mathematical definition as a number, not a range of numbers. This is the definition we use.

central buffer node

An object node in an activity that accepts inputs from multiple object nodes or produces outputs into multiple object nodes or both. Flows from central buffer nodes do not directly connect to actions.

Semantics

A central buffer node models a traditional buffer that can hold values from various sources and deliver the values to various destinations. There is no predefined ordering of values within the node but, as it is a kind of object node, the various ordering options of object node can be applied.

Notation

It is drawn as the object node symbol (a rectangle) with the «centralBuffer» keyword (Figure 14-43).

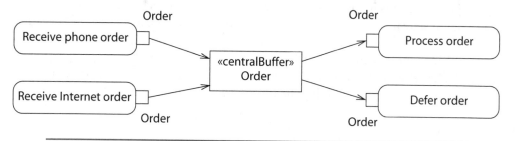

Figure 14-43. *Central buffer node*

change event

The event of a Boolean expression becoming satisfied because of a change to one or more of the values it references. A change event attached to a transition is a change trigger.

See also guard condition.

change trigger

A trigger on a state machine transition that becomes enabled if a specified change event occurs.

Semantics

A change trigger specifies a change event by a Boolean expression. There are no parameters to the event. The change event occurs when the condition becomes true (after having been false) because of a change to one or more variables on which the condition depends. When the event occurs, the change trigger fires and enables its transition, provided any attached guard condition is true.

A change trigger implies a continuous test for the condition. In practice, however, by analyzing the times at which the inputs to the condition can change, an implementation can often perform the test at well-defined, discrete times so that continuous polling is usually not required.

The event occurs when the value of the expression changes from false to true (a positive-going state change). The event occurs once when this happens and does not recur unless the value first becomes false again.

It is a semantic variation point whether a change trigger remains active if the underlying condition becomes false before the trigger enables a transition.

Note the difference from a guard condition. A guard condition is evaluated *once* whenever the event on its transition occurs. If the condition is false, then the transition does not fire and the event is lost (unless it triggers some other transition). A change event is implicitly evaluated continuously and occurs once at the time when the value becomes true. At that time, it may trigger a transition or it may be ignored. If it is ignored, the change event does not trigger a transition in a subsequent state just because the condition is still true. The change event has already occurred and been discarded. The condition must become false and then true again to cause another change event.

The values in the Boolean expression must be attributes of the object that owns the state machine containing the transition or values reachable from it.

Notation

Unlike signals, change events do not have names and are not declared. They are simply used as the triggers of transitions. A change trigger is shown by the keyword **when** followed by a Boolean expression in parentheses. For example:

```
when (self.waitingCustomers > 6)
```

Discussion

A change trigger is a test for the satisfaction of a condition. It may be expensive to implement, although there are often techniques to compile it so that it need not be tested continuously. Nevertheless, it is potentially expensive and also hides the direct cause-and-effect relationship between the change of a value and the effects that are triggered by it. Sometimes this is desirable because it encapsulates the effects, but change triggers should be used with caution.

A change trigger is meant to represent the test for values visible to an object. If a change to an attribute within an object is meant to trigger a change in another object that is unaware of the attribute itself, then the situation should be modeled as a change trigger on the attribute's owner that triggers an internal transition to send a signal to the second object.

Note that a change event is not explicitly sent anywhere. If an explicit communication with another object is intended, a signal should be used instead.

The implementation of a change trigger can be done in various ways, some of them by making tests within the application itself at appropriate times and some of them by means of underlying operating system facilities.

changeability

A property that indicates whether the value of an attribute or link can change.

Semantics

The read-only flag is a Boolean constraint on a property, that is, an association end or an attribute. If true, the property may not be modified after its initialization. A read-only association end must be navigable (otherwise there would be no point to it). If false, the property can be modified (unless otherwise prohibited).

Notation

The keyword {readOnly} is placed on a property that cannot be modified. For clarity, the keyword {unrestricted} may be placed on a property that can be modified, although usually it is assumed that the absence of {readOnly} implies changeability.

History

In UML1, degrees of changeability could be specified, such as the ability to add elements to a set but not remove or modify them.

Discussion

This concept is imprecisely defined. Clearly, a property must be modifiable initially while it is initialized, but the concept of initialization is not defined in UML. Probably a range of values, as in UML1 but with additional choices, would be better than a simple Boolean value.

child

The more specific element in a generalization relationship. Called subclass for a class. A chain of one or more child relationships is a descendant. Antonym: parent.

Semantics

A child element inherits the features of its parent (and indirectly those of its ancestors) and may declare additional features of its own. It also inherits any associations and constraints that its ancestors participate in. A child element obeys the substitutability principle—that is, an instance of a descriptor satisfies any variable declaration classified as one of the ancestors of the descriptor. An instance of a child is an indirect instance of the parent.

The descendant relationship is the transitive closure of the child relationship. An instance of a descendant is an indirect instance of the ancestor.

Discussion

Note that *child, parent, ancestor,* and *descendant* are not official UML terms, but we use them in this book for convenience because UML does not seem to have good simple terms that cover all the uses of the concepts.

choice

A node in a state machine at which a dynamic evaluation of subsequent guard conditions is made. See branch.

Semantics

A state machine transition may be structured into several segments using junction nodes to separate segments. Only one segment may have a trigger, but each segment may have its own guard condition and effects. Semantically, however, all of the guard conditions along an entire path are evaluated before the path is chosen or any effects are executed, so the segmentation is just for convenience. The junction nodes should not be considered as states in any sense.

A choice node also divides a transition into two segments, the first of which may have a trigger. In the case of a choice node, however, the first segment is enabled without regard to any subsequent segments, and any effects on it are executed before any subsequent guard conditions are evaluated. When the choice node is reached, the guard conditions of outgoing segments are dynamically evaluated, including any changes caused by the execution of the first segment. One of the outgoing segments whose guard condition evaluates true then fires. If no outgoing segment is true, the model is ill formed. To avoid this possibility, the guard condition [else] can be applied to one of the segments; it is chosen if all other guard conditions evaluate false.

A choice node may be considered a real state with the restriction that any outgoing transition must be enabled immediately using guard conditions only.

Notation

A choice node is shown as a diamond. Outgoing segments must have guard conditions but no triggers (Figure 14-44).

For the common case in which all of the guard conditions are comparisons to the same value, the value may be placed inside the diamond and the guard conditions may be written as expressions omitted the shared first value. The saving in space is unlikely to overcome the loss in clarity, however.

History

Dynamic choices within transitions are new in UML2.

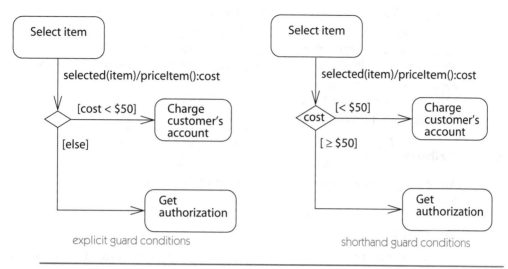

Figure 14-44. *Choice node*

class

The descriptor for a set of objects that share the same attributes, operations, methods, relationships, and behavior. A class represents a concept within the system being modeled. Depending on the kind of model, the concept may be real-world (for an analysis model), or it may also contain algorithmic and computer implementation concepts (for a design model). A classifier is a generalization of class that includes other class-like elements, such as data type, actor, and component.

Semantics

A class is the named description of both the data structure and the behavior of a set of objects. A class is used to declare variables. An object that is the value of a variable must have a class that is compatible with the declared class of the variable—that is, it must be the same class as the declared class or a descendant of it. A class is also used to instantiate objects. A creation operation produces a new object that is an instance of the given class.

An object instantiated from a class is a direct instance of the class and an indirect instance of the ancestors of the class. The object contains a slot to hold a value for each attribute; it accepts all the operations and signals of its class, and it may appear in links of associations involving the class or an ancestor of the class.

Some classes may not be directly instantiated, but instead are used only to describe structure shared among their descendants; such a class is an abstract class. A class that may be instantiated is a concrete class.

A class may also be regarded as a global object. Any class-scope attributes of the class are attributes of this implicit object. Such attributes have global scope, and each has a single value across the system. A class-scope operation is one that applies to the class itself, not to an object. The most common class-scope operations are creation operations.

In UML, a class is a kind of classifier. *Classifier* includes a number of class-like elements, but it finds its fullest expression in *class*.

class attribute

An attribute whose value is shared by all instances of a class. Also called static feature.

Semantics

A class attribute (or static attribute, for C++ or Java users) is an attribute for which one slot is shared by all instances of a class (but not part of any one of them specifically). Such an attribute is therefore not a property of an instance at all but rather a property of the class. Access to a class attribute does not require an instance, although some programming languages provide a syntax that uses an instance for convenience. For most purposes, a class attribute is a global variable in the namespace of a class.

A default value for a class attribute represents the value of the attribute when the class itself is initialized. The time when this happens is not defined by UML.

A class attribute is modeled as an attribute for which the **isStatic** flag is true.

Notation

A class attribute is shown in the attribute section of a class box using the syntax for an ordinary attribute with the entire attribute string underlined. See Figure 14-45.

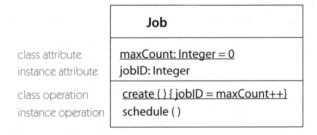

Figure 14-45. *Class features*

class diagram

A class diagram is a graphic presentation of the static view that shows a collection of declarative (static) model elements, such as classes, types, and their contents and relationships. A class diagram may show a view of a package and may contain symbols for nested packages. A class diagram contains certain reified behavioral elements, such as operations, but their dynamics are expressed in other diagrams, such as statechart diagrams and communication diagrams.

See also classifier, object diagram.

Notation

A class diagram shows a graphic presentation of the static view. Usually several class diagrams are required to show an entire static view. Individual class diagrams do not necessarily indicate divisions in the underlying model, although logical divisions, such as packages, are natural boundaries for forming diagrams.

Discussion

The UML specification distinguishes among class diagrams and component diagrams, collectively called structure diagrams. Most users will likely call them all class diagrams with no loss of semantics. There is no rigid line between different kinds of diagrams anyway.

The UML class diagram was heavily influenced by the entity-relationship (E-R) diagram of P. P. Chen, through UML predecessor notations such as Shlaer-Mellor, Booch, OMT, Coad-Yourdon, and others. It is the most important object modeling diagram.

class feature

A feature of a class itself, rather than the individual instances. See class attribute and class operation. Also called static feature.

Notation

A class feature is a text string with the same syntax as the corresponding instance feature, except the string is underlined. See Figure 14-45.

class-in-state

A combination of a class and a state applicable to that class.

See also activity.

Semantics

A class with a state machine has many states, each of which characterizes the behavior, values, and constraints of instances that are in the state. In some cases, certain attributes, associations, or operations are valid only when an object is in a certain state or set of states. In other cases, an argument to an operation must be an object in a particular state. Often, these distinctions are simply part of the behavioral models. But sometimes, it is useful to treat the combination of class and state as constraining the value of an object, variable, parameter, or substate. The combination of class and state, treated as a kind of type, is a class-in-state.

If the state machine of the class has orthogonal states, the state specification may be a set of substates that an object of the class can hold simultaneously.

Class diagram. A class-in-state is equivalent to a subclass, provided dynamic classification is allowed. By modeling it as a class, it may be used as the type of a variable or of a parameter. It may participate in associations that are valid only for objects in the given state. In Figure 14-46, consider the association **Assignment** between **SubmittedPaper** and **ConferenceSession**. This association is valid for a **Submitted-Paper** in the **accepted** state (target multiplicity one) but not in the **rejected** state. For any **SubmittedPaper**, the target multiplicity is zero-or-one, because the class includes both **accepted** and **rejected** papers. However, if the association is modeled between **SubmittedPaper** in state **accepted** and **ConferenceSession**, it has target multiplicity exactly one.

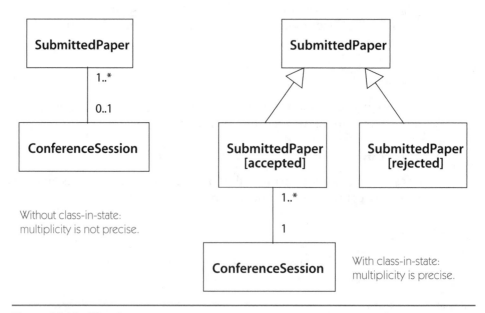

Figure 14-46. *Class-in-state*

Sequence diagram. An assertion, called a state invariant, may be placed at a point on a lifeline to specify a constraint on the object represented by the lifeline at that point in the execution. The constraint can specify the state of the object or a Boolean expression on its values. This is an assertion, not an executable action, and the model is ill formed if the assertion is violated.

Activity diagram. An object node has a type. It can also specify a state, which indicates that the corresponding object must have the given type and state at that point in the activity.

Notation

Class diagram. A class-in-state can be shown as a class symbol in which the name of the class is followed by its state name within brackets (Classname[statename]). The brackets may also contain a comma-separated list of names of concurrent states to indicate that an object holds several of them. The class should be shown as a subclass of the plain class. (Note that this is a naming convention, not official UML notation.) See Figure 14-46.

Sequence diagram. A state invariant is shown as a rounded box on the lifeline with a Boolean constraint inside the box. If constraint is that the object must be in a given state, the name of the state may be shown in the box (Figure 14-47). A comma-separated list of state names may be used if the state of the object involves multiple concurrent states.

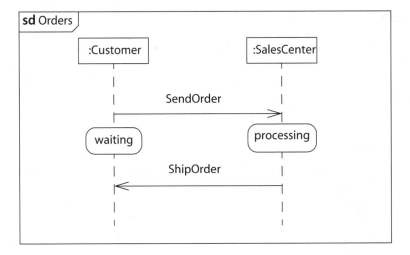

Figure 14-47. *State invariants in sequence diagram*

Figure 14-48. *Object node with state constraint*

Activity diagram. An object node is shown as a rectangle containing the name of a class. The class name may optionally be followed by a state name in brackets (Classname[statename]). This indicates that the value produced at that point in the computation must have the given type and be in the given state.

See Figure 14-48.

Discussion

Class-in-state and dynamic classification are two ways to accomplish the same goal of allowing changes to the structure of an object during its life. Depending on the implementation environment, one or the other may be the more convenient mechanism.

The notation suggested for class-in-state in a class diagram is not defined in the UML specification. Perhaps it would be useful to add this capability to UML, but modelers who want to show class-in-state can use the suggested naming convention, with the understanding that it is a convention.

class name

Each class (or, in general, classifier) must have a non-null name that is unique among classifiers within its container (such as a package or containing class). The scope of a name is its containing package and other packages that can see the containing package.

See name for a full discussion of naming and uniqueness rules.

Notation

The class name is shown in the top compartment of a class rectangle. The name compartment may also contain a keyword or stereotype name (Figure 14-49).

Figure 14-49. *Name compartment*

An optional stereotype keyword may be placed above the class name within guillemets, and/or a stereotype icon may be placed in the upper-right corner of the compartment. The stereotype name must not match a predefined keyword, such as **enumeration**.

The name of the class appears next. The class name is centered horizontally in boldface. If the class is abstract, its name appears in italics. But any explicit specification of generalization status in braces (such as {abstract} or {concrete}) takes precedence over the name font.

By default, a class shown within a package is assumed to be defined within that package. To show a reference to a class defined in another package, use the syntax

```
Package-name::Class-name
```

as the name string in the name compartment (Figure 14-50). A full qualified name can be specified by chaining together package names separated by double colons (::). The same class name can be used for different classes in different packages, provided qualified names are used to distinguish them, but this duplication of names can lead to error and should be used with caution.

References to classes also appear in text expressions, most notably in type specifications for attributes and variables. In text expressions, a reference to a class is indicated simply by using the name of the class itself, including a possible package name, subject to the syntax rules of the expression.

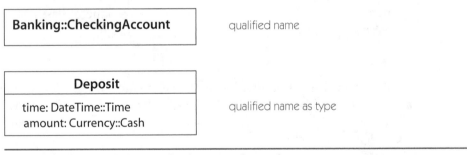

Figure 14-50. *Qualified names for classes in other packages*

class operation

An operation whose access is tied to a class, rather than to an instance of a class. See also static feature.

Semantics

A class operation is a global operation in the namespace of a class. It can be invoked without an instance of the class. Its methods have access to the features of the class.

Class operations are typically used to construct new instances of a class. They are also sometimes used to access class attributes of a class.

A class operation is modeled as an attribute for which the isStatic flag is true.

Notation

A class operation is shown in the operation section of a class box using the syntax for an ordinary class with the entire operation string underlined. See Figure 14-45.

classification action

An action whose execution determines whether an object is classified by a given class.

See action.

classifier

A model element that describes behavioral and structural features. Kinds of classifiers include actor, association, behavior, class, collaboration, component, data type, interface, node, signal, subsystem (as a stereotype), and use case. Classes are the most general kind of classifier. Others can be intuitively understood as similar to classes, with certain restrictions on content or usage, although each kind of classifier is represented by its own metamodel class. Most properties of classes apply to classifiers, in general, with certain restrictions for each kind of classifier.

See also static view.

Semantics

Classifier is an abstraction that includes several kinds of modeling elements that have structural and behavioral descriptions. A classifier describes a set of instances and can be the type of a variable or parameter. Classifiers can be organized into generalization hierarchies.

In UML, a class is a kind of classifier. *Classifier* includes a number of class-like elements, but it finds its fullest expression in *class.*

Some of the contents of a classifier can be redefined in a descendant. See redefinition.

Structure

A classifier has a class name and lists of attributes and operations. A classifier may participate in association, generalization, dependency, and constraint relationships. A classifier is declared within a namespace, such as a package or another class, and has various properties within its namespace, such as multiplicity and visibility. A classifier has various other properties, such as whether it is abstract or an active class. A classifier may be specified as a leaf, that is, one that may not be specialized. It may have a state machine that specifies its reactive behavior—that is, its response to the reception of events. A classifier may declare the set of events (including exceptions) that it is prepared to handle. It may provide the realization of the behavior specified by zero or more interfaces or types by providing an implementation for the behavior. An interface lists a set of operations that a classifier realizing the interface promises to support.

A classifier contains a list of attributes and a list of operations that each form a namespace within the classifier. Inherited attributes and inherited operations also appear within the respective namespaces. The namespace for attributes also includes other properties, such as rolenames of associations leaving the class and internal parts. Each name must be declared only once within the classifier and its ancestors. Otherwise there is a conflict, and the model is ill formed. Operation names may be reused with different signatures. Otherwise they represent redefinition of the same operation, for example, to declare the operation abstract or concrete in a subclass.

A classifier may own behaviors, such as methods and interactions, that implement or describe its operations. A classifier may optionally have one attached behavior, such as a state machine, that describes the overall dynamics of an instance of the classifier. The attached behavior starts when an instance is created and stops when it is destroyed. An instance responds to events that it recognizes. If an event corresponds to a trigger in the attached behavior, it is place in an event pool. For example, a signal that triggers a state machine transition is a triggered effect. Events are taken from the pool one at a time and the triggered effects are allowed to run to completion before another event is selected. In general, selection of events is unordered, although profiles may define priority ordering. If an event does not correspond to a trigger in the attached behavior but does correspond to an operation, the operation resolves to a behavior that is executed immediately and concurrently with other executions, independently of the attached behavior. For example, a normal method execution is an immediate effect.

A classifier is also a namespace and establishes the scope for nested classifier declarations. Nested classifiers are not structural parts of instances of the classifier. There is no data relationship between objects of a class and objects of nested classes. A nested class is a declaration of a class that may be used by the methods of the outer class. Classes declared within a class are private to it and are not accessible outside the class unless explicitly made visible. There is no visual notation to show nested class declarations. The expectation is that they will be made accessible within a tool by hyperlinks. Nested names must be referenced using qualified names.

Notation

A classifier is shown as a solid-outline rectangle with three compartments separated by horizontal lines. The top compartment holds the class name and other properties that apply to the entire class. The middle compartment holds a list of attributes. The bottom compartment contains a list of operations. The middle and bottom compartments can be suppressed in a class symbol.

Usage. Classes, interfaces, signals, and associations are declared in class diagrams and used in many other diagrams. Various other kinds of classifiers, such as use cases and collaborations, appear in special kinds of diagrams, although many of them can also appear in class diagrams. UML provides a graphical notation for declaring and using classifiers, as well as a textual notation for referencing classifiers within the descriptions of other model elements. The declaration of a classifier in a class diagram defines the contents of the classifier: its attributes, operations, and other properties. Other diagrams define additional relationships and attachments to a classifier.

Figure 14-51 shows a basic class declaration with attributes and operations. This format is applicable to other kinds of classifiers with the kind of classifier shown in guillemets above the classifier name, for example, «controller». Certain kinds of classifier have their own icons. These include associations, collaborations, actors, and use cases.

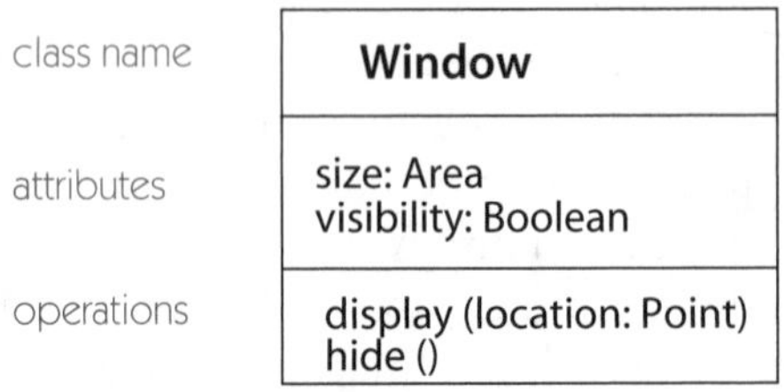

Figure 14-51. *Basic class declaration*

Figure 14-52 shows the same class declaration with additional detail, much of it information of an implementation nature, such as visibility, class-level creation operations, and implementation-dependent operations.

All internal information about the class is suppressed in Figure 14-53. The information is still present in the internal model and would usually be shown on at least one diagram.

Suppressing compartments. Either or both of the attribute and operation compartments may be suppressed (Figure 14-54). A separator line is not drawn for a missing compartment. If a compartment is suppressed, no inference can be drawn about the presence or absence of elements in it. Note that an empty compartment (that is, one with separator lines but no content) implies that there are no elements

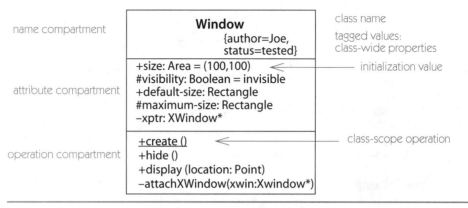

Figure 14-52. *Detailed class declaration with visibilities of features*

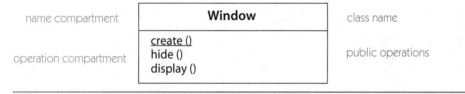

Figure 14-53. *Class symbol with all details suppressed*

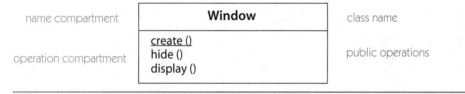

Figure 14-54. *Class declaration with attributes and non-public operations suppressed*

in the corresponding list. If some kind of filtering is in effect, then there are no elements that satisfy the filter. For example, if only public operations are visible, then the presence of an empty operation compartment indicates that there are no public operations. No conclusion can be drawn about private operations.

Additional compartments. Additional compartments may be supplied to show other predefined or user-defined model properties—for example, to show business rules, responsibilities, variations, signals handled, exceptions raised, and so on. An additional compartment is drawn with a compartment name at the top, shown in a distinctive font to identify its contents (Figure 14-55).

The standard compartments (attribute, operation) do not require compartment names, although they may have names for emphasis or clarity if only one compartment is visible. Most compartments are simply lists of strings, in which each string encodes a property. Note that "string" includes the possibility of icons or embedded documents, such as spreadsheets and graphs. More complicated formats are

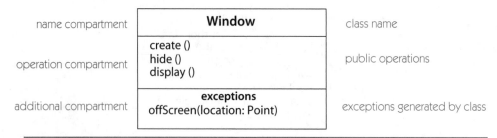

name compartment — Window — class name

operation compartment — create () / hide () / display () — public operations

additional compartment — exceptions / offScreen(location: Point) — exceptions generated by class

Figure 14-55. *Class declaration additional named compartment*

possible, but UML does not specify such formats. They are a user and tool responsibility. If the nature of the compartment can be determined from the form of its contents, then the compartment name may be omitted.

See font usage, string.

Stereotype. A stereotype is shown as a text string in guillemets (« ») above the class name (Figure 14-56). Instead of the text string, an icon can be placed in the upper right corner of the name compartment. A class symbol with a stereotype icon may be "collapsed" to show just the stereotype icon, with the name of the class either inside or below the icon (Figure 14-262). Other contents of the class are suppressed. See stereotype.

«signal» / **Cancel** / priority: Integer — full declaration

«signal» / **Cancel** — details suppressed

Figure 14-56. *Class with stereotype*

Style guidelines

- Center a stereotype name in normal typeface within guillemets above the class name.
- Center or left-justify a class name in boldface.
- Left-justify attributes and operations in normal typeface.
- Show the names of abstract classes or the signatures of abstract operations in italics.
- Show the attribute and operation compartments when needed (at least once in the diagram set) and suppress them in other contexts or in references. It is useful to define a "home" location for a class once in a set of diagrams and to give its full description there. In other locations, the minimal form is used.

Discussion

The concept of classifier applies to a range of usages in logical modeling, as well as implementation. In UML, under certain semantic variation points, an instance may have multiple types, as well as be able to change its type at run time. Various more restrictive notions of class found in most programming languages can be thought of as special kinds of classifiers.

classifier role

This UML1 concept has been superseded by role and connector within structured classifier. The syntax and semantics have changed considerably.

client

An element that requests a service from another element. The term is used to describe a role within a dependency. In the notation, the client appears at the tail of a dependency arrow. Antonym: supplier.

See dependency.

collaboration

A specification of a contextual relationship among instances that interact within a context to implement a desired functionality.

A collaboration is a description of structure. Collaborations are forms of structured classifiers. The behavior of a collaboration may be specified by interactions that show message flows in the collaboration over time.

See also connector, role, interaction, message.

Semantics

Behavior is implemented by groups of objects that exchange messages within a context to accomplish a purpose. To understand the mechanisms used in a design, it is important to focus on patterns of collaboration involved in accomplishing a purpose or a related set of purposes, projected from the larger system within which they fulfill other purposes as well. An arrangement of objects and links that work together to accomplish a purpose is called a collaboration; a sequence of messages within a collaboration that implements behavior is called an interaction. A collaboration is a description of a "society of objects." It is a kind of commentary on a fragment of a class model, explaining how a set of objects work together to carry out a particular purpose in ways that are unique to the particular situation.

For example, a commercial sale represents an arrangement of objects that have certain relationships to each other within the transaction. The relationships are not meaningful outside the transaction. The roles of a sale include buyer, seller, and broker. To perform a specific interaction, such as selling a house, participants playing the various roles exchange a certain sequence of messages, such as making an offer or signing a contract.

The message flows within the collaboration may optionally be specified by interactions, which specify legal behavior sequences. The messages in an interaction are exchanged among roles over connectors within the collaboration.

A collaboration consists of roles. A role is a description of a participant in an interaction. Structurally, it is a slot that may be bound to an instance of a classifier within an instance of the collaboration. A role may have a type that constrains the instances that can be bound to it. The same classifier may play different roles in the same or different collaborations; each would be filled by a different object. (It is also possible for one object to play multiple roles in one or many collaboration instances.) For example, within a commercial transaction, one party may be the seller and the other may be the buyer, even though both participants are companies. The **seller** and **buyer** are roles of type **Company** within the collaboration **Sale**. Roles are meaningful only within a collaboration; outside a particular collaboration they have no meaning. Indeed, in another collaboration, the roles may be reversed. An object may be a **buyer** in one instance of collaboration and a **seller** in another. The same object may play multiple roles in different collaborations. Contrast the restricted scope of a role with an association. An association describes a relationship that is globally meaningful for a class in all contexts, whether or not an object actually participates in the association. A collaboration defines relationships that are restricted to a context and that are meaningless outside of that context.

A connector is a relationship between two roles within a particular collaboration. It is a relationship that exists only within the collaboration. Connectors may have types, which must be associations that constrain the connector to be implemented as a link of the given association. If no type is given for a connector, it represents a transient connection within the context of the connection, which might be implemented by a parameter, local variable, or other mechanism. For example, in the real estate transaction mentioned previously, the seller and buyer are related by virtue of their participation in the same sale. They do not have any permanent relationship outside the real estate collaboration.

A collaboration describes the context for an operation, a use case, or other kinds of behavior. It describes the context in which the implementation of an operation or use case executes—that is, the arrangement of objects and links that exist when the execution begins, and the instances that are created or destroyed during execution. The behavior sequences may be specified in interactions, shown as sequence diagrams or communication diagrams.

A collaboration may also describe the implementation of a class. A collaboration for a class is the union of the collaborations for its operations. Different collaborations may be devised for the same class, system, or subsystem; each collaboration shows the subset of attributes, operators, and related objects that are relevant to one view of the entity, such as the implementation of a particular operation.

Patterns. A parameterized collaboration represents a design construct that can be reused in various designs. Usually the base classifiers are parameters. Such a parameterized collaboration captures the structure of a pattern.

See template.

A design pattern is instantiated by supplying actual classifiers for the base classifier parameters. Each instantiation yields a collaboration among a specific set of classifiers in the model. A pattern can be bound more than once to different sets of classifiers within a model, avoiding the need to define a collaboration for each use. For example, a model-view pattern defines a general relationship among model elements; it can be bound to many pairs of classes that represent model-view pairs. Each pair of actual model-view classes represents one binding of the pattern. One such pair would be a house and a picture of the house, another pair would be a stock and a graphic showing the current price of the stock.

Note that a pattern also involves guidelines for use and explicit advantages and disadvantages. These can be put in notes or in separate text documents.

Layers of collaborations. A collaboration may be expressed at various levels of granularity. A coarse-grained collaboration may be refined to produce another collaboration that has a finer granularity. This is accomplished by expanding one or more operations from a high-level collaboration into distinct lower-level collaborations, one for each operation.

Collaborations may be nested. A collaboration may be implemented in terms of subordinate collaborations, each of which implements part of the overall functionality. The subordinate collaborations are indirectly connected by their participation in the outer collaboration—their definitions are independent but the output of one is the input of another.

Run-time binding. At run time, objects and links are bound to the roles and connectors of the collaboration. A collaboration instance does not own the instances bound to its roles (unlike an instance of a structured class, which does own its parts). It merely references them and establishes a contextual relationship among the objects bound to its roles for the duration of the collaboration instance. The objects playing the roles must exist previously. They must be compatible with the declared types of the roles to which they are bound.

Links corresponding to connectors are often created as part of the creation of a collaboration instance, especially when the connector does not have an underlying association.

An object can be bound to one or more roles, usually in different collaborations. If an object is bound to multiple roles, then it represents an "accidental" interaction between the roles—that is, an interaction that is not inherent in the roles themselves, but only a side effect of their use in a wider context. Often, one object plays roles in more than one collaboration as part of a larger collaboration. This is an "inherent" interaction between the roles. Such overlap between collaborations provides an implicit flow of control and information between them.

Notation

A collaboration definition is shown as a dashed ellipse with two compartments: the top compartment shows the name of the collaboration and the bottom compartment shows its structure as a set of role icons connected by connectors. A role icon is shown as a rectangle containing the name of the role and its type, in the form:

name : Type [multiplicity]

The multiplicity is optional; if it is omitted, the default is one.

A connector is shown as a solid line or path connecting two role icons. See Figure 14-57.

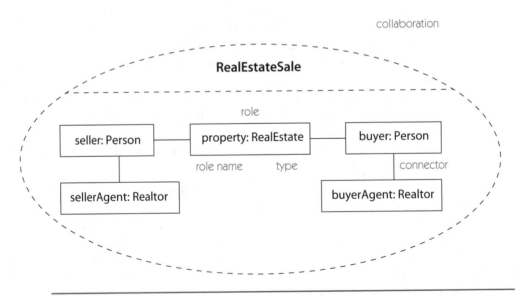

Figure 14-57. *Collaboration notation*

An alternate notation may be used when there are no connectors. The collaboration is shown as a dashed ellipse with a single compartment containing the name of the collaboration definition. For each role, a dashed line is drawn to the class rectangle representing the type. The line is labeled by the name of the role on the end near the type rectangle. Often a note is attached to the collaboration ellipse to show constraints. See Figure 14-58.

Figure 14-58. *Alternate collaboration notation*

See sequence diagram for the use of collaborations to establish the lifelines of an interaction.

History

Although the overall intent is roughly the same as in UML1, the concept of collaboration has been considerably rearranged in UML2. There is now a separation between the static structure, the collaboration, and the dynamic structure, the interaction. Internally, collaboration is treated as a kind of structured classifier, in which the parts represent roles, so the parameterization of UML1 is no longer necessary. The terms *classifier role*, *association role*, and *association end role* have been retired. Concepts such as internal generalizations are no longer necessary either.

Discussion

The UML specification does not use the word *instance* for collaborations, probably from a misguided idea that instances must correspond to C++ classes. We use the word because it is the usual word for the concept, and there is little danger of confusion as long as readers keep in mind that instantiation does not imply a particular implementation. In most cases, collaborations do not correspond to implementation classes. They are an emergent concept, but that does not mean that they do not have instances once the word is properly understood.

collaboration diagram

A diagram showing the definition of a collaboration. In UML2, a collaboration diagram is a kind of composite structure diagram. Note that collaboration definitions and uses may also be shown on class diagrams.

collaboration occurrence

See collaboration use.

Discussion

The term was used for collaboration use but this confuses the meaning of occurrence, which is otherwise used to mean a temporal happening. The word *use* is preferable to describe the appearance of a static entity in a context.

collaboration role

A slot for an object or link within a collaboration. It specifies the kind of object or link that may appear in an instance of the collaboration.

See connector, collaboration.

collaboration use

The use of a collaboration as bound to specific parts within a context.

Semantics

A collaboration is the definition of a context involving several roles. A collaboration can be used by binding the roles to classifiers within a particular context, such as the internal structure of a class or the definition of a larger collaboration. Such a bound collaboration is called a collaboration use. A collaboration may be used many times in different collaboration uses.

A classifier bound to a role must be compatible with the type of the role, if any. A classifier is compatible if it is the same as the type or a descendant of the type. It must also obey any constraints on the role.

A collaboration use may also occur in an object model. The class of each object must be compatible with the type of the corresponding role. Such a collaboration use represents a set of objects that interact to fulfill the purposes of the collaboration. Such a usage is usually within some context, such as the specification of a procedure, but the context may not always be explicit.

A collaboration use may appear within the definition of a larger collaboration. In this context, its roles are bound to roles of the larger collaboration, rather than classifiers. The types of the roles of the larger collaboration must be compatible with the types of the roles of the collaboration used in the use. When the larger collaboration is bound, an object bound to a role of the larger collaboration is automatically bound to the matching role of the inner collaboration.

A collaboration use may connect a classifier to a collaboration to indicate that the collaboration expresses an aspect of the behavior of the collaboration. There may be many such collaboration uses. A classifier may have one collaboration use to show the collaboration that represents the main behavior of the entire classifier.

Notation

A collaboration use is shown as a dashed ellipse containing a name string:

useName : Collaboration

where useName identifies the particular use and Collaboration is the name of the collaboration definition. The useName string may be omitted. For each role of the collaboration, a dashed line is drawn from the ellipse to the rectangle symbol of the classifier bound to the role. The name of the role is placed by the end of the line near the classifier symbol.

A collaboration use may be used to attach a collaboration to a classifier for which it shows an aspect of behavior. This is shown by a dashed arrow from a collaboration use to a classifier symbol. If the collaboration represents the overall behavior of the classifier (rather than just an aspect of it), the keyword «represents» is placed on the arrow (). See Figure 14-59.

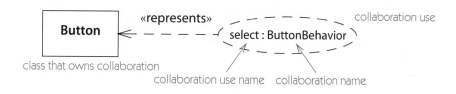

Figure 14-59. *Class behavior represented by collaboration*

Example

Figure 14-60 shows the definition of a very general collaboration representing any sale. It has three roles, a buyer, a seller, and an item. The buyer and sellers must be agents, which include persons and companies. An interaction could be attached to the collaboration showing the process of negotiation, payment, and so on.

Figure 14-61 shows the use of this collaboration in an object diagram representing a particular sale, the Louisiana Purchase. Napoleon and Thomas Jefferson are of type Executive, which is a kind of Agent. Louisiana is of type Land, which is a kind of property. The bindings are compatible with the types of the roles.

Figure 14-60. *Collaboration definition*

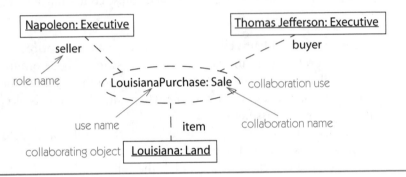

Figure 14-61. *Collaboration use in object diagram*

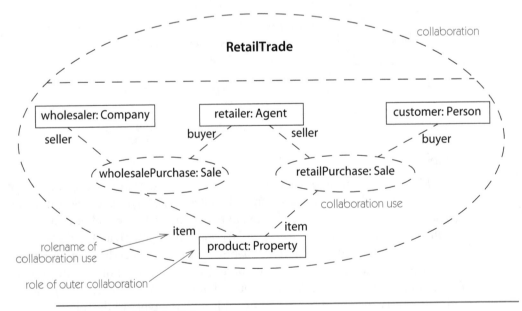

Figure 14-62. *Nested collaborations*

Figure 14-62 shows the use of the Sale collaboration within a larger collaboration representing retail trade as a chain of sales. This collaboration has four roles: a wholesaler, a retailer, a customer, and a product. The relationship between the wholesaler and the retailer is the same as the relationship between the retailer and the customer—both of them are uses of the Sale collaboration. Note that the product role is bound to the item role in both of the nested collaborations. This collaboration shows how a single product passes through the sales chain, so it is important that both item roles be bound to the same product role.

The wholesaler is of type Company, which is a kind of Agent. The customer is of type Person, which is also a kind of Agent. Although the Sale collaboration only requires the buyer and seller to be of type Agent, the roles in the RetailTrade collaboration are more specific. The retailer is of type Agent; it has been kept general.

This example shows how large collaborations may be built from smaller ones.

Discussion

The term *collaboration occurrence* was used, but a cleanup of terminology distinguishes occurrence as an instance of an event, that is, something in the temporal domain, whereas a collaboration use is in the static domain.

combined fragment

A construct within an interaction that comprises an operator keyword and one or more interaction operands, each of which is a fragment of an interaction. It is shown as a nested region within a sequence diagram.

Semantics

Interactions include a number of constructs for representing contingent behavior, such as conditionals, loops, and so on. Because many of these constructs share structural information, they are grouped together as kinds of combined fragments. A combined fragment has a keyword that specifies which construct it is.

Depending on the keyword, there are one or more embedded operands, each of which is a structured subfragment of the overall interaction.

A combined fragment may also have zero or more gates, which specify the interface between the combined fragment and other parts of the interaction.

The keyword may be one of the following:

alt	A conditional has multiple operands. Each operand has a guard condition. The absence of a guard implies a true condition. The condition **else** is true if no other guard evaluates true. Exactly one operand whose guard evaluates true is executed, unless no guard is true. If more than one operand evaluates true, the choice may be nondeterministic.

assert

An assertion has one subfragment. If the execution reaches the beginning of the construct, then the behavior of the subfragment must occur. This is often combined with ignore or consider to assert the behavior of a particular kind of message.

break

A break construct has one subfragment with a guard condition. The subfragment is executed if the guard is true and the remainder of the enclosing interaction fragment is not executed. Otherwise execution continues normally.

consider

A consider construct has one subfragment and a list of message types. Only the listed message types are represented within the subfragment. This means that other types can occur in the actual system but the interaction is an abstraction that ignores them. Opposite of the ignore construct.

critical

A critical region has one subfragment. A sequence of events on a single lifeline in the critical region must not be interleaved with any other events in other regions. There is no constraint on events on other lifelines, so this does not preclude concurrent activity that does not affect the critical region. This construct overrides a parallel construct that would otherwise permit interleaving.

ignore

An ignore construct has one subfragment and a list of message types. Only the listed message types are represented within the subfragment. This means the declared types can occur in the actual system but the interaction is an abstraction that ignores them. For example, any constraints on the types within the larger activity do not apply to actual appearances of the types in the ignore fragment, because the types are invisible for modeling purposes in the fragment. Opposite of the consider construct.

loop

A loop construct has one subfragment with a guard. The guard may have a minimum and maximum count as well as a Boolean condition. The subfragment is executed as long as the guard condi-

	tion evaluates true, but it is executed at least the minimum count and no more than the maximum count. If the guard is absent, it is treated as true and the loop depends on the repetition count.
neg	A negative construct has one subfragment. The subfragment defines execution sequences that may not occur. In many cases, the model may not list all sequences that are forbidden, so it is risky to draw conclusions about the absence of a negative construct.
opt	A optional construct has one subfragment with a guard condition. The subfragment is executed if the guard is true and is not executed otherwise. This construct is equivalent to a conditional with a single guarded subfragment and an empty else clause).
par	A parallel construct has two or more subfragments that are executed concurrently. The execution order of individual elements in parallel subfragments may interleave in any possible order (unless prohibited by a critical construct). The concurrency is logical and need not be physical; the concurrent executions may be interleaved on a single execution path.
seq	A weak sequencing construct has two or more subfragments. It is the same as parallel execution, except that events on the same lifeline from different subfragments are ordered in the same order as the subfragments within the enclosing weak sequencing fragment. Events on different lifelines that do not appear in multiple subfragments may interleave in any order.
strict	A strict sequencing construct has two or more subfragments. The subfragments are executed in the order they appear within the construct. Events on different lifelines are ordered according to the subfragments, unlike the case with a parallel construct.

See each kind of construct for more information and notation.

Notation

The general notation for a combined fragment in a sequence diagram is a rectangle with a small pentagon in the upper left corner containing the keyword for the construct. If the fragment has more than one subfragment, they are separated by horizontal dashed lines. The rectangle is nested within its containing fragment or within the sequence diagram as a whole.

As a shorthand, the pentagon may contain multiple keywords to indicate nested constructs. The keyword on the left indicates the outermost construct. For example, **sd strict** indicates a sequence diagram containing a strict sequencing construct.

Parameters. A few of the constructs take arguments after the keyword, as follows:

The ignore and consider constructs take a comma-separated list of message names enclosed in braces, for example:

consider {start, stop}

The loop construct may contain a lower bound and an upper bound in parentheses, for example:

loop (2, 5)

If the upper bound is omitted, it is the same as the lower bound:

loop (2)

To show an unlimited upper bound, an asterisk (*) may be used:

loop (1,*)

If no bound is shown, then the lower bound is zero and the upper bound is unlimited.

History

The use of structured constructs such as combined fragment was a major reason for the replacement of the UML1 sequence diagram notation by the current notation based largely on MSC (Message Sequence Chart) notation.

comment

An annotation attached to an element or a collection of elements. A comment has no direct semantics, but it may display semantic information or other information meaningful to the modeler or to a tool, such as a constraint or method body.

See also note.

Semantics

A comment contains a text string, but it may also include embedded documents if a modeling tool permits. A comment may be attached to a model element, a presentation element, or a set of elements. It provides a text description of arbitrary information, but it has no semantic impact. Comments provide information to modelers and may be used to search models.

Notation

Comments are displayed in note symbols, which are shown as rectangles with bent upper-right corners ("dog ears") attached by a dashed line or lines to the element or elements that the comment applies to (Figure 14-63). Modeling tools are free to provide additional formats for displaying comments and browsing them, such as pop-ups, special fonts, and so on.

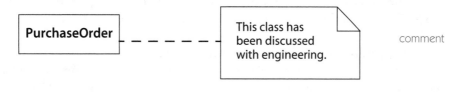

Figure 14-63. *Comment*

communication

Objects communicate by transmitting messages to other objects.

Semantics

Communication among objects and execution threads is specified by an abstract model of message transmission among objects. Communication is initiated by broadcast, call, send, and reply actions. The target of a transmission may be explicit (call and send actions), dependent on execution context (reply), or implicit in the execution environment. On a broadcast, call, or send, the arguments of the action are copied and formed into a message for transmission to the target or targets. All transmissions obey copy semantics; that is, an object itself is not transmitted, and two messages with identical arguments have no individual identity and are not distinguishable. However, references to objects may be transmitted. The exact form of the message transmission is not specified by UML and is not accessible to a user program (except insofar as a profile makes implementation information accessible). In particular, additional implementation-dependent information may be included in the transmission for purposes of the execution environment. Furthermore, the encoding of information is not specified, permitting various implementations. For example, there is no distinction in UML between a local procedure call and a remote procedure call; if an implementation requires marshalling and unmarshalling of arguments, that is its own business and not part of the UML model (or, hopefully, of the programming language as technology matures). One piece of information is explicitly required without specification of a particular implementation: On a synchronous call, sufficient information must be encoded so that a subsequent return or reply action can transmit the reply information to the correct execution thread. Because this information is opaque, the receiving activity cannot manipulate it except by replying. The encoding of this information is heavily dependent on the execution environment, yet in a logical sense the encoding is irrelevant.

The speed and transmission path of a message is unspecified in the UML specification. If there are multiple concurrent messages, no assumptions can be made about the order of their reception. If synchronization is required, it should be modeled explicitly. Profiles may make such information explicit, for example, in a real-time profile.

Ordinary calls behave as procedure calls, in that they do not really require any action on the part of the target object; an execution is created when the call is received. The definition of "received" and the resources within which the execution is performed are details of implementation, but not part of the logical model. A send action or a call that triggers a state machine transition, however, must be handled by the execution thread of the target object itself. The execution thread can be modeled as an ongoing activity with accept actions or as an attached state machine with transitions. In any case, the messages must be collected somehow and processed one at a time. The UML specification mandates some kind of event pool that collects events, including received messages, but it does not impose any constraints on how the events are handled, except that they must be processed one at a time. A profile can add constraints typical of a reactive system, such as FIFO (first-in first-out) processing, priorities, or time limits on response.

The basic communications model in UML is meant to be very general and to accommodate a wide range of implementation choices, but it is nevertheless practical in identifying the essential qualities of communication and forcing models to explicitly state underlying assumptions about the execution environment.

Notation

Notation is discussed under various topics, such as action, communication diagram, and sequence diagram.

communication diagram

A diagram that shows interactions organized around the parts of a composite structure or the roles of a collaboration. Unlike a sequence diagram, a communication diagram explicitly shows the relationships among the elements. On the other hand, a communication diagram does not show time as a separate dimension, so the sequence of messages and the concurrent threads must be determined using sequence numbers. Sequence diagrams and communication diagrams both express interactions, but show them in different ways.

See collaboration, pattern, sequence diagram.

Notation

A communication diagram is a structured class or a collaboration together with messages that form an interaction. It is shown as a graph whose nodes are rectangles representing parts of a structured class or roles of a collaboration. The nodes correspond to the lifelines in an interaction, but they are shown within their structural context. Lines between parts show connectors that form communication paths. The lines may be labeled with their contextual name and/or the name of the underlying association, if any. Multiplicities may be shown on connectors. Messages between parts are shown by labeled arrows near connector lines. Typically, an interaction represents the implementation of an operation or use case.

A communication diagram shows the slots for objects involved as lifelines in an interaction. The lifelines have the syntax rolename : classname. Either the rolename or the class name may be omitted, but the colon is required if the rolename is omitted. A diagram also shows the connectors among the objects. These represent associations as well as transient links representing procedure arguments, local variables, and self-links. An arrow next to a line indicates a message flowing in the given direction over the link. An arrow on a connector represents a communication path in a single direction (optional notation extrapolated from, but not explicitly found in, the UML specification).

Implementation of an operation

A communication diagram that shows the implementation of an operation includes symbols for the target object role and the roles of other objects the target object uses, directly or indirectly, to perform the operation. Messages on connectors show the flow of control in an interaction. Each message shows a step within the method for the operation.

A communication diagram describing an operation also includes role symbols representing arguments of the operation and local variables created during its execution. Objects created or destroyed during the execution may be labeled by notes.

Objects without a keyword exist when the operation begins and still exist when it is complete.

The internal messages that implement a method are numbered, starting with number 1. For a procedural flow of control, the subsequent message numbers use "dot" sequences nested in accordance with call nesting. For example, the second top-level step is message 2; the first subordinate step inside that step is message 2.1. For asynchronous messages exchanged among concurrent objects, all the sequence numbers are at the same level (that is, they are not nested).

See message for a full description of message syntax including sequencing.

A complete collaboration diagram shows the roles of all the objects and links used by the operation. If an object is not shown, the assumption is that it is not used. It is not safe to assume that all the objects on a collaboration diagram *are* used by the operation, however.

Example

In Figure 14-64, an operation **redisplay** is called on a **Controller** object. At the time when the operation is called, it already has a link to the **Window** object, where the picture will be displayed. It also has a link to a **Wire** object, the object whose image will be displayed in the window.

The top-level implementation of the **redisplay** operation has only one step—the calling of operation **displayPositions** on the **wire** object. This operation has sequence number 1, because it is the first step in the top-most method. This message flow passes along a reference to the **Window** object that will be needed later.

The **displayPositions** operation calls the **drawSegment** operation on the same **wire** object. The call, labeled with sequence number 1.1, is dispatched along the implicit **self** link. The star indicates an iterative call of the operation; the details are supplied in the brackets.

Each **drawSegment** operation accesses two **Bead** objects, one indexed by qualifier value **i-1** and one by value **i**. Although there is only one association from **Wire** to **Bead** within the context of this operation, two links to two **Bead** objects are needed. The objects are labeled **left** and **right** (which are the classifier roles in the collaboration). One message is dispatched along each link. The messages are labeled 1.1.1a and 1.1.1b. This indicates that they are steps of operation 1.1; the letters at the end indicate that the two messages can be dispatched concurrently. In a normal implementation, they would probably not be executed in parallel, but because they are declared as concurrent, they can be executed in any convenient sequential order.

When both values (**r0** and **r1**) have been returned, the next step following the operation 1.1 can proceed. Message 1.2 is a create message sent to a **Line** object. Actually, it goes to the **Line** class itself (in principle, at least), which creates a new **Line** object linked to the sender.

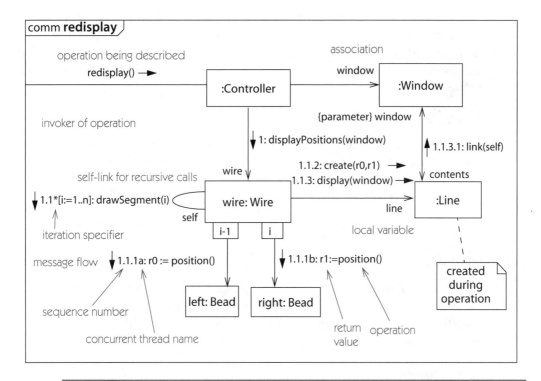

Figure 14-64. *Communication diagram syntax with message flows*

Step 1.3 uses the newly created link to send a **display** message to the newly created **Line** object. The pointer to the **window** object is passed along as an argument, making it accessible to the **Line** object as a link. Note that the **Line** object has a link to the same **window** object that is associated with the original **Controller** object; this is important to the operation and it is shown by the diagram. In the final step 1.3.1, the **Window** object is requested to create a link to the **Line** object.

The final state of the system can be observed by mentally erasing all the temporary links. There is a link from **Controller** to **wire** and from **wire** to its **Bead** parts, from **Controller** to **window** and from **window** to its **contents**. Once the operation is complete, however, a **Line** has no access to the **Window** that contains it. The link in that direction is transient and disappears when the operation is complete. Similarly, a **Wire** object no longer has access to the **Line** objects used to display it.

Discussion

The UML specification is somewhat unclear on what is allowed in communications diagrams. We have interpreted them to allow overlaying messages on internal structure, otherwise they would be superfluous.

The specification indicates the tag **sd** for all diagrams showing interactions. This seems confusing and useless; either you can tell by looking what kind of diagram it is, in which case no tag is necessary, or you can't, in which case a distinction among diagrams is necessary. Therefore we have used the tag **comm** on these diagrams.

History

This was called a collaboration diagram in UML1, which was confusing because collaborations were static structures, but the diagram included messages.

communication path

A kind of association that allows nodes to exchange signals and messages.

compartment

A graphical subdivision of a closed symbol, such as a class rectangle divided vertically into smaller rectangles. Each compartment shows properties of the element that it represents. Compartments come in three kinds: fixed, lists, and regions.

See also class, classifier.

Notation

A *fixed compartment* has a fixed format of graphical and text parts to represent a fixed set of properties. The format depends on the kind of element. An example is a class name compartment, which contains a stereotype symbol and/or name, a class name, and a property string that shows various class properties. Depending on the element, some of the information may be suppressible.

A *list compartment* contains a list of strings that encode constituents of the element. An example is an attribute list. The encoding depends on the constituent type. The list elements may be shown in their natural order within the model, or they may be sorted by one or more of their properties (in which case, the natural order will not be visible). For example, a list of attributes could be sorted first on visibility and then on name. List entries can be displayed or suppressed based on the properties of the model elements. An attribute compartment, for instance, might show only public attributes. Stereotypes and keywords may be applied to individual entries by prepending them to the list entry. A stereotype or keyword may be applied to all subsequent entries by inserting it as a list entry by itself. They affect all subsequent list entries until the end of the list or another such running declaration. The string «constructor» placed on a separate line in an operation list would stereotype the subsequent operations as constructors, but the string «query» further down the list would revoke the first declaration and replace it by the «query» stereotype.

A *region* is an area that contains a graphic subpicture showing substructure of the element, often potentially recursive. An example is a nested state region. The nature of the subpicture is peculiar to the model element. Including both regions and text compartments in a single symbol is legal, but it can be messy. Regions are often used for recursive elements, and text is used for leaf elements with no recursive substructure.

A class has three predefined compartments: name, a fixed compartment; attributes, a list compartment; and operations, another list compartment. A modeler can add another compartment to the rectangle and place its name at the head of the compartment, in a distinctive font (for example, small boldface). Names may be placed on the attribute and operation compartments, if desired.

The graphical syntax depends on the element and the kind of compartment. Figure 14-65 shows a compartment for signals. Figure 14-242 shows a compartment for responsibilities.

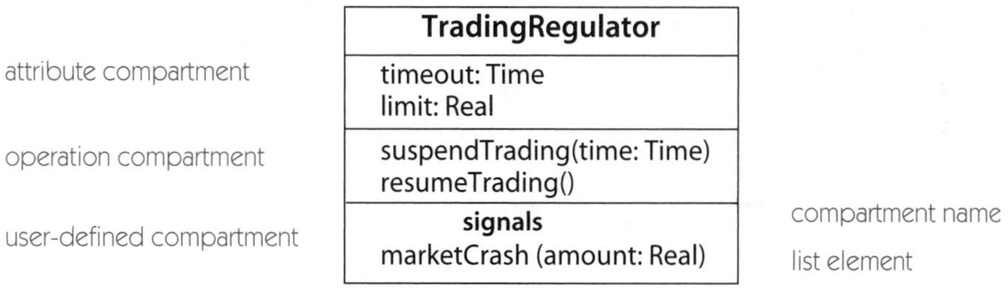

attribute compartment	**TradingRegulator**	
	timeout: Time limit: Real	
operation compartment	suspendTrading(time: Time) resumeTrading()	
user-defined compartment	**signals** marketCrash (amount: Real)	compartment name list element

Figure 14-65. *Named compartment in a class*

compile time

Refers to something that occurs during the compilation of a software module.
See modeling time, run time.

complete

Keyword for a generalization set whose subtypes cover all possible cases of the supertype.
See generalization set.

completion transition

A transition that lacks an explicit trigger event and is triggered by the completion of activity in the source state.
See also do activity, transition, trigger.

Semantics

A completion transition is represented as a transition that has no explicit trigger event. The transition is triggered implicitly when its source state (including nested states) has completed any activity. Completion can be one of the following:

- Termination of an entry action and a contained do activity, if any
- Reaching a final state within a nonorthogonal composite state
- Reaching the final states of all regions of an orthogonal state
- Reaching an unlabeled exit point or final state within a referenced submachine

An exit activity on a state is executed when the completion transition fires, before any actions of the transition itself.

A completion transition may have a guard condition and an effect. Usually, it is undesirable to have an isolated guarded completion transition, because if the guard condition is false, the transition will never fire (because the implicit trigger occurs only once). Occasionally, this may be useful to represent some kind of failure, provided a triggered transition eventually pulls the object out of the dead state. More commonly a set of guarded completion transitions have conditions that cover all possibilities so that one of them will fire immediately when the state terminates.

Completion transitions are also used to connect initial states and history states to their successor states, because these pseudostates may not remain active after the completion of activity.

A completion event takes precedence over normal events. If a completion event occurs, an enabled completion transition fires immediately without being placed in the normal event pool. A completion event may therefore be considered more of a special kind of control construct rather than a normal event.

Notation

A completion transition is shown by a transition arrow without a trigger event. The arrow may have a guard condition in square brackets and it may have an effect expression following a slash (/). Often it has no label at all.

Example

Figure 14-66 shows a state machine fragment of ticket-ordering application. The **Selecting** state remains active as long as the customer keeps picking dates. When the customer presses the "done" button, then the **Selecting** state reaches its final state. This triggers the completion transition, which goes to the **Selected** state.

complex port

A port that has multiple interfaces.

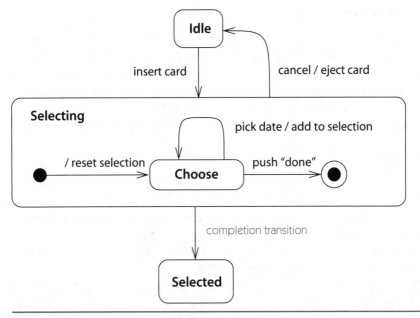

Figure 14-66. *Completion transition*

Semantics

A port may have multiple interfaces. These include both provided interfaces and required interfaces.

Notation

A complex port is shown by connecting multiple interface symbols to the port symbol. If desired, the port symbol can be drawn an a rectangle rather than a square, so that the interface symbols may be connected more easily. See Figure 14-67.

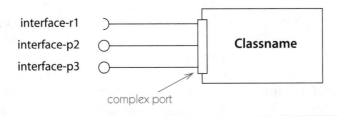

Figure 14-67. *Complex port*

complex transition

A transition with more than one source state and/or more than one target state. It represents a response to an event that causes a change in the amount of concurrency. It is a sychronization of control, a forking of control, or both, depending on the number of sources and targets. (This term is presented here for convenience because no equivalent term is defined in the UML2 specification.)

See also branch, composite state, fork, join, merge, orthogonal region.

Semantics

At a high level, a system passes through a series of states, but the monolithic view that a system has a single state is too restrictive for large systems with distribution and concurrency. A system may hold multiple orthogonal states at one time. The set of active states is called the active state configuration. If a nested state is active, then all states that contain it are active. If the object permits concurrency, then more than one orthogonal region may be active.

In many cases, the activity of a system can be modeled as a set of threads of control that evolve independently of each other or that interact in limited ways. Each transition affects, at most, a few states in the active state configuration. When a transition fires, unaffected active states remain active. The progress of the threads at a moment can be captured as a subset of states within the active state configuration, one subset for each thread. Each set of states evolves independently in response to events. If the number of active states is constant, the state model is nothing but a fixed collection of state machines that interact. In general, however, the number of states (and therefore the number of threads of control) can vary over time. A state can transition to two or more concurrent states (a fork of control), and two or more concurrent states can transition to one state (a join of control). The number of concurrent states and their evolution is controlled by the state machine for the system.

A complex transition is a transition into or from an orthogonal state. The vertices in one side of the transition must include one state from each orthogonal region in the orthogonal state. A complex transition has more than one source state and/or target state. If it has multiple source states, it represents a join of control. If it has multiple target states, it represents a fork of control. If it has multiple source and target states, it represents a synchronization of parallel threads.

If a complex transition has multiple source states, all of them must be active before the transition is a candidate for triggering. The order in which they become active is irrelevant. If all the source states are active and the trigger event occurs, the transition is enabled and may fire if its guard condition is true. Each complex transition has a single trigger, even if there are multiple source states. The concept of simultaneous occurrence of events is not supported by UML; each event must trigger a separate transition and then the resultant states can be followed by a join.

If a complex transition with multiple source states lacks a trigger event (that is, if it is a completion transition) then it is triggered when all its explicit source states become active. If its guard condition is satisfied at that time, it fires.

When a complex transition fires, all the source states and all their peers within the same composite state cease to be active, and all the target states and all their peers become active.

In more complicated situations, the guard condition may be expanded to permit firing when some subset of the states is active; this capability can easily lead to ill-formed models and should be avoided or used with extreme care.

The UML metamodel does not include complex transition as a metaclass. A complex transition is modeled as a set of single-source, single-target transitions connected by fork or join pseudostates, but the effect is the same as a complex transition with multiple sources or targets.

Example

Figure 14-68 shows a typical concurrent composite state with complex transitions entering and leaving it. Figure 14-69 shows a typical execution history of this machine (the active states are shown in blue). The history shows the variation in number of active states over time.

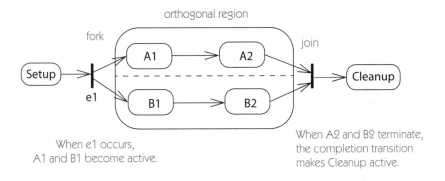

Figure 14-68. *Fork and join*

Orthogonal states

Unless a state machine is carefully structured, a set of complex transitions can lead to inconsistencies, including deadlocks, multiple occupation of a state, and other problems. The problem has been extensively studied under Petri net theory, and the usual solution is to impose well-formedness rules on the state machine to avoid the danger of inconsistencies. These are "structured programming" rules for state machines. There are a number of approaches, each with advantages and disadvantages. The rules adopted by UML require that a state machine decompose

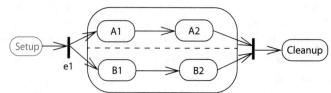

e1 occurs

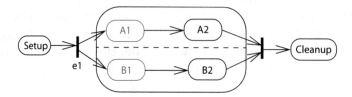

A1 completes

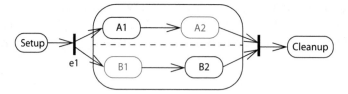

B1 completes

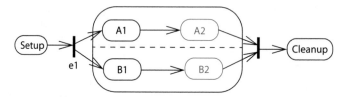

A2 and B2 complete

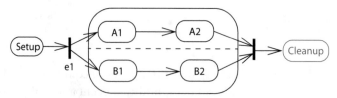

(Active states shown in blue)

Figure 14-69. *History of active states in a state machine with orthogonal regions*

into finer states using an *and-or* tree. The advantage is that a well-nested structure is easy to establish, maintain, and understand. The disadvantage is that certain meaningful configurations are prohibited. On balance, this is similar to the trade-off in giving up goto's to get structured programming.

A composite state may be decomposed into a set of mutually exclusive substates (an "or" decomposition, if it has exactly one region) or into a set of orthogonal regions, each of which contains mutually exclusive substates (an "and" decomposition followed by an "or" decomposition, if it has more than one region). The structure is recursive. Generally, "and" layers alternate with "or" layers. An "and" layer represents orthogonal decomposition—all of the substates are active concurrently. An "or" state represents a sequential decomposition—one substate is active at a time. A legal set of orthogonal states can be obtained by recursively expanding the nodes in the tree, starting with the root. Replace an "and" state by all of its children; replace an "or" state by one of its children. This corresponds to the nested structure of statecharts.

Example

Figure 14-70 shows an and-or tree of states corresponding to the state machine in Figure 14-68. A typical set of concurrently active states is colored in blue. This corresponds to the third step in Figure 14-69.

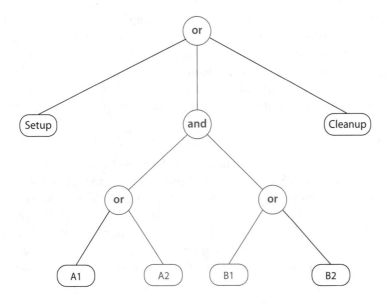

(Typical set of active states shown in blue)

Figure 14-70. *And-or tree of nested states*

If a transition enters an orthogonal state (one with more than one region), it enters all the orthogonal subregions. If a transition enters a nonorthogonal state (one with a single region), it enters exactly one substate. The active state within a nonorthogonal state or a region can change. With an orthogonal state, a state in each orthogonal region remains active as long as the orthogonal state is active. A state in an orthogonal region can be further decomposed.

Therefore, a simple transition (one that has one input and one output) must connect two states in the same nonorthogonal region or two states separated by or-levels only. A complex transition must connect all the subregions within an orthogonal state with a state outside the orthogonal state (we omit more complicated cases, but they must follow the principles above). In other words, a transition entering an orthogonal state must enter a state in each subregion; a transition leaving an orthogonal state must leave each subregion.

A shortcut representation is available: If a complex transition enters an orthogonal state but omits explicit transitions to one or more of the subregions, then there is implicitly a transition to the initial state of each unlisted subregion. If a subregion has no initial state, the model is ill formed. If a complex transition leaves an orthogonal state, there is an implicit transition from each unlisted subregion. If a complex transition fires, any activity within a subregion is terminated—that is, it represents a forced exit. A transition can be connected to the enclosing orthogonal state itself. It implies a transition to the initial state of each subregion—a common modeling situation. Similarly, a transition from an enclosing orthogonal state implies the forced exit of each subregion (if it has an event trigger) or waiting for each subregion to complete (if it is triggerless, that is, if it is a completion transition).

The rules on complex transitions ensure that meaningless combinations of states cannot be active concurrently. A set of orthogonal subregions is a partition of the enclosing composite state. All of them are active or none of them is active.

Notation

A complex transition is shown as a short heavy bar (a synchronization bar, which can represent synchronization, forking, or both). The bar may have one or more solid transition arrows from states to the bar (the states are the source states); the bar may have one or more solid arrows from the bar to states (the states are the target states). A transition label may be shown near the bar, describing the trigger event, guard condition, and actions, as described under transition. Individual arrows do not have their own transition strings; they are merely part of the overall single transition.

Example

Figure 14-71 shows the state machine from Figure 14-68 with an additional exit transition. It also shows an implicit fork from state **Setup** to the initial states in

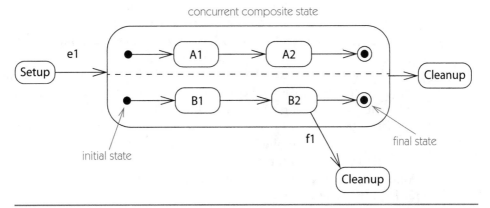

Figure 14-71. *Complex transitions (fork, join)*

each subregion and an implicit join from the final states in each subregion to state
Cleanup.

If event **f1** occurs when state **B2** is active, then the transition to state **Cleanup** occurs. This transition is an implicit join; it terminates state **A2** as well as state **B2**.

component

A modular part of a system design that hides its implementation behind a set of
external interfaces. Within a system, components satisfying the same interfaces
may be substituted freely.

Semantics

A component describes a modular piece of a logical or physical system whose externally visible behavior can be described much more concisely than its implementation. The externally visible behavior is represented as a set of interfaces, possibly
with attached behaviors, such as protocol state machines or use cases, for additional detail. A system specifies its implementation using slots that hold components satisfying specific interfaces. Any component that satisfies the set of
interfaces can be substituted in a slot. The separation between external interfaces
and internal implementation allows the development of systems and their parts to
be cleanly separated, permitting the substitution of different components into a
given system slot and the use of the same component within different systems.
This modularity increases the reusability of both system frameworks and components.

Components have two aspects. They define the external face of a piece of a system, and they implement the functionality of a system. Components without implementation are an abstract type. They are used to specify the requirements of a

given system slot. Components with implementation may be subtypes of an abstract component. Concrete components may substitute for their ancestors. (They may substitute in any place where they satisfy the interfaces, but a child component is guaranteed to satisfy its parent's interfaces.)

A component may or may not be directly instantiated at run time. An indirectly instantiated component is implemented, or realized, by a set of classifiers. The component itself does not appear in the implementation; it serves as a design that an implementation must follow. The set of realizing classifiers must cover the entire set of operations specified in the provided interface of the component. The manner of implementing the component is the responsibility of the designer.

A directly instantiated component specifies its own encapsulated implementation. The implementation of a component may be specified as a structured classifier containing parts and connectors. When the component is instantiated, its internal structure is instantiated also. The relation between the component and its implementation is explicit. The parts may themselves be specified by other components, so components may form a recursive assembly.

The relationships between components may be specified by dependencies among their interfaces. The interfaces of a component describe the functionality that it supports. Interfaces may be provided interfaces or required interfaces. A provided interface describes the operations that a component guarantees to make available to other components. Each operation in the interface must eventually map to an implementation element supported by the component. The component may supply additional operations, but it must at least supply all the operations in a provided interface. A required interface describes the functionality that it needs from other components. The component may not always use all of the listed operations, but it is guaranteed to work if the components that it uses at least supply all the listed operations. Behaviors attached to interfaces may specify additional constraints on the ordering of messages among components.

For additional precision in specification and interconnection, the interfaces of a component may be localized into ports. Each port bundles a set of required and provided interfaces, and optionally includes an attached behavior specifying the interactions through the port. Messages to a component with ports are directed to specific ports, and the implementation of the component can determine which port messages arrive on and depart from.

The internal "wiring" of a component is specified with assembly connectors and delegation connectors. Within the implementation of a component, assembly connectors connect ports of different subcomponents. (A subcomponent is a part whose type is a smaller component.) A message sent on a port of one component is received on a connected port of another component. A set of subcomponents may be wired together through their ports. A subcomponent need not know anything about other subcomponents, except that they exist and satisfy the constraints on connected ports. In many frameworks, if the modeler connects components correctly, no additional code is needed. Communication among components is modeled by their ports. The ports might exist in the physical code, or they might be compiled away.

A delegation connector connects an external port of a component with a port on one of its internal subcomponents. A message received by the external port is passed to the port on the internal component; a message sent by the internal port is passed to the external port and thence to the component connected to it. Assembly connectors permit the assembly of components at one level into a high-level component. Delegation connectors permit the implementation of high-level operations by low-level components.

Concrete components may also have artifacts, that is, physical pieces of implementation, such as code, scripts, hypertext elements, and so on. These are the physical manifestation of the model on a specific computation platform. Each artifact may manifest one or several model elements.

A component is also a namespace that may be used to organize design elements, use cases, interactions, and code artifacts.

There are several predefined stereotypes of component, including subsystem, specification, and realization.

Artifacts. An artifact is a physical unit of the construction of a system. The term includes software code (source, binary, or executable) or equivalents, such as scripts or command files. Artifacts exist in the implementation domain—they are physical units on computers that can be stored, moved, and manipulated. Models may show dependencies among components and artifacts, such as compiler and run-time dependencies or information dependencies in a human organization. An artifact may also be used to show implementation units that exist at run time, including their location on node instances. Artifacts may be deployed onto physical nodes.

Example

For example, a spelling checker may be a component within a text editor, E-mail system, and other frameworks. The provided interface might consist of an operation that checks a block of text and an operation that adds words to the exception dictionary for a document. The required interface might consist of access to a standard dictionary plus an exception dictionary. Different spelling checkers might have different user interfaces or performance characteristics, but any of them could be substituted in any appropriate slot without damaging the containing application.

Structure

A component has a required interface and a provided interface.

A component may be directly or indirectly implemented.

A component has a set of references to classifiers that realize its behavior. This set may be empty if the component provides a direct implementation.

A component may have operations and attributes, which must cover the specification of its provided interfaces.

A component may own a set of elements within its namespace, much like a package. These elements may include artifacts.

As a structured class, a component may have a set of parts and connectors that compose its direct implementation. It may also have external ports that organize its interfaces.

Notation

A component is displayed as a rectangle with the keyword «component». Instead of or in addition to the keyword, it may contain a component icon in its upper right corner. This icon is a small rectangle with two smaller rectangles protruding from its side. The name of the component (as a type) is placed inside the outer rectangle (Figure 14-72).

Figure 14-72. *Component notation (alternatives)*

Operations and attributes available to outside objects may be shown directly in compartments of the rectangle. In most cases, however, these are suppressed in favor of the interfaces of the component.

Interfaces may be listed in a compartment of the rectangle. The keywords «provided» and «required» may be placed on individual interface names or they may be placed on lines without interface names, in which case they apply to the following list of names.

Alternately, interfaces may be shown by attaching interface icons to the boundary of the rectangle. A provided interface is shown as a small circle attached to the rectangle by a line. A required interface is shown as a small semicircle attached to the rectangle by a line. See Figure 14-73.

Interfaces may also be shown in a fully explicit form (Figure 14-74): An interface is shown as a rectangle with the keyword «interface». A compartment in the rectangle holds a list of operations. A component is connected to a provided interface by a dashed line with a triangular arrowhead. A component is connected to a required interface by a dashed line with an open arrowhead and the keyword «use».

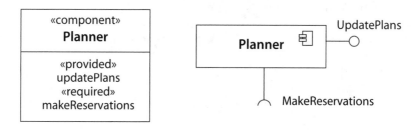

Figure 14-73. *Component interface notation (alternatives)*

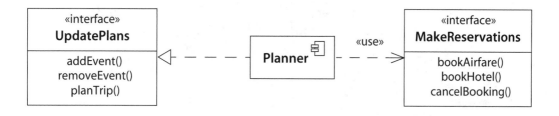

Figure 14-74. *Explicit interface notation*

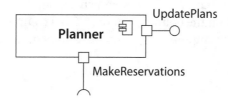

Figure 14-75. *Component port notation*

A port is shown as a small rectangle on the boundary of the component rectangle (Figure 14-75). The name of the port is placed near the small rectangle. One or more interface symbols (provided and/or required) may be attached to the small rectangle by solid lines.

Classes and artifacts that realize the implementation of a component may be connected to the component by dependency arrows (a dashed line with an open arrowhead). Alternately, they may be nested within the component rectangle.

The direct implementation of a component is shown as an internal structure diagram of parts and connectors nested within the component rectangle (Figure 14-76). The types of the parts may be classes or subcomponents.

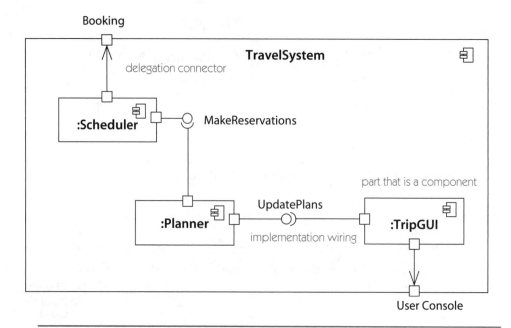

Figure 14-76. *Component internal structure*

Subcomponents may be connected by adjoining the half-circle of a required interface to the circle of a compatible provided interface in a "ball and socket" notation. Delegation connectors are shown by solid arrows with open arrowheads between a port on the boundary of the overall component and an interface symbol or port of a subcomponent. The keyword «**delegate**» may optionally be placed on the arrow.

History

The focus of components has been redirected away from the physical view of UML1 toward a more logical concept of a component as a tightly encapsulated unit. Components have been separated from the physical concept of artifact so that they can be used in conceptual models. The distinction between a structured class and a component is somewhat vague and more a matter of intent than firm semantics.

component diagram

A diagram that shows the definition, internal structure, and dependencies of component types. There is no sharp line between component diagrams and general class diagrams.

See component for examples of component diagrams.

composite aggregation

See composition.

composite class

A class that is related to one or more classes by a composition relationship.
See composition, structured classifier.

composite object

An instance of a composite class.
See composition, structured classifier.

Semantics

A composite object has a composition relationship to all of its composite parts. This means that it is responsible for their creation and destruction, and that no other object is similarly responsible. In other words, there are no garbage collection issues with the parts; the composite object can and must destroy them when it dies, or else it must hand over responsibility for them to another object.

The composition relationship is often implemented by physical containment within the same data structure as the composite object itself (usually a record). Physical containment ensures that the lifetime of the parts matches the lifetime of the composite object.

Notation

A composite object may be connected to each of its parts by a composition link, that is, a line with a filled diamond on the end attached to the composite object (Figure 14-77).

An instance of a structured class is shown as a rectangle whose internal objects and connectors may be nested within a graphic compartment inside the object symbol. The graphic compartment may be shown as an additional compartment below the attribute compartment, although usually the attribute compartment is suppressed.

Example

Figure 14-78 shows a structured object, namely a desktop window, composed of various parts. It contains multiple instances of the ScrollBar class. Each instance has its own name and role within the composite object. For example, the horizontalBar and the verticalBar are both scrollbars, but they behave differently within the composite. They are labeled by their roles within the structured object.

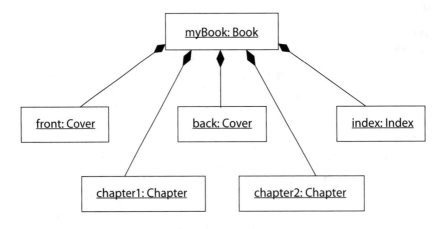

Figure 14-77. *Composite object*

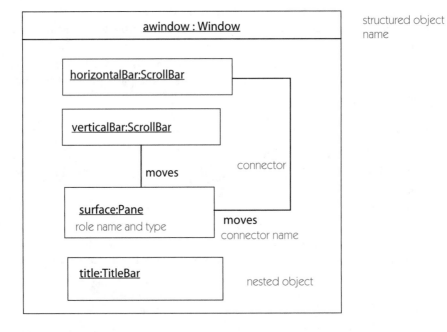

Figure 14-78. *Structured object*

composite state

A state that contains one or more regions, each containing one or more direct substates.

See also complex transition, orthogonal region, orthogonal state, region, simple state, state.

Semantics

A composite state is a state with substates. A composite state can be decomposed, using *and*-relationships, into one or more regions, each of which is decomposed, using *or*-relationships, into one or more mutually exclusive direct substates. If a composite state is active, exactly one direct substate in each of its regions is active. The net effect is an *and-or tree* of active states. Each state machine has a top-level state, which is a composite state.

A composite state with exactly one region is a nonorthogonal state. If it is active, exactly one direct substate is active. It adds a layer of substructure but does not add additional concurrency.

A composite state with more than one region is an orthogonal state. Its regions are called orthogonal regions. If it is active, exactly one direct substate in each orthogonal region is active. It introduces concurrency equal to the number of orthogonal regions, as well as a layer of substructure within each orthogonal region.

A system may hold multiple states at one time. The set of active states is called the active state configuration. If a nested state is active, then all composite states that contain it are active. If the object permits concurrency, then more than one orthogonal state may be active.

See complex transition for a discussion of concurrent execution; Figure 14-70 shows an and-or tree.

A group transition is a transition that directly leaves a composite state. If it is a completion transition, it is enabled when the final state of each region is reached.

Each region of a composite state may have, at most, one initial state and one final state. Each region may also have, at most, one shallow history state and one deep history state.

A newly created object starts in its initial state, which the outermost composite state must have. The event that creates the object may be used to trigger a transition from the initial state. The arguments of the creation event are available to this initial transition. An object that transitions to its outermost final state is destroyed and ceases to exist.

Notation

A composite state is a state with subordinate detail. It has a name compartment, an internal transition compartment, and a graphic compartment that contains a nested diagram showing the subordinate detail. All of the compartments are optional. For convenience and appearance, the text compartments (name and internal transitions) may be shrunk as tabs within the graphic region, instead of spanning it horizontally.

An expansion of an orthogonal composite state into orthogonal regions is shown by tiling the graphic compartment of the state using dashed lines to divide it into subregions. A nonorthogonal composite state has a single subregion. Each subregion may have an optional name and must contain a nested state diagram with direct substates. The name compartment and other text compartments of the entire state are separated from the regions by a solid line. Alternately, the name of the composite state may be placed in a small tab attached to the overall state symbol so that the name compartment does not look like a region.

An initial state is shown as a small, solid-filled circle. In a top-level state machine, the transition from an initial state may be labeled with the event that creates the object. Otherwise, it must be unlabeled. If it is unlabeled, it represents any transition to the enclosing state. The initial transition may have an action. The initial state is a notational device. An object may not be *in* such a state but must transition to an actual state.

A final state is shown as a circle surrounding a small, solid-filled circle (a bull's eye). It represents the completion of activity in the enclosing state, and it triggers a transition on the enclosing state labeled by the implicit activity completion event (usually displayed as an unlabeled transition).

Example

Figure 14-79 shows a nonorthogonal composite state containing two direct substates, an initial state, and a final state. When the composite state becomes active, the substate **Start** (the target of the initial state) is activated first.

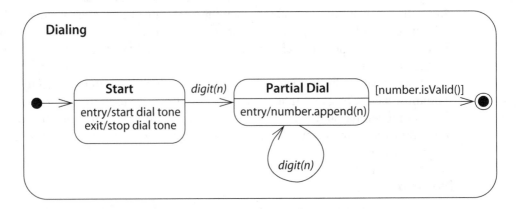

Figure 14-79. *Nonorthogonal composite state*

The contents of a composite state may be hidden in a particular view. A hidden region is shown by a small icon representing two linked state symbols. Figure 14-80 shows an outer composite region whose decomposition is shown. The decomposition of its two substates is hidden.

Figure 14-81 shows an orthogonal composite state containing three orthogonal subregions. Each orthogonal subregion is further decomposed into direct substates. When the composite state **Incomplete** becomes active, the targets of the initial states become active. When all three subregions reach the final state, then the completion transition on the outer composite state **Incomplete** fires and the **Passed** state becomes active. If the **fail** event occurs while the **Incomplete** state is active, then all three orthogonal subregions are terminated and the **Failed** state becomes active.

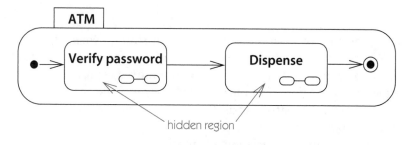

Figure 14-80. *Hidden region in composite state*

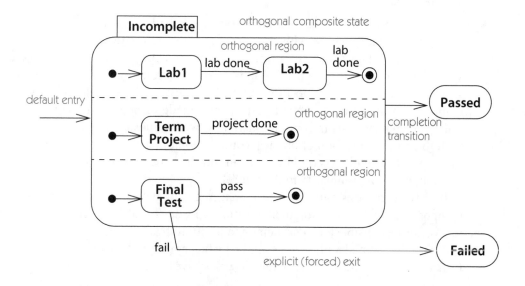

Figure 14-81. *Orthogonal composite state*

composite structure

Composite structure describes the interconnection of objects within a context to form an entity with an overall purpose. Composite structures include structured classifiers and collaborations.

See structured classifier, collaboration, connector, structured part, port.

composite structure diagram

A diagram that shows the internal structure (including parts and connectors) of a structured classifier or a collaboration. There is no rigid line between a composite structure diagram and a general class diagram.

composition

A strong form of aggregation association with strong ownership of parts by the composite and coincident lifetime of parts with the composite. A part may belong to only one composite at a time. Parts with nonfixed multiplicity may be created after the composite itself. But once created, they live and die with it (that is, they share lifetimes). Such parts can also be explicitly removed before the death of the composite. Composition is recursive.

See also aggregation, association, composite object.

Semantics

There is a strong form of aggregation association called composition. A composite is an aggregate association with the additional constraints that an object may be part of only one composite at a time and that the composite object has sole responsibility for the management of all its parts. As a consequence of the first constraint, the set of all composition relationships (over *all* associations with the composition property) forms a forest of trees made of objects and composition links. A composite part may not be shared by two composite objects. This accords with the normal intuition of physical composition of parts—one part cannot be a direct part of two objects (although it can indirectly be part of multiple objects at different levels of granularity in the tree).

By having responsibility for the management of its parts, we mean that the composite is responsible for their creation and destruction. In implementation terms, it is responsible for their memory allocation. In a logical model, the concept is less rigidly defined and must be applied when appropriate. During its instantiation, a composite must ensure that all its parts have been instantiated and correctly attached to it. It can create a part itself or it can assume responsibility for an existing part. But during the life of the composite, no other object may have responsibility for it. This means that the behavior for a composite class can be designed with the knowledge that no other class will destroy or deallocate the parts. A composite may add additional parts during its life (if the multiplicities permit), provided it assumes sole responsibility for them. It may remove parts, provided the multiplicities permit and responsibility for them is assumed by another object. If the composite is destroyed, it must either destroy all its parts or else give responsibility for them to other objects.

Under some circumstances, a class may permit other objects to create or destroy composite parts of one of its instances, but it retains ultimate responsibility for them. In particular, it must create all necessary parts on its initialization and it must destroy all remaining parts on its destruction.

This definition encompasses most of the common logical and implementation intuitions of composition. For example, a record containing a list of values is a common implementation of an object and its attributes. When the record is allocated, memory for the attributes is automatically allocated also, but the values of the attributes may need to be initialized. While the record exists, no attribute can be removed from it. When the record is deallocated, the memory for the attributes is deallocated also. No other object can affect the allocation of a single attribute within the record. The physical properties of a record enforce the constraints of a composite.

This definition of composition works well with garbage collection. If the composite itself is destroyed, the only pointer to the part is destroyed and the part becomes inaccessible and subject to garbage collection. Recovery of inaccessible parts is simple even with garbage collection, however, which is one reason for distinguishing composition from other aggregation.

Note that a part need not be implemented as a physical part of a single memory block with the composite. If the part is separate from the composite, then the composite has responsibility for allocating and deallocating memory for the part, as needed. In C++, for example, constructors and destructors facilitate implementation of composites.

An object may be part of only one composite object at a time. This does not preclude a class from being a composite part of more than one class at different times or in different instances, but only one composition link may exist at one time for one object. In other words, there is an or-constraint among the possible composites to which a part might belong. Also, one object may be part of different composite objects during its life, but only one at a time.

Structure

The aggregation property on an association end or property may have the following values.

none   The attached classifier is not an aggregate or composite.

shared   The attached classifier is a potentially shared aggregate. The other end is a part.

composite   The attached classifier is a composite. The other end is a part.

At least one end of an association must have the value none.

Notation

Composition is shown by a solid-filled diamond adornment on the end of an association path attached to the composite element (Figure 14-82). The multiplicity may be shown in the normal way. It must be 1 or 0..1.

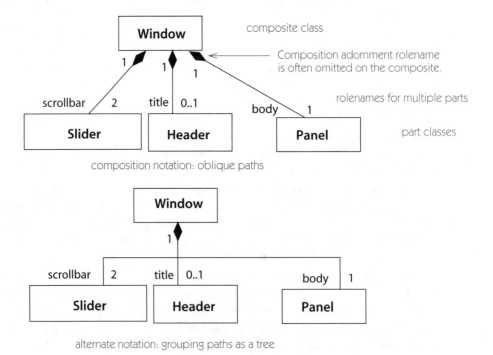

Figure 14-82. *Composition notation*

Alternately, composition may be shown by graphically nesting the symbols of the parts within the symbol of the composite (Figure 14-83). This is the notation for a structured classifier. A nested element may have a rolename within the structured class. The name is shown in front of its type in the syntax

rolename : classname

A nested classifier may have a multiplicity within its composite element. The multiplicity is shown by a multiplicity string in the upper-right corner of the symbol for the part or by placing the multiplicity in square brackets after the classifier name. If the multiplicity mark is omitted, the default multiplicity is one.

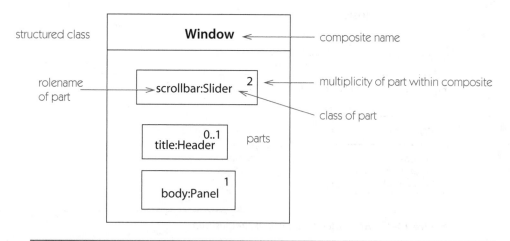

Figure 14-83. *Composition of structured class as graphical nesting*

A line drawn entirely within a border of a structured class is considered to be part of the composition. Any objects connected by a single link of the association must belong to the same composite. An association drawn so that its path breaks the border of the composite is not considered to be part of the composition. It represents an ordinary association. Any objects on a single link of the association may belong to the same or different composites (Figure 14-84).

Note that attributes are usually treated as composition relationships between a class and the classes of its attributes (Figure 14-85). They may represent references to other classes, that is, associations. In general, however, attributes should be reserved for primitive data values (such as numbers, strings, and dates) and not references to classes, because any other relationships to the referenced classes cannot be seen in the attribute notation. In cases where a class is widely referenced but navigation in the reverse directions is unimportant, the use of attributes containing references may be useful, however.

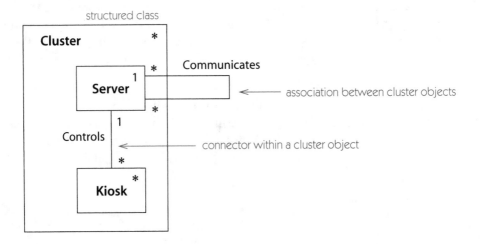

Figure 14-84. *Association within and among structured class*

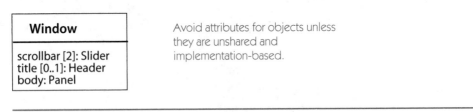

Figure 14-85. *Attributes are a form of composition*

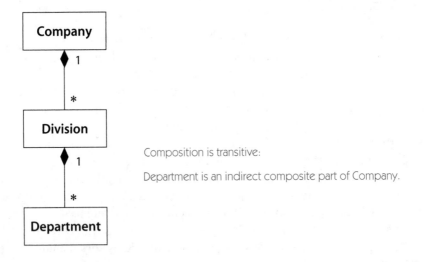

Figure 14-86. *Multilevel composition*

Note that the notation for composition resembles the notation for collaboration. A collaboration is a kind of structured classifier in which the parts are related by the collaboration rather than being physical pieces of it.

Figure 14-86 shows multilevel composition.

Discussion

(See also the discussion under aggregation for guidelines on when aggregation, composition, and plain association are appropriate.)

Composition and aggregation are metarelationships—they transcend individual associations to impose constraints in the entire set of associations. Composition is meaningful across composition relationships. An object may have at most one composition link (to a composite), although it might potentially come from more than one composition association. In other words, a class might show more than one composition association to other classes, but a particular object can be part of only one other object at a time chosen from one of those classes. The entire graph of composition and aggregation links and objects must be acyclic, even if the links come from different associations. Note that these constraints apply to the instance domain—the aggregation associations themselves often form cycles, and recursive structures always require cycles of associations.

Consider the model in Figure 14-87. Every **Authentication** is a composite part of exactly one **Transaction**, which can be either a **Purchase** or a **Sale**. Every **Transaction** need not have an **Authentication**, however. From this fragment, we have enough information to conclude that an **Authentication** has no other composition associations. Every authentication object must be part of a transaction object (the multiplicity is one); an object can be part of at most one composite (by definition); it is already part of one composite (as shown); so **Authentication** may not be part of any other composition association. There is no danger that an **Authentication** may have to manage its own storage. A **Transaction** is always available to take the responsibility, although not all **Transactions** have **Authentications** that they need to manage. (Of course, the **Authentication** can manage itself if the designer wants.)

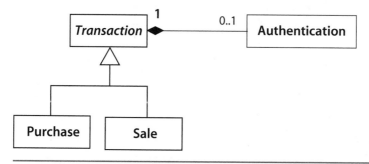

Figure 14-87. *Composition to an abstract composite class*

Figure 14-88. *Shared part class*

In Figure 14-88, an **Autograph** may optionally be part of either a **Transaction** or a **Letter**. It can't be part of both at one time (by the rules of composition). This model does not prevent an **Autograph** from starting as part of a **Letter** and then becoming part of a **Transaction** (at which time it must cease being part of the **Letter**). In fact, an **Autograph** need not be part of anything. Also, from this model fragment, we cannot preclude the possibility that **Autograph** is optionally part of some other class that is not shown on the diagram or that might be added later.

What if it is necessary to state that every **Autograph** must be part of either a **Letter** or a **Transaction**? Then the model can be reformulated, as in Figure 14-87. A new abstract superclass over **Letter** and **Transaction** can be added (**Document**) and the composition association with **Autograph** moved to it from the original classes. At the same time, the multiplicity from **Autograph** to **Document** is made one.

There is one minor problem with this approach: The multiplicity from **Document** to **Autograph** must be made optional, which weakens the original mandatory inclusion of **Autograph** within **Transaction**. The situation can be modeled using generalization of the composition association itself, as in Figure 14-89. The composition association between **Autograph** and **Transaction** is modeled as a child of the composition association between **Autograph** and **Document**. But its multiplicities are clarified for the child. (Note that they remain consistent with the inherited ones, so the child is substitutable for the parent.) This situation can be modeled using redefinition of the parent association by the child association. Alternately, the original model can be used by adding a constraint between the two compositions that one of them must always hold.

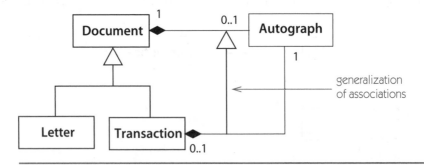

Figure 14-89. *Generalization of composition association*

compound transition

A transition represented by several segments connected by pseudostates.

Semantics

A compound transition is an implicit transition composed of several segments connected by join, junction, fork, or choice pseudostates. The transition must be executed in its entirety. It is not possible to execute some segments and leave one of the pseudostates active.

A compound transition may involve branches through junctions or choices. If none of the pseudostates are choice vertices, then all of the guard conditions on all possible paths through the segments are evaluated before the transition fires, and the transition fires only if at all of the conditions on at least one path evaluate true. Any actions performed during execution of the transition do not affect the guard conditions or alter the selected path. If no valid path exists at the time of evaluation, then the transition does not fire.

If some of the paths involve choice vertices, then the evaluation of guard conditions proceeds only as far as any choice vertices (or to target states on paths that have no choice vertices). If at least one such path evaluates true, a path is selected and the transition fires. Any actions on such paths are performed. When a choice vertex is encountered, the conditions on outgoing paths are reevaluated using the results of execution up to that point. An outgoing path for which all conditions evaluate true (up to any subsequent choice vertices) is selected and execution continues on the selected path, and so forth until a target state is encountered and the compound transition is complete.

If a choice vertex is encountered and no outgoing path evaluates true, the model is ill formed. A choice vertex may not remain active. A choice vertex is a guarantee by the modeler that at least one outgoing path will satisfy its guard conditions. If the guard conditions cannot easily be examined to ensure that they cover all possibilities, the use of an **else** condition on one outgoing path will guarantee that a valid choice always exists.

History

The choice vertex has been added in UML2.

concrete

A generalizable element (such as a class) that can be directly instantiated. Of necessity, its implementation must be fully specified. For a class, all its operations must be implemented (by the class or an ancestor). Antonym: abstract.

See also direct class, instantiation.

Semantics

Only concrete classifiers can be instantiated. Therefore, all the leaves of a generalization hierarchy must be concrete. In other words, all abstract operations and other abstract properties must eventually be implemented in some descendant. (Of course, an abstract class might have no concrete descendants if the program is incomplete, such as a framework intended for user extension, but such a class cannot be used in an implementation until concrete descendants are provided.)

Notation

The name of a concrete element appears in normal type. The name of an abstract element appears in italic type.

concurrency

The performance of two or more activities during the same time interval. There is no implication that the activities are synchronized. In general, they operate independently except for explicit synchronization points. Concurrency can be achieved by interleaving or simultaneously executing two or more threads.

See complex transition, composite state, thread.

Discussion

UML treats concurrency as a normal characteristic that is inherent in computation, unlike its second-hand status in many programming languages. Objects, messages, events, and executions are naturally concurrent. Actions and activities include the possibility of low-level concurrency among different threads of execution. There is no assumption of a universal clock—synchronization is accomplished by exchange of messages. In its treatment of concurrency, UML takes an Einsteinian view that is consistent with the distributed nature of modern computers, systems, and networks.

concurrency kind

Specification of the ability of an operation to accept simultaneous calls.

Semantics

The execution of each call to a passive operation is independent. Because operations may access shared resources in an object, however, there is sometimes a need to prevent multiple operations from executing concurrently. The concurrency property on an operation can have the following values:

concurrent   No restrictions on simultaneous invocation of op-
                  erations on the same object.

sequential   Simultaneous invocation of operations on the same
                  object may cause problems. The modeler is respon-
                  sible to ensure that simultaneous invocations do
                  not occur. If they do occur, the system is ill formed.

guarded   Simultaneous invocation of operations on the same
                  object may occur, but they are dynamically caught
                  and managed by the execution environment so that
                  only one invocation at a time may execute. When
                  an execution completes, a blocked invocation is al-
                  lowed to proceed, if one exists. There is no guaran-
                  tee that invocations will be executed in any
                  particular order (such as the order in which they
                  were called). The modeler is responsible to ensure
                  that deadlocks over shared resources do not cause
                  an invocation to wait indefinitely, preventing other
                  invocations on the same object from proceeding
                  (and potentially clearing the blockage).

Discussion

This property appears to be an Ada remnant that mixes logical concepts with implementation concerns, not entirely successfully. The specification is ambiguous
about whether it applies to multiple invocations of the same operation or to invocations of different operations on the same object. The choices do not cover all the
possibilities of a transaction-management system. There are no rollback provi-
sions, for example. To include full transaction processing would be beyond the
scope of a universal model such as UML, in any case. It would probably be better
for modelers to avoid this concept entirely and accomplish serialization using active objects, rather than hiding synchronization under a deceptively complicated
property.

concurrent substate

This UML1 term does not appear in UML2. Concurrency is now modeled using
orthogonal regions. See orthogonal region, orthogonal state.

conditional

One of the basic constructs of computation, a dynamic choice among several alternatives based on run-time values. Conditionals appear in each of the dynamic views in UML:

- In an interaction, a combined fragment within an interaction that involves a run-time choice among several alternatives. See conditional fragment.
- In an activity, a node that involves a run-time choice among several output arcs. See conditional node.
- In a state machine, a transition with a guard condition and no trigger. See conditional transition.

In each of the views, the basic concept of a conditional is the same, but there are differences in detailed specification.

conditional fragment

A combined fragment in an interaction that represents a dynamic choice among several operand subfragments. It is called *alternative* within the interaction specification.

Semantics

A conditional in an interaction is represented as a combined fragment with the keyword **alt**. A conditional has multiple operands, each a subfragment. Each operand has a guard condition. The absence of a guard implies a true condition. The condition **else** is true if no other guard evaluates true. Exactly one operand whose guard evaluates true is executed, unless no guard is true. If more than one operand evaluates true, the choice may be nondeterministic.

Notation

A conditional is shown as a rectangular region with the tag **alt** within a small pentagon on the upper left corner (Figure 14-90). The region is divided into subregions by horizontal dashed lines. Each subregion represents one operand of the conditional. A constraint representing a successful condition may be placed on the lifeline of the object whose values are being tested, at the top of the subregion. Usually the conditions for all the regions will be on the same lifeline. In lieu of a constraint, the pseudoconstraint [else] may be placed on the lifeline to indicate a branch that is taken if no constraint is true.

History

The conditional fragment notation based on MSC is a major improvement in power and clarity over the UML1 notation for branching in a sequence diagram.

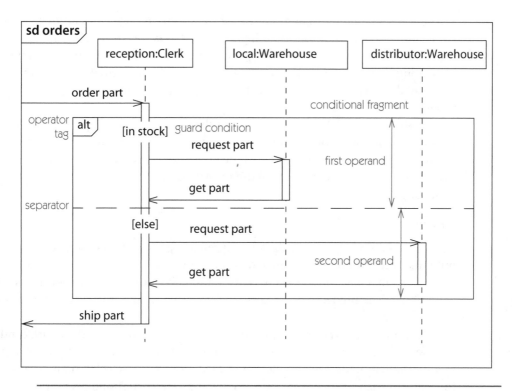

Figure 14-90. *Conditional (alt) fragment*

conditional node

A structured control node in an activity that represents a dynamic choice among several clauses.

Semantics

A conditional node is a control construct within an activity containing one or more clauses. Each clause has a test and a body section. When the condition node is executed, the test sections of the clauses are executed in an unspecified, possibly concurrent, order. If one or more test sections yield true values, the body section corresponding to one of the true test sections is executed. If more than one test section yields a true value, exactly one single body section is executed. The choice among multiple true tests is nondeterministic.

It is not guaranteed that all test sections will be executed before a choice is selected. It is possible that test sections will be executed concurrently and that some may be partially complete when a choice is made. Modelers should avoid tests that create side effects, otherwise there may be additional nondeterminacy resulting from the indeterminate execution order of tests.

The testing sequence may be controlled by specifying priorities among clauses. No clause will be tested unless all higher-priority clauses have tested false. There may be multiple clauses of the same priority, in which case indeterminacy is possible among them. If the clauses are totally ordered, the potential indeterminacy is eliminated. Note, however, that indeterminacy can sometimes be a useful thing to model.

Values created in a test may be used in the corresponding body section. Their use outside the conditional involves stringent restrictions and is discouraged.

An else clause is executed if none of the other clauses evaluate true. It is modeled as a clause with a true condition whose priority is lower than all other clauses.

See any trigger, else.

Structure

A conditional node has two subnodes representing the test and the body. An output pin of the test node is designated as the test result.

A clause may have predecessor clauses and successor clauses within the same conditional. The predecessor-successor relationship defines the evaluation priorities of the tests.

If the body of any clause has output pins, then each clause and the entire conditional itself must have an identical set of output pins (identical in number, type, and multiplicity). On the completion of execution of the selected body fragment, the value of each of its output pins is copied to the corresponding output pin of the entire conditional. The set of pins on each clause must match, otherwise some output pins of the conditional might lack values after execution of certain clauses.

The **assured** flag is an assertion by the modeler that at least one test will succeed. This is necessary if subsequent actions use the outputs of the conditional, for example.

The **determinate** flag is an assertion by the modeler that no more than one test will succeed concurrently. This may be used to assert deterministic behavior.

The **assured** and **determinate** flags are modeling assertions, not executable statements. They are useful when human intelligence exceeds the capability of theorem provers, but if incorrect they may lead to errors.

Notation

No notation is specified in the UML document. It is expected that structured activities will often use textual syntax in some action language.

For simple situations, a conditional can be represented by a decision node with several outcomes. This form does not capture the nested structure of a conditional fully, but it is satisfactory for simple situations.

For most complex situations, a variation on the conditional fragment notation might be used: Enclose the conditional in a rectangle with an **alt** tag, divide it into regions with dashed lines, and begin each region with a test expression in brackets, with the remainder of the region being an activity graph of the body. Although a test is also potentially shown as an activity graph, it becomes graphically messy to show both tests and bodies in graphical form.

conditional transition

The use of guards to choose among firing of multiple state machine transitions.

Semantics

A state machine transition includes a guard condition. When a trigger event for a transition occurs, the guard is evaluated. If it evaluates true, the transition may fire.

State machine transitions may be used to represent conditionals in the following ways:

- A set of transitions leaving a source state have completion events as their triggers and guard conditions that together cover all possibilities. When the source state becomes active and its entry or do activities are completed, one of the transitions will be chosen. This situation is very much like a traditional conditional construct in a programming language.

- A set of transitions leaving a source state all have the same trigger event and guard conditions that together cover all possibilities. When the trigger event occurs, one of the transitions will be chosen. This situation can also be modeled using junction states to avoid repeating the trigger. A segment from the source state to the junction state has the trigger event, and a set of transitions leaving the junction state have guard conditions but no triggers. In both cases, the guard conditions are evaluated after the event occurs but before a transition is selected.

- A transition segment goes from a source state to a choice pseudostate, and a set of transition segments leaves the choice pseudostate. Each of them has a guard condition but no trigger. In this case, an action on the initial transition segment may affect the values appearing in the guards. The guards are evaluated after the initial segment fires. One of them must evaluate true or the model is ill formed. The choice pseudostate is equivalent to an anonymous state followed by a set of completion transitions.

Notation

See notation for choice, guard condition, transition.

conflict

Most generally, a situation in which some potential ambiguity exists between different elements of a model. Depending on the case, there may be rules to resolve the conflict or the presence of the conflict may create an ill-formed model.

Semantics

Conflict is a situation of contradictory specifications, for example, when the same-named attribute or operation is inherited from more than one class, or when the same event enables more than one transition, or any similar situation in which the normal rules yield potentially contradictory results. Depending on the semantics for each kind of model element, a conflict may be resolved by a conflict resolution rule, it may be legal but yield a nondeterministic result, or it may indicate that the model is ill formed.

The following kinds of conflict may occur in UML:

• The same name is defined in multiple, different ways in the same namespace, often because of inheritance or imports.

For example, the same name may be used for elements in different levels of the same namespace or in different namespaces imported into a third namespace. This may be resolved by using qualified names. Duplicate names for the same kind of element defined in the same namespace are prohibited because there is no way to distinguish them.

Duplicate names among attributes in a classifier are prohibited and make the model ill formed. Duplication can occur through inheritance. Name duplication among operations does not cause a conflict if the signatures differ. If the signatures are the same, a method in a descendant class overrides a method in an ancestor class, but there are tight restrictions on any changes to the signature of operations in descendant classes.

• Actions that access the same shared resource (such as a variable or a device) may execute concurrently.

Concurrency brings with it the possibility of conflicting access to the same resources. If one concurrent thread can modify a resource and one or more others can read or modify it, the state of the read or the final state of the resource may be indeterminate. This is not necessarily a problem; sometimes indeterminacy is harmless or even desirable. If multiple modifications on a resource from different threads can interleave, the final state of the resource may even be inconsistent or totally meaningless. Access conflicts can be resolved in various ways: by ensuring that concurrent actions do not share resources; by isolating a set of actions on a resource to ensure that the final result is consistent, if not deterministic; by funneling all actions on a given resource through a single gatekeeper object; or by removing the concurrency. There are a number of elements in UML for performing the various resolutions. See concurrency kind, isolation flag.

• Inconsistent specifications apply to two related elements.

Two parts of the model may specify inconsistent things. Sometimes priority rules are given to resolve the conflict. For example, a substate may defer an event while a composite state consumes it. This conflict is resolved in accordance with priorities for triggering transitions. On the other hand, if conflicting constraints are specified for the same element (often through inheritance), the model is ill formed.

• Multiple choices are enabled.

The various conditional constructs allow multiple branches to be enabled concurrently. They also specify that only one branch will execute. If the conflict is not resolved by priority rules, the choice is nondeterministic. This is not a model error and may in fact model useful behavior. Similarly, multiple methods may be inherited for an operation. If all the methods are defined in classes that form a single path through the generalization hierarchy, the overriding rules resolve the conflict. If, however, two methods for the same operation are inherited from different ancestral paths, the methods are in conflict and the model is ill formed.

Discussion

It is possible to avoid conflicts by defining them away with conflict resolution rules, such as: If the same feature is defined by more than one superclass, use the definition found in the earlier superclass (this requires that the superclasses be ordered). UML does not generally specify rules for resolving conflict on the principle that it is dangerous to count on such rules. They are easy to overlook and frequently are the symptom of deeper problems with a model. It is better to force the modeler to be explicit rather than depend on subtle and possibly confusing rules. In a tool or programming language, such rules have their place, if only to make the meaning deterministic. But it would be helpful for the tools to provide warnings when rules are used so that the modeler is aware of the conflict.

connectable element

A kind of element that can be part of the implementation of a structured classifier and can be attached to a connector.

Semantics

This abstract metaclass includes attributes, parameters, parts, ports, and variables. Because it is so broadly defined, this metaclass does not really limit things very much.

A more intuitive definition is: A part may represent an instance or a value in the context of a structured class or collaboration. The part may be an inherent structural piece of the whole or it may represent a transient entity, such as a parameter or a value.

connection point

A reference to an entry point or exit point of a state machine, used with a reference to the state machine by a submachine state within another state machine.

Semantics

A state machine can be defined with the intent that it be referenced from other state machines as a kind of state machine subroutine. Such a reference is a submachine state. If the submachine is always entered through its initial state and always exits through its final state, no additional interfaces need be defined. Sometimes, however, a submachine has multiple entry points or exit points that must be made visible to state machines within which it is referenced. A entry point is an additional place at which a state machine may begin execution. An exit point is an additional place at which a state machine may terminate execution. Entry and exit points are pseudostates in the state machine.

A connection point is a reference to an entry point or an entry point of a state machine when the state machine is used within another state machine. When the state machine is referenced by a submachine state in another state machine, transitions may connect to named connection points on the submachine state that correspond to the connection points defined in the referenced state machine. Although connection points represent flow of control, they perform the same kind of parameterization as parameters and arguments in procedures.

See submachine state.

Notation

An entry point is shown as a small empty circle. An exit point is shown as a small circle with an 'X' inside. The name of the entry point or exit point is placed near the circle. The entry point or exit point is placed within the outer boundary of the state machine to which it applies. An entry point can appear wherever an initial state can appear, and an exit point can appear wherever a final state can appear.

A connection point is shown as a small empty circle or a small circle containing an 'X'; it is drawn on the border of the rounded box representing a submachine state (Figure 14-91). Within the rounded box is the name of the submachine state and a colon followed by the name of the referenced state machine. Transitions of the enclosing state machine may connect to the connection points (with an entry point as a target and an exit point as a source).

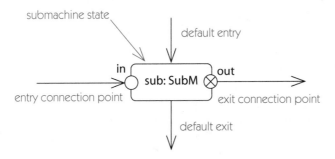

Figure 14-91. *Connection points*

An alternate notation eliminates the circles and shows the connection point by placing on the transition arrow a text label of the form:

(via connection-name)

As the circle notation is both clear and intuitive, the alternate notation is best avoided.

History

UML1 had a concept of stub states to show entries and exits to submachines. The new connection point notation is clearer and is parallel to a similar notation for parameters.

connector

The connection of two structured parts within a structured classifier or a collaboration; a specification of a contextual association that applies only in a certain context, such as the objects within a classifier or objects satisfying a collaboration.

See also association, collaboration, component, delegation connector, structured classifier.

Semantics

A connector is a contextual association that is meaningful and defined only in the context described by a structured classifier or a collaboration. It is a relationship that is part of the context but not an inherent relationship in other situations. Connectors are the key structural part of collaborations. They permit the descriptions of contextual relationships. They often represent communications paths among the parts of a structured classifier.

Within a classifier, a structured part denotes an individual appearance of another classifier, distinct from other appearances of that classifier and from the classifier declaration itself. Similarly, a connector represents an association that is used in a particular context, sometimes a restricted use of a normal association and sometimes another mechanism, such as a parameter or a local variable of a procedure. A connector connects two parts. When a structured class is instantiated, its parts and connectors are created as part of the instantiation.

To establish an instance of a collaboration, objects must be bound to roles (parts in the collaboration) and links must be bound to the connectors. The links are often created as part of the instantiation of the collaboration. In many cases, the links among objects define a collaboration. One object can play (be bound to) more than one role.

A connector connects two or more parts within a structured classifier or roles within a collaboration (Figure 14-92). It may include a reference to an association that specifies the links that implement the connector. If the connector is to be implemented by other mechanisms, such as parameters, local variables, global values, or implicit relationships between the parts of a single object, the association is omitted.

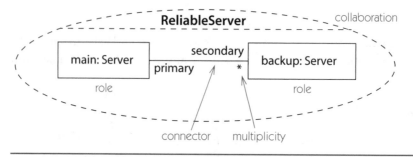

Figure 14-92. *Connector in a collaboration*

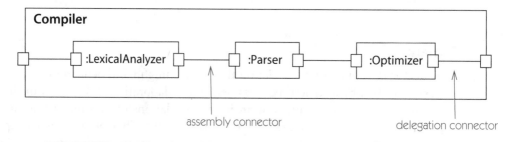

Figure 14-93. *Connectors in a structured class*

One or both ends of a connector may be connected to ports on internal parts (Figure 14-93). A connector between two internal ports is an assembly connector. The ports must be of complementary types. A message sent on one port is received on the other. One end of a connector may be connected to an external port of the structured classifier. A connector between an external port and an internal port is a delegation connector. The ports must be of the same type. A message received on the external port is received by the internal port; a message sent on the internal port is sent on the external port.

A connector has a multiplicity on each end indicating how many objects may be connected to a single object (including any ordering or uniqueness constraints). If a connector is connected to a port and no multiplicity is specified, the multiplicity of the connector is the same as the multiplicity of the port.

In some cases, a connector can be regarded as uses of a general association between the participating classes. In that case, the collaboration shows one way of using the general association for a particular purpose within the collaboration.

In other cases, the connections among parts or roles have no validity outside the context of the structured classifier or collaboration. If a connector has no explicit association, then it defines an implicit ("transient") association valid only within the collaboration.

Notation

A connector is displayed in the same way as an association—namely, as a solid line between two part or role symbols (Figure 14-92 and Figure 14-93). The fact that it is a connector is clear because it involves parts or roles. It may have a label with the syntax:

```
connector-name :Association-name
```

The association name (including colon) may be omitted if there is no underlying association, that is, if the connector represents a transient contextual relationship.

An end name and a multiplicity may be placed on an end of a connector.

History

In UML1, contextual relationships had to be modeled as either associations or links, neither of which was correct in most cases. There was a idea that an aggregation could own both classes and associations, but that idea was not worked out correctly. The UML2 concept of a context as the internal structure of a classifier models contextual relationships explicitly.

consider

A combined fragment in an interaction that filters messages so that only those of specified message types are shown.

Semantics

A consider construct has a list of message types and a subfragment, which is an interaction fragment. Within the subfragment, only messages whose types appear in the list are represented. This indicates that messages of other types may occur but they are not represented in the interaction, which is therefore an abstraction of the actual system. This construct is often combined with assertion to indicate that a certain message must follow another message.

Notation

A consider construct is shown in a sequence diagram as a region with the keyword **consider** followed by a list of message names.

Figure 14-94 shows a consider construct containing an assertion. It states that only start or stop messages will be considered. The assertion therefore applies to only start or stop messages. It essentially means that a start message must be followed by a stop message and not another start message, but that messages of any other type can occur because they are ignored by the assertion.

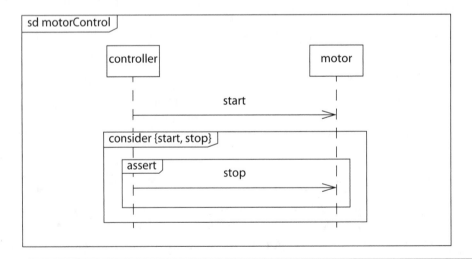

Figure 14-94. *Consider combined fragment*

constraint

A semantic condition or restriction represented as text in natural language or a specified formal language.

Semantics

A constraint is a semantic condition or restriction expressed as a linguistic statement in some textual language.

In general, a constraint can be attached to any model element or list of model elements. It represents semantic information attached to a model element, not just to a view of it. Each constraint has a body and a language of interpretation. The body is a string encoding a Boolean expression for the condition in the constraint language. A constraint applies to an ordered list of one or more model elements. Note that the specification language may be a formal language or it may be a natural language. In the latter case, the constraint will be informal and not subject to automatic enforcement (which is not to say that automatic enforcement is always practical for all formal languages). UML provides the constraint language OCL [Warmer-99], but other languages can also be used.

Some common constraints have names to avoid writing a full statement each time they are needed. For example, the constraint **xor** between two associations that share a common class means that a single object of the shared class may belong to only one of the associations at one time.

A constraint is an assertion, not an executable mechanism. It indicates a restriction that must be enforced by correct design of the system. How to guarantee a constraint is a design decision.

Run-time constraints are meant to be evaluated at moments when an instantiated system is "stable"—that is, between the execution of operations and not in the middle of any atomic transactions. During the execution of an operation, there may be moments when the constraints are temporarily violated. Since models may have several levels of granularity, invariants—that is, constraints that are always true—always have some amount of informality. By contrast, preconditions and postconditions are constraints that are evaluated at well-determined times, at the invocation of an operation and at its completion, so they are not subject to concerns about partially completed changes.

A constraint cannot be applied to itself.

An inherited constraint—a constraint on an ancestor model element or on a stereotype—must be observed even though additional constraints are defined on descendants. An inherited constraint may not be set aside or superseded. Such a model is poorly constructed and must be reformulated. An inherited constraint can be tightened, however, by adding additional restrictions. If constraints inherited by an element conflict, then the model is ill formed.

Notation

A constraint is shown as a text string enclosed in braces ({ }). The text string is the encoded body written in a constraint language. If a constraint has a name, the name is shown as a string followed by a colon, all preceding the constraint text.

Tools are expected to provide one or more languages in which formal constraints may be written. One predefined language for writing constraints is OCL. Depending on the model, a computer language such as C++ may be useful for some constraints. Otherwise, the constraint may be written in natural language, with interpretation and enforcement remaining human responsibilities. The language of each constraint is part of the constraint itself, although the language is not generally displayed on the diagram (the tool keeps track of it).

For a list of elements represented by text strings in a compartment (such as the attributes within a class): A constraint string may appear as an entry in the list (Figure 14-95). The entry does not represent a model element. It is a *running constraint* that applies to all succeeding elements of the list until another constraint list element or the end of the list. The running constraint may be replaced by another running constraint later in the list. To clear the running constraint, replace it by an empty constraint. A constraint attached to an individual list element does not replace the running constraint but may augment it with additional restrictions.

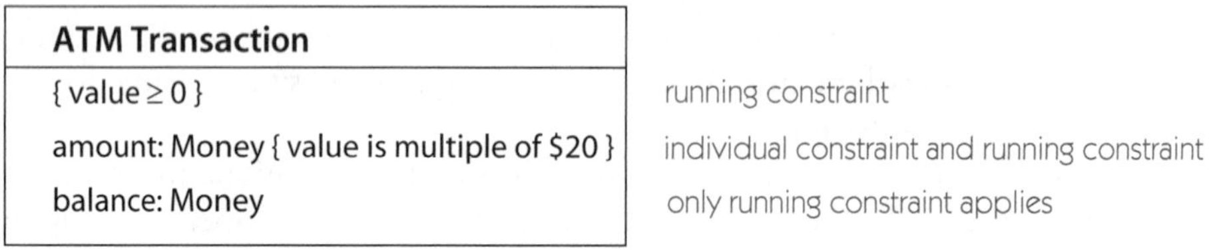

ATM Transaction	
{ value ≥ 0 }	running constraint
amount: Money { value is multiple of $20 }	individual constraint and running constraint
balance: Money	only running constraint applies

Figure 14-95. *Constraints within lists*

For a single graphical symbol (such as a class or an association path): The constraint string may be placed near the symbol, preferably near the name of the symbol, if any.

For two graphical symbols (such as two classes or two associations): The constraint is shown as a dashed arrow from one element to the other element labeled by the constraint string (in braces). The direction of the arrow is relevant information within the constraint (Figure 14-96).

For three or more graphical symbols: The constraint string is placed in a note symbol and attached to each symbol by a dashed line (Figure 14-96). This notation may also be used for the other cases. For three or more paths of the same kind (such as generalization paths or association paths), the constraint may be attached

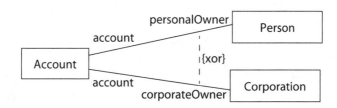

binary constraint: attached to dashed arrow

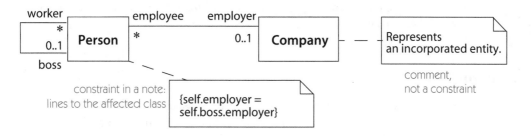

Figure 14-96. *Constraint notation*

to a dashed line crossing all the paths. In case of ambiguity, the various lines may be numbered or labeled to establish their correspondence to the constraint.

The language of a constraint is usually not shown. It may be shown by placing the name of the language inside braces, all within the braces for the constraint itself and preceding the body of the constraint.

Discussion

A constraint makes a semantic statement about the model itself, whereas a comment is a text statement without semantic force and may be attached to either a model element or a presentation element. Both constraints and comments may be displayed using notes. In principle, constraints are enforceable by tools. In practice, some may be difficult to state formally and may require human enforcement. In the broad sense of the word, many elements in a model are constraints, but the word is used to indicate semantic statements that are difficult to express using the built-in model elements and that must be stated linguistically.

Constraints may be expressed in any suitable language or even in human language, although a human-language constraint cannot be verified by a tool. The OCL language [Warmer-99] is designed for specifying UML constraints, but under some circumstances a programming language may be more appropriate.

Because constraints are expressed as text strings, a generic modeling tool can enter and maintain them without understanding their meaning. Of course, a tool or an add-in that verifies or enforces the constraint must understand the syntax and semantics of the target language.

A list of constraints can be attached to the definition of a stereotype. This indicates that all elements bearing the stereotype are subject to the constraint.

Enforcement. When the model contains constraints, it does not necessarily tell what to do if they are violated. A model is a declaration of what is supposed to happen. It is the job of the implementation to make it happen. A program might well contain assertions and other validation mechanisms, but a failure of a constraint must be considered a programming failure. Of course, if a model can help to produce a program that is correct by construction or can be verified as correct, then it has served its purpose.

construction

The third phase of a software development process, during which the detailed design is made and the system is implemented and tested in software, firmware, and hardware. During this phase, the analysis view and the design view are substantially completed, together with most of the implementation view and some of the deployment view.

See development process.

constructor

An operation that creates and initializes an instance of a class. May be used as an operation stereotype.

See creation, instantiation.

container

An object that exists to contain other objects, and which provides operations to access or iterate over its contents, or a class describing such objects. For example, arrays, lists, and sets.

See also aggregation, composition.

Discussion

It is usually unnecessary to model containers explicitly. They are most often the implementation for the "many" end of an association. In most models, a multiplicity greater than one is enough to indicate the correct semantics. When a design model is used to generate code, the container class used to implement the association can be specified for a code generator using tagged values.

context

A view of a set of modeling elements that are related for a purpose, such as to execute an operation or form a pattern. A context is a piece of a model that constrains or provides the environment for its elements. A collaboration provides a context for its contents.

As a specific term in the metamodel, the word is used for:

- The namespace in which a constraint is evaluated.

- The classifier that directly owns a behavior or that indirectly owns an action within the behavior.

See structured classifier.

continuation

A label in an interaction that allows conditionals to be broken into two pieces and semantically combined.

Semantics

A continuation is a label that may appear as the final element in an operand of a conditional fragment in a sequence diagram. The same label may appear as the first element of an operand of a different conditional fragment. Intuitively, if control reaches the label at the end of the region in the first conditional, it may resume at the corresponding label at the beginning of the region in the second conditional.

The labels in the two conditionals effectively connect the two conditionals into a single virtual conditional. The construct is useful if one of the conditionals is embedded in a referenced subdiagram and therefore cannot be combined with the second conditional.

Notation

A continuation is shown as the same symbol as a state, that is, a rectangle with rounded corners containing the name of the continuation. A pair of corresponding continuations must cover the same set of lifelines.

Example

Figure 14-97 shows matching continuations at the end and beginning of conditionals. Figure 14-98 expands the example to show an equivalent model that has the same meaning.

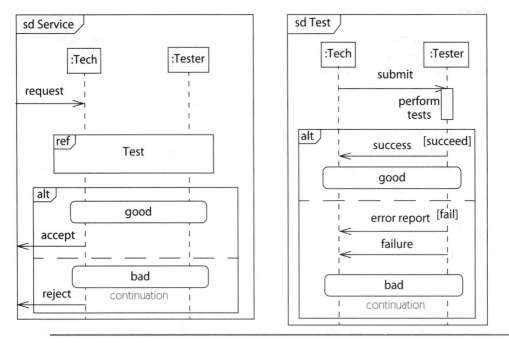

Figure 14-97. *Continuations*

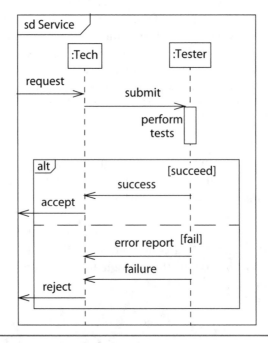

Figure 14-98. *Interpretation of continuations*

control flow

A sequencing constraint on the execution of activity nodes.
See also data flow.

Semantics

An activity is a graph of activity nodes and activity edge. An activity node is a basic action, an object node, a control node, or a higher-level grouping of nodes. An activity edge is a relationship that governs the flow of data and control between two nodes. A node may have input and output edges. A node may begin execution only when all the prerequisites specified by its input edges are satisfied.

A control flow is an edge that specifies flow of control rather than data. If a node has an input control flow, it may begin execution only after the node at the other end of the edge has completed execution. (Certain kinds of control nodes may begin execution when a designated subset of nodes has tokens.) The control flow is an outgoing edge of the other node. In other words, when a node completes execution, a control token is placed on each of its output control flows. If control flow serves as an input edge of another node, the node becomes enabled after all of its input edges contain tokens. If a node has several input edges, the node synchronizes execution of all of its input threads. Some kinds control nodes execute when a subset of their input edges contain tokens; the enabling rules are described for each kind of control node.

A control flow may be regarded as a degenerate data flow edge without any data, so the sequencing rules can be expressed in terms of tokens on edges.

Notation

Control flow in an activity diagram is shown as a solid arrow from one node to another. The control flow is an output of the node at the tail of the arrow and an input of the node at the arrowhead.

Example

In Figure 14-99, **receive order** has two output control flows. When it completes, **ship order** and **bill customer** become enabled because they each have a single input control flow. These activities may execute concurrently. When both of them complete, **send confirmation** becomes enabled.

History

Control flow and data flow have been added as part of the greatly expanded activity model of UML2.

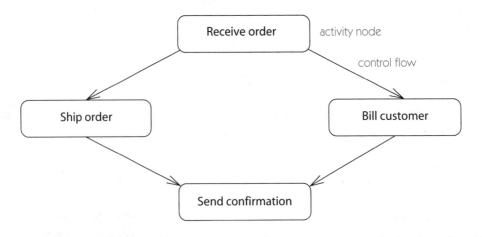

Figure 14-99. *Control flows*

control node

A activity node in an activity whose purpose is to coordinate control flows and object flows among other nodes; a specific flow-of-control construct.

See also activity.

Semantics

In an activity, simple flow of control from one node to another is modeled using control flow edges and data flow edges. An action begins execution when it receives tokens on all its input edges; when it completes execution, it produces tokens on all its output edges. More complex forms of control are modeled using control nodes, some of which do not require or produce tokens on all of their edges. Control nodes model decisions, concurrent forks, and starting and stopping an activity. Structured conditionals and loops are modeled using structured activity nodes. (These are not called control nodes in the UML2 metamodel, but they also model complex flow of control).

Kinds of control nodes

The following are the kinds of activity nodes that model complex control:

Decision. A decision node has one input edge and multiple output edges. Usually the output edges have guards. When the input edge is enabled, an output edge whose guard is true is enabled. Only one output is enabled even if more than one guard is satisfied. For convenience, one output of the decision may be labeled with the keyword **else**. This flow is taken if no other guard is satisfied. If no guard is true, the model is ill formed.

Usually a decision is paired with a subsequent merge (to form a conditional) or a previous merge (to form a loop), although decisions and merges may be used to form patterns of control that are not possible using fully nested control structures. Care should be taken, however, to avoid meaningless configurations.

A decision is notated as a diamond with one input arrow and two or more output arrows. Each output is labeled with a guard condition (Figure 14-100).

Merge. A merge is a place at which two or more alternate paths of control come together. It is the inverse of a decision. When any input edge is enabled, the output edge becomes enabled.

A diamond is the symbol for either a decision or merge. It is a decision if there are multiple output arrows; it is a merge if there are multiple input arrows (Figure 14-100).

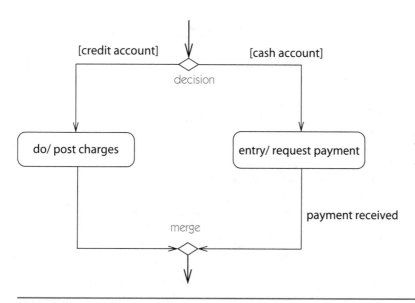

Figure 14-100. *Decision and merge*

Fork. A fork node has one input edge and multiple output edges. When the input edge is enabled, all of the output edges become enabled. In other words, a fork increase the amount of concurrent activity.

Usually a fork is paired with a subsequent join node so that the amount of concurrency eventually balances, but more complicated situations are possible and useful. Care should be taken, however, to avoid meaningless situations in which excess activity tokens are created and not properly joined.

A fork is shown as a heavy line with one input arrow and two or more output arrows (Figure 14-101).

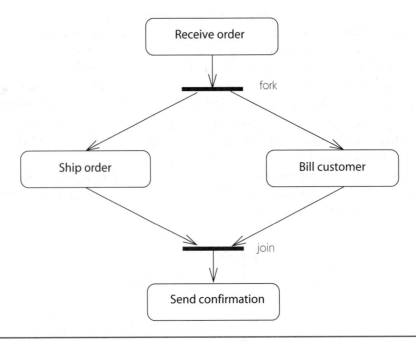

Figure 14-101. *Fork and join*

Join. A join node has two or more input edges and one output edge. When all of the input edges are enabled, the output edge becomes enabled. In other words, a join decreases the amount of concurrency.

A join is shown as a heavy line with two or more input arrows and one output arrow (Figure 14-101).

A join and a fork can be combined by drawing a heavy line with multiple input arrows and multiple output arrows.

Forks and joins are not necessary in simpler situations, because multiple edges leaving or entering a node are equivalent to a fork or a join, but using them makes the concurrency obvious. (Also note that the convention on multiple edges to a node has changed since UML1, therefore showing explicit forks/joins and decisions/merge avoids any danger of misunderstanding.)

Initial. An initial node has no input edge and one output edge. An initial node represents the default starting point for a transition to the containing activity. When the activity is invoked, the output of the initial node becomes enabled.

An initial node is shown as a small filled circle with an arrow leaving it (Figure 14-102).

Activity final. An activity final node has one or more input edges and no output edge. If any of the input edges are enabled, the execution of the enclosing activity is terminated and any active nodes or flows are aborted. Any outputs produced by

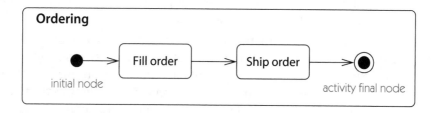

Figure 14-102. *Initial and activity final nodes*

the activity are organized into a return packet. If the activity was invoked by a synchronous call, a return message is transmitted to the caller with any output values.

It is possible to have multiple activity final nodes. The first one enabled terminates all activity.

An activity final is shown as a small hollow circle containing a smaller filled circle (a bull's eye or target symbol) with arrows entering it (Figure 14-102).

Flow final. A flow final node has one or more input edges and no output edge. If any of the input edges are enabled, their tokens are consumed. This provides a way to eliminate activity on the exit of a stand-alone loop. However, in most cases it is cleaner to explicitly join the tokens into another node, so this construct should be used carefully if at all.

A flow final is shown as a small hollow circle with a small X crossing the circle. It has one or more arrows entering it (Figure 14-103).

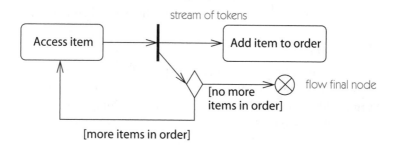

Figure 14-103. *Flow final node*

Conditional. A conditional node is a structured control construct with one or more input edges, one or more output edges, and two or more embedded clauses, which are subordinate activity fragments. When all the input edges are enabled, the tests of the clauses are evaluated and exactly one clause is selected for execution. When the clause completes execution, its output values become the output values of the conditional itself, and the output edges of the conditional become enabled. For full details, see conditional node.

Loop. A loop node is a structured control construct with one or more input edges, one or more output edges, and three embedded activity fragments, one each for setup, testing, and loop body. When all the input edges are enabled, the setup part is executed, then the body part is executed repeatedly as long as the test part yields a true output value. When the test is false, the output values from the body become the output values of the loop itself, and the output edges of the conditional become enabled. See loop node for full details.

Other constructs. In addition to the preceding, some other constructs that are not considered control nodes perform functions that have control aspects.

See exception handler, expansion region, interruptible activity region.

copy

The copy stereotype from UML1 has been retired.

coregion

A notational convenience in which an area of a lifeline may be bracketed to indicate that the order of events in that area is unconstrained.

Semantics

A coregion is equivalent to a parallel construct in which each event on a lifeline belongs to a separate concurrent region of the parallel construct.

Notation

A coregion is indicated by a matched pair of square brackets on a lifeline, with the coregion being the section of the lifeline between the concave sides of the brackets. Events within the bracketed region may occur in any order, even though they are ordered along the line itself

Example

Figure 14-104 shows a referee and two players. The referee notifies both players to get ready. Each player must acknowledge with a ready message. It does not matter which order the messages are received by the referee. Both messages must be received before proceeding. Therefore, the receipt of the ready messages is placed within a coregion. After both messages are received, the referee instructs the players to go.

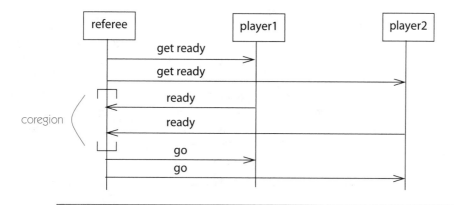

Figure 14-104. *Coregion*

create (stereotype of BehavioralFeature)

A behavioral feature that creates an instance of the classifier containing the feature.
See creation, usage.

create (stereotype of Usage Dependency)

A dependency denoting that the client classifier creates instances of the supplier
classifier.
See creation, usage.

create action

An action whose execution creates a new object of a given type. The properties of
the object are not initialized by the action.
See action.

creation

The instantiation and initialization of an object or other instance (such as a use
case instance). Antonym: destruction.
See also instantiation.

Semantics

Creation of an object is the result of an action that instantiates the object. Creation
may be modeled at different levels: a raw creation action or a higher-level operation that invokes the action and then initializes the new object. A creation operation may have parameters that are used for initialization of the new instance. At

the conclusion of the creation operation, the new object obeys the constraints of its class and may receive messages.

A creation operation, or constructor, may be declared as a class-scope operation. The target of such an operation is (conceptually, at least) the class itself. In a programming language such as Smalltalk, a class is implemented as an actual run-time object and creation is therefore implemented as a normal message to such an object. In a language such as C++, there is no actual run-time object. The operation may be thought of as a conceptual message that has been optimized away at run time. The C++ approach precludes the opportunity to compute the class to be instantiated. Otherwise, each approach can be modeled as a message sent to a class. (This assumes that a class can be treated as an object, which is a semantic variation point.)

The initial value expressions for the attributes of a class are (conceptually) evaluated at creation, and the results are used to initialize the attributes. The object creation action does not explicitly evaluate the expressions, but some UML profiles automatically invoke them on creation. The code for a creation operation can explicitly replace these values, so initial value expressions should be regarded as overridable defaults.

Creation may be treated at two levels: the creation of a raw object with the correct type and property slots but without initialization of values, and the creation of a fully formed object that satisfies all constraints. The former may be modeled by a create action. The latter may be modeled with an operation that includes a create action as well as actions to initialize the property values of the object. Although both levels could be included in a model, most models will probably use one level or the other.

Within a state machine, the parameters of the creation operation that created an object are available as an implicit current event on the transition leaving the top-level initial state.

Notation

In a class diagram, a creation operation (constructor) declaration is included as one of the operations in the operation list of the class. It may have a parameter list, but the return value is implicitly an instance of the class and may be omitted. As a class-scope operation, its name string must be underlined (Figure 14-105). If an instance-scope operation of a class creates an instance of another class, its name string is not underlined.

A prototype of the created instance may be shown as an object symbol (rectangle with underlined name). A dashed arrow with open arrowhead goes from the object symbol to the creation operation. The arrow has the stereotype «create».

A creation operation execution within a sequence diagram is shown by drawing a message arrow, with its open arrowhead on a lifeline top rectangle. Below the

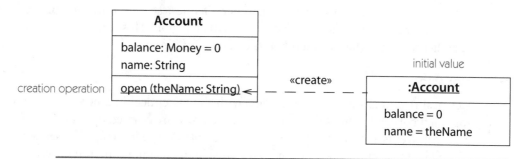

Figure 14-105. *Creation operation*

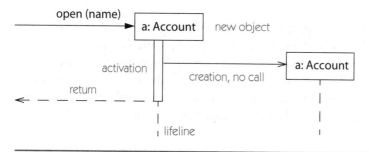

Figure 14-106. *Creation sequence diagram*

rectangle is the lifeline for the object (dashed line or double solid line, depending on whether it is active), which continues until the destruction of the object or the end of the diagram. If a synchronous call creates an object and then transfers control to it, however, a filled arrowhead is used (Figure 14-106).

See also communication diagram and sequence diagram for notation to show creation within the implementation of a procedure.

critical

Keyword for a critical region construct.

critical region

A combined fragment in an interaction whose events may not be interleaved with events from concurrent regions.

Semantics

A critical region has one subfragment. A sequence of events on a single lifeline in the critical region must not be interleaved with any other events in other regions.

There is no constraint on events on other lifelines, so this does not preclude concurrent activity that does not affect the critical region. This construct overrides a parallel construct that would otherwise permit interleaving.

Notation

A critical region is shown as a rectangle with the tag **critical** in a pentagon in the upper left corner. Lifelines that traverse the rectangle are covered by the critical region. All events within the rectangle are part of the noninterruptible sequence defined by the region. Events on lifelines outside the rectangle are not covered by the region, therefore their order is not constrained by the critical region.

Example

Figure 14-107 shows part of a DVD player sequence diagram (with much detail omitted). In the main loop, the player repeatedly displays frames. At any time (because it is within a parallel construct), the user can send a pause message to the player. After the user sends a pause message, the user sends a resume message. Because the pause-resume sequence is within a critical region, no display frame messages may intervene. The player therefore stops displaying frames until the resume message occurs.

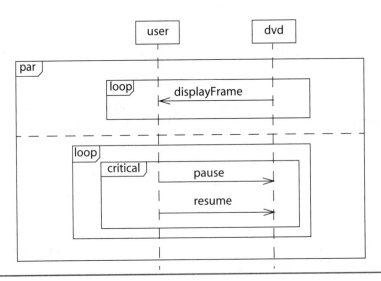

Figure 14-107. *Critical region*

current event

The event that triggered a run-to-completion step in the execution of a state machine.

See also run-to-completion, state machine, transition.

Semantics

A state machine may traverse several connected transition segments in response to an event. All but the final transition segment go to pseudostates—that is, dummy states whose purpose is to help structure the state machine, but which do not wait for outside events. In principle, all the segments could be gathered into one transition, but the separation into multiple segments using pseudostates permits common subsequences to be shared among multiple transitions.

The execution of a chain of transition segments is part of a single run-to-completion step that may not be interrupted by an outside event. During the execution of such a chain of transitions, actions and guard conditions attached to segments have implicit access to the event that triggered the first segment and to the parameters of that event. This event is known as the current event during a transition.

The current event is particularly useful for the initial transition of a new object to obtain the creation parameters. When a new object is created, the event creating it becomes the current event and its parameters are available during the initial transition of the new object's state machine.

Notation

Parameters of the current event may use the format:

    event-name . attribute name

Example

Figure 14-108 shows a transition from the Idle state to the Purchase state triggered by the request event. The entry action of Purchase calls the setup operation, which uses the product parameter of the current event.

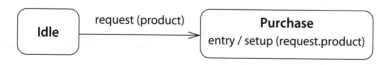

Figure 14-108. *Use of current event*

data flow

A relationship in an activity between activity nodes that supply and consume data values and, implicitly, the control sequencing constraint implied by the relationship.

Semantics

An activity is a graph of activity nodes and activity edges. An activity node is a basic action or a higher-level group of actions. An activity edge is a relationship that governs the flow of data and control between two nodes. A node may have input and output edges. An node may begin execution only when all the prerequisites specified by its input edges are satisfied, including the presence of all required data values and all required control tokens. Actions require tokens on all input edges. Some kinds of control nodes require inputs on a designated subset of input edges.

A object flow edge specifies the flow of data rather than just control. If a node has an input object flow edge, the data value is an input parameter of the node. The node may begin execution only after a data value has been produced by the node at the supplier end of the edge. The object flow edge is an outgoing edge of the other node. In other words, when a node completes execution, a data token is placed on each of its output object flow edges. If a successor node uses the object flow edge as an input parameter, the node becomes enabled after data values are available on all of its input object flow edges and control tokens are available on all of its input control flow edges (with the exception of certain kinds of control nodes that explicitly join flow of control from one of several inputs).

Data values on edges are individual copies that are not shared or stored in a central repository. Values may include references to objects, but in that case the object is separate from the value and not part of the data token. A target of an object flow edge uses the value by consuming it.

Data flow implies control flow, because a node may not execute until all of its data input values are available. A control flow may be regarded as a degenerate object flow edge without any data, so the sequencing rules can be expressed in terms of tokens on edges.

Notation

Data flow is shown by a solid arrow with a stick arrowhead between pins on activity nodes. Alternately, it may also shown by an object node symbol (rectangle) between two activity nodes, with a solid arrow from the source node to the object node and another solid arrow from the object node to the target node. See Figure 14-109.

See object flow, object node, and pin for notation and examples.

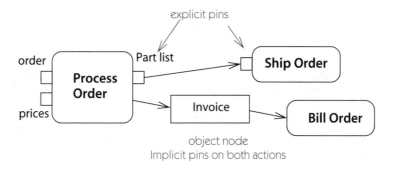

Figure 14-109. *Data flows*

History

Control flow and data flow have been added as part of the greatly expanded activity model of UML2.

data store node

A central buffer node for persistent information.

Semantics

A data store node is an object node that can accept input values from various sources and can send output values to various destinations. Usually the input flows and the output flows are disconnected. In other words, a value is deposited in the data store by one thread of control and removed later by a different thread of control. In a data store, the persistence of the data may exceed the life of the thread that created the data. If the containing activity terminates or executes an activity final node, the tokens in the data store are destroyed.

Notation

A data store node is shown as a rectangle containing the keyword «datastore» above the name of the data store. Data store instance nodes may also be shown by underlying the name string of the node.

Example

Figure 14-110 shows a bank account that accepts deposits and withdrawals. The two actions occur independently in different threads of control in the same activity. They need not correspond.

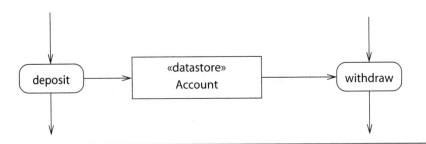

Figure 14-110. *Data store node*

data type

A descriptor of a set of values that lack identity (independent existence and the possibility of side effects). Data types include primitive predefined types and user-definable types. Primitive types include numbers, strings, and Boolean values. User-definable types are enumerations. Anonymous data types intended for implementation in a programming language may be defined using language types within profiles.

See also classifier, identity.

Semantics

Data types are the predefined primitives needed as the foundation of user-definable types. Their semantics are mathematically defined outside the type-building mechanisms in a language. Numbers are predefined. They include integers and reals. Strings are also predefined. These data types are not user-definable.

Enumeration types are user-definable finite sets of named elements that have a defined ordering among themselves but no other computational properties. An enumeration type has a name and a list of enumeration constants. The enumeration type **Boolean** is predefined with the enumeration literals **false** and **true**.

Operations may be defined on data types, and operations may have data types as parameters. Because a data type has no identity and is just a pure value, operations on data types do not modify them; instead, they just return values. It makes no sense to talk of creating a new data type value, because they lack identity. All data type values are (conceptually) predefined. An operation on a data type is a query that may not change the state of the system but may return a value.

A data type may also be described by a language type—a data type expression in a programming language. Such an expression designates an anonymous data type in a target programming language. For example, the expression **Person* (*) (String)** denotes a type expression in C++ that does not correspond to a simple data type with a name. Language types are not defined in the UML specification, but they would have to be added by a profile for a particular language.

data value

An instance of a data type, a value without identity.
See also data type, object.

Semantics

A data value is a member of a mathematical domain—a pure value. Two data values with the same representation are indistinguishable; data values have no identity. Data values are passed by value in a programming language. It makes no sense to pass them by reference. It is meaningless to talk about changing a data value; its value is fixed permanently. In fact, it *is* its value. Usually, when one talks of changing a data value, one means changing a variable that holds a data value so that it holds a new data value. But data values themselves are invariable.

decision

A control node in an activity. See decision node.

decision node

A control node in an activity that passes control and data to one of several outputs.
See also branch, merge.

Semantics

A decision node has one input and two or more outputs. The input value is used to evaluate guard conditions on each of the outputs. If a guard condition evaluates true, the corresponding output is eligible for selection. Exactly one eligible output is chosen to receive a copy of the input value. If more than one guard condition evaluates true, the choice of output is nondeterministic. If no guard condition is true, the model is ill formed.

One of the guard conditions may have the special condition **else**. An output with an else condition is selected if no other condition is true.

A decision input behavior may be attached to the node. This behavior has one input and one output. The input must be the same type as the input of the decision node. When the decision node receives a value, the decision input behavior is invoked with the input value of the decision node as its argument. The output value of the behavior may be referenced in guard conditions on the outputs of the decision node. The behavior may be invoked multiple times, therefore it must not have any side effects.

Notation

A decision node is shown as a diamond with one input arrow and two or more output arrows. Usually most of the output arrows have guard conditions in square brackets. The special guard condition [else] may be placed on one output arrow.

A decision input behavior is shown as a note symbol (dog-eared rectangle) with the keyword «decisionInput» above a string for the expression for the behavior.

Example

Figure 14-111 shows a decision node operating on the output of a previous activity. Figure 14-112 shows the same example using a decision input expression to avoid repeating a calculation in each branch.

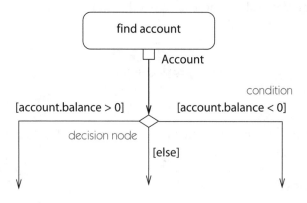

Figure 14-111. *Decision node*

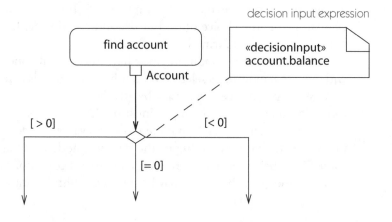

Figure 14-112. *Decision node with decision input expression*

default value

A value supplied automatically for a parameter if no argument value is provided. See parameter.

Also used (somewhat misleadingly) to mean an initial value for an attribute of a newly created object. See initial value.

See also unspecified value.

Notation

A default value for an operation or an attribute is specified by placing an equal sign (=) followed by an expression string after the specification for the element. For example:

makeRectangle (center: Point, width: Real, height: Real, angle: Real = 0)

deferrable event

An event whose recognition may be deferred while a state is active.
See deferred event.

deferred event

An event whose occurrence has been deferred because it has been declared to be a deferrable event in the active state. See also state machine, transition.

Semantics

A state may designate a set of events as *deferrable*. If an event occurs while an object is in a state for which the event is deferrable and the event does not trigger a transition, the event is deferred: The event has no immediate effect; it is saved until the object enters a state in which the given event is not deferred. If other events occur while the state is active, they are handled in the usual way. When the object enters a new state, deferred events that are no longer deferrable then occur one at a time and may trigger transitions in the new state (the order of occurrence of previously deferred events is indeterminate, and it is risky to depend on a particular order of occurrence). If no transition in the undeferrable state is triggered by an event, it is ignored and lost.

Deferrable events should be used with care in ordinary state machines. They can often be modeled more directly by a concurrent state that responds to them while the main computation is doing something else. They can be useful to allow computations to be sequentialized without losing asynchronous messages.

If a state has a transition triggered by a deferrable event, then the transition overrides the deferral and the event triggers the transition, notwithstanding the deferrable specification.

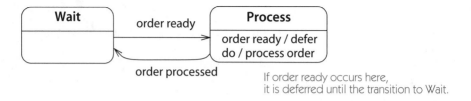

Figure 14-113. *Deferrable event*

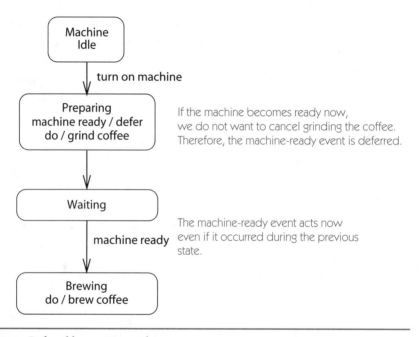

Figure 14-114. *Deferrable event example*

Notation

A deferrable event is indicated by an internal transition on the event with the reserved word **defer** in place of the action. The deferral applies to the state and its nested substates (Figure 14-113).

Figure 14-114 shows steps in making a pot of coffee. The sequence starts when the machine is turned on. The coffee drinker has to grind the coffee and wait for the machine to heat up before brewing the coffee. These might complete in either order. In this model, we treat grinding the coffee as a do activity. In case the machine is ready before the coffee has been ground, the **machine ready** event is deferred in the **Preparing** state. Otherwise the coffee grinding would be interrupted by the **machine ready** event. When grinding is complete, the do activity terminates and the completion transition takes the system to the **Waiting** state. After grinding the coffee, it is necessary to wait until the machine is ready. If the **machine ready** event has already occurred during the previous state, it will trigger the **machine ready** transition immediately when the **Waiting** state is entered, otherwise the system will remain in the **Waiting** state until the event occurs.

A deferrable event is a way to model a necessary event that might arrive before or after another necessary event.

delegation

The ability of an object to issue a message to another object in response to a message. Delegation can be used as an alternative to inheritance. In some languages (such as *self*), it is supported by inheritance mechanisms in the language itself. In most other languages, such as C++ and Smalltalk, it can be implemented with an association or aggregation to another object. An operation on the first object invokes an operation on the second object to accomplish its work. Contrast: inheritance.

Although most models assume a traditional view of inheritance, the UML resolution mechanism that determines the effect of invoking an operation is written in a general way so that behavior such as delegation can be used if desired. The inclusion of delegation in UML would therefore be a semantic variation point.

See also delegation connector.

delegation connector

A connector between an external port of a structured classifier or component and an internal part. Connections to the external port are treated as going to the element at the other end of the delegation connector.

Semantics

A delegation connector connects an external port of a component with a port on one of its internal subcomponents. A message from an external source received by the external port is passed to the port on the internal component; a message from an internal source received by an internal port is passed to the external port and thence to the component connected to it. Delegation connectors permit the implementation of high-level operations by low-level components.

Delegation connectors must match elements of the same polarity, that is, required elements to required elements or provided elements to provided elements. The interface of the element receiving a delegated message must include the message types that can be produced by the element producing a delegated message. An external port may delegate to a set of elements that together cover the element types of the external port. At run time, the delegated message is delivered to any and all delegation elements that match the run-time message type.

Notation

A delegation connector is shown as a line between the external port and the internal port or component. An arrow may be drawn in the direction of message transmission, that is, from an external provided port to an internal provided element or from an internal required port or element to an external required port. If a port represents a complex interface (both required and provided interfaces), a simple line is used.

Example

Figure 14-115 shows the internal decomposition of a television. It has 3 external ports: set channel, set volume, and display settings. The external port set channel delegates to a port on the internal component of type Tuner. The external port set volume delegates to a port on the internal component of type Amplifier. Internal ports for display settings on both the Tuner and the Amplifier components delegate to the external port display settings.

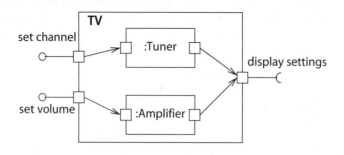

Figure 14-115. *Delegation connectors*

dependency

A relationship between two elements in which a change to one element (the supplier) may affect or supply information needed by the other element (the client). This is a term of convenience that groups together several different kinds of modeling relationships.

See relationship (Table 14-3) for a full chart of UML relationships.

Semantics

A dependency is a statement of relationship between two elements in a model or different models. The term, somewhat arbitrarily, groups together several different kinds of relationships, much as the biological term *invertebrate* groups together all phyla except *Vertebrata*.

In a case in which the relationship represents an asymmetry of knowledge, the independent elements are called *suppliers* and the dependent elements are called *clients*.

A dependency may have a name to indicate its role in the model. Usually, however, the presence of the dependency itself is sufficient to make the meaning clear, and a name is redundant. A dependency may have a stereotype to establish the precise nature of the dependency, and it may have a text description to describe itself in full detail, albeit informally.

A dependency between two packages indicates the presence of at least one dependency of the given kind between an element in each of the packages (except for access and import that relate packages directly). For example, a usage dependency between two classes may be shown as a usage dependency between the packages that contain them. A dependency among packages does not mean that all elements in the packages have the dependency—in fact, such a situation would be rare. See package.

Dependencies are not necessarily transitive.

Note that association and generalization fit within the general definition of dependency, but they have their own model representation and notation and are not usually considered to be dependencies. Template binding also has its own representation. Element import also has its own representation.

Dependency comes in several varieties that represent different kinds of relationships: abstraction, permission, and usage.

Abstraction. An abstraction dependency represents a shift in the level of abstraction of a concept. Both elements represent the same concept in different ways. Usually one of the elements is more abstract, and the other is more concrete, although situations are possible when both elements are alternative representations at the same level of abstraction. From least specific to most specific relationships, abstraction includes the stereotypes trace dependency, refinement (keyword **refine**), realization (which has its own metaclass and special notation), derivation (keyword **derive**), and substitution (a special case of realization).

Permission. A permission dependency (keyword **permit**) relates an element, such as a package or class, to another element to which it is granted permission to use the private contents. For example, the C++ friend construct could be modeled as a permission dependency between an operation and a class.

Usage. A usage dependency (keyword «**use**») connects a client element to a supplier element, the change of which may require a change to the client element. Usage often represents an implementation dependency, in which one element makes use of the services of another element to implement its behavior. Stereotypes of usage include call, creation (keyword **create**), instantiation (keyword **instantiate**), and send. This is an open list. Other kinds of usage dependency may occur in various programming languages.

Notation

A dependency is shown as a dashed arrow between two model elements. The model element at the tail of the arrow (the client) depends on the model element at the arrowhead (the supplier). The arrow may be labeled with an optional keyword, to indicate the kind of dependency, and an optional name (Figure 14-116).

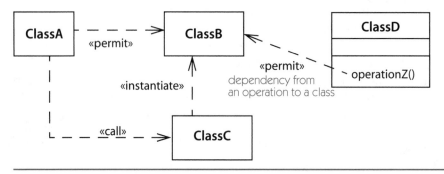

Figure 14-116. *Some dependencies among classes*

Several other kinds of relationships use a dashed arrow with a keyword, although they do not fit the definition of dependency. These include binding, use case extend and include, and the attachment of a note or constraint to the model element that it describes. If a note or constraint is one of the elements, the arrow may be suppressed because the note or constraint is always the source of the arrow.

deployment

The assignment of software artifacts to physical nodes during execution.

Semantics

Artifacts model physical entities, such as files, scripts, database tables, text documents, and web pages. Nodes model computational resources, such as computers and disk drives. A deployment is the assignment of an artifact or set of artifacts to a node for execution.

A manifestation dependency relates an artifact to the logical element that it implements.

Device and execution environment are kinds of nodes. The distinction among kinds of nodes is rather vague and could probably be ignored.

A communication path is an association between nodes allowing them to exchange messages and signals. Networks can be modeled as nodes connected by communication paths.

For components, a deployment may own a set of deployment specifications, each of which contains a string specification of a deployment location within the node and an execution location. This concept is a hook that requires extension in profiles to be useful.

Notation

Deployment is shown by the graphical nesting of an artifact symbol within a node symbol Figure 14-117. Alternately, a dashed arrow may be drawn from the artifact symbol to the node symbol with the keyword «**deploy**». Deployments may be shown at the type level or the instance level by the use of classifier or instance specification symbols (nonunderlined or underlined name strings, respectively).

A deployment specification is shown as a rectangle symbol with the keyword «**deploymentSpec**». Values of particular parameters can be listed. A dashed arrow is drawn from the rectangle to the artifact whose deployment it describes.

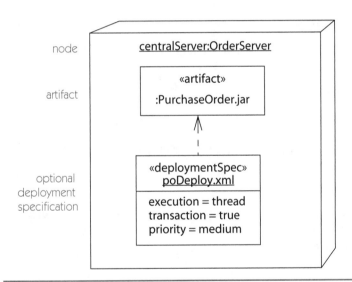

Figure 14-117. *Deployment*

History

Deployment has been repositioned in UML2 to apply to artifacts rather than model elements. The concept of manifestation relates model elements to artifacts.

deployment (phase)

That phase of development that describes the configuration of the running system in a real-world environment. For deployment, decisions must be made about configuration parameters, performance, resource allocation, distribution, and concurrency. The results of this phase are captured in configuration files as well as the deployment view. Contrast analysis, design, implementation, and deployment (phase).

See development process, stages of modeling.

deployment diagram

A diagram that shows the configuration of run-time processing nodes and the artifacts that live on them. A deployment diagram may be at the class level or the instance level. See deployment.

deployment specification

A detailed specification of the parameters of the deployment of an artifact to a node. See deployment.

deployment view

A view that shows the nodes in a distributed system, the artifacts that are stored on each node, and the components and other elements that the artifacts manifest.

derivation

A relationship between an element and another element that can be computed from it. Derivation is modeled as a stereotype of an abstraction dependency with the keyword **derive**.

See derived element.

derive (stereotype of Abstraction dependency)

A dependency, the source and target of which are elements, usually, but not necessarily, of the same type. A derive dependency specifies that the source may be computed from the target. Although the source is logically redundant, it may be implemented for design reasons, such as efficiency.

See derivation, derived element.

derived element

A element that can be computed from other elements and is included for clarity or for design purposes even though it adds no semantic information.

See also constraint, dependency.

Semantics

A derived element is logically redundant within a model because it can be computed from one or more other elements. The formula for computing a derived element may be given as a constraint.

A derived element may be included in a model for several reasons. At the analysis level, a derived element is semantically unnecessary, but it may be used to provide a name or a definition for a meaningful concept, as a kind of macro. It is important to remember that a derived element adds nothing to the semantics of a model.

In a design-level model, a derived element represents an optimization—an element that could be computed from other elements but is physically present in the model to avoid the cost or trouble of recomputing it. Examples are an intermediate value of a computation and an index to a set of values. The presence of a derived element implies the responsibility to update it if the values it depends on change.

Notation

A derived element is shown by placing a slash (/) in front of the name of the derived element, such as an attribute, a rolename, or an association name (Figure 14-118).

The details of computing a derived element can be specified by a dependency with the stereotype «derive». Usually, it is convenient in the notation to suppress the dependency arrow from the constraint to the element and simply place a constraint string near the derived element, although the arrow can be included when it is helpful.

Discussion

Derived associations are probably the most common kind of derived element. They represent virtual associations that can be computed from two or more fundamental associations. In Figure 14-118, for instance, derived association WorksForCompany can be computed by composing WorksForDepartment with the employer composition. An implementation might explicitly include WorksForCompany to avoid recomputing it, but it does not represent any additional information.

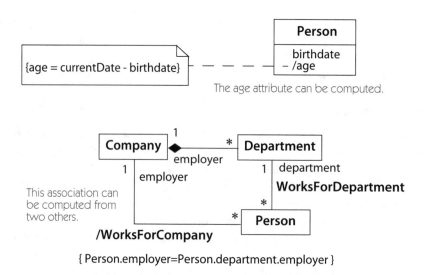

Figure 14-118. *Derived attribute and derived association*

There is a difference with association generalization (Figure 14-33), which represents two levels of detail for an association. It would not usually be implemented at both levels. Usually only the child associations would be implemented. Sometimes only the parent association would be implemented, with the child associations constraining the kinds of objects that can be related.

derived union

A property that is specified as the union of all of the other properties that are declared as subsets of it.

Semantics

It is often useful to define an abstract property, such as an association end name, as the union of a set of specific properties. For example, a family relative could be defined as a sibling, a child, or a spouse. Such a declaration is called a derived union. It indicates that the derived property is equal to the union of all its explicitly declared subset properties and no more.

A derived union is specified by setting the derived union flag on the abstract property. Each constituent property is specified with the subset relationship to the derived union property.

Notation

A derived union property is shown using the property string {union} after its name. If the property is an association end name, the string may be placed near the end of the path representing the association. Each subset property is shown using a property string of the form {subsets uname}, where uname is the name of the union property.

Example

Figure 14-119 shows the derivation of the relative association from the subset relationships child-parent, husband-wife, and sibling. Because sibling and relative are symmetric, we only show one role name; there is no way to declare that an association is symmetric. We could build a more complete real world model by adding additional kinds of relatives, such as cousins.

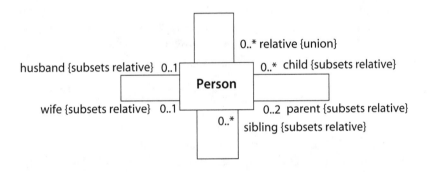

Figure 14-119. *Derived union*

descendant

A child or an element found by a chain of child relationships; the transitive closure of the specialization relationship. Antonym: ancestor.

See generalization.

descriptor

A model element that describes the common properties of a set of instances, including their structure, relationships, behavior, constraints, purpose, and so on. Contrast: instance.

Semantics

The word *descriptor* characterizes model elements that describe sets of individuals, including instances in the broadest sense. Most of the elements in a model are descriptors—classes, associations, states, use cases, collaborations, events, and so on. Sometimes, the word *type* is used in this meaning, but that word is often used in a more narrow sense to mean only class-like things. The word *descriptor* is meant to include every kind of descriptive element. A descriptor has an intent and an extent. The structure description and other general rules are the intent. Each descriptor characterizes a set of instances, which are its extent. There is no assumption that the extent is physically accessible at run time. The major dichotomy in a model is the descriptor-instance distinction.

An instance model shows elements that are not descriptors.

Notation

The relationship between a descriptor and its instances is usually reflected by using the same geometric symbol for both, but underlining the name string of an instance. A descriptor has a name, whereas an instance has both an individual name and a descriptor name, separated by a colon, and the name string is underlined.

design

That stage of a system development that describes how the system will be implemented, at a logical level above actual code. For design, strategic and tactical decisions are made to meet the required functional and quality requirements of a system. The results of this stage are represented by design-level models, especially the static view, state machine view, and interaction view. Contrast: analysis, design, implementation, and deployment (phase).

See stages of modeling, development process.

design model

A model constructed for exploring architecture and implementation choices, as opposed to understanding domain requirements. Contrast with analysis model, implementation model. (This is not an official UML term.)

design time

Refers to what occurs during a design activity of the software development process. Contrast: analysis time.

See modeling time, stages of modeling.

design view

A view of a model that contains a static declaration of the classes, collaboration, and components in a system, their dependencies, and their internal implementation at a level above a programming language. The design view is concerned with issues such as flow of control, data structures, computational complexity, visibility, and model decomposition for work by multiple teams.

destroy

To eliminate an object and reclaim its resources. Usually this is an explicit action, although it may be the consequence of another action, or of a constraint, or of garbage collection. See action, destruction.

destroy (stereotype of BehavioralFeature)

A stereotype denoting that the designated behavioral feature destroys an instance of the classifier containing the feature.

destruction

The elimination of an object and the reclaiming of its resources. Conceptually, the destruction of a composite object leads to the destruction of its composite parts. Destruction of an object does not automatically destroy objects related by ordinary association or even by aggregation, but any links involving the object are destroyed with the object.

See also composition, final state, instantiation.

Semantics

Like creation, destruction can be modeled at two levels: a low level action that destroys the identity and storage for the object, and a higher-level operation that destroys composite parts owned by the object as well as performing other kinds of clean up implied by the semantics of a particular class. Both levels can exist within a model, although most models will probably use one or the other.

Notation

On a sequence diagram, the destruction of an object is shown by a large X on the lifeline of the object (Figure 14-120). It is placed at the message that causes the object to be destroyed or at the point where the object terminates itself. A message that destroys an object may be shown with the stereotype «destroy».

See sequence diagram (Figure 14-248) for notation to show destruction within the implementation of a procedure.

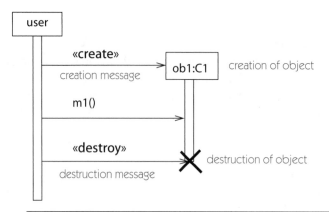

Figure 14-120. *Creation and destruction*

determinacy

The characteristic of a computation that yields the same value or effect every time it is executed.

Semantics

Determinacy is often, but not always, a desirable characteristic. In dealing with real-world interactions, indeterminacy is often an essential part of the semantics. Even within internal computations, indeterminacy can sometimes be useful, for example, in producing a game-playing application with unpredictable behavior. Other times indeterminacy may be harmless because various outcomes may be equally good and the an indeterminate program may be simpler and faster.

Indeterminacy is related to concurrent behavior in which concurrent threads share access to the same resource, with at least one thread modifying the resource. In UML, concurrent behavior can arise from state machines containing orthogonal states, activities with concurrent nodes, or interactions with concurrent lifelines. Indeterminacy can also arise from overlapping guard conditions on transitions or conditionals, that is, from a set of guard conditions on a single state or activity node for which certain values satisfy more than one condition. According to UML semantics, only one branch will be chosen, but the choice is indeterminate. The indeterminacy can be removed by ordering the conditions, but sometimes it does not matter which branch is chosen, and the program is simpler and often faster if the choice is unconstrained.

Sometimes there is an apparent indeterminacy that cannot occur in practice because of the actual run-time values. In such cases, the modeler should note the fact in comments or with assertions so that the intent is clear.

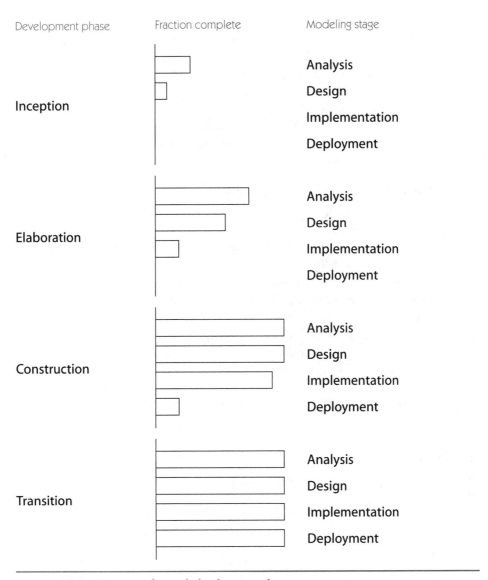

Figure 14-121. *Progress after each development phase*

development process

A set of guidelines and a partially ordered set of work activities intended to produce software in a controlled, reproducible manner. The purpose of a software development process is to ensure the success and quality of a finished system.

See also stages of modeling.

Discussion

UML is a modeling language, not a process, and its purpose is to describe models that may be produced by various development processes. For standardization, it is more important to describe the resultant artifacts of a development than the process of producing them. That's because there are many good ways of building a model, and a finished model can be used without knowing how it was produced. Nevertheless, UML is intended to support a wide range of processes.

For details of an iterative, incremental, use-case-driven, architectural-centric development process that the authors of this book endorse, see [Jacobson-99].

Relationship of modeling stages and development phases

The stages of modeling fit within an iterative development process, which has the phases inception, elaboration, construction, and transition phase. The phases are sequential within one release of an application, but each phase includes one or more iterations. Within an iteration, individual model elements are moved along the path from analysis toward deployment, each at its own appropriate pace. Although the development phases and the modeling stages are not synchronized, there is a correlation. In the earlier development phases and the earlier iterations of a phase, there is more emphasis on the earlier model stages.

Figure 14-121 shows the balance of effort during successive phases and iterations. During inception, the focus is mainly on analysis, with a skeleton of elements progressing toward design and implementation during elaboration. During construction and transition, all the elements must eventually be moved to completion.

device

A physical computational resource with processing capability upon which artifacts may be deployed for execution. A device is a kind of node. See node.

Semantics

There is no great difference between a node and a device. Devices are intended to represent physical computation devices, although the guidelines are vague. The distinction might be more significant in a profile that defines particular kinds of devices within a certain execution environment.

Notation

A device is shown as a node symbol (cube image) with the keyword «device» above the name of the device.

diagram

A graphical presentation of a collection of model elements, most often rendered as a connected graph of arcs (relationships) and vertices (other model elements). UML supports a number of kinds of diagram.

See also background information, font usage, hyperlink, keyword, label, package, path, presentation element, property string.

Semantics

A diagram is not a semantic element. A diagram shows presentations of semantic model elements, but their meaning is unaffected by the way they are presented.

Notation

Most UML diagrams and some complex symbols are graphs that contain shapes connected by paths. The information is mostly in the topology, not in the size or placement of the symbols (there are some exceptions, such as a timing diagram). There are three important kinds of visual relationships: connection (usually of lines to 2-dimensional shapes), containment (of symbols by 2-dimensional closed shapes), and visual attachment (one symbol being "near" another one on a diagram). These geometric relationships map into connections of nodes in a graph in the parsed form of the notation.

UML notation is intended to be drawn on 2-D surfaces. Some shapes are 2-D projections of 3-D shapes, such as cubes, but they are still rendered as icons on a 2-D surface. In the near future, true 3-D layout and navigation may be possible on desktop machines but it is not currently common.

There are four kinds of graphical constructs used in UML notation: icons, 2-D symbols, paths, and strings.

An icon is a graphical figure of a fixed size and shape. It does not expand to hold contents. Icons may appear within area symbols, as terminators on paths, or as stand-alone symbols that may or may not be connected to paths. For example, the symbols for aggregation (a diamond), navigability (an arrowhead), final state (a bull's eye), and object destruction (a large X) are icons.

Two-dimensional symbols have variable height and width, and they can expand to hold other things, such as lists of strings or other symbols. Many of them are divided into compartments of similar or different kinds. Paths are connected to 2-D symbols by terminating the path on the boundary of the symbol. Dragging or deleting a 2-D symbol affects its contents and any paths connected to it. For example, the symbols for class (a rectangle), state (a rounded rectangle), and note (a dog-eared rectangle) are 2-D symbols.

A path is a sequence of line or curve segments whose endpoints are attached. Conceptually, a path is a single topological entity, although its segments may be manipulated graphically. A segment may not exist apart from its path. Paths are always attached to other graphic symbols at both ends (no dangling lines). Paths may have terminators—that is, icons that appear in a sequence on the end of the path and that qualify the meaning of the path symbol. For example, the symbols for association (solid lines), generalization (solid lines with a triangle icon), and dependency (dashed lines) are paths.

Strings present various kinds of information in an "unparsed" form. UML assumes that each usage of a string in the notation has a syntax by which it can be parsed into underlying model information. For example, syntaxes are given for attributes, operations, and transitions. These syntaxes are subject to extension by tools as a presentation option. Strings may exist as the content of a compartment, as elements in lists (in which case the position in the list conveys information), as labels attached to symbols or paths, or as stand-alone elements on a diagram. For example, class names, transition labels, multiplicity indications, and constraints are strings.

A diagram may be presented as a frame containing the graphical contents. The frame includes the name of the diagram and establishes its extent. A frame is drawn as a rectangle with a small pentagon (called the name tag) in the upper left corner. The pentagon contains the type and name of the diagram in the format:

tag name parameters$_{opt}$

The *tag* is a word that indicates the kind of diagram. The *name* is the individual name of a particular diagram, by which it can be located in a browser. Diagram names are hierarchical within their package structure. A fully qualified name is shown as a sequence of names separated by double colons (::), for example:

Acme-Company::Purchasing::OrderEntry.

Certain kinds of diagrams have parameters.

The frame may be omitted when the context is clear and no information is shown on the boundary. It is an optional presentation capability.

Figure 14-122 shows a package diagram using the frame and tag notation.

Table 14-1 shows UML diagram types and tags.

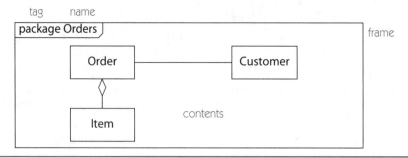

Figure 14-122. *Diagram with frame*

Table 14-1: *Diagram tags and diagram types*

Tag	Name
activity	activity diagram
class	class diagram
comm	communication diagram
component	component diagram
class	composite structure diagram
deployment	deployment diagram
intover	interaction overview diagram
object	object diagram
package	package diagram
state machine	state machine diagram
sd	sequence diagram
timing	timing diagram
use case	use case diagram

Discussion

The UML specification does not consistently describe the tags for each kind of diagram, so we have had to extrapolate. The interactions chapter uses **sd** for all kinds of interaction diagrams, which is useless if the different kinds of diagram cannot be otherwise distinguished and pointless if they can, so we have made adjustments.

direct class

The class that most completely describes an object.

See also class, generalization, inheritance, multiple classification, multiple inheritance.

Semantics

An object may be an instance of many classes—if it is an instance of a class, then it is also an instance of the ancestors of the class. The direct class is the most specific description of an object, the one that most completely describes it. An object is a direct instance of its direct class and an indirect instance of the ancestors of the direct class. An object is not an instance of any descendants of the direct class (by definition).

If multiple classification is allowed in a system, no single direct class may completely describe an object. The object may be the combined direct instance of more than one class. An object is a direct instance of each class that contains part of its description, provided no descendant also describes the object. In other words, none of the direct classes of an object have an ancestor relationship to each other.

If a class is instantiated to produce an object, the object is a direct instance of the class.

direct instance

An instance, such as an object, whose most specific descriptor, such as a class, is a given class. Used in a phrase like, "Object O is a direct instance of class C." In this case, class C is the direct class of object O.

See direct class.

direct substate

With respect to a composite state, a state contained by it without being contained by an intermediate state; a top-level state within a region of a composite state.

See composite state, indirect substate, region, state.

Semantics

A composite state contains one or more regions. Each region directly contains one or more states. A top-level state of a region is called a *direct substate* of the composite state containing the region. The phrase can also be used with respect to a region. If a composite state is active, exactly one direct substate from each region is active.

Direct substates themselves may include composite states. Their substates are called indirect substates of the original composite state. Because some of the direct or indirect substates may have multiple regions, a state may have multiple active indirect substates per region.

disjoint

Keyword for a generalization set whose subtypes are incompatible.

See generalization set.

disjoint substate

This UML1 term does not appear in UML2. See direct substate.

distribution unit

A set of objects or components that are allocated to an operating-system process or a processor as a group. A distribution unit can be represented by a run-time composite or by an aggregate. This is a design concept in the deployment view.

do activity

Ongoing execution of a behavior that occurs within a state. Contrast: effect, entry activity, exit activity.

See also completion transition, state.

Semantics

A do-activity is the execution of behavior within a state machine that is based on holding a given state. The activity starts when the state is entered and continues until the activity completes on its own or the state is exited. A transition that forces an exit from the state aborts the do activity. A do-activity is not terminated by the firing of an internal transition, because there is no change of state. The action of the internal transition may explicitly terminate it.

A do-activity is an exception to the normal run-to-completion semantics of a state machine, in that it may continue execution even when the direct execution of an effect has completed and the state machine handles another event.

Notation

A do activity uses the notation for an internal transition with the reserved word **do** in place of the event name:

do / activity-expression

Example

Figure 14-123 shows an alarm system that illustrates the difference between a transition effect and a do-activity. When the event **detect intrusion** occurs, the system fires a transition. As part of the transition firing, the effect **summon police** occurs.

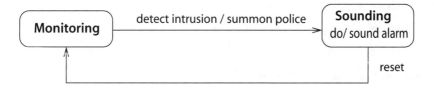

Figure 14-123. *Do-activity*

No events may be accepted while the action is being executed. After the activity is performed, the system enters the **Sounding** state. While the system is in this state, it performs the **sound alarm** activity. A do-activity takes time to complete, during which events might occur that interrupt the do-activity. In this case, the **sound alarm** activity does not terminate on its own; it continues as long as the system is in the **Sounding** state. When the **reset** event occurs, the transition fires and takes the system back to the **Monitoring** state. When the **Sounding** state ceases to be active, its activity **sound alarm** is terminated.

document (stereotype of Component)

A component representing a document; a file that is not a source file or an executable.

See component.

duration

A specification of the elapsed time between two events.

duration constraint

A constraint on a duration.

Notation

A duration constraint on a sequence diagram may be shown by drawing a vertical line with open arrowheads at both ends between the vertical position of two events. An expression for the duration is placed in braces over the center of the arrow. The constraint may also be shown as a text expression in braces. Figure 14-124 shows an example.

duration observation action

An action that returns the value of a duration at run time.

Notation

The duration of a message transmission may be shown on a message as:

    name = duration

Figure 14-124 shows an example.

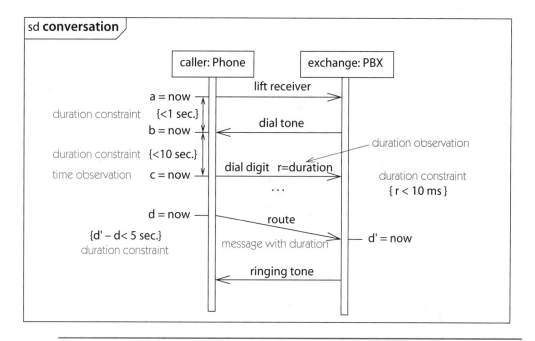

Figure 14-124. *Duration constraint*

Discussion

Although this is stated as an action in the UML specification, in most cases modelers would want to make assertions about time without executing run-time actions. It is probably best to regard this as simply a definition of a name that can be used in a constraint expression, rather than a real action.

The basic model of interactions make the assumption that time on different lifelines is independent (an "Einsteinian" assumption). Measuring the duration of a message transmission requires that the time scales of the two lifelines be the same, however. In most cases in which issues such as message transmission are a modeling issue, some kind of global time scale can be assumed. In cases where the time skew of different clocks in a real-time system is important, the simple UML time model is inadequate and a more elaborate time model must be used. It is expected that real-time profiles will provide various time models.

dynamic classification

A semantic variation of generalization in which an object may change type or role. Contrast: static classification.

See also multiple classification.

Semantics

In many programming languages, an object may not change the class from which it is instantiated. This static classification restriction simplifies implementation and optimization of compilers, but it is not a logical necessity. For example, under the static classification assumption, an object instantiated as a circle must remain a circle; it may not be scaled in the x-dimension, for example. Under the dynamic classification assumption, a circle that is scaled in one dimension becomes an ellipse. This is not regarded as a problem.

Either assumption may be used in a UML model. This is an example of a semantic variation point. The choice affects surprisingly little of a model, although the differences are important for execution. The same classes must be defined in either case, but the operations they support may differ in the two cases.

dynamic concurrency

This UML1 concept has been replaced by expansion region.

dynamic view

That aspect of a model dealing with the specification and implementation of behavior over time, as distinguished from static structure found in the static view. The dynamic view is a grouping term that includes the use case view, state machine view, activity view, and interaction view.

edge

See activity edge.

effect

An action or activity that is executed when a transition fires. The execution has run-to-completion semantics; that is, no additional events are processed during the execution.

See transition.

elaboration

The second phase of a software development process, during which the design for the system is begun and the architecture is developed and tested. During this phase, most of the analysis view is completed, together with the architectural parts of the design view. If an executable prototype is constructed, some of the implementation view is done. See development process.

element

A constituent of a model. This book describes elements that may be used in UML models—model elements, which express semantic information, and presentation elements, which provide graphic presentations of model-element information.

Element is the most abstract class in the UML metamodel. An element can own and be owned by other elements, and it can own comments.

See also diagram, model element.

else

A keyword indicating a pseudocondition on a branch that is true if and only if no other condition is true. It guarantees that a conditional will have at least one valid choice.

Semantics

The else pseudocondition may be specified on any of the UML branching constructs, including: (for activities) conditional node, decision node; (for interactions) conditional fragment; (for state machines) choice node.

Notation

The else pseudocondition is expressed by the string [else].

enabled

A transition whose prerequisites have been satisfied that is eligible for execution.

Semantics

Before a transition can fire, the owning object must hold the source state of the transition or one of its descendants and must satisfy the trigger of the transition. The trigger is satisfied if the object has received and not yet processed an event occurrence that matches the trigger. A signal trigger is satisfied by a signal that is a descendant of the transition trigger. If these conditions occur, the guard condition of the transition is evaluated in the current context. If the guard condition evaluates true (or if it is absent), the transition is enabled. If the transition has multiple source states (that is, if it is a join node), the current state configuration must include all of them.

It may happen that multiple transitions are enabled by the same event. In that case, one and only one transition will fire. The selection may be nondeterministic.

When a transition is selected for firing, any other enabled transitions cease to be enabled.

If a transition contains multiple segments that do not include a choice pseudostate, then all triggers and guard conditions on all segments must be satisfied for the transition to be enabled. The transition does not become enabled one segment at a time.

A choice pseudostate effectively breaks a transition into two separate transitions. The transition is enabled if the triggers and guard conditions on all segments before the choice pseudostate are satisfied. The transition remains enabled at the choice pseudostate. No triggers are allowed past the choice pseudostate. At least one outgoing segment must satisfy its guard condition so that the transition can successfully transfer to a target state.

An activity whose prerequisites have been satisfied is also said to be enabled. In the case of conditional nodes or conflicts over input tokens, multiple activities may become enabled simultaneously, but only one will be selected for execution unless their inputs are disjoint.

entity (stereotype of Component)

A persistent information component representing a business concept.

Discussion

This stereotype might have been inspired by the term *Entity Bean* from the Enterprise Java Beans (EJB) community. It is a narrow use of a common word, however, and conflicts with the use of the word *entity* in other areas, such as the Entity-Relationship (ER) model familiar in data bases.

entry activity

An action performed when a state is entered.

See also exit activity, run-to-completion, state machine, transition.

Semantics

A state may have an optional entry activity attached to it. Whenever the state is entered in any way, the entry activity is executed after any activities attached to outer states or transitions and before any activities attached to inner states. The entry activity may not be evaded by any means. It is guaranteed to have been executed whenever the owning state or a state nested within it is active.

Execution order. On a transition between two states with exit and entry activity in which the transition also has an attached activity, the execution order is: Any exit activities are executed on the source state and its enclosing states out to, but not including, the state that encloses both the source and target states. Then the activity attached to the transition is executed, after which the entry activities are executed (outermost first) on the enclosing states inside the common state, down to and including the target state. Figure 14-170 shows some transitions that have multiple activities.

Notation

An entry activity is coded using the syntax for an internal transition with the dummy event name **entry** (which is therefore a reserved word and may not be used as an actual event name).

entry / activity

Only one entry activity may be attached to a state, but the activity may be a sequence so no generality is lost.

Discussion

Entry and exit activities are not semantically essential (the entry action could be attached to all incoming transitions) but they facilitate the encapsulation of a state so that the external use of it can be separated from its internal construction. They make it possible to define initialization and termination activities, without concern that they might be avoided. They are particularly useful with exceptions, because they define activities that must be performed even if an exception occurs.

An entry activity is useful for performing an initialization that must be done when a state is first entered. One use is to initialize variables that capture information accumulated during a state. For example, a user interface to allow keypad input of a telephone number or an account number would clear the number on entry. Resetting an error counter, such as the number of password failures, is another example. Allocating temporary storage needed during the state is another use for an entry action.

Often, an entry activity and an exit activity are used together. The entry activity allocates resources, and the exit activity releases them. Even if an external transition occurs, the resources are released. This is a good way to handle user errors and exceptions. User-level errors trigger high-level transitions that abort nested states, but the nested states have an opportunity to clean up before they lose control.

History

This has been renamed from *action* to *activity*, with the understanding that its execution may require time, but otherwise it is not much changed from UML1.

entry point

Within a state, an externally visible pseudostate that can be the target of an external transition. It specifies an internal state within the state that becomes the effective target state of any such transition.

Semantics

An entry point is an encapsulation mechanism. It allows the definition of alternate initial states within a state for use by external transitions. They are used when there is more than one way to enter a state and the default initial substate will not suffice. Each entry point designates an internal state within the owning state. Entry points have names that are visible externally. An external transition may have an entry point as its target. A transition connected to an entry point is effectively connected to the designated state as its target, but the external transition need not know about the internal details of the state in making the connection. This mechanisms is particularly useful with submachines, in which the transition references the submachine and a direct connection to an inner state would not be possible without making a recursive copy of the submachine.

Note that the initial substate of a state may be considered equivalent to an entry point with an empty name.

Regardless of how a state is entered, whether through an entry point, an initial state, or an explicit transition to an internal substate, the entry activity of the state is executed before the transfer to the internal state occurs.

Notation

An entry point is shown as a small circle on the boundary of the state symbol. The name of the entry point is placed near the circle. A solid arrow is drawn from the circle to the designated internal state within the state symbol.

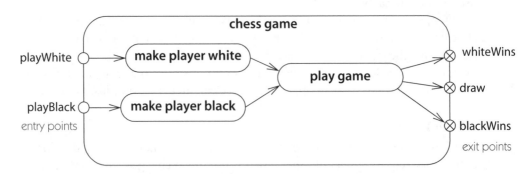

Figure 14-125. *Entry and exit points*

Figure 14-125 shows a state representing the playing of a computerized chess game. Initially the player can choose to play white or black pieces, each of which is modeled as an entry point. Because of the symmetry, there is no default initial state. The state also has three exit points, corresponding to a win by white or black or to a draw.

History

Entry and exit points replace UML1 stubs in a much cleaner UML2 formulation.

enumeration

A data type whose instances form a list of named literal values. Usually, both the enumeration name and its literal values are declared.

See also classifier, data type.

Semantics

An enumeration is a user-definable data type. It has a name and an ordered list of enumeration literal values, each of which is a value in the range of the data type—that is, it is a predefined instance of the data type.

For example, RGBColor = {red, green, blue}, in which the data type is RGBColor and its possible values are red, green, and blue. The data type Boolean is a predefined enumeration with the literals false and true.

Enumeration literals can be compared for equality or for relative position in the list of literals. They are atomic and have no substructure. The enumeration type may define operations that take literals as arguments and return literals as results. For example, the various Boolean operations are defined over the values false and true.

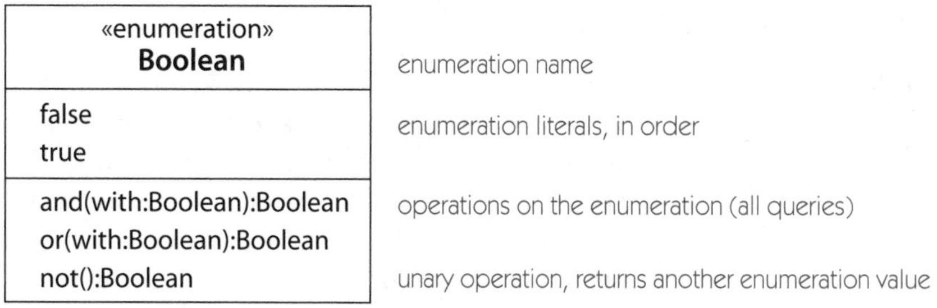

«enumeration» **Boolean**	enumeration name
false true	enumeration literals, in order
and(with:Boolean):Boolean or(with:Boolean):Boolean not():Boolean	operations on the enumeration (all queries) unary operation, returns another enumeration value

Figure 14-126. *Enumeration declaration*

Notation

An enumeration is shown as a rectangle with the keyword «enumeration» above the name of the enumeration type in the upper compartment (Figure 14-126). The second compartment contains a list of enumeration-literal names. The third compartment (if present) contains a set of operations on the type. They must all be queries (which, therefore, do not need to be explicitly declared as such).

enumeration literal

An instance value of an enumeration type. It has a name and a relative position within the list of literals of its enumeration type. See enumeration.

event

A type of noteworthy occurrence that has a location in time and space.
See also state machine, transition, trigger.

Semantics

An event is something that happens during execution of a system that is worth modeling. Within a state machine, an occurrence of an event can trigger a state transition. An event has a (possibly empty) list of parameters that convey information from the creator of the event to its receiver. The time at which the event occurred is implicitly a parameter of every event. Other parameters are part of the definition of an event.

An occurrence (instance) of an event has an argument (actual value) corresponding to each event parameter. The value of each argument is available to an action attached to a transition triggered by the event.

Note that events do not explicitly appear in models. A trigger on a state machine transition specifies an event whose occurrence enables the transition.

There are four kinds of events that can be used in triggers:

call event	The receipt of a request to invoke an operation, that is, the receipt of a call. The expected result is the execution of the operation by triggering a transition in the receiver. The trigger specifies the operation. The parameters of the event are the parameters of the operation and, implicitly, a return pointer. The caller regains control when the transition is complete (or immediately if no transition fires).
change event	The satisfaction of a Boolean condition specified by an expression in the event. The trigger specifies a Boolean condition as an expression. There are no parameters of

the event. This kind of event implies a continuous test for the condition. The event occurs when the condition changes from false to true. In practice, however, the times at which the condition can be satisfied can often be restricted to the occurrence of other events, so that polling is usually not required.

signal event

The receipt of a signal, which is an explicit named entity intended for explicit communication between objects. The trigger specifies the signal type. The parameters of the event are the parameters of the signal. A signal is explicitly sent by an object to another object or set of objects. A general broadcast of an event can be regarded as the sending of a signal to the set of all objects, although in practice, it might be implemented differently for efficiency. The sender explicitly specifies the arguments of the signal at the time it is sent. A signal sent to a set of objects may trigger zero or one transition in each of them.

Signals are explicit means by which objects may communicate with each other asynchronously. To perform synchronous communication, two asynchronous signals must be used, one in each direction of communication, or else a synchronous call may be used.

Signals are generalizable. A child signal is derived from a parent signal; it inherits the parameters of the parent and may add additional parameters of its own. A child signal satisfies a trigger that specifies one of its ancestors.

time event

The satisfaction of a time expression, such as the occurrence of an absolute time or the passage of a given amount of time after an object enters a state. The trigger specifies the time expression. Note that both absolute time and elapsed time may be defined with respect to a real-world clock or a virtual internal clock (in which case, it may differ for different objects).

There are also various kinds of formal occurrences that might be considered events from some viewpoints, including initiation of execution, completion of execution, creation, and destruction.

Notation

See the specific kind of trigger associated with an event for details on notation.

event occurrence

See occurrence, occurrence specification.

Discussion

This term was used for both occurrence and occurrence, which are different. It may be used as a synonym for *occurrence*, but the word *event* is redundant.

exception

An indication of an unusual situation raised in response to behavioral faults by the underlying execution machinery or explicitly raised by an action. The occurrence of an exception aborts the normal flow of control and causes a search for an exception handler on an enclosing activity node.

Semantics

An exception is an indication that an abnormal situation has occurred that prevents normal execution from occurring. An exception is usually generated implicitly by underlying implementation mechanisms in response to a failure during execution. For example, an attempt to use an invalid array index to access an array element may be treated as an exception. An exception can also be explicitly raised by an action. Such "soft exceptions" can be used to indicate troublesome situations that are not well handled by the normal processing sequence.

In order that a program can respond correctly to an exception, it is necessary to know which exception occurred and, in many cases, additional parameters of the exception. Both of these needs are met by modeling exceptions as objects. The type of the exception object indicates the nature of the exception. The attributes of the exception object represent the parameters of the exception. Because different object types have different attributes, exceptions can represent exactly as much information as needed (unlike mechanisms in some older programming languages in which exceptions were limited to single values). Because exception types are ordinary classifiers, they can form generalization hierarchies.

Some actions cause exceptions if specified conditions occur during the execution of the actions. For example, an attempt to access the attribute of a null object might be specified to raise a "null reference" exception. For each kind of predefined exception type, the conditions that cause it must be specified, together with an exception type and list of attribute values that are supplied by the execution machinery if the exception occurs.

There is also an explicit **RaiseException** action that permits a modeler to raise an arbitrary exception. The argument to this action is a single object. The type of this object represents the kind of exception, and its attributes represent the exception parameters. Any class can potentially be used as an exception type, although some implementations may require that exception types be descended from a designated root exception class.

When an exception occurs, the execution of the current action is abandoned without generation of output values. An exception token is created to represent the parameters of the exception.

A search is performed by the execution machinery to find an exception handler able to handle the exception. Exception handlers are attached to activity nodes. Each exception handler designates an exception type that it handles. First, the action that raised the exception is examined to see if it has an exception handler. If so, the body of the exception handler is executed with the exception token as input value. When the exception handler body completes execution, the output values of the exception handler replace the (not-yet-generated) output values of the original action, and execution of the action is considered complete. The exception handler must have the same number and types of outputs as the action it protects. After the completion of exception handling, execution of subsequent actions proceeds as if the original action completed normally.

An exception handler catches an exception whose type is the same as or a descendant of the type designated by the handler. In other words, an exception handler can ignore distinctions among subtypes when it catches exceptions.

If a handler for the exception is not found on the original action, the exception propagates to the activity node containing the original action, and so on to successive nested nodes until an activity node is found with an exception handler that catches the given exception. Each time the exception propagates outward, the execution of the current activity node is terminated and normal output values are not generated. If there are concurrent tokens active in an activity node, propagation cannot occur until they are eliminated. The UML specification does not specify a mechanism for eliminating concurrent tokens, and several semantically different mechanisms are compatible with the exception-handling mechanism, including waiting for concurrent activity to finish, automatically aborting all concurrent activity, or providing some kind of interrupt mechanism to allow the model to terminate concurrent activity in a controlled manner. These choices are semantic variation points in the UML specification. The default assumption is that concurrent activity is aborted by the exception.

Once a handler for the exception type is found, its body is executed in the fashion described previously. The outputs of the exception handler replace the original outputs of the protected activity node, and execution proceeds with successive nodes (but execution of embedded levels has already been irrevocably aborted).

If an exception propagates to the top level of an activity without being handled, execution of the entire activity is abandoned. If the activity was invoked asynchronously, no further effects occur and the exception handling is complete. If the activity was invoked synchronously, the exception is returned to the execution frame of the caller, where the exception is reraised in the scope of the call action, where it may be handled or may propagate further.

If an exception propagates to the root of a system, the system architect has probably done a poor job of design and the system will probably crash.

An operation may declare the exceptions that it might raise (including exceptions propagated from other called operations). The exceptions represent part of its complete signature.

Notation

The occurrence of an exception within an activity can be shown as an output pin on the boundary of the activity box with a small triangle near it. The output pin symbol is labeled with the type of the exception (Figure 14-127).

An exception handler attached to an activity node is shown by drawing a jagged arrow ("lighting bolt") from the protected node to an input pin symbol on the boundary of the activity symbol for the handler. The input pin is labeled with the type of the exception (Figure 14-128).

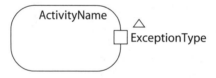

Figure 14-127. *Exception raised by activity*

Figure 14-128. *Exception handler on activity*

There does not seem to be a defined notation for the declaration of an exception potentially raised by an operation.

Example

Figure 14-129 shows a matrix computation protected by two exception handlers. If exception **SingularMatrix** occurs, one answer is substituted. If exception **Overflow** occurs, another answer is substituted. If no exception occurs, the computed answer is used. In any case, the final result is printed.

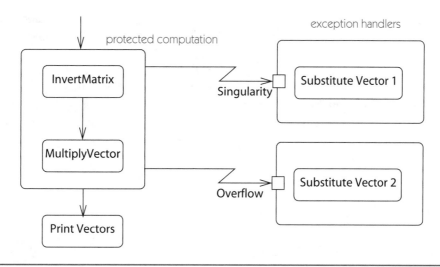

Figure 14-129. *Exception handlers on computation*

History

In UML1, a exception was regarded as a kind of signal sent between independent objects. Although this was a reasonable way to model messaging among concurrent objects, it did not match the concept of exception that existed in many programming languages for many years, in which exception handling was a mechanism to break out of the normal flow of control to handle unusual situations without confusing the main logic of a program. UML2 shifted to the standard concept of exception found in languages such as C++.

There is still a bit of residual language describing an exception as a signal. This is likely an oversight by the writers that should be ignored.

exception handler

An executable activity node responsible for assuming control if an exception of a given type occurs during the execution of the activity node attached to the exception handler.

Semantics

An exception handler is attached to an activity node to protect the node against exceptions of a given type that might occur during execution of the protected node. If an exception occurs that is the same as or a descendant of the given type, execution of the protected node is abandoned and execution of the exception handler begins. An exception token is created whose attribute values capture the parameters of the exception. The exception handler has one designated input location, which receives the exception token as its value. The exception handler shares scope with the node that it protects and has access to all values and objects that the protected node could access. An exception handler must have the same number and types of output pins as the node that it protects. When execution of the handler is complete, the output values produced by the exception handler substitute for the original output values of the protected node, and execution of subsequent nodes proceeds as if the exception had not occurred. The purpose of an exception handler is to produce a situation in which execution can proceed without concern for whether an exception occurred.

Notation

See exception for details of notation.

executable (stereotype of Artifact)

A program file that can be executed on a computer system.
See artifact, file.

executable node

An activity node that can be executed and that can have an exception handler.

Semantics

Executable nodes are those that can have exception handlers that can catch exceptions caused by the node or one of the nodes nested within it. Executable nodes include actions, conditional nodes, loop nodes, and expansion regions.

execution

The run-time processing of a behavior specification to modify the state of a system within a particular execution environment.

Semantics

The concept of behavior execution is part of the dynamic semantics of UML, but it is not part of a UML model, because a UML model describes the specification of the behavior itself. When the model is executed, the use of the behavior is a behavior execution.

A run-time model can be constructed using interactions. An execution specification models the occurrence of a behavior execution during a behavior trace.

execution environment

A kind of deployment node that represents a particular kind of execution platform, such as an operating system, a workstation engine, a database management system, and so on.

Also (and more commonly) used informally to describe the context within which execution of a model occurs.

Semantics

An execution environment models a hardware-software environment that supplies a set of standard services for use by application components. Examples include operating systems, database management systems, workflow engines, and so on. Components can be deployed on the execution environment. The execution environment is usually part of another node that models the computing hardware.

Notation

An execution environment is shown as a node symbol (a cube image) with the keyword «executionEnvironment».

execution occurrence

See execution specification.

Discussion

The term execution occurrence was used, but it conflicts with the use of occurrence to denote an event instance. The term execution specification is consistent with the use of the terms object specification, occurrence specification, and value specification to model groups of run-time entities within a context.

execution specification

The specification of the execution of an activity, operation, or other behavior unit within an interaction. An execution (sometimes known as focus of control) represents the period during which an object performs a behavior either directly or through a subordinate behavior. It models both the duration of the execution in time and the control relationship between the execution and its invokers. In a conventional computer and language, the execution itself corresponds to a value of the stack frame.

See call, sequence diagram.

Semantics

An execution specification models the execution of a behavior or operation, including the period during which an operation calls other subordinate operations (see call). An execution specification has two associated events, representing its start and its completion. Usually the starting event is the target of an invocation message, and the completion event may be the source of a return message.

Notation

An execution specification is shown on a sequence diagram as a tall, thin rectangle (a vertical hollow bar), the top of which is aligned with its initiation event and whose bottom is aligned with its completion event (Figure 14-130). The behavior being performed is shown by a text label next to the execution specification symbol or in the left margin, depending on style. Alternately, the incoming message symbol may indicate the behavior. In that case, the label may be omitted on the execution specification itself. If the flow of control is procedural, then the top of the execution specification symbol is at the tip of the incoming message arrow that initiates the operation execution and the bottom of the symbol is at the tail of a return message arrow.

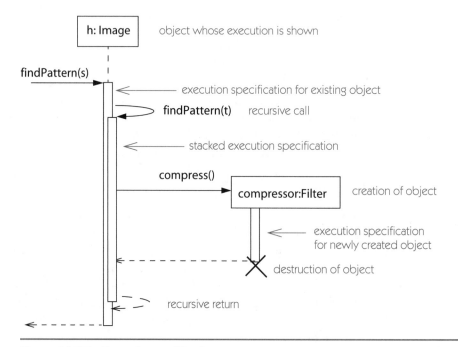

Figure 14-130. *Execution specifications*

If there is concurrent activity by multiple objects, then each execution specification shows the execution of one concurrent object. Unless the objects communicate, the concurrent executions are independent and their relative execution times are irrelevant.

In the case of procedural code, an execution specification shows the duration during which a procedure is active in the object or a subordinate procedure called by the original procedure is active, possibly in some other object. In other words, all the active nested procedure execution specifications are shown simultaneously. This set of simultaneous nested executions corresponds to the stack frame of the computation in a conventional computer. In the case of a second call to an object with an existing execution specification, the second execution specification symbol is drawn slightly to the right of the first one, so that they appear to "stack up" visually. Stacked calls may be nested to an arbitrary depth. The calls may be to the same operation (a recursive call) or to different operations on the same object.

It is possible (although often unnecessary) to distinguish the period during which an execution specification is blocked because it has called a subordinate operation. The rectangle can be colored black when the execution specification represents direct execution and white when it represents a call to a subordinate operation. This is not official notation, but the notation does support two colors for some unstated reason, so modelers could adopt conventions for their use.

Discussion

It was called *execution occurrence*, but that term conflicts with the general naming pattern that *specification* qualifies the name of a run-time entity when it describes a group of entities within a context.

exit activity

An activity performed when a state is exited.

See also entry activity, run-to-completion, state machine, transition.

Semantics

A state may have an optional exit activity attached to it. Whenever the state is exited in any way, the exit activity is executed after any activities attached to inner states or transitions and before any activities attached to outer states. The exit activity may not be evaded by any means. It is guaranteed to be executed before control leaves the owning state.

Entry and exit activities are not semantically essential; the exit activity could be attached to all outgoing transitions. However, they facilitate the encapsulation of a state so that the external use of it can be separated from its internal construction. They make it possible to define initialization and termination activities, without concern that they might be avoided. They are particularly useful with exceptions, because they define effects that must be performed even if an exception occurs.

Notation

An exit activity is coded using the syntax for an internal transition with the dummy event name **exit** (which is, therefore, a reserved word and may not be used as an actual event name).

> exit / activity

Only one exit activity may be attached to a state. But the activity may be a sequence, so no generality is lost.

Discussion

An exit activity is useful for performing a cleanup that must be done when a state is exited. The most significant use of exit activities is to release temporary storage and other resources allocated during execution of the state (usually, a state with nested detail).

Often, an entry activity and an exit activity are used together. The entry activity allocates resources, and the exit activity releases them. Even if an exception occurs, the resources are released.

exit point

Within a state, an externally visible pseudostate that can be the source of an external transition. It represents a final state within the state that may be connected to an external transition.

See also entry point.

Semantics

An exit point is an encapsulation mechanism. It allows the definition of alternate final states within a state for use by external transitions. They are used when there is more than one way to complete a state and the default final state will not suffice. Each exit point represents a named final state within the owning state. Exit points have names that are visible externally. An external transition may have an exit point as its source. A transition connected to an exit point is effectively connected to the designated internal named final state as its source, but the external transition need not know about the internal details of the state in making the connection. This mechanism is particularly useful with submachines, in which the transition references the submachine and a direct connection to an inner state would not be possible without making a recursive copy of the submachine.

Note that the default final state of a state may be considered equivalent to an exit point with an empty name.

Regardless of how a state is exited, whether through an exit point, a default final state, or an explicit transition to an external state, the exit activity of the state is executed before the transfer to the external state occurs.

Notation

An exit point is shown as a small circle on the boundary of the state symbol. The name of the exit point is placed near the circle. Transitions from internal states may be connected to the exit point as target.

Figure 14-125 shows a state representing the playing of a computerized chess game. Initially the player can choose to play white or black pieces, each of which is modeled as an entry point. Because of the symmetry, there is no default initial state. The state also has three exit points, corresponding to a win by white or black or to a draw.

expansion region

A structured activity node that executes once for each element within an input collection.

Semantics

An expansion region is a mechanism to apply a computation repeatedly to each of the elements within a collection of values. It is a "for all" construct. Outside the region, inputs and outputs are modeled as tokens whose values are collections, such as sets, bags, and lists. Inside the region, the collections are expanded into individual elements, and the region is executed once for each group of elements chosen, one from each input and output collection. All the input collections must have the same size and must be of the same kind (set, bag, list, and so on). The output collections are constructed as part of the execution of the expansion region; their size will be the same as the size of the input collections. The collections need not hold the same type of element, although each collection will hold elements of a given type (but they can vary within a collection with polymorphism).

The purpose of an expansion region is to expand each collection into a collection of individual group of elements, each group containing one element from each collection. The computation within the expansion region is written in terms of inputs and outputs that represent individual elements, not collections. Each group of elements is a "slice" from the overall group of collections. The expansion region executes once for each slice of values, mapping input elements to output elements. In other words, the expansion region takes apart the collections into slices of individual values, executes the computation in the region once for each slice of values, and reassembles the output values into collections.

The collection inputs and outputs of an expansion region are explicitly identified as expansion nodes. The activity within an expansion region can also read values from the outer context. These inputs that do not pass through expansion nodes have the same fixed value for each execution of the region. It is not possible to connect outputs of internal actions outside the region because it would mismatch a collection of values to a single value. A collection of values must be reassembled through an output expansion node.

Normally an expansion region operates in parallel for all elements. There should be no conflict among different executions so that the result does not depend on execution order, which is unspecified and may be concurrent. Optionally, an expansion region may be specified to execute iteratively. If the input collection is ordered, the elements are delivered for execution in the same order. An iterative execution makes possible the accumulation of results over the entire collection of values. Because the executions are sequential, access can be made to shared resources or values. It is also possible to specify that the execution will use streams of internal values.

Notation

An expansion region is shown as a dashed rounded box. One of the keywords «parallel», «iterative», or «stream» may be shown to indicate the execution style. The collection inputs and outputs (expansion nodes) are shown on the boundary of the box as small rectangles divided into a sequence of smaller compartments (that is, it is supposed to look like a sequence of slots). An activity graph fragment may be shown within the box. The fragment may take inputs from the input expansion node symbols and deliver outputs to the output expansion node symbols. Within the expansion region, the types of the object flows correspond to individual elements of the collections. Outside the expansion region, data flow arrows may be connected to the expansion nodes. The types of these data flows correspond to collections of values.

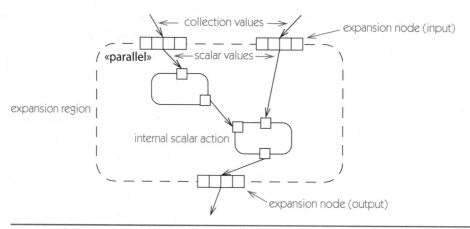

Figure 14-131. *Expansion region*

As a shorthand, expansion node symbols may be placed directly on an action symbol to indicate the execution of a single action within an expansion region.

Figure 14-131 shows an expansion region with two collection inputs and one collection output. It contains two internal actions that take two input values and produce one output value, which is reassembled into an output collection.

Example

Figure 14-132 shows the FFT (Fast Fourier Transform) algorithm as an expansion region. This represents one pass through the main loop of the algorithm, which is executed *log(n)* times during the entire algorithm. The input to the algorithm is an

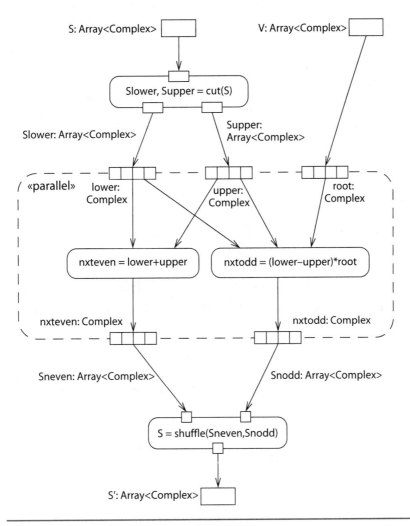

Figure 14-132. *FFT as expansion region*

array of complex values S. The input array is split into two subarrays by the *cut* operation, which operates on arrays. Outside the expansion region, it is convenient to express the algorithm in terms of operations on entire arrays. The two subarrays and an array of complex roots are the collection inputs to the expansion region. The inside of the expansion region represents the so-called butterfly operation. It takes a pair of values, one from each subarray, and a complex root value, and computes two new subarray values for the next pass. The expansion region is executed once for each slice of input values. The two output values are reassembled into two output subarrays, which are combined together into a single full-size array using the *shuffle* array operation. (It interleaves elements from the two inputs.)

The expansion region allows operations on entire arrays and operations on individual elements of arrays to be shown together on the same diagram. It allows two levels of detail to be used together.

History

Expansion regions replace a much clumsier UML1 mechanism for expressing actions on sets of values.

export

In the context of packages, to make an element accessible outside its enclosing namespace by adjusting its visibility. Contrast with access and import, which make outside elements accessible within a package.

See also access, import, visibility.

Semantics

A package exports an element by setting its visibility to a level that permits it to be seen by other packages (public for packages importing it, protected for its own children).

expression

A structured tree that denotes a value (possibly a set) when evaluated in an appropriate context.

Semantics

An expression is a tree of symbols that evaluates to a (possibly empty) set of instances or values when executed in a context. An expression should not modify the environment in which it is evaluated. An expression has a type. The result value or values are of the given type.

An expression comprises a symbol and a list of operands, which may be literal values (such as Boolean values or numbers), instances, or subexpressions. An expression is therefore a tree whose leaves are literal values, instances, or expression strings in a specific language.

An operand can also be an opaque expression, that is, a string that is to be evaluated in the syntax of a specified language. The language may be a constraint-specification language, such as OCL; it may be a programming language, such as C++ or Smalltalk; or it may be a human language. Of course, if an expression is written in a human language, then it cannot be evaluated automatically by a tool and it must be purely for human consumption.

Various subclasses of expressions yield different types of values. These include Boolean expressions, integer expressions, and time expressions.

Expressions appear in actions, constraints, guard conditions, and other places.

Notation

An expression is displayed as a string defined in a language. The syntax of the string is the responsibility of a tool and a linguistic analyzer for the language. The assumption is that the analyzer can evaluate strings at run time to yield values of the appropriate type or can yield semantic structures to capture the meaning of the expression. For example, a Boolean expression evaluates to a true or false value. The language itself is known to a modeling tool but is generally implicit on the diagram under the assumption that the form of the expression makes its purpose clear. The name of the language may be placed in braces before the string.

Example

self.cost < authorization.maxCost

{OCL} i > j and self.size > i

Discussion

The set of operator symbols is not specified in the UML document, therefore the concept of expression is not completely specified.

extend

A relationship from an *extension* use case to a *base* (extended) use case, specifying how the behavior defined for the extension use case can be inserted into the behavior defined for the base use case. The extension use case incrementally modifies the base use case in a modular way.

See also extension point, include, use case, use case generalization.

Semantics

The extend relationship connects an extension use case to a base use case (Figure 14-133). The extension use case in this relationship is not necessarily a separate instantiable classifier. Instead, it consists of one or more segments that describe additional behavior sequences that incrementally modify the behavior of the base use case. Each segment in an extension use case may be inserted at a separate location in the base use case. The extend relationship has a list of extension point names, equal in number to the number of segments in the extension use case. Each extension point must be defined in the base use case. When the execution of a use case instance reaches a location in the base use case referenced by the extension point and any condition on the extension is satisfied, then execution of the instance may transfer to the behavior sequence of the corresponding segment of the extension use case; when the execution of the extension segment is complete, control returns to the original use case at the referenced point. See Figure 14-134 for an example of behavior sequences.

Multiple extend relationships may be applied to the same base use case. An instance of a use case may execute more than one extension during its lifetime. If several use cases extend one base use case at the same extension point, then their relative order of execution is nondeterministic. There may even be multiple extend relationships between the same extension and base use cases, provided the extension is inserted at a different location in the base. Extensions may even extend other extensions in a nested manner.

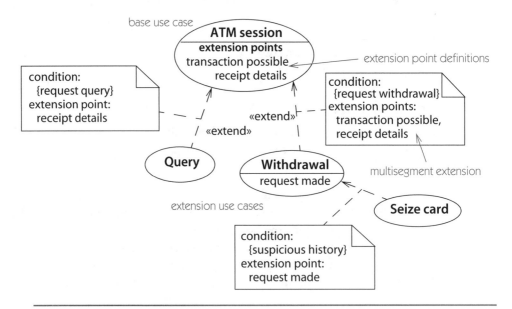

Figure 14-133. *Extend relationship*

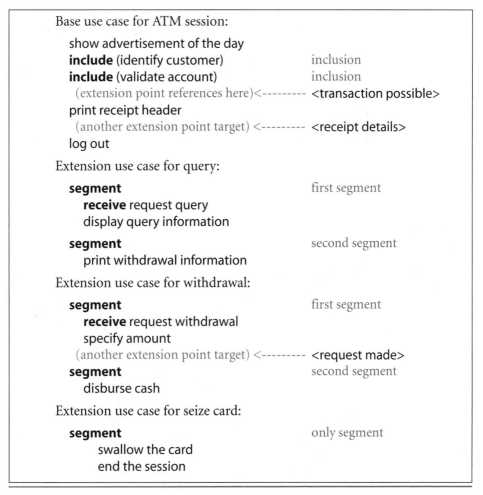

Base use case for ATM session:

    show advertisement of the day
    include (identify customer)   inclusion
    include (validate account)   inclusion
      (extension point references here)<---------- \<transaction possible>
    print receipt header
      (another extension point target) <---------- \<receipt details>
    log out

Extension use case for query:

    segment   first segment
      receive request query
      display query information
    segment   second segment
      print withdrawal information

Extension use case for withdrawal:

    segment   first segment
      receive request withdrawal
      specify amount
      (another extension point target) <---------- \<request made>
    segment   second segment
      disburse cash

Extension use case for seize card:

    segment   only segment
      swallow the card
      end the session

Figure 14-134. *Behavior sequences for use cases*

An extension use case in an extend relationship may access and modify attributes defined by the base use case. The base use case, however, cannot see the extensions and may not access their attributes or operations. The base use case defines a modular framework into which extensions can be added, but the base does not have visibility of the extensions. The extensions implicitly modify the behavior of the base use case. Note the difference with use case generalization. With extension, the effects of the extension use case are added to the effects of the base use case in an instantiation of the base use case. With generalization, the effects of the child use case are added to the effects of the parent use case in an instantiation of the child use case, whereas an instantiation of the parent use case does not get the effects of the child use case.

An extension use case may extend more than one base use case, and a base use case may be extended by more than one extension use case. This does not indicate any relationship among the base use cases.

An extension use case may itself be the base in an extend, include, or generalization relationship.

Structure (of extension use case)

An extension use case contains a list of one or more *insertion segments*, each of which is a behavior sequence.

Structure (of base use case)

A base use case defines a set of extension points, each of which references a location or set of locations in the base use case where additional behavior may be inserted.

Structure (of extend relationship)

The extend relationship has a list of extension point names, which must be present in the base use case. The number of names must equal the number of segments in the extension use case.

The extend relationship may have a condition, an expression in terms of attributes of the base use case or the occurrence of events such as the receipt of a signal. The condition determines whether the extension use case is performed when the execution of a use case instance reaches a location referenced by the first extension point. If the condition is absent, then it is deemed to be always true. If the condition for an extension use case is satisfied, then execution of the extension use case proceeds. If the extension point references several locations in the base use case, the extension use case may be executed at any one of them.

The extension may be performed more than once if the condition remains true. All segments of the extension use case are executed the same number of times. If the number of executions must be restricted, the condition should be defined accordingly.

Execution semantics

When a use case instance performing the base use case reaches a location in the base use case that is referenced by an extend relationship, then the condition on the extend relationship is evaluated. If it is true or if it is absent, then the extension use case is performed. In many cases, the condition includes the occurrence of an event or the availability of values needed by the extension use case segment itself—for example, a signal from an actor that begins the extension segment. The condition may depend on the state of the use case instance, including attribute values of the base use case. If the event does not occur or the condition is false, the execution of the extension use case does not start. When the performance of an extension segment is complete, the use case instance resumes performing the base use case at the location at which it left off.

Additional insertions of the extension use case may be performed immediately if the condition is satisfied. If the extension point references multiple locations in the base use case, the condition may be satisfied at any of them. The condition may become true at any location within the set.

If there is more than one insertion sequence in an extension use case, then the extension is executed if the condition is true at the first extension point. The condition is not reevaluated for subsequent segments, which are inserted when the use case instance reaches the corresponding locations within the base use case. The use case instance resumes execution of the base between insertions at different extension points. Once started, all the segments must be performed.

Note that, in general, a use case is a nondeterministic state machine (as in a grammar) rather than an executable procedure. That is because the conditions may include the occurrence of external events. To realize a use case as a collaboration of classes may require a transformation into explicit control mechanisms, just as the implementation of a grammar requires a transformation to an executable form that is efficient but harder to understand.

Note that *base* and *extension* are relative terms. An extension can itself serve as a base for a further extension. This does not present any difficulty, and the previous rules still apply—the insertions are nested. For example, suppose use case B extends use case A at extension point x, and suppose use case C extends use case B at extension point y (Figure 14-135). When an instance of A comes to extension point x, it begins performing use case B. When the instance then comes to extension point y within B, it begins performing use case C. When the execution of C is complete, it resumes performing use case B. When the execution of B is complete, it resumes performing A. It is similar to nested procedure calls or any other nested construct.

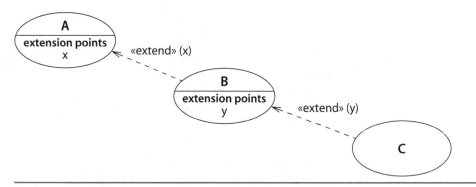

Figure 14-135. *Nested extends*

Table 14-2: *Comparison of Use Case Relationships*

Property	Extend	Include	Generalization
Base behavior	Base use case	Base use case	Parent use case
Added behavior	Extension use case	Inclusion use case	Child use case
Direction of reference	Extension use case references the base use case.	Base use case references the inclusion use case.	Child use case references the parent use case.
Base modified by the addition?	The extension implicitly modifies the behavior of the base. The base must be well formed without the extension, but if the extension is present, an instantiation of the base may execute the extension.	The inclusion explicitly modifies the effect of the base. The base may or may not be well formed without the inclusion, but an instantiation of the base executes the inclusion.	The effect of executing the parent is unaffected by the child. To obtain the effects of the addition, the child, not the parent, must be instantiated.
Is the addition instantiable?	Extension is not necessarily instantiable. It may be a fragment.	Inclusion is not necessarily instantiable. It may be a fragment.	Child is not necessarily instantiable. It may be abstract.
Can the addition access attributes of the base?	The extension may access and modify the state of the base.	The inclusion may access the state of the base. The base must provide appropriate attributes expected by the inclusion.	The child may access and modify the state of the base (by the usual mechanisms of inheritance).
Can the base see the addition?	The base cannot see the extension and must be well formed in its absence.	The base sees the inclusion and may depend on its effects, but it may not access its attributes.	The parent cannot see the child and must be well formed in its absence.
Repetition	Depends on condition	Exactly one repetition	Child controls its own execution.

Notation

A dashed arrow is drawn from the extension use case symbol to the base use case symbol with a stick arrowhead on the base. The keyword «extend» is placed on the arrow. A list of extension point names may appear in parentheses after the keyword.

Figure 14-133shows use cases with extend relationships. There is no official notation for specifying behavior sequences. Figure 14-134 is merely suggestive.

Discussion

The extend, include, and generalization relationships all add behavior to an initial use case. They have many similarities, but it is convenient to separate them in practice. Table 14-2 compares the three viewpoints.

Note that segment and location are not precise terms, so they must be considered semantic variation points subject to implementation.

extension

The attachment of a stereotype to a metaclass, thereby extending the definition of the metaclass to include the stereotype.

Semantics

An extension is a relationship from a stereotype to a UML metaclass (a class in the definition of the UML model itself, such as Class or Operation). It indicates that the properties defined in the stereotype may be applied to instances of the metaclass that bear the stereotype. Note that an instance of a metaclass is an ordinary class as defined in a user model, so defining an extension to a metaclass means that a user-model element of the given metaclass has additional modeling-time properties whose values the modeler can specify. An extension may be optional or required. If an extension is required, all instances of the metaclass must bear the extension. If an extension is optional, instances of the metaclass may or may not bear the extension. Furthermore, an instance of the metaclass can add or remove the extension during its lifetime.

Notation

An extension is shown by a solid arrow from the stereotype rectangle to the metaclass rectangle with a filled black arrowhead on the class end of the arrow. The keyword {required} is used to indicate a required extension; otherwise the extension is optional. The keyword «metaclass» may be placed in the metaclass rectangle.

Example

Figure 14-136 shows the extension of the metaclass **Class** by the **Authorship** stereotype, which defines the properties **author** and **creation** date. Extension of **Class** indicates that a class defined in a user model can bear the stereotype **Author**. Because the {required} keyword is absent, the use of the stereotype is optional. The model defining such a class can then define values for these properties. For example, they may identify the person who created the class and the date it was created.

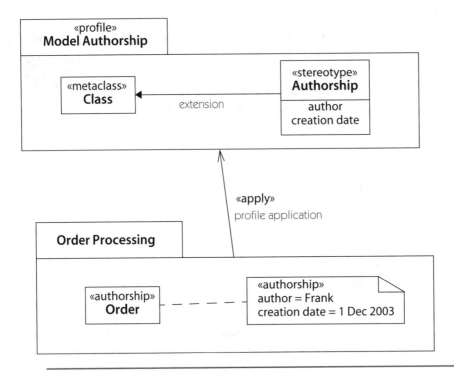

Figure 14-136. *Extension of metaclass by stereotype*

Discussion

The word *extension* is used variously for the extend relationship of use cases, the extension of classes by stereotypes, and the run-time instances of a class. This overlap is somewhat confusing because these are not the same concepts.

extension point   516

A named marker that identifies a location or set of locations within the behavioral sequence for a use case, at which additional behavior can be inserted. An extension point declaration opens up the use case to the possibility of extension. An insertion segment is a behavior sequence in an extension use case (a use case related to a base use case by an extend relationship). The extend relationship contains a list of extension point names that indicate where the insertion segments from the extension use case insert their behavior.

See also extend, use case.

Semantics

An extension point has a name. It references a set of one or more locations within a use case behavior sequence. The concept of location is not defined within UML, therefore it is a semantic variation point dependent on implementation.

A location may correspond to a state within a state machine description of a use case, or the equivalent in a different description—between two statements in a list of statements or between two messages in an interaction.

An extend relationship contains an optional condition and a list of extension point references equal in number to the number of insertion segments in the extension use case. An insertion segment may be performed if the condition is satisfied while a use case instance is executing the base use case at any location in the extension point corresponding to the insertion segment.

The location of an extension point can be changed without affecting its identity. The use of named extension points separates the specification of extension behavior sequences from the internal details of the base use case. The base use case can be modified or rearranged without affecting the extensions. Moreover, an extension point can be moved within the base without affecting the relationship or the

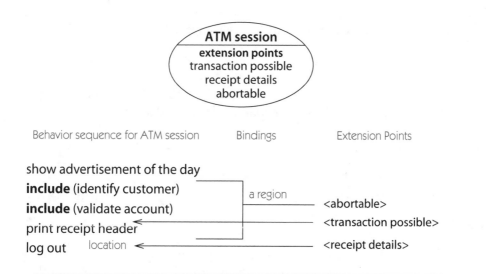

Figure 14-137. *Extension point declarations*

extension use case. As with all kinds of modularity, this independence requires a good choice of extension points and is not guaranteed under all circumstances.

Notation

The extension points for a use case may be listed as strings in a compartment named **extension points** (Figure 14-137).

Note that there is no standard text language for behavior sequences, therefore the syntax for describing extension points or locations is not precisely defined. The notation in Figure 14-137 is merely suggestive.

extent

The set of instances described by a classifier. Also sometimes called *extension*.

Contrast: intent.

Semantics

A classifier, such as a class or an association, has both a description (its intent) and a set of instances that it describes (its extent). The purpose of the intent is to specify the properties of the instances that compose the extent. There is no assumption that the extent is physically manifest or that it can be obtained at run time. For example, a modeler should not assume that the set of objects that are instances of a class can be obtained even in principle.

facade

The facade stereotype from UML1 has been retired.

feature

A property, such as operation or attribute, which is encapsulated as part of a list within a classifier, such as an interface, a class, or a datatype.

file (stereotype of Artifact)

A physical file in the context of the target system.

See artifact.

final node

An abstract kind of node in an activity graph which stops activity. The subtypes of final node are activity final node, which terminates all activity within the graph, and flow final node, which terminates the thread of activity containing the node but does not affect concurrent activity.

final state

A special state that, when entered, indicates that the execution of the containing region has been completed. The state containing the region is completed if all other contained regions (if any) have also completed. When a composite state completes, a completion transition leaving the composite state is triggered and may fire if its guard condition is satisfied.

See also do activity, completion transition, destruction.

Semantics

To promote encapsulation, it is desirable to separate the outside view of a composite state from the inside details as much as possible. From the outside, the state is viewed as an opaque entity with an internal structure that is hidden. From the outside viewpoint, transitions go to and from the state itself. From the inside viewpoint, they connect to substates within the state. An initial state or a final state is a mechanism to support encapsulation of states.

A final state is a special state that indicates that the activity of a region within the composite state is complete and that a completion transition leaving the composite state is enabled. If there are multiple regions in the composite state, all of them must reach completion. A final state is not a pseudostate. A final state may be active for a period of time, unlike an initial state that immediately transitions to its successor. Control may remain within a final state while waiting for the completion of other orthogonal regions of the composite state—that is, while waiting for sychronization of multiple threads of control to join together. Outgoing event-triggered transitions are not allowed from a final state, however (otherwise, it is just a normal state). A final state may have any number of incoming transitions from within the enclosing composite state, but no transitions from outside the enclosing state. The incoming transitions are normal transitions and may have the full complement of triggers, guard conditions, and actions.

If an object reaches its top-level final state, the state machine terminates and the object is destroyed.

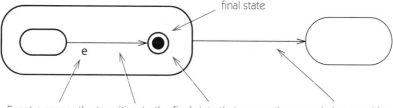

Event e causes the transition to the final state that causes the completion transition.

Figure 14-138. *Final state*

Notation

A final state is displayed as a bull's-eye icon—that is, a small, filled black disk surrounded by a small circle. The symbol is placed inside the enclosing composite state whose completion it represents (Figure 14-138). Only one final state may occur (directly) within each orthogonal region of a composite state. Additional final states may occur, however, within nested composite states. For convenience, the final state symbol may be repeated within a state, but each copy represents the same final state.

fire

To execute a transition.

See also run-to-completion, trigger.

Semantics

When an event required by a transition occurs, and the guard condition on the transition is satisfied, the transition performs its action and the active state changes.

When an object receives an event, the event is saved in a pool if the state machine is executing a run-to-completion step. When the step is completed, the state machine handles an event from the pool, if any. A transition is *triggered* if its event is handled while the owning object is in the state containing the transition or is in a substate nested inside the state containing the transition. An event satisfies a trigger event that is an ancestor of the occurring event type. If a complex transition has multiple source states, all of them must be active for the transition to be enabled. A completion transition is enabled when its source state completes activity. If it is a composite state, it is enabled when all its direct substates have completed or reached their final states.

When the event is handled, the guard condition (if any) is evaluated. If the Boolean expression in the guard condition evaluates to true, then the transition is said to *fire*. The action on the transition is executed, and the state of the object becomes the target state of the transition (no change of state occurs for an internal transition, however). During the state change, all exit activity and entry activity effects on the minimal path from the original state of the object to the target state of the transition are executed. Note that the original state may be a nested substate of the source state of the transition.

If the guard condition is not satisfied, nothing happens as a result of this transition, although some other transition might fire if its condition is satisfied.

Conflicts. If more than one transition is eligible to fire, only one of them will fire. A transition in a nested state takes precedence over a transition in an enclosing state. Otherwise, the choice of transitions is undefined and may be nondeterministic.

This is often a realistic real-world situation, and nondeterminism may sometimes be desirable.

As a practical matter, an implementation may provide an ordering of transitions for firing. This does not change the semantics, as the same effect could be achieved by organizing the guard conditions so that they do not overlap. But it is often simpler to be able to say, "This transition fires only if no other transition fires."

Deferred events. If the event or one of its ancestors is marked for deferral in the state or in an enclosing state, and the event does not trigger a transition, the event is a deferred event until the object enters a state in which the event is not deferred. When the object enters a new state, any previously deferred events that are no longer deferred become *pending* and they are handled in an indeterminate order. If the first pending event does not cause a transition to fire, it is discarded and another pending event occurs. If a previously deferred event is marked for deferral in the new state, it may trigger a transition, but it remains deferred if it fails to trigger a transition. If the occurrence of an event causes a transition to a new state, any remaining pending and deferred events are reevaluated according to the deferral status of the new state and a new set of pending events is established.

An implementation might impose stricter rules on the order in which deferred events are processed or supply operations to manipulate their order.

flag

This term is used in this book to indicate a Boolean value that specifies a structural constraint on a model element. Depending on the situation, a flag is sometimes modeled as a true-false statement and sometimes as a two-choice enumeration.

flow

A generic term used to describe among sources and targets of various kinds of information, including data and locus of execution (control). The activity model provides concepts and notation to model data flow and control flow explicitly. Other models provide ways to model flow of information implicitly.

Discussion

UML2 contains a stand-alone information flow model that is meant to add a rudimentary data flow modeling capability which we do not recommend. The activity model provides a much more complete flow modeling capability that is properly integrated with the rest of UML.

flow final node

A node in an activity that destroys all tokens that reach it. It has no other effect on the execution of the activity.

Semantics

A flow final node will destroy tokens that reach it. This might be useful to terminate a thread of control that can execute independently that has no further effect on the rest of the activity.

Notation

A flow final node is shown as a circle with an X in it (Figure 14-139).

Discussion

The UML2 document shows an example of a flow final used to terminate a loop that has been spewing out concurrent executions of a subactivity. This construct should probably be avoided, if possible, in favor of a structured loop with an explicit merge of control, as its semantics are suspect.

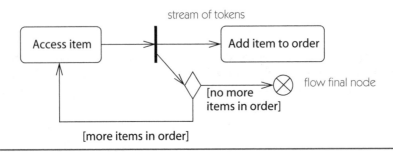

Figure 14-139. *Flow final node*

focus (stereotype of Class)

A class that defines core logic or control in conjunction with one or more auxiliary classes that support it by providing subordinate mechanisms.
    See auxiliary.

focus of control

A symbol on a sequence diagram that shows the period of time during which an object is performing an action, either directly or through a subordinate procedure. In UML2, it is now called *execution specification*.
    See execution specification.

font usage

Text may be distinguished through the use of different fonts and other graphic markers.

See also graphic marker.

Discussion

Italics are used to indicate an abstract class, attribute, or operation. Other font distinctions are primarily for highlighting or to distinguish parts of the notation. It is recommended that names of classifiers and associations be shown in boldface and subsidiary elements, such as attributes, operations, rolename, and so on, be shown in normal type. Compartment names should be shown in a distinctive font, such as small boldface, but the choice is left to an editing tool. A tool is also free to use font distinctions for highlighting selected elements, to distinguish reserved words and keywords, and to encode selected properties of an element, or it may enable the use of such distinctions under user control. Similar considerations apply to color, although its use should be optional because many persons are color blind. All such uses are convenience extensions to the canonical notation described in this book, which is sufficient to display any model.

fork

In a state machine, a complex transition in which one source state is replaced by two or more target states, resulting in an increase in the number of active states. In an activity, a node that copies a single input token onto multiple concurrent outputs. Antonym: join.

See also complex transition, composite state, join.

Semantics

In a state machine, a fork is a transition with one source state and two or more target states. (Actually it is a pseudostate, but that is an internal detail that is unimportant in most cases.) If the source state is active and the trigger event occurs, the transition action is executed and all the target states become active. The target states must be in different regions of a composite state.

In an activity, a fork node is a node with one input and multiple outputs. An input token is copied onto each of the outputs, increasing the amount of concurrency. The outputs may have guards, but this usage introduces considerable danger of ill-formed models; we recommend that decisions and forks be separated.

In both state machines and activities, forks increase the amount of concurrent threads of execution. A fork is usually matched to a later join that decreases the amount of concurrency.

Notation

In a state machine diagram or an activity diagram, a fork is shown as a heavy bar with one incoming transition arrow and two or more outgoing transition arrows. It may have a transition label (guard condition, trigger event, and action). Figure 14-140 shows an explicit fork into a concurrent composite state.

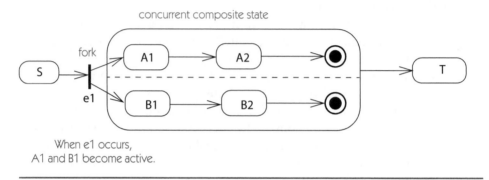

Figure 14-140. *Fork*

fork node

A kind of control node in an activity that copies a single input onto multiple concurrent outputs.

See fork.

formal argument

See parameter.

framework (stereotype of Package)

A generic architecture that provides an extensible template for applications within a domain. A framework is the starting point for constructing an architecture. Typically, elements are modified, specialized, and extended to tailor the generic architecture to a specific problem.

See package.

friend

This UML1 dependency has been removed in UML2.

full descriptor

The complete implicit description of a direct instance. The full descriptor is implicitly assembled by inheritance from all the ancestors.

See also direct class, inheritance, multiple classification.

Semantics

A declaration of a class or other model element is, in fact, only a partial description of its instances; call it the *class segment*. In general, an object contains more structure than described by the class segment of its direct class. The rest of the structure is obtained by inheritance from the ancestor classes. The complete description of all its attributes, operations, and associations is called the full descriptor. The full descriptor is usually not manifest in a model or program. The purpose of inheritance rules is to provide a way to automatically construct the full descriptor from the segments. In principle, there are various ways to do this, often called *meta-object protocols*. UML defines one set of rules for inheritance that cover most popular programming languages and are also useful for conceptual modeling. Be aware, however, that other possibilities exist—for example, the CLOS language.

Discussion

The UML specification does not actually define the rules for inheritance. The actual mapping of an operation to a method is dependent on a resolution mechanism that is not completely defined in the specification. Most modelers (and most tools) will assume inheritance rules compatible with Smalltalk or Java, but the specification permits wider definitions of inheritance, such as those found in self or CLOS.

functional view

A view dealing with the breakdown of a system into functions or operations that provide its functionality. A functional view is not usually considered object-oriented and can lead to an architecture that is hard to maintain. In traditional development methods, the data flow diagram is the heart of the functional view. UML does not directly support a functional view, although an activity has some functional characteristics.

gate

A connection point in an interaction or interaction fragment for a message that comes from or goes to outside the interaction or fragment.

Semantics

A gate is a parameter that represents a message that crosses the boundary of an interaction or interaction fragment. Messages within the interaction can be connected to the gate. If the interaction is referenced within another interaction, messages may be connected to its gates. When the interaction is executed, messages connected through gates will be delivered properly.

Notation

In a sequence diagram, a gate is simply a point on the boundary of the sequence diagram or interaction fragment that is connected to the head or tail of a message arrow. The name of the connected message arrow is the name of the gate (Figure 14-141).

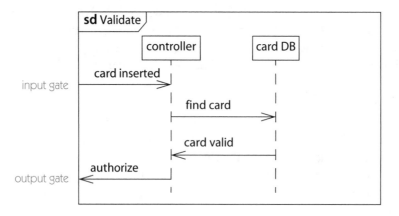

Figure 14-141. *Gates*

general ordering

An constraint that the time of one occurrence specification precedes the time of another occurrence specification in an interaction.

Semantics

Usually occurrence specifications in interactions are ordered by their relative positions on lifelines and by ordering constraints implied by messages (the source event of a message occurs before the target event). Occurrence specifications that are not constrained by lifelines and messages (including indirect constraints from multiple events) are assumed to be concurrent. Sometimes a modeler wishes to specify an ordering constraint among two otherwise unordered occurrence specifications. A general ordering is a constraint that one occurrence specification precedes the other.

Notation

A general ordering is shown as a dotted line between two occurrence specifications (usually the intersections between messages and lifelines). The line contains a solid arrowhead somewhere along its path (not at an end). The arrow points toward the occurrence specification that occurs later.

Example

Figure 14-142 shows an example in which two users exchange messages with a server. In the absence of the general ordering, the following ordering constraints (and their closures) can be assumed:

a < b, c < d, b < d, d < e, e < f, e < g, g < h

By applying multiple constraints, we can infer that c < f, for example. It is not possible to determine the relative ordering of a and c, because they are unrelated by a chain of constraints. The addition of the general ordering between a and c explicitly specifies that a < c. The relative ordering of b and c is still unspecified, however. Similarly, the relative ordering of f and g is unspecified.

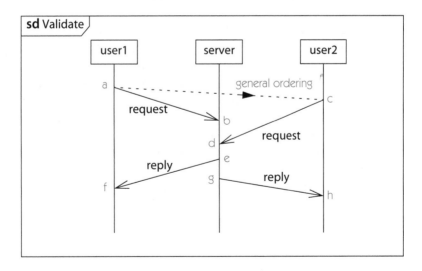

Figure 14-142. *General ordering of occurrence specifications*

Discussion

Explicit ordering constraints should be avoided, if possible. Often they represent the absence (in the model or in the actual system) of necessary synchronization messages.

generalizable element

This UML1 element has been retired in UML2. Most of its semantics have been moved into classifier. Classifiers now include associations, so they are generalizable. Behaviors, including interactions and state machines, are also generalizable.

generalization

A taxonomic relationship between a more general element and a more specific element. The more specific element is fully consistent with the more general element and contains additional information. An instance of the more specific element is an indirect instance of the more general element and inherits its characteristics.

See also association generalization, generalization set, inheritance, multiple inheritance, substitutability principle, use case generalization.

Semantics

A generalization relationship is a directed relationship between two classifiers of the same kind, such as classes, use cases, or associations. One element is called the parent, and the other is called the child. For classes, the parent is called the superclass and the child is called the subclass. The parent is the description of a set of (indirect) instances with common properties over all children; the child is a description of a subset of those instances that have the properties of the parent but that also have additional properties peculiar to the child.

Generalization is a transitive, antisymmetric relationship. One direction of traversal leads to the parent; the other direction leads to the child. An element related in the parent direction across one or more generalizations is called an ancestor; an element related in the child direction across one or more generalizations is called a descendant. No directed generalization cycles are allowed. A class may not have itself for an ancestor or descendant. An instance of a classifier is an indirect instance of all of the ancestors of the classifier.

In the simplest case, a class (or other generalizable element) has a single parent. In a more complicated situation, a child may have more than one parent. The child inherits structure, behavior, and constraints from all its parents. This is called multiple inheritance (it might better be called multiple generalization). A child element references its parent and must have visibility to it.

Behavior elements are classes, therefore they may participate in generalization, similar to state machines and interactions.

Each kind of classifier has its own generalization semantics. For the application of generalization to associations, see association generalization. For the application of generalization to use cases, see use case generalization. Nodes and components are much like classes, and generalization applied to them behaves the same as it does for classes.

A child inherits the attributes, associations, operations, and constraints of its parent. By default, they are unchanged, but in some cases they may be redefined in the child. See redefinition.

Types and substitutability

Normally generalization implies that a child element can be used wherever a parent element is defined, for example, to substitute for a parameter of a given type. Such a generalization is said to be substitutable. Substitutable generalizations support polymorphism, because any semantics of the parent element can be guaranteed for any child element.

Close modeling of programming language constructs sometimes requires generalizations that are not substitutable. In other words, it cannot be assumed that a child element can be used anywhere a parent element is defined. This may occur because internal constituents are overridden or redefined, for example. UML permits the definition of a generalization as substitutable or nonsubstitutable. While occasional use of nonsubstitutable generalizations may be convenient for sharing structure, they defeat the larger purpose of generalization and should be avoided as much as possible.

Generalization sets

A set of classifiers sharing a common parent may be grouped into a generalization set. Each generalization set represents a distinct dimension or aspect on which the supertype can be specialized. See generalization set.

Notation

Generalization between classifiers is shown as a solid-line path from the child element (such as a subclass) to the parent element (such as a superclass), with a large hollow triangle at the end of the path where it meets the more general element (Figure 14-143). The lines to the parent may be combined to produce a tree (Figure 14-144).

Generalization may be applied to associations, as well as to classifiers, although the notation may be messy because of the multiple lines. An association can be shown as an association class for the purpose of attaching generalization arrows.

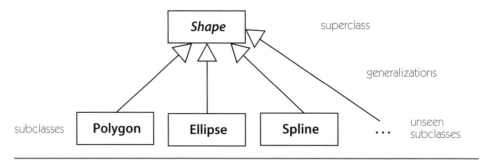

Figure 14-143. *Generalization*

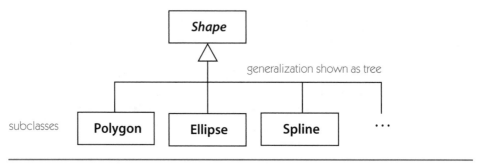

Figure 14-144. *Generalization using tree style*

A text label following a colon placed on a generalization line indicates that the generalization belongs to a generalization set of the given name. If two generalizations with the same parent have the same name, they are in the same generalization set.

Presentation options

A group of generalization paths for a given superclass may be shown as a tree with a shared segment (including triangle) to the superclass, branching into multiple paths to each subclass. This is merely a notational device that does not indicate an *n*-ary relationship. In the underlying model, there is one generalization for each subclass-superclass pair. There is no semantic difference if the arcs are drawn separately.

If a text label is placed on a generalization triangle shared by several generalization paths to subclasses, the label applies to all the paths. In other words, all the subclasses share the given properties.

Discussion

The parent element in a generalization relationship can be defined without knowledge of the children, but the children must generally know the structure of their parents in order to work correctly. In many cases, however, the parent is designed to be extended by children and includes more or less knowledge of the expected children. One of the glories of generalization, however, is that new children are often discovered that had not been anticipated by the designer of the parent element, leading to an expansion in power that is compatible in spirit with the original intent.

The realization relationship is like a generalization in which only behavior specification is inherited rather than structure or implementation. If the specification element is an abstract class with no attributes, no associations, and only abstract operations, then generalization and realization are roughly equivalent as there is nothing to inherit but behavior specification. Note that realization does not actually populate the client, however; therefore, the operations must be in the client or inherited from some other element.

History

In UML2, generalization is restricted to classifiers, but because most everything is a classifier, not much is lost.

generalization set

A set of generalizations that compose one dimension or aspect of the specialization of a given classifier.

See also generalization, powertype.

Semantics

A classifier can often be specialized along multiple dimensions, each representing a different aspect of the structure and semantics of the concept. Because these dimensions are orthogonal ways of viewing a classification hierarchy, it is useful to partition the children of a classifier according to the aspect of the parent that they represent. A set of generalizations representing such a dimension is called a generalization set. The parent element of all the generalizations in the set must be the same.

Usually each dimension characterized by a generalization set represents only part of the semantics of the original classifier. To obtain a complete child classifier, it is necessary to combine (using multiple inheritance) one classifier from each orthogonal generalization set.

For example, a geometric shape might be specialized according to whether its edges are straight or curved and according to whether its boundary is intersecting or nonintersecting. A curved shape could be specialized into conic sections or splines. A complete subclass would require a choice from each dimension. For example, a star is a shape that has straight edges and is intersecting.

Each generalization set represents an abstract quality of the parent, a quality that is specialized by the elements in the set. But a parent with multiple generalization sets has multiple dimensions, all of which must be specialized to produce a concrete element. Therefore, classifiers within a generalization set are inherently abstract. Each of them is only a partial description of the parent, a description that emphasizes one quality and ignores the rest. For example, a subclass of geometric shape that focuses on straightness of edges ignores self-intersections. A concrete element requires specializing all the dimensions simultaneously. This can occur by multiple inheritance of the concrete model element from a classifier in each of the generalization sets, or by multiple classification of an instance by a classifier in each of the generalization sets. Until all the generalization sets are combined, the description remains abstract.

For example, consider two generalization sets on a vehicle: means of propulsion and venue (where it travels). The propulsion generalization set includes wind-powered, motor-powered, gravity-powered, and muscle-powered vehicles. The venue generalization set includes land, water, and air vehicles. An actual vehicle must have a means of propulsion and a venue. A wind-powered water vehicle is a sailboat. There is no particular name for an animal-powered air vehicle, but instances of the combination exist in fantasy and mythology.

A powertype is a classifier associated with a generalization set. It is a metaclass whose instances are the classifiers in a generalization set. It represents the quality that is being selected in the generalization.

Generalization set constraints

A constraint may be applied to the elements in a generalization set. The following properties can be specified. See powertype.

disjoint	The classifiers in the set are mutually exclusive. No instance may be a direct or indirect instance of more than one of the elements.
overlapping	The classifiers in the set are not mutually exclusive. An element may be an instance of more than one of the elements.
complete	The classifiers in the set completely cover a dimension of specialization. Every instance of the supertype must be an instance of at least one of the classifiers in the set.
incomplete	The classifiers in the set do not completely cover a dimension of specialization. An instance of the supertype may fail to be an instance of one of the classifiers in the set.

Notation

A generalization set is shown as a text label following a colon on a generalization arrow. Figure 14-145 shows a specialization of **Employee** on two dimensions: employee **status** and **locality**. Each generalization set has a range of possibilities represented by subclasses. But both dimensions are required to produce an instantiable subclass. **Liaison**, for example, is a class that is both a **Supervisor** and an **Expatriate**.

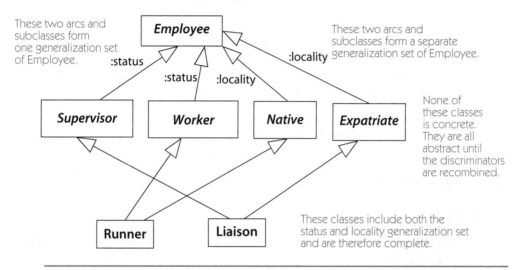

Figure 14-145. *Generalization sets*

Several generalization arrows may be combined into a single tree with one arrowhead. The name of the generalization set may be placed on the arrowhead so that it need not be repeated on each subclass. Constraints on generalization sets may be placed on an arrowhead that branches to multiple subclasses, or they may be placed on a dashed line that crosses a set of generalization arrows that compose a generalization set. Figure 14-146 shows the declaration of constraints on generalizations. It illustrates both the "tree style" of notation, in which the generalization paths are drawn on an orthogonal grid and share a common arrowhead, as well as the "binary style," in which each parent-child relationship has its own oblique arrow.

History

UML2 generalization sets replace UML1 discriminators with roughly equivalent capability.

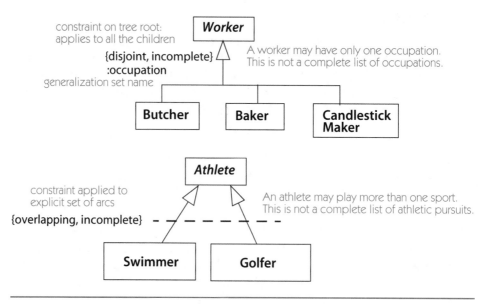

Figure 14-146. *Generalization set constraints*

graphic marker

A notational element such as geometry, texture, fill pattern, font, color, and so on. See also font usage.

Notation

Symbols for notation are constructed from various graphic markers. No one graphic marker has semantic significance by itself, but the goal of notation is to use graphic markers in a consistent and orthogonal way as much as possible.

Some graphic markers are used to construct predefined UML symbols, while other graphic markers are not used in the canonical notation. For example, no meaning has been assigned to color because many printers do not render it and some people cannot distinguish all colors. Unassigned graphic markers, such as colors, can be used within editing tools for whatever purpose the modeler or tool wishes. Often such usage is modifiable and carries no fixed meaning. Modelers should use such capabilities with care if the model may be used in another context where the graphic marker might be unavailable (such as a monochrome copy).

UML permits limited graphical extension of its notation. A graphic icon or a graphic marker (such as texture or color) can be associated with a stereotype. The UML does not specify the form of the graphic specification. But many bitmap and stroked formats exist and might be used by a graphical editor (although their portability is a difficult problem).

More general forms of icon specification and substitution are conceivable, but we leave these to the ingenuity of tool builders—with the warning that excessive use of extensibility capabilities may lead to loss of portability among tools.

group transition

A transition whose source is a composite state.

Semantics

A transition whose source is a composite state is called a *group transition* (or a *high-level transition*). It applies whenever the active state configuration includes one or more substates contained (directly or indirectly) by the composite state. If the trigger of the group transition is satisfied and no transition on a state nested within the composite state is satisfied, the firing of the group transition forces the termination of activity within the composite state. Any terminated threads of activity execute their exit activities until all the direct substates of the composite state reach completion. If the target state is exterior to the composite state, the exit activity of the composite state is executed. Then any further activities encountered on the path to the target state(s) are executed, and the active state configuration is updated by replacing the terminated states with the new target state or states.

guard condition

A condition that must be satisfied in order to enable an associated transition to fire.
See also any trigger, branch, junction, transition.

Semantics

A guard condition is a Boolean expression that is part of the specification of a transition. When a signal is received, it is saved until the state machine has completed any current run-to-completion step. When any run-to-completion step is completed, the triggers of transitions leaving the current state (including containing states) are examined to find those eligible to fire. The guard conditions of eligible transitions are evaluated, not necessarily in a fixed order. If the condition of at least one eligible transition is satisfied, the transition is enabled to fire (but if more than one transition is enabled, only one will fire and the event is consumed, possibly removing satisfaction of other triggers). The test occurs as part of the trigger evaluation process. If the guard condition evaluates to false when the event is handled, it is not reevaluated unless the trigger event occurs again, even if the condition later becomes true.

A guard condition must be a query—that is, it may not modify the value of the system or its state; it may not have side effects.

A guard condition may appear on a completion transition. In that case, it selects one arm of a branch.

Notation

A guard condition is part of the string for a transition. It has the form of a Boolean expression enclosed in square brackets.

```
[ boolean-expression ]
```

Names used within the expression must be available to the transition. They are either parameters of the trigger event, attributes of the owning object, or property names reachable by navigation starting from the such names.

guillemets

Small double angle marks (« ») used as quotation marks in French, Italian, Spanish, and other languages. In UML notation they are used to enclose keywords and stereotype names. For example: «bind», «instanceOf». Guillemets are available in most fonts, so there is really no excuse for not using them, but the typographically challenged often substitute two angle brackets (<< >>) instead.

See also font usage.

high-level transition

See group transition.

history state

A pseudostate that indicates that the enclosing composite state remembers its previously active substate after it exits.

See also composite state, pseudostate, state machine, transition.

Semantics

A history state allows a composite state to remember the last substate that was active in it prior to the most recent exit from the composite state. A transition to the history state causes the former active substate to be made active again after executing any specified entry activity or activities on the path to the substate. Incoming transitions may be connected to the history state from outside the composite state or from the initial state.

A history state may have one outgoing unlabeled transition. This transition indicates the initial default history state. It is used if a transition to the history state occurs when no stored state is present. The history state may not have incoming transitions from other states within the composite state because it is already active.

A history state may remember *shallow history* or *deep history*. A shallow history state remembers and reactivates a state at the same nesting depth as the history state itself. If a transition from a nested substate directly exited the composite state, the enclosing substate at the top level within the composite state is activated, but not any nested substates. A deep history state remembers a state that may have been nested at some depth within the composite state. To remember a deep state, a transition must have taken the deep state directly out of the composite state. If a transition from a deep state goes to a shallower state, which then transitions out of the composite state, then the shallower state is the one that is remembered, because it is the source of the most recent exit. A transition to a deep history state restores the previously active state at any depth. In the process, entry activities are executed if they are present on inner states containing the remembered state. A composite state may have both a shallow history state and a deep history state. An incoming transition must be connected to one or the other.

If a composite state reaches its final state, then it loses its stored history and behaves as if it had not been entered for the first time.

Notation

A shallow history state is shown as a small circle containing the letter H, as in Figure 14-147. A deep history state is shown as a circle containing the letters H*.

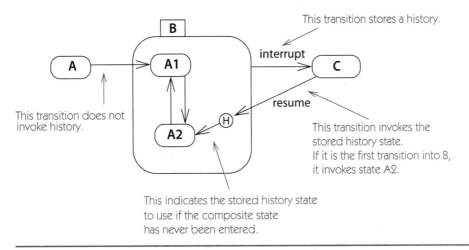

Figure 14-147. *History state*

hyperlink

An invisible connection between two notation elements that can be traversed by some command.

See also diagram.

Notation

A notation on a piece of paper contains no hidden information. A notation on a computer screen, however, may contain additional invisible hyperlinks that are not apparent in a static view but that can be invoked dynamically to access some other piece of information, either in a graphical view or in a textual table. Such dynamic links are as much a part of a *dynamic* notation as the visible information, but the UML specification does not prescribe their form. They are a tool responsibility. The UML specification attempts to define a *static* notation for UML, with the understanding that some useful and interesting information may show up poorly or not at all in such a view. On the other hand, it is not the intent to specify the behavior of all dynamic tools nor to stifle innovation in dynamic presentation. Eventually, some dynamic notations may become well enough established to standardize, but more experience is needed.

identity

An object's inherent property of being distinguishable from all other objects.

See also data value, object.

Semantics

Objects are discrete and distinguishable from each other. The identity of an object is its conceptual handle, the inherent characteristic that allows it to be identified and referenced by other objects. Conceptually, an object does not need an internal value to identify itself; such mechanisms should not be included in logical models, as they can be generated automatically. In an implementation, identity may be implemented by addresses or keys, but they are part of the underlying implementation infrastructure and need not be explicitly included as attributes in most models. Pure values, on the other hard, have no identity, and two identical values are indistinguishable in all respects.

Identity is only meaningful if an object can be modified. Two references to an object have the same identity if a change to the object using one reference is visible to the other reference. A read-only object is therefore indistinguishable from a pure value.

There is a test identity action that determines if two values are the same object.

ignore

A tag on a combined fragment in an interaction that indicates that certain message types are suppressed in the model within the fragment, regardless of their actual occurrence during execution. This tag is equivalent to a **consider** tag that lists all the other message types. See consider.

Semantics

Certain constraints in interactions are most easily expressed by focusing on a subset of the message types that participate in the constraints. In such cases, it may be useful to suppress other message types in the model because they are not relevant to the given constraint or because they are discarded in practice. The **ignore** tag on a combined fragment indicates that the listed message types will not be shown within the fragment and that any constraints should filter them out before being applied.

For example, an interaction might state that a message of type A is always immediately followed by a message of type B and not another of type A, but messages of type C might occur independently without regard to messages of type A or B. This can be modeled by ignoring message type C within the fragment that requires B to follow A.

Notation

The keyword **ignore** is followed by a comma-separated list of message type names. The entire string is placed in the rectangular tab on the boundary of a fragment.

ill formed

Designation of a model that is incorrectly constructed, one that violates one or more predefined or model-specified rules or constraints. Antonym: well formed.

See also conflict, constraint.

Semantics

A model that violates well-formedness rules and constraints is not a valid model and therefore has inconsistent semantics. To attempt to use such a model may yield meaningless results. It is the responsibility of a modeling tool to detect ill-formed models and prevent their use in situations that might be troublesome. Because the use of some constructs extends the built-in UML semantics, automatic verification may not be possible in all cases. Also, automatic checking cannot be expected to verify consistency of operations, because that would involve solving the halting problem. Therefore, in practical situations, a combination of automatic verification and human verification is necessary.

Although a finished model must be well formed, intermediate versions of a model will likely be ill formed at times during development because they might be incomplete fragments of a final model. Editing a valid model to produce another valid model may require passing through intermediate models that are ill formed. This is no different from editing computer programs—the final program given to a compiler must be valid, but working copies in a text editor are often invalid. Therefore ill-formed models must be editable and storable by support tools.

implementation

1. A definition of how something is constructed or computed. For example, a method is an implementation of an operation. Contrast: specification. The realization relationship relates an implementation to its specification.

See realization.

2. That stage of a system that describes the functioning of the system in an executable medium (such as a programming language, database, or digital hardware). For implementation, low-level tactical decisions must be made to fit the design to the particular implementation medium and to work around its limitations (all languages have some arbitrary limitations). If the design is done well, however, the implementation decisions will be local and none of them will affect a large portion of the system. This stage is captured by implementation-level models, especially the static view and code. Contrast analysis, design, implementation, and deployment (phase).

See development process, stages of modeling.

implementation (stereotype of Component)

A component that provides the implementation for a separate specification to which it has a dependency.

See implementation, specification.

implementation class (stereotype of Class)

A class that provides a physical implementation, including attributes, associations to other classes, and methods for operations. An implementation class is intended for a traditional object-oriented language with fixed single classification. An object in such a system must have exactly one implementation class as its direct class. Contrast with type, a stereotype for a class that permits multiple classification. In a conventional language, such as Java, an object can have one implementation class. and many interfaces. The implementation class must be consistent with the interfaces.

See type.

implementation dependency

A realization relationship between an interface and a class in which the class conforms to the contracts specified by the interface.

Semantics

A provided interface is an interface that describes the externally available operations that a class makes available. An implementation dependency models the realization relationship between the interface and the class. A class may have multiple implementation dependencies to multiple interfaces, and multiple classes can implement the same interface.

Notation

A solid line is drawn from a provided interface to the boundary of a class that implements it (Figure 14-148).

Figure 14-148. *Implementation dependency*

implementation inheritance

The inheritance of the implementation of a parent element—that is, its structure (such as attributes and operations) and its code (such as methods). By contrast, interface inheritance involves inheritance of interface specifications (that is, operations) but not methods or data structure (attributes and associations). Implementation inheritance (the normal meaning of generalization in UML) includes the inheritance of *both* interface and implementation.

See also generalization, inheritance.

import   i120 i124 s9

A directed relationship that adds the names of elements to a namespace.

See access, qualified name, visibility.

Semantics

The names of elements defined within a package (or other namespace) may be used within textual expressions (such as OCL constraints) found in the package.

Elements from other packages can be referenced using their qualified names, that is, the sequence of names of the nested namespaces containing the element starting from the system root. In many cases, a modeler wishes to treat an element or group of element as if they had been defined locally, so that simple names can be used instead of qualified names. A package (the client) that imports an element from another package (the supplier) may use the simple name of the imported element to refer to it within expressions. Elements may be imported only if they are visible to the importing package. For example, an element that is private within its package cannot be imported by another package. The import relationship specifies the import visibility within the importing package as public or private. If it is public, the imported element is visible to any element that can see the importing package (and the element can therefore be imported by another package). If the visibility is private, the imported element is not visible outside the importing package.

An imported element may be given an alias, which is the name by which the imported element may be directly referenced within the importing package. If an alias is given, the original name of the imported element does not appear in the importing package.

A package implicitly gains access to all packages imported by any package within which it is nested (that is, nested packages can see everything that their containing packages see). If there is a clash of names, a name defined or imported by an inner package hides a name defined or imported by an outer package. The name in the outer package must be referenced using its qualified name.

Elements of different kinds, such as an attribute and an operation, do not clash. Some elements use additional parameters besides the name in determining whether names clash. For example, operations with distinct signatures do not clash even if they have identical names.

If the names of two imported elements clash, neither name is added to the namespace. If the name of an imported element clashes with a name defined within the importing namespace, the internal name takes precedence and the imported name is not added to the namespace.

An element in a package has access to all elements that are *visible within the package* (or other namespace). The visibility rules may be summarized as follows.

- An element defined in a package is visible within the same package.

- If an element is visible within a package, then it is visible within all packages nested inside the package.

- If a package imports another package with public visibility, then all elements defined with public visibility in the imported package are visible within the importing package.

- If a package is a child of another package, then all elements defined with public or protected visibility in the parent package are visible within the child package. Protected elements are invisible externally to the child package.

- Access and import dependencies are not transitive. If A can see B and B can see C, it does not necessarily follow that A can see C.

- An element defined in a nonpackage namespace is visible within the nearest enclosing package, but is invisible externally to that package.

One consequence is that a package cannot see inside its own nested packages unless it imports them and unless their contents of the nested packages are public.

The following are some further rules on visibility.

- The contents of a classifier, such as its attributes and operations as well as nested classes, are visible within the package if they have public visibility in the classifier.

- The contents of a classifier are visible within a descendant classifier if they have public or protected visibility in the classifier.

- All contents of a classifier are visible to elements within the classifier, including within methods or state machines of the classifier.

The normal simple case concerns elements in packages that are peers. In that case, an element can see all the elements in its own package and all the elements with public visibility in those packages imported by its package. A class can see the public features in other classes that it can see. A class can also see protected features in its ancestors.

Notation

An import dependency is shown by a dashed arrow, drawn with its tail on the client package and its head on the supplier package. The arrow uses the keyword «import» as a label. If the import is private, the keyword «access» is used instead.

An alias name may be shown before or after the keyword.

Alternately, an import may be shown as a text string within the importing package using the following syntax:

{ import qualifiedName }

Example

Figure 14-149 shows an example of package import among two peer packages. Package P imports package Q. Classes K and L in package P can use M as an unqualified name to reference public class M in package Q, but they cannot see private class N at all. Classes M and N in package Q can use qualified name P::K to reference public class K in package P, but they cannot see class L at all.

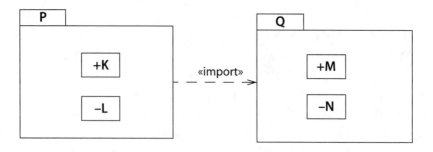

Figure 14-149. *Package import*

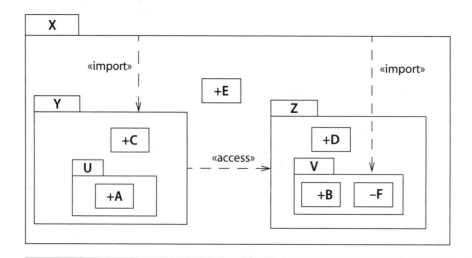

Figure 14-150. *Access rules*

Figure 14-150 shows a more complicated case of visibility and access declarations. The symbol in front of an element name represents the visibility of the element outside its own container: + for public, – for private (not visible outside).

Class A can see C and E and use their unqualified names because they are in enclosing packages Y and X.

Classes C and A can see D and use its unqualified name because package Y imports package Z. Class A is nested inside package Y and can therefore see everything Y can see.

Classes A, C, and E can see B and use its unqualified name because they are nested in package X, which imports package V containing B. They cannot see F, however, because it has private visibility within its package V. Class F, therefore, cannot be seen outside package V.

Class E can see D but must use the qualified name Z::D, because D is in package Z, which has not been imported by package X. The import of package Z by package Y has private visibility (keyword access), therefore the import of package Y by package X does not confer visibility on the contents of package Z.

Class C and class E can see A but must use the qualified name (U::A), because class A is in package U, which has not been imported by another package. Package Y has been imported by package X, so class E does not need to include Y in the qualified name.

Classes B and F can see classes D and E and use their unqualified names, because they are found in enclosing packages. They can also see C and use its unqualified name, because C is in package Y, which is imported by enclosing package X, which ultimately contains B and F. The fact that F is private does not prevent it from seeing other classes, but other classes cannot see F.

Classes B and F can see each other and use their names because they are in the same package. Class F is private to classes in outer packages, not to classes in its own package.

History

UML1 used access and import dependencies to grant permission to reference elements from other packages. That overprotective concept has been dropped. Import now only determines the appearance of an imported name in the importing namespace. If an element can be seen, it can be referenced directly, and its qualified name can always be used within expressions.

Discussion

Note that importing is only about use of names in text expressions. It is not needed to construct models themselves. An element from another package can always be explicitly referenced in a diagram, because relationships are direct references not dependent on names. Also note that the use of the names in namespaces is largely dependent on extensions to UML by tools.

inactive

A state that is not active; one that is not held by an object.

inception

The first phase of a software development process, during which the initial ideas for a system are conceived and evaluated. During this phase, some of the analysis view and small portions of other views are developed.

See development process.

include

A relationship from a *base* use case to an *inclusion* use case, specifying that the behavior defined for the inclusion use case is to be inserted into the behavior defined for the base use case. The base use case can see the inclusion and can depend on the effects of performing the inclusion, but neither the base nor the inclusion may access each other's attributes.

See also extend, use case, use case generalization.

Semantics

The include relationship connects a base use case to an inclusion use case. The inclusion use case in this relationship is not a separate instantiable classifier. Instead, it explicitly describes an additional behavior sequence that is inserted into a use case instance that is executing the base use case. Multiple include relationships may be applied to the same base use case. The same inclusion use case may be included in multiple base use cases. This does not indicate any relationship among the base use cases. There may even be multiple include relationships between the same inclusion base case and base use cases, provided each insertion is at a different location in the base.

The inclusion use case may access attributes or operations of the base use case. The inclusion represents encapsulated behavior that potentially can be reused in multiple base use cases. The base use case sees the inclusion use case, which may set attribute values in the base use case. But the base use case must not access the attributes of the inclusion use case, because the inclusion use case will have terminated when the base use case regains control.

Note that additions (of all kinds) may be nested. An inclusion, therefore, may serve as the base for a further inclusion, extension, or generalization.

The inclusion is an explicit statement within the behavior sequence of the base use case. The location is therefore implicit, unlike the situation with the extend relationship.

Notation

A dashed arrow is drawn from the base use case symbol to the inclusion use case symbol with a stick arrowhead on the inclusion. The keyword «include» is placed on the arrow (Figure 14-151). The location can be attached to the arrow as a property list in braces, but usually it is referenced as part of the text for the base use case and need not be shown on the diagram. Figure 14-152 shows the behavior sequences for these use cases.

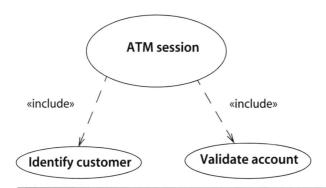

Figure 14-151. *Include relationship*

Base use case for ATM session:

show advertisement of the day	behavior step
include identify customer	inclusion
include validate account	another inclusion
print receipt header	behavior step
log out	behavior step

Inclusion use case for **Identify Customer:**

get customer name
include verify identity
if verification failed **then** abort the session
obtain account numbers for the customer

Inclusion use case for **Validate Account:**

establish connection with account database
obtain account status and limits

Figure 14-152. *Behavior sequences for use cases*

incomplete

Keyword indicating that the subtypes of a generalization set do not cover all cases of the supertype.

See generalization set.

incremental development

The development of a model and other artifacts of a system as a series of versions, each complete to some degree of precision and functionality, but each adding incremental detail to the previous version. The advantage is that each version of the model can be evaluated and debugged based on the relatively small changes to the previous version, making it easier to make changes correctly. The term is closely allied with the concept of iterative development.

See development process.

indeterminacy

The property that execution might produce more than one possible outcome.
See determinacy.

indirect instance

An entity that is an instance of an element, such as a class, and is also an instance of a child of the element. That is, it is an instance but not a direct instance.

indirect substate

With respect to a composite state, a state contained by it that is also contained by another substate of the composite state, and which is therefore not a direct substate of the composite state; a nested state at other than the top level.

See composite state, direct substate.

information flow

A declaration that information is exchanged between objects of given types.

Semantics

An information flow specifies a source and a target classifier and one or more classifiers that represent types of information that may be sent from an object of the source type to an object of the target type.

Notation

It is shown as a dashed arrow (a dependency) with the keyword «flow».

Discussion

The concept of information flow and information item are so vague as to question their usefulness. A more robust model of control and data flow is found in the activity model.

information item

An information item represents a type of information that can be exchanged over information flows.

inheritance

The mechanism by which more specific elements incorporate structure and behavior defined by more general elements.

See also full descriptor, generalization, redefinition

Semantics

Inheritance allows a full description of a classifier to be automatically constructed by assembling declaration fragments from a generalization hierarchy. A generalization hierarchy is a tree (actually, a partial order) of declarations of model elements, such as classes. Each declaration is not the declaration of a complete, usable element, however. Instead, each declaration is an incremental declaration describing what the element declaration adds to the declarations of its ancestors in the generalization hierarchy. Inheritance is the (implicit) process of combining those incremental declarations into full descriptors that describe actual instances.

Think of each classifier as having two descriptions, a segment declaration and a full descriptor. The segment declaration is the incremental list of features that the element declares in the model—the attributes and operations declared by a class, for example. The segment declaration is the additional structure that a classifier declares compared to its parents. The full descriptor of a classifier includes the new structure as well as the structure of the parents. The full descriptor does not appear explicitly within the model. It is the full description of an instance of the element—for example, the complete list of attributes and operations held by an object of a class. The full descriptor is the union of the contents of the segment declarations in an element and all its ancestors.

That is inheritance. It is the incremental definition of an element. Other details, such as method lookup algorithms, vtables, and so on, are merely implementation mechanisms to make it work in a particular language, not part of the essential definition. Although this description may seem strange at first, it is free of the implementation entailments found in most other definitions, yet is compatible with them.

Conflicts

If the same feature appears more than once among the set of inherited segments, there may be a conflict. Unless it is explicitly redefined, no attribute may be declared more than once in an inherited set. If a multiple definition occurs, the declarations conflict and the model is ill formed. (This restriction is not essential for logical reasons. It is present to avoid the certain confusion that would occur if attributes had to be distinguished by pathnames.)

The same operation may be declared more than once, provided the declaration is exactly the same (the methods may differ, however) or a child declaration strengthens an inherited declaration (for example, by declaring a child to be a query or increasing its concurrency status). A method declaration on a child replaces (overrides) a method declaration on an ancestor. There is no conflict. If distinct methods are inherited from two different ancestors that are not themselves in an ancestor relationship, then the methods conflict and the model is ill formed.

Discussion

The words *generalization* and *inheritance* are often used interchangeably, but there are actually two related but distinct concepts. Generalization is a taxonomic relationship among modeling elements. It describes what an element *is*. Inheritance is a mechanism for combining shared incremental descriptions to form a full description of an element. In most object-oriented systems, inheritance is based on generalization, but inheritance can be based on other concepts, such as the delegation pointer of the Self language. Basing the inheritance mechanism on the generalization relationship enables factoring and sharing of descriptions and polymorphic behavior. This is the approach taken by most object-oriented languages and by UML. But keep in mind that there are other approaches that could have been taken and that are used by some programming languages.

initial node

A control node indicating the place where execution begins when the activity is invoked.

Semantics

An initial node is a control node with no inputs and one output. When the activity containing the initial node is invoked, a control token is placed in the initial node and the activity is allowed to execute.

An activity may have multiple initial nodes, in which case a control token is placed in each of them. This would represent a situation with concurrency.

Notation

A initial node is shown as a small solid black circle with no input arrows and one output arrow. See Figure 14-13.

initial state

A pseudostate that indicates the default starting state of the enclosing region. It is used when a transition targets the boundary of a composite state.

See also composite state, creation, entry activity, entry point, exit point, initialization, junction.

Semantics

To promote encapsulation, it is desirable to separate the outside view of a composite state from the inside details as much as possible. From the outside, the state is viewed as an opaque entity with hidden internal structure. From the outside viewpoint, transitions go to and from the state itself. From the inside viewpoint, they connect to substates within the state.

An initial state is a dummy state (pseudostate) that designates the default starting state of the containing region. Rather, it is a syntactic means of indicating where the control should go. An initial state must have an outgoing triggerless transition (a transition with no event trigger, therefore automatically enabled as soon as the initial state is entered). The transition connects to a real state in the composite state. The transition may have an action on it.

When an external transition to the boundary of the enclosing composite state fires, the following behavior occurs, in order: Any action on the external transition is executed; each orthogonal subregion of the composite state is activated; for a given subregion, any entry activity is executed; the initial state of the subregion is activated and causes its outgoing transition to be taken; any action on the outgoing transition is executed; the default starting state of the subregion becomes active; the execution of the transition is now complete. At the completion of the transition, one state will be active in each subregion of the composite state.

The entry action of the composite state and the completion transition on the initial state may access the implicit current event—that is, the event that triggered the first segment in the transition that ultimately caused the transition to the initial state.

The transition on an initial state may not have an event trigger. An initial state is a pseudostate and may not remain active.

Most often the transition from the initial state is unguarded. In that case, it must be the only transition from the initial state. A set of outgoing transitions may be provided with guard conditions, but the guard conditions must completely cover all possible cases (or, more simply, one of them can have the guard condition else). The point is that control must leave the initial state immediately. It is not a real state, and some transition must fire.

The initial state in the top-level state of a class represents the creation of a new instance of the class. When the transition leaving the initial state fires, the implicit current event is the creation event of the object and has the argument values passed by the constructor operation. These values are available within actions on the outgoing transition.

Object creation

The initial state of the topmost composite state of a class is slightly different. It may have a trigger with the stereotype «create», together with a named event trigger with parameters. There may be multiple transitions of this kind with different triggers. The signature of each trigger must match a creation operation on the class. When a new object of the class is instantiated, the transition corresponding to its creation operation fires and receives the arguments from the call to the creation operation.

Notation

An initial state is displayed as a small filled black circle inside the symbol of its composite state. Outgoing transition arrows may be connected to it. Only one initial state may occur (directly) within a composite state. However, additional initial states may occur within nested composite states.

Example

In Figure 14-153, we start in state X. When event e occurs, the transition fires and action a is performed. The transition goes to state Y. Entry action b is performed, and the initial state becomes active. The outgoing transition immediately fires, performing action c and changing to state Z.

Instead, if event f occurs when the system is in state X, then the other transition fires and action d is performed. This transition goes directly to state Z. The initial state is not involved. Because control passes into state Y, action b is performed, but action c is not performed in this case.

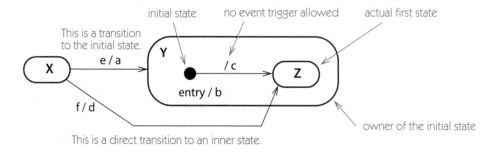

Figure 14-153. *Initial state*

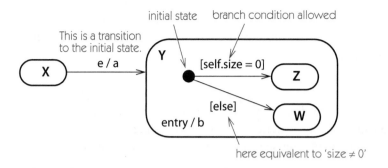

Figure 14-154. *Initial state with branch*

In Figure 14-154, the initial state has a branch. Again, suppose the system starts in state **X**. When event **e** occurs, actions **a** is performed, the system changes to state **Y**, and the entry action **b** is performed. Control goes to the initial state. The size attribute of the owning object is tested. If it is 0, control goes to state **Z**; if it is not 0, control goes to state **W**.

initial value

An expression specifying the value that an attribute in an object holds just after it has been initialized.

See also default value, initialization.

Semantics

An initial value is an expression attached to an attribute. The expression is a text string that also designates a language for interpreting the expression. When an object holding the attribute is instantiated, the expression is evaluated according to the given language and the current value of the system. The result of the evaluation is used to initialize the value of the attribute in the new object.

The initial value is optional. If it is absent, then the attribute declaration does not specify the value held by a new object (but some other part of the overall model may supply that information).

Note that an explicit initialization procedure for an object (such as a constructor) may supersede an initial value expression and overwrite the attribute value.

The initial value of a class-scope attribute is used to initialize it once at the beginning of execution. UML does not specify the relative order of initialization of different class-scope attributes.

Notation

An initial value for an attribute is shown as a text expression following an equal sign (=). See attribute.

Discussion

In UML2, the initial value for an attribute has been confusingly renamed *default value*. You will probably be better understood if you ignore this renaming, which is also used (and makes better sense) for parameters with omitted arguments.

initialization

Setting the value of a newly created object—namely, the values of its attributes, links of associations that it belongs to, and its control state.

See also instantiation.

Semantics

Conceptually, a new object is created complete in one step. It is easier, however, to think about the instantiation process in two steps: creation and initialization. First, a new empty shell object is allocated with the proper structure of attribute slots, and the new raw object is given identity. Identity can be implemented in various ways, such as by the address of the memory block containing the object or by an integer counter. In any case, it is something that is unique across the system and can be used as a handle to find and access the object. At this point, the object is not yet legal—it may violate the constraints on its values and relationships. The next step is initialization. Any declared initial value expressions for attributes are evaluated, and the results are assigned to the attribute slots. The creation method may explicitly calculate the values for attributes, thereby overriding the default initial values. The resultant values must satisfy any constraints on the class. The creation method may also create links containing the new object. They must satisfy the declared multiplicity of any associations that the class participates in. When the initialization is complete, the object must be a legal object and must obey any constraints on its class. After initialization is complete, attributes or associations whose changeability property is **frozen** or **addOnly** may not be altered until the object is destroyed. The entire initialization process is atomic and may not be interrupted or interleaved.

The semantics of initialization depend greatly on the concreteness of the modeling view. At a conceptual level, the object simple acquires a value. At a concrete level close to implementation, the mechanisms available in a particular execution environment become important. It is not possible to enforce a single view of initialization across all possible uses.

inout parameter

A parameter used to supply arguments to the called procedure and also to return values to the caller using side effects on the parameter itself.

Semantics

A parameter can have a direction, which can include in, out, inout, and return. An inout parameter is a parameter intended to directly represent parameters in certain programming languages that both supply argument values and permit assignments to parameter variables within the bodies of procedures, with the assigned values available to the caller.

Notation

The keyword inout may be placed before the name of an out parameter. Parameters without keywords are in parameters.

See out parameter.

instance

An individual entity with its own identity and value. A classifier specifies the form and behavior of a set of instances with similar properties. An instance has identity and values that are consistent with the specification in the classifier. Instances appear in models as instance specifications.

See also classifier, identity, instance specification, link, object.

Semantics

The UML specification document does not include a clear specification of the run-time environment that models describe. Without such a specification, models lack meaning. The following discussion probably should have been included in the specification. It represents the commonly accepted background without which models make little sense.

An instance is an entity in a run-time system. The purpose of models is to describe the possible configurations and history of instances. Instances do not appear in models—instances are "out there" in the actual system. A model contains descriptions of instances. A description may characterize a set of instances without regard to the individual context of each instance; a classifier is such a description. A description may describe a individual instance in more or less detail, including its value, its relationships to other instances, and its history; an instance specification is such a description.

An instance has identity. In other words, at different times during the execution of a system, the instance can be identified with the same instance at other times, even though the value of the instance changes. At any time, an instance has a value expressible in terms of data values and references to other instances. A data value is a degenerate case. Its identity is the same as its value; or considered from a different viewpoint, it has no identity. Identity represents a handle with which an instance can be referenced and manipulated. It is distinct from the value of the instance. It may be implemented using addresses, keys, or other mechanisms, but it is an abstract concept distinct from its possible implementations.

A value is an immutable entity from some mathematical type. Values cannot be changed; they simply exist. Operations can be defined on values that yield other values, but such operations do not change values; only (mutable) instances can be changed.

In addition to identity and value, each instance has a descriptor that constrains the values that the instance can have. A descriptor is a model element that describes instances. This is the descriptor-instance dichotomy. Most modeling concepts in UML have this dual character. The main content of most models is descriptors of various kinds. The purpose of the model is to describe the possible values of a system in terms of its instances and their values.

Each kind of descriptor describes one kind of instance. An object is an instance of a class; a link is an instance of an association. A use case describes possible use case instances; a parameter describes a possible argument value; and so on. Some instances do not have familial names and are usually overlooked except in very formal settings, but they nevertheless exist. For example, a state describes possible occurrences of the state during an execution trace.

A model describes the possible values of a system and its behavior in progressing from value to value during execution. The value of a system is the set of all instances in it and their values. The system value is valid if every instance is the instance of some descriptor in the model, and if all the explicit and implicit constraints in the model are satisfied by the set of instances.

The behavior elements in a model describe how the system and the instances in it progress from value to value. The concept of identity of instances is essential to this description. Each behavioral step is the description of the change of the values of a small number of instances in terms of their previous values. The remainder of the instances in the system preserve their values unchanged. For example, a local operation on one object can be described by expressions for the new values of each attribute of the object without changes to the rest of the system. A nonlocal function can be decomposed into local functions on several objects.

Note that the instances in an executing system are not model elements. They are not part of the model at all. Anything in a model is a *description* of something in the executing system. An instance specification is a description of an instance or group of instances. It may be more or less specific—it may describe a single instance with its complete value in a very specific scenario, or it may describe a set of instances with some ambiguity in a range of possible situations.

Direct instance. Each object is the direct instance of some class and the indirect instance of the ancestors of the class. This is also the case for instances of other classifiers. An object is a direct instance of a class if the class describes the instance and no descendant class also describes the object. In the case of multiple classification, an instance may be a direct instance of more than one classifier, none of which is an ancestor of any of the others. Under some execution semantics, one of the classifiers is designated the implementation class and the others are designated types or roles. The full descriptor is the implicit full description of an instance—all its attributes, operations, associations, and other properties—whether obtained by an instance from its direct classifier or from an ancestor classifier by inheritance. In case of multiple classification, the full descriptor is the union of the properties defined by each direct classifier.

Creation. See instantiation for a description of how instances are created.

Notation

Instances only exist in the "real world", therefore they do not appear in models. Instance specifications appear in models. This is a subtle but important semantic distinction. When you describe the instances a running system, you are building a model of it—an instance model. Instance specifications are the elements in such a model. See instance specification for their notation.

instance of

Relationship between an instance and its descriptor. Modeled in an instance specification by a set of classifiers.

See instance, instance specification.

instance specification

A description in a model of an instance or group of instances. The description may or may not describe all details of the instance.

Semantics

An instance specification is the description of an individual instance in the context of its participation in a system and its relationship to other instances. Unlike an instance, which exists as only as a concrete individual in an executing system, an instance specification can be more or less precise. At one extreme, it can describe a single object in a single execution of a system in full detail. More often, it describes some aspects of the run-time instance and omits others that are not of interest in a certain view. It can also represent multiple objects over many executions of a particular scenario, so the type of an instance specification may be abstract, even though every run-time object necessarily has a concrete type. Keep in mind that the instance specification, as a description, can be an abstraction of actual instances.

An instance specification is both like and unlike a classifier. Like a classifier, it constrains the instances that it describes. Unlike a classifier, it describes an individual instance and can have a contextual relationship to other instances and to the system in which it is embedded.

Structure

classifier	A classifier or classifiers that characterize the instance. The type of the instance may be the same or a descendant. If multiple classifiers are given, the type of the instance must be a descendant of all of them. The classifiers may be abstract. The instance may also have classifiers in addition to those listed, unless this is explicitly proscribed.
specification	An optional description of how to compute, derive, or construct the instance. This may be informal or it may be in a formal language. It may also be complete or incomplete (and therefore abstract). Usually the specification and values for the slots are mutually exclusive.
slots	There may be one slot for each attribute of the classifier or classifiers, but not every attribute must be included (in which case the description is abstract). Each slot contains a value specification for the attribute within the instance. A value specification may be a literal value, an expression tree, an expression string, or another instance specification.

Notation

Although classifiers and instance specifications are not the same, they share many properties, including the same form (because the descriptor must describe the form of the instances). Therefore, it is convenient to choose notation for each classifier-instance pair so that the correspondence is visually obvious. There are a limited number of ways to do this, each with its advantages and disadvantages. In UML, the classifier-instance distinction is shown by using the same graphic symbol for each pair of elements and by underlining the name string of an instance element. This visual distinction is easily apparent without being overpowering even when an entire diagram contains instance elements.

For an instance specification, the classifier name is replaced by an instance name string of the form:

$$\underline{name : Type_{list,}\ \lfloor = specification \rfloor_{opt}}$$

The name is the name of the instance. It may be omitted but the colon must be present. The name of a classifier or a list of names of classifiers may be present or omitted. The specification is optional. It is given as an expression. The form of the expression is implementation dependent. It is usually absent if values are given for slots. The specification may also be listed on its own line below the name string. In that case, the equal sign is omitted.

In addition to the name compartment, an instance specification may have an attribute slot compartment corresponding to the attribute compartment of a classifier. One slot may be included for each attribute (included inherited attributes) of any of the given types. A slot specification has the form:

$$name \lfloor : type \rfloor_{opt} = value$$

The name is the name of the attribute. The type of the attribute may be included for convenience, but it is not needed because it is known from the classifier. The value is given as a text expression.

The operation compartment is not part of an instance specification, because all objects of a given type share the same operations specified in the classifier.

Although Figure 14-155 shows object specifications, the underlining convention can be used for other kinds of instances, such as use case instances, component instances, and node instances.

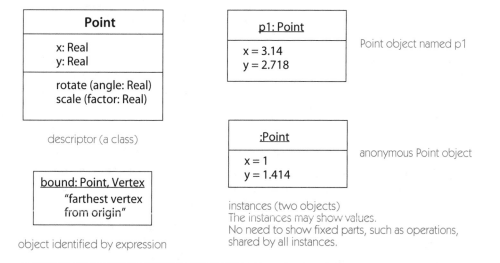

Figure 14-155. *Descriptor and instances*

Link specifications (association instances) are shown as solid paths connecting object symbols. It is unnecessary to underline the names because a line connecting two object symbols is automatically a link specification. A link symbol can have the same adornments as an association (aggregation, navigability, association end names). Multiplicity is not appropriate as a link specification connects individual instance specifications. There can be multiple link symbols with the same association name or end name. If the links are ordered, a dashed arrow with the keyword **ordered** can be drawn across the link symbols in order; otherwise the link symbols or the link ends can be numbered. In principle, both ends of an association can be ordered, but this is tricky to use and difficult to display; use it with reluctance.

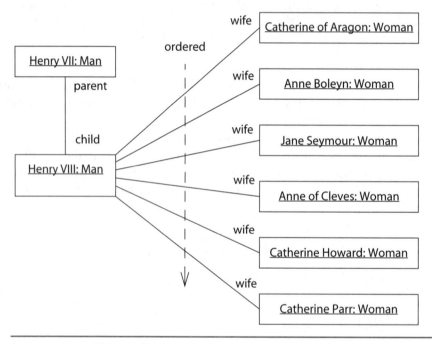

Figure 14-156. *Link specification*

Because instances appear in models as instance specifications, usually only details relevant to a particular example are included. For example, the entire list of attribute values need not be included; or the entire list of values can be omitted if the focus is on something else, such as message flow between objects.

Instance of structured class. An instance of a structured class is shown using a rectangle with a graphic compartment. To show an instance of a contained part, a rectangle is drawn. The name string has the syntax:

name⌊/ role-name⌋list :⌊Type-name⌋list,

The various elements are optional (including colon if type is omitted).

A connector is drawn as a solid path between part rectangles. The name of the connector (if any) is underlined.

Attribute values for a part may be shown in an attribute compartment with the syntax:

```
name = value
```

Figure 14-157 shows an instance of a structured classifier.

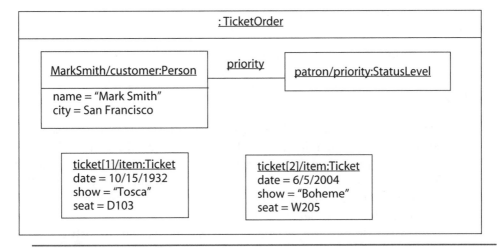

Figure 14-157. *Instance of structured class*

History

In UML2, a clear distinction has been made between instance specifications and instances, a subtle but important difference the lack of which caused endless semantic confusion in UML1.

instantiable

Able to have direct instances. Synonym: concrete.

See also abstract, direct instance, generalizable element.

Semantics

Generalizable elements may be declared as abstract or instantiable. If they are instantiable, then direct instances can be created.

instantiate

To create an instance of a descriptor.
See instantiation.

instantiate (stereotype of Usage dependency)

A dependency among classifiers indicating that operations on the client create instances of the supplier.
See instantiation, usage.

instantiation

The creation of new instances of model elements.
See also initialization.

Semantics

Instances are created at run time as a result of primitive create actions or creation operations. First an identity is created for the new instance; then its data structure is allocated as prescribed by its descriptor; and then its property values are initialized as prescribed by the descriptor and the creation operator. Conceptually, all of this happens at once, but it is convenient for modeling and implementation to break instantiation into several stages.

The instantiation usage dependency shows the relationship between an operation that creates instances or a class containing such an operation and the class of objects being instantiated.

Objects. When a new object is instantiated (created), it is created with identity and memory and it is initialized. The initialization of an object defines the values of its attribute, its association, and its control state.

Usually, each concrete class has one or more class-scope (static) constructor operations, the purpose of which is to create new objects of the class. Underlying all the constructor operations is an implicit primitive operation that creates a new raw instance that is then initialized by the constructor operations. After a raw instance has been created, it has the form prescribed by its descriptor, but its values have not yet been initialized, so they may be semantically inconsistent. An instance is therefore not available to the rest of the system until it has been initialized, which occurs immediately after creation of the raw instance.

Links. Similarly, links are created by creation actions or operations, usually by instance-scope operations attached to one of the participating classes, rather than by constructor operations on the association element itself (although this is a possible implementation technique under some circumstances). Again, there is an underlying implicit primitive operation that creates a new link among a specific tuple of objects. This operation has no effect if a link of the same association already exists among the tuple of objects (unless the association has a bag on one of its ends). With an ordinary association, there is nothing more to do. A link of an association class, however, requires initialization of its attribute values.

Use case instances. The instantiation of a use case means that a use case instance is created, and the use case instance begins executing at the beginning of the use case controlling it. The use case instance may temporarily follow another use case related by extend or include relationships before it resumes executing the original use case. When the use case instance comes to the end of the use case it is following, the use case instance terminates.

Other instances. Instances of other descriptors may be created in a similar two-step process: First perform a raw creation to establish identity and to allocate data structure, then initialize the values of the new instance so that it obeys all relevant constraints. For example, an activation is created implicitly as the direct consequence of a call to an operation.

The exact mechanisms of creating instances are the responsibility of the runtime environment.

Notation

An instantiation dependency is shown as a dashed arrow from the operation or class performing the instantiation to the class being instantiated; the stereotype «instantiate» is attached to the arrow.

On a sequence diagram, the instantiation of a new instance is shown by placing a rectangle at the head of a message arrow. The lifeline for the new instance is drawn beneath its head rectangle.

Discussion

Instantiation is sometimes used to mean binding a template to produce a bound element, but binding is more specific for this relationship.

intent

The formal specification of the structural and behavioral properties of a descriptor. Sometimes called *intension*. Contrast: extent.

See also descriptor.

Semantics

A descriptor, such as a class or an association, has both a description (its intent) and a set of instances that it describes (its extent). The purpose of the intent is to specify the structural and behavioral properties of the instances in an executable manner.

interaction

A specification of how messages are exchanged over time between roles within a context to perform a task. An interaction specifies a pattern of behavior. The context is supplied by a classifier or collaboration. In an instance of an interaction, objects are bound to its roles and a particular trace of messages among objects must be consistent with the specification.

Semantics

A reusable arrangement of connected objects can be specified using a structured classifier or a collaboration. Each object is a part within a well-defined context.

Objects or other instances communicate within a context to accomplish a purpose (such as performing an operation) by exchanging messages. The messages may include signals and calls, as well as implicit interactions through conditions and time events. A pattern of message exchanges to accomplish a specific purpose is called an interaction.

Traces. An interaction describes a set of possible traces. A trace is a particular execution history. It comprises a partially ordered set of event occurrences, including the sending or receiving ends of messages. In simple cases, the event occurrences (and even the messages) are usually totally ordered; in more complicated cases, there may be overlap.

For example, one trace involving banking might be "insert bank card, supply password, request withdrawal, receive cash, remove card". An interaction can describe multiple traces. For example, another trace for the same interaction might include "insert bark card, supply password, bank rejects card because of invalid password". The semantics of an interaction can be defined by the traces that it allows and those that it prohibits.

Structure

An interaction describes the behavior of a structured classifier or a collaboration. An interaction contains a set of lifelines. Each lifeline corresponds to an internal part of a classifier or a role of a collaboration. Each lifeline represents an instance or set of instances over time. The interaction describes the internal activity of the parts and the messages they exchange.

An interaction is structured as a tree of nested interactions whose leaves are occurrence specifications, execution specifications, and constraints on the state of the target instance and its parts. Constructs that build larger interactions out of smaller ones include structured control constructs (loop, conditional, parallel, and others). The nested nodes of the tree are called interaction fragments. Most of the syntactic structure of interactions is described within articles about various kinds of interaction fragments.

Within a primitive interaction, occurrence specifications partition a lifeline into successive time segments. An occurrence specification is a point on a lifeline that represents an interesting piece of behavior that impinges on an instance, such as the sending or receipt of a message or a change of state of the instance.

Messages connect pairs of occurrence specifications on different lifelines (or occasionally, on the same lifeline). A message can be identified by two occurrence specifications: one that represents sending the message by one instance and one that represents receiving the message by the other instance. A message also has parameters that describe the type of message and its argument values.

Execution specifications are regions of a lifeline that represent execution activity by the instances described by the lifeline. Execution activity includes primitive actions as well as execution of operations that may span multiple nested layers of structure.

For further details, see combined fragment, interaction fragment, occurrence specification, message, execution specification.

Notation

Interactions are shown as sequence diagrams or as communication diagrams.

Sequence diagrams explicitly show sequencing of occurrence specifications, messages, and representations of method activations. However, sequence diagrams show only the participating objects and not their relationships to other objects or their attributes. Therefore, they do not fully show the contextual view of a collaboration.

Communication diagrams show the full context of an interaction, including the objects and their relationships to other objects within the interaction. Communications diagrams specify message sequencing by nested tags, so they do not provide a visual image of the overall time sequences.

Sequence diagrams are often better for understanding user interactions and designing use cases, while communication diagrams are often better for understanding algorithms on circular data structures and also for planning algorithms involving navigations within object networks.

See interaction diagram.

History

In UML2, interactions were heavily influenced by Message Sequence Charts (MSC) of the International Telecommunication Union (ITU). They have many similar constructs but they are not completely identical. The inclusion of these constructs may influence the ITU standard, and the two sets of constructs may converge in the future.

The UML2 interactions are a major improvement on the UML1 interactions, which were weak in building more complicated constructs, such as conditionals, loops, and concurrent threads. The combined fragment construct from UML2 interactions (and originally from MSC) handles structured constructs in a clean and powerful way. The UML1 constructs are obsolete and should not be used.

interaction diagram

A generic term that applies to several types of diagrams that emphasize object interactions. These include communication diagrams and sequence diagrams. Closely related are activity diagrams.

More specialized variants include timing diagrams and interaction overview diagrams.

See also collaboration, interaction.

Notation

A pattern of interaction among objects is shown on an interaction diagram. Interaction diagrams come in various forms all based on the same underlying information but each emphasizing one view of it: sequence diagrams, communication diagrams, and interaction overview diagrams.

A sequence diagram shows an interaction arranged in time sequence. In particular, it shows the objects participating in the interaction by their lifelines and the messages they exchange, arranged in time sequence. A sequence diagram does not show the links among the objects. Sequence diagrams come in several formats intended for different purposes.

A communication diagram shows an interaction arranged around the objects that perform operations. It is similar to an object diagram that shows the objects and the links among them needed to implement a higher-level operation.

The time sequence of messages is indicated by sequence numbers on message flow arrows. Both sequential and concurrent sequences can be shown using appropriate syntax. Sequence diagrams show time sequences using the geometric order of the arrows in the diagram. Therefore, they do not require sequence numbers, although sequence numbers may be included for convenience or to permit switching to a collaboration diagram.

Sequence diagrams and collaboration diagrams express similar information but show it in different ways. Sequence diagrams show the explicit sequence of messages and are better for real-time specifications and for complex scenarios. Collaboration diagrams show the relationships among objects and are better for understanding all the effects on an object and for procedural design.

A timing diagram allows a numerical time axis to be defined rather than just specifying relative message sequences. They also allow visual representation of state changes to be shown for each lifeline provided there only a handful of states. Timing diagrams may be useful for real-time situation, but they are not needed in most conceptual design.

An interaction overview diagram is a strange mixture of interaction diagrams and activity diagrams whose usefulness is unclear.

Discussion

Interactions and activities both model behavior, but from different viewpoints. A sequence diagram shows primarily sequences of events for each role, with messages connecting the roles. The focus is on the roles and the flow of control between the roles, not the processing. An activity diagram shows the procedural steps involved in performing a high-level operation. It shows the flow of control between procedural steps rather than the flow of control between objects. A number of constructs in activity diagrams and interaction diagrams are closely related and sometimes (but not always) use the same icons.

interaction fragment

A structural piece of an interaction.

Semantics

An interaction fragment is a piece of an interaction, one of:

combined fragment	A structured part of an interaction that may include one or more operands (subfragments). There are many kinds of combined fragments with different syntax and semantics, distinguished by their interaction operation parameter. These include loop, conditional, parallel, and other constructs.
continuation	A label that allows conditionals to be broken into two pieces and semantically combined.
occurrence specification	A notable point in the sequence of activity of an interaction.
execution specification	A region of time during which an action or operation is being executed.
interaction	The body of an interaction is a fragment.
interaction use	A parameterized reference to an interaction within another interaction.
interaction operand	A constituent piece of a combined fragment.
state invariant	A constraint on the state or values of a lifeline.

Notation

See sequence diagram and communication diagram for notation.

interaction occurrence

See interaction use.

Discussion

The term was used but it conflicts with the use of occurrence to mean an instance of an event. The word *use* appears in other places to mean the reference to a defined element to be used within a particular context. The term *interaction reference* might work equally well.

interaction operand

A structural piece of a combined fragment; a subfragment.

Semantics

A combined fragment is a structured interaction construct. Each fragment comprises one or more interaction operands, each a subfragment of the interaction. The number of operands depends on the type of combined fragment. For example, a loop has one operand (the loop body) and a conditional has one or more operands (the branches of the conditional). An operand is a nested fragment of an interaction. Each operand covers the lifelines covered by the combined fragment or a subset of them.

Notation

A combined fragment is shown as a rectangle divided into multiple subfragments by horizontal lines. In most cases, the ordering of the subfragments in the diagram does not imply either temporal sequence or order of testing.

See combined fragment.

interaction overview diagram

A variation on an activity diagram incorporating sequence diagram fragments together with flow of control constructs.

Notation

An interaction overview diagram contains sequence diagram notation, primarily references and nested sequence diagrams, with decision and fork notation from activity diagrams. The control symbols show the high level flow of control among the nested symbols, which can contain sequences including messages.

Figure 14-158 shows an example of a student who has been accepted into a university. First the student must accept or decline admission. After accepting, the student must both register for classes and apply for housing. After both of those are complete, the student must pay the registrar. If payment is not received in time, the student is excluded by the registrar.

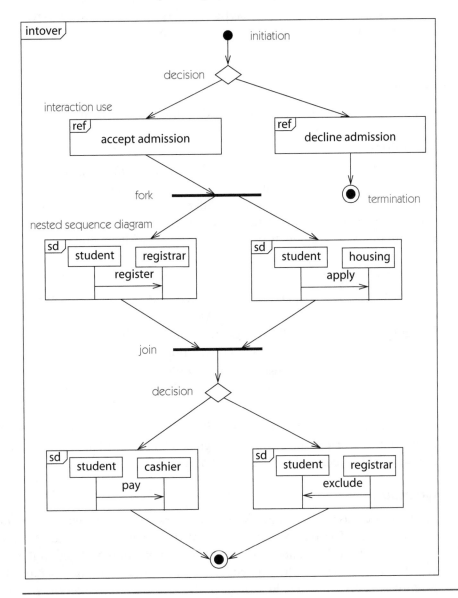

Figure 14-158. *Interaction overview diagram*

Discussion

This is a strange mixture of concepts from activity diagrams and sequence diagrams. It tries to mix the control flow mechanism among activity nodes from activity diagrams with the sequence of messages among lifelines from sequence diagrams. Some critics feel that it adds little new.

The UML specification states that the tag **sd** is used on all diagrams representing interactions, but that seems confusing, so we have used the tag **intover** to indicate an interaction overview diagram.

interaction use

A reference to an interaction within the definition of another interaction.

Semantics

An interaction use is a parameterized reference to an interaction within the body of another interaction. As with any modular reference, such as procedures, this allows the reuse of a definition in many different contexts. When an interaction use is executed, the effect is the same as executing the referenced interaction with the substitution of the arguments supplied as part of the interaction use.

Structure

referent	A reference to a target interaction that is executed when the interaction use is executed.
arguments	A list of arguments that are substituted for the parameters of the target interaction.
gates	A list of gates in the enclosing interaction that are matched to the parameterized gates of the target interaction.

The interaction use must cover all the lifelines that appear within the referenced interaction and that occur within the original interaction. (The referenced interaction might add lifelines that occur only within itself.)

Notation

An interaction use is shown in a sequence diagram as a rectangle with the tag **ref** (for reference). The rectangle covers the lifelines that are included in the referenced interaction. The name of the referenced interaction is placed in the rectangle. Any parameters of the reference are placed in a comma-separated list in parentheses after the name. Return values (if any) are placed after the parentheses with a colon (:) before the list of values.

The full syntax of the name string is:

$\lfloor$return-attribute-name $=\rfloor_{opt}$ $\lfloor$collaboration-use .$\rfloor_{opt}$
     interaction-name $\lfloor$(arguments$_{list,}$)$\rfloor_{opt}$ $\lfloor$: return-value $\rfloor_{opt}$

where return-attribute-name is the name of an attribute that receives the return value, collaboration-use is the name of a collaboration use within a structured classifier (rare), interaction-name is the name of the referenced interaction, the arguments are a comma-separated list, and the return-value is assigned to the return attribute. The full form is not needed in simple examples.

Figure 14-159 shows two interaction uses, one with an argument and one without arguments.

Discussion

It was called *interaction occurrence*, but this conflicts with the meaning of occurrence as an instance of an event.

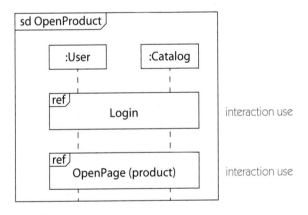

Figure 14-159. *Interaction uses*

interaction view

A view of a model that shows the exchange of messages among objects to accomplish some purpose. It consists of collaborations and interactions and is shown using communication diagrams and sequence diagrams.

interface

A declaration of a coherent set of public features and obligations; a contract between providers and consumers of services.

See also classifier, realization.

Semantics

An interface is a classifier for the externally visible properties, operations, and receptions of an implementation classifier, without specification of internal structure. An interface may constrain the way in which its operations are invoked and may impose pre- and postconditions on its operations. Each interface often specifies only a limited part of the behavior of an actual class. An interface should define a coherent set of capabilities, whereas an implementation class often combines several purposes. A class may support many interfaces, either disjoint or overlapping in their effect. An interface has no private aspect; all of its contents are public.

Interfaces may have generalization relationships. A child interface includes all the contents of its ancestors but may add additional content. An interface is essentially equivalent to an abstract class with no attributes and no methods and only abstract operations. All the features in an interface have public visibility (otherwise, there would be no point to including them, as an interface has no "inside" that could use them).

An interface has no direct instances. An interface represents a contract to be fulfilled by instances of classifiers that realize the interface. An interface specifying the behavior made available by a classifier to other, unspecified classifiers is called a provided interface. An interface specifying behavior requested by a classifier from other, unspecified classifiers is called a required interface.

A classifier that implements an interface need not have the exact same structure as the interface; it must simply deliver the same services to external requestors. For example, an attribute in an interface may be implemented by operations in the implementation or the names of operations in the implementation may be implementation-specific (but many modelers will expect the exact operation to be provided by the implementation).

An interface represents a declaration of services made available to or required from anonymous classifiers. The purpose of interfaces is to decouple direct knowledge of classifiers that must interact to implement behavior. Instances may call on instances of classifiers that implement required interfaces, without needing direct associations among the implementing classifiers.

Structure

An interface may have the following structure:

attributes	State values to be maintained by the implementing classifier, not necessarily as attribute values.
operations	Services that unspecified, anonymous objects can invoke of an implementing object. An interface may not provide methods to implement its operations.

receptions	Signals that anonymous objects can send to an implementing object.
constraints	Preconditions, postconditions, or other constraints on the invocation of services of an implementing object.
nested	Nested interfaces that must be supported by classifiers implementing the interface. The concept is not well explained in the official UML document.
protocol	A protocol state machine specifying the order in which services of the implementing object may be invoked.

An interface may have associations to other interfaces. This means that a conforming association must exist between instances of classifiers that realize the interfaces. Each interface is a provided interface of the other interface.

An interface may have an associations to a classifier. This means that a conforming association must exist between instances of classifiers realizing the interface and instances of the classifier. The interface is a provided interface of the classifier.

Implementation

If a classifier implements an interface, then it must declare or inherit all the operations in the interface or provide equivalent behavior. It may contain additional operations (see realization). If the classifier realizes more than one interface, it must contain each operation found in any of its interfaces. The same operation may appear in more than one interface. If their signatures match, they must represent the same operation or they are in conflict and the model is ill formed. (An implementation may adopt language-specific rules for matching signatures. For example, in C++, parameter names and return types are ignored.)

Attributes must be implemented in some way in the classifier, but UML is somewhat vague on what constitutes implementation. Presumably an implementation that implements attributes by some collection of operations is also free to rename and reshape operations during design. If an interface is regarded as a specification of the exact operations to be provided by a classifier, then it is best to either avoid declaring attributes in the interface or to expect them to appear directly in the implementation also.

The UML2 specification defines implementation as a special case of realization, but the distinction between realization and implementation appears minimal.

Notation

An interface is a classifier and may be shown using the rectangle symbol with the keyword «interface». A list of attributes and operations defined by the interface is placed in the attribute or operation compartment. All features are public. Signals bearing the «signal» keyword may also be included in the operation compartment, or they may be listed in a separate compartment with the name signals.

The realization (provided interface) relationship is shown by a dashed line with a solid triangular arrowhead (a "dashed generalization symbol") from a classifier rectangle to an interface rectangle. It is also possible to use a dependency arrow (a dashed line with a stick arrowhead) with the keyword «interface». The classifier provides the interface to others.

The required relationship is shown by a dependency arrow from a classifier rectangle to an interface rectangle. The keyword «use» may optionally be included, but it is not necessary.

Associations between two interfaces may be shown by a solid association line. If the association is bidirectional, the line has no arrowheads. If the association is directed, place a stick arrowhead on the end near the target interface.

A more compact notation is available for showing provided and required interfaces of classifiers in places where it is unnecessary to show the contents of the interface. To show a provided interface of a classifier, an interface may be displayed as a small circle attached by a solid line to classifiers that provide the interface. The name of the interface is placed below (or otherwise near) the circle. The circle notation does not show the list of features that the interface supports. Use the full rectangle symbol to show the list of features.

To show a required interface of a classifier, an interface may be displayed as a small half circle attached by a solid line to classifiers that require the interface. The name of the interface is placed below (or otherwise near) the half circle.

To show that two classifiers share an interface, use the same name. For visual emphasis, a dependency arrow may be drawn from a required interface to the matching provided interface.

In the case of external ports on components, a provided or required interface symbol may be connected directly to the port symbol. A complex port, that is, one that has both provided and required interfaces, is shown by connecting multiple interface symbols to a single port symbol.

Example

Figure 14-160 shows a simplified view of financial classes that deal with prices of securities. The FinancialPlanner is a personal finance application that keeps track of investments, as well as personal expenses. It needs the ability to update securities prices. The MutualFundAnalyzer examines mutual funds in detail. It needs the ability to update the prices of the underlying securities, as well as the prices of the funds. The ability to update securities prices is shown by the interface Update-Prices. There are two classes that implement this interface, shown by the solid lines connecting them to the interface symbol. Class ManualPriceEntry allows a user to manually enter prices of selected securities. Class QuoteQuery retrieves security prices from a quote server using a modem or the Internet.

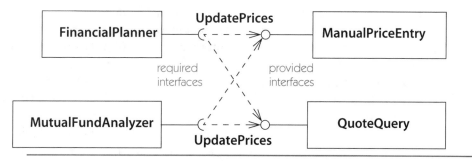

Figure 14-160. *Interface suppliers and clients*

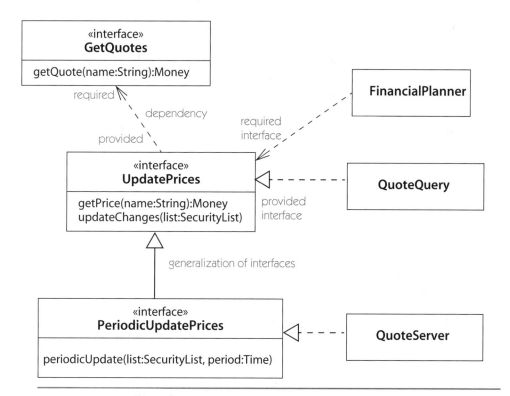

Figure 14-161. *Full interface notation*

Figure 14-161 shows the full notation for an interface as a keyword on a class symbol. We see that this interface involves two operations—asking the price of a security and getting a value, and submitting a list of securities and receiving a list of prices that have changed. In this diagram, the **QuoteQuery** class is connected to the interface using a realization arrow and **FinancialPlanner** is connected by a dependency arrow, but it is the same relationship shown in the previous diagram, just a more explicit notation.

This diagram also shows a new interface, **PeriodicUpdatePrices**, which is a child of the original interface. It inherits the two operations and adds a third operation that submits a request for a periodic, automatic update of prices. This interface is realized by the class **QuoteServer**, a subscription service. It implements the same two operations as **QuoteQuery** but in a different way. It does not share the implementation of **QuoteQuery** (in this example) and therefore does not inherit implementation from it.

Figure 14-161 shows the difference between interface inheritance and full inheritance. The latter implies the former, but a child interface may be implemented in a different way than the parent interface. **QuoteServer** supports the interface that **QuoteQuery** implements, namely **UpdatePrices**, but it does not inherit the implementation of **QuoteQuery**. (In general, it is convenient to inherit implementation, as well as interface, so the two hierarchies are often identical.)

A dependency between a provided and a required interface is shown as a dashed arrow from the provided to the required interface.

An interface may also contain a list of the signals it handles (Figure 14-162).

Interfaces are used to define the behavior of classes, as well as components, without restricting the implementation. This permits distinguishing interface inheritance, as declared in Java, from implementation inheritance.

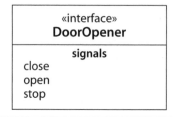

Figure 14-162. *Interface with signals*

interface specifier

This UML1 construct is obsolete in UML2.

interleaving semantics

The semantics of interactions that events from different traces may come in any relative order when the traces are merged, although the events on each trace preserve their ordering in the merge. There is no sense in which unrelated events from different traces may occur at the "same time"; the concept of "same time" has no meaning for independent events.

See interaction, trace.

internal activity

An activity attached to a state that is executed when the state is entered, active, or exited.

See also internal transition.

Semantics

Internal activities are attached to a state. An internal activity may be an entry activity, an exit activity, or a do activity. An entry activity is executed when a state is entered. It is executed after any entry activities on enclosing states and before any entry activities on nested states. An exit activity is executed when a state is exited. It is executed after any exit activities on nested states and before any exit activities on enclosing states.

A do activity is executed as long as the state is active. It is initiated when the state is entered but after any entry activity attached to the state. Unlike other activities attached to states or transitions, a do activity may continue execution for an extended time. If a transition causes an exit from the state and the do activity is still executing, it is forcibly terminated before any exit activity of the state is executed. If the do activity terminates by itself while the state is still active, the state satisfies its completion condition and may trigger a completion transition. The do activity is not restarted unless the state is exited and reentered.

Notation

An internal activity is shown as a text string in a compartment in the state symbol with the syntax:

    keyword / activity-expression

The keyword is **entry, exit,** or **do.** The activity expression is implementation dependent, but in many cases the name of a defined activity with a list of arguments will suffice.

Example

Figure 14-163 shows a state that is entered when a password is requested. The entry action is executed when the state is entered; it turns off the typing echo before password typing begins. The exit action is executed when the state is exited; it restores the typing echo after the password has been typed. The other entry is an internal transition that is executed if the help function is requested while the state is active.

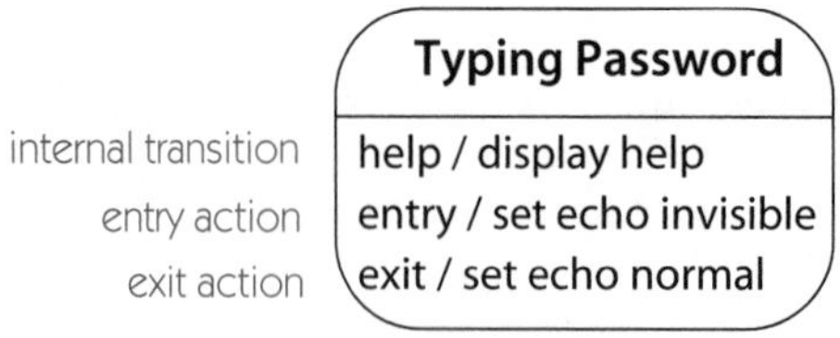

```
                    ╭──────────────────────╮
                    │   Typing Password     │
                    ├──────────────────────┤
internal transition │ help / display help   │
      entry action  │ entry / set echo invisible │
       exit action  ╲ exit / set echo normal │
                    ╰──────────────────────╯
```

Figure 14-163. *Internal transition and internal activity syntax*

Discussion

The UML2 document states that internal activities and internal transitions may be placed in separate compartments, but two compartments are superfluous and inconsistent with examples in the document.

internal structure

The interconnected parts, ports, and connectors that compose the contents of a structured classifier.

See structured classifier.

internal transition

A transition attached to a state that has an action but does not involve a change of state.

See also state machine.

Semantics

An internal transition allows an event to trigger an activity without a change of state. An internal transition has a source state but no target state. If the trigger is satisfied while the state is active, the transition fires, its activity is executed, but the state does not change even if the internal transition is attached to and inherited from an enclosing state of the current state. Therefore, no entry activity or exit activity are executed. In this respect, it differs from a self-transition, which causes the exit of nested states and exit and reentry of the source state, with the execution of exit and entry activities.

Notation

An internal transition is shown as a text entry within a compartment of a state symbol. The entry has the same syntax as the text label for an external transition. Because there is no target state, there is no need to attach it to an arrow.

event-name / activity-expression

The event names **entry, exit,** and **do** are reserved words and may not be used as event names. These reserved words are used to declare an entry activity, an exit activity, and the execution of an do activity. For uniformity, these special activities use internal transition syntax to specify the action. They are not internal transitions, however, and the reserved words are not event names.

Figure 14-163 shows the notation. If the **help** signal is generated while the state is active, the **display help** activity is performed. The **Typing Password** state remains active.

Discussion

An internal transition may be thought of as an "interrupt" that causes an action but does not affect the current state, and therefore does not invoke exit or entry actions. Attaching an internal transition to a composite state is a good way to model an action that must occur over a number of states but must not change the active state—for example, displaying a help message or counting the number of occurrences of an event. It is not the right way to model an abort or an exception. These should be modeled by transitions to a new state, as their occurrence invalidates the current state.

interrupt

The occurrence of an event that terminates a region of execution and initiates execution intended to deal with the occurrence.

Semantics

Interrupts deal with the situation in which activity cannot always be allowed to complete execution when certain events occur, such as a time-out, a request to abort a transaction, or the occurrence of an event that renders a partial computation irrelevant.

An interruptible activity region is a set of nodes and edges within which activity can be interrupted by the occurrence of a specified event. The interrupting event trigger is specified as part of an interruptible activity region. A target activity node, outside the region, is also specified. This represents the interrupt handler (this is not an official UML term). If the specified event occurs while there is activity in the region, all activity in the region is terminated and control is transferred to the interrupt handler activity node. There is no possibility to resume the original execution after an interrupt. The interrupt handler replaces the execution of the original activity node and can transfer control where it likes when it is complete. Activity outside the interruptible activity region is unaffected by the interrupt and continues concurrently with the execution of the interrupt handler.

Low-level details, such as whether terminated activities have a final opportunity to clean up before terminating and how details of the interrupting event are communicated to the interrupt handler, are unspecified in the UML2 document but may be added in profiles.

Notation

An interruptible activity region is shown on an activity diagram as a dashed rectangle with rounded edges (Figure 14-164). The interrupt handler is shown as an activity symbol disjoint from the interruptible region. An interrupting edge is shown as a jagged "lighting bolt" arrow from inside the interruptible region to the boundary of the interrupt handler. The interrupting event name is placed near the jagged arrow. Take care to start the arrow within the interruptible region, otherwise it may be confused with an exception.

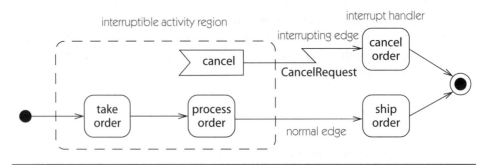

Figure 14-164. *Interrupt*

Discussion

UML2 has provided rudimentary support for interrupts, but much broader capability might be expected in the future, perhaps in a profile.

interrupt handler

An activity that gains control when an interrupt occurs. (This is not an official UML term.) See interrupt.

interruptible activity edge

The specification of an event whose occurrence terminates all activity within a designated region and transfer of control to a designated interrupt handler activity. See interrupt.

interruptible activity region

A set of activity nodes and edges within which activity is terminated if a designated event occurs. See interrupt.

interval

The range of values between two designated values.

Semantics

Intervals are often used for multiplicities (using integers) and time (using time expressions).

Notation

An interval is shown as a text string with the minimum value or expression followed by a double period (..) followed by the maximum value or expression. For example:

1..3

31 May 2002..30 June 2002

invariant

A constraint that must be true at all times (or at least at all times when no operation is incomplete), or at least at all times during a specified time interval or when specified conditions are true.

Semantics

An invariant is a Boolean expression that must be true at all times when specified conditions are true. It is not expected to be true below a certain granularity, for example, during the execution of an operation that updates the values on which the constraint depends. The exact granularity is often implied rather than stated formally. An invariant is an assertion, not an executable statement. If it fails, the model is ill formed; it is not intended to specify a corrective action (although bug-checking software might well take emergency action to avoid system damage in an implementation). Depending on the exact form of the expression, it might or might not be possible to verify it automatically in advance.

See also precondition, postcondition.

Structure

An invariant is specified as a constraint. Its usage depends upon its context within another modeling construct.

invocation

The request to execute a designated parameterized behavior element or behavioral feature.

Semantics

An invocation request is an action that specifies a behavior element or behaviorally feature and a list of argument values. For many kinds of invocation, it also designates a target object. The types of the values in the argument list must match the corresponding parameters in the behavior element. Depending on the kind of invocation, the request is either asynchronous or synchronous. For an asynchronous request, the action forms the target object, behavior element designation, and argument values into a request packet that is transmitted to the target object (or to the targets implied by the specific action). The invoking thread is then free to continue without waiting for the completion, or indeed the initiation, of the invoked execution.

For a synchronous request, the invoking thread is blocked from further execution while the invocation request is transmitted to the target and the requested execution proceeds. The invocation request packet includes sufficient information to allow a subsequent return action to return control to the invoking thread; this return information is opaque and inaccessible to the target execution except to perform a return. When the invoked execution completes, any return values are transmitted to the invoking execution, which is unblocked and allowed to continue execution.

Invocation actions have the following varieties, each with its own parameters:

broadcast	Sends a signal to an implicit set of target objects. The objects are intended to represent all objects within a specified region of a system. The signal type and argument list are parameters. Always asynchronous.
call operation	Executes a method found by mapping an operation using system-specific resolution rules. The target object, operation, argument list, and synchronicity are parameters.
call activity	Invokes an activity directly from another activity. The invoked activity, argument list, and synchronicity are parameters. Other kinds of behavior, such as state machines, can also be invoked.
send signal	Sends a signal to a target object. The target object, signal type, and argument list are parameters. Always asynchronous.
send object	Sends a signal object to a target object. The target object and signal object are parameters. Always asynchronous.

Notation

There is no defined syntax for actions, but the operation or signal name followed by a list of arguments in parentheses will work for all informal uses and many formal ones. The keywords **broadcast**, **call**, or **send** will usually clarify ambiguous situations.

isolation flag

A flag that ensures that the execution of an activity node will not conflict with the execution of other nodes that share access to the same objects.

Semantics

Multiple concurrent executions have no sequencing dependencies if the objects they access are disjoint, because a change in the relative order of their execution will not change the results. If different activity nodes share access to the same objects, the relative order of execution may affect the results. Indeterminacy can be avoided by totally ordering the execution sequence. Sometimes, however, execution is determinate if each activity node is allowed to execute completely without interleaving execution of the other activity nodes, regardless of which activity node executes first. For example, consider two fragments that each increment the value of a counter. The result is determinate if any one increment is executed in its entirety, but may be faulty if two activities each access the variable simultaneously and then write back the incremented value.

Setting the isolation flag is an executable statement that an activity node is to be executed so that no interleaving executions of other executions occur. It is not an assertion; it has executable effect. It does not require that the executions be sequential, provided that the result is not affected by any concurrent execution. In actual practice, implementing the isolation flag efficiently might involve some preanalysis of potential execution sequences to identify sources of conflict and only sequentializing the potentially conflicting activities.

iteration expression

A specification within an interaction of the range of number of iterations of a loop.

Semantics

On a loop within an interaction, the range of iterations can be specified by a minimum and maximum count.

Notation

Sequence diagram. In a sequence diagram, the bounds on the number of iterations of a loop are included in parentheses as part of the tag after the keyword loop:

loop   Minimum = 0, unlimited maximum

loop (repeat)   Minimum = maximum = repeat

loop (minimum, maximum) Explicit minimum and maximum bounds

In addition to the bounds, a Boolean expression can be included as a guard on a lifeline. The loop will continue to iterate if the expression is true, but it will iterate at least the minimum count and no more than the maximum count, regardless of the guard expression.

Figure 14-163 shows a loop with bounds and a guard condition.

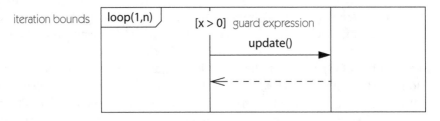

Figure 14-165. *Iteration bounds in loop*

Communication diagram. An iteration expression may appear after the number or name that represents a nesting level in the sequence number. The iteration expression represents conditional or iterative execution. It represents the execution of zero or more messages depending on the conditions involved. The choices are

* [iteration-clause]   An iteration

[condition-clause]   A branch

An iteration represents a sequence of messages. The iteration-clause shows the details of the iteration variable and test, but it may be omitted (in which case the iteration conditions are unspecified). The iteration-clause is meant to be expressed in pseudocode or an actual programming language. UML does not prescribe its format. An example would be

*[i := 1..n]

A condition guards a message whose execution is contingent on the truth of the condition-clause. The condition-clause is meant to be expressed in pseudocode or a programming language. UML does not prescribe its format. An example would be:

[x > y]

Note that a branch is notated the same as an iteration without a star. You can think of it as an iteration restricted to a single occurrence.

The iteration notation assumes that the messages in the iteration will be executed sequentially. There is also the possibility of executing them concurrently. That notation is a star followed by a double vertical line, for parallelism (*||). For example,

*[i:=1..n]|| q[i].calculateScore ()

Note that in a nested control structure, the iteration expression is not repeated at inner levels of the sequence number. Each level of structure specifies its own iteration within its enclosing context.

Example

For example, a full sequence number might be:

3b.1*[i:=1..n].2

which means:

> the third step of the outer procedure
>
> the second concurrent thread within that step
>
> the first step within that thread, which is a loop from 1 to n
>
> the second step within the loop

Figure 14-166 shows a simple communication diagram in which the iterations of the loop are to be executed concurrently.

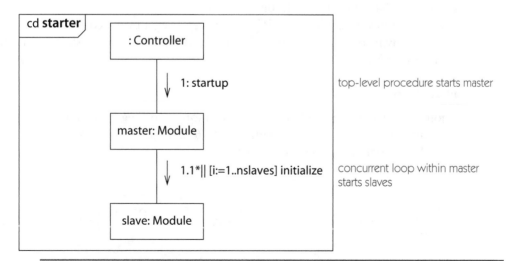

Figure 14-166. *Interaction expression in communication diagram*

iterative development

The development of a system by a process broken into a series of steps, or iterations, each of which provides a better approximation to the desired system than the previous iteration. The result of each step must be an executable system that can be executed, tested, and debugged. Iterative development is closely allied with the concept of incremental development. In iterative incremental development, each iteration adds incremental functionality to the previous iteration. The order of adding functionality is chosen to balance the size of the iterations and to attack potential sources of risk early, before the cost of fixing problems is large.

See development process.

join

A place in a state machine, activity diagram, or sequence diagram at which two or more concurrent threads or states combine to yield one thread or state; an and-join or "unfork." Antonym: fork. See complex transition, composite state.

Semantics

A join is a pseudostate in a complex transition with two or more source states and one target state. If all the source states are active and the trigger event occurs, the transition effect is executed and the target state becomes active. The source states must be in different orthogonal regions of a composite state.

The individual input edges of the join may not have guard conditions. The overall join may have a guard condition.

A transition segment leaving a join may have a trigger provided no previous segment on any incoming path has a trigger. The trigger must be satisfied before the transition fires.

Notation

A join is shown as a heavy bar with two or more incoming transition arrows and one outgoing transition arrow (Figure 14-167). It may have a transition label (guard condition, trigger event, and action).

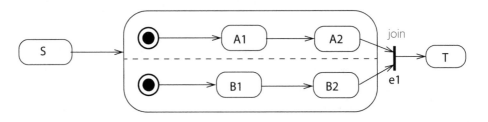

Figure 14-167. *Join*

Discussion

See merge for discussion.

join node

A control node in an activity that synchronizes multiple flows.

Semantics

A join node has multiple incoming edges and one outgoing edge. When a token is available on each input edge, the input tokens are consumed and a token is placed on the output edge. This has the effect of reducing the number of concurrent tokens in the execution.

A join specification may be placed on the node to specify conditions under which the node may fire without waiting for tokens to be present on all nodes. The join specification has complicated semantics and introduces a serious danger of constructing ill-formed models with dangling tokens. The danger can be greatly reduced by placing the node within an interruptible region and treating the output of the node as an interrupting edge.

Data tokens are joined by outputting them as a sequence on the output edge.

Notation

A join is shown as a heavy bar with two or more incoming flow arrows and one outgoing flow arrow (Figure 14-168).

Note that a fork and a join have the same notation but different numbers of inputs and outputs. It is possible to combine them into one symbol with multiple input and output arrows.

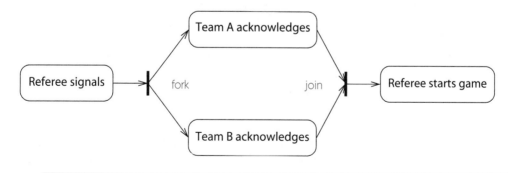

Figure 14-168. *Fork and join nodes*

Discussion

Joining of data values is a controversial area and might be handled in various other ways. Joining a single data value with one or more control values is straightforward, although the specification does not explicitly permit it.

junction

A pseudostate that is part of a single overall transition in a state machine. It does not break a single run-to-completion step in the execution of a transition or introduce the possibility of a dynamic choice based on actions executed during the transition.

See also branch, merge.

Semantics

A transition in a state machine can cross several composite state boundaries from the source state to the target state. In executing such a transition, one or more entry activity or exit activity executions may be invoked. Sometimes, it is necessary to interleave one or more actions on the transition with the entry activities and exit activities attached to the nested states. This is not possible with a simple transition, which has a single action attached.

It is also convenient to allow several triggers to have a single outcome, or to allow a single trigger to have several possible outcomes with different guard conditions.

A junction state is a pseudostate that makes it possible to build a single overall transition from a series of transition fragments. A junction state may have one or more incoming transition segments and one or more outgoing transition segments. It may not have an internal do activity, a submachine, or any outgoing transitions with event triggers. It is a dummy state to structure transitions and not a state that can be active for any finite time.

A junction state is used to structure a transition from several segments. Only the first segment in a chain of junction states may have an event trigger, but all of them may have guard conditions. Subsequent segments must be triggerless. The effective guard condition is the conjunction of all the individual guard conditions. The transition does not fire unless the entire set of conditions is met before the transition fires. In other words, the state machine may not remain at the junction state.

If multiple transitions enter a single junction state, they may each have a different trigger or may be triggerless. Each path through a set of junction states represents a distinct transition.

An outgoing transition may have a guard condition. If there are multiple outgoing transitions, each must have a distinct guard condition. This is a branch.

An outgoing transition may have an effect attached. (The junction state may have an internal action, but this is equivalent to attaching an action to the outgoing transition, which is the preferred form.) The action is executed provided all guard conditions are satisfied, even those found in subsequent segments. A transition may not "partially fire" so that it stops at a junction state. It must reach a normal state.

When an incoming transition fires, the outgoing transition fires immediately. Any attached action is then executed. The execution of the incoming transition and the outgoing transition are part of a single atomic step (a run-to-completion step)—that is, they are not interruptible by an event or other actions.

If a compound transition crosses into a state, any actions on segments outside the state are executed before the entry activity, and any actions on segments inside the state are executed after the entry activity. An action on a segment that crosses the boundary is considered to be outside the state. A similar situation exists for transitions crossing out of a state.

Note that a choice pseudostate also connects multiple segments into a compound transition, but it has different rules for guard conditions. When a path contains a choice vertex, the guard conditions on the path before the choice vertex are evaluated before the transition fires. Guard conditions on the path after the choice vertex are evaluated dynamically after any actions on the initial segments have been performed. The modeler must guarantee that a valid subsequent path will then exist. Unless one segment from each choice vertex contains an else condition or can otherwise be guaranteed to cover all possible results, there is the danger of an invalid execution scenario. There is no such danger with a junction vertex because all of the conditions are evaluated in advance before the transition fires. Junction vertices and choice vertices each have their place.

Notation

A junction pseudostate is shown in a state machine as a small filled circle. It has no name. It may have incoming and outgoing transition arrows.

Example

Figure 14-169 shows a (somewhat contrived) example illustrating the equivalent effects of junction pseudostates. The two incoming segments and two outgoing segments multiply to produce four equivalent complete transitions. Note that in each case, all of the guard conditions are evaluated before any of the transitions fire or any actions are executed. If the values of the guard conditions change during execution of the actions, it has no effect on the firing of the transition.

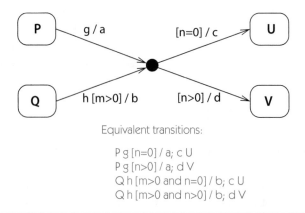

Equivalent transitions:

P g [n=0] / a; c U
P g [n>0] / a; d V
Q h [m>0 and n=0] / b; c U
Q h [m>0 and n>0] / b; d V

Figure 14-169. *Junction pseudostates with multiple paths*

Figure 14-170 shows two complete transitions from state S to state T—a single-segment transition triggered by event **f**, and a multisegment transition triggered by event **e**, which is structured using two junction states. The annotations show the interleaving of the transition actions with the exit and entry actions.

Note that the placement of the action label along the transition line has no significance. If action **d** had been placed inside state X, it would nevertheless be executed after state X is exited and before state Y is entered. Therefore, it should be drawn at the outermost location along the transition.

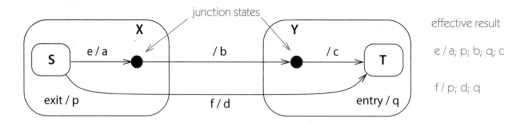

Figure 14-170. *Junction pseudostates with multiple actions*

For other examples, see Figure 14-284.

See also control node for other shortcut symbols that may be included in statechart diagrams and activity diagrams.

keyword

A keyword is a textual adornment that categorizes a model element that lacks its own distinct syntax. They are not a semantic category.

See also graphic marker, stereotype.

Semantics

Keywords are not a semantic category. They are used for stereotype notation, but they are used for the notation of certain other elements as well.

Notation

Keywords are used for built-in model elements that lack a unique notation, as well as for user-definable stereotypes. The general notation for the use of a keyword is to enclose it in guillemets (« »).

«keyword»

When the keyword is part of an area symbol, such as a class rectangle, the keyword is placed within the symbol boundary.

Some predefined keywords are described in the text of this document and are treated as reserved words in the notation. Other names are available for users to employ as stereotype names. The use of a stereotype name that matches a predefined keyword is not allowed.

Discussion

The number of easily distinguishable visual symbols is limited. The UML notation therefore makes use of text keywords to distinguish variations on a common theme, including metamodel subclasses of a base class, stereotypes of a metamodel base class, and groups of list elements. From the user's perspective, the metamodel distinction between metamodel subclasses and stereotypes is often unimportant, although it is, of course, important to tool builders and others who implement the metamodel.

label

A term for a use of a string on a diagram. It is purely a notational term.

See also diagram.

Notation

A label is a graphic string that is logically attached to another symbol on a diagram. Visually, the attachment is usually a matter of containing the string in a closed region or placing the string near the symbol. For some symbols the string is placed in a definite position (such as below a line), but for most symbols the string must be "near" a line or icon. An editing tool can maintain an explicit internal graphic linkage between a label and a graphic symbol so that the label remains logically connected to the symbol even if they become separated visually. But the final appearance of the diagram is a matter of aesthetic judgment and should be made so that there is no confusion about which symbol a label is attached to. Although the attachment may not be obvious from a visual inspection of a diagram, the attachment is clear and unambiguous at the graphic structure level (and therefore poses no ambiguity in the semantic mapping). A tool may visually show the attachment of a label to another symbol using various aids (such as a colored line or flashing of matched elements) as a convenience.

language type

An anonymous data type defined in the syntax of a programming language.
   See also data type.

Semantics

A language type is an construct following syntax rules of a particular programming language, usually expressed as a string. In UML2, it would be a kind of data type. When modeling programming language constructs closely, it might be used as the type of an attribute, variable, or parameter.
   For example, the C++ data type "**Person* (*)(Contract*, int)**" could be defined as a C++ language type.
   UML does not contain a generic data type variant suitable for declaring programming language data types. If they are needed, they must be added in profiles for a particular programming language.

layer

An architectural pattern of grouping packages in a model at the same level of abstraction. Each layer represents a virtual world at some level of reality.

leaf

A generalizable element that has no children in the generalization hierarchy. It must be concrete (fully implemented) to be of any use.
   See also abstract, concrete.

Semantics

The leaf property declares that an element *must* be a leaf. The model is ill formed if it declares a child of such an element. The purpose is to guarantee that a class cannot be modified, for example, because the behavior of the class must be well established for reliability. The leaf declaration also permits separate compilation of parts of a system by ensuring that methods cannot be overridden and facilitating inlining of method code. An element for which the property is false may indeed *be* a leaf at the moment, but children might be added in the future if the model is modified. Being a leaf or being constrained to be a leaf are not fundamental semantic properties but rather are software engineering mechanisms to control human behavior.

library (stereotype of Artifact)

An artifact representing a static or dynamic library.
   See artifact.

lifeline

A role in an interaction that represents a participant over a period of time and, by extension, the participant itself. In a sequence diagram, it is shown as a vertical line, parallel to the time axis, with a head symbol showing its name and type.

Semantics

A lifeline represents a participant in an interaction. An interaction is based on a context in which objects interact. The context can be a structured classifier or a collaboration. The parts of the classifier or the roles of a collaboration have relationships to each other by which they exchange messages. A lifeline represents one of those parts or roles.

Because a part or role may have multiplicity greater than one, it may represent multiple objects during execution. A lifeline represents only one of those objects, therefore one general role may map into multiple lifelines in a particular interaction. If the multiplicity is greater than one, an optional selector expression on each lifeline specifies which object out of the set it represents.

A lifeline indicates the period during which an object exists. An object is active if it owns a thread of control—that is, if it is the root of the thread. A passive object is temporarily active during the time when it has a thread of control passing through it—that is, during the period of time during which it has a procedure call outstanding. The latter is called an execution specification (or activation). It includes the time during which a procedure is calling a lower-level procedure. This distinction is only useful in considering nested procedure calls; for systems of concurrent interacting objects that interact asynchronously, all of them may be considered active all the time in many cases.

A lifeline contains an ordered list of occurrence specifications, each of which models the occurrence of an event. The order represents the time sequence in which the events occur. The relative ordering of occurrence specifications on different lifelines is meaningful only if messages connect them or explicit sequencing dependencies are inserted, otherwise they are considered concurrent and can appear in any actual relative order.

Notation

In a sequence diagram, a lifeline is shown on as a vertical dashed line. (The line can be solid but it is usually dashed.) The vertical line represents the existence of the object over a particular period of time (Figure 14-171).

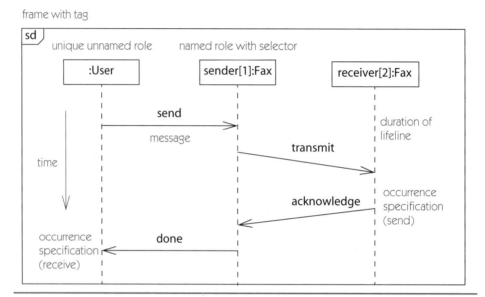

Figure 14-171. *Lifelines*

The creation of the object is shown by a head symbol, that is, a rectangle at the top of the lifeline at the point at which the object is created. If the rectangle is at the top of the sequence diagram, then the object is assumed to be created already when the interaction begins. The name and type of the participant are shown as a text string in the rectangle, in the following syntax:

$$name_{opt} \lfloor [\, selector \,] \, \rfloor_{opt} \lfloor : Type \rfloor_{opt}$$

where name is the name of the individual participant (usually assigned by the modeler of the interaction for convenience), selector is an expression to identify a particular object when the role has multiplicity greater than one, and Type is the type of the object. The name is often omitted when there is only one object of a given type in an interaction.

The string **self** can be used to denote the instance of the classifier that owns the interaction.

Arrows between lifelines indicate messages between objects. The lifeline on the tail of the arrow is the sending of the message; the lifeline on the head of the arrow is the receiver of the message (for example, the provider of an operation). The intersection of a message arrow with a lifeline is an occurrence specification, the sending or receiving of a message. The vertical ordering of occurrence specifications on a lifeline indicates the relative time order of sending or receiving the messages. The receipt of a message by the receiver follows its sending by the sender. There is no ordering among occurrence specifications on different lifelines unless there is a message path between them. Occurrence specifications that are unrelated are concurrent and can occur in any relative order during execution.

Other kinds of occurrence specifications include state constraints, creation, destruction, and the beginning and ending of execution (although the latter often corresponds to the receipt of messages).

If the object is created or destroyed during the period of time shown on the diagram, then its lifeline starts or stops at the appropriate point. Otherwise, it goes from the top to the bottom of the diagram. An object symbol is drawn at the head of the lifeline. If the object is created during the time shown on the diagram, then the object symbol is drawn at the head of the message that creates it. Otherwise, the object symbol is drawn above any message arrows.

If the object is destroyed during the diagram, then its destruction is marked by a large *X*, either at the arrowhead of the message that causes the destruction or (in the case of self-destruction) just below the final return message from the destroyed object. An object that exists when the transaction starts is shown at the top of the diagram (above the first arrow). An object that exists when the transaction finishes has its lifeline continue beyond the final arrow.

The period of time during which an object is permanently or temporarily active may be shown by a thin rectangle (a solid double line) that hides the lifeline. A second double line may be overlaid, slightly shifted, to show recursion. See execution specification for more details. Showing execution specifications is only useful in understanding flow of control in procedure calls. Because all object in an asynchronous system are always active, the double lines are usually omitted because they add no information in such cases.

See Figure 14-130 for an example showing creation, destruction, and recursive activations.

In a combined fragment, such as a conditional fragment, lifelines may overlap several operands. In this case, the different operands represent alternate execution histories, and the relative order of the operands does not represent time sequencing. The portion of a lifeline within a particular operand, however, does represent a time sequence of occurrence specifications.

In a conditional or loop construct, a guard condition may be placed at the top of a lifeline within an operand in a combined fragment. The guard condition determines whether the given branch is chosen or whether another iteration is performed. The condition is an expression on the object represented by the lifeline. It is shown as a text expression in square brackets in the form:

[Boolean-expression]

See Figure 14-90 for an example of a conditional and Figure 14-165 for an example of a loop.

A state constraint is a condition that must be true at a particular time during an interaction. It is shown as a text expression in braces on the lifeline at the relative point at which it applies. It must be satisfied immediately before the next event on the lifeline.

A lifeline may be interrupted by a state symbol to show a change of state. An arrow may be drawn to the state symbol to indicate the message that caused the change of state, or the state symbol may simply appear on the line if it represents a change during an internal computation. See Figure 14-249 for an example.

A coregion indicates a set of events that may occur in any order, regardless of their actual positioning on a lifeline. See Figure 14-104 for an example.

link

A tuple of object references that is an instance of an association or of a connector.

Semantics

A link is an individual connection among two or more objects. It is a tuple (ordered list) of object references. It is an instance of an association. The objects must be direct or indirect instances of the classes at corresponding positions in the association. An association may contain duplicate links from the same association—that is, two identical tuples of object references—only if one of the ends is specified as a bag (including a list).

A link that is an instance of an association class may have a list of attribute values in addition to the tuple of object references. Duplicate links with the same tuple object references are not permitted, even if their attribute values are distinct, unless the association has a bag on one of its ends. The identity of a link comes from its tuple of object references, which must be unique.

A link may be used for navigation. In other words, an object appearing in one position in a link may obtain the set of objects appearing in another position. It may then send them messages (called "sending a message across an association"). This process is efficient if the association has the navigability property in the target direction. Access may or may not be possible if the association is nonnavigable, but it will probably be inefficient. Navigability in opposite directions is specified independently.

Within a collaboration, a connector is a contextual, often transient, relationship between classifiers. An instance of a connector is also a link, but typically one whose life is limited to the duration of the collaboration. Such a transient association is usually not called an association; the word is usually reserved for noncontextual relationships.

Notation

Precisely speaking, objects and links appear in the "real world" and not in models or diagrams. Models of objects and links appear in some (possibly implied context) as instance specifications and connectors. For convenience in this discussion, we use the words *object* and *link* to mean the models of the actual entities, but they implicitly appear as parts within a context.

A binary link is shown as a path between two objects—that is, one or more connected line segments or arcs. In the case of a reflexive association, the path is a loop, with both ends on a single object.

See association for details of paths.

A rolename may be shown at each end of a link. An association name may be shown near the path. It is unnecessary to underline the name to indicate an instance, because a path between two objects must also be an instance. Links do not have instance names. They take their identity from the objects they relate. Multiplicity is *not* shown for links because instances do not have multiplicity; multiplicity is a property of the association that limits how many instances can exist. To show multiplicity, simply show multiple links from the same association. (As always, an instance diagram can never show the general case.) Other association adornments (aggregation, composition, and navigation) may be shown on the link roles.

A qualifier may be shown on a link. The value of the qualifier may be shown in its box. Figure 14-172 shows both ordinary and qualified links.

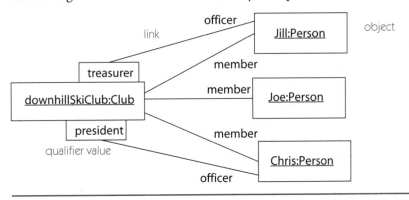

Figure 14-172. *Links*

Other adornments on links can show properties of their associations, including directionality of navigation, aggregation or composition, implementation stereotypes, and visibility.

N-ary link. An *n*-ary link is shown as a diamond with a path to each participating object. The other adornments on the association and the adornments on the roles have the same possibilities as the binary link.

Discussion

How should a dependency be shown on an object diagram? In general, a dependency represents a relationship among classes, not among objects, and belongs on a class diagram, not an object diagram. What about procedure arguments, local variables of procedures, and the caller of an operation? These must exist as actual data structures, not simply dependencies. Therefore, they can be shown as links. The caller of a procedure requires a reference to the target object—this is a link. Some links may be instances of association roles in collaborations, such as most parameters and local variables. Remaining dependencies are relevant to the class itself and not its individual objects.

link end

An instance of an association end.

Liskov substitution principle

See substitutability principle.

list

An ordered variable-length collection of model elements owned by and nested within another model element; an ordered bag.
See also classifier, multiplicity, state.

Semantics

The word list is a shorthand for an ordered bag, that is, an ordering sequence of values in which the same value may appear more than once (formally, a mapping from a subset of the positive integers to the elements of a set). It corresponds to setting the multiplicity properties isUnique=false and isOrdered=true. A set without duplicates whose elements have a relative ordering is called an *ordered set*. The word *list* implies that duplicate values may occur.

A classifier contains several lists of subordinate elements, including attributes, operations, and methods. A state contains a list of internal transitions. Other kinds of elements contain lists of other elements. Each kind of list is described individually. This article describes the properties of embedded lists, in general. In addition to lists of attributes and operations, optional lists can show other predefined or user-defined values, such as responsibilities, rules, or modification histories. UML does not define these optional lists. The manipulation of user-defined lists is tool-dependent.

An embedded list and the elements in the list belong exclusively to the containing class or other container element. Ownership is not shared among multiple containers. Other classes may be able to access the list elements—for example, by inheritance or association—but ownership of the contained lists for model editing belongs to the immediate container. Owned elements are stored, copied, and destroyed along with their containers.

The elements in a list have an order determined by the modeler. The order may be useful to the modeler—for example, it may be used by a code generator to generate a list of declarations in a programming language. If the modeler doesn't care about the order, maybe because the model is in the analysis stage or because the language ignores the ordering, then the order still exists in the model but can simply be ignored as irrelevant.

Notation

As a constituent on a multiplicity specifier, use the word list in braces: {list}, {seq}, or {sequence}.

An embedded list in a classifier rectangle appears within its own compartment as a list of strings, one string per line for each list element. Each string is the encoded representation of a feature, such as an attribute, operation, internal transition, and so on. The nature of the encoding is described in the article for each kind of element.

Ordering. The canonical order of the strings is the same as for the list elements within the model, but the internal ordering may be optionally overridden and the strings sorted according to some internal property, such as name, visibility, or stereotype. Note, however, that the items maintain their original order in the underlying model. The ordering information is merely suppressed in the view.

Ellipsis. An ellipsis (. . .) as the final element of a list or the final element of a delimited section of a list indicates that there are additional elements in the model that meet the selection criteria but are not shown in that list. In a different view of the list, such elements may appear.

Stereotype. A stereotype may be applied to a list element. A stereotype keyword enclosed in guillemets («») precedes the element string.

Property string. A property string may specify a list of properties of an element. A comma-separated list of properties or constraints, all enclosed in braces ({ }), follows the element.

Group properties. Stereotypes and other properties may also be applied to groups of list elements. If a stereotype, keyword, property string, or constraint appears on a line by itself, then the line does not represent a list element. Instead, the restrictions apply to each successive list element as if they had been placed directly on each line. This default applies until another group property line occurs in the list. All group properties can be cancelled by inserting a line with an empty keyword («»), but it is generally clearer to place all entries that are not subject to group properties at the head of the list. Figure 14-173 shows the application of stereotypes to multiple list elements.

Note that group properties are merely a notational convenience and that each model element has its own distinct value for each property.

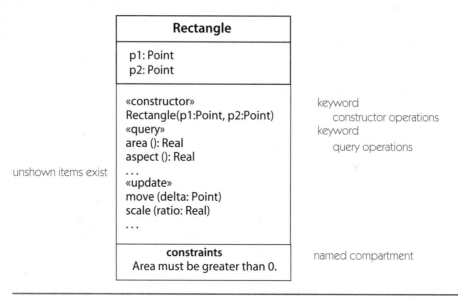

Figure 14-173. *Stereotype keyword applied to groups of list elements*

Compartment name. A compartment may display a name indicating which kind of compartment it is. The name is displayed in a distinctive font (such as boldface or in a smaller size) centered at the top of the compartment. This capability is useful if some compartments are omitted or if additional user-defined compartments are added. For a class, the predefined compartments are named **attributes** and **operations**. An example of a user-defined compartment might be **requirements**. The name compartment in a class must always be present and therefore does not require or permit a compartment name. Figure 14-173 and Figure 14-174 show named compartments.

Presentation options

Ordering. A tool may present the list elements in a sorted order. In that case, the inherent ordering of the elements is not visible. A sort is based on some internal property and does not indicate additional model information. Typical sort rules include alphabetical order, ordering by stereotype (such as constructors, destructors, then ordinary methods), ordering by visibility (public, then protected, then private), and so on.

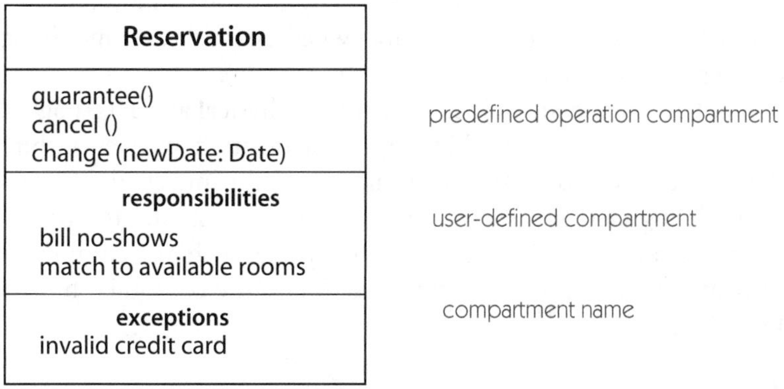

Reservation
guarantee() cancel () change (newDate: Date)
responsibilities bill no-shows match to available rooms
exceptions invalid credit card

predefined operation compartment

user-defined compartment

compartment name

Figure 14-174. *Compartments with names*

Filtering. The elements in the list may be filtered according to some selection rule. The specification of selection rules is a tool responsibility. If a filtered list shows no elements, there are no elements that meet the filter criterion, but the original list may or may not contain other elements that do not meet the criterion and are therefore invisible. It is a tool responsibility whether and how to indicate the presence of either local or global filtering, although a stand-alone diagram should have some indication of such filtering if it is to be understandable.

If a compartment is suppressed, no inference can be drawn about the presence or absence of its elements. An empty compartment indicates that no elements meet the selection filter (if any).

Note that attributes may also be shown by composition (see Figure 14-85).

location

The physical placement of an artifact, such as a file, within a distributed environment. In UML, location is discrete and the units of location are nodes.

See also artifact, node.

Semantics

The concept of location requires the concept of a space within which things can exist. UML does not model the full complexity of the three-dimensional universe. Instead, it supports a topological model of spaces connected by communications paths. A node is a computing resource at which a run-time entity can live. Nodes are connected by communications paths modeled as associations. Nodes may contain deployments of artifacts, which means that a copy of the artifact is stored on or executed on the node. Deployment may be specified on a type or instance level. A type-level model would specify that certain kinds of nodes hold certain kinds of artifacts. An instance-level model would specify that certain node instances hold certain artifact instances. Deployments are owned by the nodes, and the same artifact can be deployed on many nodes.

Deployment and deployment locations are for physical artifacts. Logical modeling elements may be implemented by physical artifacts. This relationship is called manifestation (see the entry). We might have the following chain of relationships: A logical modeling element, such as a component, is manifested by an artifact, such as a program file, which is deployed on a node, such as a computer. There is no direct relationship between the component and the computer, but there is an indirect relationship.

Notation

The location of an artifact (such as a file) deployed onto a node may be shown by nesting the artifact symbol within the node symbol, as shown in Figure 14-175. Deployment may also be shown by a dependency arrow (dashed line) from the artifact to the node with the keyword «deploy». The deployment relationship may be shown at the type level or the instance level by using classifier (no underlining) or instance specification (underlined name string with name and type) symbols.

Figure 14-175 shows deployment locations at the type level. PostScript files can live on printers. Figure 14-176 shows an instance version of the previous diagram. In this example, printer pr1 holds two instances of PostScript files, a header file and a job file.

History

In UML2, location has been restricted to artifacts, rather than all model elements.

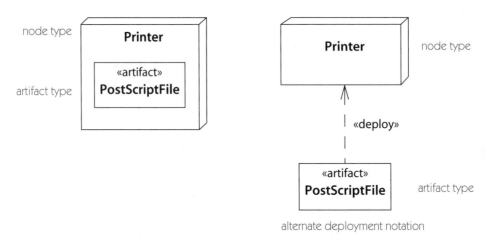

Figure 14-175. *Deployment locations at type level*

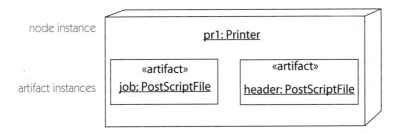

Figure 14-176. *Deployment locations at instance level*

loop

A behavioral construct in which a piece of behavior is executed repeatedly while a specified condition remains true. This article covers loops in interaction models.

See also loop node for loops in activity models.

Semantics

In an interaction, a loop is a variety of combined fragment in which the single body fragment is executed as long as a guard condition is true. A loop fragment may have a lower and upper limit on number of repetitions, as well as a Boolean condition using values from one of the lifelines in the fragment. The body of the loop is executed repeatedly while the Boolean condition evaluates true at the beginning of each repetition, but it is always executed at least the minimum count and it is never executed more than the maximum count. If the minimum count is absent, it is assumed to be zero. If the maximum count is absent, it is assumed to be unlimited.

Note that a loop fragment in an interaction is somewhat simpler than the loop node in an activity, which has initialization, update, and body sections.

Notation

A loop is shown as a rectangle with the tag loop in the upper left corner. The keyword loop may be followed by the bounds on the number of iterations of a loop in the syntax:

loop	Minimum = 0, unlimited maximum
loop (repeat)	Minimum = maximum = repeat
loop (minimum, maximum)	Explicit minimum and maximum bounds, with minimum ≤ maximum

In addition to the bounds, a Boolean expression can be included as a guard on a lifeline. The loop will continue to iterate if the expression is true, but it will iterate at least the minimum count and no more than the maximum count, regardless of the guard expression.

Lifelines that traverse the rectangle are available to the loop. Those that are outside the rectangle are inaccessible to it.

Figure 14-177 shows a loop with bounds and a guard condition. This loop must execute at least once, therefore the condition is not evaluated the first time. The loop terminates with the first success or after three failures, and the final status is available as the result.

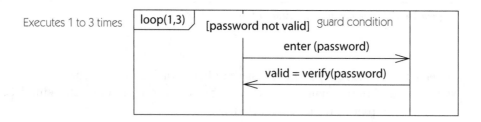

Figure 14-177. *Loop in sequence diagram*

loop node

A structured activity node that executes repeatedly while a condition evaluates true. This entry discusses loops in activity models. See also loop for loops in interaction models.

Semantics

In an activity model, a loop node is a kind of structured control node. It has three parts that are each smaller activity model fragments:

setup
: A fragment that computes initial values for loop variables before the first execution of the body.

test
: A fragment that evaluates a condition for performing another iteration of the loop before the first execution of the body (optionally) and before each subsequent execution. This fragment should not produce side effects. One Boolean value in the test subactivity is designated as the test result. The loop node also has a flag indicating whether the test is to be performed before the first iteration of the body or whether there is at least one iteration of the body.

body
: A fragment that performs the main work of the loop on each iteration. It may have side effects.

To permit execution of loops without side effects using a data flow approach, a loop may also define and update a set of loop variables:

loop variables	A set of pins in the loop that hold values that are computed initially, are available within the test and loop body, and are updated after each iteration of the loop body.
loop inputs	A set of values from outside the loop that are used to initialize the loop variables.
loop updates	A set of results from the loop body that are used to update the values of the loop variables for the next iteration. Within an iteration, the loop variables do not change their values. Their new values are computed in the loop update values but are not placed in the loop variables until completion of the loop body.
results	A set of values from the loop body that represent the output values of the overall loop. They may include loop variables. If the test is performed before the first iteration (that is, if the loop might have zero iterations), the output values can only come from the loop variables, which are the only loop values that have values initially.

Notation

There is no official graphic notation for a loop node. The feeling of the UML developers was that this construct is best expressed textually in many cases. Undoubtedly various notations will be proposed, and one of them may eventually be adopted. Until then, a text description can be placed in an activity symbol (rectangle with rounded corners).

manifestation

The physical implementation of a model element as an artifact.

Semantics

In software, models are eventually implemented as a set of artifacts, such as files of various kinds. Artifacts are the entities that are deployed onto physical nodes, such as computers or storage units. It is important to track the mapping of model elements to their implementation in artifacts. A manifestation is the relationship between a model element and the artifact that implements it. This is a many-to-many relationship. One model element may be implemented by multiple artifacts, and one artifact may implement multiple elements, although some design approaches attempt more of a one-to-one mapping (but only for "major" model elements, however "major" is defined).

Notation

A manifestation relationship is shown as a dependency arrow—a dashed line with a stick arrowhead—from an artifact to a model element. The keyword «manifest» is placed on the arrow. An artifact may have multiple manifestation arrows leaving it and a model element may have multiple manifestation arrows entering it.

In Figure 14-178 three classes are manifested by one header file, purchasing.h, but each class is manifested by its own code file.

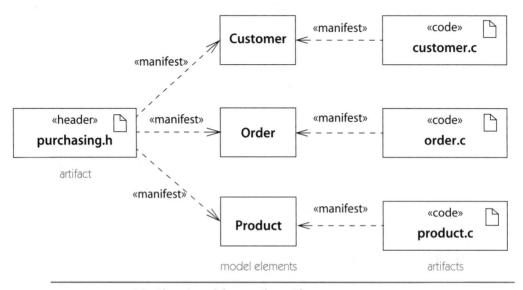

Figure 14-178. *Manifestation of elements by artifacts*

many

An abbreviation for the multiplicity 0..*—that is, zero or more without limit. In other words, the cardinality of a collection with this multiplicity can be any non-negative integer.

See multiplicity.

member

Name for a named structural inheritable constituent of a classifier, either an attribute, owned association end, operation, reception, or method. Each classifier may have a list of zero or more of each kind of member. A list of members of a given kind is notated as a list of strings within a compartment of the classifier symbol.

See also list.

merge

A place in a state machine or activity diagram where two or more alternate control paths come together; an "unbranch." Antonym: branch. See also junction.

Semantics

A merge is simply a situation in which two or more control paths come together. It does not change the amount of concurrency.

In a state machine, a state may have more than one input transition. No special model construct is required or provided to indicate a merge. It may be indicated by a junction if it is part of a single run-to-completion path. If control arrives at a state through any input transition, the state becomes active.

In an activity, a merge is indicated by a merge node (Figure 14-179). A merge node has two or more input flows and one output flow. If a token arrives on any input, it is copied to the output immediately.

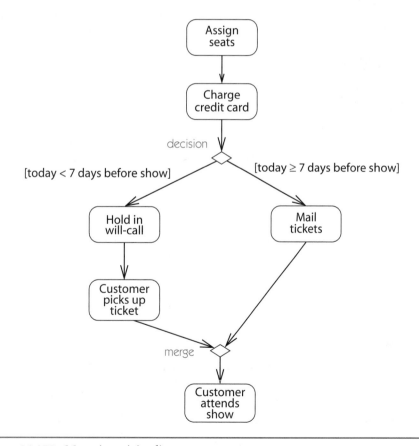

Figure 14-179. *Merge in activity diagram*

In an interaction, unstructured flows of control are not supported. A merge happens implicitly at the end of a conditional fragment.

Notation

A merge may be indicated in an activity diagram by a diamond with two or more input transitions and a single output transition. No conditions are necessary; a merge happens automatically when a token appears on any input. Figure 14-179 shows an example.

A diamond is also used for a branch (the inverse of a merge), but a branch is clearly distinguished because it has one input transition and multiple output transitions, each with its own guard condition. The use of the same symbols shows the symmetry between a branch and a merge.

A combination branch and merge is legal but of limited usefulness. It would have multiple input transitions and multiple, labeled output transitions.

A branch and merge are usually paired in a nested fashion.

In a state machine diagram, a merge is shown by simply drawing multiple transition arrows that enter the same state. No merge icon is necessary.

Discussion

Be sure to distinguish merge and join. Merge combines two or more alternate paths of control. In any execution, only one path will be taken at a time. No synchronization is necessary.

Join combines two or more concurrent paths of control. In any execution, all the paths will be taken, and the join will fire only when all of them have reached the source states of the join.

message

The conveyance of information from one role to another as part of an interaction within a context; at the instance level, a communication from one object to another. A message may be a signal or the call of an operation. The sending and the receipt of a message are occurrence specifications.

See also call, collaboration, interaction, operation, send, signal.

Semantics

A message is the transmission of a signal from one object (the *sender*) to one or more other objects (the *receivers*), or it is the call of an operation on one object (the *receiver*) by another object (the *sender* or *caller*). The implementation of a message may take various forms, such as a procedure call, explicit raising of events, interprocess communication between active threads, and so on. At a logical level, sending a signal and calling an operation are similar. They both involve a communication from a sender to a receiver that passes information by value that the receiver uses to determine what to do. A call can be considered a pattern of signals that involves a send with an implicit return pointer argument that is later used to send a return signal to the caller. A call can be modeled as two messages, a call message and a later return message. At an implementation level, signals and calls have different properties and detailed behavior, so they are distinguished as UML elements. A message is owned by an interaction, and the sender and receiver are lifelines of the interaction.

The receipt of a signal may trigger a state machine transition. The sending of a signal is asynchronous; the sender continues execution after sending it.

The receipt of an operation call may invoke a procedure or may trigger a state machine transition or both. A call may be asynchronous or synchronous. If the call is synchronous, the caller waits until the invoked execution responds. A synchronous operation may return values as part of the response. When execution of the procedure is complete, then the caller resumes control and receives any return values.

Note that a direct call of an activity is simply a flow-of-control construct within the model and does not correspond to a message, because only a single object is involved.

A message represents a single transmission between one sender and one receiver. A message has a send occurrence specification and a receive occurrence specification. The broadcast action sends a set of messages, one for each object in the implicit target set. Other actions send one message, but they can appear in loops or expansion regions to send sets of messages.

A message has argument values, which must agree in number and types with the parameters of the specified operation or the attributes of the specified signal. The return values, if any, must match the return types of the specified signal. Any return values for an asynchronously called operation are ignored and do not generate a reply message.

A time constraint is placed on the occurrence specifications that identify a message, rather than the message itself. A duration constraint can be placed on the message.

There is no absolute time scale that relates events on different lifelines. Unless otherwise constrained, events on different lifelines are concurrent. A message establishes a temporal ordering among the sending and received events. The events on a single lifeline are temporally ordered. Any chain of messages that returns to the same lifeline must finish at a later point than the beginning of the chain (that is, reverse time travel is prohibited except in science fiction novels).

Structure

interaction	The interaction that owns the message.
send event	The occurrence specification of sending the message. The lifeline owning this occurrence specification is the sender of the message.
receive event	The occurrence specification of receiving the message. The lifeline owning the occurrence specification is the receiver of the message.
signature	The signal or operation defining the type of the message.
arguments	A list of argument values compatible with the signature. The arguments must be accessible to the sender; that is, they must be properties of the sender or the owner of the interaction, parameters of the interaction invocation, constants, or values reachable from the preceding items.
connector	(optional) The connector over which the message is transmitted.
synchronicity	Either signal (always asynchronous), synchronous call, or asynchronous call. Must match the signature.
kind	Whether the message is complete (default, includes sender and receiver), lost (no receiver), or found (no sender). Lost and found messages are used in advanced modeling situations for noisy systems or systems with incomplete knowledge. They are unnecessary in most models.

A message in the model may not cross the boundary of a combined fragment, such as a conditional branch or loop. To model a message instance that crosses a boundary, use a gate on the boundary to combine two messages that each remain within one fragment. During execution, one message instance will correspond to the chain of messages in the model.

Notation

The notation for sequence diagrams and communication diagrams is different.

Sequence diagrams

On a sequence diagram, a message is shown as a solid arrow from the lifeline of one object, the sender, to the lifeline of another object, the target (Figure 14-180). Officially, time scales on different lifelines are independent, so the angle of the arrow has no semantic significance. However, some modelers assume a uniform

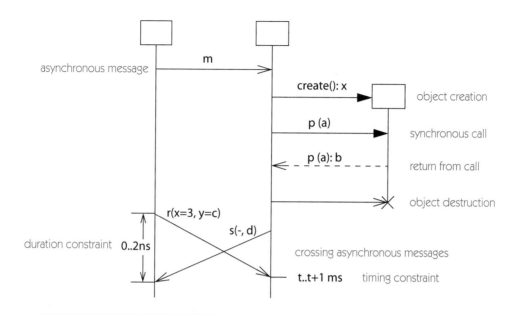

Figure 14-180. *Message notation in sequence diagram*

time scale across all lifelines, so that an arrow perpendicular to the lifelines implies instantaneous (or at least fast) message transmission, and a slanted arrow implies that the duration of transmission is observable. Such assumptions are not reflected in the semantic model unless timing constraints are inserted. In case of a message from an object to itself, the arrow may start and finish on the same lifeline. The message arrows are arranged in sequential order from top to bottom, vertically. Unless the sending point of one message follows the receiving point of another message on the same lifeline (or there is a chain of intermediate messages that connect the two), the two messages are concurrent, and their relative order is not significant. Messages may have sequence numbers, but because the relative order of messages in shown visually, the sequence numbers are often omitted. (Also, sequence numbers are not useful if there are concurrent messages.)

A message arrow may be labeled with the syntax:

$\lfloor$ attribute = $\rfloor_{opt}$ name $\lfloor$ (argument$_{list,}$) $\rfloor_{opt}$ $\lfloor$: return-value $\rfloor_{opt}$

where name is the name of the signal or operation, and attribute is the optional name of an attribute (of the lifeline) to store the return value.

Argument values can be replaced by a dash (–), which indicates that any argument value is compatible with the model. The entire name string can be replaced by an asterisk (*), which indicates that any message is compatible with the model.

As an option, a parameter name may be included with an argument value, so an argument may have one of the following syntaxes:

```
argument-value
parameter-name = argument-value
```
—

If parameter names are used and some parameters are missing, any values are acceptable for the missing parameters.

Synchronicity. An asynchronous message is shown by an open (stick) arrowhead. A synchronous call is shown by a filled black arrowhead. The return from a synchronous call is shown by a dashed line with an open (stick) arrowhead.

If a diagram contains primarily synchronous calls with activation regions shown, the return messages may be omitted and the return values shown on the original call messages. The return is implicit at the end of the called activation region. This convention reduces the number of arrows in the diagram but causes more mental effort for the reader, so many modelers choose to always show returns.

A message that creates (or causes the creation of) an object is shown by placing the header box for a lifeline at the head of the arrow. A message that destroys (or causes the destruction of) an object is shown by placing a large X on the arrowhead. The messages may be synchronous or asynchronous.

A lost or found message is shown by placing a small black circle at the end of the arrow at which the object is not known.

Transmission delay. Usually message arrows are drawn horizontally, indicating the duration required to send the message is atomic—that is, it is brief compared with the granularity of the interaction and that nothing else can "happen" during the message transmission. This is the correct assumption within many computers. If the message requires some time to deliver, during which something else can occur (such as a message in the opposite direction), then the message arrow may be slanted downward so that the arrowhead is below the arrow tail. Unless two messages cross, however, no actual conclusions can be drawn from slanting messages.

Communication diagrams

On a communication diagram, a message is shown as a small labeled arrow attached to a path between the sender and the receiver objects. The path is the connector used to access the target object. The arrow points along the path in the direction of the target object. In the case of a message from an object to itself, the message appears on a path looping back to the same object and the keyword «self» appears on the target end. More than one message may be attached to one link, in the same or different directions. The message arrow is labeled with the name of the message (operation or signal name) and its argument values.

The relative order of messages is shown by the sequence number portion of the message label. Unlike sequence diagrams, in which sequencing is shown graphically, sequence numbers are needed in communication diagrams. A message may also be labeled with a guard condition.

Synchronicity. The same arrow types may be used as those in sequence diagrams.

Message label. The label has the following syntax:

    sequence-expression_{opt} message

where message is the message syntax described previously under sequence diagrams, and the sequence expression combines ordering and conditionality as described below.

Sequence expression. The sequence-expression is a dot-separated list of sequence-terms followed by a colon (':'). Each term represents a level of procedural nesting within the overall interaction. If all the control is asynchronous, then nesting does not occur and a simple one-level numbering system is used. Each sequence-term has the following syntax.

    label iteration-expression_{opt}

where label is

    integer

or

    name

The integer represents the sequential order of the message within the next higher level of procedural calling. Messages that differ in one integer term are sequentially related at that level of nesting. An example is: Message 3.1.4 follows message 3.1.3 within activation 3.1.

The name represents a concurrent thread of control. Messages that differ in the final name are concurrent at that level of nesting. An example is: Message 3.1a and message 3.1b are concurrent within activation 3.1. All threads of control are equal within the nesting depth.

The iteration expression represents conditional or iterative execution. This represents zero or more messages that are executed, depending on the conditions. The choices are

*[iteration-clause]	an iteration
[condition-clause]	a branch

An iteration represents a sequence of messages at the given nesting depth. The iteration-clause may be omitted (in which case, the iteration conditions are unspecified).

The iteration-clause is meant to be expressed in pseudocode or an actual programming language; UML does not prescribe its format. An example would be:

*[i := 1..n].

A condition represents a message whose execution is contingent on the truth of the condition clause. The condition-clause is meant to be expressed in pseudocode or an actual programming language; UML does not prescribe its format. An example would be: [x > y].

Note that a branch is notated the same as an iteration without a star. One might think of it as an iteration restricted to a single occurrence.

The iteration notation assumes that the messages in the iteration will be executed sequentially. There is also the possibility of executing them concurrently. The notation for this is to follow the star with a double vertical line, for parallelism (*||).

Note that in a nested control structure, the recurrence symbol is not repeated at inner levels. Each level of structure specifies its own iteration within the enclosing context.

Example

The following are samples of control message label syntax.

2: display (x, y)	Simple message
1.3.1: p= find(specs):status	Nested call with return value
1b.4 [x < 0] : invert (x, color)	Conditional within second concurrent thread
3.1*[i:=1..n]: update ( )	Iteration

Activity diagrams

Signal receipt. The receipt of a signal may be shown as a concave pentagon that looks like a rectangle with a triangular notch in its side (either side). The signature of the signal is shown inside the symbol. An unlabeled transition arrow is drawn from the previous action state to the pentagon, and another unlabeled transition arrow is drawn from the pentagon to the next action state. This symbol replaces the event label on the transition, which fires when the previous activity is complete and the event then occurs (Figure 14-181).

Signal sending. The sending of a signal may be shown as a convex pentagon that looks like a rectangle with a triangular point on one side (either side). The signature of the signal is shown inside the symbol. An unlabeled transition arrow is drawn from the previous action state to the pentagon, and another unlabeled transition arrow is drawn from the pentagon to the next action state. This symbol replaces the send-signal label on the transition (Figure 14-182).

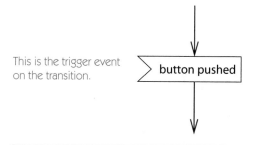

This is the trigger event on the transition.

button pushed

Figure 14-181. *Signal receipt*

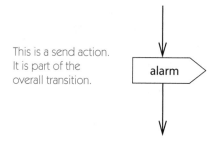

This is a send action. It is part of the overall transition.

alarm

Figure 14-182. *Signal send*

Example

In Figure 14-183, **EnterCreditCardData** and **ChargeCard** are activities. When they are completed, processing moves on to the next step. After **EnterCreditCardData** is completed, there is a branch on the amount of the request; if it is greater than $25, authorization must be obtained. A signal **request** is sent to the credit center. On a plain state machine, this would be shown as an action attached to the transition leaving **EnterCreditCardData**; they mean the same thing. **AwaitAuthorization** is a real wait state, however. It is not an activity that completes internally. Instead, it must wait for an external signal from the credit center (**authorize**). When the signal occurs, a normal transition fires and the system goes to the **ChargeCard** activity. The trigger event could have been shown as a label on the transition from **AwaitAuthorization** to **ChargeCard**. It is merely a variant notation that means the same thing.

History

The concept of message has been considerably broadened in UML2. The content can now be any object. Calls and signal sending have been brought within a common overall approach.

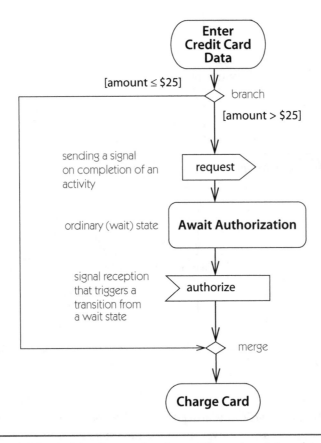

Figure 14-183. *Activity diagram showing sending and receiving of signals*

metaclass (stereotype of Class)

A class whose instances are classes. Metaclasses are typically used to construct metamodels. A metaclass can be modeled as a stereotype of a class using the keyword «metaclass». See Figure 14-184.

See powertype, profile, stereotype.

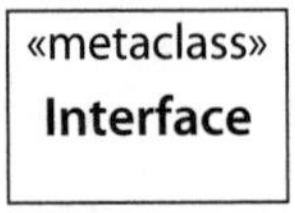

«metaclass»
Interface

Figure 14-184. *Metaclass*

metametamodel

A model that defines the language for expressing a metamodel. The relationship between a meta-metamodel and a metamodel is analogous to the relationship between a metamodel and a model. This level of indirection is usually relevant only to tool builders, database builders, and the like. UML is defined in terms of a meta-metamodel, called the Meta-Object Facility (MOF).

metamodel (stereotype of Model)

A model that defines the language for expressing other models; an instance of a metametamodel. The UML metamodel defines the structure of UML models. Metamodels usually contain metaclasses.

metaobject

A generic term for all entities in a metamodeling language. For example, metatypes, metaclasses, meta-attributes, and meta-associations.

metaobject facility

See MOF.

metarelationship

A term grouping relationships that connect descriptors to their instances. These include the instance relationship and the powertype relationship.

method

The implementation of an operation. It specifies the algorithm or procedure that produces the results of an operation.

See also concrete, operation, realization, resolution.

Semantics

A method is an implementation of an operation. If an operation is not abstract, it must have a method or trigger a state machine transition, either defined on the class with the operation or inherited from an ancestor. A method is specified as a procedural expression, a linguistic string in a designated language (such as C++, Smalltalk, or a human language) that describes an algorithm. The language must be matched to the purpose, of course. A human language, for instance, may be adequate for early analysis but not suitable for code generation.

An operation declaration implies the presence of a method unless the operation is declared as abstract. In a generalization hierarchy, each repeated declaration of the operation implies a new method that overrides any inherited method of the same operation. Two declarations represent the same operation if their signatures match.

Note that a method is an executable procedure—an algorithm—not simply a specification of results. A before-and-after specification is not a method, for example. A method is a commitment to implementation and addresses issues of algorithm, computational complexity, and encapsulation.

In some respects, a method may have stricter properties than its operation. A method can be a query even though the operation is not declared as a query. But if the operation is a query, then the method must be a query. Similarly, a method may strengthen the concurrency property. A sequential operation may be implemented as a guarded or concurrent method. In these cases, the method is consistent with the declarations of its operation. It just strengthens the constraints.

Notation

The presence of a method is indicated by an operation declaration that lacks the abstract property (Figure 14-185). If the operation is inherited, the method can be shown by repeating the operation declaration in normal (nonitalic) text to show a concrete operation. The text of the method body may be shown as a note attached to the operation list entry, but usually method bodies are not shown at all on diagrams. They remain hidden for a text editor to show on command.

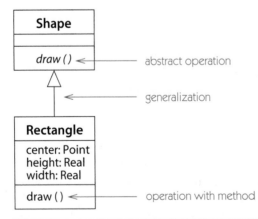

Figure 14-185. *Method on nonabstract operation*

Discussion

The UML specification does not actually define how operations are mapped into methods on an operation call. The specification assumes that some resolution mechanism is present, but the specification does not define the precise mechanism. This allows UML models to be used with a wide range of programming languages having different forms of method lookup, but it unfortunately leaves a model somewhat ambiguous. In practice, a specific resolution mechanism will be assumed for most of the models of a given organization. In many cases, resolution will be the traditional object-oriented method lookup, in which a search is made for a method on a given operation starting at the target class and working toward more general levels of the class hierarchy. Other resolution mechanisms are possible, however, and may be supported by appropriate tools.

See resolution.

model

A semantically complete description of a system.

See also package, subsystem.

Semantics

A model is an abstraction of a system from a particular viewpoint. It describes the system or entity at the chosen level of precision and viewpoint. Different models provide more-or-less independent viewpoints that can be manipulated separately.

A model may comprise a containment hierarchy of packages in which the top-level package corresponds to the entire system. The contents of a model are the transitive closure of its containment (ownership) relationships from top-level packages to model elements.

A model may also include relevant parts of the system's environment, represented, for example, by actors and their interfaces. In particular, the relationship of the environment to the system elements may be modeled. A system and its environment form a larger system at a higher level of scope. Therefore, it is possible to relate elements at various levels of detail in a smooth way.

Elements in different models do not directly affect each other, but they often represent the same concepts at different levels of detail or stages of development. Therefore, relationships among them, such as trace dependency and refinement, are important to the development process itself and often capture important design decisions.

Notation

A model can be shown as a package symbol (rectangle with a small rectangular tab on the upper left) with the keyword «model». Instead of the keyword, a small triangle may be placed in the body of the symbol or in the tab. See Figure 14-186.

There is little notational detail to show about models, however. Tools can show lists of models, but models have few relationships among themselves. Most useful is the ability to traverse from a model name to its top package or to a map of its overall contents.

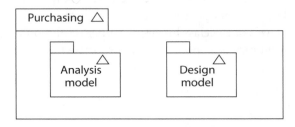

Figure 14-186. *Model notation*

Discussion

No one view of a system, or indeed no system itself, is ever complete in and of itself. There are always connections to the wider world, and a model always falls short of reality. Therefore, the concept of a closed model is always an approximation in which arbitrary lines must be drawn for practical work.

A UML model is represented as a package hierarchy that emphasizes one view of a system. Each model may have its own leveling hierarchy that may be similar or different to the leveling hierarchy of other views of the system.

model element

An element that is an abstraction drawn from the system being modeled. Contrast with presentation element, which is a (generally visual) presentation of one or more modeling elements for human interaction. In the UML2 specification, however, only model elements are described, so they are simply called elements.

Semantics

All elements that have semantics are model elements, including real-world concepts and computer-system implementation concepts. Graphic elements whose purpose is to visualize a model are presentation elements. They are not model elements, as they do not add semantics to the model. The UML2 specification does not describe them.

Model elements may have names, but the use and constraints on names vary by kind of model element and are discussed with each kind. Each model element belongs to a namespace appropriate to the kind of element. All model elements may have the following attached properties.

constraint   Zero or more constraints may be attached to a model element. Constraints are restrictions that are expressed as linguistic strings in a constraint language.

comment   A text string adding information meaningful to the modeler. This is often used to explain the reasons for design choices.

In addition, model elements may participate in dependency relationships. Depending on their specific type, model elements may own other model elements and may be owned by other model elements. All model elements are indirectly owned by the root of the system model.

model management view

That aspect of a model dealing with the organization of the model itself into structured parts—namely, packages and models. The model management view is sometimes considered to be a part of the static view and is often combined with the static view on class diagrams.

modeling time

Refers to something that occurs during a modeling activity of the software development process. It includes analysis and design. Usage note: When discussing object systems, it is often important to distinguish between modeling-time and run time concerns.

See also development process, stages of modeling.

modelLibrary (stereotype of Package)

A package containing model elements intended to be reused by other packages, but without defining stereotypes to extend the metamodel (as in a profile).

module

A software unit of storage and manipulation. Modules include source code modules, binary code modules, and executable code modules. The word does not correspond to a single UML construct, but rather includes several constructs.

See component, package, subsystem.

MOF

The Meta-Object Facility, a specification by the Object Management Group intended for use in specifying modeling languages, such as UML and CWM (Common Warehouse Metamodel). The MOF has repository mechanisms suitable for storing and accessing models in various languages. MOF defines a modeling language that is identical to a subset of UML. A UML user does not need to learn the MOF to build UML models, because UML concepts are sufficient for UML use. MOF may be useful to the developer writing tools to exchange models. Ordinary users will simply use such tools and need not understand their internal formats.

multiobject

This UML1 concept has been eliminated from UML2.

Discussion

A multiobject was intended to allow modeling a set in two complementary ways: as a single object that can have operations over the entire set and as a set of individual objects that have their own operations. The concept can be modeled in UML2 using a structured class instead of a multiobject. The structured class contains a set of objects. Another class can have associations to both the structured class and to its parts.

Figure 14-187 shows an example.

To perform an operation on each object in a set of associated objects requires two messages: an iteration to the cluster (the multiobject) to extract links to the individual objects, then a message sent to each object using the (temporary) link.

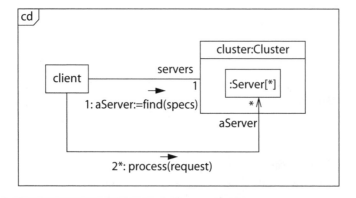

Figure 14-187. *Communication diagram with multiobject*

This may be elided on a diagram by combining the messages into one that includes an iteration and an application to each object. The target rolename takes a *many* indicator (∗) to show that many links are implied. Although this may be written as a single message, in the underlying model (and in any actual code) it requires the two layers of structure (iteration to find links, message using each link) mentioned previously.

multiple classification

A semantic variation of generalization in which an object may belong directly to more than one class.

Semantics

This is a semantic variation point under which an object may be a direct instance of more than one class. When used with dynamic classification, objects may acquire and lose classes during run time. This allows classes to be used to represent temporary roles an object may play.

Although multiple classification matches logic and everyday discourse well, it complicates implementation of a programming language and is not supported by the popular programming languages.

multiple inheritance

A semantic variation point of generalization in which an element may have more than one parent. This is the default assumption within UML and is necessary for proper modeling of many situations, although modelers may choose to restrict its use for certain kinds of elements. Some programming languages avoid it or restrict its use. Contrast: single inheritance.

multiplicity

A specification of the range of allowable cardinality values—the sizes—that a collection may assume. Multiplicity specifications may be given for association ends, attributes, parts within composite classes, repetitions of messages, and other purposes. In principle, a multiplicity is a (possibly infinite) subset of the non-negative integers. In practice, it is an integer interval. If multiplicity is greater than one, it includes an indication of whether the elements are ordered and unique.

Contrast: cardinality.

See also multiplicity (of association), multiplicity (of part).

Semantics

Cardinality range. Multiplicity is a constraint on the cardinality (size) of a collection. In principle, it is a subset of the nonnegative integers. In practice, it is usually a single interval with a minimum and a maximum value. Any collection (in UML) must be finite, but the upper bound on all collections can be finite or unbounded (an unbounded multiplicity is called "many"). The upper bound must be greater than zero; or, at any rate, a multiplicity comprising only zero is not very useful, as it permits only the empty set. Multiplicity is coded as a string.

In UML, the multiplicity range is specified as an integer intervals. An interval is a set of contiguous integers characterized by its minimum and maximum values. Some infinite sets cannot be specified this way—for example, the set of even integers—but usually little is lost by simply including the gaps. For most design purposes, a major purpose of the multiplicity is to bound the amount of storage that might be needed.

See multiplicity (of association) and multiplicity (of part) for specific details of using multiplicity with these elements.

Ordering and uniqueness. If the upper bound is greater than one, multiplicity also includes indicators for ordering and uniqueness. A set is ordered if its elements can be traversed in a fixed sequence. The elements are unique if no two elements have the same value; otherwise duplicate elements are allowed. A collection that allows duplicates is called a bag.

Notation

Multiplicity range is specified by a text expression for an integer interval in the form

    minimum..maximum

where minimum and maximum are integers, or maximum can be a "∗" which indicates an unbounded upper limit. An expression such as 2..∗ is read "2 or more."

An interval can also have the form

    number

where number is an integer representing an interval of a single size. It is equivalent to the expression **number..number**.

The multiplicity expression consisting of a single star

    ∗

is equivalent to the expression **0..∗**—that is, it indicates that the cardinality is unrestricted ("zero or more, without limit"). This frequently encountered multiplicity is read "many."

Ordering and uniqueness are shown by keywords in braces. Ordering can be **ordered** or **unordered**. The default is unordered and need not be shown. Uniqueness can be **unique** or **nonunique**. The default is unique and need not be shown.

The following keywords may be used for the combinations of properties:

set	unordered, unique elements (default)
bag	unordered, nonunique elements
ordered set	ordered, unique elements
list (or sequence)	ordered, nonunique elements

Example

0..1	optional value
1	exactly one
0..*	any number of elements, unordered, unique
* {list}	any number of elements, ordered, duplicates
1..* {ordered}	one or more, ordered, unique
1..6 {bag}	between 1 and 6, unordered, duplicates

History

In UML1, ordering was a separate property from multiplicity. Because ordered sets may not contain duplicates, many UML models of lists were subtly incorrect.

In UML2, it was recognized that ordering and uniqueness are intimately related to multiplicity, so they were combined into one concept.

Discussion

A multiplicity expression can include variables, but they must resolve to integer values when the model is complete—that is, they must be parameters or constants. Multiplicity is not meant to be dynamically evaluated within a run-time scope like a dynamic array bound. It is meant to specify the possible range of values (worst case) a set might assume and the application must therefore accommodate in its data structures and operations. It is a model-time constant. If the bound is variable at run time, then the proper choice of multiplicity is *many* (0..*).

The multiplicity may be suppressed on a diagram, but it exists in the underlying model. In a finished model, there is no meaning to an "unspecified" multiplicity. Not knowing the multiplicity is no different from saying that it is many, because in the absence of any knowledge, the cardinality might take any value, which is just the meaning of many.

See unspecified value.

multiplicity (of association)

The multiplicity specified on an association end.
See multiplicity.

Semantics

The multiplicity attached to an association end declares how many objects may fill the position defined by the association end.

For a binary association, the multiplicity on the target end constrains how many objects of the target class may be associated with a given single object from the other (source) end. Multiplicity is typically given as a range of integers. (See multiplicity for a more general definition.) Common multiplicities include exactly one; zero or one; zero or more, without limit; and one or more, without limit. The phrase "zero or more, without limit" is usually called many. If the multiplicity is greater than one, it also contains indicators of whether the collection of associated elements is ordered and whether the elements in the set are unique.

In an *n*-ary association, the multiplicity is defined with respect to the other *n-1* ends. For example, given a ternary association among classes (A, B, C), then the multiplicity of the C end states how many C objects may appear in association with a particular pair of A and B objects. If the multiplicity of this association is (many, many, one), then for each possible (A, B) pair, there is a unique value of C. For a given (B, C) pair, there may be many A values, however, and many values of A, B, and C may participate in the association.

See *n*-ary association for a discussion of *n*-ary multiplicity.

Notation

The multiplicity is shown by a multiplicity string near the end of the path to which it applies (Figure 14-188). A range of numbers has the form n1..n2. Keywords in braces show ordering and uniqueness.

See multiplicity for further details on syntax and more general forms for specifying it (although these are probably more general than needed for most practice).

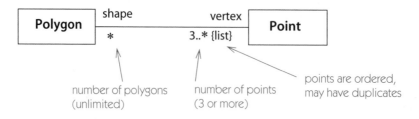

Figure 14-188. *Multiplicity of association*

multiplicity (of attribute)

The possible number of values of an attribute in each object.

Semantics

The multiplicity attached to an attribute declares how many values may be held by an object having the attribute. If the maximum count is greater than one, it also indicates whether the elements are ordered and whether their values may be duplicated.

The usual multiplicity is exactly one (1..1), meaning that every object has one value for the attribute. Other common multiplicities include zero or one (an optional, or "nullable," value); zero or more, without limit (a set of values); and one or more, without limit (a nonempty set of values). The phrase "zero or more, without limit" is usually called many.

Notation

The multiplicity is shown by a multiplicity range string in brackets after the attribute type (Figure 14-189). If there are no brackets, then the multiplicity is exactly one (a scalar value, the default). Keywords indicating ordering and uniqueness are placed in braces after the brackets.

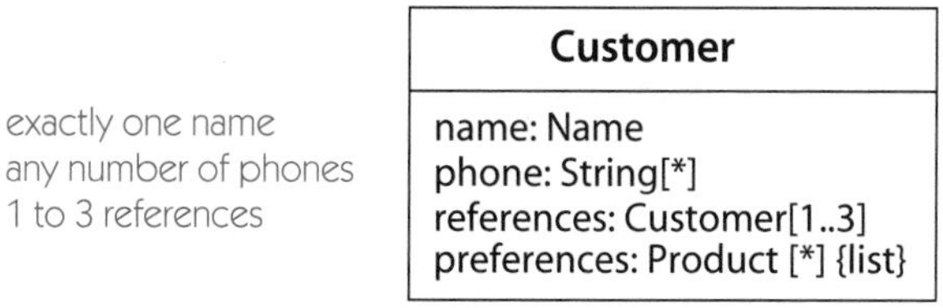

```
                              ┌──────────────────────────────┐
                              │         Customer             │
                              ├──────────────────────────────┤
exactly one name              │ name: Name                   │
any number of phones          │ phone: String[*]             │
1 to 3 references             │ references: Customer[1..3]    │
                              │ preferences: Product [*] {list}│
                              └──────────────────────────────┘
```

Figure 14-189. *Multiplicity of attributes*

multiplicity (of part)

The range of possible cardinalities of the instances within a context—that is, how many instances may legitimately exist at one time.

Semantics

When applied to a part within a structured classifier or collaboration, multiplicity declares how many instances of the part may exist within one instance of the container. The usual default is one, but other values can be declared.

Notation

The multiplicity indicator may be placed in line with the name, using the syntax for multiplicity (of attribute), or it may be placed in the upper right corner of the part rectangle (Figure 14-190). The indicator may be omitted if the multiplicity is exactly one.

Figure 14-190. *Multiplicity of part*

n-ary association

An association among three or more classes. Contrast: binary association.

Semantics

Each instance of the association is an *n*-tuple of values, one from each of the respective classes. A single class may appear in more than one position in the association, but the values in the different positions are independent and need not be the same object. A binary association is a special case with its own simpler notation and certain additional properties that are meaningless (or at least hopelessly complicated) for an *n*-ary association.

Multiplicity for *n*-ary associations may be specified but is less obvious than binary multiplicity. The multiplicity on an association end represents the potential number of values at the end, when the values at the other *n-1* ends are fixed. Note that this definition is compatible with binary multiplicity.

Aggregation (including composition) is meaningful only for binary associations. An *n*-ary association may not contain the aggregation or composition marker on any role.

There is no semantic difference between a binary association and an *n*-ary association with two ends, regardless of representation. An association with two ends is deemed to be a binary association, and one with more than two ends is deemed to be an *n*-ary association.

Notation

An *n*-ary association is shown as a large diamond (that is, large compared with a terminator on a path), with a path from the diamond to each participant class. The name of the association (if any) is shown near the diamond. Adornments may appear on the end of each path as with a binary association. Multiplicity may be indicated, but qualifiers and aggregation are not permitted.

An association class symbol may be attached to the diamond by a dashed line. This indicates an *n*-ary association that has attributes, operations, and/or associations.

Example

Figure 14-191 shows the record of a team in each season with a particular goal-keeper. It is assumed that the goalkeeper might be traded during the season and might have a record with different teams. In a record book, each link would be a separate line.

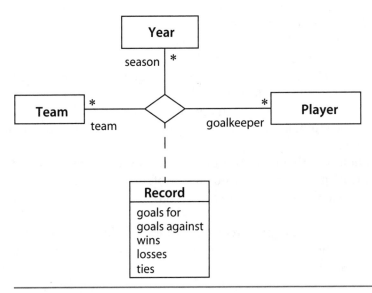

Figure 14-191. *Ternary association that is also an association class*

Style guidelines

Usually, the lines are drawn from the points on the diamond or from the midpoint of a side.

Discussion

In an *n*-ary association, the multiplicity is defined with respect to the other *n-1* ends. For example, given a ternary association among classes (A, B, C), the multiplicity of the C end states how many C objects may appear in association with a particular pair of A and B objects. If the multiplicity of this association is (many, many, one), then for each possible (A, B) pair there is a unique C value. For a given

(B, C) pair, there may be many A values, however, and individually many values of A, B, and C may participate in the association. In a binary association, this rule reduces to the multiplicity of each end defined with respect to the other end.

There is no point in defining multiplicity with respect to one end only (as some authors have proposed) because the multiplicity would be many for any meaningful *n*-ary association. If not, the association could be partitioned into a binary association between the single class and an association class that includes all the remaining classes, with a gain in both precision and efficiency of implementation. In general, it is best to avoid *n*-ary associations, because binary associations are simpler to implement and they permit navigation. Generally, *n*-ary associations are useful only when all the values are needed to uniquely determine a link. An *n*-ary association will almost always be implemented as a class whose attributes include pointers to the participant objects. The advantage of modeling it as an association is the constraint that there can be no duplicate links within an association.

Consider the example of a student taking a course from a professor during a term (Figure 14-192). A student will not take the same course from more than one professor, but a student may take more than one course from a single professor, and a professor may teach more than one course. The multiplicities are shown in the diagram. The multiplicity on **Professor** is optional (0..1); the other multiplicities are many (0..*).

Each multiplicity value is relative to a pair of objects from other ends. For a (course, student) pair, there is zero or one professor. For a (student, professor) pair, there are many courses. For a (course, professor) pair, there are many students.

Note that if this association is reified into a class, then it would be possible to have more than one copy of the same (student, course, professor) combination, which is not desirable.

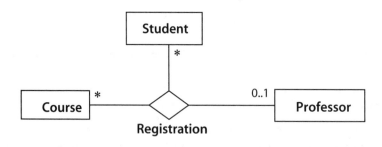

Figure 14-192. *Multiplicity on n-ary association*

name

A string used to identify a model element.

See also namespace.

Semantics

A name is an identifier—a sequence of characters from a finite, predefined alphabet in some defined language. An implementation may impose restrictions on the form of names, such as the exclusion of certain characters (for example, punctuation marks), restrictions on initial characters, and so on. In particular, it is assumed that names are usable as selectors and search keys within various data sets. For example, names from the Roman alphabet usually include upper and lower case letters; numerals; and one or more separators, such as underscore and hyphen, while other punctuation marks are implementation-dependent.

Tools and languages may impose reasonable limits on the length of strings and the character set they use for names, possibly more restrictive than those for arbitrary strings, such as comments.

Names are defined within a namespace, such as a package or class. Within a namespace, a name must be unique within its own semantic group, such as classifiers, states, attributes, and so on, but names of different groups may coincide (although this should be avoided to prevent confusion). Each namespace, except the entire system, is contained within another namespace. The names of all the nested namespaces and the final element name are composable into a single qualified name string.

Note that the absence of a name is not equivalent to an empty string and sometimes implies an anonymous element. Two elements lacking names are not necessarily the same element.

Notation

A name is displayed as a string. A name is usually displayed on a single line and contains only nonprintable characters. The canonical notation for names includes alphabetic characters, numerals, and underscores. If additional characters are allowed within a particular implementation, then it is possible that certain characters may have to be encoded for display to avoid confusion. This is an implementation responsibility of a tool.

Individual names from a namespace hierarchy separated by double colons may be composed into a qualified name.

namespace

A part of the model in which names may be defined and used. Within a namespace, each name has a particular meaning.

Semantics

All named elements are declared in a namespace, and their names have scope within it. The top-level namespaces are packages, containers whose purpose is to group elements primarily for human access and understandability, and also to organize models for computer storage and manipulation during development. Primary model elements, including classes, associations, state machines, and collaborations, act as namespaces for their contents, such as attributes, association ends, states, and collaboration roles. The scope of each model element is discussed as part of its description. Each of these model elements has its own distinct namespace.

Names defined within a namespace must be unique for a given element type. Some elements are anonymous and must be found by relationship to named elements. Namespaces can be nested. It is possible to search inward over a list of nested namespaces by giving their names.

Within a namespace, there may be multiple groups of elements of the same or similar types. Names of elements within one group must be unique, but the same name can be reused in a different group. The formation of the subgroups is somewhat uneven. In any case, the use of repeated names within a single namespace is dangerous, regardless of whether they can be distinguished by element type.

The concept of uniqueness may vary by type. For example, operations in some programming languages are identified by their entire signature, including the name of the operation and the types of their parameters. The signature is the effective name within the operation namespace.

To gain access to names in other namespaces, a package can access or import another package.

The system itself defines the outermost namespace that provides the base for all absolute names. It is a package, usually with packages nested within it to several levels until primitive elements are finally obtained. The list of names from the root to a particular element is called the qualified name; it identifies a particular element.

Notation

The notation for a qualified name, a path over several nested namespaces, is obtained by concatenating the names of the namespaces (such as packages or classes) separated by pairs of double colons (::).

UserInterface::HelpFacility::HelpScreen

navigability

Navigability on an association end is a Boolean quality that indicates whether it is possible to use an association at run time to find the value or values (depending on the multiplicity of the end) of the type specified by the end, given one value for each of the other ends. An attribute is always navigable.

See also navigation efficiency.

Semantics

Navigability describes whether it is possible to traverse an association at run time. At run time, the extent of an association is a set of tuples (links), each tuple containing one value corresponding to each end of the association. Navigability means that, given values for all but one of the association ends, the tuples containing all of those values can be obtained; the result is usually stated as the set of values for the remaining association end. The cardinality of the set of tuples and the equivalent set of values is constrained by the multiplicity on that association end.

In the case of a binary association, navigability on an end (the *target* end) means that it is possible to obtain the set of values for the end associated with a single value of the type specified on the other end (the *source* end).

Lack of navigability does not mean that there is no way to traverse the association. If it is possible to traverse the association in the other direction, it may be possible to search all the instances of the other class to find those that lead to an object, thereby inverting the association. This approach may even be practical in small cases.

An attribute may or may not also be modeled as an association, and vice versa. In any case, attributes are always navigable. In other words, given an instance of a class, it is possible to obtain the value or values specified by the attribute.

Notation

A navigable association direction is shown with an arrowhead on the end of the association path attached to the target class. The arrow indicates the direction of traversal (Figure 14-193). The navigability adornment may be suppressed (usually, on all associations in a diagram). Arrowheads may be attached to zero, one, or both ends of a binary association or to any number of ends attached to classes in an n-ary association. Adornments are never placed on line ends attached to the diamond in an n-ary association.

A nonnavigable association direction can be shown with a small X on the end of the association attached to the class that cannot be reached.

As a convenience, the arrowheads may be omitted on associations that are navigable in all directions. In theory, this can be confused with an association that is not navigable in any direction, but such an association is unlikely in practice and can be explicitly noted if it occurs.

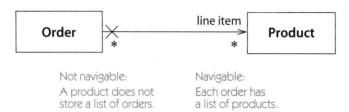

Not navigable:
A product does not
store a list of orders.

Navigable:
Each order has
a list of products.

You can find the orders for a product, but you must search for them external to Product.

Figure 14-193. *Navigability*

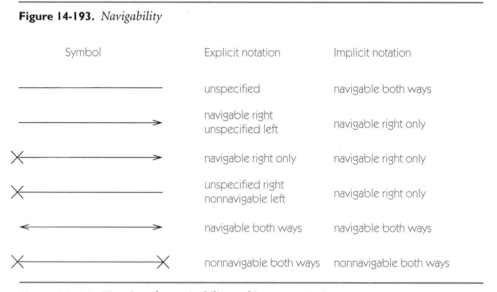

Symbol	Explicit notation	Implicit notation
	unspecified	navigable both ways
	navigable right unspecified left	navigable right only
	navigable right only	navigable right only
	unspecified right nonnavigable left	navigable right only
	navigable both ways	navigable both ways
	nonnavigable both ways	nonnavigable both ways

Figure 14-194. *Notations for navigability on binary association*

Alternately a lack of annotation indicates "undecided" navigability, and all navigability must be shown as arrows or Xs. The interpretation of unmarked ends is a convention that must be agreed to by the modelers and modeling tools.

Figure 14-194 shows the various combinations of navigability markings on binary associations. The explicit notation requires navigability to be shown explicitly. The implicit notation treats a single arrow as one-way navigable and no arrows as two-way navigable.

Discussion

The phrase "obtain values" is deliberately somewhat vague. Often it implies navigation efficiency (see the entry). Often it also implies that the traversal can be performed using an action (see read action), using syntax in a programming language, or using an OCL expression (such as object.aname).

Navigability is distinct from the ownership of a property by a class or an association. An association end that is owned by a class is an attribute of the class at the opposite end of the association, and it can therefore be used in methods of the class to traverse the association. class. However, the end may be navigable even if it is not owned by a class. In that case, if the association is not visible from the class itself, the end would not be visible within the class, and a method of the class would not be able to traverse the association, but it would be possible to traverse the association from a method (of some other class) that has visibility to the association.

navigable

An association or link that can be traversed in an expression. Its navigability property is **true**. Such a link is often implemented as a pointer or set of pointers, but it may be implemented in other ways, such as a database table.

See navigability, navigation efficiency.

navigation

To traverse connections in a graph, especially to traverse links and attributes in an object model to map an object into a value. In the latter case, the navigation path can be expressed as a sequence of attribute names or rolenames.

See navigability.

navigation efficiency

Indicates whether it is possible to efficiently traverse an association to obtain the object or set of objects associated with a value or tuple of values from the other end or ends. Navigation efficiency is usually implied by navigability but is not its defining property.

See also navigability.

Semantics

Navigation efficiency can be defined in a general manner so that it is applicable to abstract design as well as to various programming languages. An association is efficiently navigable if the average cost of obtaining the set of associated objects is proportional to the number of objects in the set (*not* to the upper limit on multiplicity, which may be unlimited) plus a fixed constant. In computational complexity terms, the cost is $O(n)$. If the multiplicity is one or zero-one, then the access cost must be constant, which precludes searching a variable-length list. A slightly looser definition of navigation efficiency would permit a minimum cost of $log(n)$.

Although a navigable association of multiplicity one is usually implemented using a pointer, an external implementation is possible using hash tables, which have a constant average access cost. Thus, an association can be implemented as a look-up-table object external to the participating classes and can still be considered navigable. (In some real-time situations, the worst-case cost rather than the average cost must be limited. This doesn't require a change to the basic definition other than substituting the worst-case time, but probabilistic algorithms such as hash tables may be ruled out.)

If an association is not navigable in a given direction, it does not mean that it cannot be traversed at all but that the cost of traversal may be significant—for example, requiring a search through a large list. If access in one direction is infrequent, a search may be a reasonable choice. Navigation efficiency is a design concept that allows a designer to design object access paths with an understanding of the computational complexity costs. Usually, navigability implies navigational efficiency.

It is possible (if somewhat rare) to have an association that is not efficiently navigable in any direction. Such an association might be implemented as a list of links that must be searched to perform a traversal in either direction. It would be possible but inefficient to traverse it. Nevertheless, the use for such an association is small.

Note that efficient navigation does not require implementation as pointers. A database table may implement an association. The association is efficiently navigable if indexing avoids the need for brute force searches.

Discussion

Navigation efficiency indicates the efficiency of obtaining the set of related objects to a given object or tuple. When the multiplicity of a binary association is 0..1 or 1, then the obvious implementation is a pointer in the source object. When the multiplicity is many, then the usual implementation is a container class containing a set of pointers. The container class itself may or may not reside within the data record for an object of the class, depending on whether it can be obtained at constant cost (the usual situation for pointer access). The container class must be efficient to navigate. For example, a simple list of all the links for an association would not be efficient, because the links for an object would be mixed with many other uninteresting links and would require a search. A list of links stored with each object would be efficient, because no unnecessary search is required.

In a qualified association, a navigable setting in the direction away from the qualifier usually indicates that it is efficient to obtain the object or set of objects selected by a source object and qualifier value. This is consistent with an implementation using hash tables or perhaps a binary tree search indexed by the qualifier value (which is exactly the point of including qualifiers as a modeling concept.

An n-ary association is usually implemented as a standalone object. It might have indexes on various combinations of ends to permit efficient navigation.

neg

Keyword for negative construct in an interaction.

negative

A combined fragment in an interaction that specifies execution sequences that must not occur.

Semantics

A negative fragment describes sequences that may not occur, that is, those that are prohibited by the interaction. It is obviously of no use if all permitted sequences are explicitly described. It is useful if the general description is incomplete but certain sequences are to be explicitly excluded.

Notation

The keyword **neg** is placed in the tag of a combined fragment. The body of the fragment describes the prohibited sequences.

node

A node is a run-time physical object that represents a computational resource, which generally has at least a memory and often processing capability. Run-time artifacts may be deployed on nodes.

The word *node* is also used (confusingly) to denote a composite control structure within an activity. See activity node.

See also artifact, deployment, location.

Semantics

Nodes include computing devices but also (in a business model, at least) human resources or mechanical processing resources. Nodes may be represented as types and as instances. A node defines a location at which an artifact may reside.

Physical nodes have many additional properties, such as capacity, throughput, and reliability. UML does not predefine these properties, as there are a great number of possibilities, but they can be modeled in UML using stereotypes and tagged values.

Nodes may be connected by associations to show communication paths. The associations can be given stereotypes to distinguish various kinds of communication paths or various implementations of them.

A node is inherently part of the implementation view and not the analysis view. Node instances rather than node types generally appear in deployment models.

Although node types are potentially meaningful to show the types of artifacts that can be deployed, the types of the individual nodes often remain anonymous.

A node is a classifier and may have attributes. Most of the time, node instances are shown in deployment diagrams. Node types have a more limited use.

There are a number of kinds of nodes but they are all singularly lacking in added semantics, so distinguishing them can be regarded as little more than comments.

Notation

A node is shown as a figure that looks like an off-center projection of a cube (Figure 14-195).

A node type has a name as a classifier:

Node-type

where Node-type is a classifier name.

A node instance has a name and a type name. The node may have an underlined name string in it or below it. The name string has the syntax

name:Node-type

The name is the name of the individual node (if any). The Node-type says what kind of a node it is. Either or both elements are optional.

Dependency arrows (dashed arrows with the arrowhead on the component) may be used to show the ability of a node type to support a component type. A stereotype may be used to state the precise kind of dependency.

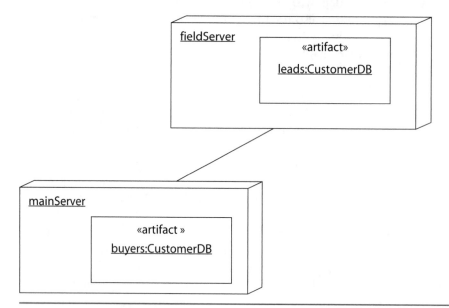

Figure 14-195. *Nodes and artifacts*

Artifact types may be shown within node type symbols. This indicates that artifact instances of the given types may reside on node instances of the given types. Artifact instances may be shown within node instance symbols. This indicates that the artifact instances reside on the node instances.

Nodes may be connected by association symbols to other nodes. An association between two nodes indicates a communication path between them. The association may have a stereotype to indicate the nature of the communication path (for example, the kind of channel or network).

Example

Figure 14-195 shows two connected nodes containing two databases.

nonorthogonal state

A composite state with a single region. See composite state.

Semantics

A composite state with a single region is an "and" decomposition into direct substates. When the composite state is active, exactly one of its direct substates is active. If a direct final state is reached, the nonorthogonal state containing it is complete and a completion transition leaving it may be triggered.

note

A symbol for displaying a comment or other textual information, such as a method body or a constraint.

Notation

A note is a dog-eared rectangle with its upper-right corner bent over. It contains text or extended text (such as an embedded document) that is not interpreted by UML. A note can present information from various kinds of model elements, such as a comment, a constraint, or a method. The note does not usually explicitly indicate the kind of element represented, but that is generally apparent from its form and usage. Within a modeling tool, the underlying element will be explicit in the model. A note can be attached with a dashed line to the element that it describes. If the note describes multiple elements, a dashed line is drawn to each of them.

A note may have a keyword in guillemets to clarify its meaning. The keyword «constraint» indicates a constraint.

Example

Figure 14-196 shows notes used for several purposes, including a constraint on an operation, a constraint on a class, and a comment.

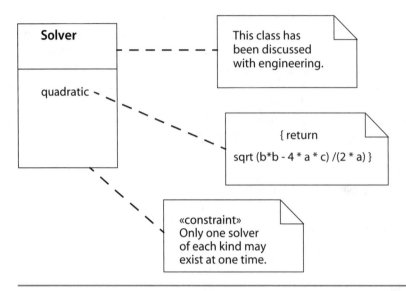

Figure 14-196. *Notes*

null

The explicit lack of a value, either because none exists or because none is shown.

object

A discrete entity with a well-defined boundary and identity that encapsulates state and behavior; an instance of a class.

See also class, identity, instance, object flow.

Semantics

An object is an instance of a class, which describes the set of possible objects that can exist. An object can be viewed from two related perspectives: as an entity at a particular point in time with a specific value and as a holder of identity that has different values over time. Both views can coexist in a model, but not in the same object or class. The first view is appropriate to a snapshot, which represents a system at a point in time. An object in a snapshot has values for each of its attributes. An object is attached to a collection of links that connect it to other objects.

Each object has its own unique identity and may be referenced by a unique handle that identifies it and provides access to it. The view of an object as an identity is appropriate to a collaboration instance, in which the object has run-time relationships to other objects that it uses to exchange message instances.

An object contains one attribute slot for each attribute in its full descriptor—that is, for each attribute declared in its direct class and in every ancestor class. When instantiation and initialization of an object are complete, each slot contains a value that is an instance of the classifier declared as the attribute type. As the system executes, the value in an attribute slot may change unless the attribute changeability property forbids it to change. At all times between the execution of operations, the values in an object must satisfy all implicit and explicit constraints imposed by the model. During execution of an operation, constraints may be temporarily violated.

If multiple classification is allowed in an execution environment, then an object may be the direct instance of more than one class. The object contains one attribute slot for each attribute declared in any of its direct classes or any of their ancestors. The same attribute may not appear more than once, but if two direct classes are descendants of a common ancestor, only one copy of each attribute from the ancestor is inherited, regardless of the multiple paths to it.

If dynamic classification is allowed, an object may change its direct class during execution. If attributes are gained in the process, then their values must be specified by the operation that changes the direct class.

If both multiple classification and dynamic classification are allowed, then an object may gain and lose direct classes during execution. However, the number of direct classes may never be less than one (it must have some structure, even if it is transient).

An object may be called to execute any operation that appears in the full descriptor of any direct class—that is, it has both direct and inherited operations.

An object may be used as the value of any variable or parameter whose declared type is the same class or an ancestor of the direct class of the object. In other words, an instance of any descendant of a class may appear as the value of a variable whose type is declared to be the class. This is the substitutability principle. This principle is not a logical necessity but exists to simplify the implementation of programming languages.

Notation

Object diagrams

An object diagram shows a configuration of objects. An object is an instance of a class. An object is modeled as an instance specification, which may represent a single object or a set of objects satisfying given conditions. The general rule for the notation for instance specifications is to use the same geometrical symbol as the descriptor but to underline the name of the instance specification to distinguish it as an individual. The instance specification may include values or constraints for attributes, but properties shared by all instances are notated only in the descriptor.

Operations, for example, only appear in the class; there is no need to show them for each object of the class, because all objects share the same operations.

The canonical notation for an object specification is a rectangle with two compartments. The top compartment contains the object name and class, and the bottom compartment contains a list of attribute names and values (Figure 14-197). There is no need to show operations because they are the same for all objects of a class.

The top compartment shows the name of the object and its class, all underlined, using the syntax

objectname : classname

The classname can include the full pathname of the enclosing package, if necessary. The package names precede the classname and are separated by double colons. For example

displayWindow: WindowingSystem::GraphicWindows::Window

A stereotype for the class may be shown textually (in guillemets above the name string) or as an icon in the upper-right corner. The stereotype for an object must match the stereotype for its class.

To show multiple classes of which the object is an instance, use a comma-separated list of classnames. Some of the classes can be transient roles that the object plays during a collaboration. For example

aPerson: Professor, Skier

The type of an object specification can be abstract. Any actual object satisfying the specification must have a concrete class that is a descendant of the abstract class.

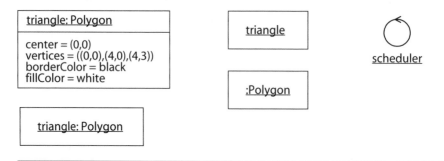

Figure 14-197. *Object notation*

The second compartment shows the attributes for the object and their values as a list. Each value line has the syntax

attributename : type = value

The type is redundant with the attribute declaration in the class and may be omitted. The value is specified as a string that represents the value. The attribute names are not underlined.

The name of the object may be omitted. In this case, the colon should be kept with the class name. This represents an anonymous object of the class, given identity by its relationships. Each symbol that contains an anonymous object denotes a distinct object distinguished by its relationships to other objects.

The class of the object may be suppressed (together with the colon), but it should be shown when possible to avoid confusion.

The attribute value compartment as a whole may be suppressed.

Attributes whose values are not of interest may be suppressed.

The attribute value may be a constraint, rather than a single value. This means that the object value must satisfy the constraint. A constraint in a note symbol (dog-eared rectangle) can be attached to the attribute name by a dashed line.

Sequence diagrams

In a sequence diagram, a lifeline represents an object or a set of objects of a type. A lifeline is shown as a vertical line or thin rectangle headed by a rectangle containing the name and type of the object. The header rectangle has the same syntax as given above under *object diagram*. See lifeline for syntax. Figure 14-171 shows an example.

To show the presence of an object in a particular state of a class, a state constraint may be placed on the lifeline. This is shown as the name of the state enclosed in a small rounded rectangle. A comma-separated list of state names may be used. The constraint is effective at the time when the next event may be received. Figure 14-47 shows an example.

To show a change of class (dynamic classification), there must be at least two state constraints on a lifeline, separated by at least one event (such as the receipt of a message that changes the state).

A constraint may also be placed on the values of attributes. This is shown as a text string in braces placed on the lifeline. The constraint must be valid when the next event is received.

Activity diagrams

In an activity diagram, the flow of an object as a value may be shown as an object flow. This has a different emphasis from objects in object or sequence diagrams, in which the objects are the subjects of interest. See object flow.

Object Constraint Language

See OCL.

object diagram

A diagram that shows objects and their relationships at a point in time. An object diagram may be considered a special case of a class diagram in which instance specifications, as well as classes, may be shown. Also related is a communication diagram, which shows roles within a context.

See also diagram.

Notation

Tools need not support a separate format for object diagrams. Class diagrams can contain object specifications, so a class diagram with objects and no classes is an "object diagram." The phrase is useful, however, to characterize a particular usage achievable in various ways.

Discussion

An object diagram models the objects and links that represent the state of a system at a particular moment. It contains object specifications, which can show single objects from a particular execution or prototypical objects with some range of values. To show a general pattern of objects and relationships that can be instantiated many times, use a collaboration.

An object diagram does not show the evolution of the system over time. For that purpose, use a communication diagram or a sequence diagram to represent an interaction.

object flow

A kind of activity edge in an activity that represents the flow of values between two activity nodes.

See also control flow, object node.

Semantics

An object flow is a kind of activity edge connecting two activity nodes, usually an executable node and an object node. (To be precise, they connect to pins on executable nodes, but in effect they connect the nodes.) It represents the production of a value by a source action or the consumption of a value by the target action. It can also connect two object nodes. See object node for details.

A multicast connects one object node to multiple activity nodes; a multireceive connects multiple activity nodes to one object node. These are intended to support publish-subscribe architectures, but they would appear to be generally usable.

Notation

An object flow is shown as a solid arrow connecting two activity nodes. It may have a guard condition, in which case the flow can occur only if the condition is satisfied.

The keywords «multicast» and «multireceive» (but not both together) can be applied to the arrow.

object flow state

This UML1 concept is obsolete in UML2. It has been replaced by object node.

object lifeline

See lifeline.

Object Management Group

See OMG.

object node

A kind of activity node that represents the existence of an object produced by one action in an activity and used by other actions.

See also control flow, object flow.

Semantics

An activity mainly models the flow of control among actions and control constructs. It can also model the flow of values among the actions.

An object node represents an object value that exists at a point within a computation. The object may be the output of one activity node and the input of other activity nodes. An object node has an input object flow connected to a source action (or other activity node). When the source action completes, an object token is generated and placed on the object node. This represents the creation of on object of the class or a new object value as a result of a computation. If an object node has multiple input flows, values can come from any one of them.

An object node has a connection to an output pin on a source action (or other activity node). A value is placed in the object node whenever the action executes. If the object node is connected to input pins on multiple actions, they may contend for values in the object node.

An object node has a type. The absence of a type means that any type is allowed. The types of objects in the node must be the same or descendants of the node type. If an object node is the input or output of an action, the types must be identical.

An object node may have an upper bound on the number of values it can hold. If the node is full, it will not accept additional tokens from input flows, which may in turn block preceding actions. If no bound is specified, the capacity of the node is unlimited.

By default, the values in an object node are ordered by their arrival. An object node may have a selector behavior that determines which value is selected next. For convenience, the predefined behaviors FIFO (first in-first out) and LIFO (last in-first out) may be specified, but any ordering may be implemented by an appropriated behavior. The selector behavior must be free of side effects.

An object node symbol represents the existence of an object value in a certain state at a particular point within the execution of an activity. Different object nodes may represent the same value at different stages of its lifetime. Object nodes can also represent intermediate values in computations, even those that are never stored in memory.

Notation

An object node is shown on an activity diagram as a rectangle with object flow arrows as inputs and outputs. The name of the object value type is placed in the rectangle. The object may be constrained to be in a specific state or set of orthogonal states. The name of a state or list of states may be enclosed in square brackets and placed after or beneath the type name. Additional constraints on the node are placed in braces, either inside or below the rectangle. The full syntax is:

Classname [Statename] {Constraint}

In addition, the following special forms may be placed outside the rectangle:

{ upperBound = integer }

{ ordering = rule }

where rule may be the name of a user-defined selection behavior or it may be one of:

FIFO }

LIFO

Unless otherwise specified, an object node is unlimited and FIFO.

Example

Figure 14-198 shows object nodes in an activity diagram. An object value is created by the completion of an action or invoked activity. For example, a value with class and state **Order[Placed]** is created by the completion of invoked activity **Request Service**. Because that activity has two successor activities, the object flow state **Order[Placed]** is an output of a fork symbol. State **Order[Entered]**, on the other hand, is the result of completing activity **Take Order**, which has no other suc-

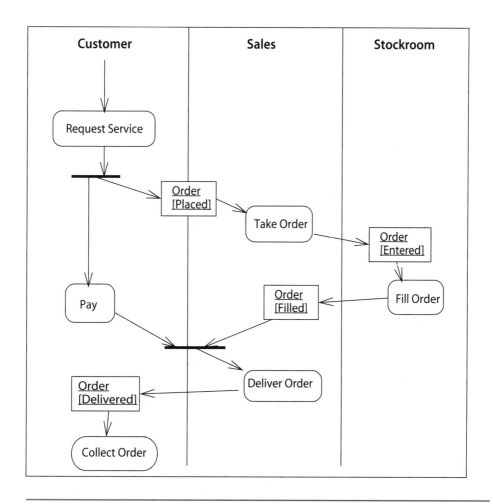

Figure 14-198. *Object nodes in an activity diagram*

cessor activities, so no fork symbol is required. In this example, all of the object nodes would likely be mapped into a single object whose value is modified by each activity invocation.

Figure 14-199 shows a portion of an activity diagram concerned with building a house. When the frame has been built, the carpenter is free to work on the roof and the house is ready for the plumbing to be installed. These events are modeled as signals—**Carpenter free** and **Frame ready**—from one activity node to the others. The diagram shows the special syntax for a signal. This does not necessarily imply that the execution processes communicate directly; there may be communication objects that are not shown in the model. As a result of these signals, the roof can be built and the plumbing can be installed. Signal notation is only needed to model communication between distinct objects or the processes running on them.

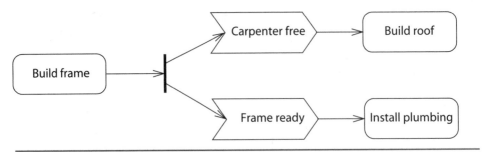

Figure 14-199. *Signals in activity diagram*

Discussion

An object node represents the data flow view of a computation. Unlike traditional data flow, however, it exists at a definite point within a flow of control. This places it squarely into an object-oriented framework. Object orientation unites the data structure, control flow, and data flow viewpoints into a single model.

object specification

The use of an object of a given type within a context.

Semantics

An object is a unique individual. Therefore, objects can rarely be used directly within models or programs, which represent reusable patterns applicable to many objects. A class describes many objects with similar characteristics, but it has no context. An object specification is the description of the use of an object of a given type within a particular reusable context. For example, the value of an attribute may be an object of a certain class. The attribute doesn't have a fixed object as its value; each instance containing the attribute has a different object as its value. The value of the attribute is therefore an object specification; it describes a family of objects within a specific context, an instance containing the attribute.

An object specification is a kind of value specification.

OCL

Object Constraint Language, a text language for specifying constraints and queries. OCL is not intended for writing actions or executable code.

Semantics

The Object Constraint Language (OCL) is a text language for writing navigation expressions, Boolean expressions, and other queries. It may be used to construct expressions for constraints, guard conditions, actions, preconditions and postconditions, assertions, and other kinds of UML expressions. The OCL is defined by the OMG in a companion specification to UML. A complete description of the OCL syntax and semantics can be found in the specification on the OMG Web site. A summary can be found in [Warmer-99]. The following selected summary contains the most useful OCL syntax for creating navigation expressions and Boolean conditions. The full language contains a large number of predefined operators on collections and on primitive types.

Notation

Syntax for some common navigation expressions is shown below. These forms can be chained together. The left-most element must be an expression for an object or a collection of objects. The expressions are meant to work on collections of values when applicable. For more details and syntax, see the OCL description.

item . selector

> selector is the name of an attribute in the item or the name of a role of the target end of a link attached to the item. The result is the value of the attribute or the related object(s). The result is a value or a collection of values, depending on the multiplicities of the item and the association.

item . selector (argument$_{list,}$)

> selector is the name of an operation on the item. The result is the return value of the operation applied to the item.

item . selector [qualifier-value]

> selector designates a qualified association that qualifies the *item*. qualifier-value is a value for the qualifier attribute. The result is the related object or collection selected by the qualifier. Note that this syntax is applicable to array indexing as a form of qualification.

collection -> collection-property

> collection-property is the name of a built-in OCL function on collections. The result is the property of the collection. Illegal if collection-property is not a predefined OCL function. Several of the properties are listed below.

collection -> select (boolean-expression)

> boolean-expression is written in terms of objects within the collection. The result is the subset of objects in the collection for which the expression is true.

collection -> size

> The number of elements in the collection.

| self | Denotes the current object (may be omitted if the context is clear). |
| operator | The usual arithmetic and Boolean operators:
= < > <= >= <> + – * / not |

Example

flight.pilot.training_hours >= flight.plane.minimum_hours

The collection of pilots who have enough training hours.

company.employees–>select (title = "Boss" and self.reports–>size > 10)

The number of bosses who have more than 10 reports.

occurrence

Something notable that happens during the execution of a system; an instance of an event. Sometimes called *event occurrence*, but the word *event* is redundant.

Semantics

An occurrence is something that happens in space and time, just as an object is something that exists with a well-defined boundary. For example, "King Louis XIV died in Versailles on 1 September 1715" is an occurrence. An event is the descriptor of a group of potential occurrences that share common traits, just as a class is the descriptor of a group of potential objects that share common traits. For example, "king dies" is an event that is interesting because of its many consequences and is therefore worth identifying as a category of occurrences. Objects and occurrences are unique run-time entities, whereas classes and events are model elements that describe run-time entities. An object is an instance of a class, and an occurrence is an instance of an event. (Precisely speaking, the word *instance* applies only to classifiers, that is, static structure, but the relationship is really the same.) In any case, we have the relationship:

object is to class as occurrence is to event

Objects and occurrences do not usually appear in models. Histories (traces in UML terminology) describe unique objects and occurrences, but models are concerned with repeatable patterns that apply to many objects and occurrences. For example, an occurrence of event "king dies" may trigger consequences such as a state funeral, potential successors fighting for the job, and the coronation of a new king. In UML, a state machine could model these consequences; its transitions would be triggered by events.

An event is a type, that is, a category of occurrences with similar characteristics. A model often needs to model the occurrence of a given event in a particular context, such as a sequence of events of specific kinds. For example, we might have the sequence "When an event 'king dies' occurs, then the event 'state funeral' occurs, then 'crown new king' occurs." The model is not referring to a particular occurrence, such as "Louis XIV dies", but to any occurrence of the event "king dies". This kind of model element is an occurrence specification. It describes many potential occurrences of a given event within a specific context.

Notation

Individual occurrences rarely appear in models, therefore there is no defined notation. Usually occurrence specifications appear in models to show event sequences.

occurrence specification

The specification of the occurrence of an event during the execution of a system.

Semantics

An occurrence specification is a model element representing a set of potential occurrences within a specific context. An occurrence is a unique individual, whereas an occurrence specification represents many occurrences. An occurrence specification has a location within a sequence, therefore it is more specific than an event, which describes all occurrences of a given kind without locating them within a sequence. Occurrence specifications are modeled within interactions. A lifeline represents a sequence of occurrence specifications. The model of the sending or receipt of a message by an object is an occurrence specification, therefore a message connects two occurrence specifications on two lifelines. The execution of an activity may be modeled by two occurrence specifications (the beginning and end of execution) on the same lifeline.

Notation

An occurrence specification usually is not explicitly shown as a separate concept. It is usually shown by the intersection of a message arrow and a lifeline. A stand-alone occurrence specification on a lifeline can be shown by drawing a small tic on the lifeline and labeling it with text.

See sequence diagram for examples.

Discussion

Occurrence specification was called *event occurrence*, but that term does not distinguish the run-time entity (occurrence) from the model element (specification). The new terminology has the correspondence:

object : object specification : class :: occurrence : occurrence specification : event.

OMG

The Object Management Group, Inc., a not-for-profit corporation intended to facilitate the specification of software technology through open consortiums of interested companies, universities, associations, and other parties. The OMG is the owner of the specifications of UML, MOF, OCL, and other related technologies. Information about the OMG, the official UML specifications, and other work may be found on the web site www.omg.org.

opaque expression

A text string expressed in a specific language that, when evaluated, yields a value.

Semantics

An opaque expression is an escape convention to allow expressions in other languages to be used in UML where values are needed. Because the other languages are, by definition, outside of UML, they are opaque with respect to UML. All that is known is that, when evaluated, they produce values; a type may be optionally specified for the values.

The UML model includes a text string and the name of the target language. The OCL language is explicitly permitted; other languages, such as programming languages, may be used at the discretion of the modeling tool.

An important language (family of languages, really) is natural language. This is a good way to express higher-level models to be communicated to humans.

Notation

An opaque expression is expressed in the syntax of the target language. Often the target language is implicit within a particular user's model, but it can be stated by placing the name of the language (the official name as expressed in its defining standard) in braces in front of the text expression. For example, a UML constraint is often placed in braces, so an example of an OCL constraint might be:

{ {OCL} self.size > 0 and self.size < n }

operand

One of the nested subfragments of a combined fragment in an activity. Each kind of combined fragment has a specified configuration of operands.

See combined fragment.

operation

An operation is a specification of a transformation or query that an object may be called to execute.

See also call, method, resolution.

Semantics

An operation specifies a transformation on the state of the target object (and possibly the state of the rest of the system reachable from the target object) or a query that returns a value to the caller of the operation. It has a name and a list of parameters, including return parameters. It may impose constraints on parameters or the target object before or after invocation.

An operation is invoked by a call, which suspends the caller until the execution of the operation is complete, after which the caller resumes control beyond the point of the call, receiving a return value if one is supplied by the operation. A call may be synchronous or asynchronous. Only a synchronous call may receive a return value.

An operation specifies the result of a behavior, not the behavior itself. A call to an operation undergoes a resolution step to choose the behavior to be invoked based on the operation and characteristics of the target object, such as its type. The behavior can be a method, a state machine transition, or something else.

A method is a procedure that implements an operation. It has an algorithm or procedure description. A call that resolves to a method causes the execution of the procedure.

A state machine transition may have an operation as its trigger. A call that resolves to a transition causes the firing of the transition.

An operation is declared in a class. The declaration is inherited by the descendants of the class. An operation may be redefined in a descendant class. The redefinition must have the same number of argument and result parameters, and their types must conform (descendants are permitted). If two operations that are not related by redefinition have matching signatures (including conforming signatures), the declarations conflict and the model is ill formed. Two operations may have the same name if their signatures do not conform. The definition of conformance may vary among systems.

The operation declaration that is the common ancestor of all other declarations of it is called the *origin* (after Bertrand Meyer). It represents the governing declaration of the operation that is inherited by the others.

An operation may be abstract or concrete. A concrete operation must resolve to a behavior (such as method or transition trigger) in the owning class. An abstract operation need not, and usually will not, have a resolved behavior.

Structure

An operation has the following main constituents.

abstract
: An operation may be abstract or concrete. A concrete operation must resolve to a behavior. An abstract operation must resolve to behaviors in concrete descendants only.

concurrency
: The semantics of concurrent calls to the same passive instance, an enumeration. Possible values are:

sequential
: Callers must coordinate so that only one call to an object (on any sequential operation) may execute at once. If concurrent calls occur, then the semantics and integrity of the system cannot be guaranteed.

guarded
: Multiple calls from concurrent threads may occur simultaneously to one object (on any guarded operation), but only one is allowed to commence at a time. The others are blocked until the execution of the first operation is complete. It is the responsibility of the modeler to ensure that deadlocks do not occur because of simultaneous blocks. Guarded operations must perform correctly (or block themselves) in the case of a simultaneous sequential operation, or guarded semantics cannot be claimed.

concurrent
: Multiple calls from concurrent threads may occur simultaneously to one object (on concurrent operations). All of them may proceed concurrently with correct semantics. Concurrent operations must be designed so that they perform correctly in the case of a concurrent, sequential, or guarded operation on the same object. Otherwise, concurrent semantics cannot be claimed.

constraints
: Operations may have preconditions, postconditions, and body conditions. Preconditions must be true when an operation is called, otherwise the call is in error and the operation may fail. The caller must ensure that preconditions are met. Postconditions are asserted to be true when invoked behavior completes execution, otherwise the

implementation of the behavior is in error. The implementor of the behavior must ensure that postconditions are met. Body conditions are postconditions on return values. Preconditions and postconditions are inherited by subclasses and may not be overridden. Body conditions are inherited by subclasses but they may be overridden in subclasses.

leaf
: Whether the operation may be redefined by descendant classes. If true, the implementation cannot be redefined. The default is false.

exceptions
: A list of exceptions that the operation may raise during execution.

query
: Whether the execution of the operation leaves the state of the system unchanged—that is, whether it is a query. If true, the operation returns a value, but it has no side effects. If false, it may alter the state of the system, but a change is not required. The default is false.

name
: The name of the operation, a string. The name, together with the list of parameter types (not including parameter names), is called the matching signature of the operation. The inclusion of return types varies among implementations. The matching signature must be unique within the class and its ancestors. If there is a duplication, it must be a redefinition of the operation; otherwise the model is ill formed.

parameter list
: The list of declarations of the parameters of the operation. See parameter list.

return results
: A list of the types of the values returned by a call of the operation, if any. If the operation does not return values, then this property has the value null. Note that many languages do not support multiple return values, but it remains a valid modeling concept that can be implemented in various ways, such as by treating one or more of the parameters as output values.

static
: Whether the operation applies to individual objects (nonstatic) or to the class itself (static). Static operations are often used for constructors. The default is nonstatic.

visibility
: The visibility of the operation by classes other than the one defining it. See visibility.

A method is a behavior procedure that implements an operation. A method is attached to a class. The operation must be defined in the same class or an ancestor of the class containing the method. The parameters of the behavior must match the parameters of the operation it implements. A method may have preconditions and postconditions. It may weaken the preconditions or strengthen the postconditions with respect to the operation it implements.

A call trigger is a trigger that enables a transition based on the receipt of a call. The call trigger is defined for the class owning the state machine declaration. The call trigger makes available its argument values to any behaviors attached to the transition. Any return parameters of the operation are ignored by the call trigger.

An operation may be redefined. See redefinition (operation).

Notation

An operation is shown as a text string that can be parsed into properties of the operation. The default syntax is

$$\lfloor \text{«stereotype»} \rfloor_{opt} \ \text{visibility}_{opt} \ \text{name (parameter-list)} \lfloor : \text{return-type} \rfloor_{opt}$$
$$\lfloor \text{\{ property-string \}} \rfloor_{opt}$$

The stereotype, visibility, return-type, and property string are optional (together with their delimiters). The parameter list may be empty. Figure 14-200 shows some typical operations.

Name. A string that is the name of the operation (not including parameters).

Parameter list. A comma-separated list of parameter declarations, each comprising a direction, name, and type. The entire list is enclosed in parentheses (including an empty list). See parameter list and parameter for full details.

```
+display (): Location
+hide ()
«constructor» +create ()
-attachXWindow(xwin:Xwindow*)
```

Figure 14-200. *Operation list with a variety of operations*

Return type. A string containing a comma-separated list of names of classifiers (classes, data types, or interfaces). The type string follows a colon (:) that follows the parameter list of the operation. The colon and return-type string are omitted if the operation does not return any values (e.g., C++ **void**). Some, but not all, programming languages support multiple return values.

Exceptions. Exceptions potentially raised by the operation may be shown as a property string of the form:

exception $\text{name}_{list,} \text{x}$

Visibility. The visibility is shown as one of the punctuation marks '+', '#', '–', or '~' representing **public, protected, private,** or **package.** Alternately, visibility can be shown as a keyword within the property string (for example, {visibility=private}). This form must be used for user-defined or language-dependent choices.

Abstract. An abstract operation is shown by placing the name in italics. Otherwise the operation is concrete. Abstract may also be indicated by the property string **abstract.**

Query. The choice is shown by a property string of the form **isQuery=true** or **isQuery=false.** The choice **true** may also be shown by the keyword **query.** The absence of an explicit choice indicates the choice **false**—that is, the operation may alter the system state (but it does not guarantee to alter it).

Leaf. The choice is shown by a property string of the form **isPolymorphic=true** (overridable) or **isPolymorphic=false** (not overridable). The absence of an explicit choice indicates the choice **true**—that is, overridable. The string **isPolymorphic** alone indicates a true value.

Static. An instance-scope (nonstatic) operation is indicated by not underlining the operation string. A class-scope (static) operation is indicated by underlining the name string. A static operation can alternately be indicated by a property string **static.**

Concurrency. The choice is a property string of the form **concurrency=**value, where the value is one of the keywords **sequential, guarded,** or **concurrent.**

Constraints. A constraint may be shown as a text string in braces within a note symbol (dog-eared rectangle). The note symbol is connected to the operation string by a dashed line. The keywords «**precondition**», «**postcondition**», and «**bodyCondition**» can be used to distinguish the kind of constraint.

Method. There is no specified notation to indicate the presence of a method. The following convention can be used to indicate the presence of methods: A declaration of a concrete operation necessarily implies the presence of a behavior to implement the behavior. A declaration of an abstract operation implies no behavior. To show the presence of a concrete behavior on a subclass, redefine the operation in the subclass as a concrete operation.

Method body. The body of a method may be shown as a string within a note attached to an operation declaration. The keyword «**method**» may be used to indicate a method declaration.

Signals. To indicate that a class accepts a signal (a reception), the keyword «**signal**» is placed in front of an operation declaration within the list of operations. The parameters are the attributes of the signal. The declaration must not have a return type. The response of the object to the reception of the signal is shown within a state machine attached to a class.

Redefinition. See redefinition (operation).

Presentation options

The argument list and return type may be suppressed (together, not separately).

A tool may show the visibility indication in a different way, such as by using a special icon or by sorting the elements by group.

The syntax of the operation signature string can be that of a particular programming language, such as C++ or Smalltalk. Specific tagged properties may be included in the string.

Style guidelines

Operation names typically begin with a lowercase letter.

opt

Keyword for optional combined fragment in an interaction.

optional

A combined fragment in an interaction that represents a dynamic choice about whether to execute the operand.

Semantics

A optional construct has one operand with a guard condition. The operand is executed if the guard is true and is not executed otherwise. This construct is equivalent to a conditional with an empty else clause.

Notation

An optional fragment is shown as a rectangular region with the tag **opt** within a small pentagon on the upper left corner. The region contains the body of the optionally executed operand (Figure 14-201).

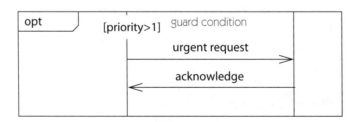

Figure 14-201. *Optional (opt) fragment*

ordering

A property of a set of values, such as the set of objects related to an object across an association, stating whether the set is ordered or unordered.

See also association, association end, multiplicity.

Semantics

If the multiplicity upper bound on an attribute or association end is greater than one, then a set of objects is associated with the attribute slot or the end of an association. The ordering property declares whether the set is ordered or unordered. If it is unordered, the objects in the set have no explicit order; they form an ordinary set. If it is ordered, the elements in the set have an explicitly imposed order. The element order is part of the information represented by the association—that is, it is additional information beyond the information in the elements themselves. The elements can be obtained in that order. When a new link is added to the association, its position in the sequence must be specified by the operation adding it. The position may be an argument of the operation or it may be implicit. For example, a given operation may place a new link at the end of the existing list of links, but the location of the new link must be specified somehow.

Note that an ordered set is not the same as a set whose elements are sorted by one or more attributes of the elements. A sorting is totally determined by the values of the objects in the set. Therefore, it adds no information, although it may certainly be useful for access purposes. The information in an ordered association, on the other hand, is additional to the information in the elements themselves.

An ordered relationship may be implemented in various ways, but the implementation is usually stated as a language-specified code generation property. An implementation extension might substitute the data structure to hold the elements for the generic specification **ordered**.

A sorted set requires a separate specification of the sorting rule itself, which is best given as a constraint. A sorted set should not be declared as ordered.

Notation

Ordering is specified by a keyword in braces near the end of the path to which it applies (Figure 14-202). The absence of a keyword indicates unordered. The keyword {ordered} indicates an ordered set. For design purposes, the keyword {sorted} may be used to indicate a set arranged by internal values.

For an attribute with multiplicity greater than one, one of the ordering keywords may be placed after the attribute string, in braces, as part of a property string.

The list of requests is ordered.   The set of reservations is unordered.

Figure 14-202. *Ordered and unordered sets*

If a set is both ordered and may have duplicate values (a bag), the keyword list or sequence may be used.

If an ordering keyword is omitted, then the set is unordered.

Discussion

An ordered set has information in the ordering, information that is additional to the entities in the set itself. This is real information. Therefore, it is not derivable but must be specified when an entity is added. In other words, on any operation that adds an entity, its position within the list of entities must be specified. Of course, an operation can be implemented so that the new entity is inserted in an implicit location, such as the beginning or the end of the list. And just because a set is ordered does not mean that any ordering of entities will be allowed. These are decisions that the modeler must make. In general, the position of the new entity within the list is a parameter of the creation operation.

Note that the ordering of a binary association must be specified independently for each direction. Ordering is meaningless unless the multiplicity in a direction is greater than one. An association can be completely unordered, it can be ordered in one direction and not the other, or it can be ordered in both directions.

Assume an association between classes A and B that is ordered in the B direction. Then, usually, a new link will be added as an operation on an A object, specifying a B object and a position in the list of existing B objects for the new link. Frequently, an operation on an A object creates a new B object and also creates a link between A and B. The list must be added to the list of links maintained by A. It is possible to create a new link from the B side, but generally the new link is inserted at a default position in the A-to-B list, because the position within that list has little meaning from the B end. Of course, a programmer can implement more complicated situations if needed.

An association that is ordered in both directions is somewhat unusual, because it can be awkward to specify the insertion point in both directions. But it is possible, especially if the new links are added at default locations in either direction.

Note that a sorted set does not contain any extra information beyond the information in the set of entities. Sorting saves time in an algorithm, but it does not add information. It may be regarded as a design optimization and need not be included in an analysis model. It may be specified as a value of the ordering property, but it does not require that an operation specify a location for a new entity added to the set. The location of the new entity must be determined automatically by the method by examining the attributes on which the list is sorted.

orthogonal region

A region of an orthogonal state. If an orthogonal state is active, each of its regions is concurrently active.

See composite state, orthogonal state, region.

orthogonal state

A composite state that contains more than one region. If the composite state is active, one substate from each region is active. Concurrently active substates of different regions are independent of each other.

See complex transition, composite state, orthogonal region, region.

Semantics

A composite state has one or more regions. If a composite state is active, one substate in each region must be active. If there is more than one region, substates from different regions are concurrently active. For convenience, a composite state with a single region is called a nonorthogonal state; a composite state with more than one region is called an orthogonal state. Any complex transition into or out of an orthogonal state involves a fork or a join that changes the number of active states in the active state configuration. Such a transition must (explicitly or implicitly) include at least one state from each region of an orthogonal state.

History

The concept of regions was added in UML2 to make the decomposition of states more uniform than in UML1, but with equivalent power.

otherwise

See else.

out parameter

A parameter that communicates values to the caller using side effects on the parameter calling mechanism.

See also inout parameter.

Semantics

A parameter can have a direction, which can include in, out, inout, and return. An out parameter is a parameter intended to directly represent parameters in certain programming languages that permit assignments to parameter variables within the bodies of procedures, with the assigned values available to the caller. An inout parameter is a parameter that can be used both for input and output values.

Notation

The keyword **out** may be placed before the name of an out parameter. The keyword **inout** may be placed before the name of an inout parameter. Parameters without keywords are in parameters.

Discussion

The use of out parameters and inout parameters is present only to provide low-level compatibility with detailed programming. They has no place in modeling and should be avoided by all prudent modelers. A clean distinction between in parameters and return parameters is common to most modern programming languages with a few unfortunate exceptions.

overlapping

Keyword indicating that the subtypes of a generalization set are compatible; that is, an object can be an instance of more than one simultaneously.
See generalization set.

owner scope

This UML1 term has been deleted. See static feature for the equivalent capability.

package

A general-purpose mechanism for organizing elements into groups, establishing ownership of elements, and providing unique names for referencing elements.
See also access, dependency, import, model, namespace, subsystem.

Semantics

A *package* is a grouping of model elements and diagrams. Every model element that is not part of another model element must be declared within exactly one namespace; the namespace containing the declaration of an element is said to *own* the element. A package is a general-purpose namespace that can own any kind of model element that is not restricted to a particular kind of element. A package may contain nested packages and ordinary model elements. Usually there is a single root package that owns the entire model for a system.

Packages are the basis for configuration control, storage, and access control. Each element is owned either by another model element or by a single package, so the ownership hierarchy is a strict tree. Model elements (including packages) can reference other elements in other packages, so the usage network is a directed graph rather than a tree.

A model is a kind of package.

Packages may have dependency relationships to other packages. In most cases these summarize dependencies among the contents of the packages. A usage dependency between two packages means that there exists at least one usage dependency between elements of the two packages (not that every pair of elements has the dependency).

A package is a namespace for its elements. A named element can be uniquely determined by its qualified name, which is the series of names of packages or other namespaces from the root to the particular element. To avoid the need for qualified names, a package can import elements or the contents of another package into its own namespace. An element within the importing package can then use the name of the imported element as if it had been defined directly in the package.

A nested package has access to any elements directly contained in outer packages (to any degree of nesting), without needing to import them. A package must import its contained packages to add them to its direct namespace, however. A contained package is, in general, an encapsulation boundary.

A package specifies the visibility of its elements. Visibility indicates whether other elements can access the element or its contents. When a package imports elements from other packages, it can further restrict the visibility of the imported elements to its own clients.

A package defines the visibility of its contained elements as **private** or **public**. Public elements are available to other elements of the owning package or one of its nested packages and to packages importing the package. Private elements are not available at all outside the owning package.

Contents of other element types (such as attributes and operations) may also have the visibility **protected** or **package**. Protected elements are available only to descendants of the classifier owning the feature. Package elements are available to all elements within the same package as the classifier owning the feature.

Profile application is a relationship between a package and a profile indicating that the stereotypes defined in the profile may be applied to elements within the package.

See import for a full description of the visibility rules for elements in various packages.

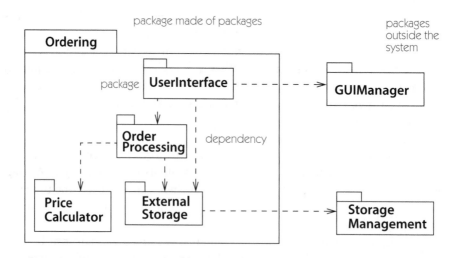

Figure 14-203. *Packages and their relationships*

Notation

A package is shown as a large rectangle with a small rectangle (a "tab") attached on one corner (usually, the left top of the large rectangle). It is meant to suggest a file folder. The contents of the package may be shown within the large rectangle (Figure 14-203).

If contents of the package are not shown, then the name of the package is placed within the large rectangle. If contents of the package are shown, then the name of the package may be placed within the tab.

A keyword string may be placed above the package name. Keywords may include model. User-defined stereotypes are also notated with keywords, but they must not conflict with any predefined keywords.

The visibility of a package element outside the package may be indicated by preceding the name of the element by a visibility symbol ('+' for public, '–' for private).

Dashed arrows may be drawn between package symbols to show relationships that occur among at least some of the elements in the packages. For example, a dependency with the keyword «use» implies a usage dependency between at least one element in one package and one element in another package.

Profile application is shown by a dashed arrow from a package to a profile (package symbol with the keyword «profile»). The arrow has the keyword «apply».

Presentation options

A tool may also show visibility by selectively displaying those elements that meet a chosen visibility level, for instance, all the public elements only.

A tool may show visibility by a graphic marker, such as color or font.

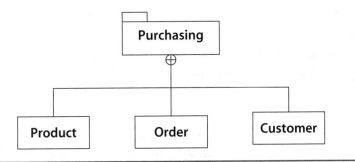

Figure 14-204. *External notation for package contents*

It is expected that packages with large contents will be shown as simple icons with names, in which the contents may be dynamically accessed by "zooming" to a detailed view. Instead of showing the contents of a package as nested icons, a branching line may be drawn from the package to the icons of its elements. A small cross in a circle is attached to the line on the package end. See Figure 14-204. (The same notation can be used for any nested namespace, including classes declared in the scope of other classes.)

Example

Figure 14-203 shows the package structure of an order-processing subsystem. The top-level package contains several low-level packages. The dependencies among the packages are shown by dashed arrows. The figure also shows some external packages on which the subsystem depends. These may be off-the-shelf components or library elements.

Discussion

Packages are primarily intended as access and configuration control mechanisms to permit developers, particularly in large work groups, to organize large models and evolve them without getting in each other's way. Inherently, they mean what the developers want them to mean. More practically, packages should follow some kind of semantic boundary if they are to be useful. Because they are intended as configuration control units, they should contain elements that will likely evolve together. Packages also group elements that must be compiled together. If a change to one element forces the recompilation of other elements, then they might also be placed in one package.

Every model element must be owned by exactly one package or other model element. Otherwise, model maintenance, versioning, and configuration control become impossible. The package that owns a model element controls its definition. It can be referenced and used in other packages, but a change to it requires access permission and update rights to the package that owns it.

package diagram

A structure diagram whose content is primarily packages and their relationships. There is no rigid line between the different kinds of structure diagrams, so the name in merely a convenience without semantic significance.

package merge

A mechanism for merging the contents of packages, including rules for importing elements and resolving name conflicts using specialization and redefinition. This is an advanced modeling feature intended primarily for metamodel builders forced to reuse the same model for several different, divergent purposes. Its use can lead to confusion and should be avoided if possible. It is not intended for use by the ordinary modeler. See the UML2 specification document for the semantics, which are complex and tricky.

package visibility

A visibility value indicating that the given element (usually a feature) is not visible outside the package containing the classifier owning the element.

packageable element

An element that can be owned directly by a package.

Semantics

Packageable elements, including classifiers, dependencies, constraints, instance specifications, and other packages, can be contained as direct elements of packages. Other elements cannot appear on their own but must be owned by particular kinds of elements. For example, attributes and operations are parts of classifiers, and states and transitions are parts of state machines.

par

The keyword indicating a parallel combined fragment in an interaction diagram. See parallel.

parallel

An combined fragment that specifies multiple interaction operands (subfragments) whose behavior is to be executed concurrently (in parallel).

Semantics

A single interaction fragment imposes a linear ordering on the events that occur on each lifeline. In general, there is no restriction on the ordering of events on different lifelines. Even though sequence diagrams appear to have a vertical time dimension, the timelines of different lifelines are not synchronized, and no conclusion can be drawn from the relative position of two events on different lifelines. Messages between lifelines do impose an ordering: The events preceding the sending event on one lifeline precede the events following the receiving event on the other lifeline.

A parallel construct has two or more operands (subfragments). Within each operand, the events are ordered on lifelines and by messages. Events in parallel operands, however, have no relative ordering and may be interleaved in any order consistent with the ordering imposed by each operand separately.

Notation

A parallel combined fragment in a sequence diagram is shown as a rectangular outline with a small pentagon in the upper left corner containing the tag **par** (Figure 14-205). The rectangle covers the lifelines that exchange messages within the fragment. The rectangle is divided vertically into two or more sections by horizontal dashed lines. Each section contains a sequence diagram fragment containing messages among lifelines. Within each section, the ordering of events along a lifeline is significant. The ordering of the sections within the overall rectangle is not significant, and no ordering is expressed or implied among the events from different sections.

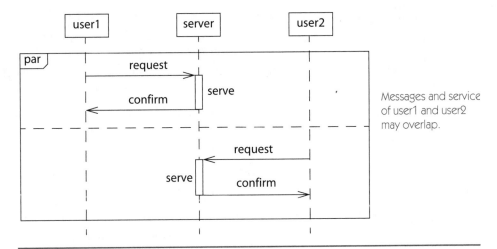

Figure 14-205. *Parallel combined fragment in sequence diagram*

Example

Figure 14-205 shows an interaction with two users and one server. Each user makes a request, the server performs the service, and replies to the user. In this example, there is no specified ordering among the two interaction sequences. The first sequence may precede the second, or follow it, or the two sequences may be interleaved in various ways. For example, the second sequence might start first but finish last. The processing of the two requests might or might not overlap. No assumptions at all may be made about the two sequences.

If two interaction sequences might occur in either order, but no interleaving of sequences may occur, the critical region construct may be used together with the parallel construct.

parameter

The specification of a variable that can be changed, passed, or returned. A parameter may include a name, type, and direction. Parameters are used for operations, messages, events, and templates. Contrast: argument.

A parameter usage dependency relates an operation having a parameter or a class containing such an operation to the class of the parameter.

See also argument, binding.

Semantics

A parameter is a placeholder for a value that is bound to it when the enclosing element is used. It constrains the values that the argument can take. It has the following parts.

default value	An expression for a value to be used if no argument is supplied for the parameter. The expression is evaluated when the parameter list is bound to arguments.
direction	The direction of information flow of the parameter, an enumeration with the following values:
in	An input parameter passed by value. Changes to the parameter are not available to the caller. This is the default.
out	An output parameter. There is no input value. The final value is available to the caller.
inout	An input parameter that may be modified. The final value is available to the caller.

return   A return value of a call. The value is available to the caller. Semantically, no different from an out parameter, but the result is available for use in an in-line expression.

The preceding choices may not all be directly available in every programming language, but the concept behind each of them makes sense in most languages and can be mapped into a sensible implementation.

name   The name of the parameter. It must be unique within its parameter list.

type   A reference to a classifier (a class, data type, or interface in most procedures). An argument bound to the parameter must be an instance of the classifier or one of its descendants.

Notation

Each parameter is shown as a text string that can be parsed into the various properties of a parameter. The default syntax is

$$\text{direction}_{opt} \text{ name} : \text{type} \lfloor \text{multiplicity} \rfloor_{opt} \lfloor = \text{default-value} \rfloor_{opt}$$

Direction. The direction is shown as a keyword preceding the operation name. If the keyword is absent, then the direction is in. The choices are in, out, inout, and return. Return parameters are usually shown following a colon in the operation signature, where they need not be marked for direction.

Name. The name is shown as a string.

Type. The type is notated as a string that is the name of a class, an interface, or a data type.

Default value. The value is shown as an expression string. The language of the expression would be known by (and specifiable to) a tool but is not shown in the canonical format.

Static. A static operation (one that applies to the entire class, rather than a single object) is indicated by underlining the signature string. If the string is not underlined, the operation applies to the target object (the default).

Parameter dependency. A parameter dependency is shown as a dashed arrow from the operation having the parameter or the class containing the operation to the class of the parameter; the arrow has the stereotype «**parameter**» attached.

Example

Matrix::transform (**in** distance: Vector, **in** angle: Real = 0): **return** Matrix

All of the direction labels here may be omitted.

parameter list

A specification of the values that an operation or template receives. A parameter list is an ordered list of parameter declarations. The list may be empty, in which case the operation is called with no parameters.

See parameter.

Notation

A parameter list is a comma-separated list of parameter declarations enclosed in parentheses.

(parameter$_{list,}$)

The parentheses are shown even if the list is empty.

( )

parameter set

A complete set of inputs or outputs for a behavior, in alternation with other complete sets of inputs or outputs for the behavior.

Semantics

Usually all of the parameters of a behavior are required by it (for inputs) or produced by it (for outputs) on any execution. In data flow terms within an activity, control is a join (an "and") of inputs and a fork of outputs.

Sometimes, however, a behavior has alternative inputs or outputs. A parameter set is a complete list of input or output parameters. Each entry is a parameter. A behavior may have multiple input or output parameter sets. On any one execution of the behavior, exactly one complete set of inputs and one complete set of outputs will be produced. On different executions, different parameter sets may be used.

What happens if a behavior receives a complete set of inputs as well as partial inputs to other parameter sets is not specified.

Notation

In an activity diagram, a parameter set is shown by enclosed one or more parameter symbols (squares on the boundary of an activity node) within a rectangle. An activity node may have multiple parameter sets on its boundary.

Figure 14-206 shows an example of parameter sets on an activity node. On any one execution of the node, either (i1 and i2), or (i3), or (i4, i5, and i6) will have input values. On any one execution, either (o1), or (o2, o3, o4, and o5) will get output values. The choice of output set does not depend on the choice of input set (or, in any case, we can't tell from this model).

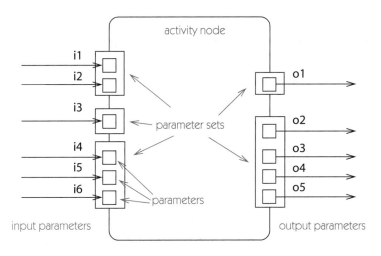

Figure 14-206. *Parameter sets*

Discussion

The notation is a bit unfortunate, because it uses double nesting to change an "and" situation into an "or" situation. It might have been better to have some kind of mark that connects the alternative input sets.

parameterized element

See template.

parent

The more general element in a generalization relationship. Called superclass for a class. A chain of one or more parent relationships (that is, the transitive closure) is an ancestor. The opposite is child.

See generalization.

Discussion

Note that *child, parent, ancestor,* and *descendant* are not official UML terms, but we use them in this book for convenience because UML does not seem to have good simple terms that cover all the uses of the concepts.

part

See structured part.

participates

Informal term for the attachment of a model element to a relationship or to a reified relationship. For example, a class participates in an association, and a classifier role participates in a collaboration.

partition

The division of a set into disjoint subsets. See activity partition for an important kind of partition used in activities.

passive object

An object that does not have its own thread of control. Its operations execute under a control thread anchored in an active object.

See also active class, active object.

Semantics

An active object is one that owns a thread of control and may initiate control activity. A passive object is one that has a value but does not initiate control. However, an operation on a passive object may send messages while processing a request that it has received on an existing thread.

A passive class is a class whose instances are passive objects. A passive class may not declare receptions because its objects do not receive signals.

Notation

An active class is shown by doubling the left and right sides of the class rectangle. A passive class is shown by the absence of doubling. The same distinctions may be shown on object symbols.

In many cases, the presence of active classes is not shown. No conclusions should be drawn from the symbols unless at least some active classes or objects are shown.

path

A connected series of graphic segments that connects one symbol to another, usually used to show a relationship.

Notation

A *path* is a chain of connected graphical symbols that represents a single semantic concept. Paths are used in the notation for relationships of various kinds, such as associations, generalizations, and dependencies. The endpoints of two connected

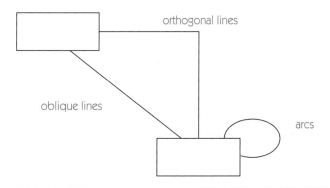

Figure 14-207. *Paths*

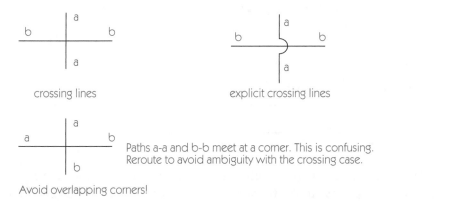

Figure 14-208. *Path crossings*

segments coincide. A segment may be a straight line segment, an arc, or some other shape (such as a spline), although many tools support only lines and arcs (Figure 14-207). Lines can be drawn at any angle, although some modelers or tools prefer to restrict lines to orthogonal angles and possibly force them onto a regular grid for appearance and ease of layout.

Generally, the routing of a path has no significance, although paths should avoid crossing closed regions, because crossing the boundary of a graphic region may have semantic significance. (For example, an association between two classes in a collaboration should be drawn within the collaboration region to indicate an association between objects from the same collaboration instance, whereas a path that made an excursion from the region would indicate an association between objects from different collaboration instances.) More precisely, a path is topological. Its exact routing has no semantics, but its connection to and intersection with other symbols may have significance. The exact layout of paths matters greatly to understandability and aesthetics, of course, and may subtly connote the importance of

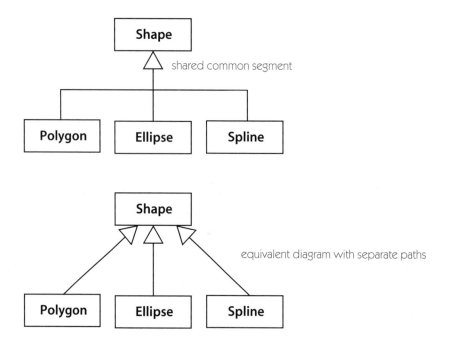

Figure 14-209. *Paths with shared segment*

relationships and real-world affinities. But such considerations are for humans and not computers. Tools are expected to support the easy routing and rerouting of paths.

On most diagrams, the crossing of lines has no significance. To avoid ambiguity about the identity of crossing lines, a small semicircle or gap can be drawn in one of them at the crossing point (Figure 14-208). More commonly, modelers just treat a crossing as two independent lines. Modelers should avoid routings that might be mistaken as crossings.

In some relationships (such as aggregation and generalization), several paths of the same kind may connect to a single symbol. If the properties of the various model elements match, then the line segments connected to the symbol can be combined into a single symbol with a base and branches. The base, which is connected to the shared symbol, branches as a tree into paths to each symbol (Figure 14-209). This is purely a graphical presentation option. Conceptually, the individual paths are distinct. This presentation option may not be used when the modeling information on the various segments is not identical.

pathname

See qualified name.

pattern

A parameterized collaboration that represents a set of roles for parameterized classifiers, relationships, and behavior that can be applied to multiple situations by binding elements from the model (usually classes) to the roles of the pattern. It is a collaboration template.

Semantics

A pattern represents a parameterized collaboration that can be used multiple times within one or more systems. To be a pattern, the collaboration must be usable in a wide range of situations to justify giving it a name. A pattern is a solution that has been shown to work in a number of situations. It is not necessarily the only solution to a problem, but it is a solution that has been effective in the past. Most patterns have advantages and disadvantages that depend on various aspects of the wider system. The modeler must consider these advantages and disadvantages before making a decision to use a pattern.

A UML parameterized collaboration represents the structural and behavioral views of certain kinds of patterns. Patterns involve other aspects that are not modeled directly by UML, such as the list of advantages and disadvantages and examples of previous use. Many of these other aspects can be expressed in words. See [Gamma-95] for a fuller treatment of patterns, as well as a catalog of some proven design patterns.

Generating collaborations from patterns. A collaboration can be used to specify the implementation of design constructs. The same kind of collaboration may be used many times by parameterizing its constituents. A pattern is a parameterized collaboration. Generally, the classes of the roles in the collaboration are parameters. A pattern is instantiated as a collaboration by binding values, usually classes, to its parameters. For the common case of parameterized roles, the template is bound by specifying a class for each role. Typically, the connectors in a pattern are not parameterized. When the template is bound, they represent implicit associations between the classes bound to the collaboration—that is, the binding of the template to make a collaboration generates additional associations.

Notation

Figure 14-210 shows the Observer pattern from [Gamma-95]. We have modified the structure shown in the *Design Patterns* book to specify a pattern as a collaboration to indicate the collaborative nature of most patterns.

The binding of a pattern to produce a collaboration is shown as a dashed ellipse containing the name of the pattern (Figure 14-211). A dashed line is drawn from the pattern binding symbol to each of the classes (or other model elements) that participate in the collaboration. Each line is labeled by the name of the parameter.

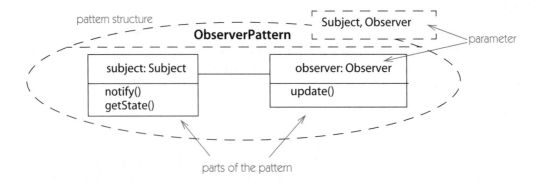

Figure 14-210. *Pattern definition*

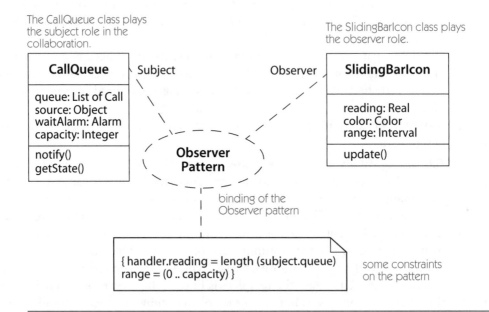

Figure 14-211. *Binding of a pattern to make a collaboration*

In most cases, the name of a role in the collaboration can be used as a parameter name. Therefore, a pattern binding symbol can show the use of a design pattern, together with the actual classes that occur in that use of the pattern. The pattern binding usually does not show the internal structure of the collaboration that is generated by the binding. This is implied by the binding symbol.

permission

A kind of dependency that grants the client element permission to use the contents of the supplier element, regardless of the visibility declarations of the content elements.

Semantics

Permission is a kind of dependency that makes the internal elements of the supplier accessible to the client, even if they have been declared private. This has the same effect as the friend construct in C++.

Notation

A permission dependency is shown as a dashed arrow from the client (the element gaining permission) to the supplier (the element granting permission) with the keyword «permit» attached to the arrow.

Example

In Figure 14-212, the PrintManager can delete any job and reset the printer, even though those operations are private.

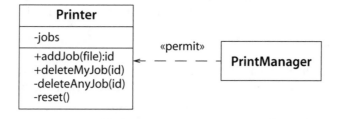

Figure 14-212. *Permit dependency*

persistent object

An object that exists after the thread that created it has ceased to exist.
See data store node.

Semantics

UML2 does not provide support for declaring persistence as a generic concept. Persistence is a complicated concept that must be considered in a particular execution environment. Profiles are expected to provide this kind of capability.

Petri net

A formalism for computation that emphasizes concurrent, distributed, asynchronous computation with explicit synchronization points, rather than the sequential, monolithic model characteristic of Turing machines and most traditional automata theory. They were invented by German computer scientist Carl Adam Petri in his Ph.D. thesis in 1962 and have engendered an entire field of research. The UML2 activity model is loosely based on Petri nets.

pin

A connection point on an action for input and output values.

Semantics

A pin is an object node that represents a connection point for input and output values of an action. There is one input pin for each input parameter and one output pin for each output parameter. The pins of an action are ordered so they can be matched to parameters. Pins have names and types.

Pins will not usually be implemented as distinct mechanisms. They are just part of the modeling formalism of actions.

Various special-purpose declarations can be attached to a pin, such as the ability to accept streams of data and the ability to output exception objects.

Notation

A pin is shown as a small rectangle attached to the outside of the border of an action symbol (a rounded box). A name can be placed near the pin symbol, or the full parameter notation can be used (Figure 14-213).

If a pin accepts data streams, the keyword {stream} is placed near the symbol.

If a pin produces exception objects, a small triangle is placed near the symbol.

If an action is shown disconnected from other actions, small arrows may be placed inside the pin symbol to distinguish input and output pins.

Numbers (starting with 1) may be placed near the pin symbol to show the ordering of pins. Usually the names are sufficient to establish the implicit ordering, so numbers are rarely used.

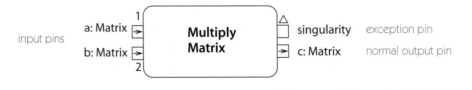

Figure 14-213. *Pin notation*

Various presentation options are available, but they seem unnecessary and less intuitive than the normal notation, so we do not encourage their use.

Example

Figure 14-214 shows several activity nodes connected through pins. The inputs to the activity nodes are object nodes representing data.

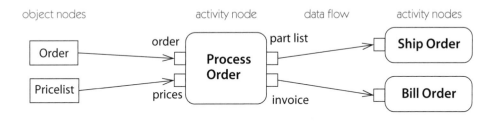

Figure 14-214. *Nodes connected through pins*

polymorphic

Indicates an operation whose implementation (a method or state machine triggered by a call event) may be supplied by a descendant class. An operation that is not polymorphic is a leaf operation.

See also abstract operation, generalization, inheritance, method.

Semantics

If an operation is polymorphic, then a method may be supplied for it in a descendant class (whether or not a method has already been supplied in the original class). Otherwise, a method must be available for the operation in the class declaring the operation, and the method cannot be overridden in a descendant class. A method is available if it is declared by a class or inherited from an ancestor. An abstract operation must be polymorphic (because it has no direct implementation). An operation is nonpolymorphic if it is declared to be a leaf operation.

If an operation is declared polymorphic in a class—that is, if it is not declared as a leaf—it may be declared to be a leaf in a descendant class. This prevents it from being overridden in a further descendant. A leaf operation may not be declared polymorphic in a descendant class. It may not be overridden at any depth.

UML does not mandate the rules for method combination if a method is declared in a class and overridden in a descendant class. Mechanisms, such as declaring before, after, and around methods, may be handled in a language-specific manner using tagged values. Actions such as explicitly calling the inherited method are, of course, dependent on the action language in any case.

Notation

A nonpolymorphic operation is declared using the keyword {leaf}. Otherwise, it is assumed to be polymorphic.

Discussion

An abstract operation is necessarily polymorphic. Otherwise, it could not be implemented at all. Bertrand Meyer calls this a deferred operation, because its specification is defined in a class but its implementation is deferred to subclasses. This is an essential, probably the most essential, use of inheritance in both modeling and programming. Using inheritance, operations can be applied to sets of objects of mixed classes. The caller need not know or determine the class of each object. It is only necessary that all of the objects conform to an ancestor class defining the desired operations. The ancestor class need not implement the operations. It must simply define their signatures. The caller need not know even the list of possible subclasses. This means that new subclasses can be added later, without disrupting polymorphic operations on them. Source code that invokes operations need not change when new subclasses are added. The ability to add new classes after the original code is written is one of the key pillars of object-oriented technology.

A more problematic use of polymorphism is the replacement (overriding) of a method defined in a class by a different method defined in a subclass. This is often cited as a form of sharing, but it is dangerous. Overriding is not incremental, so everything in the original method must be reproduced in the child method, even to make a small change. This kind of repetition is error-prone. In particular, if the original method is changed later, there is no guarantee that the child method will be changed also. There are times when a subclass can use a completely different implementation of an operation, but many experts would discourage such overriding because of the inherent danger. In general, methods should be either completely inherited without overriding or deferred; in the latter case there is no implementation in the superclass, so there is no danger of redundancy or inconsistency.

To permit a subclass to extend the implementation of an operation without losing the inherited method, most programming languages provide some form of method combination that uses the inherited method but allows additional code to be added to it. In C++, an inherited method must be explicitly invoked by class and operation name, which builds the class hierarchy into the code rigidly—not a very robust approach. In Smalltalk, a method can invoke an operation on **super**, which causes the operation to be handled by the inherited method. If the class hierarchy changes, then the inheritance still works, possibly with a method from a different class. However, the overriding method must explicitly provide a call to **super**. Errors can and do happen, because programmers forget to insert the calls when a change occurs. Finally, CLOS provides very general and complicated automatic method combination rules that may invoke several methods during the execution of a single operation call. The overall operation is implemented from several fragments rather than being forced to be a single method. This is very general but harder to manage for the user.

UML does not force a single method combination approach. The UML2 specification assumes that resolution of operations to behavior is specified somehow, but does not restrict it or provide a uniform way of specifying it. Method combination is a semantic variation point. Any of these approaches may be used. If the programming language is weak on method combination, then a modeling tool may be able to provide help in generating the appropriate programming-language code or in warning about possible oversights if method overriding is used.

port

A structural feature of a classifier that encapsulates interaction between the contents of the classifier and its environment.

See interface, structured classifier, structured part.

Semantics

A port is a connection point between a classifier and its environment. Connections from the outside world are made to ports according to provided and required interfaces declared on a port. The outside clients of the classifier have no visibility or direct interaction with the contents or implementation of the classifier. When a classifier is implemented, ports on internal parts are connected to its external ports in accordance with the declared interfaces. The use of ports permits the internal structure of a classifier to be modified without affecting the external clients, provided the interfaces on the ports are correctly supported. Ports permit encapsulated parts to be "wired together" to form the implementation of a classifier.

The behavior of a port is specified by its provided and required interfaces.

Ports are created as part of the instantiation of their classifier and destroyed with it. They may not be created or destroyed during the life of an object.

A port may be specified with multiplicity. If the multiplicity is not a single integer, the cardinality must be specified when the classifier is instantiated. A separate port instance is created for each value in the multiplicity set. If the multiplicity is ordered, the ports can be identified by their index positions.

A call to an object may be made using a specific port, if the provided interface for the port supports the operation. The behavior for the classifier can determine which port received a call and can use this information in the method or to select a method to implement the call. If a port is a behavior port, calls are implemented by the behavior of the classifier. If a port is not a behavior port, calls are forwarded to the internal part owning the port for implementation.

Structure

A classifier may have any number of ports. Each port has a set of provided interfaces and a set of required interfaces. A provided interface declares a service that the classifier is prepared to provide for an anonymous outside client. It is not necessary for the client to have a predefined relationship with the classifier. A required interface declares a service that the classifier requires from an anonymous outside provider. Another classifier connected to the port may request the provided services from the owner of the port but must also be prepared to supply the required services to the owner.

Two implementation properties may be declared on ports:

service port
If false, the port is used only in the internal implementation of the classifier and is not required by its environment, therefore it can be deleted or altered without affecting the use of the classifier. The default is true (the port is needed).

behavior port
If true, requests on the port are implemented directly by the declared behavior implementation (such as a state machine or procedure) of the classifier. If false, the port is a *delegation* port that must be connected to a port on an internal part, and an external request will be transmitted to the internal part for implementation. Delegation ports permit larger classifiers to be "wired together" from smaller parts without additional behavior specification, but eventually at the innermost nesting level behavior must implemented directly.

visibility
A port may be public, private, or protected.

There is no assumption about how a port is implemented. It might be implemented as an explicit object, or it might merely be a virtual concept that does not explicitly appear in the implementation.

If several connectors are attached to a port from the inside, it is a semantic variation point whether requests will be forwarded on all connectors or whether one connector will somehow be selected for each request.

Notation

Declaring ports on structured classifiers

A port is shown as a small square straddling the boundary of a classifier rectangle. The name of the port is placed near the square. The square may be placed just inside the classifier rectangle to indicate a port with restricted visibility, such as a service port; these should be rare, because the main purpose of ports is to encapsulate communication with the environment.

The type of a port may be shown following a colon, using the syntax:

name : Type [multiplicity]

The various parts of this syntax are optional. Multiplicity can be used to declare a set of ports of the same type. All ports of a given type have the same interfaces.

Instead of declaring port types, the interfaces for the port may be shown using interface symbols. A provided interface is shown by a small circle connected to the port square by a line. A required interface is shown by a small semicircle connected to the port square by a line. The name of an interface is placed near the circle, semicircle, or line. Multiple interfaces of either kind may be attached to the same port.

Example

Figure 14-215 shows a camcorder declaration with its ports. The camcorder has two input ports: an TV input and a microphone input. These are shown as provided interfaces, because the camcorder accepts their inputs and acts on them. The camcorder has one kind of output port, an audio output, but there are two instances of this port in each camcorder instance. This is shown as a required interface, because the camcorder requires the services of another device (such as an amplifier or a headphone) to process the outputs.

The camcorder is also shown with one mixed port, the IEEE 1394 (Firewire) port. This port handles both input and output at the same time. This is shown by connecting both a provided and required interface to it. (This approach is not really satisfactory for complex protocols. See discussion for recommendations.)

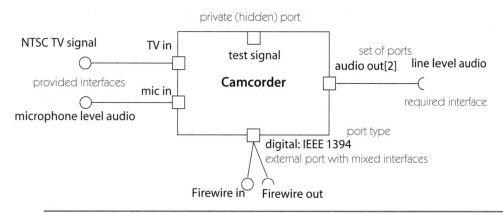

Figure 14-215. *Structured classifier with ports*

Using ports within structured classifiers

A classifier with ports may be used as part of another structured classifier. Each use of the classifier as a part of a structured classifier is shown by a rectangle inside the declaration of the structured classifier. The internal rectangle has a small square for each port in the declaration of its type. If one of the ports was declared with multiplicity, one square is shown for each instance of the port in the particular part. An index number may be used in brackets to distinguish the multiple instances of the same port declaration:

```
name[integer]
```

The ports on the internal parts may be connected to ports on other internal parts or to delegation ports (nonbehavior ports) on the boundary of the structured classifier. Connectors are shown by solid line paths. A delegation port and an internal port connected to it must be of the same type, because a request received on one is also received on the other. Two internal ports connected together must be of complementary types, because a request sent by one is serviced by the other. Two types are complementary if the required services of each are a subset of the provided services of the other. In the simplest case, the provided interfaces of one will be the same as the required interface of the other.

A behavior port on the structured classifier (one that is implemented directly by the structured classifier) is shown by a line from the port to a small state symbol (a rectangle with rounded corners). This is meant to suggest a state machine, although other forms of behavior implementation are also permitted.

Figure 14-216 shows the notation for internal ports and connectors.

A port may be connected by multiple connectors to parts or other ports. The meaning of multiple connections is a semantic variation point: either a message is copied to each connector or a message goes to exactly one connector. This capability is only useful within an implementation environment that provides support for the specification.

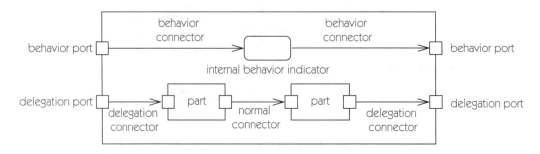

Figure 14-216. *Internal ports in a structured classifier*

Example

Figure 14-217 shows a book formatting program (greatly simplified) built from smaller modules. It accepts a raw text without a table of contents or index and produces a formatted book with a table of contents in front and an index in back. The original input is cloned into 3 copies. One is passed to a component that extracts the entries for the table of contents, one is passed to a component that extracts index entries, and the third is passed unchanged to the final combination. The entry lists are formatted and then passed to the combiner module, which merges them into a single output text.

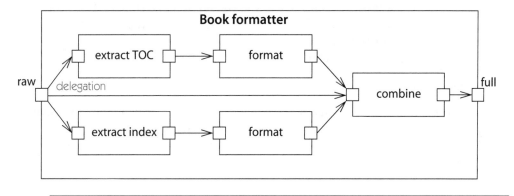

Figure 14-217. *Ports and connectors within a structured class*

History

Ports and structured classifiers in UML2 are a major enhancement that greatly improves the ability to build structured models.

Discussion

The specification of interfaces as either provided or required is a restrictive concept based in traditional programming thinking of interfaces as sets of operations that are called independently and then reply. While these are adequate in simple cases, large systems are often constructed from parts that interact according to well-defined sequences of messages. A well-defined interaction sequence is called a *protocol*. Protocols can be specified by grammars, interactions, or protocol state machines. UML2 does not explicitly support declaration of protocols, but a port type can be identified with a protocol. To show a protocol as an interface symbol, the distinction between provided and required interfaces can simply be ignored (because it is meaningless in complex systems), and the ball-and-socket symbols can be used to represent the complementary halves of a complex protocol, with no assumption that the protocol can be reduced to a set of simple operations.

postcondition

A constraint that must be true at the completion of an operation.

Semantics

A postcondition is a Boolean expression that must be true after the execution of an operation completes. It is an assertion, not an executable statement. Depending on the exact form of the expression, it might be possible to verify it automatically in advance. It can be useful to test the postcondition after the operation, but this is in the nature of debugging a program. The condition is supposed to be true, and anything else is a programming error. A postcondition is a constraint on the implementor of an operation. If it is not satisfied, then the operation has been implemented incorrectly.

See also invariant, precondition.

Structure

A postconditions is a constraint that can be attached to an action, an activity, an operation, a behavior, or a transition in a protocol state machine.

Notation

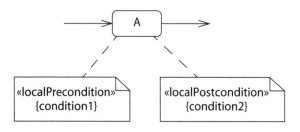

Figure 14-218. *Conditions on action*

Action

A postcondition is shown as text in a note with the keyword «localPostcondition». The note is attached to the action symbol by a dashed line (Figure 14-218).

Activity

A postcondition is shown as a text string within the activity node boundary in the upper right, preceded by the keyword «Postcondition» (Figure 14-219).

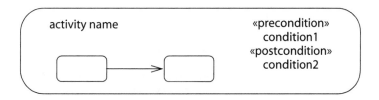

Figure 14-219. *Conditions on activity*

Operation

A postcondition can be shown as text in a note with the keyword «**postcondition**». The note is attached to the text string of the operation by a dashed line (Figure 14-220).

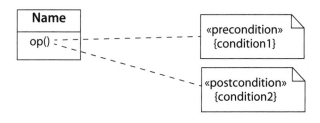

Figure 14-220. *Conditions on operation*

Transition in a protocol state machine

The transition arrow has a text string with the syntax:

[precondition] event / [postcondition]

This syntax applies to protocol state machines, not to behavioral state machines (Figure 14-221).

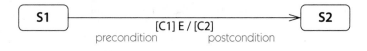

Figure 14-221. *Conditions on protocol state machine transition*

Example

Figure 14-222 shows a postcondition on an array sort operation. The new value of the array (a') is related to the original value (a). This example is expressed in structured natural language. Specification in a more formal language is also possible.

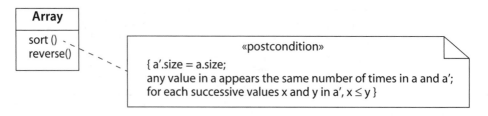

Figure 14-222. *Postcondition*

powertype

A metaclass whose instances are subclasses of a given class.

See also generalization, generalization set, metaclass.

Semantics

The subclasses of a given class may themselves be considered instances of a meta-class. Such a metaclass is called a powertype. For example, class **Tree** may have sub-classes **Oak, Elm,** and **Willow.** Considered as objects, those subclasses are instances of metaclass **TreeSpecies. TreeSpecies** is a powertype that ranges over **Tree.**

The instances of a powertype are all subclasses of a single superclass, so the set of generalization relationships constitutes a generalization set. A superclass can have multiple generalization sets and therefore multiple powertypes. Powertypes and generalization sets are alternate ways of looking at the same quality. A powertype adds the ability to declare properties that apply to individual classes in the generalization set. These properties apply to the classes themselves, not to the objects that are instances of the classes. For example, **TreeSpecies** might have properties such as **geographic distribution** and **average lifetime.**

Notation

A powertype is shown as a class with the keyword «**powertype**» (Figure 14-223). The name of a powertype can be used as a label for the generalization set on a generalization arrow (see generalization set).

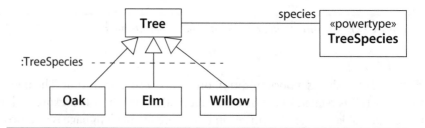

Figure 14-223. *Powertype*

precondition

A constraint that must be true when an operation is invoked.
See also postcondition.

Semantics

A precondition is a Boolean expression that must be true when an operation is called. It is the responsibility of the caller to satisfy the condition. The receiver should not have to check the condition. A precondition is not a guard condition. It is a condition that *must* be true, not a way to optionally execute an operation. As an implementation practice, it can be useful to test the precondition at the beginning of the operation, but this is in the nature of debugging a program. The condition is supposed to be true, and anything else is a programming error. If the condition is not satisfied, no statement can be made about the integrity of the operation or the system. It is liable to utter failure. In practice, explicitly checking preconditions by the receiver may detect many errors.
See also invariant, postcondition.

Structure

A precondition is a constraint that can be attached to an action, an activity, an operation, a behavior, or a transition in a protocol state machine.

Notation

A precondition has the same notation as a postcondition with the appropriate substitution of keyword. See postcondition for diagrams.

Action

A precondition is shown as text in a note with the keyword «localPrecondition». The note is attached to the action symbol by a dashed line (Figure 14-218).

Activity

A precondition is shown as a text string preceded by the keyword «Precondition». The text string is placed within the activity symbol boundary in the upper right (Figure 14-219).

Operation

A precondition can be shown as text in a note with the keyword «precondition». The note is attached to the text string of the operation by a dashed line (Figure 14-220).

Transition in a protocol state machine

The transition arrow has a text string with the syntax:

[precondition] event / [postcondition]

This syntax applies to protocol state machines, not to behavioral state machines (Figure 14-221).

Example

Figure 14-224 shows a precondition on a matrix product operator.

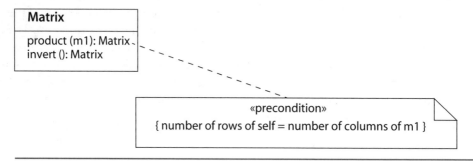

Figure 14-224. *Precondition*

presentation element

A textual or graphical representation of one or more model elements.
　See also diagram.

Semantics

Presentation elements (sometimes called view elements, although they include nongraphical forms of presentation) present the information in a model for human perception. They are the notation. They show part or all of the semantic information about a model element. They may also add aesthetic information useful to humans, for example, by grouping conceptually related elements together. But the added information has no semantic content. The expectation is that a presentation element is responsible for maintaining itself correctly despite changes to the underlying model elements, whereas the model elements need not be aware of presentation elements to operate correctly.

　The descriptions of UML notation in this book define the mapping from model elements to graphical presentations on a screen. The implementation of presentation elements as objects is the responsibility of a tool implementation.

primitive function

The declaration of a mathematical function that accepts a (possibly empty) list of input values and produces a (nonempty) list of output values without side effects or access to any objects.

Semantics

UML2 does not have a predefined set of primitive functions, such as arithmetic functions. This surprises many people, but no two programming languages have exactly the same set of primitive functions, and there have been many bitter fights about which are the "correct" set of primitive functions. For example, few languages implement (even within the limits of memory) integer arithmetic; almost all implement modulo-arithmetic with various bases. UML2 assumes that a particular environment will have a predefined set of primitive functions. Because primitive functions are totally self-contained and may not interact with the environment, they do not add any interesting modeling semantics, and failing to enumerate a preferred predefined set is no handicap. A profile for a particular execution environment or programming language should declare a set of primitive functions as part of its contents.

The apply action applies a primitive function to a set of input values to generate a set of output values. Because primitive functions are totally self-contained, this action imposes no constraints whatsoever on implementation and can be totally concurrent with all other executions in the environment.

It is the intention that primitive functions may not be decomposed or analyzed within UML itself. They are assumed to be implemented directly by the execution environment as atomic actions.

primitive type

A predefined basic data type, such as an integer, Boolean, or string.
See also enumeration.

Semantics

Instances of primitive types do not have identity. If two instances have the same representation, then they are indistinguishable and can be passed by value with no loss of information.

Primitive types include numbers, strings, and possibly other system-dependent data types, for example, dates and money, whose semantics are predefined outside UML. Additional primitive types may be added by profiles. Primitive types will usually correspond closely to those found in the target programming language.

See also enumerations, which are user-definable data types that are not predefined primitive types.

private

A visibility value indicating that the given element is not visible outside its own namespace even to descendants of the namespace.

procedure

An algorithm expressed in a form that can be executed, usually with parameters that can be supplied on invocation.

Semantics

Procedure is an informal term for an executable parameterized algorithm, usually expressed as a list of steps that are executed according to the rules of a given language. UML does not restrict the form that procedures can take. A state machine could be considered a procedure, and any procedure could be modeled by a state machine, so UML already deals with the semantic issues that procedures have. UML has the metaclass **Behavior**, which is somewhat more general than procedure in that it permits imprecise specifications as well as fully executable ones.

process

1. A heavyweight unit of concurrency and execution in an operating system. See thread, which includes heavyweight and lightweight processes. If necessary, an implementation distinction can be made using stereotypes.
2. A software development process—the steps and guidelines by which to develop a system.
3. To execute an algorithm or otherwise handle something dynamically.

process (stereotype of Component)

A transaction-based component.
   See active class, process, thread.

profile

The definition of a set of limited additions to a base metamodel to adapt it to a specific platform or domain.

Semantics

A profile is a package that identifies a subset of an existing base metamodel (possibly including all of it) and defines stereotypes and constraints that may be applied to the selected metamodel subset. The purpose is to allow limited modifications of

UML metamodels without requiring or permitting arbitrary changes to the metamodel. If full first-class extensibility is required, a new metamodel can be defined using MOF, but the result may or may not be much like UML.

A profile may also contain model elements or have a dependency to a package containing model elements. Such a package in a model library. The elements in the package become available to an package that applies the profile.

A profile designates a base metamodel (such as the standard UML metamodel) and selects elements from it using element import or package import. The selected elements may be a subset that are relevant to a particular platform or domain, so that tools or modelers need not deal with unwanted UML capabilities.

A profile contains a set of stereotype and constraint declarations. The stereotypes may be extensions of metamodel elements in the selected set. A stereotype declaration defines tags—essentially additional metaattributes—of existing metamodel elements. In a user model, the stereotype can be applied to an element of the given metatype and the additional metaattributes can be given values by the modeler. The model values may be used for communication among humans, or they may be used by tools to generate code. A stereotype may add metaattributes, but it may not remove existing ones.

A constraint may be applied to a given metaclass. Elements of the metaclass in user-defined models are subject to the constraint. Constraints may be added in profiles, but existing constraints may not be removed or weakened. A model with a profile remains a UML model and must satisfy all of the UML constraints.

A profile is made available to a user model by profile application.

Notation

A profile is shown as a package symbol (rectangle with large tab) with the keyword «profile» above the name of the package. The package symbol contains metamodel elements selected into the profile, declared stereotypes with extension arrows to their base metamodel elements, and constraints that apply to metamodel elements.

A profile may import type declarations that may be used as the types of stereotype tags. Any imported types may also be used in user models, similar to predefined types such as Integer and String.

A profile may have a dependency arrow to a model library, that is, a package containing model element declarations. The model elements are available to packages that apply the profile.

Example

Figure 14-225 (from the UML specification document) shows the definition of a simple profile for an EJB environment.

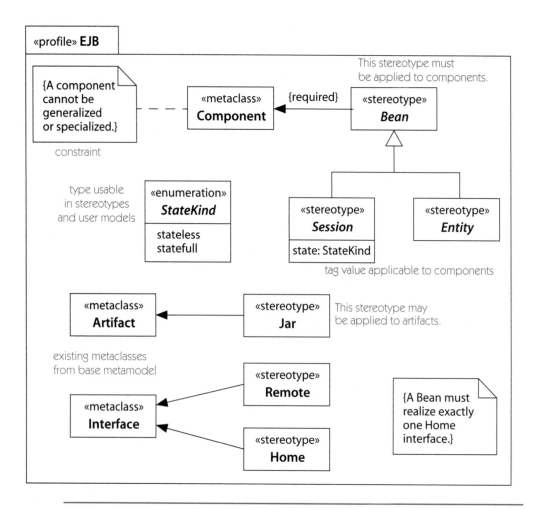

Figure 14-225. *Profile definition*

profile application

The specification that the stereotypes and constraints declared in a given profile may be applied to model elements within a given package.

Semantics

A profile defines stereotypes and constraints that refer to a designated subset of a UML base metamodel (by default, the entire UML standard metamodel). Many different profiles may be defined, possibly with conflicting definitions. Profile application makes a given profile available for use within a given package in a user model.

One or more profiles may be applied to a given package. The constraints from the profile have effect on model elements of the given metatype within the user package. Multiple profiles may be applied to the same package provided their constraints do not conflict. If an applied profile depends on another profile, both profiles must be applied to the user-model package.

Applying a profile to a package makes available the stereotypes declared in the profile for use within the package on model elements on which the stereotype is defined. A stereotype must be applied to a model element explicitly. If the stereotype bears the {required} constraint, it must be applied to all elements of the given metatype, but it is still best to be explicit about it.

Notation

Profile application is shown by a dashed dependency arrow with a stick arrowhead from the user package to the profile symbol. The keyword «apply» is placed on the arrow. Multiple profiles may be applied to the same package, and the same package may be applied to multiple packages.

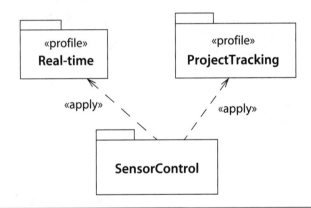

Figure 14-226. *Profile application*

projection

A mapping from a set to a subset of it. Most models and diagrams are projections from the full set of information that is potentially available.

property

A structural feature of a classifier. In particular, attributes and association ends are properties. A structured part in a structured classifier is also a property.

See also association, association end, attribute, redefinition (property).

Semantics

The main structural constituent of both associations and classifiers is a description of values that occur in instances of the elements. In classifiers, structural properties are called attributes; they represent values that occur in instances of classifiers. In associations, structural properties are called association ends; they represent values that are connected by associations. An association is a relationship among classifiers in which no one classifier is dominant. An attribute is a relationship among classifiers in which one classifier is the owner and the other appears in the attribute. It is possible to describe the same relationship as an attribute, an association, or both simultaneously.

Structure

A structural property is owned by either a classifier or an association. If it is owned by a classifier, it is an attribute of the classifier and is navigable from the classifier to the value held in the attribute. An attribute may additionally be modeled as an association end that is not owned by the association. If an end is owned by an association, it may or may not be navigable. The semantic difference between an attribute and an association end is small, and a given relationship can be modeled as an attribute, an association, or both simultaneously. The distinction enables different packaging strategies: Attributes must be managed with their owning classifiers, whereas association ends can be freely added without modifying the participating classifiers.

A structural property has the following settings. See the individual entries for more information.

aggregation kind	Whether the set of values is an aggregate or composite; an enumeration with the values {none, shared, composite}. If the value is not none, the association is called an aggregation. A shared aggregation permits more than one whole for a given part and does not imply management of the part by the whole. A composite aggregation (composition) allows only a single whole for a given part and implies management of the part by the whole. The default is none. Only a binary association can be an aggregation or composition; only one end can be an aggregate of any kind, and the other end (value of none) marks the parts. If both ends have value none, the association is not an aggregation. See aggregation.
changeability	Whether the value of the property may change after initialization. The choice is changeable or read only. The default is changeable. The definition of initialization is vague and likely to be implementation-dependent. Only a navigable property may be read only.

default value

An expression for the initial value of an attribute evaluated and assigned to the attribute when the owning classifier is instantiated. This setting is optional. If it is absent, no initial value is specified (but some other part of the model, such as a creation operation, may specify a value).

derived

A flag specifying whether the property is computable from other values and therefore does not represent a degree of freedom. The computation itself must be specified as a constraint, if desired. A derived property is often read only; if it is changeable, semantics of updating its value are implementation specific (best avoided in most modeling).

derived union

A flag specifying whether the property (and, in an association, the association itself) is defined as the union of all the properties that are specified as subsetting it. If true, then any instance of an association is necessarily an instance of one of the subsetting associations. The derived setting is true for a derived union.

multiplicity

The possible number of values of the attribute or association end that can exist simultaneously in one object having the property. It is specified as an integer range. The most common value for attributes is "exactly one" denoting a scalar attribute. The value "zero or one" denotes a property with an optional value. A missing value is distinguishable from any value in the domain of the property type. (In other words, the absence of a value is different from the value zero or null.) If the upper bound is greater than one, the ordering and uniqueness settings are relevant. See multiplicity.

name

The name of the property, that is, the name of the attribute or association end, an identifier string. This name identifies an attribute within a classifier and an association end within an association (possible both for a given property). The name must be unique within an association and also among direct and inherited property elements (attributes and association ends visible to the class) of the source class. The same name can be used in redefinitions within descendant classifiers, but the UML specification should be consulted for restrictions on usage.

navigability	A flag indicating whether it is possible to traverse an association to obtain the object or set of objects at one end associated with a value or tuple of values from all of the other ends. The default is **true** (navigable). An attribute is always navigable. An association may be navigable even if its end are not owned by classes.
ordering	Whether (and potentially how) the set of related objects is ordered, an enumeration with the values {unordered, ordered}. Part of the multiplicity specification.
qualifier	A list of attributes used as selectors for choosing objects within a set of values. If a qualifier is present, then the multiplicity constrains the cardinality of the set of values including the qualifier values; the unqualified multiplicity is assumed to be many unless otherwise specified. See qualifier.
redefinition	An association end may redefine a property defined in an ancestor classifier or association. The redefined property may or may not have the same name and visibility. See redefinition.
rolename	The name of the association end, an identifier string. The term *rolename* is informal.
static	A Boolean setting. If true, the value of the property is shared by all instances of the classifier; alternately, it may be considered a property of the classifier itself. If false, each instance of the classifier has its own value of the property. The default is false (nonstatic).
subsetting	A property may be marked as a subset of another specified property. The set of values associated with an object by the property must be the same as or a subset of the set of values associated with the object by the specified property. For example, this allows an association to be defined and then divided into more specialized associations, such as an employee association into worker and manager associations. A subset property may have a more restrictive type and multiplicity than the original property. See subsetting.
type	The type of value indicated by the property. As an attribute, this is the type of the attribute value; as an association end, this is the type of the attached object.

uniqueness	Whether the collection of objects related to a given object may contain duplicates. If true, no duplicates are allowed and the collection is a set (if unordered) or an ordered set (if ordered); if false, duplicates are allowed, and the collection is a bag (if unordered) or a list (if ordered). Part of the multiplicity specification.
visibility	Whether the property is accessible to other classifiers. In an association, the visibility is placed on the target end, that is, the end opposite from the classifier owning the property. Each direction of traversal across an association has its own visibility value.

Notation

The end of an association path is connected to the edge of the rectangle of the corresponding class symbol. Association end properties are shown as adornments on or near the end of the path at which it attaches to a classifier symbol (Figure 14-32). See association.

Attribute settings are shown as substrings within the entire attribute string. See attribute for the full attribute string syntax.

Text properties are shown within braces at the end of an attribute string or near the association end. Text labels on an association end are placed near the association end so that they cannot be confused with labels on the entire association, but there is no specified relative positioning of multiple text labels. They can be moved around to make a neat diagram.

The following list is a brief summary of adornments for each modeling setting. See the individual articles for more details.

aggregation kind	A small diamond on the association end representing the whole, a hollow diamond for a shared aggregate, a filled diamond for a composition aggregate. No adornment for a part or a nonaggregation. The string {shared} or {composite} can also be placed near an end or in an attribute string. There does not appear to be a way to mark an attribute that represents a part without including an association.
changeability	The text property {addOnly} near the target end, usually omitted for {changeable} but permitted for emphasis.
default value	For an attribute, shown as a text string expression following an equal sign. A default value is rarely shown for an association.

derived	For a derived attribute, shown as a slash (/) in front of the attribute name. For a derived association, shown as a slash in front of the association name (a slash by itself is allowed if there is no association name).
derived union	The property string {union} is placed in the attribute string or near the association end.
multiplicity	For an attribute, the multiplicity interval in square brackets after the type name, for example, **vertex: Point[3..*]**. In the absence of a string, the default is exactly one. For an association end, a text label near the end of the path, in the form min..max (without any brackets). In the absence of a label, the multiplicity is usually unspecified, but other conventions are sometimes adopted.
name	For an attribute, the name is shown as a text string preceding the type (if any). If a single name is shown, it is the attribute name, and the type is unspecified. For an association end, the name is shown as a text string near the end of the association path attached to the target classifier symbol.
navigability	For an attribute, navigability is always true and need not be shown. For an association end, an arrowhead on the end of a path shows navigability in that direction. A small **X** on the end of a path shows nonnavigability in that direction. Often the following convention is adopted: An arrow on one end and no arrow on the other ends indicates nonnavigability on the unmarked ends. If no end has an arrowhead, the association is navigable in all directions (because there is little need for associations that are not navigable in any direction). A different convention is that unmarked ends have unspecified navigability. In any case, the same convention should be used for an entire diagram and, preferably, for all diagrams in a model.
ordering	The property string {ordered} on the attribute string or near the target end indicates an ordered set; the property {seq}, {sequence}, {list}, or {ordered bag} indicates an ordered bag, that is, an ordinary list with possible duplicates. The absence of a mark indicates an unordered set.
qualifier	A small rectangle between the end of the path and the source class in a traversal. The rectangle contains one or more attributes of the association—the qualifiers.

redefinition	The property string {**redefined** original} indicates a redefinition of property original.
rolename	A text label near the target end
subsetting	The property string {**subsets** original} indicates a subsetting of property original. A comma-separated list of names is allowed.
type	For an attribute, the type is shown as a text string after a colon (:). For an association, the association path line is attached to the rectangle symbolizing the type.
uniqueness	The property string {**bag**} in the attribute string or near the target end indicates a nonunique collection (bag). The property string {**list**}, {**ordered bag**}, {**seq**}, or {**sequence**}, indicates an ordered nonunique collection (sequence). The absence of a mark indicates a set.
visibility	Visibility symbol (+ # − ~) prefixed to rolename.

Discussion

Note that the term *property* is also used in a general sense to mean any value attached to a model element.

property string

A text syntax for showing a value or value attached to an element, especially tagged values, but also including built-in attributes of model elements.

Notation

One or more comma-separated property specifications enclosed in braces ({ }). Each property declaration has the form

    property-name = value

or

    property-literal

where the property literal is a unique enumerated value whose appearance implies a unique property name.

Example

    { abstract, author=Joe, visibility=private }

Presentation options

A tool may present property specifications on separate lines with or without the enclosing braces, provided they are appropriately marked to distinguish them from other information. For example, properties for a class might be listed under the class name in a distinctive typeface, such as italics or a different font family. This is a tool issue.

Note that property strings may be used to display built-in attributes, as well as tagged values, but such usage should be avoided if the canonical form is simple.

protected

A visibility value indicating that the given element is visible outside its own namespace only to descendants of the namespace.

protocol conformance

The declaration that a specific state machine conforms to the protocol defined by a general protocol state machine.

Semantics

A protocol state machine defines rules on the invocation of operations or exchange of messages that a behavioral state machine or procedure may perform. A protocol conformance relationship requires that a behavioral state machine or a more specialized protocol state machine obey every rule imposed by the general protocol state machine.

protocol state

The state of a protocol state machine.

Semantics

A protocol state may not have an entry activity, exit activity, or do activity.
The full range of composite states and submachine states is allowed.

Notation

The notation is the same as a behavioral state, that is, a rounded rectangle containing the name of the state.

protocol state machine

A state machine used to specify the legal sequences of operation calls and signals received by an object.

Semantics

A behavioral state machine is an executable specification that converts events recognized by an object into a sequence of effects. Any sequence of events produces an outcome. By contrast, a protocol state machine specifies the legal sequences of events that may occur within the context of a classifier. It is not responsible for ensuring that a legal sequence occurs; the responsibility may lie with the caller or may be distributed over the design of a system. A protocol state machine merely defines the legal sequences, often to facilitate the design of the overall system that ensures that valid sequences occur. In language theory terms, a protocol state machine is an acceptor or a grammar for valid sentences.

A protocol state machine differs from a behavioral state machine as follows:

• Transitions do not have effects. The purpose of a transition is to specify the legal messages. Effects must be specified elsewhere in the design, possible as operations on classes or as transitions of a behavioral state machine that might be constructed later in the design process.

• The transition may have a precondition that must be true if the event occurs. This is interpreted as a precondition on the associated operation, if any.

• A transition may have a postcondition. The postcondition indicates the state of the owning object after the transition is complete. Although protocol transitions do not have effects, the postcondition may impose constraints on the results of the called operation or on effects that may be needed as part of the eventual implementation.

If a sequence of events (operation calls or signals) leads to a valid path through the protocol state machine, that sequence of events is legal and must be accepted by the system design. The postconditions may impose constraints on the implementation.

If a sequence of events does not lead to a valid path, it may not occur. There are two possible consequences for the designer: If the creation of the events is under the control of the rest of the system, the designer must ensure that invalid sequences are not generated, but then the target class need not handle such invalid sequences. Otherwise, the protocol state machine may be an assertion that the invalid sequences cannot occur (for whatever reasons) and that the system need not handle them. (A wise designer will check for invalid sequences anyway and generate graceful error failures if necessary.)

Notation

A protocol state machine is shown by the keyword {**protocol**} after the name of the state machine.

A protocol transition has the following syntax for its label:

$\lfloor$[precondition]$\rfloor_{opt}$ message-name $\lfloor$(parameter-list)$\rfloor_{opt}$
    $\lfloor$[postcondition]$\rfloor_{opt}$

The message name must be the name of an operation or signal.

Example

Figure 14-227 shows the rules for bidding in contract bridge as a protocol state machine.

History

In UML2, the previously informal concept of protocol state machine has been formalized.

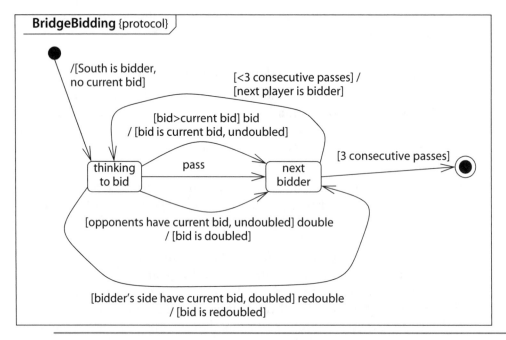

Figure 14-227. *Protocol state machine for bridge bidding*

protocol transition

A transition in a protocol state machine.

Semantics

Protocol transitions specify legal sequences of events. They do not specify effects.

Notation

See protocol state machine.

provided interface

An interface that declares the services that a classifier offers to provide to anonymous requestors.

See interface, port, required interface.

Semantics

A provided interface is a relationship between an interface and a classifier (rather than a kind of interface) that declares the class can be invoked to provide the services described in the interface. A required interface is the complementary relationship that a classifier requires the services described in the interface. If one class declares a provided interface and the other class requires the same interface, the classes can interact over the interface with no additional structure.

Notation

A provided interface relationship is shown by a small circle attached to a classifier (or a port on a classifier) by a line (Figure 14-228). The circle is not a separate part of the symbol, and it does not represent the interface itself. The name of the interface is placed near the circle. Alternately, a provided interface can be shown using realization notation.

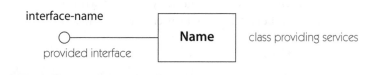

Figure 14-228. *Provided interface notation*

pseudostate

A vertex in a state machine that has the form of a state but has special behavior.

Semantics

A pseudostate is a transient state that structures the details of a transition. When a pseudostate is active, a state machine has not completed its run-to-completion step and will not process events. Pseudostates are used to chain transition segments, and a transition to one implies a further automatic transition to another state without requiring an event.

Pseudostates include choice, entry point, exit point, fork, history state, initial state, join, junction, and terminate.

A final state is not a pseudostate. It may remain active when a state machine has completed its run-to-completion step, but it has restrictions on the transitions that can depart from it.

Notation

Each kind of pseudostate has its own notation.

public

A visibility value indicating that the given element is visible outside its own namespace.

qualified name

A string composed by concatenating the names of the nested namespaces containing an element, starting from the implicit unnamed namespace that contains the entire system and ending with the name of the element itself.

Semantics

A qualified name uniquely identifies a model element, such as an attribute or a state, within a system and may be used within an expression to reference an element. Not every kind of element has a name.

Notation

A qualified name is displayed as a list of nested namespace and element names separated by double colons (::). A namespace is a package or an element with nested declarations. For example:

Accounting::Personnel::Employee::address

A qualified name references an element in the package named by the path prefix.

qualifier

A slot for an attribute or list of attributes on a binary association, in which the values of the attributes select a unique related object or a set of related objects from the entire set of objects related to an object by the association. It is an index on the traversal of an association.

See association class, association end.

Semantics

A binary association maps an object to a set of related objects. Sometimes it is desirable to select an object from the set by supplying a value that distinguishes the objects in the set. This value could be an attribute of the target class. In general, however, the selector value may be part of the association itself, an association attribute whose value is supplied by the creator when a new link is added to the association class. Such an attribute on a binary association is called a qualifier. An object, together with a qualifier value, determines a unique related object or (somewhat less often) a subset of related objects. The value qualifies the association. In an implementation context, such an attribute has been called an index value.

A qualifier is used to select an object or objects from the set of objects related to a object (called the *qualified object*) by an association (Figure 14-229). The object selected by the qualifier value is called the *target object*. A qualifier always acts on an association whose multiplicity is *many* in the target direction. In the simplest case, each qualifier value selects a single object from the target set of related objects. In other words, a qualified object and a qualifier value yield a unique related target object. Given a qualified object, each qualifier value maps into a unique target object.

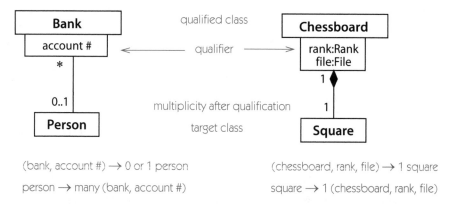

Figure 14-229. *Qualified associations*

Many kinds of names are qualifiers. Such a name within a context maps to a unique value. The qualified object supplies the context, the qualifier is the name, and the target object is the result. Any ID or other unique code is a qualifier; its purpose is to uniquely select a value. An array can be modeled as a qualified association. The array is the qualified object, the array index is the qualifier, and the array element is the target object. For an array, the qualifier type is an integer range.

A qualifier may be used in a navigation expression to select a subset of objects related to an object across an association—namely, those bearing a particular value for the qualifier attribute value or list of values. The qualifier serves as a selector within the set of objects related by the association. It partitions the set into subsets by qualifier value. In most cases, the purpose of a qualifier is to select a unique object from the set of related objects so that a qualified association behaves like a lookup table.

Structure

Qualifier. A qualifier attribute is an optional part of a binary association end. The qualifier qualifies the class attached to the association end. An object of the class and a qualifier value select an object or set of objects from the class at the other end of the binary association. It is possible for both ends of a binary association to have qualifiers, but it is rare.

A qualifier is an association attribute or list of attributes. Each attribute has a name and a type but no initial value, as qualifiers are not freestanding objects, and each qualifier value must be explicit when a link is added to the association.

Qualifiers are not used with *n*-ary associations.

Multiplicity. The multiplicity of the qualified relationship is placed on the opposite end of the binary association from the qualifier. (The mnemonic is that the qualified class and qualifier together form a composite value that is related to the target class.) In other words, the qualifier is attached to the "near end" of the association, and the multiplicity and rolename are attached to the "far end."

The multiplicity attached to the target association end denotes how many target objects might be selected by a (source object, qualifier value) pair. Common multiplicity values include 0..1 (a unique value may be selected, but every possible qualifier value does not necessarily select a value), 1 (every possible qualifier value selects a unique target object, therefore the domain of qualifier values must be finite), and * (the qualifier value is an index that partitions the target objects into subsets).

In the majority of cases, the multiplicity is zero-or-one. This choice means that an object and qualifier value may yield, at most, one related object. A multiplicity of one means that every possible qualifier value yields exactly one object. This obviously requires the qualifier type to be a finite domain (in a computer implementation anyway). This multiplicity can be useful for mapping finite enumerated types—for example, a **Pixel** qualified by **PrimaryColor** (enumeration of red, green, and blue) would yield the red-green-blue value triplet for each pixel in an image.

The multiplicity of the unqualified association is not stated explicitly. But it is usually assumed to be many, or at least more than one. Otherwise, there would be no need for a qualifier.

A multiplicity of many on a qualified association has no significant semantic impact, because the qualifier does not reduce the multiplicity of the target set. Such a multiplicity represents a design statement that an index to traverse the association must be provided. In that case, the qualifier partitions the set of target objects into subsets. Semantically, this adds nothing beyond having an association attribute, which also (implicitly) partitions the links. The design connotation of a qualifier in a design model is that the traversal should be efficient—that is, it must not require a linear search among all the target values. Usually it is implemented by some kind of lookup table. An index in a database or data structure is properly modeled as a qualifier.

In the reverse direction across a qualified association (that is, going from the target class to the qualified object), the multiplicity indicates the number of (qualified object, qualifier) pairs that can relate to a target object, not the number of qualified objects. In other words, if several (qualified object, qualifier) pairs map into the same target object, then the reverse multiplicity is many. A reverse multiplicity of one from target to qualifier means that there is exactly one pairing of qualified object and qualifier value that relates to the target object.

Notation

A qualifier is shown as a small rectangle attached to the end of an association path between the final path segment and the symbol of the qualified class. The qualifier rectangle is part of the association path, not part of the class. The qualifier is attached to the class that it qualifies—that is, an object of the qualified class, together with a value of the qualifier, uniquely selects a set of target class objects on the other end of the association.

Qualifier attributes are listed within the qualifier box. There may be one or more attributes in the list. Qualifier attributes have the same notation as class attributes, except that initial value expressions are not meaningful.

Presentation options

A qualifier may not be suppressed. It provides essential detail, the omission of which would modify the inherent character of the relationship.

A tool may use a thinner line for qualifier rectangles than for class rectangles to distinguish them clearly.

The qualifier rectangle, preferably, should be smaller than the class rectangle to which it is attached, although this is not always practical.

Discussion

The multiplicities on a qualified association are treated as if the qualified object and the qualifier are a single entity, a composite key. In the forward direction, the multiplicity on the target end represents the number of objects related to the composite value (qualified object + qualifier value). In the reverse direction, the multiplicity describes the number of composite values (qualified object + qualifier) related to each target object, not the number of qualified objects related to each target object. This is why the qualifier is placed on the very end of the association path adjacent to the class symbol—you can think of the association path connecting the composite value to the target class.

There is no provision for specifying the multiplicity of the unqualified relationship. In practice, however, it is usually many in the forward direction. There is no point to have a qualified association unless many target objects are related to one qualified object. For logical modeling, the purpose of the qualifier is to reduce the multiplicity to one by adding the qualifier so that a query can be assured of returning a single value rather than a set of values. The uniqueness of the qualifier value is frequently a crucial semantic condition that is difficult to capture without qualifiers. Almost all applications have many qualified associations. Many names are really qualifiers. If a name is unique within some context, it is a qualifier, and the context should be identified and modeled appropriately. Not all names are qualifiers. Names of persons, for example, are not unique. Because personal names are ambiguous, most data processing applications use some kind of identification number, such as a customer number, a Social Security number, or an employee number. If an application requires the lookup of information or the retrieval of data based on search keys, the model should generally use qualified associations. Any context in which names or identification codes are defined to select things out of sets should usually be modeled as a qualified association.

Note that the qualifier value is a property of the link, not of the target object. Consider a Unix file system, in which each directory is a list of entries whose names are unique within the directory, although the same names can be used in other directories. Each entry points to a file, which may be a data file or another directory. More than one entry can point to the same file. If this happens, the file has several aliases. The Unix directory system is modeled as a many-to-one association in which the directory qualified by the filename yields a file. Note that the filename is not part of the file; it is part of the relationship between a directory and a file. A file does not have a single name. It may have many names in many directories (or even several names in the same directory). The filename is not an attribute of the file.

A major motivation for qualified associations is the need to model an important semantic situation that has a natural and important implementation data structure. In the forward direction, a qualified association is a lookup table—for a qualified object, each qualifier value yields a single target object (or a null value if the qualifier value is absent in the set of values). Lookup tables are implementable by data structures, such as hash tables, b-trees, and sorted lists that provide much greater efficiency than unsorted lists, which must be searched linearly. In almost all cases, it is poor design to use a linked list or other unsorted data structure for searches on names or codes, although, sadly, many programmers use them. Modeling appropriate situations with qualified associations and using efficient data structures to implement them is crucial to good programming.

For a logical model, there is little point in having a qualified association with a multiplicity of many in the forward direction, because the qualifier does not add any semantic information that an association attribute could not show. In a model intended for the design of algorithms and data structures, however, a qualifier carries an additional connotation—namely, the intent that the selection be efficient. In other words, a qualified association denotes an indexed data structure optimized for lookup on the qualifier value. In this case, a multiplicity of many can be useful to represent a set of values that must be accessible together under a common index value, without having to search other values.

A qualifier attribute should, generally, not be included as an attribute of the target class, as its presence in the association is sufficient. In case of an index value, however, it may be necessary to take a value that is inherently an attribute of the target class and make it a redundant qualifier value. Index values are inherently redundant.

Constraints

Some complicated situations are not straightforward to model with any set of nonredundant relationships. They are best modeled using qualified associations to capture the basic access paths with additional constraints stated explicitly. Because these situations are uncommon, it was felt that trying to include them in a notation that could capture all possible multiplicity constraints directly was not worth the added complexity.

For example, consider a directory in which each filename identifies a unique file. A file may correspond to multiple directory-filename pairs. This is the basic model we have seen before. This model is shown in Figure 14-230.

Now, however, we wish to add additional constraints. Suppose that each file must be in just one directory, but within that directory it could have many names—that is, there is more than one way to name the same file. This can be modeled with a redundant association between **File** and **Directory**, with multiplicity one in the **Directory** direction (Figure 14-231). The redundancy of the two associations is indicated by the constraint {same}, which implies that the two elements are the same but at different levels of detail. Because these associations are redundant, only the qualified association would be implemented; the other would be treated as a run-time constraint on its contents.

Figure 14-230. *Simple qualifier*

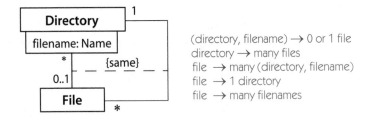

Figure 14-231. *File with multiple names in one directory*

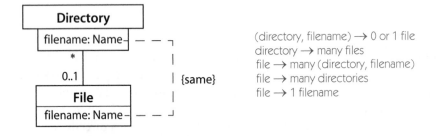

Figure 14-232. *File with same name in all directories*

A similar constraint is that each file may appear in multiple directories, but it always has the same name wherever it appears. Other files can have the same name, but they must be in different directories. This can be modeled by making **filename** an attribute of **File** but constraining the class attribute and the qualifier to be the same (Figure 14-232). This pattern occurs frequently as a search index, although in a general index the multiplicity of the qualified target would be many. This situation, therefore, has more semantic content than an index, which is an implementation device.

A third case would allow a file to appear in multiple directories under various names, but the file could appear only once within a single directory. This could be

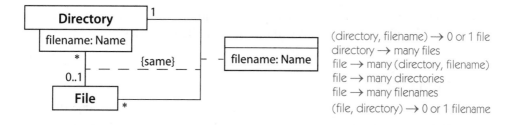

Figure 14-233. *File with at most one name in any directory*

modeled with redundant qualified association and association class that share the same attribute **filename** (Figure 14-233).

These examples have been shown with redundant relations to illustrate the nature of the constraints. In practice, however, it is usually satisfactory to state the constraint textually, with the qualified association shown graphically.

query

An operation that returns a value but does not alter the state of the system; an operation without side effects.

Semantics

An operation (but not a reception) may be declared to be a query. A query does not alter the state of the environment; it only returns a value to the caller. The behavior implementing the operation must obey the constraint.

raise exception action

An action whose execution produces an exception of a given type. As a result of the exception, the execution of the action is terminated and the exception handling mechanism operates.

See action, exception, exception handler.

read action

A family of actions whole execution outputs the value of an attribute, association end, qualifier, extent, or other value.

See action.

realization

The relationship between a specification and its implementation; an indication of the inheritance of behavior without the inheritance of structure.

See also interface.

Semantics

A specification describes the behavior or structure of something without determining how the behavior will be implemented. An implementation provides the details about how to implement behavior in an effectively computable way. The relationship between an element that specifies behavior and one that provides an implementation is called realization. In general, there are many ways to realize a specification. Similarly, an element can realize more than one specification. Realization is therefore a many-to-many relationship among elements.

The meaning of realization is that the client element must support all the behavior of the supplier element but need not match its structure or implementation. A client classifier, for example, must support the operations of the supplier classifier, and it must support all state machines that specify external behavior of the supplier. But any attributes, associations, methods, or state machines of the supplier that specify implementation are irrelevant to the client. Note that the client does not actually inherit the operations from the supplier. It must declare them itself or inherit them from an ancestor so that all the operations of the supplier are covered. In other words, the supplier in a realization indicates which operations must be present in the client, but the client is responsible for providing them. In the most general sense of realization, the names of the operations need not match, only their total behavior.

Certain kinds of elements, such as interfaces and use cases, are intended for specifying behavior, and they contain no implementation information. Other kinds of elements, such as classes, are intended for implementing behavior. They contain implementation information, but they can also be used in a more abstract way as specifiers. Usually, realization relates a specification element, such as a use case or an interface, to an implementation element, such as a collaboration or a class. It is possible to use an implementation element, such as a class, for specification. It can be placed on the specification side of a realization relationship. In this case, only the specification parts of the supplier class affect the client. The implementation parts are irrelevant for the realization relationship. More precisely, then, realization is a relationship between two elements in which the external behavior specification parts of one constrain the implementation of the other. It might be thought of as inheritance of behavior specification without inheritance of structure or implementation (and with the need to actually declare the operations by the client).

A component may be realized by a set of classes that together implement the behavior specified by the provided and required interfaces of the component.

If the specification element is an abstract class with no attributes, no associations, and only abstract operations, any specialization of the abstract class implicitly realizes the abstract class, as there is nothing to inherit but specification.

The implementing element must support all of the behavior included in the specifying element. For example, a class must support all the operations of the interfaces that it realizes, with semantics that are consistent with all the specifications required by the interfaces. The class can implement additional operations, and the implementation of the operations can do additional things, provided the operation specifications of the interfaces are not violated.

Notation

The realization relationship is shown by a dashed path with a closed triangular arrowhead on the end adjacent to the element supplying the specification and with its tail on the element supplying the implementation (Figure 14-234).

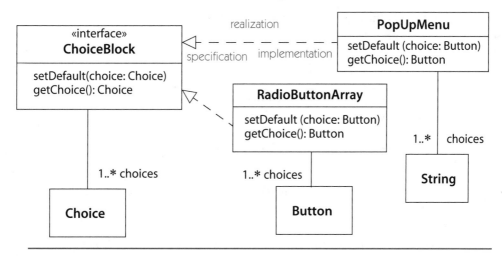

Figure 14-234. *Realization relationship*

Discussion

Another important case is the realization of a use case by a collaboration (Figure 14-235). A use case specifies externally visible functionality and behavioral sequences, but it does not supply an implementation. A collaboration describes the objects that implement the use case behavior and the way that they interact to do it. Usually, one collaboration implements one use case, but a collaboration can be implemented using subordinate collaborations, each of which does part of the job. The objects and classes used to implement a collaboration usually appear in other collaborations as well. Each class in the collaboration devotes part of its functionality to the use case being implemented. Therefore, a use case is eventually implemented by slices through several classes.

Figure 14-235. *Realization of use case by collaboration*

realization (stereotype of Classifier)

A classifier that specifies the physical implementation of a domain. Contrast with specification.
See realization.

realize

To provide the implementation for a specification element.
See realization.

receive

To handle a message instance passed from a sender object.
See receiver, sender, substitution.

Semantics

The reception of a message by an object is an event. If the message represents a call, it is a call event; if the message represents a signal send, it is a signal event. If an operation (in the case of a call) or a reception (in the case of a signal) is declared by the classifier of the owning object, the receipt of the message by an object may resolve to an effect, such as the execution of a procedure or the triggering of a transition. (The declaration of the reception may be implicit if the reception resolves to a trigger.)

Instead of declaring an effect for a given kind of reception, an object may execute an accept action, in which case the object waits until an event of a specified kind is handled by the object.

receive action

See accept action.

receive event

The receipt of a message (usually a signal) by an object.
    See signal event.

receiver

The object that handles a message instance passed from a sender object. The receipt of a message is usually intended to cause an effect in the receiver.

reception

A declaration that a classifier is prepared to react to the receipt of a signal. A reception is a feature of a classifier.

Semantics

A reception is a declaration that an instance of a classifier is prepared to handle and react to the receipt of an instance of a signal. A reception is similar (in spirit) to an operation. It declares the signal type that the classifier accepts and specifies the effect of the receipt of an instance of the signal.

The receipt of a signal may trigger a state machine transition, it may cause the execution of a procedure, or it may have another effect specified by the resolution mechanism. If a signal receipt causes the execution of a synchronous procedure, any attempt to return is ignored.

Notation

A reception may be shown in the operation list of a class or interface using the syntax for an operation with the keyword «signal» in front of the signal name. The parameters correspond to the attributes of the signal; they must all be in-only parameters.

Alternately, a list of signal signatures may be placed in its own compartment; the compartment has the name Signals. Both ways are shown in Figure 14-236.

record type

A traditional record type may be represented in UML as a data type with attributes.

redefinable element

An element within a classifier whose specification can be redefined within a specialization of the classifier. See redefinition.

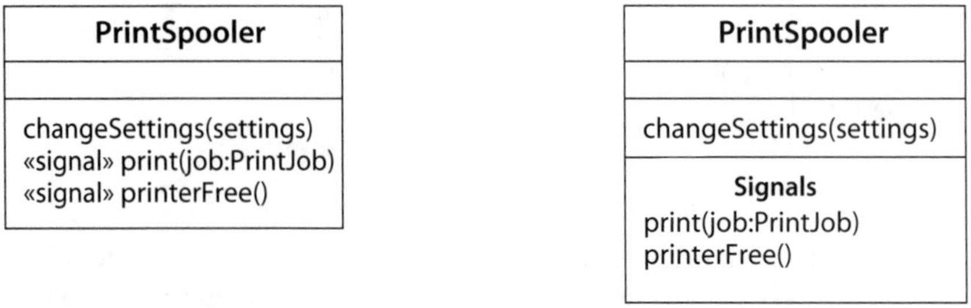

PrintSpooler
changeSettings(settings) «signal» print(job:PrintJob) «signal» printerFree()

PrintSpooler
changeSettings(settings)
Signals print(job:PrintJob) printerFree()

Figure 14-236. *Two ways to notate signal reception*

Semantics

Ordinarily, an element defined within the context of a classifier specification is simply inherited by descendants of the classifier without modification. This unchangeability supports polymorphism by ensuring that all the descendants of a classifier share the same definition of its elements.

Sometimes, however, it is desirable to be able to modify the definition of an element by making it more specific or by adding constraints in the new context. Invariant constraints on the original definition must be respected, however.

The following kinds of elements can be redefined: activity edge, activity node, classifier, extension point, feature, region, state, transition. The semantics of redefinition vary among different kinds of elements.

The *leaf* flag indicates that a redefinable element cannot be further redefined.

redefines

Keyword indicating the redefinition of a feature in a classifier.

See redefinition (operation), redefinition (property).

redefinition

A modification of the specification of an element defined within the context of a classifier specification to a new specification within the context of a descendant classifier.

Semantics

A redefinable element defined in a classifier can be redefined in a descendant classifier. The redefinition references the original definition and the classifier within which it was defined. The redefinition may augment, constrain, or override the original specification. The substitutability principle may be violated by redefinition, because the redefinition may invalidate a constraint from an ancestor.

Notation

Notation depends on the kind of element being redefined.

See redefinition (behavior), redefinition (classifier), redefinition (operation), redefinition (property), redefinition (state machine), redefinition (template).

History

Redefinition is a new UML2 concept.

Discussion

Redefinition should be used sparingly and with care, because it can produce obscure models.

redefinition (behavior)

Semantics

A behavior may redefine another behavior. The type of behavior may be changed. For example, a state machine could be replaced by a procedure.

If it implements a behavioral feature, the redefinition replaces the original behavior in the specialized classifier.

If it implements a classifier (as a classifier behavior), the redefinition extends the original definition but does not replace it.

An interaction may be substituted for another interaction in the specialization of an owning classifier.

Notation

See redefinition (operation), redefinition (state machine).

redefinition (classifier)

Semantics

A classifier declared within another classifier can be redefined within a specialization of the containing classifier. The specification does not seem to indicate what changes are allowed in the redefined classifier, however. Presumably attributes and operations can be added; it is unclear whether or how existing attributes and operations can be modified. Possibly the same kinds of changes permitted in a subclass are permitted in a redefined classifier.

redefinition (operation)

Semantics

An operation may be redefined in a specialization of a class. This redefinition may specialize the types of the formal parameters or return results, add new preconditions or postconditions, add new raised exceptions, or otherwise refine the specification of the operation.

The BodyCondition (a constraint on the return value) may be overridden in a redefinition. The postcondition can only be strengthened in a redefinition.

Notation

The new operation is included in the subclass with the following string appended:

{ redefines operation-name }

redefinition (property)

Semantics

A property (attribute or association end) can be redefined in a descendant classifier. Among the characteristics of a property that can be redefined are name, type (may be specialized), default value, derivation status, visibility, multiplicity, and constraints on values.

Interaction of association specialization with association end redefinition and subsetting is undefined.

Notation

A redefinition has the syntax

{ redefines property-name }

where property-name is the name of the attribute or association end that is being redefined. The string is placed after the attribute string or near the end of an association line with the defining property. The name of the new property may be different from the original property.

Example

Figure 14-237 shows several redefinitions of attributes and association ends.

Discussion

A property with the same name as a property that would have been inherited is assumed to be a redefinition without the need for the **redefines** keyword. This is a

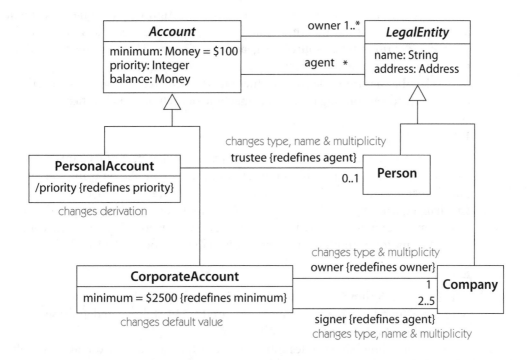

Figure 14-237. *Redefinition of properties*

dangerous rule, as it can easily lead to subtle and gross errors. Don't use it. Always be explicit about redefinition, as it is confusing enough on its own.

redefinition (state machine)

In specializing a classifier, the behavior state machines specifying the classifier and its methods may be redefined. (The document uses the word *extended* in referring to redefinition of state machines.). When a state machine is redefined, its states, regions, and transitions may be redefined.

States may be redefined. A simple state can become a composite state by adding a region. A composite state can add regions, vertices, transitions, entry/exit/do activities, and transitions to regions inherited from the original state machine. If a state is part of a region, a redefinition of the state must be part of a redefinition of the region. A redefinition of a submachine state can replace the submachine reference, provided it has the same entry and exit points as the original submachine reference. The new submachine reference may have additional entry and exit points.

A region may be redefined. The redefinition may add vertices and transitions, and states and transitions may be redefined.

A transition may be redefined. A redefined transition may redefine its content and target state, but not its source state or trigger. A redefined transition must be uniquely identified by a (source, target, trigger) tuple. This excludes transitions that differ only in guard condition from being redefined.

If a classifier has multiple parents, the state machine redefinition has an orthogonal region corresponding to the state machine of each parent classifier.

Notation

A redefined state machine has the keyword {**extended**} as part of its name tag.

In a redefined state machine, additions and changes are shown using solid lines. States, regions, and transitions that are not shown are assumed to be inherited (unchanged from the original state machine). Inherited states, regions, and transitions may be drawn using dashed lines if they are needed to establish the context for additions, for example, if they are involved in transitions.

Example

Figure 14-238 shows a state machine for a vending machine. This serves as the base for a state machine redefinition. Figure 14-239 shows a redefinition of the state machine for the vending machine.

The dashed lines show states inherited from the base definition, and the solid lines show states and transitions added in the redefinition. Note that some states,

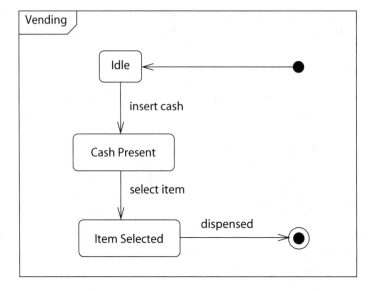

Figure 14-238. *Original state machine for redefinition*

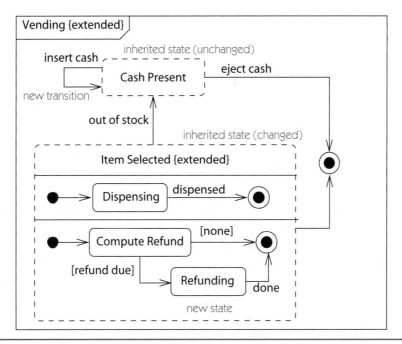

Figure 14-239. *State machine redefinition*

such as the initial state and **Idle**, are not shown because they have not changed. The transitions from **Idle** to **Cash Present** and from **Cash Present** to **Item Selected** are not shown because they have not changed.

The simple state Item Selected has been extended to be a composite state with two regions. It has an additional transition to **Cash Present** triggered by **out of stock**. Note that the transition triggered by **dispensed** is still present, but it is overridden by a transition with the same trigger within the composite state.

redefinition (template)

Semantics

A redefined template signature may add additional template parameters.

Presumably the element on which the template is based (such as classifier) may be specialized in the usual way, with other legal redefinitions.

Notation

None specified.

Discussion

It is probably a bad idea to actually redefine a template, because too many things would be happening simultaneously. The experience of C++ shows the danger of mixing templates, overloading, and inheritance.

reference

A denotation of a model element; often called a *pointer*, but no implementation should be assumed, in general.

Semantics

Model elements are connected by two metarelationships: ownership and reference. Ownership is the relationship between an element and its constituent parts, the parts that are defined within it and owned by it. The ownership relationship forms a strict tree. The contained elements are subordinate to the container element. Ownership, configuration control, and storage of models are based on the containment hierarchy.

Reference is a relationship between elements at the same level of detail or between elements in different containers. For example, reference is the relationship between an association and its participant classes, between an attribute and the class or data type that is its type property, or between a bound template and its argument values. For a reference to be possible, the element performing the reference must have visibility to the element being referenced. This requires that the element being referenced have a visibility setting that allows it to be seen outside its package, unless the source of the reference is in the same package.

Note that reference is an internal metamodel relationship, not a user-visible relationship; it is used to construct the other relationships.

refine (stereotype on Abstraction dependency)

A stereotype on dependency that denotes a refinement relationship.
See refinement.

refinement

A relationship that represents a fuller specification of something that has already been specified at a certain level of detail or at a different semantic level.
See abstraction.

Semantics

A refinement is a historical or computable connection between two elements with a mapping (not necessarily complete) between them. Often, the two elements are in different models. For example, a design class may be a refinement of an analysis class; it has the same logical attributes, but their classes may come from a specific class library. An element can refine an element in the same model, however. For example, an optimized version of a class is a refinement of the simple but inefficient version of the class. The refinement relationship may contain a description of the mapping, which may be written in a formal language (such as OCL or a programming or logic language). Or it may be informal text (which, obviously, precludes any automatic computation but may be useful in early stages of development). Refinement may be used to model stepwise development, optimization, transformation, and framework elaboration.

Structure

Refinement is a kind of abstraction dependency. It relates a client (the element that is more developed) to a supplier (the element that is the base for the refinement).

Notation

A refinement is indicated by a dependency arrow (a dashed arrow with its head on the more general element and tail on the more specific element) with the keyword «refine». The mapping may be attached to the dependency path by a dashed line connected to a note. Various kinds of refinement have been proposed and can be indicated by further stereotyping. In many cases, refinement connects elements in different models and will therefore not be visible graphically.

Example

Optimization is a typical kind of refinement. Figure 14-240 shows a chessboard that has a simple representation in the analysis model, but it has a much more elaborate and obscure representation in the design model. The design class is not a specialization of the analysis class, because it has a totally different form. The class in the analysis model and the one in the design model have the same name, because they represent the same concept at two different semantic levels.

Discussion

The distinction between refinement and realization is not clear in the UML specification, and it may be that refinement is an unnecessary redundancy without precise semantics.

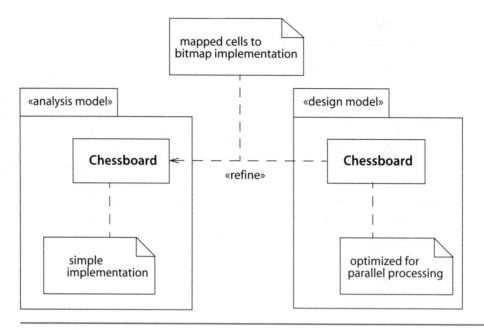

Figure 14-240. *Refinement*

region

A direct constituent of a composite state or a state machine, containing vertices (substates and pseudostates) and transitions forming a nested fragment of a state machine.

See composite state, state machine, transition, vertex.

Semantics

A region is a nested fragment of a state machine containing a connected set of states, pseudostates, and transitions. Transitions to and from other regions are also allowed. Regions are the direct constituents of composite states and state machines, so they are the structure permitting nested composition of state machines.

The direct substates of a region are mutually exclusive. If a region is active, exactly one direct substate is active. If a region contains (directly or indirectly) composite states, an active region may have multiple active indirect substates at deeper nesting levels.

If a region is part of a nonorthogonal state, it represents a sequential decomposition of the state. Only one direct substate may be active at once.

If a region is part of an orthogonal state, it represents a concurrent decomposition of the state. The other regions of the same orthogonal regions are its peer orthogonal regions. One direct substate from each orthogonal region is active when the orthogonal state is active.

Notation

The contents of a region are shown as a connected graph of state symbols and transition arrows. For a nonorthogonal state, the contents of its single region are simply nested within its state symbol. For an orthogonal state, its state symbol is divided into sections by dashed lines and each section shows the contents of a different region. The name of the region may be included in its section. See composite state for examples of notation.

Discussion

Compared to traditional state automata from computer science, regions provide the ability to define nested states and nested transitions, greatly reducing the number of transitions needed in complex systems. This ability was added by David Harel in his *statecharts*, which provide the foundation of most of the UML state machine concepts.

reification

The act of reifying something.
See reify.

reify

To treat as an object something that is not usually regarded as an object.

Discussion

Reification has a long-standing philosophical and literary meaning. It is used to describe the characterization of abstract concepts as things or persons in mythology and poetry. For example, the god Thor was a reification of thunder. Plato's theory of ideals turned things around from the prevalent perception. He regarded pure concepts, such as Beauty, Good, and Courage, as the true eternal reality, and regarded the physical instantiations as imperfect copies—reification carried to its ultimate limit.

Reification is one of the most useful ideas for object orientation, and it underlies almost every aspect of modeling. Building a model in the first place requires the imposition of objects onto a continuous world. Humans do this naturally in every sentence they speak—a noun is a reification of a thing and a verb is a reification of an action. Reification is particularly useful when applied to things in models or programs that do not start out treated as objects, such as dynamic behavior. Most persons think of an operation as an object, but what about the execution (the word itself is a reification) of an operation? Generally, people think of that as a process. But reify it and give it a name—call it an activation—and you can suddenly give it properties, form relationships to other objects, manipulate it, and store it. Reification of behavior transforms dynamic processes into data structures that can be stored and manipulated. This is a powerful concept for modeling and programming.

relationship

A reified semantic connection among model elements. This includes association and various kinds of directed binary relationships.

Semantics

Table 14-3 shows the various kinds of UML relationships. The first column (kind) shows the groupings under which they are arranged in the metamodel. The second column (variety) shows the different kinds of relationships. The third column (notation) shows the base notation for each relationship: Association is a solid path, dependency is a dashed arrow, and generalization is a solid path with triangular arrowhead. The fourth column (keyword) shows the text keywords and additional syntax for those relationships that require it.

reply action

An action whose execution passes values and restores control to the execution of a previous call action.
    See action.

repository

A storage place for models, interfaces, and implementations; part of an environment for manipulating development artifacts.

request

A data object sent to a target object as a signal.
    See send, signal.

Table 14-3: *UML Relationships*

Kind	*Variety*	*Notation*	- - - → *Keyword or Symbol*
abstraction	derivation	dependency	«derive»
	manifestation	dependency	«manifest»
	realization	realization	- - - - ▷
	refinement	dependency	«refine»
	trace dependency	dependency	«trace»
association		association	─────
binding		dependency	«bind» (parameter$_{list,}$)
deployment		dependency	«deploy» or physical nesting
extend		dependency	«extend» (extension point$_{list,}$)
extension		extension	──────▶
generalization		generalization	─────▷
import	private	dependency	«access»
	public	dependency	«import»
include		dependency	«include»
information flow		dependency	«flow»
package merge		dependency	«merge»
permission		dependency	«permit»
protocol conformance			none specified
substitution		dependency	«substitute»
usage	call	dependency	«call»
	creation	dependency	«create»
	instantiation	dependency	«instantiate»
	responsibility	dependency	«responsibility»
	send	dependency	«send»

required interface

See interface, port, provided interface.

Semantics

A required interface is a relationship between an interface and a classifier that de-clares the classifier requires the services described in the interface. The services must be made available by another classifier, usually as one of its provided inter-faces. Required and provided interfaces are complementary. If one class declares a provided interface and the other class requires the same interface, the classes can interact over the interface with no additional structure.

Notation

A required interface relationship is shown by a small half circle attached to a classi-fier (or a port on a classifier) by a line. The half circle is not a separate symbol, and it does not represent the interface itself. The name of the interface is placed near the half circle.

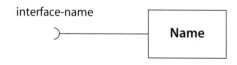

Figure 14-241. *Required interface notation*

requirement

A desired feature, property, or behavior of a system.

Semantics

A text requirement may be modeled as a comment.

Discussion

The term *requirement* is a natural language word that corresponds to a variety of UML constructs that are intended to specify the desired characteristics of a system. Most commonly, requirements corresponding to user-visible transactions will be captured as use cases. Nonfunctional requirements, such as performance and qual-ity metrics, may be captured as text statements that eventually trace to elements of the final design. UML comments and constraints may be used to represent non-functional requirements.

resolution

The mechanism of determining a behavioral effect for a call based on an operation and a target object.

Semantics

UML permits a wide range of processes for determining the effect of an event. The traditional object-oriented inheritance mechanisms of Smalltalk, C++, and Java are most familiar, but the definition of UML is intended to be broad enough to support alternate mechanisms, such as the object-based delegation of *self* or the multivariate polymorphism of CLOS. This generality is achieved by assuming a mechanism that converts the call of an operation on a target object into the determination of a behavior to be executed. This mechanism is called *resolution*. It is assumed that any specific UML model will provide a resolution mechanism, although no formal means is provided to define the mechanism within UML itself. The specific resolution mechanism is a semantic variation point of the modeling and execution environment.

The UML specification provides the following rules: The receipt of a call or a signal by an object is an event. The occurrence of an event may enable a transition of the state machine of the owning object if a trigger for the event appears in a transition leaving a state in the active state configuration. In addition to or instead of triggering a transition, an event may cause the execution of a behavior, such as a procedure. The outcome of the resolution process may produce a behavior that is to be executed with the parameters of the event.

The UML specification defines the rules of the *object-oriented resolution process,* which is the default resolution process and the one that corresponds to traditional object-oriented languages for calls of operations: The class of the target object is examined to find a method declaration attached to the called operation. A method is a behavior. If such a method is found in the class, the behavior is executed with the arguments of the call. If no method is found corresponding to the operation, the parent class is examined for a method corresponding to the operation, and so on upward in the generalization hierarchy until no method is found in the root class, in which case there is an error unless an accept action is outstanding for the operation. If any class has multiple parent classes, all of them are examined for matching methods, and if more than one method is found, there is an error. If the same method is found by searching along multiple paths due to multiple parents, however, it is not an error.

If a call both triggers a transition and resolves to a method, the method is executed and allowed to return values to the caller, and then the transition is allowed to fire asynchronously.

resolve

To undergo the resolution process when an event is handled by an object to produce a behavioral effect.
See resolution.

responsibility

A contract or obligation of a class or other element.

Semantics

Responsibility is an informal concept. A responsibility can be represented as a stereotype on a comment. The comment is attached to a class or other element that has the responsibility. The responsibility is expressed as a text string.

Notation

Responsibilities can be shown in a named compartment within a classifier symbol rectangle (Figure 14-242).

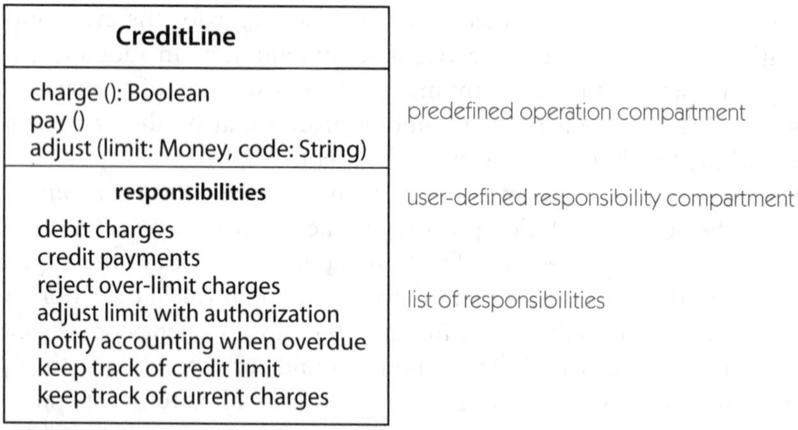

CreditLine
charge (): Boolean pay () adjust (limit: Money, code: String)
responsibilities
debit charges credit payments reject over-limit charges adjust limit with authorization notify accounting when overdue keep track of credit limit keep track of current charges

predefined operation compartment

user-defined responsibility compartment

list of responsibilities

Figure 14-242. *Compartment for responsibilities*

responsibility (stereotype on Usage)

A dependency expressing a contract or obligation of an element.
See responsibility.

return

There is no explicit return action. The return action is implicit. At the termination of execution of the behavior invoked by a synchronous call, output values of the behavior execution are assembled into a message that is conveyed to the execution of the call action, restoring control to it and providing return values.

See action.

return parameter

A parameter representing information produced as during the execution of a behavior and conveyed to the invoker of the behavior after completion of execution.

Semantics

The default parameter kinds are in (only) and return. Each of these passes information in a read-only by-value way.

Discussion

The use of out and inout parameters is a convenience for specific programming languages and should be avoided in modeling, because it causes tight linkage between the internal details of a behavior and the calling environment.

reuse

The use of a preexisting artifact.

Discussion

Reuse is often claimed to be the purpose of object-oriented technology, but this claim is overstated. Concepts such as polymorphic operations and encapsulation of internal structure are actually much more important benefits. Bear in mind that reuse can occur through other means than inheritance, including copying of code. One of the great errors in modeling is to force inappropriate generalization in an attempt to achieve reuse, which instead often causes confusion.

role

A constituent element of a structured classifier that represents the appearance of an instance (or, possibly, set of instances) within the context defined by the structured classifier.

See collaboration, connector, structured classifier.

Semantics

A role is the appearance of an individual within the context defined by a structured classifier. An instance of a collaboration does not own the objects that appear in its context; it merely references them, and they may appear in multiple collaboration contexts. An instance of a structured class does own its parts; they exist within its context and may not be part of another structured class.

A role differs from an association in that a role is tied to a particular classifier, and all the roles of a single classifier are implicitly related. The implicit relationship among roles within a given structured classifier may be explicitly modeled using connectors.

rolename

A name for a particular association end within an association.

The UML1 term *rolename* is not actually used in UML2, but as the official term *association end name* is somewhat unwieldy, we will continue to use the UML1 term for convenience, as many users undoubtedly will do.

Semantics

A rolename provides a name to identify an association end within an association, as well as to navigate from one object to another using the association. Because a rolename can be used in these two complementary ways, the name must be unique in two namespaces simultaneously.

All the rolenames in an association must be different. Within a self-association (an association involving the same class more than once), rolenames are necessary to disambiguate the ends attached to the same class. If there are multiple unnamed associations between a pair of classes, rolenames are needed to distinguish the associations, and they are needed in any case for navigation. Otherwise, rolenames are optional, because the class names can be used to disambiguate the ends. However, they are necessary for writing navigation expressions in languages such as OCL.

A rolename is also used to navigate from an object to neighboring related objects. Each class "sees" the associations attached to it and can use them to find objects related to one of its instances. By convention, the rolename on the association end attached to a neighboring class is used to form a navigation expression to access the object or collection of objects related by that association. In Figure 14-243, consider class B that is associated to class A by a one-to-many association and to class C by a one-to-one association. Given an object bb of class B, the expression bb.theA yields a set of objects of class A, and the expression bb.theC yields an object of class C. In effect, the rolename on the far side of a navigable association is an

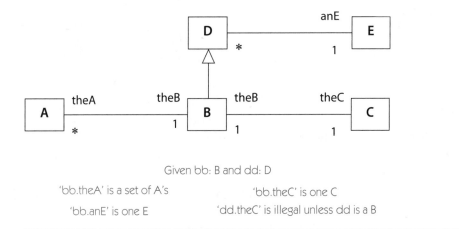

Given bb: B and dd: D

'bb.theA' is a set of A's   'bb.theC' is one C

'bb.anE' is one E   'dd.theC' is illegal unless dd is a B

Figure 14-243. *Navigation over associations*

attribute of a class—that is, it may be used as a term in an access expression to traverse the association.

Because a rolename can be used like an attribute name to extract values, a rolename enters the namespace of the class on the far side of the association. It goes in the same namespace as attribute names. Both attribute names and rolenames must be unique within that namespace. Attributes and association rolenames are inherited, and the attribute names and pseudoattribute names must be unique among inherited names also. A rolename attached to an ancestor class can be used for navigation in a descendant. In Figure 14-243, the expression **bb.anE** is legitimate, because class **B** inherits the rolename **anE** from class **D**.

Rolenames and association names are optional if each association can be uniquely identified. Either an association name or the rolenames on its ends can identify an association. It is not necessary to have both, although it is permitted to do so. If it is the only association between two classes, both the association name and the rolenames may be omitted. In principle, a rolename is required for a navigation expression. In practice, a tool may provide a default rule for creating implicit rolenames from the names of the associated classes.

Notation

A rolename is shown by a graphic string placed near the end of an association path, at which it meets a class box. If it exists, the rolename may not be suppressed.

The rolename may bear a visibility marker—an arrowhead—that indicates whether the element at the far end of the association can see the element attached to the rolename.

run time

The period of time during which a computer program executes. Contrast: modeling time.

run-to-completion

A transition or series of actions that must be completed in its entirety.
See also action, state machine, transition.

Semantics

A state machine conceptually undergoes a series of discrete steps over time in which it handles one occurrence at a time from a pool of events recognized by the object that owns the state machine. Occurrences of events recognized by the object are placed into the event pool. In general, the event occurrences in the pool are unordered, although profiles are free to define execution environments with various ordering or priority rules. During each step, the state machine selects an event from the pool (in the general case, nondeterministically) and then carries out the consequences of handling that event. The execution step may contain substeps, including concurrency. During an execution step, no other event is selected from the pool until the execution of the step in complete. Because one event at a time is processed until the effected behavior is complete, the execution step is call a *run-to-completion* step. If additional events occur during the run-to-completion step, they are placed into the event pool but they do not interrupt the execution step.

When a run-to-completion step starts, an event occurrence is selected from the event pool. In the general case, the occurrence is selected nondeterministically.

The event is matched against states in the active state configuration to enable transitions to fire. If multiple states are active, up to one transition per direct region of an orthogonal region may be enabled to fire. If multiple transitions are enabled within the same region, one of them is selected (nondeterministically) to fire.

Multiple transitions from orthogonal regions may fire concurrently. There is no assumption that they are serialized, and their actions may interleave. Good modeling ensures that orthogonal transitions do not interact.

The firing of each transition comprises the following steps:

1. The *common enclosing state* is the most specific state that contains both the source state and the target state of the transition. The current state is exited as a series of substeps until the current state is just inside the common enclosing state. During each change of state, the exit activity of the state being exited is executed.

2. Then the effect attached to the transition is executed.

3. Then states are entered as a series of substeps until the target state is reached. During each change of state, the entry activity of the state being entered is executed.

The transition is now complete.

When all transitions that fire are complete, the run-to-completion step is complete, and another event occurrence may be handled from the event pool.

Transition segments and pseudostates

A transition may be composed of multiple segments arranged as a chain and separated by pseudostates. Several chains may merge together or branch apart, so the overall model may contain a graph of segments separated by pseudostates. Only one segment in a chain may have a trigger event. The transition is triggered when the trigger event is handled by the state machine. If the guard conditions on all the segments are satisfied, the transition is enabled, and it fires, provided no other transition fires. The actions on the successive segments are executed. Once execution begins, the actions on all of the segments in the chain must be executed before the run-to-completion step is complete.

During execution of a run-to-completion transition, the trigger event that initiated the transition is available to actions as the current event. Entry and exit activities can therefore obtain the arguments of the trigger event. Various events may cause execution of an entry or exit activity, but an activity can discriminate the type of the current event.

Because of the run-to-completion semantics of transitions, they should be used to model assignments, testing flags, simple arithmetic, and other kinds of bookkeeping operations. Long computations should be modeled as interruptible activities or separate threads.

scenario

A sequence of actions that illustrates behavior. A scenario may be used to illustrate an interaction or the execution of a use case instance.

scope

The UML1 concept of owner scope and target scope has been simplified in UML2. Owner scope is modeled by the static feature flag on attributes and operations. Target scope has been abandoned as a concept.

script (stereotype of Artifact)

A file containing text that can be interpreted by a computer system.
See artifact.

sd

Tag on a diagram frame indicating a sequence diagram.

segment

A transition fragment that may include a pseudostate.

Semantics

A segment is a transition fragment that can include pseudostates. A compound transition is a transition between two states. It may be composed of a chain of segments. During execution of a system, a change of state must involve an entire compound transition. It is not possible for a pseudostate to remain active. Segments are therefore syntactic units to construct compound transitions and are transitions in name only.

self-transition

A transition in which the source state and the target state are the same. It is considered a state change. When it fires, the source state is exited and reentered, therefore exit actions and entry actions are invoked. It is not equivalent to an internal transition, in which no change of state occurs.

semantic variation point

A point of variation in the semantics of a metamodel. It provides an intentional degree of freedom for the interpretation of the metamodel semantics.

Discussion

The same execution semantics are not suitable for all possible applications. Different programming languages and different purposes require variations in semantics, some subtle, some gross. A semantic variation point is an issue on which various modelers or various execution environments disagree about the specific semantics, often for good reasons. By simply identifying and naming semantic variation points, arguments about the "right" semantics of a system can be avoided.

For example, the choice of whether to permit multiple classification or dynamic classification is a semantic variation point. Each choice is a semantic variation. Other examples of semantic variation points include whether a call can return more than one value and whether classes exist at run time as actual objects.

semantics

The formal specification of the meaning and behavior of something.

send

To create a message containing an object (often a signal) created by a sender object and to transfer it to a receiver object in order to convey information.

See also action, message, signal.

Semantics

A send action is an action that an object can perform as part of the execution of a behavior. It specifies a signal to send, a list of arguments or an object for the signal value, and a target object to receive the signal.

An object sends an object to another object. In many cases, the object is a signal, but any kind of object can be sent. The sender can embed the send action in a loop or expansion region to send a message to a set of objects. A broadcast action sends a message to the set of all objects, although, in practice, the set of target objects may be implementation dependent and may vary from node to node.

A send action is asynchronous. Once the message is launched toward the target object, the sender is free to continue execution concurrently with the transmission and subsequent handling of the message by the target object. There is no return information as part of a send message, because the sender continues execution and its state would be unknown. A call action should be used in situations where the sending object needs to block until a return value is received. The receiver of a message can later send a message to the original sending object if it has a handle to the object, but there is no inherent relationship between the two messages.

Messages are sent by value. A send parameter may only be an "in" parameter.

A send usage dependency is a stereotype of a usage dependency from the action or operation sending the signal to the type of the signal.

Create as send

Creating a new object may be regarded (conceptually) as sending a message to a factory object, such as a class, which creates the new instance and then passes the message to it as its "birth event." This provides a mechanism for a creator to communicate with its creation—the birth event may be regarded as going from the creator to the new object, with the side effect of instantiating the new object along the way. Figure 14-244 shows creation of an object using both text syntax and graphical syntax. This is an informal use of the send action and not officially approved.

This model can be used even if the target language, such as C++, does not support classes as run-time objects. In that case, the creation action is compiled (which imposes some restrictions on its generality—for example, the name of the class must be a literal value) but the underlying intent is the same.

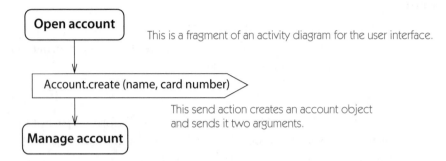

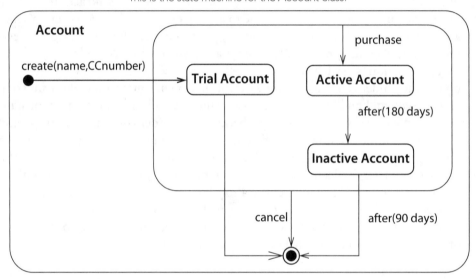

Figure 14-244. *Creation of new object by sending a message*

Text notation

Within a transition, sending a signal is an action that can be expressed in a specific expression language. For examples in this book, we use the syntax:

send target-object . signal-name (argument$_{list,}$)

Example

This internal transition selects an object within a window using the cursor location, and then it sends a **highlight** signal to it. The syntax is informal:

right-mouse-down (location) [location **in** window]
/ object := pick-object (location) ; **send** object.highlight ()

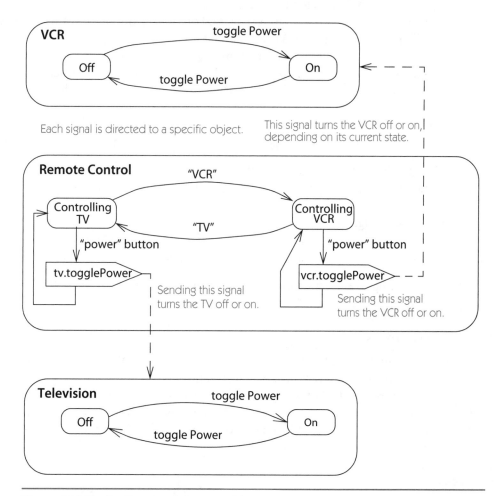

Figure 14-245. *Send action notation*

Figure 14-246. *Sending signals between objects*

Diagram notation

There is a graphical syntax to show a send action in a state machine or in an activity diagram. A convex pentagon containing the name of the signal may be included as part of a chain of actions connected by transition arrows (Figure 14-245).

In the UML specification, no syntax is given to specify the target object, but in this book we use the syntax:

target-object . signal-name (argument$_{list,}$)

There is no official graphical notation to show the target object, but we suggest the following use of the dependency notation: Sending a message between state machines may be shown by drawing a dashed dependency arrow from the send action to the receiving state machine. Figure 14-246 contains state diagrams showing the sending of signals between three objects.

Note that this notation may also be used on other kinds of diagrams to show the sending of events between classes or objects.

In a sequence diagram, sending a message is shown by drawing an arrow from the lifeline of the sending object to the lifeline of the receiving object. The arrowhead is open. The name and arguments of the signal are placed near the arrow. See message for examples.

send (stereotype of Usage dependency)

A dependency, the source of which is an operation or a classifier and the target of which is a signal, specifying that the client sends the signal to some unspecified target.

See send, signal.

send event

The sending of an event (usually a signal) by an object.

See signal event.

Semantics

Events can represent both the sending and the receipt of messages. Both kinds of events appear in interactions. As triggers, however, send events are less interesting than receipt events, because the sender can simply perform necessary actions are part of sending a message. Explicit implementation of send events might be useful, however, if behavior is to be triggered automatically without modifying the sending code.

sender

The object passing a message instance to a receiver object.

See call, send.

seq

1. Tag for a combined fragment within a sequence diagram representing weak sequencing.

2. Keyword on a multiplicity specification indicating that the elements of the set form an ordered sequence.

sequence diagram

A diagram that shows object interactions arranged in time sequence. In particular, it shows the objects participating in an interaction and the sequences of messages exchanged.

See also activation, collaboration, lifeline, message.

Semantics

A sequence diagram represents an interaction—a set of communications among objects arranged visually in time order. Unlike a communication diagram, a sequence diagram shows time sequences explicitly but does not include object relationships. It can exist in a descriptor form (describing all possible scenarios) and in an instance form (describing one actual scenario). Sequence diagrams and collaboration diagrams express similar (although not identical) information, but they show it in different ways.

Notation

A sequence diagram is shown in a rectangular frame with the string **sd** name in a small pentagon in the upper left corner. The name is the name of the interaction shown by the diagram. If the interaction has parameters, they are shown as a comma-separated list in parentheses following the name.

A sequence diagram has two dimensions: the vertical dimension represents time; the horizontal dimension represents objects participating in the interaction (Figure 14-247 and Figure 14-248). Generally, time proceeds down the page (the axes may be reversed if desired). Often, only the sequences of messages are important, but in real-time applications, the time axis can be an actual metric. There is no significance to the horizontal ordering of the objects.

Each participant is shown in a separate column called a lifeline. Each lifeline is a role within the interaction. During each execution of the interaction, the lifeline represents an object or set of objects. A rectangle is placed at the top of the diagram (if the object exists when the interaction begins) or at the point during the interaction where the object is created, at the end of a message arrow for the creation action. A line is drawn from the object symbol to the point at which the object is destroyed (if that happens during the time shown by the diagram). This line is called the lifeline. A large X is placed at the point at which the object ceases to exist, either at the head of the arrow for the message that destroys the object or at the point at which the object destroys itself. For any period during which the object is active, the lifeline is broadened to a double solid line. This includes the entire life of an active object or an activation of a passive object—a period during which an operation of the object is in execution, including the time during which the operation waits for the return of an operation that it called. If the object calls

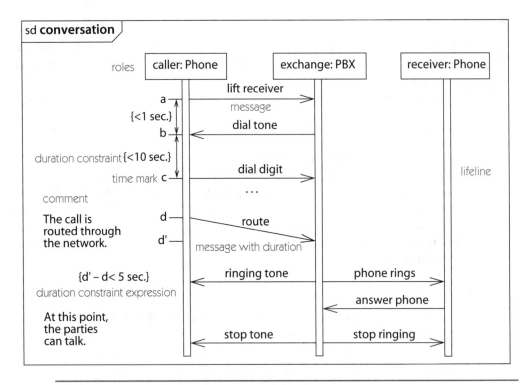

Figure 14-247. *Sequence diagram with asynchronous flow of control*

itself recursively, directly or indirectly, then another copy of the double solid line is overlapped on it to show the double activation (potentially it could be more than two copies). The relative ordering of objects has no significance, although it is helpful to arrange them to minimize the distance that message arrows must cover. A comment about the activation may be placed in the margin near it.

In the rectangle at the top of the lifeline, a string is placed with the syntax:

name⌊selector⌋$_{opt}$: Type

Either the name or the type (but not both) may be omitted. The name is the name of the role within the interaction. The selector is an expression to identify one element from a set if the multiplicity is greater than one; it is omitted if the multiplicity is one. The type is the type of the object.

To indicate a lifeline that is decomposed into an interaction, append the string:

ref interaction-name

to the string in the lifeline rectangle.

Each message is shown as a horizontal arrow from the lifeline of the object that sent the message to the lifeline of the object that received the message. A label may be placed in the margin opposite an arrow to denote the time at which the message is sent or received. The time label have a horizontal hash mark to show its exact location in the diagram.

In many models, messages are assumed to be instantaneous, or at least atomic. If a message requires some time to reach its destination, then the message arrow may be drawn diagonally downward so that the receiving end is lower than the sending time. Both ends can have labels to denote the time the message was sent or received.

For asynchronous flow of control among active objects, the objects are represented by double solid lines and the messages are shown as arrows. Two messages can be sent simultaneously, but two messages cannot be received simultaneously—there is no way to guarantee simultaneous reception. Figure 14-247 shows an asynchronous sequence diagram.

Figure 14-248 shows procedural flow of control on a sequence diagram. When modeling procedural flow of control, an object yields control on a call until a subsequent return. A synchronous call is shown with a solid filled arrowhead. The head of a call arrow may start an activation or a new object. A return is shown with a dashed line. The tail of a return arrow may finish an activation or an object.

Various flow-of-control constructs, such as conditionals, loops, and concurrent execution, may be shown by embedding a diagram fragment within the overall diagram. The diagram fragment includes a subset of the lifelines. It has an operator tag to indicate its purpose. Some kinds of fragments, such as conditionals, are divided into subregions by horizontal dashed lines. Each region is a subdiagram, and the relationship among the subregions is indicated by the fragment tag. For example, in a conditional, each branch is shown in a separate region. See combined fragment for a list of fragment kinds.

A state or condition of the lifeline may be shown as a small state symbol (rectangle with rounded corners) placed on the lifeline. The state or condition must be true at the time of the next event on the lifeline. Figure 14-249 shows the states during the life of a theater ticket. A lifeline may be interrupted by a state symbol to show a change of state. An arrow may be drawn to the state symbol to indicate the message that caused the change of state.

A state diagram can be parameterized so that it can be referenced from other state diagrams. A gate is a connection point on a state diagram for messages from outside. See Figure 14-141 for an example.

An interaction use is a reference to a state diagram within another state diagram. The reference can include a subset of the lifelines in the referencing diagram. See Figure 14-159 for an example. If the referenced state diagram has gates, the referencing diagram can connect messages to the interaction use symbol.

History

Much of the UML2 sequence diagram notation is drawn directly from the ITU Message Sequence Chart (MSC) notation, although it has been extended.

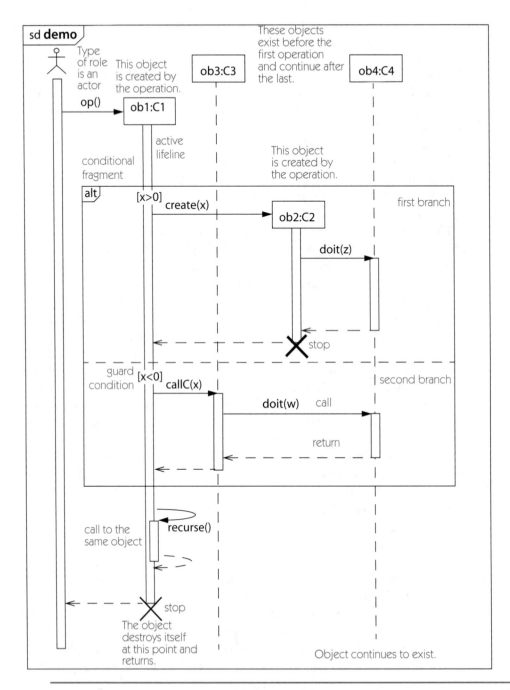

Figure 14-248. *Sequence diagram with procedural flow of control*

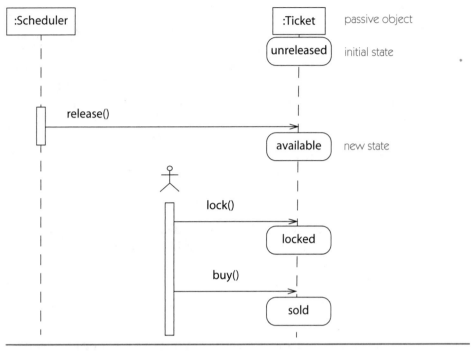

Figure 14-249. *Object states on a sequence diagram*

sequence number

A text part of a message label on a communication diagram that indicates the relative execution order of the messages in an interaction. A sequence number may show the location of the message within a nested calling sequence, the name of a thread of control, and a specification of conditional and iterative execution.

See collaboration, message.

service (stereotype of Component)

A stateless, functional component that returns a value rather than performing a side effect.

See component.

shared aggregation

An aggregation that does not represent ownership.

Semantics

One end of a binary association can be marked as being an aggregation, meaning that an instance of the class connected to the end is considered to be composed of parts that are instances of the class at the other end. An aggregation can be composite or shared. A composite aggregation conveys the sense of ownership. An object may be part of at most one composite aggregation. A shared aggregation does not have this restriction. An object can belong to many shared aggregations.

There are no precise semantics to shared aggregation except for the restriction that chains of aggregation links may not form a cycle. Modelers use shared aggregation in various ways to represent various semantic concepts.

Notation

Shared aggregation is shown by a hollow diamond on the end of an association line that is connected to the class representing the aggregate object (as opposed to its parts).

See association for details.

side effect

A computation that modifies the state or value of a system, as opposed to one that merely returns a value without making any permanent changes (a query).

signal

The specification of a block of information to be communicated asynchronously between objects. Signals have parameters expressed as attributes.

See also event, message, send.

Semantics

A signal is an explicit named classifier intended for explicit communication between objects. It has attributes that constitute its information. It is explicitly sent by an object to another object by a send action. A broadcast action sends a signal to the set of all objects—although, in practice, it would be implemented differently for efficiency. The sender specifies the attributes of the signal at the time it is sent, either as an argument list or by supplying a signal object whose attributes have already been initialized. Once a signal has been sent, the sender resumes execution concurrently with the transmission of the signal to the target. The receipt of a signal by its target object is an event that is intended to trigger transitions in the receiver's state machine or invoke asynchronous methods. A signal sent to a set of objects may trigger zero or one transition in each object independently. Signals are explicit means by which objects may communicate with each other asynchronously. To perform synchronous communication, two signals must be used, one in each direction.

Signals are classifiers. A signal may have a supertype. It inherits the attributes of the supertype and may add additional attributes of its own. A signal triggers any transition declared to use one of its ancestor signals.

A signal declaration has scope within the package in which it is declared. It is not restricted to a single class. Signals are declared independently of classes.

A class or interface may declare the signals it is prepared to handle. Such a declaration is a reception. A reception may specify a method to be executed on receipt of a signal.

A signal is a classifier and may have operations that may access and modify its attributes. These operations may be used by the sender to construct the signal object and by the receiver to access its value.

Notation

The stereotype keyword «signal» within an operation compartment indicates the declaration of a reception. The name of the signal may be followed by a list of its parameters (attributes) in parentheses. The declaration may not have a return type.

The declaration of a signal type may be expressed as a stereotype of a class symbol. The keyword «signal» appears in a rectangle above the name of the signal. The signal's parameters appear as attributes within the attribute compartment. The operation compartment may contain access operations.

A signal parameter is declared as an attribute that may have an initial value, which can be overridden during initialization or sending. The initial value is used if a signal instance is created, initialized, and then sent as an object. If a signal is sent using operation-calling syntax, the initial values of the signal's attributes are default values of the parameters in the call action.

Figure 14-250 shows the use of generalization notation to relate a child signal to its parent. The child inherits the parameters of its ancestors and may add additional parameters of its own. For example, the **MouseButtonDown** signal has the attributes **time**, **device**, and **location**.

To use a signal as a trigger of a transition, use the syntax

signal-name (parameter$_{list,}$)

A parameter has the syntax

parameter-name : type-expression

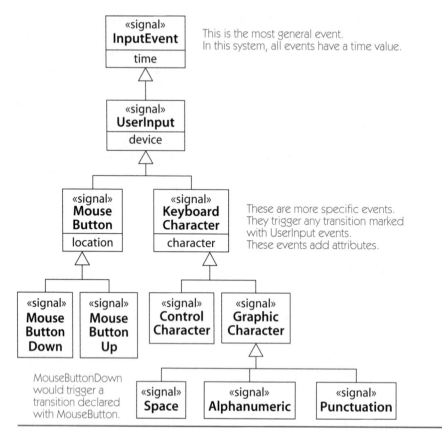

Figure 14-250. *Signal declarations*

Discussion

A signal is the most fundamental communication among objects, having simpler and cleaner semantics than do procedure calls. A signal is inherently a one-way asynchronous communication from one object to another in which all information is passed by value. It is a suitable model for communication in distributed, concurrent systems.

To build synchronous communication, use pairs of signals, one in each direction. A call may be viewed as a signal with an implicit return pointer parameter, although it embodies a fairly complicated mechanism.

signal event

An event that is the receipt by an object of a signal sent to it, which may trigger a transition in its state machine.

Semantics

More precisely, there are receive events and send events. The term *signal event* is often used loosely to mean *receive event* because state machines usually act on the receipt of messages from other objects. Both kinds of signal event are possible, however, under certain styles of systems.

signal trigger

A trigger whose event is a signal event.

signature

The name and parameter properties of a behavioral feature, such as an operation or signal. A signature may include optional return types (for operations, not for signals).

Semantics

The signature of an operation is part of its declaration. Some (but not all) of the signature is used for matching operations and methods to check for conflict or overriding. The details of what is included for matching and what is excluded may be language specific. If two signatures match but the remaining properties are inconsistent (for example, an **in** parameter corresponds to an **out** parameter), then the declarations conflict and the model is ill formed.

simple state

A state that has no nested states within it. A set of nested states forms a tree and the simple states are the leaves. A simple state has no substructure. It may have internal transitions, an entry activity, an exit activity, and a do activity. Contrast: composite state, submachine state.

simple transition

A transition with one source state and one target state. It represents a response to an event with a change of state within a region of mutually exclusive states. The amount of concurrency does not change as a result of executing it.

Contrast: complex transition, compound transition.

single classification

An execution regime in which each object has exactly one direct class. This is the execution model in most object-oriented programming languages. Whether to allow single classification or multiple classification is a semantic variation point.

single inheritance

A semantic variation of generalization in which an element may have only one parent. Whether to allow single inheritance or multiple inheritance is a semantic variation point. The default is to allow multiple inheritance.

singleton

A class that has (by declaration) exactly one instance. A singleton is a way to represent global knowledge in an application, yet keep it within an object-oriented framework.

Semantics

Every application must have at least one singleton class (often implicitly) to establish the context for the application. Often, the singleton class equates to the application itself and is implemented by the control stack and address space on a computer.

A singleton must exist within a context declaring its scope, such as a structured class or component. Often the context is a structured class representing the complete system.

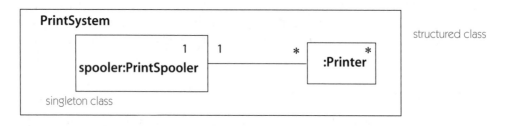

Figure 14-251. *Singleton class*

Notation

A singleton is shown as a class symbol with a small '1' in the upper right corner (Figure 14-251). This value represents the multiplicity of the class within the cotext. A singleton must exist within a context. The notation can be used within a class diagram with the understanding that there is an implied execution context.

slot

A place in an object or other instance for a value.

snapshot

A collection of objects, links, and values that forms the configuration of a system at an instant during its execution.

source (stereotype of Artifact)

A file containing the text of a program that can be compiled into executable code. See file.

source scope

This UML1 concept has been replaced by static feature.

source state

The state within a state machine from which a transition departs. The transition applies to the source state. If the active state configuration includes the source state or a state nested within it, then the transition is a candidate for firing.

specialization

To produce a more specific description of a model element by adding features, relationships, constraints, and other items to an original model element. The opposite relationship is generalization, which is also used as the name of the relationship between the more specific element and the more general element, as there is no good term for the relationship that is undirected. A child element is the specialization of a parent element. Conversely, the parent is the generalization of the child.
See generalization.

specification

A declarative description of what something is or does. For example, a use case or an interface is a specification. Contrast: implementation.

specification (stereotype of Classifier)

A classifier that describes a domain of objects without providing a physical implementation. Typically it describes interfaces or constraints on the objects without listing their features. See realization, specification.

stages of modeling

Development states an element or a model goes through during the process of designing and building a system.

See also development process.

Discussion

The overall development effort can be divided into activities focused on different ends. These activities are not performed in sequence; rather, they are performed iteratively during the phases of the development process. Analysis deals with capturing requirements and understanding the needs of a system. Design deals with devising a practical approach to the problem within the constraints of data structures, algorithms, and existing system pieces. Implementation deals with constructing the solution in an executable language or medium (such as a data base or digital hardware). Deployment deals with putting the solution into practice in a specific physical environment. These divisions are somewhat arbitrary and not always clear, but they remain useful guidelines.

These views of development should not be equated with sequential phases of the development process, however. In the traditional Waterfall Process they were indeed treated as distinct phases. In a more modern iterative development process, however, they are not distinct phases. At a given point in time, development activities may exist at various levels, and they may best be understood as different tasks that need to be performed on each element of the system, not all at the same time.

Think of a group of buildings, each with a foundation, walls, and roof; all of them must be completed for all of the buildings, but not all at the same time. Usually, the parts of each building are completed more or less in order. Sometimes, however, the roof can be started before all the walls are complete. Occasionally, the distinction between walls and roof is lost—consider a dome set on the ground.

UML contains a range of constructs suitable for various stages of development. Some constructs (such as association and state) are meaningful at all stages. Some constructs (such as navigability and visibility) are meaningful during design but represent unnecessary implementation detail during analysis. This does not preclude their definition at an early stage of work. Some constructs (such as specific programming-language syntax) are meaningful only during implementation and impair the development process if introduced prematurely.

Models change during development. A UML model takes a different form at each stage of development, with a varying emphasis on different UML constructs. Modeling should be performed with the understanding that not all constructs are useful at all stages.

See development process for a discussion of the relationship of modeling stages and development phases.

start owned behavior action

An action whose execution starts execution of the main behavior attached to an object. See action.

state

A condition or situation during the life of an object during which it satisfies some condition, performs some do activity, or waits for some event.

See also action, activity, composite state, do activity, entry activity, exit activity, final state, internal transition, pseudostate, state machine, submachine state, transition.

Semantics

An object holds a series of states during its lifetime. When an object satisfies the condition of a state, the state is said to be active. The active state configuration is the set of states that are active at any point in time. If it contains more than one state, there is concurrency within the object. The number of active states can change during the life of an object due to forks or joins of control.

An object remains in a state for a finite (noninstantaneous) time. Dummy states may be introduced for convenience, which perform trivial actions and exit. But these are not the main purpose of states, and dummy states can, in principle, be eliminated, although they are useful for avoiding duplication.

States are contained in a state machine that describes how the history of an object evolves over time in response to events. Each state machine describes the behavior of the objects of a class. Each class may have a state machine. A transition describes the response of an object in a state to the occurrence of a an event: The object executes an optional activity attached to the transition and changes to a new state. Each state has its own set of transitions.

An activity may be attached to a transition. When the trigger of the transition is satisfied, the transition fires and the activity is executed, then the source state is deactivated and the target state is activated. An activity may contain nested activities, ultimately being composed of atomic actions.

An ongoing do activity may be associated with a state. The do activity is executed as long as the state is active. Alternately, ongoing activity may be modeled by a pair of actions, an entry activity that starts the do activity on entry to the state, and an exit activity that terminates the do activity on exit from the state.

A state may be a simple state, a composite state, or a submachine state. A simple state has no nested substates. A composite state contains one or more regions, each of which has one or more nested substates. A submachine state has a reference to a state machine definition, which is conceptually expanded in place of the submachine state.

States may be grouped together into composite states. Any transition on a composite state applies to all of the states nested within it, so events that affect many substates can be modeled by a single transition. A composite state has one or more regions, each of which contains one or more substates. If a composite state is active, each of its regions is active. A composite state can be nonorthogonal or orthogonal. A nonorthogonal state has a single region. Only one direct substate of a nonorthogonal state is active at a time. One direct substate from each region of an orthogonal state is active concurrently. An orthogonal state models concurrency.

To promote encapsulation, a composite state may contain initial states and final states. These are pseudostates, the purpose of which is to help structure the state machine. A transition to the composite state is equivalent to a transition to the initial state of each of its regions, but the state can be used externally without knowledge of its internal structure.

A transition to a final state of a region of a composite state represents the completion of activity in the region. In an orthogonal state, each of its regions must reach their final states for the execution of the entire state to be complete. Completion of activity in a composite state triggers a completion transition on the enclosing state to fire. A completion transition is a transition with no explicit trigger event (or, more precisely, one with the completion event as its implicit trigger, although it is not explicitly modeled). Completion of the outermost state of an object corresponds to its death.

If a state is an orthogonal state, then all its regions must complete before the completion event on the composite state occurs. In other words, a completion transition from a composite concurrent state represents a join of control from all its concurrent subthreads. It waits for all of them to complete before proceeding.

In a protocol state machine, a state represents the quiescent interval between the execution of operations. The activity of a state indicates the operations that may legally be called at that point in the protocol.

Structure

A state has the following parts.

Name. The name of the state, which must be unique within the enclosing state. The name can be omitted, producing an anonymous state. Any number of distinct anonymous states can coexist. A nested state can be identified by its qualified name (if all the enclosing states have names).

Substates. If a state machine has nested substructure, it is called a composite state. A composite state contains one or more regions, each of which contains one or more direct substates. A state with no substructure (except possible internal actions) is a simple state. A state that references another state machine definition is a submachine state.

Entry and exit activities. A state may have an entry activity and an exit activity. The purpose of these activities is to encapsulate the state so that it can be used externally without knowledge of its internal structure. An entry activity is executed when the state is entered, after any activity attached to the incoming transition and before any internal do activity. An exit action is executed when the state is exited, after the completion of any internal do activity and before any activity attached to the outgoing transition. On a transition that crosses several state boundaries, several exit and entry actions may be executed in a nested fashion. First, exit activities are executed, starting with the innermost state and progressing to the outermost state; then the activity on the transition is executed; and then entry activities are executed, starting with the outermost and finishing with the innermost. Figure 14-252 shows the result of firing a transition across state boundaries. Entry and exit activities may not be evaded by any means, including the occurrence of exceptions. They provide an encapsulation mechanism for the specification of state machine behavior, with a guarantee that necessary activities will be performed under all circumstances.

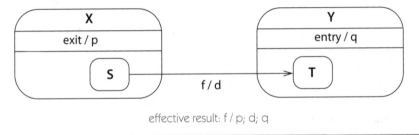

effective result: f / p; d; q

Figure 14-252. *Transition across state boundaries, with exit and entry actions*

Internal do activity. A state may contain an internal do activity described by an expression. When the state is entered, the do activity begins after the entry activity is complete. If the do activity terminates, the state is complete. A completion transition that departs the state is then triggered. Otherwise, the state waits for a triggered transition to cause a change of state. If a transition fires while the do activity is being performed, the do activity is terminated and the exit activity on the state is executed.

Internal transitions. A state may have a list of internal transitions, which are like normal transitions except that they do not have target states and do not cause a change of state. If its event occurs while an object is in the state owning the transition or a nested substate of it, then the action on the internal transition is executed, but no change of state occurs nor are entry or exit actions executed. There is no change of state even if the active state is nested within the state containing the internal transition.

This differentiates it from a self-transition, modeled as an external transition from a state to the same state. In this case, if the active state is a substate of the state with the self-transition, the final state is the target state of the transition, which forces the execution of each exit activity of the states nested within the state with the self-transition, the execution of its exit activity, and the execution of its entry activity. The actions are executed even on a self-transition to the current state, which is exited and then reentered. If a self-transition on an enclosing state of the current state fires, then the final state is the enclosing state itself, not the current state. In other words, a self-transition may force an exit from a nested state, but an internal transition does not.

Submachine. The body of a state may represent a copy of a separate state machine referenced by name. The referenced state machine is called a submachine because it is nested within the larger state machine, and the state making the reference is called a submachine state. A submachine may be attached to a class that provides the context for actions within it, such as attributes that may be read and written. A submachine is intended to be reused in many state machines to avoid repetition of the same state machine fragment. A submachine is a kind of state machine subroutine.

Within the submachine state, the submachine is referenced by name with a possible argument list. The name must be the name of a state machine that has an initial and final state or explicit entry point and exit point states. If the submachine has parameters on its initial transition, then the argument list must have matching arguments. When the submachine state is entered, its entry action is performed first, then execution of the submachine begins with its initial state. When the submachine reaches its final state, any exit action in the submachine state is performed. The submachine state is then considered completed and may take a transition based on implicit completion of activity.

A transition to a submachine state activates the initial state of the target submachine. But sometimes a transition to a different state in the submachine is desired. A entry point is a pseudostate placed within a submachine that identifies a state within the submachine. Transitions can be connected to a connection point on the submachine state that matches the entry point in the state machine definition. The transition actually goes to the internal state identified by the entry point, but the external transition need know nothing about the internal structure of the state machine. Similar connections can be made to entry points.

A submachine represents nested, interruptible activity within a state. It is equivalent to replacing the submachine state with a unique copy of the submachine. Instead of supplying a state machine, a procedural expression can be attached to the submachine (this is a do activity). A do activity can be regarded as defining a series of states, one per primitive expression, that is interruptible and can accept events between any two steps. It is not the same as an effect attached to a transition, which has substructure but does not accept events during execution because it obeys run-to-completion semantics.

Deferrable events. A deferrable event is an event whose recognition in the state is postponed if it does not trigger a transition, so that it is not lost. This allows a limited critical region capability, in which certain events can be processed without losing other events. The recognition of a deferred event is postponed as long as the active state declares it as deferrable. When the active state configuration includes a state in which the event is not deferred, it is processed. The implementation of such deferred events would involve an internal queue of events.

Redefined states. States may be defined when defining a state machine for a subclass. See redefinition (state machine).

Notation

A state is shown as a rectangle with rounded corners. It may have one or more compartments. The compartments are optional. The following compartments may be included.

Name compartment. Holds the (optional) name of the state as a string. States without names are anonymous and are all distinct. It is undesirable to repeat the same named state symbol twice in the same diagram, however, as it is confusing.

The name may optionally be placed within a rectangular tab attached to the upper side of the state symbol. This notation is particularly useful with composite states, because the name is clearly distinguished from the names and contents of the nested regions.

Nested region. Shows a state diagram fragment of a region as composed of subordinate nested states. The state diagram fragment is drawn within the boundary of the outer state. Transitions may connect directly to nested states, as well as to the boundary of the outer state. Within a nonorthogonal state, the substates are drawn directly inside the composite state. In an orthogonal state, the composite state symbol is divided into regions by dashed lines (that is, it is tiled), and one state machine fragment is shown within each region.

See composite state for details and examples.

Internal transition compartment. Holds a list of internal actions or activities performed in response to events received while the object is in the state, without changing state. An internal transition has the format

$$\text{event-name}_{opt} \, \lfloor (\, \text{argument}_{list,} \,) \rfloor_{opt} \, \lfloor [\, \text{guard-condition} \,] \rfloor_{opt}$$
$$\lfloor /\, \text{activity-expression} \rfloor_{opt}$$

Activity expressions may use attributes and links of the owning object and parameters of incoming transitions (if they appear on all incoming transitions).

The argument list (including parentheses) may be omitted if there are no parameters. The guard condition (including brackets) and the action expression (including slash) are optional.

Entry and exit actions have the same form but use reserved words **entry** and **exit** that cannot be used for event names.

entry / activity-expression

exit / activity-expression

Entry and exit activities may not have arguments or guard conditions (because they are invoked implicitly, not explicitly). To obtain parameters on an entry action, the current event may be accessed by an action. This is particularly useful for obtaining the creation parameters by a new object.

The reserved activity name **defer** indicates an event that is deferrable in a state and its substates. The internal transition must not have a guard condition or actions.

event-name / defer

The reserved word **do** represents an expression for a nonatomic do activity.

do / activity-expression

Submachine state. The invocation of a nested submachine is shown by a name string of the following form:

state-name : Machine-name

An entry point connection is shown by a small circle on the boundary of the submachine state symbol (Figure 14-253). A transition can be connected from a state to the entry point connection. An exit point connection is shown by a small circle containing an X on the boundary of the state symbol. A transition can be connected from the exit point connection to another state. See connection point.

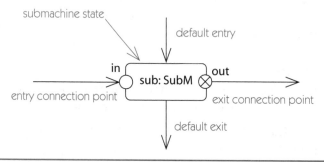

Figure 14-253. *Submachine state*

Example

Figure 14-254 shows a state with internal transitions. Figure 14-255 shows the declaration and use of a submachine.

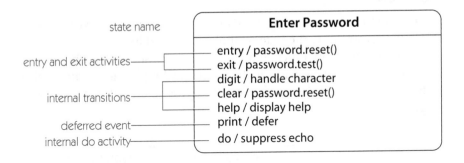

Figure 14-254. *Internal transitions, with entry and exit actions and deferred event*

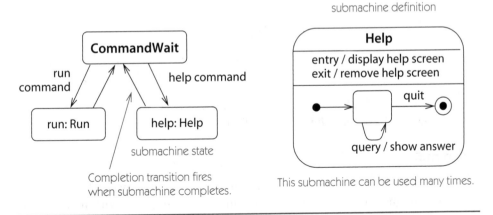

Figure 14-255. *Submachine*

state invariant

A condition that must be true when a given state is active.

Semantics

A state invariant is an assertion that a given constraint must be true when a certain state is active. If it is not true, the model is in error. The constraint may depend on the object whose state is active, as well as values reachable from the object or global values.

A state invariant may also be placed on a lifeline within an interaction. The interval between occurrence specifications is equivalent to a state. In this usage, the constraint is evaluated at the point when the next event occurs on the lifeline.

Notation

A state invariant on a state may be shown by attaching a comment containing the text of the constraint to the state symbol by a dashed line.

A state invariant on a lifeline may be shown by superimposing the text of the constraint (in curly braces) over the lifeline or by placing a state symbol (small rectangle with rounded corners) containing the name of a state on the lifeline (Figure 14-256).

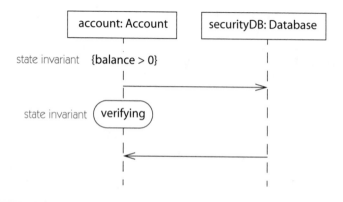

Figure 14-256. *State invariants on lifeline*

state machine

A specification of the sequences of states that an object or an interaction goes through in response to events during its life, together with its responsive effects (action and activity). A state machine is attached to a source class, collaboration, or method and specifies the behavior of the instances of the source element.

See also action, activity, composite state, event, pseudostate, state, transition.

Semantics

A state machine is a graph of states and transitions that describes the response of an instance of a classifier to the receipt of events. State machines may be attached to classifiers, such as classes and use cases, as well as to collaborations and methods. The element that the state machine is attached to is called the *owner* of the state machine.

An entire state machine is a composite state that has been decomposed recursively into substates. The innermost simple states have no substates. A state machine may include a reference to another state machine using a submachine state.

State machines can be redefined. See redefinition (state machine).

State machine execution semantics

The semantics of state machine execution are discussed in the following sections. There are many ways to implement these semantics, many of which compile away some of the explicit steps described here. Most of these semantics are described in other articles, but they are gathered here for convenience.

At any moment, one or more states are active in the active state configuration of the state machine of an object or other instance. If a state is active, then a transition leaving the state may fire, causing the execution of an action and the activation of another state or states in place of the original state. More than one active leaf state indicates internal concurrency. The structure of the state machine and its transitions impose constraints on the states that can be active concurrently. Briefly, if a composite state is active, exactly one direct substate must be active in each region of the composite state. Because a composite state may have multiple regions, a number of indirect substates may be active in the nested state machine.

Transition firing and actions

The basic assumption is that a state machine processes one event at a time and finishes all the consequences of that event before processing another event. In other words, events do not interact with other events during event processing. This is known as run-to-completion processing. It does not mean that all computation is noninterruptible. An ordinary extended computation can be broken into a series of run-to-completion steps, and the computation can be interrupted by an outside event between any steps. This is very close to the physical situation within a computer, where interrupts can occur at discrete, but small, steps.

A corollary assumption is that events are asynchronous. Two events never occur at exactly the same time—or, more precisely, if two events occur at the exact same time, it is a coincidence and they can be processed as if they had occurred in either order, with no loss of generality. The results of the different orders of execution may be different—race conditions are an essential property of concurrent systems—but you may not assume simultaneity in a distributed world. Any computation making such an assumption is logically and physically flawed. Concurrent execution requires independence in a distributed world.

Actions and activities. Conceptually, actions are instantaneous and events are never simultaneous. In an implementation, execution of actions requires some time, but the important thing is that actions are (conceptually) atomic and non-interruptible. An activity may be decomposed into subactivities and ultimately actions. Activities attached to transitions are executed using run-to-completion semantics. If an object recognizes an event while it is executing a run-to-completion step, the event occurrence is placed in an event pool until the execution of the run-to-completion step is complete. Event occurrences are removed from the event pool only when no actions are being executed. If the action of an object sends a signal to another object, then the reception of the signal is not synchronous. It is placed in the event pool and then handled like any other event, after the completion of any current run-to-completion activity attached to the current transition. A call to an operation suspends the caller until the operation has been executed. It may be implemented, at the choice of the receiver, as a method or as a call event that triggers the state machine of the receiver. To avoid problems with long periods during which events cannot be processed, effects attached to transitions should be brief. Transition activities are not intended for modeling protected regions or long interruptible computations, which can be modeled as nested do activity states. This permits event processing and permits nested computations to be interrupted. If long activities are included in real systems, events may not be processed in a timely manner. This is a consequence of a bad model. Activities must be short, compared to the required response time to events that might occur.

When a transition fires, any activity attached to it is executed. An activity may use the arguments of the triggering event, as well as attributes of the owning object or values reachable from it. An activity is completed before any additional events are processed. If a transition has multiple segments, the parameters of the trigger event are available as the implicit current event.

During the execution of a run-to-completion step, all activities have access to an implicit current event, which is the event that triggered the first transition in the run-to-completion sequence. Because there may be more than one event that could result in the execution of an activity, the activity may need to discriminate on the type of the current event to extract its values.

Event pool. New event occurrences are placed in an event pool for an object. If an object is idle and there are no event occurrences in the pool, the object waits until it receives an event and then handles it. Conceptually, an object handles a single event occurrence at a time. In an actual implementation, events might be queued in a definite order. UML semantics, however, do not specify an order of processing concurrent events, and a modeler should not assume one. If events must be processed in a certain order, the state machine should be constructed to enforce the order. A physical implementation would probably select some simple ordering rule.

Triggers. For each active state of an object, the outgoing transitions of the state are candidates to fire. A candidate transition is triggered if an event is handled whose type is the same as the trigger event on the transition. A signal that is a descendant of a signal in a transition trigger will trigger the transition. A transition is not triggered by an ancestor signal. When an event is handled and triggers a transition, the guard condition of the transition is evaluated. If the value of the guard condition is true, then the transition is enabled. The guard condition Boolean expression may involve arguments of the trigger event, as well as attributes of the object. Note that guard expressions must not produce side effects. That is, they may not alter the state of the object or the rest of the system. Therefore, the order in which they are evaluated is irrelevant to the outcome. A guard condition is evaluated only when an event is handled. If the guard condition evaluates to false, it is not reevaluated if some of its variables change value later. An event may be a candidate to trigger several transitions with different guard conditions, but if all the guard conditions fail, the event is discarded and no transition fires. Another event occurrence is then selected from the event pool.

Pseudostates. To structure complex conditions, a transition may be modeled with multiple segments. The first segment has a trigger event and is followed by a branching tree of segments with guard conditions. The intermediate nodes in the tree are pseudostates, dummy states that are present for structuring the transitions but that may not remain active at the end of a run-to-completion step. Each possible path through the tree of segments is regarded as a separate transition and is independently eligible for execution. An individual segment may not fire alone. All the guard conditions along a series of segments must be true or the transition (including any of its segments) does not fire at all. In practice, guard conditions at a branch point often partition the possible outcomes. Therefore, an implementation could process the multisegment transition one step at a time, but not always.

Usually the trigger is placed on the first segment of a path, but it may also follow a join or a junction pseudostate. A path may have at most one trigger.

There is a slight difference if one of the pseudostates is a choice pseudostate. In that case, the chain of transition segments is evaluated up to, but not including, the choice. If the guard conditions are true, the transition fires and the activities attached to the segments up to the choice pseudostate are executed and may change the values of objects in the system. The guard conditions on transition segments departing the choice pseudostate are then evaluated and one of them is selected for firing, based on the values that may include changes made by previous activities on the transition. One of the transitions must fire; if all the guard conditions are false, the model is ill formed. A choice allows the results of some actions on the transition to affect later decisions on the same transition, but all possible outcomes must be covered by the modeler.

Nondeterminism. If no transition is enabled, an event is simply ignored. This is not an error. If exactly one transition is enabled, it fires. If more than one transition from a single state is enabled, then only one of them fires. If no constraint is specified, then the choice is nondeterministic. No assumptions should be made that the choice will be fair, predictable, or random. An actual implementation may provide rules for resolving conflicts, but modelers are advised to make their intent explicit rather than rely on such rules. Whether or not any transition fires, the event is consumed.

Transitions on composite states. The transitions leaving an active state are eligible for firing. In addition, transitions on any composite state containing an active state are candidates for firing. This may be regarded as similar to the inheritance of transitions by nested states (although it is not modeled as generalization). A transition on an outer state is eligible to fire only if no transition on an inner state fires. Otherwise, it is masked by the inner transition.

Concurrently active states. At the time that an object handles an event, its active state configuration may contain one or more states. Each state receives a separate copy of the event and acts on it independently. Transitions in concurrently active states fire independently. One substate can change without affecting the others, except in the case of a complex transition, such as a fork or join (described later).

If an object has concurrent states, then they should not interact through shared memory. Concurrent states are meant to be independent and should act on different sets of values. Any interactions should be explicit by sending signals. If two concurrent states must access a shared resource, they should explicitly send signals to the resource, which can then act as an arbiter. An implementation may compile away such explicit communication, but care must then be taken to ensure that meaningless or dangerous conflicts do not ensue. If concurrent actions do access shared values, the result is nondeterministic.

If the active state configuration contains multiple states, the same process may occur independently for each state. In many cases, however, only one state from the set may be affected by a given transition.

Entry and exit activities. If a transition crosses the boundary of a composite state, the entry activity or exit activity on the composite state may be executed. A boundary crossing occurs when the source state and target state on the transition itself are in different composite states. Note that an internal transition does not cause a change of state, so it never invokes entry or exit activities.

To determine the exit and entry activities that are executed, find the current active state of the object (this might be nested within the composite state that is the source of the transition) and the target state of the transition. Then find the innermost composite state that encloses both the current state and the target state. Call this the *common ancestor*. The exit activities of the current state and any enclosing states up to, but not including, the common ancestor are executed, innermost first. Then the activity on the transition is executed. After that, the entry activities of the target state and any enclosing states up to, but not including, the common ancestor are executed, outermost first. In other words, states are exited one at a time until the common ancestor is reached, and then states are entered until the target state is reached. The exit and entry activities on the common ancestor are not executed, because it has not changed. This procedure ensures that each state is strongly encapsulated.

The activity on the transition is executed after any exit activities have been executed and before any entry activities are performed.

Note that the firing of a self-transition (a transition from a state to itself) will cause the exit of any nested states within the source state that may be active (the transition may have been inherited from an enclosing composite state). It also causes the execution of the exit activity of the source state followed by the execution of its entry activity. In other words, the state is exited and then reentered. If this effect is not desired, then an internal transition in the state should be used instead. This will not cause a change of state, even if the active state is nested within the state with the transition.

Chains of segments. A transition may be structured with several segments whose intermediate nodes are junctions. Each segment may have its own activity. The activities may be interleaved with entry and exit activity for the overall transition. With respect to entry and exit activities, each action on a transition segment occurs where it would occur if the segment were a complete transition. See Figure 14-170 for an example.

Next state. After all the activities are performed, the original current state is inactive (unless it is the target state), the target state of the transition is active, and additional events can then be processed.

Internal transitions

An internal transition has a source state but no target state. Its firing does not cause a change of state, even if the transition that fires is inherited from an enclosing state. Because the state does not change, no exit or entry activities are performed. The only effect of an internal transition is the execution of its activity. The conditions for firing an internal transition are exactly the same as for an external transition.

Note that the firing of an internal transition may mask an external transition using the same event. Therefore, there can be a purpose for defining an internal transition with no activity. As stated above, only one transition fires per event within a sequential region, and an inner transition has priority over an outer transition.

Internal transitions are useful for processing events without changing state.

Initial and final states

For encapsulation of states, it is often desirable to separate the inside of a state from the outside. It is also desirable to connect transitions to a composite state, without knowing about the internal structure of the state. This can be accomplished using initial states and final states within a composite state.

A state may have an initial and a final state. An initial state is a pseudostate—a dummy state with the connectivity of normal states—and an object may not remain in an initial state. An object may remain in a final state, but a final state may not have any explicit triggered transitions; its purpose is to enable a completion transition on an enclosing state. An initial state may not remain active; it must have an outgoing completion transition. If there is more than one outgoing transition, then they must all lack triggers and their guard conditions must partition the possible values. In other words, exactly one outgoing transition must fire when the initial state is invoked. An object may never remain in the initial state, therefore, but will immediately transition to a normal state.

If a composite state has an initial state, then transitions may be connected directly to the composite state as target. Any transition to the composite state is implicitly a transition to the initial state within the composite state. If a composite state lacks an initial state, then the composite state may not be the target of transitions; they must be connected directly to substates. A state with an initial state may also have transitions connected directly to inner states, as well as to the composite state.

If a composite state has a final state, then it may be the source of one or more outgoing completion transitions, that is, transitions that lack explicit event triggers. A completion transition is really a transition that is implicitly enabled by the completion of do activity within the state. A transition to a final state is therefore a statement that execution of the composite state is complete. When an object transitions to a final state, the completion transitions leaving its enclosing composite state are enabled to fire if their guard conditions are satisfied.

A composite state may have labeled outgoing transitions—that is, transitions with explicit event triggers. If an event occurs that causes such a transition to fire, then any ongoing activity within the state (at any nesting depth) is terminated, the exit actions of the terminated nested states are executed, and the transition is processed. Such transitions are often used to model exceptions and error conditions.

Complex transitions

A transition into an orthogonal state implies a transition into all its orthogonal regions. This can happen in two ways.

A transition may have multiple target states, one within each region of an orthogonal state. Note that such a forking transition still has a single trigger event, guard condition, and activity. This is an explicit transition into an orthogonal state that specifies each target directly. This represents an explicit fork of control into concurrent substates.

Alternately, a transition may omit targets within one or more regions of an orthogonal state, or it may have the composite state itself as the target. In this case, each omitted orthogonal region must have an initial state within it to indicate its default initial state. Otherwise, the state machine is ill formed. If the complex transition fires, the explicit target substates become active, as do the initial states of the orthogonal regions without explicit targets. In short, any transition into any orthogonal region implies a transition to the initial states of any other peer regions that do not contain explicit target states. A transition to a composite state itself implies a transition to the initial states of each of its orthogonal regions. If a composite state is active, a direct substate of each of its subregions is also active.

Similarly, a transition from a state in any orthogonal region implies a transition from all peer regions. If the occurrence of an event causes such a transition to fire, the activity in the other orthogonal regions is terminated, the exit activities of the regions are executed, the activity of the transition itself is executed, and the target state becomes active, thereby reducing the number of concurrently active states.

The transition to the final state of an orthogonal region does not force the termination of activity in other peer orthogonal regions (this is not a transition out of the region). When all the orthogonal regions have reached their final states, the enclosing composite state is deemed to have completed its activity and any completion transitions leaving the composite state are enabled to fire.

A complex transition may have multiple source states and multiple target states. In that case, its behavior is the combination of the fork and join described above.

History state

A composite state may contain a history state, which is a pseudostate. If an inherited transition causes an automatic exit from the composite state, the state "remembers" the substate that was active when the forced exit occurred. A transition to the history pseudostate within the composite state indicates that the remembered substate is to be reestablished. An explicit transition to another state or to the enclosing state itself does not enable the history mechanism, and the usual transition rules apply. However, the initial state of the composite state can be connected to the history state. In that case, a transition to the composite state does (indirectly) invoke the history mechanism. The history state may have a single outgoing completion transition without guard condition; the target of this transition is the default history state. If the state region has never been entered or if it was exited normally, then a transition to the history state goes to the default history state.

There are two kinds of history state: a *shallow history state* and a *deep history state*. The shallow history state restores states contained directly (depth one) in the same composite state as the history state. The deep history state restores the state or states that were active prior to the last explicit transition that caused the enclosing composite state to be exited. It may include states nested within the composite state to any depth. A composite state can have at most one of each kind of history state. Each may have its own default history state.

The history mechanism should be avoided if the situation can be modeled more directly, as it is complicated and not necessarily a good match to implementation mechanisms. The deep history mechanism is particularly problematic and should be avoided in favor of more explicit (and more implementable) mechanisms.

Notation

A state machine diagram shows a state machine or a nested portion of a state machine. The states are represented by state symbols (rectangles with rounded corners), and the transitions are represented by arrows connecting the state symbols. States may also contain subdiagrams by physical containment and tiling. An entire state machine diagram is placed in a rectangular frame with its name placed in a small pentagonal tag in the upper left corner. Entry and exit points may be placed on the boundary. Figure 14-257 shows an example.

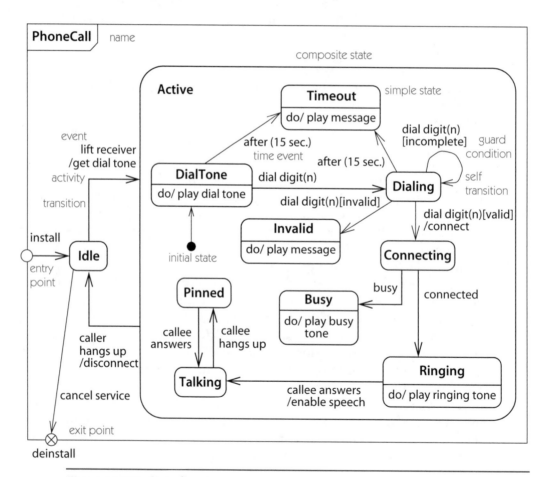

Figure 14-257. *State diagram*

The statechart notation was invented by David Harel and incorporates aspects of Moore machines (actions on entry) and Mealy machines (actions on transitions), as well as adding the concepts of nested states and concurrent states.

For more details, see state, redefinition (state machine), composite state, submachine, pseudostate, entry activity, exit activity, transition, internal transition, do activity, and redefinition (state machine). See also control node for some optional symbols intended for use within activity diagrams but that may be used in statechart diagrams.

Discussion

State machines can be used in two ways. Therefore, their meaning can be understood in either way. In one case, the state machine may specify executable behavior of its master element—typically, a class. In that case, the state machine describes the response of the master as it receives events from the rest of the universe. The response is described by transitions, each of which indicates what happens when the master receives an event while in a given state. The effect is expressed as an action and a change of state. Actions can include sending signals to other objects, which trigger their state machines. State machines provide a reductionist specification of the behavior of a system.

In the second case, the state machine may be used as a protocol specification, showing the legal order in which operations may be invoked on a class or interface. In such a state machine, transitions are triggered by call events and their actions invoke the desired operation. This means that a caller is allowed to invoke the operation at that point. The protocol state machine does not include actions to specify the behavior of the operation itself. It shows which operations can be invoked in a particular order. Such a state machine specifies valid operation sequences. This is a use of a state machine as a generator of sequences in a language (from computer science language theory). Such a machine is meant as a constraint on the design of the system. It is not directly executable and does not indicate what happens if an illegal sequence occurs—because it is not supposed to occur. It is the responsibility of the system designer to ensure that only legal sequences occur. This second usage is more abstract than the first form, which specifies, in an executable form, what happens in all cases. But it is often convenient, especially at a high level and with procedural coding.

State machines have been a part of computer science theory for many years, but the state machine model in UML is largely based on the extensions made by David Harel, who added the concept of nested states and orthogonal regions. This extension allows state machines to scale up to larger problems without excessive amounts of duplication that would otherwise be necessary. Harel has developed a precise, formal theory of his state machines. The UML model is less formal than Harel's and contains some modifications intended to enhance the usability of state machines with object-oriented models.

state machine diagram

A diagram that shows a state machine, including simple states, transitions, and nested composite states. The original concept was invented by David Harel, who called them statechart diagrams.

See state machine.

state machine view

That aspect of the system dealing with the specification of the behavior of individual elements over their lifetimes. This view contains state machines. It is loosely grouped with other behavioral views in the dynamic view.

statechart diagram

Name used by David Harel for his extension to flat state machine notation that includes nested states and concurrent states. This notation served as the basis for the UML state machine notation.

See state machine diagram.

static classification

A semantic variation of generalization in which an object may not change type or may not change role. This is the usual view in more traditional languages such as C++ or Java. The choice of static classification or dynamic classification is a semantic variation point.

static feature

A feature that is shared by an entire class, rather than applying to a single object.

Semantics

The static property indicates whether there is a distinct attribute slot for each instance of a class (nonstatic) or if there is one slot for the entire class itself (static). For an operation, the static property indicates whether an operation accesses an instance (nonstatic) or the class itself, such as a creation operator (static). Sometimes called simply *scope*. Possible values are

nonstatic
    Each classifier instance has its own distinct copy of an attribute slot. Values in one slot are independent of values in other slots. This is the default.

    For an operator, the operator applies to an individual object.

static

The classifier itself has one copy of the attribute slot. All the instances of the classifier share access to the one slot. If the language permits classes as real objects, then this is an attribute of the class itself as an object.

For an operator, the operator applies to the entire class, such as a creation operator or an operator that returns statistics about the entire set of instances.

Notation

A static attribute or operator is underlined (Figure 14-258). A nonstatic attribute or operator is not underlined (default).

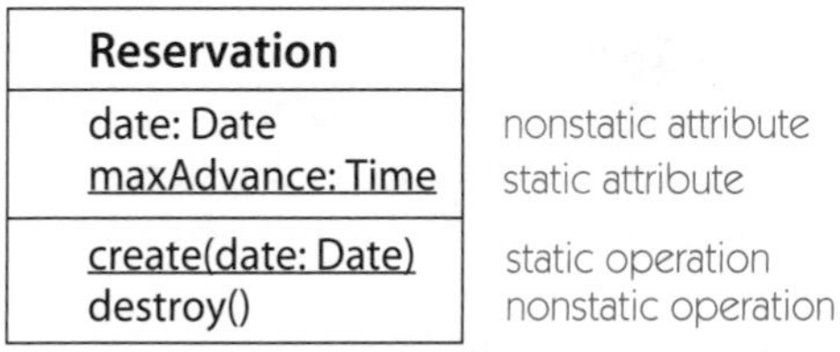

Reservation
date: Date
maxAdvance: Time
create(date: Date)
destroy()

nonstatic attribute
static attribute

static operation
nonstatic operation

Figure 14-258. *Static attribute and operation*

History

The UML1 concepts of source scope and target scope have been replaced by the more familiar concept of static features, probably with little practical loss.

Discussion

Static attributes provide global values for an entire class and should be used with care or avoided entirely, even though they are provided by most object-oriented programming languages. The problem is that they imply global information, which violates the spirit of object-oriented design. Moreover, global information becomes problematic in a distributed system, as it forces central accesses in a situation in which objects of a class may be distributed over many machines. Rather than use a class as an object with state, it is better to introduce explicit objects to hold any shared information that is needed. Both the model and costs are more apparent.

Constructors (creation operations, factory operations) are necessarily static because there is no instance (yet) on which they may operate. This is a necessary and proper use of static operations. Other kinds of static operations have the same difficulties as attributes—namely, they imply centralized global information about the instances of a class, which is impractical in a distributed system.

static view

A view of the overall model that characterizes the things in a system and their static relationships to each other. It includes classifiers and their relationships: association, generalization, dependency, and realization. It is sometimes called *class view*.

Semantics

The static view shows the static structure of a system, in particular, the kinds of things that exist (such as classes and types), their internal structure, and their relationships to other things. Static views do not show temporal information, although they may contain reified occurrences of things that have or describe temporal behavior, such as specifications of operations or events.

The top-level constituents of a static view include classifiers (class, interface, data type), relationships (association, generalization, dependency, realization), constraints, and comments. It also contains packages and subsystems as organizational units. Other constituents are subordinate to and contained within the top-level elements.

Related to the static view and often combined with it on diagrams are the design view, deployment view, and model management view.

The static view may be contrasted with the dynamic view, which complements it and builds upon it.

stereotype

A new kind of model element defined within a profile based on an existing kind of model element. It is essentially a new metaclass. Stereotypes may extend the semantics but not the structure of preexisting metamodel classes.

See also constraint, tagged value.

Semantics

A stereotype represents a variation of an existing model element with the same form (such as attributes and relationships) but with a modified intent. Generally, a stereotype represents a usage distinction. A stereotyped element may have additional constraints beyond those of the base element, as well as a distinct visual image and additional properties (metaattributes) defined through tag definitions. It is expected that code generators and other tools may treat stereotyped elements specially, by generating different code, for example. The intent is that a generic modeling tool, such as a model editor or a repository, should treat a stereotyped element for most purposes as an ordinary element with some additional text information, while differentiating the element for certain semantic operations, such as well-formedness checking, code generation, and report writing. Stereotypes represent one of the built-in extensibility mechanisms of UML.

Stereotypes are defined within profiles. Each stereotype is derived from a base model element class. All elements bearing the stereotype have the properties of the base model element class.

A stereotype can also be specialized from another stereotype. The child stereotype has the properties of the parent stereotype. Ultimately, each stereotype is based on some metamodel element class.

A stereotype may define element model-time properties through a list of tag definitions. A tag definition may have a default value that is used if no explicit tagged value is supplied. The permitted range of values for each tag may also be specified. Each element bearing the stereotype must have tagged values with the listed tags. Tags with default values are automatically implied if they are not explicit on a stereotyped element.

A tag definition is, essentially, a metaattribute for the metaclass to which the stereotype is applied. A model element bearing the stereotype may have a value for the tag definition. Note that this is a value of the model element itself, not of the instance of the model element.

A stereotype may have a list of constraints that add conditions beyond those implied by the base element. Each constraint applies to each model element bearing the stereotype. Each model element is also subject to the constraints applicable to the base element.

A stereotype is a kind of virtual metaclass (that is, it is not manifest in the metamodel) that is added within a model rather than by modifying the predefined UML metamodel. For that reason, the names of new stereotypes must differ from existing UML metaclass names or other stereotypes or keywords.

Model elements can have zero, one, or more than one stereotype.

Certain stereotypes are predefined in UML; others may be user defined. Stereotypes are one of three extensibility mechanisms in UML.

See constraint, tagged value.

Notation

Stereotype declaration. Stereotypes are defined within a profile. In such a diagram, each stereotype is shown as a class symbol (rectangle) with the «stereotype» keyword. A stereotype applies to a metaclass from the base metamodel, shown with the keyword «metaclass». The relationship is an extension relationship, shown by an arrow from the stereotype to the metaclass with a triangular filled arrowhead (Figure 14-259). If the stereotype is mandatory on all elements of the metaclass, the constraint {required} may be placed on the extension arrow. It is possible to apply more than one stereotype to the same metaclass, and the same stereotype may be applied to more than one metaclass.

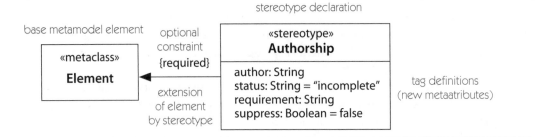

Figure 14-259. *Stereotype declaration*

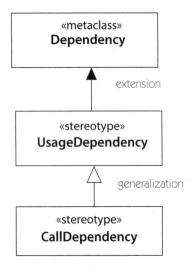

Figure 14-260. *Stereotype generalization*

A stereotype is declared using a classifier rectangle with the «stereotype» keyword above the name of the stereotype. The rectangle contains an attribute compartment in which tags are defined using attribute syntax. A default value for a tag may be shown following an equal sign. Stereotypes may show generalization (Figure 14-260).

Use of stereotype. The general notation for the use of a stereotype is to use the symbol for the base element but to place a keyword string above the name of the element (if any). The keyword string is the name of the stereotype within matched guillemets, which are the quotation mark symbols used in French and some other languages—for example: «foo. (Note that a guillemet looks like a double angle-bracket, but it is a single character in most extended fonts. Most computers have a character map utility in which special symbols can be found. Double angle-brackets are used by the typographically challenged.) The keyword string is usually

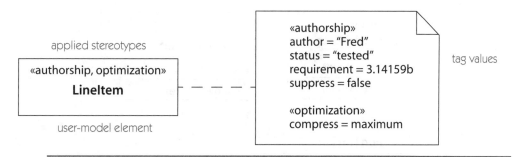

Figure 14-261. *Applying stereotypes to elements*

placed above or in front of the name of the model element being described. The keyword string may also be used as an element in a list. In that case, it applies to subsequent list elements until another stereotype string replaces it or until an empty stereotype string («») nullifies it. Note that a stereotype name should not be identical to a predefined keyword applicable to the same element type. (To avoid confusion, a predefined keyword name should be avoided for any stereotype even if it applies to separate elements and is distinguishable in principle.) If an element has multiple stereotypes, their names are included in a comma-separated list. See Figure 14-261.

The values of tags may be shown in a comment symbol attached to the model element. The name of the stereotype is placed above a list of tag values. If an element has multiple stereotypes, more than one list of values can be shown.

To permit limited graphical extension of the UML notation, a graphic icon or a graphic marker (such as texture or color) can be associated with a stereotype. UML does not specify the form of the graphic specification, but many bitmap and stroked formats exist and might be used by a graphical editor (although their portability is a difficult problem). An icon can be used in two ways. In one case, it may be used instead of or in addition to the stereotype keyword string within the symbol for the base model element on which the stereotype is based. For example, in a class rectangle it is placed in the upper-right corner of the name compartment. In this form, the normal contents of the item can be seen in its symbol. Alternately, the entire element symbol may be "collapsed" into an icon that contains the element name or has the name above or below the icon. Other information contained by the base model element symbol is suppressed. Figure 14-262 shows various ways of drawing a stereotyped class.

UML avoids the use of graphic markers, such as color, that present challenges for certain persons (the color blind) and for important kinds of equipment (such as printers, copiers, and fax machines). None of the UML symbols *require* the use of such graphic markers. Users *may* use graphic markers freely for their own purposes (such as for highlighting within a tool) but should be aware of their limitations for interchange, and they should be prepared to use the canonical forms when necessary.

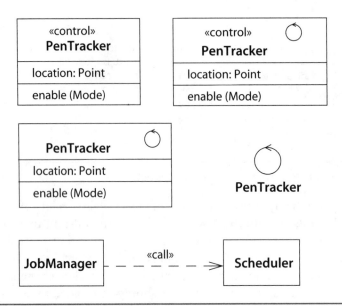

Figure 14-262. *Varieties of stereotype notation*

stop

A specification of the termination of the instance represented by a lifeline in an interaction.

Semantics

A stop indicates the destruction of the modeled instance. No occurrence specifications may follow the stop.

Notation

A stop is shown by an X on a lifeline. A message may depart from the symbol (if the object destroyed itself) or terminate on the symbol (if the object was destroyed by the action of another object).

Figure 14-248 shows examples of the stop.

strict

The keyword indicating a strict sequencing combined fragment in an interaction diagram.

See strict sequencing.

strict sequencing

An operator in a combined fragment of an interaction that indicates strict sequencing of the operands. See also weak sequencing.

Semantics

This operator indicates that the top-level operands of the combined fragment are executed strictly in order, rather than possibly being interleaved.

The distinction is subtle and unlikely to be used by most modelers. See the UML specification for more details.

string

A sequence of text characters. The details of string representation depend on implementation and may include character sets that support international characters and graphics.

Semantics

Many semantic properties, especially names, have strings as their values. A string is a sequence of characters in some suitable character set used to display information about the model. Character sets may include non-Roman alphabets and characters. UML does not specify the encoding of a string, but it assumes that the encoding is sufficiently general to permit any reasonable usage. In principle, the length of a string should be unlimited; any practical limit should be large enough to be nonrestrictive. Strings should also include the possibility of characters in various human languages. Identifiers (names) should consist entirely of characters in a finite character set. Comments and similar kinds of descriptive strings without direct semantic content might contain other kinds of media elements, such as diagrams, graphs, pictures or video clips, and other kinds of embedded documents.

Notation

A graphic string is a primitive notation element with some implementation flexibility. It is assumed to be a linear sequence of characters in some language, with the possible inclusion of embedded documents of various kinds. It is desirable to support the use of various human languages, but the details are left to editing tools to implement. Graphic strings can be one to a line, in lists, or they can be labels attached to other symbols.

Strings are used to display semantic properties that have string values and also to encode the values of other semantic properties for display. Mapping from semantic strings to notational strings is direct. Mapping of other properties to notational strings is governed by grammars, described in the articles for various elements. For example, the display notation for an attribute encodes the name, type, initial value, visibility, and scope into a single display string.

Noncanonical extensions to the encodings are possible—for example, an attribute might be displayed using C++ notation. Some of these encodings may lose some model information, however, so a tool should support them as user-selectable options while maintaining support for the canonical UML notation.

Typeface and font size are graphic markers that are normally independent of the string itself. They may code for various model properties, some of which are suggested in this document and some of which are left open for the tool or the user. For example, italics show abstract classes and abstract operations, and underlining shows static features.

Tools may treat long strings in various ways, such as truncation to a fixed size, automatic wrapping, and insertion of scroll bars. It is assumed that there is a way to obtain the full string when desired.

string value

A value that is a string.

structural feature

A static feature of a model element, such as an attribute or an operation.
The distinction from property is a bit too subtle for ordinary use.

structural view

A view of an overall model that emphasizes the structure of the objects in a system, including their types, classes, relationships, attributes, and operations.

structure diagram

A diagram that describes the static structure of a system, as opposed to its dynamic behavior. There is really no rigid line between different kinds of structure diagrams, although diagrams may be named according to the major kind of element they contain, such as class diagram, interface diagram, or package diagram.

structured classifier

A classifier containing parts or roles that form its data structure and realize its behavior.

Semantics

The internal structure of a classifier can be defined in terms of ports, parts, and connectors. Each of these kinds of elements is defined within the context provided by the definition of a structured classifier.

A structured classifier defines the implementation of a classifier. The interfaces of a classifier describe what a classifier must do. Its internal structure describes how the work is done.

Structured classifiers provide a clean way to structure the implementation of a classifier. Because the types of parts within a structure classifier may themselves be structured, the mechanism extends hierarchically.

Structured class. A structured class is the description of the internal implementation structure of a class. A structured class owns its ports, parts, and connectors. The class and its ports may have interfaces (including required interfaces and provided interfaces) to define its externally visible behavior. When an instance of a structured class is created, instances of its ports, parts, and connectors are created too. Messages on external ports can be automatically transferred to ports on internal parts, so a structure class also provides some of the behavioral description of the class. Structured classes may be hierarchical on several levels.

Collaboration. A collaboration describes a contextual relationship supporting interaction among a set of participants. A role is the description of a participant. Unlike a structured class, a collaboration does not own the instances bound to its roles. The instances of the roles exist prior to establishing an instance of the collaboration, but the collaboration brings them together and establishes links for connecting them. Collaborations describe data structure patterns.

Ports. A port is a an individual interaction point between a classifier and its environment. Messages to objects (calls and signals) may be directed to an instance of a port on an object rather than to the entire object. Actions within an object can distinguish which port a call or signal arrived on.

Within a structured classifier, ports can be connected to internal parts or to the behavior specification of the overall object. The implementation of a port involves recognizing input events and passing them to the appropriate part or behavior implementation. No further implementation description is necessary when ports are "wired" properly.

When an instance of a structured class is created, its ports are created with it. When it is destroyed, its ports are destroyed. Instances of ports are not created or destroyed during the life of an instance.

Parts. A part is a structural piece of a classifier. A part describes the role that an instance plays within a instance of the classifier.

A part has a name, a type, and a multiplicity. If the maximum multiplicity of a part exceeds one, an instance of a classifier may have multiple instances of a part, but each part instance is separate. If the multiplicity is ordered, the individual instances can be distinguished by the index of their position within the object.

Each part may have a type. The type constrains the type of the objects that may be bound to a role. The type of an object bound to a role must be the same as or a descendant of the declared type of the role.

A structured classifier is not a relationship among types, unlike an association. Each part is a distinct usage of a type in its own unique context. There may be multiple parts with the same type, each having a different set of relationships to other parts. A part is not an instance, however, but a description of all the instances that may be bound to the part. Each time the structured classifier is instantiated, a different set of objects and links may play the roles.

In the case of classes, parts are owned by a class. Instances of parts are created and destroyed along with an instance of the class. The attributes of a class may be considered parts within the class.

A part in a collaboration represents the use an instance of a type within some context. Roles instances are not owned or created by an instance of a collaboration. The instances in a collaboration exist before an instance of the collaboration is created. Creating an instance of a collaboration involves binding (referencing) existing instances to the roles of the collaboration. This creates a transient relationship among the instances bound to roles. When the collaboration is destroyed, the instances bound to its roles continue to exist but their transient contextual relationship ceases to exist.

The same object may play different roles in different collaborations. A collaboration represents a facet of an object. A single physical object may combine different facets, thereby implicitly connecting the collaborations in which it plays roles.

Connectors. A connector is a contextual relationship between the objects or other instances bound to roles in a structured classifier. It defines a communications path among the roles. A connector is only meaningful within the context of a structured classifier. Unlike an association, it is a relationship between roles, not between the classifiers that are the declared types of the roles. An association valid between the types of two roles can be bound to a connector. In a structured class, a connector more often represents a "contextual association," that is, an association valid only within the structured class. This association may be anonymous; that is, it may not correspond to a declared association. When a structured class is instantiated, a link is instantiated for each of its connectors, whether or not the connector is bound to a declared association.

Within a collaboration, a connector often represents a "transient association," that is, an association that is manifested only during the duration of the collaboration. A transient association is not usually a declared association. Such connectors correspond to parameters of a behavior, variables, global values, or the implicit relationship between parts of the same object. They are implicit within procedures and other kinds of behaviors.

A classifier role has a reference to a classifier (the base) and a multiplicity. The base classifier constrains the kind of object that can play the classifier role. The object's class can be the same as or a descendant of the base classifier. The multiplicity indicates how many objects can play the role at one time in one instance of the collaboration.

A classifier role may have a name, or it may be anonymous. It may have multiple base classifiers if multiple classification is intended.

A classifier role can be connected to other classifier roles by connectors.

Creation semantics. When a structured class is instantiated, its ports, parts, and connectors are instantiated. If a port has variable multiplicity, the cardinality of the port must be specified on instantiation of the class; ports are not dynamically created or destroyed during the life of an object. If a part has variable multiplicity, the minimum number of parts is instantiated as part of the object instantiation. If a connector has variable multiplicity, the minimum number of connectors consistent with the cardinality of parts is instantiated. If the initial configuration is ambiguous, the modeler must specify it. The modeler can explicitly specify the initial configuration on instantiation to override the implicit defaults.

Notation

A part or role is shown by using the symbol for a classifier (a rectangle) containing string label with the syntax:

$$\text{rolename}_{opt} : \text{Typename}_{opt} [\text{ multiplicity }]_{opt}$$

The name or typename may be omitted. The multiplicity (including brackets) may be omitted, in which case the default multiplicity is one. Alternatively, the multiplicity may be placed (without brackets) in the upper right of the rectangle.

A reference to an external object (that is, one that is not owned by the enclosing object) is shown by a dashed rectangle.

Figure 14-263 shows various forms that a role may take.

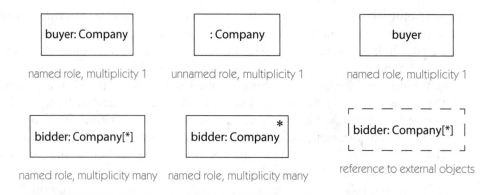

Figure 14-263. *Roles or parts*

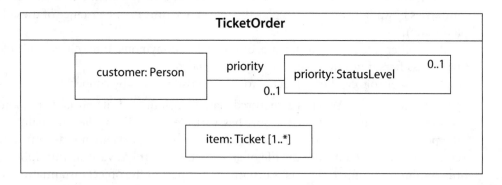

Figure 14-264. *Structured class*

Example

Figure 14-264 shows an example of a structured class. An instance of this class is shown in Figure 14-157.

History

Structured classifiers in UML1 replace semantically dubious attempts in UML1 to mark associations for local context. They are perhaps the most important added modeling feature in UML2 because they permit clear expression of multilevel models.

structured part

Within a structured classifier, an element that represents an object or set of objects within a contextual relationship.

See structured classifier.

subclass

The child of another class in a generalization relationship—that is, the more specific description. The child class is called the subclass. The parent class is called the superclass. See generalization, inheritance.

Semantics

A subclass inherits the structure, relationships, and behavior of its superclass and may add to it.

subject

The classifier whose behavior is described by a use case.

Semantics

The subject is the classifier that realizes the behavior defined by a use case. A use case need not have a subject (but then it would be a vague description of system behavior). The subject often, but not always, owns the use case. The use case has access to the features of its subject.

One classifier may have ma ny use cases. Each use case describes a facet of the classifier's overall behavior.

Notation

A subject is shown by a rectangle with its use cases drawn inside. The name of the subject is shown as a text string. Actors communicating with the use cases are drawn outside the rectangle. See Figure 14-285 for an example.

submachine

A state machine that may be invoked as part of another state machine. It is not attached to a class but instead is a kind of state machine subroutine. It has semantics as if its contents were duplicated and inserted at the state that references it.

See state, state machine, submachine state.

submachine state

A state that references a submachine (another state machine), a copy of which is implicitly part of the enclosing state machine in place of the submachine reference state. It is conceptually like a "call" on a state machine "subroutine" (but may be implemented differently). It may contain references to entry points and exit points, which identify states in the submachine.

See also state, state machine, entry point, exit point.

Semantics

A submachine state is semantically equivalent to inserting a copy of the submachine in place of the reference state. The submachine state itself has no substructure; all of the semantic structure comes from the referenced state machine.

Notation

A submachine state is drawn as a state symbol with a label of the form

    state-name : submachine-name

Transition arrows may be drawn to the submachine boundary. A transition to the
submachine state establishes the initial state of the submachine; if there is no initial
state, transitions to the boundary are not allowed. A transition may also be drawn
to a named connection point on the submachine state boundary. An entry connection point is shown as a small circle. An exit connection point is shown as a small
circle containing an X. A transition to or from a connection point is equivalent to a
transition to the corresponding entry point or from the corresponding exit point
of the submachine.

Example

Figure 14-265 shows part of a state machine containing a submachine state. The
containing state machine sells tickets to customers with accounts. It must identify
the customer as part of its job. Identifying the customer is a requirement of other
state machines, so it has been made into a separate state machine. Figure 14-266
shows the definition of state machine **Identify**, which is used as a submachine by
other state machines. The normal entry to the submachine provides for reading
the customer's card, but there is an explicit entry point that provides for manual
entry of the customer's name by the box office clerk. If the identification process is
successful, the submachine terminates at its final state. Otherwise, it goes to state
Failure.

In Figure 14-265, the submachine state is shown by a state icon with a local
name and the name of the submachine. Normal entry to the submachine is shown
by an arrow to its boundary. This transition activates the initial state of the submachine. Normal exit is shown by a completion transition from the boundary.
This transition fires if the submachine terminates normally.

Entry at entry point **ManualEntry** is shown by a transition to a connection point
on the submachine state symbol. The connection point is labeled with the name of
the entry point in the submachine. Similarly, exit from explicit state **Failure** is
shown by a transition to an exit point.

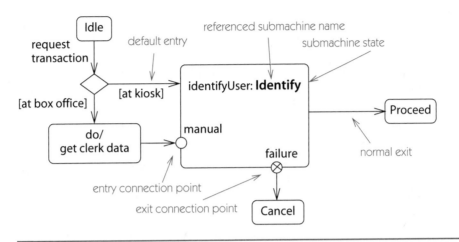

Figure 14-265. *Submachine state*

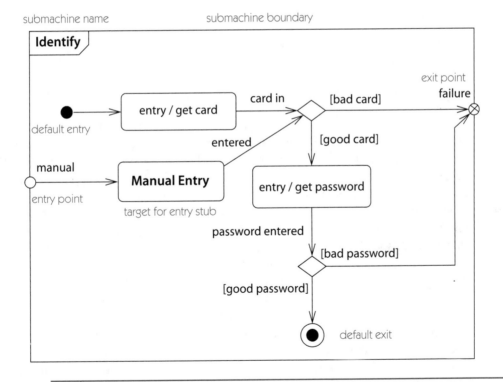

Figure 14-266. *Submachine definition*

subsets

Keyword on an association end or attribute indicating that the collection of objects that form the value is a subset of the collection of objects forming the value of another designated association end or attribute.

See also union.

Semantics

Sometimes the same property (an association end or attribute) can be modeled at more than one level of granularity, a general level covering several cases and a more specific level divided into more specific cases. If one property is declared as a subset of another property, the set of values for the first property is a subset of the values for the second property. A value for the one property will also be found among the values for the other property. Typically, the more general property is partitioned into multiple subsets that cover its entire set of values, in which case it is declared to be a union. This is not always true, however.

Notation

A subsets declaration has the form:

{ subsets other-property-name }

The declaration is placed after the declaration of the property that forms the subset and it references the property that includes the subset.

Figure 14-267 shows an example of the **subsets** and **union** declarations on associations. The association end **steering** is declared at a high level between classes **Vehicle** and **SteeringControl**. Each of these classes is specialized into several subclasses. Steering is not fully general among the subclasses, however. A car is only steered by a steering wheel, a boat is only steered by a tiller, and a horse is only steered by the reins. (OK, there are other ways to steer these things. It's just an example.) The **subsets** declaration on each of the specialized associations declares that they are special cases of the general **steering** association. The **union** declaration on the general associations declares that these are the only cases—any instance of the steering association must also be an instance of one of the associations that subsets it. Therefore, we know that you can't steer a horse with a steering wheel, although the general association would otherwise permit it.

This pattern frequently occurs when an association between general classes needs to be applied to subclasses.

If the **union** declaration on the general association did not exist, then other combinations of values might exist besides the explicit subsets.

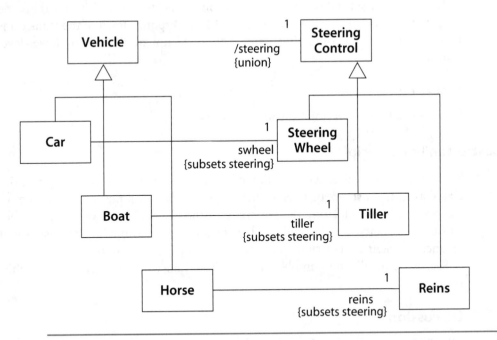

Figure 14-267. *Subsets and union*

subsetting

Definition of a property that covers a subset of the instances of another property.
See subsets.

substate

A state that is part of a composite state.
See composite state, direct substate, indirect substate, region.

Semantics

A composite state contains one or more regions. Each region contains one or more
states. Each state is a direct substate of the region that owns it and of the composite
state that owns the region. It is an indirect substate of states at a higher level.

The direct substates within a single region are mutually exclusive. If the region is
active, exactly one direct substate is active. If a composite state is active, each region is active, so exactly one direct substate from each region is active. Substates
form an "and-or" tree of activity—the decomposition of composite states into
multiple regions is an "and" of activity, while the decomposition of regions into
multiple substates is an "or" of activity.

The nested of substates within states is somewhat similar to (but not the same as) generalization of classifiers. A nested substate responds to all of the transitions that depart from its containing states if they are not overridden by lower-level transitions.

Notation

See composite state for notation and examples.

substitutability principle

The principle that, given a declaration of a variable or parameter whose type is declared as X, any instance of an class that is a descendant of X may be used as the actual value without violating the semantics of the declaration and its use. In other words, an instance of a descendant element may be substituted for an instance of an ancestor element. (Attributed to MIT Professor Barbara Liskov.)

See also generalization, implementation inheritance, inheritance, polymorphic, procedure.

Discussion

The purpose is to ensure that polymorphic operations work freely. The generalization relationship supports substitutability provided overriding and redefinition of concrete features are avoided.

The consequence of the substitutability principle is that a child may not remove or renounce properties of its parent. Otherwise, the child will not be substitutable in a situation in which a use of the parent is declared.

This is not a principle of logic but rather a pragmatic rule of programming that provides a degree of encapsulation. Nontraditional languages based on different run-time rules, such as dynamic classification, might find the principle less useful.

substitution

A dependency between classifiers that declares that the source classifier may be substituted in a place where the target classifier has been declared as a type.

Semantics

Generalization usually implies substitutability (see substitutability principle), but sometimes a classifier specifies a contract for interactions—interfaces and ports—without specifying features. Any classifier that implements the same interfaces and ports can be substituted for the original classifier, even if it does not share any of the internal structure or implementation. This relationship is expressed by the *substitution* dependency from the implementing classifier to the classifier specifying the contract. It can be used in situations where generalization is inappropriate.

Notation

Substitution is shown as a dependency drawn as a dashed arrow with the keyword «substitute».

subsystem (stereotype of Component)

A large unit of decomposition for a system. It is modeled in UML as a stereotype of component.

Semantics

A subsystem is a coherent piece of a system design. It may have its own specification and realization portions. Usually a subsystem is instantiated indirectly, that is, its behavior is realized by other classes.

The system itself constitutes the top-level subsystem. The realization of one subsystem may be written as a collaboration of lower-level subsystems. In this way, the entire system may be expanded as a hierarchy of subsystems until the bottom-level subsystems are defined in terms of ordinary classes.

A subsystem is modeled as a (large) component.

The connotations of subsystems vary widely among modeling approaches.

Notation

A subsystem is notated as a component symbol with the keyword «subsystem» (Figure 14-268).

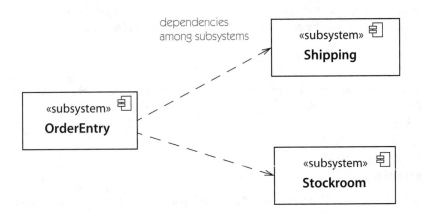

Figure 14-268. *Subsystems*

subtype

A type that is a child of another type. The more neutral term child may be used for any generalizable element.

See generalization.

summarization

To filter, combine, and abstract the properties of a set of elements onto their container in order to give a higher level, more abstract view of a system.

See package.

Semantics

Containers, such as packages and classes, can have derived properties and relationships that summarize the properties and relationships of their contents. This permits the modeler to get a better understanding of a system at a higher, less detailed level that is easier to understand. For example, a dependency between two packages indicates that the dependency exists between at least one pair of elements from the two packages. The summary has less detail than the original information. There may be one or many pairs of individual dependencies represented by package-level dependencies. In any case, the modeler knows that a change to one package *may* affect the other. If more details are needed, the modeler can always examine the contents in detail once the high-level summary has been noticed.

Similarly, a usage dependency between two classes usually indicates a dependency between their operations, such as a method on one class calling an operation (not a method!) on another class. Many dependencies at the class level derive from dependencies among operations or attributes.

In general, relationships that are summarized on a container indicate the existence of at least one use of the relationship among the contents. They do not usually indicate that all the contained elements participate in the relationship.

superclass

The parent of another class in a generalization relationship—that is, the more general element specification. The child class is classed the subclass. The parent class is called the superclass.

See generalization.

Semantics

A subclass inherits the structure, relationships, and behavior of its superclass and may add to it.

supertype

Synonym for superclass. The more neutral term parent may be used for any generalizable element.

See generalization.

supplier

An element that provides services that can be invoked by others. Contrast: client. In the notation, the supplier appears at the arrowhead of a dashed dependency arrow.

See dependency.

swimlane

See partition.

synch state

This UML1 concept has been removed from UML2. It is no longer needed because of the loosening of restrictions on activities.

synchronous action

A request in which the sending object pauses to wait for a response; a call.

Contrast: asynchronous action.

system

A collection of connected units organized to accomplish a purpose. A system can be described by one or more models, possibly from different viewpoints. The "complete model" describes the whole system.

Semantics

The system is modeled by a top-level subsystem that indirectly contains the entire set of model elements that work together to accomplish a complete real-world purpose.

systemModel (stereotype of Model)

A high-level model that contains a collection of model describing a physical system.

See model, subsystem, system.

tabular notation

The UML2 specification defines a tabular notation for sequence diagrams.

Discussion

The concept of expressing model information as tables is hardly original and the exact format given in the specification would be better included in the implementation of a tool. Its inclusion in the specification is too narrow because it is only defined for a single UML diagram.

tag definition

A property declared in a stereotype. It represents the name of a property defined at modeling time.

Semantics

A tag definition is simply an attribute of a stereotype declaration.

Notation

A tag definition is shown as an attribute in the rectangle showing the stereotype declaration.

Example

Figure 14-269 shows the declaration of stereotype **Authorship**. It applies to any element. It declares the tags **author, status, requirement,** and **suppress.** The first three are string values, the last is a Boolean.

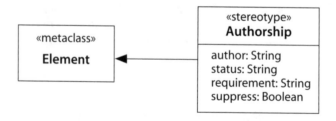

Figure 14-269. *Tag definitions in stereotype declaration*

tagged value

A tag-value pair attached to a modeling element to hold some piece of information.

See also constraint, stereotype.

Semantics

A tagged value is a name-value pair that may be attached to a model element that uses a stereotype containing a tag definition.

Tagged values represent additional modeling information beyond that defined in the UML metamodel. It is commonly used to store project management information, such as the author of an element, the testing status, or the importance of the element to a final system (the tags might be **author**, **status**, and **importance**).

Tagged values represent a modest extension to the meta-attributes of UML metaclasses. This is not a fully general extension mechanism but can be used to add information to existing metaclasses for the benefit of back-end tools, such as code generators, report writers, and simulators. To avoid confusion, tags should differ from existing metaattributes of model elements to which they are applied. This check can be facilitated by a modeling tool.

Certain tags are predefined in the UML; others may be user defined within stereotypes. Tagged values are an extensibility mechanism permitting arbitrary information to be attached to models.

Notation

Each tagged value is shown in the form

    tag = value

where tag is the name of a tag and value is a literal value. Tagged values may be included with other property keywords in a comment symbol attached to a classifier rectangle by a dashed line. The classifier must have a stereotype declaring the tag definition.

A keyword may be declared to stand for a tag with a particular value. In that case the keyword can be used alone. The absence of the tag is treated as equivalent to one of the other legal values for the tag.

    tag

Figure 14-270 shows the application of the authorship stereotype declared in Figure 14-269 to the **Customer** class. The values of each of the tags are specified for the **Customer** class.

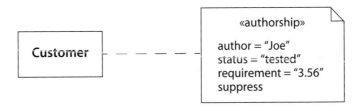

Figure 14-270. *Tagged values*

Discussion

Tagged values are a means of attaching nonsemantic project management and tracking information to models. For example, tag **author** might hold the author of an element and tag **status** might hold the development status, such as **incomplete, tested, buggy,** and **complete.**

Tagged values are also a way to attach implementation-language-dependent controls to a UML model without building the details of the language into UML. Code generator flags, hints, and pragmas can be encoded as tagged values without affecting the underlying model. Multiple sets of tags are possible for various languages on the same model. Neither a model editor nor a semantic analyzer need understand the tags—they can be manipulated as strings. A back-end tool, such as a code generator, can understand and process the tagged values. For example, a tagged value might name the container class used to override the default implementation of an association with multiplicity *many.*

The use of tags, like the use of procedures in programming language libraries, may require a period of evolution during which there may be conflict among developers. Over time, some standard uses will develop. UML does not include a "registry" of tags nor does it offer the expectation that early users of tags may "reserve" them to prevent other uses in the future.

target scope

This UML1 concept has been removed from UML2. It was not found to be very useful, and it has not been replaced.

target state

The state machine state that results from the firing of the transition. After an object handles an event that causes a transition to fire, the object is in the target state of the transition (or target states if it is a complex transition with multiple target states). Not applicable to an internal transition, which does not cause a change of state.

See transition.

template

A parameterized model element. To use it, the parameters must be bound (at model time) to actual values. Synonym: parameterized element.

See also binding, bound element.

Semantics

A template is the descriptor for an element with one or more unbound formal parameters. It defines a family of potential elements, each specified by binding the parameters to actual values. Typically, the parameters are classifiers that represent attribute types, but they can also be integers or even operations. Subordinate elements within the template definition are defined in terms of the formal parameters, so they too become bound when the template itself is bound to actual values.

Template parameterization can be applied to classifiers (such as classes and collaborations), packages, and operations. Most any kind of element can be a template parameter.

Classifiers. A template classifier is a parameterized classifier. The body of a template may contain uses of the formal parameters, usually as types of properties but also in other places. An actual classifier is produced by binding values to the parameters. Attributes and operations within the template classifier can use the formal parameters, usually as types. The template classifier can be a subtype of a regular classifier. When the template is bound, the bound classifier is a subtype of the regular classifier. Associations may be modeled using parts within a structured classifier.

A template class is not a directly usable class, because it has unbound parameters. Its parameters must be bound to actual values to create a real class. A template class may be a subclass of an ordinary class, which implies that all classes formed by binding the template are subclasses of the given class.

Other kinds of classifiers, such as use cases and signals, can be parameterized.

A bound classifier may add elements in addition to those generated by the binding. This is equivalent to generating an anonymous classifier by the binding, then making the named bound element a child of it.

A classifier may bind multiple templates at the same time. This is equivalent to generating an anonymous bound classifier for each binding, then making the named classifier a subtype of each of them.

A template parameter may be constrained to be a class that is a descendant of a specific class. A class substituted for the parameter must be a descendant of the given class. As an alternative, the parameter can be constrained to be a valid substitution for a given class, without needing to be a descendant. This permits the actual argument to satisfy the interfaces of the given class without having the same structure.

Templates can be redefined. See redefinition (template).

Collaborations. A collaboration is a classifier and may therefore be a template. Typically the types of the roles are template parameters. A template collaboration is a structural pattern. Note that a collaboration use in a class model is not the same as a bound collaboration; the latter is a collaboration (a descriptor), not a collaboration use (a reference to a collaboration).

Packages. A package may be a template. The elements of the package are often template parameters. The same package template may be bound multiple times into the same bound element. This means that the results of each individual binding are combined (using package merge) into a single resultant package. This is a way to apply the same pattern multiple times on different sets of classes.

Operations. An operation may be a template. Typically, the types of its parameters are template parameters. Constraints of the operation may also contain template parameters.

Well formedness. The contents of a template are not directly subject to the well-formedness rules of models. This is because they include parameters that do not have full semantics until they are bound. A template is a kind of second-level model element—not one that models systems directly, but one that generates model elements. The contents of a template are therefore outside the semantics of the system. The results of binding a template are ordinary model elements that are subject to well-formedness rules and are normal elements in the target system. Certain well-formedness rules for templates could be derived from the considerations that their bound results must be well formed, but we will not attempt to list them. In a sense, when a template is bound, its contents are duplicated and the parameters are replaced by the arguments. The result becomes part of the effective model as if it had been included directly.

Notation

See Figure 14-271.

Parameters. Parameters have the syntax

```
name :type =default
```

> where name is an identifier for the parameter, with scope inside the template;
>
> type is a string designating a type expression for the parameter;
>
> default is an optional expression for a default value to be used if no actual value is supplied during a binding.

If the type name is omitted, it is assumed to be a class. Other parameter types (such as IntegerExpression) must be shown explicitly and must evaluate to valid type expressions.

A parameter can be constrained to require that the argument be a descendant of a specific class. This is shown using the syntax

```
name :type <Class-name
```

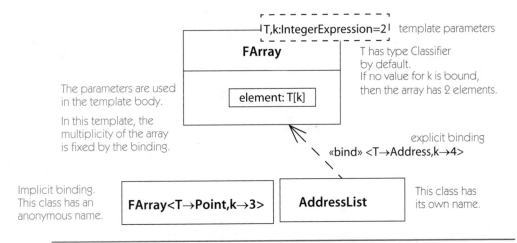

Figure 14-271. *Class template notation*

Classifiers. In a template definition, a small dashed rectangle is superimposed on the upper-right corner of the classifier rectangle. The dashed rectangle contains a list of formal parameters for the template. Each parameter has a name and a type and may include an optional default value, which is used if no actual value is supplied for the parameter in a binding. The list must not be empty (otherwise, there is no template), although it might be suppressed in the presentation. The name, attributes, and operations of the parameterized class appear as normal in the class rectangle, but the names of the formal parameters may be used in them. If the template is a structured classifier, its parts may be shown within a graphical compartment. Often the types of some of the parts are template parameters.

If features are added to the bound classifier in addition to those generated by the binding, they are shown in a feature compartment within the rectangle representing the bound classifier.

Figure 14-271 shows a class template with an integer parameter and a class parameter. The template has an association to one of its parameters.

A template can be a child of another element. This means that each bound element generated from it is a child of the given element. For example, in Figure 14-272, every class generated from **Poly** is a **Polygon**. Therefore, **Hexagon** is a child of **Shape**.

Figure 14-273 shows the addition of features to a bound class. It declares a TopTenList, a list of jokes delivered by a host on a show. The host and show date are added to the elements generated by the template. The features are shown in their usual compartment in the bound class. For a structured class, parts could be added in a graphical compartment.

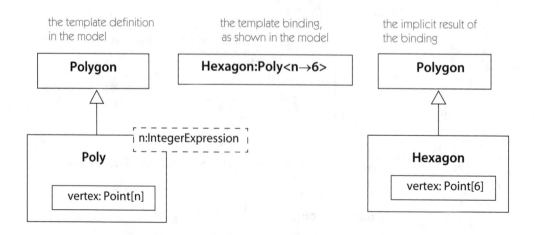

Figure 14-272. *Template subclass*

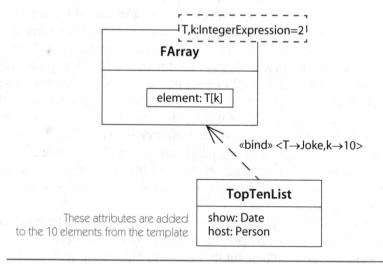

Figure 14-273. *Adding elements to a bound class*

Figure 14-274 shows the multiple binding of a bound class. **Orderlist** is both a **VArray** and a **Buffer**. Both the template parameters are bound to class **Order**. Note that the names of the parameters have nothing to do with each other, even though they are both named **T**.

A parameter can be constrained so that the actual value must be a descendant of a certain class. Figure 14-275 shows a declaration of the **Polyline** template class. A polyline is an ordered list of edges. Some polylines have straight edges, some have

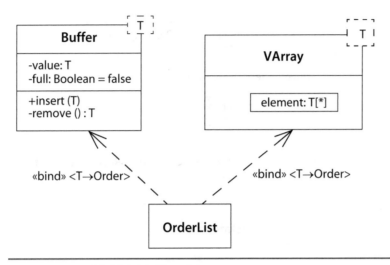

Figure 14-274. *Multiple binding of class*

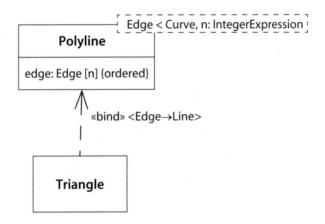

Figure 14-275. *Constrained class parameter*

curved edges. For any binding of **Polyline**, the type of edge must be a subclass of the abstract class **Curve**. For a **Triangle**, there are three straight edges.

A collaboration is a classifier and uses the same notation as a template. Figure 14-276 shows the **Sale** collaboration as a template that has three roles. The types **Property** and **Agent** are template parameters. **RealEstateSale** is a bound collaboration, in which the property must be of type real estate and the agents must be realtors.

Figure 14-276. *Collaboration template*

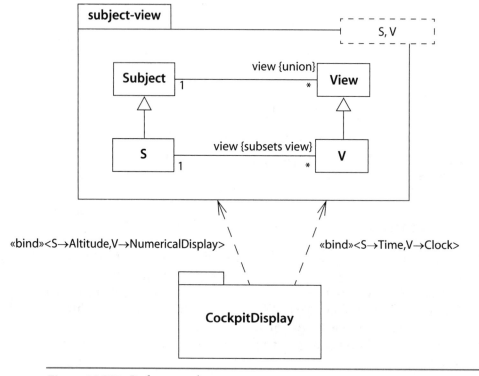

Figure 14-277. *Package template*

Packages. A package template is shown as a package symbol (rectangle with tab) with a small dashed rectangle superimposed on the upper right corner. The parameters are listed in the dashed rectangle.

Figure 14-277 shows a template that defines a subject-view paradigm. The Subject and View classes are not parameters, therefore they are copied into a template binding without change. Classes S and V are parameters. The classes bound to them become subclasses of Subject and View. The bound package is bound twice to the same template. Each binding adds a pair of classes to the package. The Subject and View classes are the same in both bindings, so they do not occur twice. Figure 14-278 shows the effective result of the package binding.

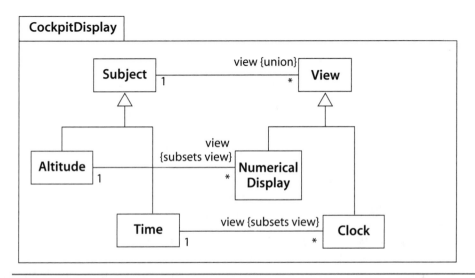

Figure 14-278. *Result of package binding*

Figure 14-279 shows the use of string substitution to model the previous example in a slightly different way. A string expression can be placed within dollar signs ($ $) to indicate that it is to be interpreted as a name. Fragments of the string expression can be template parameters enclosed in angle brackets (< >). This allows strings to be supplied as binding arguments and concatenated with literal strings to generate names for the template elements. In this example, the names of the view elements are generated from the names of the subject elements by appending the word Display. Another difference from Figure 14-277 is that the arguments are strings, rather than existing classes, which are required in the previous model. The classes are generated as part of the template expansion.

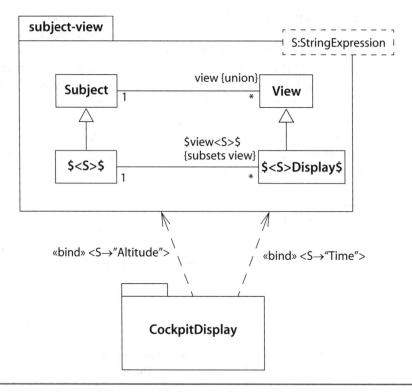

Figure 14-279. *String substitution in package template*

Operations. It is unclear if there is a notation for a parameterized operation. No example is given in the UML specification. It is probably best to avoid operation templates in any case, as they are too close to the implementation level, and their use in most programming languages is usually a mistake.

Discussion

The *effective model* is the implicit model resulting from binding all templates; it is the implicit model that describes a system. Template parameters have no meaning within the effective model itself, because they will have been bound. They may be used only within the scope of the template body itself. This is adequate to handle constituent elements contained within the parameterized element, for example, for attributes or operations within a parameterized class.

The template definition is a model fragment that is not part of the effective model. When the template is bound, the body is implicitly copied, the parameters are replaced by arguments, and the copy becomes part of the effective model. Each instantiation of the template produces an addition to the effective model.

There is more difficulty with relationships between the template and its parameters. For example, a template class might have associations or generalizations to other classes. If those classes are parameters of the template, they cannot be part of the class definition itself, because they are not features, yet they are not part of the model outside the template either. For example, an generalization might exist from a template parameter to the template element itself. This can (possibly) be modeled, but there is no notation for it, because the notation assumes that all of the parameters appear as contents of the template class itself. The template parameter cannot be drawn as a separate class outside the template class, so there appears to be no way to notate it correctly.

In principle, a template definition should include a *body* that may include elements outside the bound element. These elements could include associations and generalizations to template parameters. However, the specification does not define an explicit body, although a close reading suggests that some template parameters might be part of the body but not part of the template element itself.

A template usually cannot be a parent of another element. This would mean that each element generated by binding the template is the parent of the other element. Although someone could perhaps assign a meaning to such a situation, it seems implausible.

Two templates do not have associations to each other simply because they share the same parameter name. (Trying to do this would mean that every instantiation of the first template is related to every instantiation of the second template, which is not what is usually desired. This point has been misunderstood frequently by authors in the past.) A parameter has scope only inside its own template. Using the same name for a parameter in two templates does not make it the same parameter. Generally, if two templates have parameterized elements that must be related, one of the templates must be instantiated inside the body of the other. (Recall that a template is implicitly instantiated inside its own body. Therefore, both templates are effectively instantiated inside the body, and relationships are therefore between the instantiated elements.) Figure 14-280 shows an incorrect and a correct attempt to define such a relationship—in this case, with a parameterized "pointer" class that points to a parameterized array of the same kind.

A similar approach can be used to declare a parameterized class that is a child of another template class bound with the same parameter. Another approach is to instantiate both templates inside a third template that has a parameter. The parameter is used to bind a copy of each of the other templates. An association may then be constructed between the instantiated copies of the templates. In most practical cases, this is not needed because the relationship can be declared in the body of one of the templates.

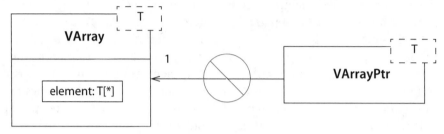

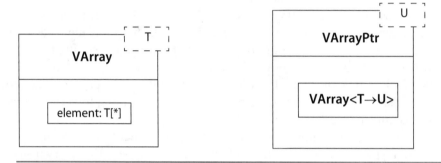

Figure 14-280. *Associations between templates*

Templates should be used sparingly. In many uses (such as in the C++ language), they perform tasks that are better done using polymorphism and generalization, in a misguided zeal for unnecessary efficiency. Because they are generators, their results are not always apparent.

terminate

A terminate whose execution terminates the execution of a state machine by the object that owns it.

Semantics

The execution of a terminate pseudostate terminates the execution of a state machine. Usually it means that the owning object is destroyed.

Under normal circumstances, a state machine terminates when it reaches a final state at the top level, therefore the terminate pseudostate is rarely needed.

Notation

A terminate pseudostate is shown as a large X.

test identity action

An action whose execution tests whether two input values have the same identity, that is, whether they are the same object.

See action.

thread

(from *thread of control*) A single path of execution through a program, dynamic model, or other representation of control flow. Also a stereotype for the implementation of an active object as a lightweight process.

See active object, complex transition, composite state, state machine, synch state.

time action

There are several actions relating to the simple time model provided by UML. More complicated models of time, such as those used in real-time systems, require UML profiles.

See action.

time constraint

A constraint on the time of an occurrence specification expressed as a time interval.

Semantics

A time constraint can refer to a single occurrence specification or to the time interval between two occurrences. It is expressed as a time interval, but the length of the interval can be zero to restrict it to a single point in time. The time can be absolute time or relative to some starting time.

Notation

A constraint on a single occurrence is shown in a sequence diagram by drawing a horizontal tick mark and placing a time expression in braces next to it.

A constraint on a time interval is shown by drawing a double-headed arrow between two tick marks and placing a time interval expression next to it.

Example

Figure 14-281 shows several time constraints. The receiver must be lifted between 7 AM and 7 PM. A dial tone must be received less than one second after the receiver is lifted. The first digit must then be dialed within ten seconds.

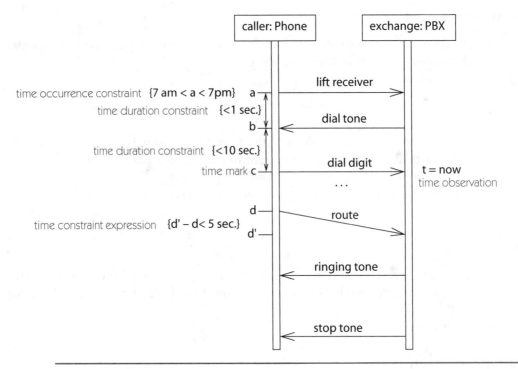

Figure 14-281. *Time constraints*

A time constraint can also be shown as a string, as shown in the last constraint, which says that the routing message must be delivered in less than five seconds.

time event

An event that denotes the satisfaction of a time expression, such as the occurrence of an absolute time or the passage of a given amount of time after an object enters a state.

Semantics

A time event is an event that depends on the passage of time and therefore on the existence of a clock. In the real world, the clock is implicit. In a computer, it is a physical entity, and there may be different clocks in different computers. The time event is (essentially) a message from the clock to the system. Note that both absolute time and elapsed time may be defined with respect to a real-world clock or to a virtual internal clock. In the latter case, it may differ for various objects.

Time events may be based on absolute time (the time of day or a clock setting within a system) or relative time (the elapsed time since the entry to a certain state or the occurrence of an event).

Notation

Time events are not declared as named events the way signals are. Instead, a time expression is simply used as the trigger of a transition.

Discussion

In any real implementation, time events do not come from the universe—they come from some clock object inside or outside the system. As such, they become almost indistinguishable from signals, especially in real-time and distributed systems. In such systems, the issue of which clock is used must also be determined—there is no such thing as the "real time." (It doesn't exist in the real universe either—just ask Einstein.)

time expression

An expression that resolves to an absolute or relative value of time. Used in defining a time event.

Semantics

Most time expressions are either elapsed time after the entry to a state or the occurrence of a particular absolute time. Other time expressions must be defined in an ad hoc way.

A time expression is defined with a minimum and maximum time. These can be the same to define a single point in time.

Notation

Elapsed time. An event denoting the passage of some amount of time after entry to the state containing the transition is notated with the keyword **after** followed by an expression that evaluates (at modeling time) to an amount of time.

after (10 seconds)

after (10 seconds since exit from state A)

If no starting point is specified, then it is the elapsed time since entry to the state containing the transition.

Absolute time. An event denoting the occurrence of an absolute time is notated with the keyword **when**, followed by a parenthetical Boolean expression involving time.

when (date = Jan. 1, 2000)

time observation action

An action that returns the current time.

Semantics

The action returns the current time.

Notation

The following syntax may be used in a sequence diagram:

```
name = now
```

Figure 14-281 shows an example.

Discussion

Unlike the duration observation action, the time observation action makes sense as an action that might be implemented and used in programs. In the UML specification, however, it is formulated in a manner inconsistent with other actions, in that it includes both an time observation and an assignment action. It is probably best for implementors to regard this as a mistake and have it merely output a value that can be assigned using the normal write actions.

In a simple system, all clocks can be regarded as identical. In a more realistic real-time system, clocks will differ and a time observation must contain the identity of the clock that is used. For modeling such systems, the simple UML time model is inadequate and a more robust real-time model must be used.

The UML specification does not define a time observation for modeling purposes, that is, one that is not meant to be executed by a user program but is meant to be used to make assertions by the modeler. We recommend the use of timing marks to attach names to times at which events occur. These are not part of the official UML specification, but they should be.

History

The UML2 timing model has lost some capability from the UML1 model, such as timing marks. Hopefully this capability will be restored in the future.

time value

A value representing an absolute or relative moment in time.
See time expression.

timing diagram

An alternate way of displaying a sequence diagram that explicitly shows changes in state on a lifeline and metric time (time units). They may be useful in real-time applications.

Notation

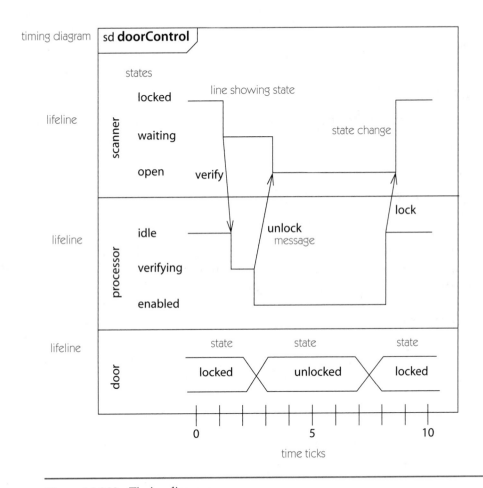

Figure 14-282. *Timing diagram*

A timing diagram (Figure 14-282) is a special form of a sequence diagram with the following differences:

• The axes are usually reversed so that time increases from left to right.

• Lifelines are shown in separate compartments arranged vertically.

- The lifeline jogs up and down to show changes in state. Each vertical position represents a different state. The ordering of states may or may not have any significance.

- Alternately, a lifeline can follow a single line with different states or values displayed on the line.

- A metric time axis may be shown. Tick marks indicate time intervals, sometimes discrete times at which changes happen.

- The times on different lifelines are synchronized.

- The value held by an object may be shown.

timing mark

A denotation for the time at which an event occurs. Timing marks may be used in constraints.

Semantics

A timing mark is the time at which an event occurs.

Notation

A timing mark is shown as a tick mark (a short horizontal line) even with an event on a sequence diagram. The name of the timing mark is placed next to the tick mark and may be used in timing expressions. See Figure 14-281 for an example.

Discussion

Note that a time observation action is not a satisfactory substitute for a timing mark. Although timing marks are not part of the official UML2 specification, we recommend their use because the capability is otherwise lacking.

token

The presence of a locus of control, including possible data values, during the execution of an activity.

Semantics

The execution semantics of activities are based on the concept of tokens as markers of activities. The concept originally comes for Petri net theory. A token is a run-time marker of the presence of a locus of control. A token may also include data values that are implied by the locus of control. An activity graph may have multiple tokens, indicating concurrent execution.

The execution rules of actions and activity nodes are based on tokens. In general, an action may begin execution when tokens are present on all its input pins. When it begins execution, it removes the tokens from the input pins and internalizes their data values. When an action completes execution, it produces tokens on each of its output pins. The tokens contain data values appropriate for the various outputs. These tokens may then enable the execution of other actions.

Activities are control constructs that include actions. Each kind of activity node has its own enabling rules. Some activities require tokens on all input pins, while some (such as merges) may be enabled by tokens on a subset of input pins. In any case, the enabling tokens are consumed before the activity begins execution, and new tokens are produced on some or all of the output pins when the activity completes execution.

The key to tokens is that they are consumed when they enable the execution of an action or activity. If two activity nodes contend for the same tokens, only one node will execute, although the selection may be nondeterministic. Because tokens combine control and data, they avoid the "action-at-a-distance" problems inherent in separating control and data. They model concurrency in an effective but natural way.

trace

A sequence of event occurrences within the execution of an interaction.

See also trace dependency for an unrelated use of the word *trace*.

Semantics

A trace is a sequence of event occurrences as the result of a particular execution of an interaction. The semantics of interactions is defined in terms of traces. An interaction defines a set of allowed traces and a set of forbidden traces. All the traces in the allowed set are definitely consistent with the interaction definition. All the traces in the forbidden set are definitely inconsistent with the interaction definition. Any other traces may or may not be consistent with the definition. It may be necessary to look at other parts of the model to determine their validity.

Several interaction constructs (such as parallel) define multiple, independent subtraces for their parts. Unless otherwise restricted, the event occurrences for each subtrace can be interleaved arbitrarily to make a single overall trace. This is the meaning of concurrency within interactions.

Two interactions are equivalent if they define the same sets of traces.

Notation

Traces are primarily a semantic concept for defining the meaning of interaction models. They represent the results of an actual execution. A sequence diagram, by contrast, is a model of an interaction definition. The sequences of event specifications in the sequence diagram are not the actual traces; rather, they are models from which traces may be derived. The best way to actually show a trace is to show a list of event occurrences in text form, but this is not often useful except as a theoretical exercise.

trace dependency (stereotype of Abstraction)

An abstraction dependency that indicates a historical development process or other extra-model relationship between two elements that represent the same concept without specific rules for deriving one from the other. This is the least specific kind of dependency, and it has minimal semantics. It is mostly of use as a reminder for human thought during development. It is intended to permit traceability of requirements across development.

See abstraction, dependency, model.

Semantics

A trace is a variety of dependency that indicates a connection between two elements that represent the same concept at different levels of meaning. It does not represent semantics within a model. Rather, it represents connections between elements with different semantics—that is, between elements from different models on different planes of meaning. There is no explicit mapping between the elements. Often, it represents a connection between two ways of capturing a concept at different stages of development. For example, two elements that are variations of the same theme might be related by a trace. A trace does not represent a relationship between run-time instances. Rather, it is a dependency between model elements themselves.

A major use of trace is for tracking requirements that have been changed throughout the development of a system. The trace dependencies may relate elements in two kinds of models (such as a use case model and a design model) or in two versions of the same kind of model.

Notation

A trace is indicated by a dependency arrow (a dashed arrow with its tail on the newer element and its head on the older element) with the keyword «trace». Usually, however, the elements are in different models that are not displayed simultaneously, so in practice, the relationship would most often be implemented in a tool as a hyperlink.

transient link

A link that exists for a limited duration, such as for the execution of an operation. See also association, collaboration, usage.

Semantics

During execution, some links exist for a limited duration. Of course, almost any object or link has a limited lifespan, if the time period is great enough. Some links, however, exist only in certain limited contexts, such as during the execution of a method. Procedure arguments and local variables can be represented by transient links. It is possible to model all such links as associations, but then the conditions on the associations must be stated very broadly, and they lose much of their precision in constraining combinations of objects. Such situations can instead be modeled using collaborations, which are configurations of objects and links that exist within special contexts.

A connector from a collaboration can be regarded as a transient link that exists only within the execution of a behavioral entity, such as a procedure. It appears within a class model as a usage dependency. For full details, it is necessary to consult the behavioral model.

Notation

A transient link may be shown as a connector within a collaboration representing the execution of a behavior.

transition

A relationship within a state machine between two states indicating that an object in the first state, when a specified event occurs and specified guard conditions are satisfied, will perform specified effects (action or activity) and enter the second state. On such a change of state, the transition is said to fire. A simple transition has a single source state and a single target state. A complex transition has more than one source state and/or more than one target state. It represents a change in the number of concurrently active states, or a fork or join of control. An internal transition has a source state but no target state. It represents a response to an event without a change of state. States and transitions are the vertices and nodes of state machines.

See also protocol state machine, state machine.

Semantics

Transitions represent the potential paths among the states in the life history of an object, as well as the actions performed in changing state. A transition indicates the way an object in a state responds to the occurrence of an event. States and transitions are the vertices and arcs of a state machine that describes the possible life histories of the instances of a classifier.

Structure

A transition has a source state, an event trigger, a guard condition, an action, and a target state. Some of these may be absent in a particular transition.

Source state. The source state is the state that is affected by the transition. If an object is in the source state, an outgoing transition of the state may fire if the object receives the trigger event of the transition and the guard condition (if any) is satisfied. The source state becomes inactive after the transition fires.

Target state. The target state is the state that becomes active after the completion of the transition. It is the state to which the master object changes. The target state is not used in an internal transition, which does not perform a change of state.

Event trigger. The event trigger is the event whose reception by the object in the source state makes the transition eligible to fire, provided its guard condition is satisfied. If the event has parameters, their values are available to the transition and may be used in expressions for the guard condition and effects. The event triggering a transition becomes the current event and may be accessed by subsequent actions that are part of the run-to-completion step initiated by the event.

A transition without an explicit trigger event is called a completion transition (or a triggerless transition) and is implicitly triggered on the completion of any internal do activity in the state. A composite state indicates its completion by reaching the final state of each of its regions. If a state has no internal activity or nested states, then a completion transition is triggered immediately when the state is entered after any entry activity is executed. Note that a completion transition must satisfy its guard condition to fire. If the guard condition is false when the completion occurs, then the implicit completion event is consumed and the transition will not fire later even if the guard condition becomes true. (This kind of behavior can be modeled instead with a change event.)

Note that all appearances of an event within a state machine must have the same signature.

Guard condition. The guard condition is a Boolean expression that is evaluated when a transition is triggered by the handling of an event, including an implicit completion event on a completion transition. If the state machine is performing a run-to-completion step when an event occurs, the event is placed in the event poll for the object owning the state machine until the step is complete and the state machine is quiescent; otherwise the event is handled immediately. If the guard expression evaluates to true, the transition is eligible to fire. If the expression evaluates to false, then the transition does not fire. If an event is handled but no transition becomes eligible to fire, the event is discarded. This is not an error. Multiple transitions having different guard conditions may be triggered by the same event. If the event occurs, all the guard conditions are tested. If more than one guard condition is true, only one transition will fire. The choice of transition to fire is nondeterministic if no priority rule is given.

Note that the guard condition is evaluated only once, at the time when the event is handled. If the condition evaluates to false and later becomes true, the transition will not fire unless another event occurs and the condition is true at that time. Note that a guard condition is not the appropriate way to continuously monitor a value. A change event should be used for such a situation.

If a transition has no guard condition, then the guard condition is treated as true and the transition is enabled if its trigger event occurs. If several transitions are enabled, only one will fire. The choice may be nondeterministic.

For convenience, a guard condition can be broken into a series of simpler guard conditions. In fact, several guard conditions may branch from a single trigger event or guard condition. Each path through the tree represents a single transition triggered by the (single) trigger event with a different effective guard condition that is the conjunction ("and") of the guard conditions along its path. All the expressions along such a path are evaluated before a transition is chosen to fire. A transition cannot partially fire. In effect, a set of independent transitions may share part of their description. Figure 14-283 shows an example.

Note that trees of guard conditions and the ability to order transitions for eligibility are merely conveniences, as the same effect could be achieved by a set of independent transitions, each with its own disjoint guard condition (but see *choice vertex* below).

Effect. A transition may contain an effect, that is, an action or activity that is executed when the transition fires. This behavior may access and modify the object that owns the state machine (and, indirectly, other objects that it can reach). The effect may use parameters of the trigger event, as well as attributes and associations of the owning object. The trigger event is available as the current event during the entire run-to-completion step initiated by the event, including later triggerless segments and entry and exit actions.

An effect is intended to be finite and should usually be fairly short, because the state machine cannot process additional events until its execution is complete. Any behavior that is intended to continue for an extended time should be modeled as a do activity attached to a state rather than a transition.

Branches. For convenience, several transitions that share the same trigger event but have different guard conditions can be grouped together in the model and notation to avoid duplication of the trigger or the common part of the guard condition. This is merely a representational convenience and does not affect the semantics of transitions.

See branch for details of representation and notation.

Choice vertex. A choice vertex permits a dynamic branch to depend on actions executed earlier in the same transition. A transition may be enabled to fire if all the guard conditions up to the choice vertex are satisfied. Guard conditions on transition segments after the choice vertex are not evaluated to determine firing. If the transition fires, its effects are executed on segments up to the choice vertex. Then the guard conditions on segments leaving the choice vertex are evaluated, including the results of the effects that have just been executed. This permits an action to affect the results of the branch. The modeler must ensure that at least one outgoing transition segment from the choice vertex will be enabled, however, or the state machine will fail. A choice vertex is a pseudostate and may not remain active. A simple way to ensure success is to include an else condition among the outgoing segments. Figure 14-284 shows an example in which the branch depends on the result of the selection operation earlier in the transition.

Completion transition. A transition that lacks an event is called a completion transition. It is triggered by the completion of activity in its source state. If the source state is a simple state, it is complete when the entry activity and do activity in the state have finished. If it is a composite state, it is complete when each of its regions have reached their final states. Although completion is called a completion event, it does not go into the event pool but is processed immediately as part of the run-to-completion step whenever it applies.

See also complex transition, fork, join, for transitions with multiple source or target states.

Notation

A transition is shown as a solid arrow from one state (the *source* state) to another state (the *target* state), labeled by a transition string. Figure 14-284 shows a transition between two states and one split into segments.

A transition has a text label of the form:

$\lfloor$ name : $\rfloor_{opt}$ event-name$_{opt}$ $\lfloor$ (parameter-list) $\rfloor_{opt}$ $\lfloor$ [guard-condition] $\rfloor_{opt}$
$\lfloor$ / effect-list $\rfloor_{opt}$

The *name* may be used to reference the transition in expressions, particularly for forming timing marks. It is followed by a colon.

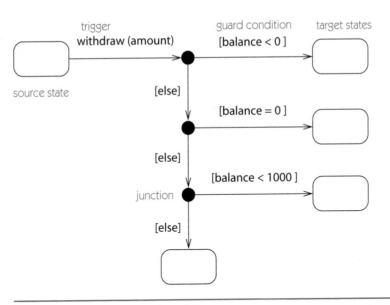

Figure 14-283. *Tree of guard conditions*

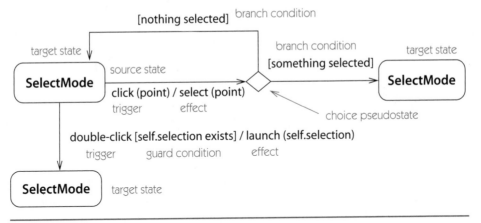

Figure 14-284. *Transitions*

The *event-name* names an event and is followed by its parameters. The parameter list may be omitted if there are no parameters. The event name and parameter list are omitted for a completion transition. The parameter-list has the format:

⌊name : type⌋list,

The *guard-condition* is a Boolean expression written in terms of parameters of the triggering event and attributes and links of the object described by the state machine. The guard condition may also involve tests of the status of concurrent states of the current machine or explicitly designated states of some reachable object—[**in** State1] and [**not in** State2] are examples. State names may be fully qualified by the nested states that contain them, yielding pathnames of the form State1::State2::State3. This may be used if the same state name occurs in different composite state regions of the overall machine.

The *effect-list* is a procedural expression that is executed if and when the transition fires. It may be written in terms of operations, attributes, and links of the owning object and the parameters of the triggering event. Actions may include call, send, and other kinds of actions. The effect-list may contain more than one action. The syntax of the expression is implementation dependent.

Internal transition. An internal transition is shown as a transition string inside a state symbol.

Branches. A transition may include a segment with a trigger event followed by a tree of junctions, drawn as small circles. This is equivalent to a set of individual transitions, one for each path through the tree, whose guard condition is the "and" of all the conditions along the path. Only the final segment of any path may have an action.

Choices. A transition may include a segment with a trigger event followed by a tree of choices, drawn as small diamonds. Any segment may have an action. The guard conditions on the segments following the choice are evaluated after any preceding effects have been executed.

Complex transitions. See complex transition for notation for transitions with multiple source or target states.

Protocol transition. See protocol state machine for notation.

Discussion

A transition represents an atomic change from one state to another, possibly accompanied by an atomic action. A transition is noninterruptible. The actions on a transition should be short, usually trivial, computations, such as assignment statements and simple arithmetic calculations.

transition phase

The fourth phase of a software development process, during which the implemented system is configured for execution in a real-world context. During this phase, the deployment view is completed, together with any of the remaining views that were not completed in previous phases.

See development process.

transmission

The transfer of control and information among objects by messages.

Semantics

A message is created as the result of a call action or send action. A message has a type (an operation or a signal) and a list of argument values. Each message is directed at a particular object. The encoding of a message and the manner of its transmission to the target object are not relevant to the UML semantics and are not visible to objects or their behaviors. The UML execution model covers a wide range of implementation possibilities, including synchronous execution within a single processor, synchronous transmission, and asynchronous transmission. In the basic UML execution model, the transmission time and sequencing relative to other messages is unknowable. Profiles aimed at particular execution environments can add this kind of information, if desired.

Asynchronous messages (from signal send actions or asynchronous calls) do not require any information about the sender. Their transmission and subsequent reception is concurrent with the ongoing execution of the object that created the message. Synchronous messages (from synchronous calls) cause the blocking of execution of the caller. They include sufficient information to identify the calling execution and to permit it to be awakened in the future and provided with return values. The encoding of this return information is explicitly opaque in the UML model; no object or action can access it, except in the act of returning control and values to the caller. This permits a wide range of implementations without biasing the form of the implementation technology. Again, profiles intended for various implementation environments may choose to specify the form of this information and make it available to user actions.

trigger

The specification of an event whose occurrence causes the execution of behavior, such as making a transition eligible to fire. The word may be used as a noun (for the event itself) or as a verb (for the occurrence of the event). It is used to describe the association of the event with the transition.

See also completion transition, transition.

Semantics

Each transition (except a completion transition that fires on the completion of internal activity) has a reference to an event as part of its structure. If the event occurs when an object is in a state containing an outgoing transition whose trigger is the event or an ancestor of the event, then the guard condition on the transition is tested. If the condition is satisfied, then the transition is enabled to fire. If the guard condition is absent, then it is deemed to be satisfied. If more than one transition is eligible to fire, only one will actually fire. The choice may be nondeterministic. (If the object has more than one concurrent state, one transition from each state may fire. But at most one transition from each state may fire.)

Note that the guard condition is tested once, at the moment when the triggering event occurs (including an implicit completion event). If no transition is enabled to fire by the occurrence of an event, the event is simply ignored. This is not an error.

The parameters of the trigger event are available for use in a guard condition or an effect attached to the transition or to an entry activity on the target state.

Throughout the execution of a run-to-completion step after a transition, the trigger event remains available to the actions of the substeps of the transition as the current event. The exact type of this event may be unknown in an entry action or in a later segment in a multiple-segment transition. Therefore, the type of event may be discriminated in an action using a polymorphic operation or a case statement. Once the exact event type is known, its parameters can be used.

The trigger event may be the reception of a signal, the reception of a call, a change event, or a time event. The completion of activity is a pseudotrigger.

Notation

The name and signature of the trigger event are part of the label on a transition.
See transition.

triggerless transition

A transition without an explicit event trigger. A triggerless transition that departs a normal state represents a completion transition, that is, a transition that is triggered by the completion of activity in the state rather than by an explicit event. When it leaves a pseudostate, it represents a transition segment that is automatically traversed when the preceding segment has completed its action. Triggerless transitions are used to connect initial states and history states to their target states.

tuple

An ordered list of values. Generally, the term implies that there is a set of such lists of similar form. (This is a standard mathematical term.)

type

A declaration of a classifier that constrains the value of an attribute, parameter, result of an operation, or variable. The actual value must be an instance of the type or one of its descendants.

type (stereotype of Class)

A specification of the general structure and behavior of a domain of objects without providing a physical implementation.

See class, implementation class, type.

Discussion

Much ink has been spilled over the distinction between type and class, mostly to justify intuitive feelings about the use of the words or programming language distinctions without a sound mathematical basis or practical need.

type expression

An expression that evaluates to a reference to one or more data types. For example, an attribute type declaration in a typical programming language is a type expression. The syntax of type expressions is unspecified in UML.

Example

In C++ the following are type expressions:

Person*

Order[24]

Boolean (*) (String, int)

uninterpreted

A placeholder for a type or types whose implementation is not specified by the UML. Every uninterpreted value has a corresponding string representation. In any physical implementation, such as a model editor, the implementation would have to be complete, so there would be no uninterpreted values.

union

A declaration that a property is defined as the union of a number of explicitly specified other properties.

See also subsets.

Semantics

Sometimes the same property (an association end or attribute) can be modeled at more than one level of granularity, where a general level covers several cases and a more specific level expands each of those cases into several more specific cases. If the high-level description is simply the union of a set of specific cases, it is called a *derived union*. The high-level description provides a way to make statements about all the specific cases, but every instance of the union must be an instance of one of the specific cases.

The high-level property is labeled with the union property. Each of its specific cases must be labeled as subsets of the high-level property. The union property is therefore defined an the union of all the properties that explicitly subset it.

Notation

A property that is a derived union is labeled by the string {union}. If the property is an association end, the label is placed near the end of the association line. If the property is an attribute, the label is placed after the attribute string.

See Figure 14-267 for an example.

uniqueness

An indicator of whether the values in a collection of multiplicity greater than one may contain duplicate values. A collection whose elements are not unique is a bag or a list.

Semantics

Uniqueness is part of the multiplicity specification. It is a Boolean flag stating whether the values of a collection must be unique. If they are unique, the collection is a set. If they are not unique, the collection is a bag. The default is unique (the collection is a set).

Notation

A multiplicity indicator may contain the following keywords:

set   The values must be unique. This is the default and the keyword may be (and usually is) omitted.

bag   The values need not be unique. Duplicates are permitted.

Uniqueness and ordering may be combined in the following ways:

	unique	*not unique*
unordered	set (default)	bag
ordered	ordered (set)	sequence or seq or list

unlimited natural

A cardinality specification that may be a nonnegative integer or the specification "many" indicating no upper bound (but still finite). Used in the specification of multiplicity.

unspecified value

A value that has not yet been specified by the modeler.

Discussion

An unspecified value is not a value at all in the proper sense and cannot appear within a complete model except for properties whose value is unnecessary or irrelevant. For example, multiplicity cannot be unknown; it must have some value. A lack of any knowledge is tantamount to a multiplicity of many. The semantics of UML therefore do not allow or deal with the absence of values or unspecified values.

There is another sense in which "unspecified" is a useful part of an unfinished model. It has the meaning: "I have not yet thought about this value, and I have made a note of it so that I will remember to give it a value later." It is an explicit statement that the model is incomplete. This is a useful capability and one that tools may support. By its very nature, such a value cannot appear in a finished model, and it makes no sense to define its semantics. A tool can automatically supply a default value for an unspecified value when a value is needed—for example, during code generation—but this is simply a convenience and not part of the semantics. Unspecified values are outside the semantics of UML.

Similarly, there is no semantic meaning to a default value for a property. A property in the model simply has a value. A tool may automatically supply values for properties of newly created elements. But again, this is just an operational convenience within the tool, not part of UML semantics. Semantically complete UML models do not have default or unspecified values; they simply have values.

usage

A dependency in which one element (the client) requires the presence of another element (the supplier) for its correct functioning or implementation—generally, for implementation reasons.

See also collaboration, dependency, transient link.

Semantics

A usage dependency is a situation in which one element requires the presence of another element for its correct implementation or functioning. All the elements must exist at the same level of meaning—that is, they do not involve a shift in the level of abstraction or realization (such as a mapping between an analysis-level class and an implementation-level class). Frequently, a usage dependency involves implementation-level elements, such as a C++ include file, for which it implies compiler consequences. A usage may be stereotyped further to indicate the exact nature of the dependency, such as calling an operation of another class or instantiating an object of another class.

Notation

A usage is indicated by a dashed arrow (dependency) with the keyword «use». The arrowhead is on the supplier (independent) element, and the tail is on the client (dependent) element.

Discussion

A usage usually corresponds to a transient link—that is, a connection between instances of classes that is not meaningful or present all the time, but only in some context, such as the execution of a subroutine procedure. The dependency construct does not model the full information in this situation, only the fact of its existence. The collaboration construct provides the capability to model such relationships in full detail.

use

Keyword for the usage dependency in the notation.

use case

The specification of sequences of actions, including variant sequences and error sequences, that a system, subsystem, or class can perform by interacting with outside objects to provide a service of value.

See also actor, classifier, subject.

Semantics

A use case is a coherent unit of functionality provided by a classifier (a system, subsystem, or class) as manifested by sequences of messages exchanged among the system and one or more outside users (represented as actors), together with actions performed by the system.

The purpose of a use case is to define a piece of behavior of a classifier (including a subsystem or the entire system), without revealing the internal structure of the classifier. The classifier whose behavior is described is called the subject. Each use case specifies a service the subject provides to its users—that is, a specific way of using the classifier that is visible from the outside. It describes a complete sequence initiated by an object (as modeled by an actor) in terms of the interaction between users and subject, as well as the responses performed by the subject. The interaction includes only the communications between the subject and the actors. The internal behavior or implementation is hidden.

The entire set of use cases of a classifier or system cover its behavior and partition it into pieces meaningful to users. Each use case represents a meaningful quantized piece of functionality available to users. Note that *user* includes humans, as well as computers and other objects. An actor is an idealization of the purpose of a user, not a representation of a physical user. One physical user can map to many actors, and an actor can represent the same aspect of multiple physical users. See actor.

A use case includes normal mainline behavior in response to a user request, as well as possible variants of the normal sequence, such as alternate sequences, exceptional behavior, and error handling. The goal is to describe a piece of coherent functionality in all its variations, including all the error conditions. The complete set of use cases for a classifier specifies all the different ways to use the classifier. Use cases can be grouped into packages for convenience.

A use case is a classifier; it describes potential behavior. An execution of a use case is a use case instance. The behavior of a use case can be specified in various ways: by an attached state machine, an activity specification, by an interaction describing legal sequences, or by pre- and postconditions. It can also be described by an informal text description. Behavior can be illustrated, but not formally specified, by a set of scenarios. But at early stages of development, this may be sufficient.

A use case instance is an execution of a use case, initiated by a message from an instance of an actor. As a response to the message, the use case instance executes a sequence of actions specified by the use case, such as sending messages to actor instances, not necessarily only to the initiating actor. The actor instances may send messages to the use case instance, and the interaction continues until the instance has responded to all input. When it does not expect any more input, it ends.

A use case is a specification of the behavior of a system (or other classifier) as a whole in its interactions with outside actors. The internal interactions among internal objects in a system that implements the behavior may be described by a collaboration that realizes a use case.

Structure

A use case is usually, but not always, owned by its subject classifier. A use case may have classifier features and relationships.

Features. A use case is a classifier and therefore has attributes and operations. The attributes are used to represent the state of the use case—that is, the progress of executing it. An operation represents a piece of work the use case can perform. A use case operation is not directly callable from the outside, but may be used to describe the effect of the use case on the system. The execution of an operation may be associated with the receipt of a message from an actor. The operations act on the attributes of the use case and indirectly on the subject classifier to which the use case is attached.

Associations to actors. An association between an actor and a use case indicates that the actor instance communicates with the subject instance to effect some result that is of interest to the actor. Actors model external users of a subject. Thus, if the subject is a system, its actors are the external users of the system. Actors of lower-level subsystems may be other classes within the overall system.

The actor end of the association may have a multiplicity that indicates how many instances of the actor may participate in a single execution of the use case. The default multiplicity is one.

One actor may communicate with several use cases—that is, the actor may request several different services of the subject—and one use case may communicate with one or more actors when providing its service. Note that two use cases that specify the same subject do not communicate with each other because each of them individually describes a complete usage of the system. They may interact indirectly through shared actors.

The use case end of the association may have a multiplicity indicating how many use case executions an instance of the actor can participate in. Participation in multiple use cases may be simultaneous or sequential.

The interaction between actors and use cases can be defined with interfaces. An interface defines the operations an actor or a use case may support or use. Different interfaces offered by the same use case need not be disjoint.

Use cases are related to other use cases by generalization, extend, and include relationships.

Generalization. A generalization relationship relates a specialized use case to the more general use case. The child inherits the attributes, operations, and behavior sequences of the parent and may add additional attributes and operations of its own. The child use case adds incremental behavior to the parent use case by inserting additional action sequences into the parent sequence at arbitrary points. It may also modify some inherited operations and sequences, but this must be done with care so that the intent of the parent is preserved. Any include or extend relationships to the child use case also effectively modify the behavior inherited from the parent use case.

Extend. An extend relationship is a kind of dependency. The client use case adds incremental behavior to the base use case by inserting additional action sequences into the base sequence. The client use case contains one or more separate behavior sequence segments. The extend relationship contains a list of extension point names from the base use case, equal in number to the number of segments in the client use case. An extension point represents a location or set of locations in the base use case at which the extension could be inserted. An extend relationship may also have a condition on it, which may use attributes from the parent use case. When an instance of the parent use case reaches a location referenced by an extension point in an extend relationship, the condition is evaluated; if the condition is true, the corresponding behavior segment of the child use case is performed. If there is no condition, it is deemed to be always true. If the extend relationship has more than one extension point, the condition is evaluated only at the first extension point prior to execution of the first segment.

An extend relationship does not create a new instantiable use case. Instead, it implicitly adds behavior to the original base use case. The base use case implicitly includes the extended behavior. The nonextended original base use case is not available in its unaltered form. In other words, if you extend a use case, you cannot explicitly instantiate the base use case without the possibility of extensions. A use case may have multiple extensions that all apply to the same base use case and can be inserted into one use case instance if their separate conditions are satisfied. On the other hand, an extension use case may extend several base use cases (or the same one at different extension points), each at its own proper extension point (or list of extension points). If there are several extensions at the same extension point, their relative execution order is nondeterministic.

Note that the extension use case is not to be instantiated, the base use case must be instantiated to obtain the combined base-plus-extensions behavior. The extension use case may or may not be instantiable, but in any case it does not include the base use case behavior.

Include. An include relationship denotes the inclusion of the behavior sequence of the supplier use case into the interaction sequence of a client use case, under the control of the client use case at a location the client specifies in its description. This is a dependency, not a generalization, because the supplier use case cannot be substituted in places at which the client use case appears. The client may access the attributes of the base to obtain values and communicate results. The use case instance is executing the client use case. When it reaches the inclusion point, it begins executing the supplier use case until it is complete. Then it resumes executing the client use case beyond the inclusion location. The attributes of the supplier use case do not have values that persist between executions.

A use case may be abstract, which means that it cannot be directly instantiated in a system execution. It defines a fragment of behavior that is specialized by or included in concrete use cases, or it may be an extension of a base use case. It may also be concrete if it can be instantiated by itself.

Behavior. The behavior sequence of a use case can be described using a state machine, activity graph, interaction, or text code in some executable language. The actions of the state machine or the statements of the code may call on the internal operations of the use case to specify the effects of execution. The actions may also indicate sending messages to actors.

A use case may be described informally using scenarios or plain text, but such descriptions are imprecise and meant for human interpretation only.

The actions of a use case may be specified in terms of calls to operations of the classifier that the use case describes. One operation may be called by more than one use case.

Realization. The realization of a use case may be specified by a set of collaborations. A collaboration describes the implementation of the use case by objects in the classifier the use case describes. Each collaboration describes the context among the constituents of the system within which one or more interaction sequences occur. Collaborations and their interactions define how objects within the system interact to achieve the specified external behavior of the use case.

A system can be specified with use cases at various levels of abstraction. A use case specifying a system, for example, may be refined into a set of subordinate use cases, each specifying a service of a subsystem. The functionality specified by the superordinate (higher-level) use case is completely traceable to the functionality of the subordinate (lower-level) use cases. A superordinate use case and a set of subordinate use cases specify the same behavior at two levels of abstraction. The subordinate use cases cooperate to provide the behavior of the superordinate use case. The cooperation of the subordinate use cases is specified by collaborations of the superordinate use case and may be presented in collaboration diagrams. The actors of a superordinate use case appear as actors of the subordinate use cases. Moreover, the subordinate use cases are actors of each other. This layered realization results in a nested set of use cases and collaborations that implement the entire system.

Notation

A use case is shown as an ellipse with the name of the use case inside or below the ellipse. If attributes or operations of the use case must be shown, the use case can be drawn as a classifier rectangle with the keyword «use case». Figure 14-285 shows a use case diagram. The subject is represented by a rectangle containing the use cases. The actors are placed outside the rectangle to show that they are external. Lines connect actors to the use cases they participate in.

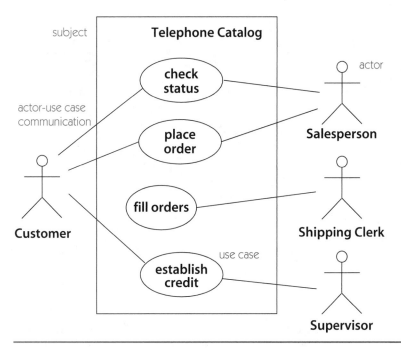

Figure 14-285. *Use cases, subject, and actors*

An extension point is a named entity within a use case that describes locations at which action sequences from other use cases may be inserted. It provides a level of indirection between the extensions and the behavior sequence text. An extension point references a location or set of locations within the behavior sequence of the use case. The reference can be changed independently of extend relationships that use the extension point. Each extension point must have a unique name within a use case. Extension points may be listed in a compartment of the use case with the heading **extension points** (Figure 14-286).

A relationship between a use case and an actor is shown using an association symbol—a solid path between the use case and the actor symbols. Generally, no name or role names are placed on the line, as the actor and the use case define the relationship uniquely.

A generalization relationship is shown by a generalization arrow—a solid path from the child use case to the parent use case, with a closed triangular arrowhead on the parent use case.

An extend relationship or an include relationship is shown by a dependency arrow with the keyword «extend» or «include»—a dashed line with a stick arrowhead on the client use case. An extend relationship also has a comment box containing a condition (on which the extension is executed) and an extension point or list of extension point names. The comment box is may be suppressed in the diagram.

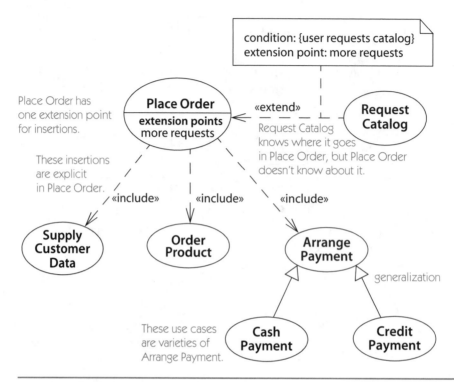

Figure 14-286. *Use case relationships*

Figure 14-286 shows various kinds of use case relationships.

Behavior specification. The relationship between a use case and its external inter-action sequences is usually represented by a hyperlink to sequence diagrams. The hyperlink is invisible but it can be traversed in an editor. The behavior may also be specified by a state machine or by programming language text attached to the use case. Natural language text may be used as an informal specification.

See extend for a sample of some behavior sequences.

The relationship between a use case and its implementation may be shown as a realization relationship from a use case to a collaboration. But because these are often in separate models, it is usually represented as an invisible hyperlink. The ex-pectation is that a tool will support the ability to "zoom into" a use case to see its scenarios and/or implementation as a collaboration.

use case diagram

A diagram that shows the relationships among actors and use cases within a system.

See actor, use case.

Notation

A use case diagram is a graph of actors, a set of use cases enclosed by a subject boundary (a rectangle), associations between the actors and the use cases, relationships among the use cases, and generalization among the actors. Use case diagrams show elements from the use case model (use cases, actors).

use case generalization

A taxonomic relationship between a use case (the child) and the use case (the parent) that describes the characteristics the child shares with other use cases that have the same parent. This is generalization as applicable to use cases.

Semantics

A parent use case may be specialized into one or more child use cases that represent more specific forms of the parent (Figure 14-287). A child inherits all the attributes, operations, and relationships of its parent, because a use case is a classifier. The implementation of an inherited operation may be overridden by a collaboration that realizes a child use case.

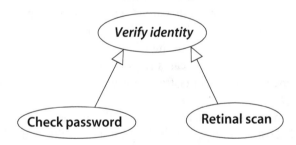

Figure 14-287. *Use case generalization*

The child inherits the behavior sequence of the parent and may insert additional behavior into it (Figure 14-288). The parent and the child are potentially instantiable (if they are not abstract), and different specializations of the same parent are independent, unlike an extend relationship, in which multiple extends all implicitly modify the same base use case. Behavior may be added to the child use case by adding steps into the behavior sequence inherited from the parent, as well as by declaring extend and include relationships to the child. If the parent is abstract, its behavior sequence may have sections that are explicitly incomplete in the parent and must be provided by the child. The child may modify steps inherited from the parent, but as with the overriding of methods, this capability must be used with care because the intent of the parent must be preserved.

Use case behavior for parent **Verify Identity:**

The parent is abstract, there is no behavior sequence.
A concrete descendant must supply the behavior as shown below.

Use case behavior for child **Check Password:**

Obtain password from master database
Ask user for password
User supplies password
Check password against user entry

Use case behavior for child **Retinal Scan**

Obtain retinal signature from master database
Scan user's retina and obtain signature
Compare master signature against scanned signature

Figure 14-288. *Behavior sequences for parent and child use cases*

The generalization relationship connects a child use case to a parent use case. A child use case may access and modify attributes defined by the parent use case.

Substitutability for use cases means that the behavior sequence of a child use case must include the behavior sequence of its parent. The steps in the parent's sequence need not be contiguous, however; the child can interleave additional steps among the steps of the behavior sequence inherited from the parent.

The use of multiple inheritance with use cases requires an explicit specification of how the behavior sequences of the parents are interleaved to make the sequence for the child.

Use case generalization may use procedure to share the implementation of a base use case without full substitutability, but this capability should be used sparingly.

Notation

The normal generalization symbol is used—a solid line from the child to the parent with a hollow triangular arrowhead on the line touching the parent symbol.

Example

Figure 14-287 shows abstract use case **Verify identity** and its specialization as two concrete use cases, whose behavior is shown in Figure 14-288.

use case instance

The execution of a sequence of actions specified in a use case. An instance of a use case. See use case.

use case model

A model that describes the functional requirements of a system or other classifier in terms of use cases.

See actor, use case.

Semantics

The use case model represents functionality of a system or other classifier as manifested to external interactors with the system. A use case model is shown on a use case diagram.

use case view

That aspect of the system concerned with specifying behavior in terms of use cases. A use case model is a model focused on this view. The use case view is part of the set of modeling concepts loosely grouped together as the dynamic view.

utility (stereotype of Class)

A stereotyped class that has no instances. It describes a named collection of non-member attributes and operations, all of which are class scope.

Discussion

More of a programming technique than a modeling concept.

value

See data value.

value specification

The specification of a value in a model.

Semantics

A value specification is not a value, but the model of a value. Unlike an actual value, which must be concrete and specific, a value specification can be more or less precise. It may specify a specific value, but it may also specify a range of values or even values of different types.

Value specifications take various forms in UML, including text expressions.

variable

A location that may hold and change values during the execution of a behavior. Variables may appear in activities and other procedural specifications.

vertex

A source or a target for a transition in a state machine. A vertex can be either a state or a pseudostate.

view

A projection of a model, which is seen from one perspective or vantage point and omits entities that are not relevant to this perspective. The word is not used here to denote a presentation element. Instead, it includes projections in both the semantic model and the visual notation.

viewpoint

A perspective from which a view is seen.

Discussion

UML incorporates a number of viewpoints, including real-world modeling, application analysis, high-level design, implementation modeling, and visual programming of existing languages. (The last is an unfortunate use of UML by many users who do not appreciate the power of abstraction and modeling.) The multiple viewpoints sometimes cause confusion because the same concepts may be used in different ways to accomplish different purposes. It is unfortunate that UML itself does not contain good ways to declare the viewpoint that a model expresses, but modelers should take care to separate different viewpoints into different models and to label each model with the viewpoint that it expresses.

visibility

An enumeration whose value (**public**, **protected**, **private**, or **package**) denotes whether the model element to which it refers may be seen outside its enclosing namespace.

See also import for a discussion of visibility rules applied to interpackage references.

Semantics

Visibility declares the ability of a modeling element to reference an element that is in a different namespace from the referencing element. Visibility is part of the relationship between an element and the container that holds it. The container may be a package, class, or some other namespace. There are three predefined visibilities.

public	Any element that can see the container can also see the indicated element.
protected	Only an element within the container or a descendant of the container can see the indicated element. Other elements may not reference it or otherwise use it.
private	Only an element within the container can see the element. Other elements, including elements in descendants of the container, may not reference it or otherwise use it.
package	This applies to elements that cannot exist freely within packages, such as features of classifiers. Only an element declared in the same package can see the element.

Additional kinds of visibility might be defined for some programming languages, such as C++ *implementation* visibility. (Actually, all forms of nonpublic visibility are language-dependent.) The use of additional choices must be by convention between the user and any modeling tools and code generators.

Notation

Visibility can be shown by a property keyword or by a punctuation mark placed in front of the name of a model element.

public	+
protected	#
private	−
package	~

The visibility marker may be suppressed. The absence of a visibility marker indicates that the visibility is not shown, not that it is undefined or public. A tool should assign visibilities to new elements even if the visibility is not shown. The visibility marker is shorthand for a visibility property specification string.

Visibility may also be specified by keywords (public, protected, private). This form is often used as an inline list element that applies to an entire block of attributes or other list elements.

Any language-specific or user-defined visibility choices must be specified by a property string or by a tool-specific convention.

Classes. In a class, the visibility marker is placed on list elements, such as attributes and operations. It shows whether another class can access the elements.

Associations. In an association, the visibility marker is placed on the rolename of the target class (the end that would be accessed using the visibility setting). It shows whether the class at the far end can traverse the association toward the end with the visibility marker.

Packages. In a package, the visibility marker is placed on elements contained directly within the package, such as classes, associations, and nested packages. It shows whether another package that accesses or imports the first package can see the elements.

weak

The keyword indicating a weak sequencing combined fragment in an interaction diagram.

See weak sequencing.

weak sequencing

An operator in a combined fragment of an interaction that indicates weak sequencing of the subfragments. See also strict sequencing.

Semantics

This operator indicates that occurrence specifications on the same lifeline in different nested operands are ordered, but that occurrence specifications on different lifelines can be interleaved.

The distinction for strict sequencing is subtle and unlikely to be used by most modelers. See the UML specification for more details.

weight

The number of tokens consumed from a particular activity edge by the execution of an activity node.

Semantics

In the basic activity model, one token is consumed from an incoming edge by each execution of an activity node. In the advanced model, a weight may be placed on an edge to allow multiple tokens to be consumed by a single execution.

The weight is a positive integer attached to an edge that specifies the minimum number of tokens to be consumed from the edge. It may also have the special value all, which indicates that all available tokens on the edge are to be consumed whenever the node begins execution.

Notation

Weight is shown by placing a string on an activity edge with the format:

{ weight = value }

where value is a positive integer or the string all, which indicates that all available tokens are consumed.

well formed

Designates a model that is correctly constructed, one that satisfies all the predefined and model-specified rules and constraints. Such a model has meaningful semantics. A model that is not well formed is called ill formed.

XMI

An external format for serializing and exchanging models across platforms and systems. It is the standard interchange format for UML. It is based on the XML language.

xor

A constraint applied to a set of associations that share a connection to one class, specifying that any object of the shared class will have links from only one of the associations. It is an exclusive-or (not inclusive-or) constraint.
See association.

write action

There is a family of actions that modify the values of various slots, including attributes, association ends, qualifiers, and variables.
See action.

Part 4: Appendices ————————

UML Definition Documents

The UML is defined by a set of documents published by the Object Management Group [UML-04]. These documents may be found on the OMG web site (www.omg.org). They may be updated from time to time by the OMG. This chapter explains the structure of the UML semantic model described in the documents.

The UML is formally defined using a metamodel—that is, a model of the constructs in UML. The metamodel itself is expressed in UML. This is an example of a metacircular interpreter—that is, a language defined in terms of itself. Things are not completely circular. Only a small subset of UML is used to define the metamodel. In principle, this fixed point of the definition could be bootstrapped from a more basic definition. In practice, going to such lengths is unnecessary.

Each section of the semantic document contains a class diagram showing a portion of the metamodel; a text description of the metamodel classes defined in that section, with their attributes and relationships; a list of constraints on elements expressed in natural language and in OCL; and a text description of the dynamic semantics of the UML constructs defined in the section. The dynamic semantics are therefore informal, but a fully formal description would be both impractical and unreadable by most.

Notation is described in a separate chapter that references the semantics chapter and maps symbols to metamodel classes.

Specification Document Structure

The UML is defined in two complementary specifications, the *UML 2.0 Infrastructure* and the *UML 2.0 Superstructure*. The infrastructure is intended to define foundational concepts that can be used in part or entirely by other specifications, for example, by the Meta-Object Specification (MOF) and Common Warehouse Metadata (CWM). It contains only the basic static concepts from UML and is oriented toward data structure description.

The UML superstructure defines the complete UML as experienced by users. There is a subset of the superstructure, called the Kernel, that incorporates in the superstructure document all the relevant parts of the infrastructure. The superstructure specification is therefore self-contained, and readers usually will not have to read the infrastructure specification unless they are concerned about configuring other specifications in parallel to UML.

The rest of this chapter describes the organization of the UML superstructure specification.

Metamodel Structure

The metamodel is divided into two main packages, structure and behavior, with two supporting packages, auxiliary elements and profiles (Figure A-1).

- The structure package defines the static structure of the UML. Within the structural package, the classes package is the foundation for everything else in UML.

- The behavior package defines the dynamic structure of the UML. Within this package, the common behavior package is not directly usable in models, but it defines the constructs shared by the other behavior subpackages.

- The auxiliary elements package defines concepts such as data types.

- The profiles package provides the ability to tailor UML

Each package is described by a chapter in the superstructure specification document. The views that we described in the overview to this book correspond roughly to the specification chapters.

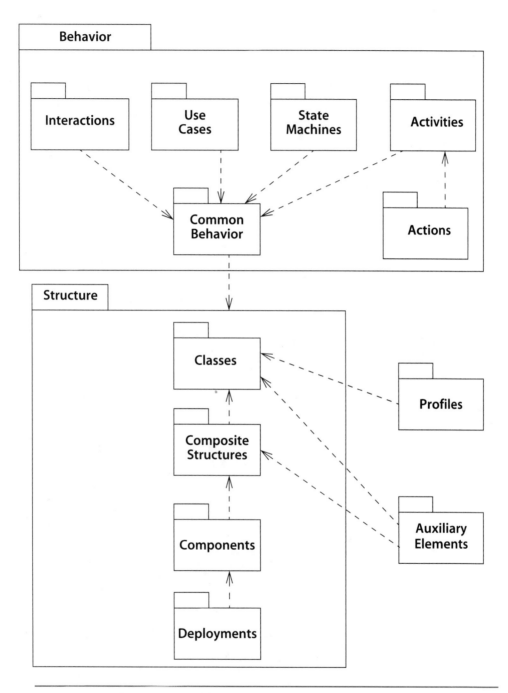

Figure A-1. *Package structure of the UML metamodel*

Appendix B
Notation Summary

This chapter contains a brief visual summary of notation. The major notational elements are included, but not every variation or option is shown. For full details, see the dictionary entry for each element.

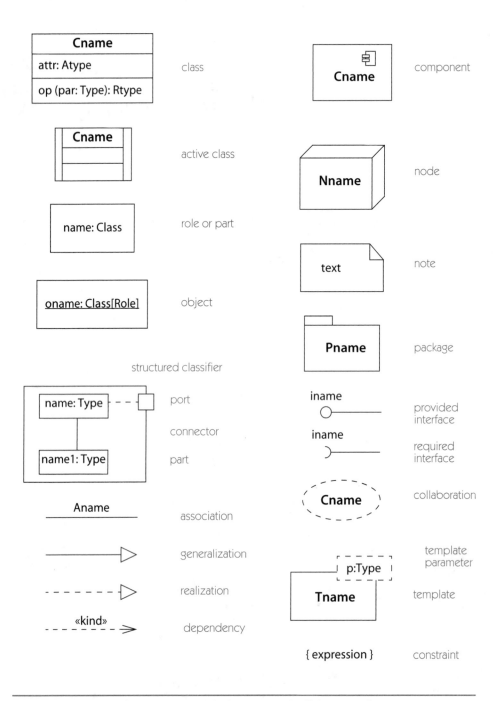

Figure B-1. *Icons on class, component, deployment, and collaboration diagrams*

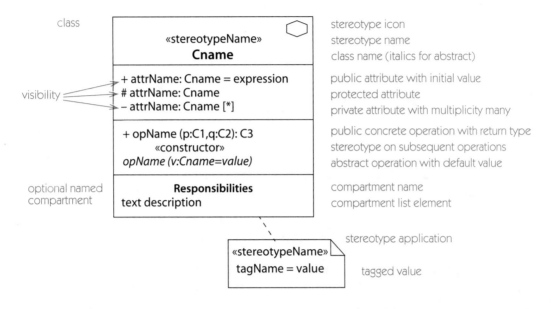

Figure B-2. *Class contents*

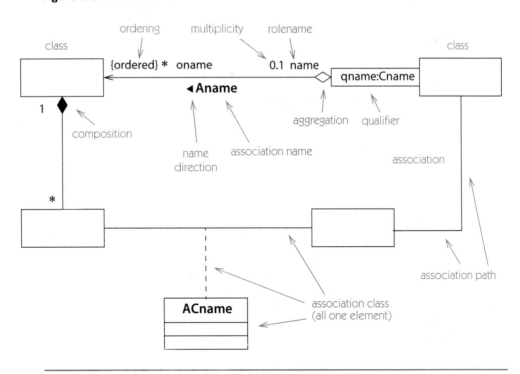

Figure B-3. *Association adornments within a class diagram*

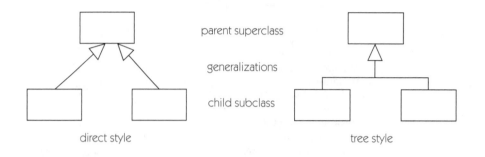

Figure B-4. *Generalization*

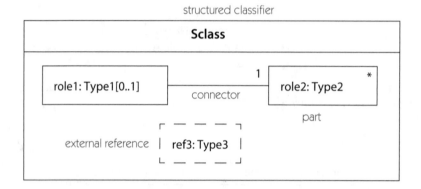

Figure B-5. *Internal structure: parts and connectors*

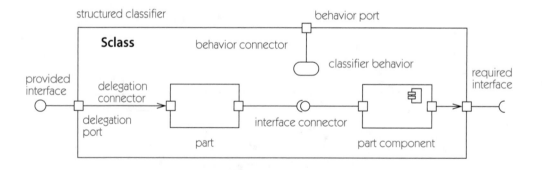

Figure B-6. *Internal structure: interfaces, ports, and internal wiring*

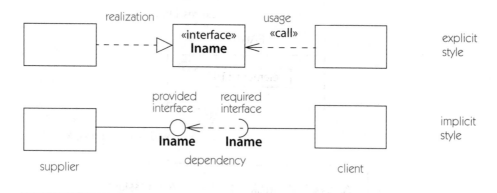

Figure B-7. *Realization of an interface*

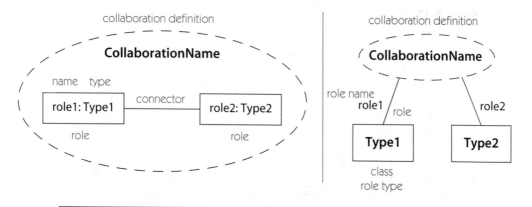

Figure B-8. *Collaboration definition—alternate notations*

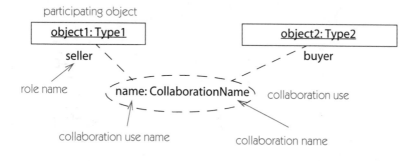

Figure B-9. *Collaboration use*

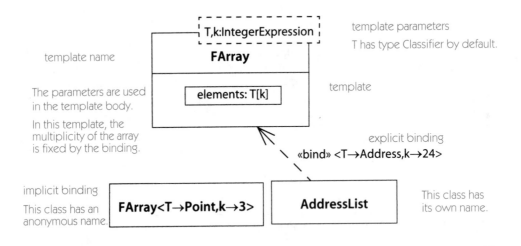

Figure B-10. *Template*

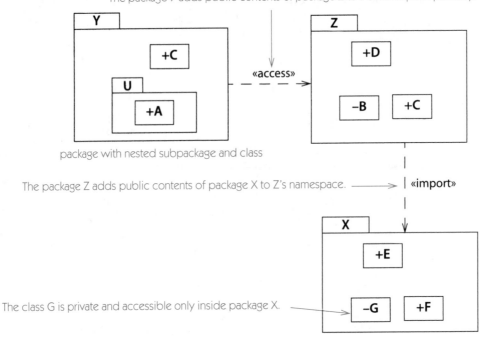

Figure B-11. *Package notation*

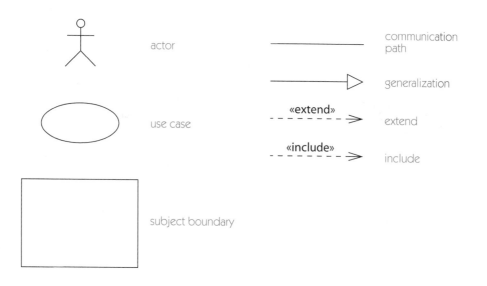

Figure B-12. *Icons on use case diagrams*

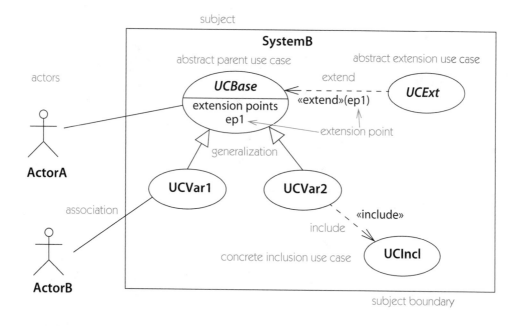

Figure B-13. *Use case diagram notation*

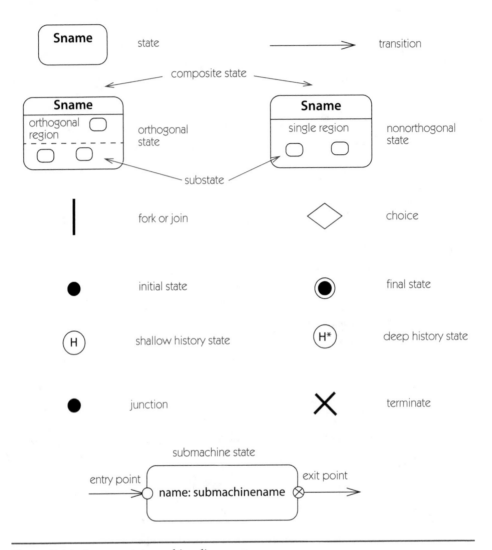

Figure B-14. *Icons on state machine diagrams*

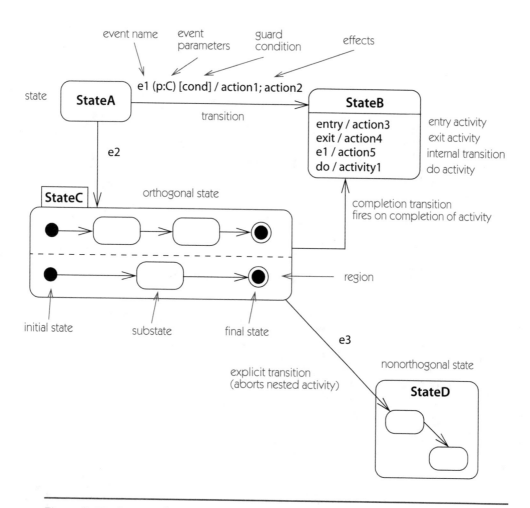

Figure B-15. *State machine notation*

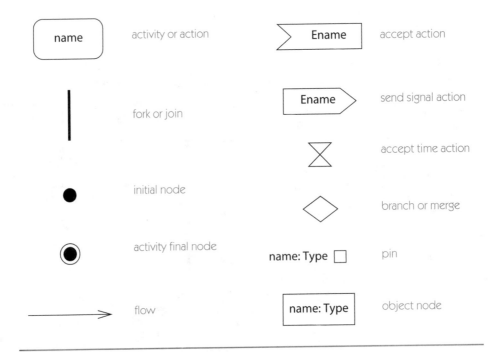

Figure B-16. *Icons on activity diagrams*

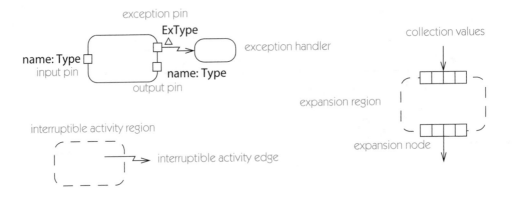

Figure B-17. *Activity groups and icons*

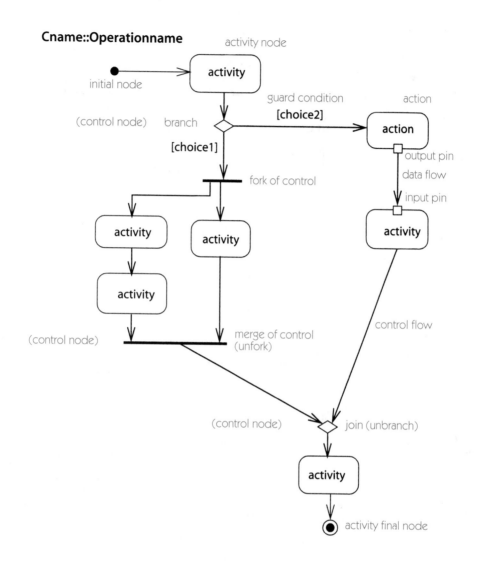

Figure B-18. *Activity diagram notation*

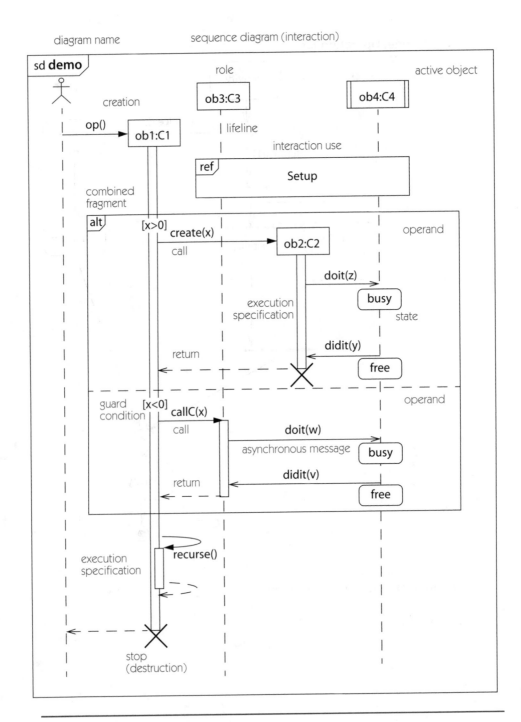

Figure B-19. *Sequence diagram notation*

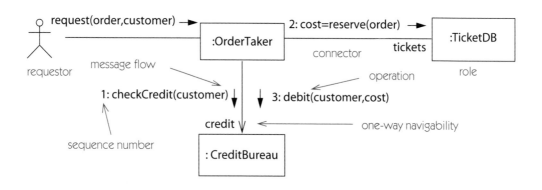

Figure B-20. *Communication diagram notation*

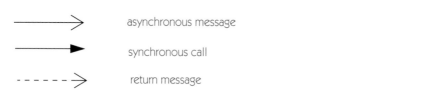

Figure B-21. *Message notation*

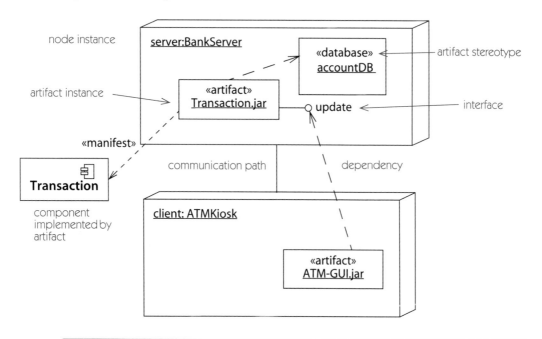

Figure B-22. *Node and artifact notation*

Bibliography

[**Birtwistle-75**] G.M. Birtwistle, O-J. Dahl, B. Myhrhaug, K. Nygaard. Simula Begin. Petrocelli/ Charter, New York, 1975.

[**Blaha-98**] Michael Blaha, William Premerlani. *Object-Oriented Modeling and Design for Database Applications.* Prentice Hall, Upper Saddle River, N.J., 1998.

[**Blaha-05**] Michael Blaha, James Rumbaugh. *Object-Oriented Modeling and Design with UML, 2nd edition.* Prentice Hall, Upper Saddle River, N.J., 2005.

[**Booch-94**] Grady Booch. *Object-Oriented Analysis and Design with Applications, 2nd ed.* Benjamin/Cummings, Redwood City, Calif., 1994.

[**Booch-99**] Grady Booch, James Rumbaugh, Ivar Jacobson. *The Unified Modeling Language User Guide.* Addison-Wesley, Reading, Mass., 1999.

[**Buschmann-96**] Frank Buschmann, Regine Meunier, Hans Rohnert, Peter Sommerlad, Michael Stal. *Pattern-Oriented Software Architecture: A System of Patterns.* Wiley, Chichester, U.K., 1996.

[**Coad-91**] Peter Coad, Edward Yourdon. *Object-Oriented Analysis, 2nd ed.* Yourdon Press, Englewood Cliffs, N.J., 1991.

[**Coleman-94**] Derek Coleman, Patrick Arnold, Stephanie Bodoff, Chris Dollin, Helena Gilchrist, Fiona Hayes, Paul Jeremaes. *Object-Oriented Development: The Fusion Method.* Prentice Hall, Englewood Cliffs, N.J., 1994.

[**Cox-86**] Brad J. Cox. *Object-Oriented Programming: An Evolutionary Approach.* Addison-Wesley, Reading, Mass., 1986.

[**ECOOP**] *ECOOP* yyyy, European *Conference on Object-Oriented Programming: Systems, Languages, and Applications* (where *yyy*=1987 and following). A series of conferences on object-oriented technology in Europe. The proceedings are published by Springer Verlag.

[**Embley-92**] Brian W. Embley, Barry D. Kurtz, Scott N. Woodfield. *Object-Oriented Systems Analysis: A Model-Driven Approach.* Yourdon Press, Englewood Cliffs, N.J., 1992.

[**Fowler-04**] Martin Fowler. *UML Distilled, 3rd ed.* Addison-Wesley, Boston, 2004.

[**Gamma-95**] Erich Gamma, Richard Helm, Ralph Johnson, John Vlissides. *Design Patterns: Elements of Reusable Object-Oriented Software.* Addison-Wesley, Reading, Mass., 1995.

[**Goldberg-83**] Adele Goldberg, David Robson. *Smalltalk-80: The Language and Its Implementation.* Addison-Wesley, Reading, Mass., 1983.

[**Harel-98**] David Harel, Michal Politi. *Modeling Reactive Systems With Statecharts: The STATEMATE Approach.* McGraw-Hill, New York, N.Y., 1998.

[**ITU-T Z.100**] International Telecommunication Union. *Specification and Description Language (SDL).* ITU-T Recommendation Z.100. Geneva, 1999.

[**ITU-T Z.120**] International Telecommunication Union. *Message Sequence Charts.* ITU-T Recommendation Z.120. Geneva, 1999.

[**Jacobson-92**] Ivar Jacobson, Magnus Christerson, Patrik Jonsson, Gunnar Övergaard. *Object-Oriented Software Engineering: A Use Case Driven Approach.* Addison-Wesley, Wokingham, England, 1992.

[**Jacobson-99**] Ivar Jacobson, Grady Booch, James Rumbaugh. *The Unified Software Development Process.* Addison-Wesley, Reading, Mass., 1999.

[**Martin-92**] James Martin, James Odell. *Object-Oriented Analysis and Design.* Prentice Hall, Englewood Cliffs, N.J., 1992.

[**Meyer-88**] Bertrand Meyer. *Object-Oriented Software Construction.* Prentice Hall, New York, N.Y., 1988.

[**OOPSLA**] *OOPSLA yyyy, Conference on Object-Oriented Programming: Systems, Languages, and Applications* (where *yyy*=1986 and following). A series of ACM conferences on object-oriented technology. The proceedings are published as special issues of *ACM Sigplan Notices.*

[**Rumbaugh-91**] James Rumbaugh, Michael Blaha, William Premerlani, Frederick Eddy, William Lorensen. *Object-Oriented Modeling and Design.* Prentice Hall, Englewood Cliffs, N.J., 1991.

[**Rumbaugh-96**] James Rumbaugh. *OMT Insights: Perspectives on Modeling from the Journal of Object-Oriented Technology.* SIGS Books, New York, N.Y., 1996.

[**Rumbaugh-99**] James Rumbaugh, Ivar Jacobson, Grady Booch. *The Unified Modeling Language Reference Manual.* Addison-Wesley, Reading, Mass., 1999. First edition of this book.

[**Selic-94**] Bran Selic, Garth Gullekson, Paul T. Ward. *Real-Time Object-Oriented Modeling.* Wiley, New York, N.Y., 1994.

[**Shlaer-88**] Sally Shlaer, Stephen J. Mellor. *Object-Oriented Systems Analysis: Modeling the World in Data.* Yourdon Press, Englewood Cliffs, N.J., 1988.

[**Shlaer-92**] Sally Shlaer, Stephen J. Mellor. *Object Lifecycles: Modeling the World in States.* Yourdon Press, Englewood Cliffs, N.J., 1992.

[**UML-98**] *Unified Modeling Language Specification, Version 1.1.* Object Management Group, Framingham, Mass., 1998. Internet: www.omg.org.

[**UML-04**] *Unified Modeling Language Specification, Version 2.0.* Object Management Group, Framingham, Mass., 2004. Internet: www.omg.org.

[**UMLConf**] *The x International Conference on the Unified Modeling Language, UML yyyy* (where *x*=an ordinal and *yyyy*=1998 and following). A series of conferences reporting research on UML. The proceedings are published by Springer-Verlag.

[**Ward-85**] Paul Ward, Stephen J. Mellor. *Structured Development for Real-Time Systems: Introduction and Tools*. Yourdon Press, Englewood Cliffs, N.J., 1985.

[**Warmer-99**] Jos B. Warmer, Anneke G. Kleppe. *The Object Constraint Language: Precise Modeling with UML*. Addison-Wesley, Reading, Mass., 1999.

[**Wirfs-Brock-90**] Rebecca Wirfs-Brock, Brian Wilkerson, Lauren Wiener. *Designing Object-Oriented Software*. Prentice Hall, Englewood Cliffs, N.J., 1990.

[**Yourdon-79**] Edward Yourdon, Larry L. Constantine. *Structured Design: Fundamentals of a Discipline of Computer Program and Systems Design*. Yourdon Press, Englewood Cliffs, N.J., 1979.

Index

Main entries are in boldface; secondary entries are in roman type; references to figures are in italics.

C

CD-ROM Warranty

Addison-Wesley warrants the enclosed CD-ROM to be free of defects in materials and faulty workmanship under normal use for a period of ninety days after purchase (when purchased new). If a defect is discovered in the CD-ROM during this warranty period, a replacement CD-ROM can be obtained at no charge by sending the defective CD-ROM, postage prepaid, with proof of purchase to:

Disc Exchange
Addison-Wesley Professional
Pearson Technology Group
75 Arlington Street, Suite 300
Boston, MA 02116
Email: AWPro@aw.com

More information and updates are available at:
http://www.awprofessional.com/